CHINATOWN OPERA THEATER IN NORTH AMERICA

MUSIC IN AMERICAN LIFE

A list of books in the series appears at the end of this book.

CHINATOWN OPERA THEATER IN NORTH AMERICA

Nancy Yunhwa Rao

Publication supported by grants from the AMS 75 PAYS Endowment of the American Musicological Society, funded in part by the National Endowment for the Humanities and the Andrew W. Mellon Foundation, and from the Li Man-Kuei Fund for Chinese Performing Arts of the Chinese Performing Arts Foundation

1 2 3 4 5 C P 5 4 3 2 1
∞ This book is printed on acid-free paper.

Library of Congress Control Number: 2016957566
ISBN 978-0-252-04056-6 (hardcover)
ISBN 978-0-252-08203-0 (paperback)
ISBN 978-0-252-09900-7 (e-book)

To my mother and father

CONTENTS

ACKNOWLEDGMENTS

In this book's long journey, it and I have incurred many debts of gratitude. I am indebted to Judith Becker for planting the seed for this intellectual engagement in Ann Arbor; to Judy Tsou for her groundbreaking paper at the 1996 conference of the Society for American Music in Washington, DC, which gave the impetus for this project; to Josephine Wright, who took an interest in this project before it had a name; and to the late Him Mark Lai, who helped me with my first inquiry about Chinese American history.

In researching Cantonese opera of the early twentieth century, I have been very lucky to have Sai-Shing Yung and Wing Chung Ng as close companions in our shared pursuit. They offered insight, shared materials, and helped open doors for me; without them, this journey would have been much too lonely. I am indebted to Chan Sau Yan for his interest and support as the director of the Chinese Opera Information Center at the Chinese University of Hong Kong. Bell Yung has been generous with support and critique at crucial points. Yu Sai Wah sent precious materials to help the research along. Helan Hon-Lun Yang was a true academic comrade, making my numerous visits to Hong Kong fun and coming to my rescue in many local matters.

The Society for American Music has been the intellectual home for this book; I have presented many of its chapters at SAM conferences. I am grateful for constant encouragement from Carol Oja, John Koegel, and Judith Tick, and I have benefited from discussions with Susan Cook, the late Catherine Parson Smith, Richard Crawford, Leta Miller, Chuck Garrett, and Beth Levy at various stages of the project. At

SAM I also met Tim Brooks and Paul Charosh, who generously shared their private record libraries and encyclopedic knowledge of the industry. This project is an unusual undertaking for one trained in music theory, but Nadine Hubbs, Kofi Agawu, Yayoi Uno Everett, Andrew Mead, and Marianne Kielien Gilbert cheered me on and offered insightful suggestions at critical points. Scholars outside music theory whose work and astute comments I have benefited from greatly include Sheetal Chhabria, Alison Isenberg, Daphne Lei, Amien Lu, Whitney Strub, Jack Tchen, Deborah Gray White, Deborah Wong, Ellen Wu, Henry Yu, and Hai Zhen. At Rutgers University, I am indebted to members of the weekly seminars at the Institute for Research on Women (2009 and 2014) and the Research Center for Historical Analysis (2011) for providing stimulating conversation and important breathing room.

This work would not have been possible without the expert assistance of the archivists who tirelessly helped me track down and retrieve files. For years, archives seemed like vacation homes for me. I owe gratitude to Suzanne A. Harris at the National Archives and Records Administration in Washington, DC, William Greene at the Pacific Region office, and Celia Cefalo at the Pacific Alaska Region office, as well as branches in New York City and elsewhere. Wei-chi Poon at the Ethnic Studies Library of the University of California, Berkeley, Judith Ng at the Hong Kong Heritage Museum, Milky Man Shan Cheung at the Chinese Opera Information Centre in Hong Kong, Bob Fisher at the Wing Luke Museum in Seattle, Wendy Nichols at the Museum of Vancouver, and George Boziwick at the Music Division of the New York Public Library offered significant assistance. At Rutgers, Glenn Sandburg helped tirelessly with countless interlibrary loans. I am also grateful for the help of staff members and librarians at the Library and Archives of Canada, the Cheung Collection at the University of British Columbia, the Him Mark Lai Collection at the University of California, Berkeley, the Special Collection at Stanford University, the Fu Sinian Memorial Library at the Academia Sinica Institute in Taipei, the archives of the China Art Research Institute in Beijing, the Special Collection at Hong Kong University, and the American Folklife Center at the Library of Congress. I began significant archival work during the year of my Faculty Research Fellowship from the National Endowment for the Humanities even though the award was for another project. I am grateful for that crucial year. I am thankful for several other fellowships and grants: the recognition conferred by the Dena Epstein Award for Archival and Library Research in American Music (from the Music Library Association) and Parsons Awards for Ethnography (from the American Folklife Center of the Library of Congress) were financially and symbolically important to me. Rutgers University provided financial support for this book in the form of sabbaticals, Faculty Council Grants, and a subvention from Dean George Stauffer of the Mason Gross School of the Arts.

Though begun late in the project, field work was a wonderful journey that shed new light on all my prior archival research. I owe the success of that segment of the project to David Lei, whose deep connection to the community led me to terrific people and their fascinating stories. They include James Lee, Tse Fook Pui, Lillian Jew, Clara Chan, Hanley Fong, Andrew Leong, Phil Choy, Bruce Quan Jr., Margaret Leung, Amien Lau, Florinda Kuan, Steven Wong, and Frederick Kwai. Phil Choy not only shared his personal collection but lent his insight as an architectural historian. Judy Yung gave personal interviews and continuing support for the project. Mui Ho kindly offered her Berkeley home on many evenings when I retreated from the archives as well as stories of growing up with Cantonese opera in Hong Kong. Andrew Li housed me on my frequent trips to Hong Kong and shared insights on architectural matters.

I am indebted to colleagues and editorial readers who read part or all of the manuscript at various stages and offered insightful comments: Eric Hung, Sai-shing Yung, Bell Yung, Taylor Atkins, Lillian Li, Judy Yung, Robert Aldridge, Kathleen Lopez, Tim Brooks, Andrew Urban, Betty Livingston Adam, John Hobbs, David McCarthy, Helan Yang, Boaz Chow, Wing Chung Ng, Jane Zanichkowsky, Vicki Low, and the anonymous readers for the University of Illinois Press. Jacqueline Thaw has my deep gratitude for designing the book cover, and I am indebted to David Wolfson for his expert setting of music examples. I am grateful for my editor at the press, Laurie Matheson, whose enthusiasm for this book was key to its completion.

My parents have been supportive of my pursuits no matter what courses they take. My attraction to Chinese classics and calligraphy stems from the scholarly atmosphere of the home they provided. My sisters Haihwa and Jessica accommodated me in ways too numerous to name over the years when I conducted research in the Bay Area, and I have long relied on their unconditioned love. My nieces Christine and Jennifer both helped my research in Berkeley during their student days there. I am also indebted to my brother Herman, both for taking care of my parents and for showing interest in the progress of the book. Karen, Erica, and Isabel have injected their unbound energy into this work, even when they did not know it. Finally, I am indebted to Nelson for his love, companionship and unwavering support for this project and everything else.

A NOTE ON CHINESE NAMES AND TERMS

Early Chinese immigrants to North America came primarily from the Pearl River delta in southern China, and their names, as well as terms and opera titles, were inevitably pronounced in Cantonese or Toisanese rather than Mandarin Chinese. In written Chinese communication this does not pose problems because the written characters are the same, but when rendering them phonetically, confusion abounds. The names of many famous Cantonese opera singers have been known in Cantonese romanization, such as actor Bak Kui Wing and actress Lee Suet Fong. However, there are many systems of romanization in Cantonese, so there are variations even on these famous names. For example, the character *bak* could be romanized as *pak* as well. Furthermore, the names of Cantonese performers of the 1920s were romanized casually by legal brokers, interpreters, or theater agents in documents such as immigration papers and journalistic accounts, or by ships' captains, immigration officers, court clerks, or journalists, few of whom spoke Chinese at all. The result is a hodgepodge of spellings and often multiple versions of the same name. Therefore, romanized Cantonese is not a reliable way to reference Chinese names in historical documents or newspapers. The study of performers posed additional difficulty. On the immigration documents they could use stage names, which often had but a tangential connection to their real names. Aliases, typically more respectful forms for prominent figures, could be used. In fact, both of the famous performers noted above used aliases on their immigration documents, Chan Shiu Bo (for Bak Kui Wing) and Lee Wan Fan (for Lee Suet Fong). Identifying performers from their romanized names is often tricky.

For the purpose of consistency, I primarily use standard Mandarin pinyin romanization for Chinese personal names and terms. The disadvantage of using pinyin, which renders unfamiliar many famous names traditionally romanized according to the Cantonese dialect, is offset by the advantages of consistency and ease of reference, both within this book and across other studies of this period.

There are exceptions, however. In all quoted texts the romanization in the original document remains intact. Also, certain spellings of names in English-language documents, such as troupe names found at the National Archives and Records Administration, are kept. The well-established Cantonese romanization of names of prominent community figures and organizations in North America are used as well, without reference to the Mandarin version in pinyin, because the latter version would be of little use. The appendix provides a list of names and terms using Chinese characters, with alternate romanizations where applicable, for reference.

In Chinese personal names, in general, a one-syllable family name is stated first, followed by a two-syllable given name. In my romanization I retain this order in translating the names of theater professionals. I also adopt the practice of closing up the two-syllable given name (for example, Li Xuefang). Stage names present some exceptions. They could contain a two-syllable name that is not the surname, followed by a one-syllable name, for example, Mudan Su (meaning Peony Su) or Gongye Chang (meaning Warrior Chang). The romanization of contemporary scholars' names, however, follows the Western practice of stating the given name followed by the family name (for example, Judy Yung).

For archival documents cited in the notes, the annotated document titles have been transcribed verbatim for the sake of accuracy for future research.

Cantonese opera titles are given in English translation; their romanized and Chinese-character names can be found in the appendix. Unless noted, all translations from Chinese to English are my own.

CHINATOWN OPERA THEATER IN NORTH AMERICA

INTRODUCTION

EVERYDAY PRACTICE AND THE IMAGINARY

THE LYRICS

The two small scraps of crumpled, yellowed paper filled with Chinese characters in a folder in the Libraries and Archives of Canada in Ottawa seemed of no importance at first.[1] They were, however, different from the other papers in the folder, correspondence dating from 1923 to the 1950s on onionskin paper or light blue airmail sheets. Such letters, mainly from southern China, were a common sight for many Chinese immigrants in the Americas. Their families, on the other side of the Pacific Ocean, moved through the cycles of life in their absence: the passing away of elderly parents, the marriages of sons or daughters, and the birth of grandchildren. Many immigrant men remained the head of their families. One wife's agitated letter scolded her husband for not having earned enough to purchase a home for the family in Hong Kong, a failure, considering his lengthy residency in North America. Earning the money to maintain and extend their paternal lineage was usually these immigrants' primary motivation.[2]

Midway through the pile of letters I found the original paper from which the small scraps had broken off. The thick paper had been tightly folded to one-eighth of its full size. The penmanship was that of a practiced hand: graceful Chinese calligraphy written with an ink brush pen. As I gingerly unfolded the fragile paper and returned the two rectangular scraps to their corner, my stomach churned. What emerged were the lyrics of a famous aria from a Cantonese opera, the genre of the region from which most Chinese emigrated before 1943. In classical verse the aria laments loved ones and the lost opportunity for a happy life together.

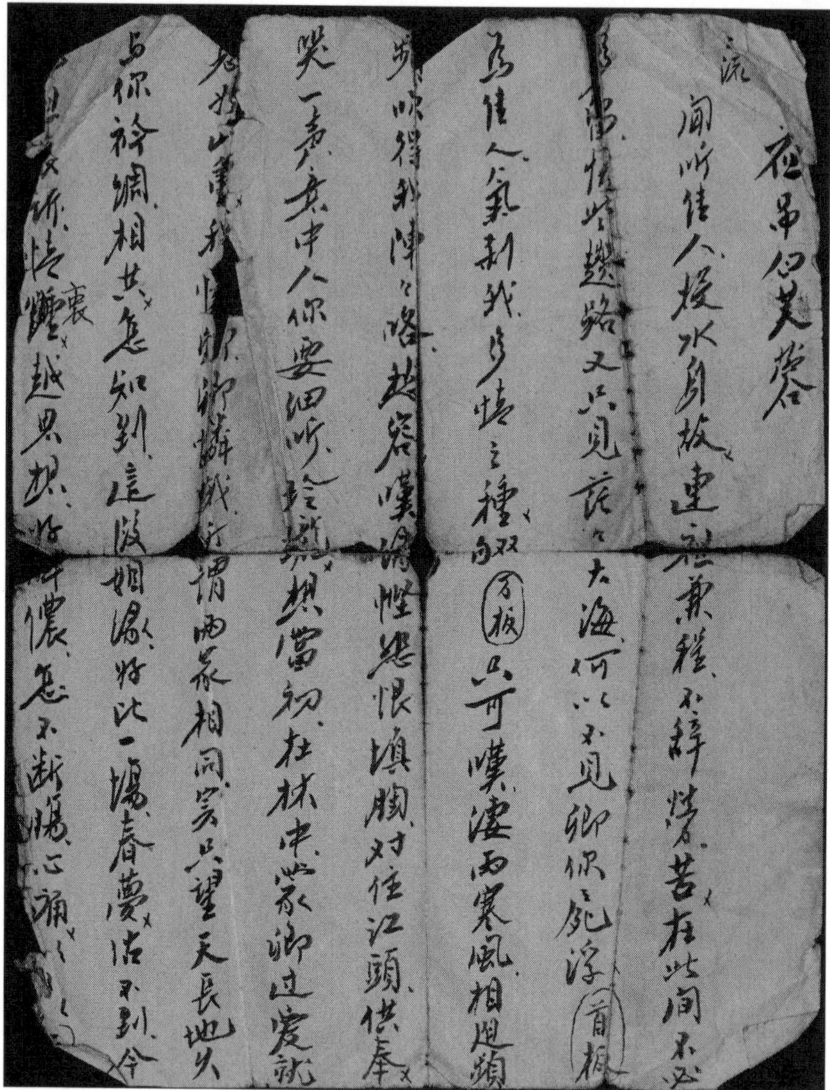

Fig. I.1. Opera lyrics (courtesy of the Library and Archives of Canada/Leung Doo Wong fonds).

The aria, a lament, is from an opera popular in the Chinese communities of North America in the 1920s and 1930s: *Nocturnal Mourning of White Lotus.* It tells of White Lotus, a young woman who meets her love, the young scholar Lu, by the river. Later she is pursued by a local tyrant, who tries to force a marriage by means of kidnapping and threats. Lu comes to her rescue many times. However, coming from an upper-class family, he is forbidden to marry her. So the devastated Lu goes into self-imposed exile. Seeing that their love is doomed, White Lotus despairs and takes her own life by jumping into the river where they first met. The despondent Lu returns to the river to mourn, and the famous lament expresses his regret and unfulfilled yearning.

The aria was fully written out in verse with annotations regarding tune types, and the lyrics in flowing calligraphy expressed musical enjoyment. (The annotation of tune types accompanying the lyrics indicates musical rendition, which can be echoed by the strokes of calligraphy.) The deep creases suggest that the folded paper had probably been carried around in a trouser or shirt pocket. It was likely intimate and personal to its owner, like the letters.[3] Here among all the letters in this archive, it quietly conveyed an inner dimension of immigrant life: that of the usually inarticulate, silent, and anonymous Chinese in North America during the Chinese exclusion era, the period from 1882 to 1943 during which immigration from China was greatly restricted. In the 1920s Cantonese opera arias, which gained great popularity through theatrical performances and recordings in North America, gave voice to Chinese immigrants' everyday stories of desires, regrets, laughter, and dreams.

This sheet might not seem to be of much value for historical research, compared to memoirs or original business papers from community organizations and kinship associations. Yet precisely because it is an imperfectly kept, hand-copied paper of very popular lyrics, it is imbued with layers of meaning. Aside from shedding light on an immigrant's self-image, it shows the deep penetration of opera into Chinese Americans' lives; during this period it constituted their primary entertainment. Also, its graceful calligraphy defies a certain stereotype of Chinatown opera theaters as rowdy, vulgar entertainment. The classical verse and calligraphy recall instead scrolls of Chinese painting and calligraphy in museums. The frayed paper, marked by repeated unfolding, offers the possibility of an analysis of what Michel de Certeau calls "imprints of acts,"[4] which allow us to "hear the tales of the repressed activity."[5] Repeated, attentive listening was pressed into the creases of the sheet of lyrics. Stumbling onto this object, the first personal memento of many such traces uncovered in my years of research, I felt a sense of relief as a student of the history of American music, because it allowed me to dream the everyday life of Cantonese opera in North America.

The lyrics of arias and songs constituted a significant part of the enjoyment of Cantonese operas. They were regularly featured on the playbills of San Francisco's Chinatown theaters in the 1920s, professionally printed and distributed to the stores daily at noon and then at the theaters at night.[6] Popular lyrics were also circulated in locally printed anthologies and pamphlets or as inserts accompanying phonograph records.[7] The page of lyrics, hand-copied with a brush pen, still a common writing device in the 1920s, is suggestive of the individual agencies of the musical process in the Chinese immigrant community. This object conveys a close engagement with the imaginary space of the opera world. As a mode of music-making, the opera lyrics are performative, affording the opportunity to enact an identity, to take on a musical persona, and to be oneself, free from society's rigidities. As a cultural artifact the paper is all the more symbolic, hidden as it was in this vast archive of documents of Canadian heritage. The paper registers the discursive processes by which Chinese immigrants' "identities were ascribed, resisted, or embraced."[8] It points to the historical process of Cantonese opera as it was sustained and developed in North America before World War II.

From the perspective of cultural circulation, at the same time, the lyrics symbolize a mobility that symbolized the ability to pass through borders, linguistic boundaries, and remote geographical places. A degree of stability allowed Cantonese opera to cross those barriers and continue to produce cultural meanings. Yet it was by no means a fixed tradition. In the 1920s Cantonese opera underwent many changes—among them the rise of virtuosity and female troupes and the development of new operas, vocal styles, and urban theaters. The genre was also very flexible, relying as it did on improvisation, with performances adjusted via appropriations and adaptations depending on historical and geopolitical situations. The scrap of lyrics, a symbol of the opera's literary, sonic, and performing space, opens the historical inquiry into the multidimensional history of Chinatown opera theaters in North America with which this book is concerned.

THE STAGE

Whereas the crumpled opera lyrics reflect the inner life of an immigrant, the thrill of the opera's stage can perhaps be seen most clearly through a toddler's eyes. Wayson Choy, recalling his experience of the early 1940s in Vancouver, wrote:

> To the right of the stage . . . an eight-man orchestra began to play. The crowd applauded. The rising notes of a dulcimer stilled the audience; the pliant notes of the two-stringed *hu chin* and the violin dispensed quivering half-melodies. Cymbals shivered; gongs and drumbeats throbbed; a pair of woodblock clacked.
>
> My all-day sucker slipped out of my hand. All at once, I felt my heart pounding to a rhythm outside of myself. I was thunder-struck. I clenched my four-year-old legs. Tightened my candy stained fists. I wanted to pee.
>
> "*Hi-lah*!" Mother said to me in Toisenese. "*Hi-lah*, look!"
>
> Balanced on the edge of her knees, feverishly swallowing the pungent air, I pushed forward, stretched my neck and *hi-lah*ed between the big heads and shoulders in front of us.
>
> The door-sized side curtain parted. A burst of color struck my eyes. In sequined costumes of forest green and gold, jolting cobalt blue and fiery red, living myths swayed onto the stage, their swords slashing the air, their open ornate fans snapping.
>
> Mother whispered into my ear who each was as, one by one, the performers made a few stylized movements to introduce their character, briefly sang their histories,

> and danced away before my amazed eyes: that's the *Hsiao-sheng*, the Scholar-Prince; there, the Princess with pretty eyes; now the grand King with his servants: last, with orchestra roars, the fierce South Wind General, his soldiers swirling behind him, tumbling like madmen.
>
> Mesmerized by the tumbling warriors, I didn't care about the growing dampness on my pant legs, but Mother made a clucking noise to signal her disgust and lifted me off her knees. I stood beside her on the box provided for children, my knees bending and straightening as if I myself were majestically stomping about the stage. . . .
>
> Guarded by two loyal servants, the Gentlewoman, played by Mah Dang Soh, stood ready to sing a challenging aria.
>
> "Oh, those opera love stories just like *Wuthering Heights*," one of Mother's oldest friends, Betty Lee, recently told me. The opera may have been *The Beauty on the Lake*, or the popular *Lay Toy Woo, The Romance at the Bridge*.
>
> The star tilted her proud, confident head to one side. The audience stirred. I was mesmerized by the lengths of pure white silk cascading from the embroidered sleeves of her emerald-green dress. Her elegant hands rose like the wings of a swan, and the silk "water sleeves" swept backwards. She seemed to be brushing tears from her eyes. Mother told me the lady lived in exile, and was aching to see again her long-lost family. . . . With long fingers now resting against her cheek, the actress began to pierce the air with her falsetto voice, and the audience—suddenly—responded with silence. We children knew we were not to run about, but to tiptoe, and not to utter even a whisper.[9]

The muscular tension and relaxation of the toddler Choy reflect not only the dynamic quality of the music and the riveting performance of the characters but also the playfulness and social order of the opera's imaginary world. The mimetic participation, explicit for this toddler though expressed in more subtle ways for the adult audience, activated an experience that became inscribed and registered on the body over time.[10] Focused listening and attentive watching formed an important part of the theater experience because, as theater scholar Diane Taylor observes, such a stage performance "provokes emotion it claims only to represent, evokes memories and grief that belong to some other body."[11] By its physical imagery audiences were transported into the world of dramatic and music narrative. (This is particularly true in Cantonese opera because the physical aspect of the performance is as important as the musical aspect, as I discuss in Chapter 4.)

The singer mentioned in Choy's reminiscence, Mah Dang Soh (Mudan Su), was familiar to Chinatown theater-goers throughout North America for more than forty years. She rose to fame in the 1920s, and she held audiences spellbound. Whether photographed in trouser roles or young female roles, her poses were always strikingly expressive of the character she portrayed. The meanings of the role types and performing bodies—encoded according to convention often passed down from mother to child—opened up a world of fantastic cultural imagination.[12] The translatability of the images into Choy's young life was so immediate that he "no longer [felt] separated from the stage." For him, as for many second-generation Chinese in North America, the opera stories strengthened the "perceptions in life [that] grew out of the fables told to" them by their mothers.[13] Similar opera-going experiences were noted by many Chinese Americans growing up in San Francisco's Chinatown at the height of live Cantonese opera performance.[14]

Choy's story provides a much-needed perspective from within the Chinese community, one different from mainstream society's reports of Chinese theater, which often described performances as incomprehensible. Those reports' caricatures of Chinese opera were so widespread in the nineteenth century that society equated strangeness with Chineseness and saw Chinese performers as not only executing weird sounds but personifying them.[15] In contrast, Choy renders the act of seeing rather than the object being seen. The effect of story-telling is powerful for children in all cultures, but here it was especially enhanced by the music, performances, costumes, and elaborate stage actions. It was as satisfying as it was meaningful.

Choy's reminiscence also shows that the theater was a unique social space and magic world during the era when the government sanctioned racism by means of exclusion laws. He writes,

> For years, Mother went regularly with her friends to the [Chinese theaters]; she thought nothing of taking me, even when I was only a few months old. Other mothers had their children with them, too, and newborns nursed indifferently at breasts wet with milk.
>
> It was many years before I understood that . . . my parents were not well off. . . . I never thought of them as a working-class, no-citizenship family, despite the fact that they were each working long hours and earning only minimum wage. Whatever daily struggles my parents faced, the Cantonese opera at night bestowed upon me such a wealth of high drama, of myth, that I lacked for nothing in the ordinary world. . . . Sometimes the thundering sounds and the imagined action were so beautiful that I nearly stopped breathing. I wanted to become what I saw before me: the General, the warriors, and the frightened guard who led the way to prison.[16]

Vancouver, the city that formed the backdrop of Choy's childhood, had a history of Cantonese opera performance that can be traced back to 1898, a decade after the city was incorporated.[17] Over the years, the theaters became important locales for cultural performances, where nightly shows retold familiar stories in endless renditions of theatrical conventions. Family opera-going facilitated what the Irish folklore historian Guy Beiner calls "social memory," in particular, the dynamic processes that "produce, convey, sustain and reconstruct collective memory."[18] The operas both transmitted and reshaped beliefs, values, and cultural symbols.

Cantonese opera served many different purposes, not least for children. For many of them the opera theater was a playground, used for activities from playing hide-and-seek in the balcony to crawling onto the edge of the stage until they were shooed away by ushers or audience. Young children were accustomed to grabbing onto the coattails of adults to enter the theaters. Each day fans eagerly awaited the playbills with pictures of their favorite performers, which they cut out and collected in treasure chests or scrapbooks.[19] Some were thoroughly immersed in the lyrical beauty and emotional intensity projected by the performances of their favorite singers.[20] Opera fan Lillian Jew, who grew up in San Francisco in the 1930s, noted, "At the Chinese school they taught historical stories, but I did not understand them until I saw them on the theater stages at the opera." The historian Judy Yung recalls using bed sheets as gowns with long flowing sleeves on a rooftop to emulate opera performance.[21] Her childhood game of impersonating opera characters, which she later learned had been a continuing amusement for a neighborhood woman, reflected the everyday role of mimicry in social memory. "The child mimics other people's actions," noted the sociologist Pierre Bourdieu, "rather than 'models.'"[22] In a form of "practical mimesis," the youth adopted the gestures, movements, and postures of opera in the environment of the theater culture with or without fully comprehending them.[23]

Bodily performances, with their amalgamation of music, lyrics, legends, and choreography, became the inspiration for games and lessons involving language, folklore, aesthetic form, and history. Opera performances transcended the immediate social context and theatrical space to become the collective identity. Choy's retelling, therefore, was an expression of that internalized world and identity, or what the anthropologist Greg Urban calls "re-externalizing," that makes apparent the internalization. Choy's description reveals the imprints of cultural imagination, identity, and social memory.[24] In many different ways, Cantonese opera as cultural and social memory was remade and reinterpreted by later generations into newer forms. Examples abound in Chinese American literature by David Henry Hwang, Maxine Hong Kingston, and Frank Chin. Kingston's *The Woman Warrior* (1976) and *Tripmaster Monkey* (1989) are but two famous examples.[25]

In spatial and symbolic terms the largest gathering places in the community, the theaters by default served as important public spaces which forged a unified voice. Warrior operas about loyalty or heart-wrenching family dramas about filial obligation shared the stage with community rallies for patriotic, political, or social causes, and the sense of duty and passion connected them. Chinatown theaters as social spaces were personal, familial, and educational, as well as political.[26] If the fantastic world of opera warriors that accompanied Choy's Vancouver childhood was more immediate to his self-image than was his family's story as hardworking non-citizens, it was the actions of musical and operatic performances that he likely had adopted as strategies for forming his identity.

LOCATING CHINATOWN THEATERS

The lyrics and vivid stage images provide a much-needed window into the golden era of Cantonese opera in North America. Though they once formed vibrant cultural scenes, Chinatown theaters' role in the North American musical landscape is little understood. Recognition of their significance has been persistently lacking in American musical and social history. To uncover this history, however, requires that we release these theaters from their repressed silence and perpetual invisibility, as well as separate them from the myths about them.

Cantonese opera followed in the steps of the first Chinese immigrants. The first troupe to arrive, Hong Fook Tong, performed in San Francisco in 1852. For the following fifty years numerous Chinese theaters staged nightly performances in that city, often with multiple theaters running concurrently. In the first golden period, the 1870s, there were four theaters in San Francisco's Chinatown. The second golden period, in the 1920s, saw the Mandarin Theater and Great China Theater opening in San Francisco for daily performances within a year of one another, each with more than seven hundred seats. Yet these theaters have been invisible to American music history. Even today, as historians begin to acknowledge their existence, Chinatown theaters are often dismissed as irrelevant. "Chinese music," runs a familiar historical narrative, "was performed . . . mostly in private and strictly within the Chinese community."[27] This narrative seems unaware of the large public performances held all through the 1920s in San Francisco. Such a description, as this book demonstrates, is false.

Invisibility is the constant state of not being seen, even when the object of study. As scholars have examined musical depictions of Chinatown in American culture, they have shown the emasculated racial stereotypes circulated in popular music and on stage, and the way these stereotypes of the other were used to reaffirm a national identity.[28] These critical studies have, by showing how the songs registered cultural attitudes toward Chinese immigrants, moved the discourse of racial politics in American music history beyond the black-white binary paradigm. Yet, though they break important new ground in racial politics, these works are not directed toward rendering audible and visible the voice and music of Chinatown theaters. In other words, interrogating the musical representation of Chinatown does not necessarily untether it from its musical stereotypes. Whether in the nineteenth century or the twenty-first, therefore, Chinatown theaters have not been part of mainstream American society's "interlocutor," as Said's famous phrase goes, "but its silent Other."[29]

The status of historical invisibility was also internalized by many in the Chinese American community. The psychological effect of negative portrayals could "work, in concrete and direct ways, to mediate the relationship between the psychic and the social."[30] It established distance between them and the theater culture, leading to dismissive comments ("authentic" corroborations of theaters' insignificance), while the social stigma associated with the theaters also gave rise to different forms of self-censorship or hesitancy to acknowledge this music history lest the stereotypes prevail and tokenism persist.[31] In order to lift the silence and undo invisibility, this book brings new attention to Chinatown theaters by considering their transnational reach and the history of an important decade in their existence. It re-centers artifacts and documents that have thus far received little scholarly attention in order to provide a narrative of the performing history, the illustrious performers, and the glory and strain of the genre.

In this book I hope to situate Chinatown theaters within a broader geopolitical framework as well. I concentrate primarily on the United States, the history of which cannot be told without the larger context of North America, and even that of the Americas to some extent. By re-orienting the angle of vision toward the transnational and studying a wider geographical area, this work traces the strong connections among Chinese across North America, the circular networks of opera performers, and the mobility of the theater world. Border crossing was an important part of Chinese theaters' business—and their greatest challenge. The transnational connection allowed the movement of capital, performers, and performance practices across boundaries both obvious and hidden, steered by the establishment of business partnerships, amorphous webs of family kinship, or the principles of urban renewal.

The period under study is the decade of the 1920s, which was chosen for several reasons. First, Chinatown theaters experienced a phenomenal rise to prominence during this period. This meant the continuing arrival of performers to maintain the vibrancy of the art. Second, Chinese theater was still the primary entertainment in the Chinese community, where not until about 1930 did other forms of entertainment such as cinema gain dominance. Third, as Chinese immigrants attained stronger standing within the community (with their own financial institutions, telephone exchange, YMCA, and so on), the number of families and their descendents grew, making social entertainment such as opera still more important. Finally, with repertory theaters putting on daily performances and the opera culture enhanced by print culture (playbills, newspapers, and anthologies of lyrics) and listening culture (recordings and radio), the theaters enjoyed great success. The 1920s therefore stand out as a golden period when Chinese theaters were deeply woven into the financial, political, social, and familial fabrics of Chinese communities in North America. The vibrant theaters continued to operate in the 1930s, although they were not as prosperous. A Works Progress Administration study of San Francisco's Chinese theaters in 1936 indicated that the troupes remained young and enthusiastic and the performances were still of excellent quality.[32]

This prosperous decade resulted in a remarkable plenitude of documents, artifacts, and even structures of Chinese theaters, such that a detailed history about them can finally be told in their own voices. As Greg Urban reminds us, the circulation of culture is only possible because "it becomes lodged, however fleetingly or enduringly, in material, perceptible, things."[33] The opera tradition in Chinatowns left its marks. Artifacts marked street corners and gathered dust in homes or stores. The glue spread over the top edges of theater playbills demonstrates their daily posting; manufacturer's marks on tattered opera drums found in Californian mining towns not only show their date and origins (late Qing Dynasty and Guangzhou) but also registered the transnational existence of opera troupes in out-of-the-way places. In many cities the opera theaters were centrally located in the Chinatown community. A few theaters of the 1920s, after multiple repurposings, still preserve the contours of the stage edge and the dual backstage doors, signatures of Cantonese opera.

As the Chinese community became more conscious of conservation in the late twentieth century, many theatrical materials and artifacts that had long been ignored or hidden increasingly were preserved and made available for study. San Francisco's Museum of Performance and Design, the Chinese Historical Society of America, the Ethnic Studies Library at the University of California, Berkeley, and Wing Luke Museum in Seattle house important playbills and stage photos. Major collections amassed by prominent merchants—the Chung and Yip Sang families in Vancouver and the Beryl Yuen family (owners of the Taiping Theater) in Hong Kong—also shed much light on historical practice. Archives kept by Chinese Americans are on the rise and have begun the institutional preservation of historical documents. Texts in Chinese, including playbills, daily advertisements, news accounts and commentaries in local Chinese newspapers, and anthologies of lyrics, are also important. In some of these collections stage photos and, more limited, historical recordings survive to form a contemporary archive of Chinatown theater performances.

Particularly revealing are immigration documents, however. The 1920s fell within the Chinese Exclusion Era, during which the U.S. government closely monitored Chinese performers and theaters. Government surveillance has often produced treasure troves of valuable materials for researchers, an irony well-known among historians in general that is especially acute in the case of Chinatown opera theaters. More than thirty years' worth of surveillance records for every Chinese person officially entering the United States as an actor, and every petition filed by theaters or troupes, today constitute primary sources for the music history of Chinese America. At the U.S. National Archives and Records Administrations, the Chinese Exclusion Act Case Files and Records contain requests, deliberations, and responses by Department of Labor and theater lawyers regarding petitions for actors' entry permits, quotas, transfers, extensions, travel, and detention and deportation. There are sizeable files for six Cantonese opera theaters or troupes for the years 1921 to 1943 and numerous files of individual performers at all ports of entry. The great volume of official documents bears witness to the ambitious scale of theatrical operations and the large number of performers present during the 1920s and allows this history of Chinatown theaters of the 1920s to emerge in fuller detail.

Nevertheless, in terms of historiography, some fundamental questions about locating Chinatown theaters remain. They are often deemed unimportant, their historical and social significance hidden in the inconsequential traces of local lore or anecdote. Chinatown was not often considered to have a musical history. How does one construct and reintroduce their history into the study of American music life, which has not been paying much attention to music in languages from the other side of the Pacific? How do we reconsider the role and the imprint of transnational figures (performers and troupes) whose continuing presence was essential to the musical culture?

Although corrective historical accounts can work to enrich the dominating narratives, it is not enough merely to provide new details and fill the gaps in the existing history. It does Chinese American music history a disservice to consider Cantonese opera in the 1920s as an innocuous foreign music tradition in multicultural America. Instead, this work situates American music as an active participant in the music practices of the trans-Pacific world. It thus offers a transnational perspective on the historiography of American music that has long focused on its transatlantic connection. By bringing attention to the performing history of Chinatown theaters in the cultural and social memory of different urban spaces, this book provides an important angle on the multivalent formation of American music history.

With its historicized notions of Chinatown theaters and opera genres, this book calls into question popular stereotypes about them. Produced by sensationalist writers for a mainstream readership, accounts in American journals and travelogues portrayed Chinatown theaters as old, unchanging, quirky, opaque, and devoid of imagination. The simplistic and routinely biased reports were long considered the only historical record, and often caricatures were taken as evidence. There has not been a history of this subject that was not constructed from these accounts. Regrettably, as Daphne Lei notes, the English-language sources concerning the nineteenth century have come to be "the best source for constructing 'local history' of Cantonese opera in San Francisco Chinatown."[34] Yet even with the aim of a legitimate portrayal of the theaters, the resulting studies could not easily escape the perspectives of their sources. This book serves to counter these long-standing stereotypes by chronicling performance practice and theater history primarily with Chinese sources. Furthermore, by resurrecting their voices and focusing on the textual traces they left, this study aims to contribute to the historical knowledge of what David Palumbo-Liu calls "a newly defined interiority" created by "the introjection of Asia into the American imaginary."[35] It is from this historically situated perspective that we can better understand the role of Chinese opera theaters in the American music landscape and its relevance to our culture and society today.

In detailing this history, I consider Chinatown theaters to be dynamic, rather than timeless, and shaped by these important factors: (1) the audiences' varied and shifting expectations of the genre; (2) the theaters' places in the community as establishments and cultural institutions; (3) Chinese performers' immigration status as the exclusion laws evolved and the ways immigration enforcement shifted; (4) the interactions between local theaters and the transnational network; and (5) individual performers and their performing styles. These five areas are traced and explored in various forms throughout this book. The individual chapters also wrestle with questions such as the following: How did theaters establish and distinguish themselves? What were their struggles and triumphs? How did rival theaters respond to competition? What constituted their repertoire, rosters of performers, and trends toward modernization? How were aspects of the theaters shaped by audience expectations?

REIMAGINING CHINATOWN THEATERS

As noted by the theater scholar Daphne Lei, Chinese opera was often a source of cultural pride for emigrant Chinese, and merchants "translated their economic success into cultural capital and psychological satisfaction."[36] Indispensable to the theater business were the merchants who sponsored it, as well as the erudite professionals with full command of the classic literary tradition of Cantonese opera. Just as important were vibrant communities that could sustain the theaters' growth. Together, different contingents of the Chinatown community shaped its opera theater. The theaters' success also relied on artists whose virtuosic performances enlivened the stages and made indelible impressions on the collective memory. Many stellar performers came from urban theaters in southern China, which were incubators for professionals who would embark on cross-Pacific journeys during the 1920s. Shanghai had several Cantonese opera theaters as well. That many performers in San Francisco's Chinese theaters were important can be corroborated by favorable reviews of them in the prominent Shanghai newspaper *Shen Bao*.

Print and visual culture played an important role. With the advancement of print media, many Chinese newspapers were published in North America (four major dailies in San Francisco alone). They contributed to the success of the theaters both by dissemination of the content—the daily advertisements of theater programs and opera recordings, reports, and laudatory poems and rhymes—and by the fact that their printing facilities, equipped with Chinese characters, also produced daily playbills and fan pamphlets.[37] A steady production of photographs of performers and stages helped shape the visual culture of Cantonese opera as well. Photography studios such as May's Studio and Suen's Studio of San Francisco, Natural Photo Studio of New York, and Yucho Chow Studio of Vancouver became partners with Chinese theaters. In turn, the contracts with opera theaters contributed to studios' success in the community.[38] May's Studio, for example, maintained a long-term business relationship with the Great China Theater and left us with hundreds of stage photos and performers' portraits. Many similar collaborations occurred between the theaters and other local businesses.

Cantonese opera recordings fostered a new listening culture. Their wide dissemination was beneficial to the theater culture and constituted an additional business opportunity for the theaters as well. New catalogues of opera arias and top singers were released regularly by transnational companies such as Victor, Columbia, and Beka. Their advertisements grew more prominent in Chinese newspapers in North American cities during the decade. Recording engineers and their equipment were sent from the United States to Hong Kong for recording sessions that included famous Cantonese opera singers, in particular those who performed in Chinatown theaters. The joint ventures of theaters and recording companies helped each prosper. Opera recordings were heard in homes, in stores and laundries, and in communities with few opera performances, thus helping foster a wider audience base. The recordings, accompanied by pamphlets containing the lyrics, reached their listeners via both local retail stores and mail order. The Lee Eng Company was the foremost advertiser of recordings in the *Chinese Nationalist Daily* in New York; the firm's advertisements were distinguished by the frequent use of photographs of stars such as Li Xuefang and Li Feifeng.[39] Eventually the theaters launched their own record labels to profit from the business. The Great China Theater, which opened in 1925 in San Francisco, collaborated with Hong Kong merchants in 1927 to start the Oriental Record Company. It was so successful that by 1930 the company had produced nearly two hundred titles in six catalogues.[40]

Affinity groups and other business and cultural organizations played significant roles in maintaining the theaters and facilitating the circulation of performers on the transnational network. These entities had the social power to help promote performers and secure their reputation within the community. The close connections were evident in that opera performers with surnames of prominent family associations received the strongest support. For example, it was unsurprising that star actress Guan Yinglian's well-known patron in San Francisco shared her family name. (See the epilogue.) Furthermore, fundraising events used the personnel and space of the theaters to mobilize community support. Such social functions were crucial, as Tong Soon Lee notes concerning a parallel situation in Singapore: "Chinese opera has served as a form of entertainment as well as an important social and religious component for the Chinese masses[;] . . . they initiated and participated in fund-raising events."[41] Generally, in the United States, as Yong Chen showed in his study of San Francisco, "Theatrical productions . . . reflected and promoted the ideological and social transformation of the community," such that one theater playbill proclaimed that the show was meant to "awaken our fellow countrymen to defend against the insult from outside."[42] Moreover, as Alison Marshall notes, opera performance was "a space to which men seeking non-religious and non-political involvements were drawn."[43] No doubt Cantonese opera provided the most iconic public face of the Chinatown community—a splendid and ideal version of Chinese culture. The performers' participation in social and cultural activities such as parades and fairs actively advanced the community's agenda. At times the local, the transnational, and the global were interwoven. Local concerns were articulated through opera theaters, which were also part of the larger transnational network, while Chinese global initiatives were championed by the theaters in search of support from local communities.

Imagining the Chinatown theaters through their multi-faceted history avoids the usual pitfalls associated with considering them merely as a re-creation of the past. Instead, it focuses on the dynamic ways the operas were presented and situated within their social-historical context and geopolitical reality, rather than as a peripheral cultural production. In fact, Chinatown theaters had a significant role in the Chinese community's creation and practice of cultural activities. As Adam McKeown puts it, "Chinese in the United States saw themselves as much more than a marginalized immigrant group in the early twentieth century. They were keenly aware of global economic and political trends and endeavored to forge a meaningful place for themselves and for China within these changes."[44] These theaters made an important contribution to creating such a place, and they offered an effective way for self-conscious Chinese merchants to shape the image of a culturally sophisticated, modern Chinatown.

In many ways, this book contributes to an understanding of what might be seen as a field of opera culture: the musically, visually, literarily, and dramatically constituted subjectivity. To understand this field of knowledge—its legends, performing styles, performing practices, audience expectations, and discourse—is to understand the Chinese American cultural space.

TRANSNATIONAL CHINATOWN THEATERS IN THE AMERICAN MUSIC SCENE

The transnational history of this cultural space invites us to, on one hand, consider border crossing and accentuate its many hitherto neglected facets, and, on the other, reconsider transnational social practices in local contexts. In *The Rise of Cantonese Opera,* Wing Chung Ng connects dots on the world canvas to relate a history that includes both South China and "theatrical sojourns in neighboring

Southeast Asia and distant North America since the mid-nineteenth century."[45] The arena of Cantonese opera in the 1920s ranged from Australia to the Americas and from Southeast Asia to England. Cantonese opera theaters and troupes were essentially transnational businesses because they relied on strong border-crossing networks, and their activities therefore involved continuing interaction between individual actors of different nations. Many performers garnered fame in Southeast Asia before gaining stardom in Hong Kong; the birthplace for top performers could as easily have been Singapore, the major hub for Cantonese opera in Southeast Asia, as South China; the cross-Pacific route was one among many in the network.

In North America the transnationality of Cantonese theaters' operation was apparent: local theaters drew financial sponsors from across the continent; sprawling networks of kinship facilitated movement on the performing circuit; prominent merchants such as Chin Lain (in San Francisco) or Yip Sang (in Vancouver) took up Cantonese opera as part of their multinational commerce, operating theaters and theatrical supply importing firms. In various American cities, theaters helped create the infrastructure of cultural life in the communities through transnational operations. The theaters secured transnational performers, as well as venues, advertisements, and local protections, to ensure the lively daily performances. The local operatic engagement was so meaningful that, though they might be considered transient by some, performers had lasting influence on the local community. Their talent, glamour, and skills were key to the community's loyalty to the theaters. Regardless of the length of their stay, their rigorous marshaling of singing, acting, dancing, and other skills established the practices of the theaters and formed the large repository of music. Furthermore, the repertoire and practices that they brought from city to city resulted in a homogeneous transnational opera culture shared by Chinese communities of this era all over North America.

In the 1920s, when they re-established themselves in American cities, Chinatown theaters entered the Roaring Twenties, a time of unprecedented prosperity in the United States and of an immense appetite for cultural novelty and diversity. Chinese themes were fashionable, in well-established and fast-rising genres, at grand commercial productions and school plays, and in metropolises and small cities. Yellowface dramas had been staged with great commercial success since late nineteenth century. Operas such as Franco Leoni's *L'Oracolo* kept the public mesmerized by depictions of Chinatown onstage. Fascination for Chinese themes helped drum up the great enthusiasm for the posthumous grand premiere of Giacomo Puccini's *Turandot* in 1926. If skits of "Chinese opera" in revues such as variety shows and vaudeville houses had been popular for the preceding decades, the audiences of the 1920s were drawn to the trope in musicals and opera of the day. Chinese topics were also popular in sheet music, troping Chinese with melodies with open fifths and pentatonicism. The trope of Chinese opera shaped commercial entertainment in various forms.

When taking part in the new scene of American entertainment, Chinatown theaters were well aware of this fascination, the consumption of the imagined, exotic Chinese as entertainment. They prepared for it as a cultural interlocutor. The earliest troupes brought bilingual playbills for mixed audiences, mobilized English-language news media to bring attention to the star actresses, and booked large revue theaters for the troupes' premieres. The stage was designed with a contemporary sensibility of realism, a reflection of the image of modern Chinatown in the 1920s. If the troupe adapted its performance for the consumption of mainstream America, it was offering serious and often grand presentation of opera with the best performers they could recruit.

Nevertheless, Cantonese opera theaters in the 1920s never became popular among mainstream Americans in the way non-Chinese ones troping Chinese opera did. The sharp difference between the two cannot be bridged. As the media scholar Sabine Haenni points out, while the Chinese community considered Cantonese opera to be its leisure culture, the mass culture appropriated all of Chinatown as its object of leisure.[46] As their playbills and stage photos show, cultural distinctiveness and sophistication were the anchors of Chinatown theaters and enticements for financial investment and audiences. So even without the mainstream society's support, the strong audience base of Chinese communities kept opera theaters prosperous and the transnational performing circuit network bustling. Over the years the professional operation grew immensely owing to the frequent appearance of many stellar performers. Furthermore, the opera theaters provided a social space that served as an intersection and point of contact where musical and theatrical representations were readily accessible to the large urban population and where intricate familial, business, and operatic networks intersected with the local community to work the magic. As such they "promoted new forms of individual and collective identity"[47] and continued to attract generations of non-Chinese spectators, musicians, actors, dancers, writers, and so on. In their work, the music and stagecraft of Chinatown theaters were recast and transformed, and they gave rise to much progressive, experimental, and influential modern American music, dance, and theater.[48]

PLAN OF THE BOOK

This book constructs a five-part narrative of the history of Chinese theaters in America during the 1920s. The first two parts provide the historical, social, and aesthetic background for the chronicle of the theaters in the latter three parts. Part I offers various historical contexts. Chapter 1 provides a discussion of the transnational, social, and cultural histories that helped shape the U.S. Chinatown theater constellation. It considers the symbolic significance of the language and the impact of transnational business networks. Chapter 2 is devoted to the complicated regulatory and cultural history of Chinese American music spaces, tracing the treatment of Chinese performers within American immigration history and its various effects. It identifies a turning point that involved the American popular entertainment industry's intervention into the Chinese exclusionary policies. It is followed by a case study in Chapter 3 that examines close-up one theater's tug-of-war with the Immigration Bureau to gain legitimacy. This chapter portrays daily life under exclusionist laws and considers the question of the performers' legal status within the nation-state. Part II focuses on the practice of Cantonese opera in the 1920s. Chapter 4 provides the genre's history and describes 1920s practice, including role types, repertoire, and music, as well as an important part of the opera production—playbills. Chapter 5 presents a study of a famous aria based on historical recordings in order to provide a glimpse of its sonic world. Transcriptions of the recordings are made to further the discussion of the lyric-melodic patterns and sonic characteristics. Although the use of Western notation in transcription is imperfect at best, it nonetheless fills the void in the documented representation of this sonic space in American music history.

Part III focuses on the Pacific Northwest connection. Chapter 6 examines the scene in Canada that led to the return of Cantonese opera to the United States in 1922. The companies and troupes commenced the golden age of Chinatown theater and would eventually give rise to the prosperous and influential Great China Theater. Chapters 7 and 8 chronicle its performing history in its various aspects: repertoire, programming, performers, theatrical professionals, and new ventures in phonograph records. Part IV considers the history of a homegrown theater. Chapters 9 and 10 trace the development of the Mandarin Theater as the first Chinese theater built in San Francisco in that decade, as well as its fierce rivalry with Great China Theater, through which it gained a reputation as a theater of actresses and staged many of the top actresses of the decade. Part V considers the spread of theaters on the transnational network, as well as the transnational operation itself. Chapter 11 traces the work of troupes and theaters in Toronto, Boston, and New York and their distinctive development on the East Coast. Chapter 12 examines theatrical companies that ventured into Honolulu, Vancouver, and Havana and brings attention to a case study of transnational network based on kinship. The book closes with an epilogue that reflects on Chinatown opera theaters' impact on the local community, as well as other aspects of American music.

PART I

TRANSNATIONAL HISTORY AND IMMIGRATION

CHAPTER 1

SHAPING FORCES, NETWORKS, AND LOCAL INFLUENCES

A focus on the transnational, with its emphasis on multiple sites and exchange, can potentially transform the figure of the "other" from a representational construct to a social actor.

—Mae Ngai, "Promises and Perils of Transnational History"

The first decades of the twentieth century constituted an important phase of cultural production for Chinese Americans of which Chinatown theaters were an important part. This chapter considers the multinational histories, transnational forces, and local influences at work that made the theaters so prosperous in the 1920s. Considering both sides of the Pacific allows us to keep in view the various social activities, historical actors, and transnational networks that affected the remarkable growth of Chinese theaters in North America in this period.

CHINESE MIGRATION AND OPERA THEATERS

The first large-scale Chinese migration to the United States came from the Pearl River Delta of Guangdong Province in the mid-nineteenth century. It was part of a global migration from southern China that included not only people following intra-Asian trade routes but also indentured servants going to Cuba and Peru and people going to Australia and the United States (primarily of their own volition and with their own money).[1] Early immigrants were attracted by the California gold rush; later they came to build railroads, develop agriculture and fisheries along the Pacific Coast, work on plantations in Hawaii, operate laundries, and work in the export-import business.[2] By 1869, when the construction of the Central Pacific Railroad was near completion, 90 percent of the workforce of ten thousand people was Chinese.[3] Between 1852 and 1882 (the year in which the Chinese Exclusion Act was passed by Congress), more than three hundred thousand Chinese entered the United States. Anti-Chinese riots, as well as the completion of the railroad, drove these Chinese immigrants to urban areas, where they formed communities. Such ethnic enclaves, while reinforcing cultural ties among residents and shielding the populace from racial hostility, did not always arise by choice: many restrictive covenants or zoning laws limited the areas where Chinese and other Asians could reside. In San Francisco, for example, Chinese residents were forced to live in one area of the city. (In 1929, the area roughly ran three blocks from Kearny Street north to Powell Street, and five blocks from Sacramento Street east to Broadway Street.)[4] The Chinese exclusion law and its extensions were not repealed until 1943.

Starting in the mid-nineteenth century, Cantonese opera troupes accompanied immigrants to the United States. Following the Hong Fook Tong troupe's 1852 debut Chinese theaters burgeoned in San Francisco, often with several theaters operating concurrently, including Hing Chuen Yuen (at the Union Theater in the 1860s), Yun Henn Choy (Royal Chinese Theater, Jackson Street, about 1874), Look Sun Fung (Peacock Theater, Washington Street, about 1877), Quan San Yoke (Gem of Mount Quan, Jackson Street, about 1878), Dam Quai Yuen (Washington Street, about 1878), Yee Quan Ying (Grand Theater, Washington Street, about 1879), and the Wing Ti Ping Company (about 1879). Because Chinese immigrants in the early days were working in gold mines in California, troupes regularly toured "the Mother Lode circuit"—smaller towns with sizable Chinese populations.[5] Chinese theaters were opened at towns such as Locke, Marysville, Nevada City, Oroville, and San Juan.[6] The Chinese community in New York, New York, likewise founded the Chinese Theater (Doyer Street, 1893).[7] Sacramento also had a very successful theater as early as 1855; Portland had a brick purpose-built theater in 1879, and by 1890, when it boasted the second largest Chinese community in America, had three theaters on its popular Second Street.[8] Unfortunately, we only have incomplete knowledge about the performances given in these theaters. Contemporary travelogues and reports noted that the audiences ranged from Chinese elite merchants to store clerks, menial laborers, and non-Chinese locals and tourists. Indeed, Chinese theaters were frequently advertised in English newspapers such as the *Sacramento Union Daily*, *Daily Alta California*, and *San Francisco Call*. And as several memoirs revealed, the theaters were also frequented by Chinese house servants or laundry workers.[9] Opera theaters invariably constituted the public face of Chinese American communities. When Hing Chuen Yuen, the first permanent Chinese theater in San Francisco, opened in 1868, the opening drew about a hundred of the city's dignitaries, including members of the legal profession, the state legislature, and the city's Board of Supervisors. When a new theater was erected in August 1874, the grand opening reportedly was viewed by eighteen hundred spectators, and attendees including judges and the chief of police were treated to a banquet and rituals.[10] Just as important, these theaters provided the performers and paraphernalia needed by the community for colorful public processions on festive occasions and holidays.

Because of changing political and social situations (in particular, the anti-Chinese movement and exclusion laws, which are discussed in Chapter 3), the fortunes of Chinatown theaters waxed and waned. The history is marked by two golden periods: the late 1870s and the 1920s.[11] The vibrancy of the theaters in the 1920s was apparent from their large casts of professional singers and musicians and daily performances of elaborate programs, in spite of the prevalence of radios, phonograph records, and later, motion pictures. During that decade Chinese theaters were established in several major U.S. cities. Many of them continued operating into the 1940s, although by the mid-1930s they were no longer at their prime. These Chinatown theaters formed a circuit for Cantonese opera performance. Nine theaters established during this decade are shown in table 1.1.

The majority were opened between 1922 and 1925. The Mandarin Theater and the Great China Theater in San Francisco were the two key players (and rivals) there, both because of their size—employing and thus bringing in the largest number of performers in the United States—and because of their political and social affiliations. The Mandarin was affiliated with the Constitutionalist Party (successor to the Chinese Empire Reform Association, which advocated for a constitutional monarchy and peaceful reform), while the Great China Theater was associated with the Nationalist Party of China (which advocated for revolution and a republic). Their operations led to offshoots in Los Angeles and Vancouver, as well as long-term engagements in Seattle, Portland, and cities as far away as Mexicali, Mexico City, and Havana. Companies also were established on the East Coast, and, though smaller, their roles in the Cantonese opera network should not be underestimated. The two theaters in New York quickly aligned themselves with the two San Francisco theaters and became important stops in the larger network, operating as a gateway to Havana for opera performers. The businesses in San Francisco and New York became intertwined with those in Canada and Cuba. While the last three theaters listed in the table no doubt also played a role in this decade, close consideration awaits a time when more historical documents about them become available.

Table 1.1. Chinese Opera Theaters in the United States in the 1920s

City	Company name	Troupe name	Location/Theater	Opening date
San Francisco	Lun On Company	Renshou Nian	Crescent Theater	October 5, 1922
Seattle	Lun Hop Company	Le Wannian	Orpheum Theater	February 1923
San Francisco	Lun Hop Company	Renshou Nian/Le Wannian	Crescent Theater	February 24, 1923
Los Angeles	Lun Hop Company	n/a	Vienna Buffet	February 1925
San Francisco	Lun Hop Company	Great China	Great China Theater	June 19, 1925
San Francisco	Mandarin Theatrical Company	Mandarin	Mandarin Theater	June 26, 1924
Los Angeles	Mandarin Theatrical Company	Mandarin	323 Jackson Street	March 1925
Boston	Lin Yick Company	Lok Tin Tsau	23 Edinboro Street	November 1922
New York	Lin Yick Company	Lok Tin Tsau	Thalia Theater	July 1925
New York		Jock Ming On	Old Bowery Theater	July 9, 1924
New York	Woh Hing Company	Yong Ni Shang	Thalia Theater	March 17, 1927
Honolulu	Kue Hing Company	Guo Fengnian	Liberty Theater	July 1923
Chicago	Tai Wing Wah (Choy Ding Quay; The Grandview Company)	Tai Wing Wah	Avenue Theatre	ca. 1924
Seattle/Portland	Tai Ping Young Company	Tai Ping Young		ca. 1924
Los Angeles	All-Star Company	All-Star		ca. 1924

SHAPING FORCES: NATIONAL, POLITICAL, AND CULTURAL

The success of Chinese theater companies in the 1920s emerged from a nexus of political, economic, social, and cultural trends that spanned continents. This section considers some of these major forces, with the exception of U.S. immigration laws, which are the focus of Chapter 2. I start with a brief historical sketch of China in late Qing Dynasty and early Republic.

Defeated by the British Empire in the First Opium War (1840), China signed the Treaty of Nanking (1842), ceding Hong Kong to Great Britain and agreeing to the importation of opium produced by British possessions. Afterward, repeated military defeats and unequal treaties with imperial powers exposed the weakness of the late imperial Qing government, giving rise to rebellions, which further weakened imperial authority, leading to its overthrow. For example, in 1900 China was invaded by the Eight-Nation Alliance, consisting of British, Japanese, Russian, Italian, German, French, U.S., and Austrian troops, who demanded further concessions from the Qing government. After the Chinese Revolution of 1911, the Republic of China was proclaimed but was soon followed by a period of shifting coalitions of competing provincial warlords. After World War I, the Treaty of Versailles awarded China's Shandong Peninsula to Japan, and the Chinese government's failure to respond touched off the May Fourth Movement in 1919. This important social movement, which marked an upsurge in Chinese nationalism and a shift toward political mobilization, modernity, and Western ideology, continued until 1921. The decade of the 1920s in China was prosperous, albeit marked by conflicts and protests against imperialism. The most significant of these was the Canton–Hong Kong Strike (June 1925 to October 1926), which paralyzed the economy in Hong Kong. During the 1925 strike, all urban Cantonese opera theaters in the region were shut down (see Chapter 7). Both the May Fourth movement and the 1925 strike had significant impacts on U.S. Chinatown theaters. The May Fourth movement propelled the cultural reform that embraced modernization and helped increase the popularity of modern spoken drama, and the 1925 strike prompted many Cantonese opera performers to turn to North America for performing opportunities in late 1925 and 1926.

The presence of foreign powers in China since the nineteenth century also resulted in the rise of transnational contact zones, bringing together the languages and social and cultural practices of different nations. Treaty ports (port cities in China opened to foreign trade and residence beginning in the mid-nineteenth century) and colonies, notably Tianjin (which contained the concessions of nine foreign countries starting in 1901), Guangzhou, Shanghai (where international settlement had existed since 1863), and Hong Kong, were both trade entrepôts and modern cosmopolitan cities. Hong Kong and Shanghai were major hubs for trans-Pacific steamships. Some of these cities were home to the earliest modern Cantonese opera theaters. In Hong Kong, for example, the Taiping Theater, opened in 1904, could accommodate one thousand people. In Guangzhou the Hai-Zhou Theater opened in 1902, and the Le-Shang Theater opened in 1905. Even in Shanghai, where many different genres of Chinese opera competed, Cantonese merchants built their own theaters, and Cantonese opera was often credited with exerting a modernizing influence on the other genres, as it led the way in incorporating electric stage props and Western instruments. The city's leading newspaper, *Shen Bao*, published frequent reviews of Cantonese opera performances between 1915 and 1930. Cross-pollination abounded among different opera genres, as well as between opera and popular music at teahouses and nightclubs in these cosmopolitan centers. These developments shaped the practices of Chinatown theaters in significant ways.

In the United States, by the end of the nineteenth century representations of Chinese culture increased in popular entertainment such as musical comedies, plays, passing shows, and musical revues. The immensely successful *The First Born* (1897) by Francis Powers and David Belasco was one of the first shows that attempted to play Chinese-sounding music throughout and depict Chinatown in a "realistic way."[12] As discussed by the historian Krystyn Moon, the show's songwriter used melodies he heard in Chinatown. In addition, the term *Chinese opera* had been used regularly to refer to popular operettas such as *The Mandarin* (1896) by Reginald De Koven or musical comedies by English lyricists and composers such as *San Toy* (1899), *A Chinese Honey Moon* (1899), and *Chin Chin* (1914). Two powerful vaudeville chains, the Pantages Circuit and the Orpheum Circuit, built theaters across the United States and Canada between 1910 and 1920 and played to people of multiple economic strata. In these shows foreign entertainers were generally popular, drawing audiences looking for exotic and novel spectacles. Popular acts included acrobats and tumblers from Japan, the Yokoi Acrobatic Troupe (1919), the Compañía Virginia Fábregas from Mexico (1917), dancers and acrobats from North Africa, and Chinese acrobats such as Ching Ling He and Tia Pen troupes. In the 1920s, which marked a period of dramatic change in favor of an urban, industrial, consumer-oriented society, genres such as musical theater gradually replaced variety shows and operettas became an important form of live performance. The growth of phonograph machines, recordings, radio and cinema, Tin Pan Alley, and jazz also came to have tremendous impact on popular entertainment. In light of this, the return of Chinatown theaters showed optimism because the 1920s embodied the cultural milieu of modern America, where the commercial success of many forms of entertainment suggests a diversity of musical taste.

Yet at the same time racial prejudice was rampant at many levels of American society. This decade was marked by the hardship and prejudice typical of the Jim Crow era, racial hostility (such as the flourishing of the Ku Klux Klan), and immigration policies that sanctioned racial hierarchy (the Immigration Act of 1924). In the name of job protection, the American Federation of Musicians and the Actors' Equity Association pushed for a ban on all foreign performers in the United States and were at the forefront of the national policy debate about restricting their entry, though they did not succeed.[13] The prejudice and unequal treatment prompted African Americans to form the Colored Actors' Union in 1921. Musical aesthetics also was not insulated from racial prejudice. Composer and educator Daniel Gregory Mason lamented that "the music of the whole world has battered our ears . . . the confusion of traditions among us is disastrously bewildering . . . Where shall we recapture our native tongue?"[14] Such a racial bias had its counterpart in the national political agenda, which in effect made Chinese performers unwelcome at the borders (as discussed in Chapter 2).

In the neighboring countries Cantonese opera was thriving with few restrictions on Chinese performers, and the theater scene was lively despite varying degrees of anti-Chinese sentiment. In Canada, the performance scene flourished in the second decade of the century. As early as 1858 the Fraser Canyon gold rush attracted an influx of miners and prospectors from North America, Europe, China, the West Indies, and elsewhere. Later, when Canadian prime minister John A. Macdonald promised to "unite Canada by rail," an even larger Chinese labor force arrived between 1881 and 1885 for the construction of the Canadian Pacific Railway (CPR).[15] The CPR hired 7,000 Chinese workers from California and 5,000 from China. Between 1881 and 1884, 17,501 Chinese from China, San Francisco, and Puget Sound landed in Victoria.[16] At the same time, anti-Chinese sentiment had been growing since the 1870s; bylaws and ordinances targeted Chinese immigrants, and riots broke out. In 1885, after the report of the Royal Commission on Chinese Immigration, the federal government passed the Chinese Immigration Act, imposing a head tax on Chinese immigrants to discourage them from entering Canada. Over time the head tax increased sharply from the initial $50 to $100 in 1900 and $500 in 1903. The high head tax did not deter Chinese communities from thriving, however. Table 1.2 shows the Chinese population in Canada by province for 1910.[17] The large population of Chinese in British Columbia prompted the arrival of opera troupes. Chinese theaters were established early on in Victoria and held regular performances. In Vancouver's Shanghai Alley, a Chinese theater was built in 1898 with five hundred seats. After 1910, however, troupes staged operas in Victoria and Vancouver and many theaters opened, holding daily performances. In Vancouver, two theaters operated concurrently well into the 1920s and provided important impetus for the development of the larger performing circuit in North America.[18]

Table 1.2. Chinese population of Canada, 1901 and 1910

Province	Major cities	1901	1910
Alberta	Calgary Edmonton Lethbridge	235	1,787
British Columbia	Cumberland Nanaimo Vancouver Victoria	14,885	19,568
Manitoba	Winnipeg	206	885
Ontario	Toronto	732	2,766
Quebec	Montreal Quebec City	1,057	1,578
Saskatchewan	Moose Jaw Saskatoon	41	957
Others		156	233
Total		17,312	27,774

Source: *Canada Year Book 1915* (Ottawa: Dominion Bureau of Statistics, Department of Trade and Commerce, 1916).

In Cuba the Chinese population reached 58,400 in 1872. But the population dwindled drastically by the early twentieth century owing to economic instability, social hostility, and exclusionary practices. A turning point came after 1914 when Cuba's sugar production expanded as a result of increasing demand in global market. The Chinese population grew from 11,217 in 1907 to 24,674 in 1931. In the mid-1920s the Chinatown in Havana emerged as an economically and culturally vibrant area called Centro Habana.[19] The large population of Chinese long relied on Chinese theaters for leisure activity. As early as 1875 a Chinese theater was established in Havana, and other cities followed suit. A three-story theater was built in 1876 in Sagua la Grande, where a company of ninety-four members played its opening night.[20] Research for this book was not conducted in Cuba, but the references encountered in the U.S. immigration documents and newspapers show that during the 1920s, theaters in Havana mostly contracted for actors directly from China or San Francisco, and Havana was a busy hub for Chinese opera performers well into the 1930s.

The lively Cantonese opera scene of these two U.S. neighbors helped North America remain a viable destination for performers, in turn greatly facilitating the return of Chinese theaters to the United States in the 1920s. Countries such as Mexico and Peru, which experienced significant Chinese migration between 1850 and 1930, also took part in this large cultural network. Music was, after all, a means of survival, and immigration documents regularly show that Chinese performers arrived in the United States from Lima, Mexicali, or Mexico City throughout the

1920s. Unfortunately, historical documents are unavailable with which to piece together either these cities' theater history or their role in the performing network.

Multifarious transnational, political, social, and cultural forces propelled the 1920s renaissance of Chinatown theaters in United States. As we will see, a dire situation in one nation could become a stimulant for another; the countries were linked in many interesting ways, and the complexity of the layers grew over time. They point to the volatile circumstances that shaped the eventual rise of the network of Chinatown opera theaters in North America, to which I now turn.

NORTH AMERICAN CITIES AND THE THEATER NETWORK

In 1890 the Chinese population in America was 107,488 of a total U.S. population of 62.9 million. More than three-quarters of them were in the cities and larger towns of northern California and the Pacific Northwest.[21] In 1910 the Chinese population, including Hawaii and Alaska, was reduced to 94,414, of a total U.S. population of 92.2 million, as the effect of Chinese exclusion could be felt.[22] Table 1.3 lists the eight areas with the highest concentration of Chinese on the U.S. mainland in 1910, 1920, and 1930. This table shows that the Chinese community in the San Francisco Bay area was by far the largest, while New York's Chinese population grew quickly. All maintained a large enough Chinese population to have Chinatowns, and all, except for Philadelphia, supported Chinese theaters during the 1920s. The Chinese population in 1930 of these cities combined was 40,341, which accounted for about 53 percent of the total Chinese population in United States (74,954).[23] That this population was concentrated in urban areas no doubt helped Chinatown theaters prosper. In addition, contrary to the common perception that it was a bachelor society, the table reveals a high proportion of native-born individuals. It reflects a sizable second generation of Chinese Americans, corroborated by the continued opening of new Chinese schools and regular meetings of Native Sons of Golden State (later renamed the Chinese American Citizens Alliance), whose goals were to fight for citizens' rights.[24] The large number of the native-born also underscores the importance of opera attendance as part of family life.

Major cities in North America were key players in facilitating the transnational network of Cantonese opera performers in the 1920s. A map showing the spatial distribution is provided in figure 1.1. From Honolulu, performers on the trans-Pacific journey traveled to major cities across North America. The network benefited from advancements in technology—speedy steamships and railroads—that expedited travel.[25] In the Pacific Northwest, the steamships of the "Triangle Route" (Victoria–Vancouver–Seattle) swiftly facilitated the return of the first troupe to the United States in 1922 (see chapter 6). The fleet known as the "Princesses of

Table 1.3. The eight areas with the highest concentration of Chinese on the U.S. mainland, 1910, 1920, and 1930

Area	City	Total			Native			Foreign-born		
		1910	1920	1930	1910	1920	1930	1910	1920	1930
Boston	Boston	1,192	1,075	1,595	376	333	636	816	742	959
	Cambridge	83	81	133	23	21	53	60	60	80
Chicago	Chicago	1,778	2,353	2,757	455	708	933	1,323	1,645	1,824
Los Angeles	Los Angeles	1,954	2,062	3,009	476	802	1,421	1,478	1,260	1,588
New York	New York	4,614	5,642	8,414	710	1,684	1,926	3,904	3,958	6,488
	Newark	231	281	647	35	59	233	196	222	414
Philadelphia	Philadelphia	997	869	1,672	122	167	649	875	702	1,023
Portland	Portland	5,608	1,846	1,416	613	609	786	5,085	1,237	630
San Francisco	Oakland	3,609	3,821	3,048	1,086	1,225	1,682	2,523	2,596	1,366
	San Francisco	10,582	7,744	16,303	3,675	3,294	7,754	6,907	4,450	8,549
Seattle	Seattle	924	1,351	1,347	207	455	621	717	896	726
Subtotal		31,572	27,125	40,341	**7,778**	**9,357**	**16,694**	**23,884**	**17,768**	**23,647**
Percentage of U.S. total		44.13%	44.0%	53.8%						
Total U.S. Chinese		71,531	61,639	74,954						

Source: U.S. Census Bureau, *Fifteenth Census of the United States* (Washington, DC: Government Printing Office, 1930).

the Canadian Pacific Railway" with ships named *Victoria*, *Adelaide*, and so on) was a primary conduit for a large number of Cantonese opera performers. On the opposite side of the continent, SS *Siboney*, *Orizaba*, and *Yucatan* and the Cuba Mail Steamship Company transported Chinese performers between New York and Havana. Immigrant documents show that the steamship lines of the Gulf of Mexico also provided popular routes between Havana, Tampico, New Orleans, and Key West, bringing Cantonese opera performers to the latter two ports.

The circulation of performers also involved other distinctive means of transportation. From Montreal, they traveled by train to enter the United States through Vermont or by water through Ellis Island. The Mexican Central Railway, finished after 1910, expedited journeys to Mexico City or Tampico from the U.S. border. Crossing the Mexican border was different on the Pacific Coast: performers often traveled between Mexicali and Calexico but were typically "on foot," according to the immigration documents. And at Los Angeles, they sometimes arrived via steamship from Lima, Peru, where Chinese theater was founded as early as 1869.[26] There were smaller venues and more occasional routes not shown here, such as Key West and New Orleans, where performers sometimes landed, and Fresno or Sacramento, where frequent performances took place. While the Chinese communities shown in figure 1.1 varied both in size and character, they were similarly entertained by opera—often by the same performers—as well as opera-related cultural activities such as literary societies (sharing poems, poetic couplets, or rhymes), community opera listening sessions held by shopkeepers, and commentaries or laudatory poems in daily Chinese-language newspapers.[27] Daily advertisements of playbills could be found in newspapers such as the *Chinese Times* (Vancouver), the *Young China*, the *World Journal*, and *Chung Sai Yat Po* (San Francisco), the *Chinese Nationalist Daily* (New York), and *Kai Ming Gong Bao* (Havana). Large circuits were formed as well: the region made up of the Pacific Northwest triangle and San Francisco saw the frequent movement of performers between Vancouver and San Francisco.[28] Further south along the coastline, the route from San Francisco to Mexicali via Los Angeles was busy as well. The rotation of artists between countries helped keep the total number of them within the official quota approved by the government, which by 1926 was 355 for the United States and Territories. This figure was based on the sum of the individual quotas for various theaters granted by the Department of Labor (see Chapter 2).

The map of the performing network shown in figure 1.1 foregrounds the effects of transnationalism on cultural production, namely, the crossings of national boundaries, the emergent meaning of such crossings, the formation of new borderlines around regions, and the forging of new cultural forms and identities grounded in North America's particular historical location. The circulation of opera performance ensured strong cultural ties between regions as well as oft-used pathways

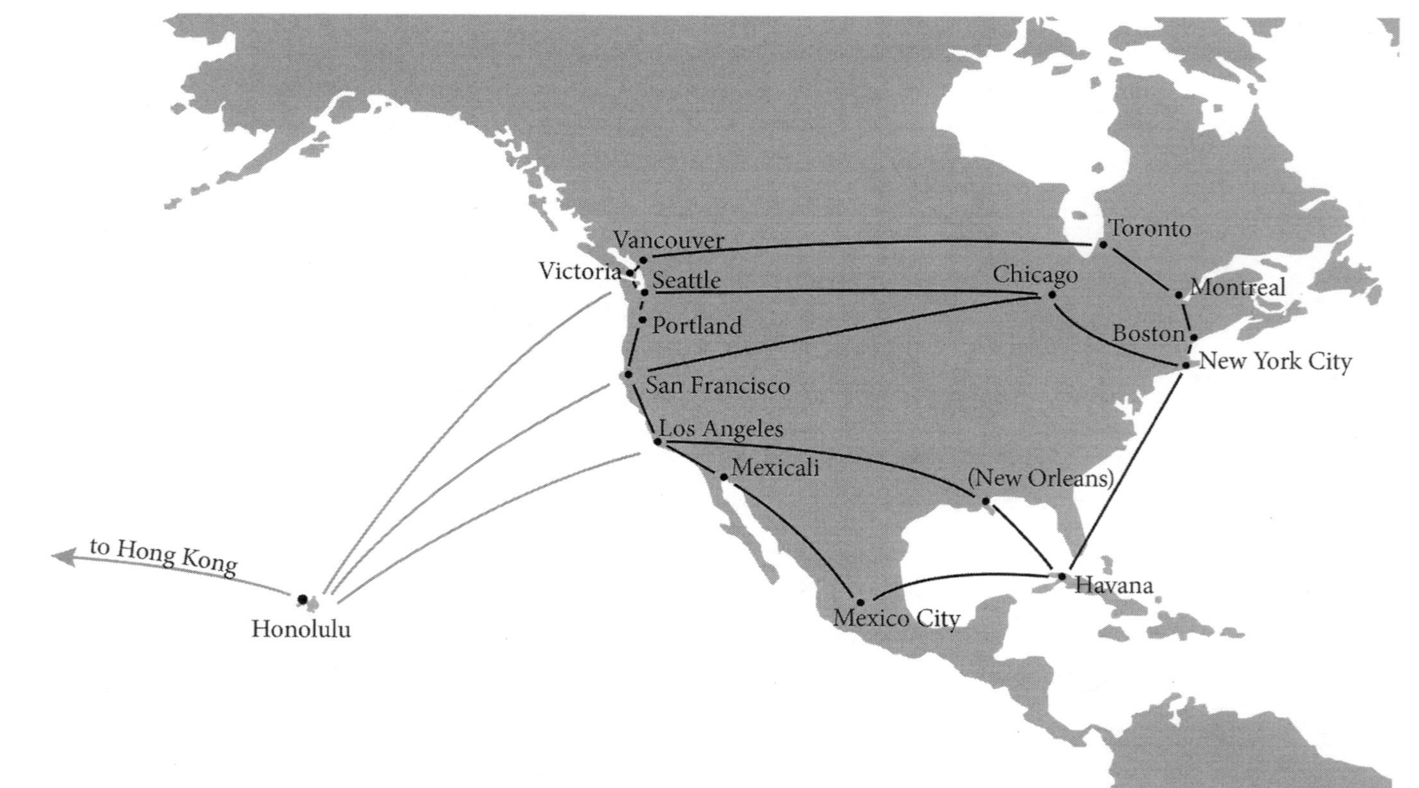

Fig. 1.1. Performing networks of Cantonese opera in North America in the 1920s.

within certain regions. This map can be read as the cartography of the mobility of Cantonese opera in Chinese America in the 1920s. When considered against the movement of better-known genres in the American musical landscape, such as the great migration of African American jazz musicians to Chicago and New York between 1910 and 1930, or the route of vaudeville performers through the chain of theaters built by dominant circuits such as the Orpheum, this map serves to connect Chinese Americans to analyses of circulation in the musical geography of North America.[29]

TRANSNATIONAL CONTACT ZONE

Figure 1.1 could also be read as adding a complex layer to the urban musical spaces of North America. Not only could every city here be considered as a node in the network of Cantonese opera performance of the 1920s, but the reverse was just as important: Cantonese opera was a constituent of these cities' urban (music) histories.[30] When Cantonese opera reappeared in lower Manhattan in 1925 at the Bowery's aging theater The Thalia, the *New York Times* reflected on the ramifications of its residency for the city's long tradition of immigrant theaters.[31] Later, the musicians were brought into institutions such as New School of Social Research when Charles Seeger and Henry Cowell offered the United States' first "world music" course in 1933.[32] They prompted many forms of creative emulation that crossed social classes in Americans' leisure time. For example, the annual Grove plays (theatrical productions) of San Francisco's famed Bohemian Club and the output of members such as Joseph Redding's *Land of Happiness* (1917) and *Fay-Yen-Fah* (1924)—the latter to be the first American opera to be staged in Europe (Monte Carlo, 1925)—were not only indebted to the city's Cantonese opera theaters. Since the Bohemian Club's founding in 1872, it had been situated at the southeast corner of Chinatown. That characteristic spatial relationship, as scholar Anthony Lee pointed out, "enabled the men to lay claim to a distinctly bohemian sensibility and identity, shaped and given substance by their trips to Chinatown."[33]

In the 1920s American cities saw a broad spectrum of diversity within their urban space. The quick rise of jazz, dancing halls, and musicals dramatically energized theater and musical entertainment. The 1927–1928 season was a high point in Broadway history, with 250 new shows.[34] That season also saw the premiere of the first successful musical, the highly influential *Show Boat*, marking a major milestone in establishing the new genre of book musicals. The reputations of blues and jazz musicians such as Bessie Smith and Louis Armstrong grew immensely, while from Tin Pan Alley still emerged many major hit songs. George Gershwin wrote *Rhapsody in Blue* (1924), and Al Jolson became the biggest star on Broadway, frequently in blackface. The different genres contested and affirmed national identities.

From Los Angeles to Chicago, Mexican theaters flourished throughout the decade, and in New York Yiddish theaters were enjoying a second golden period. Musical practices were evoked by the "transnational habitus" (a term from Bourdieu coined by Luis Guarnizo), by which people's dispositions, values, aesthetics, or choices of actions were derived from their transnational positioning and experiences.[35] In particular, Chinatown theaters employed various strategies to address local expectations, contested terrains of belonging, and identification. They were shaped both by conventions they adopted for interpreting and imagining Chinese historical legends in these urban environments, and by their existence as transnational entities.[36] In his discussion of transnationalism in Shanghai in the early years of the Republic of China, the historian Arif Dirlik points out two important senses of the term. The first is one that combines the crossing of national boundaries with the generation of new differences that produce local, heterogeneous identities. The second is one that takes note of the coming together of different nations that forges new and dynamic identities unconstrained by a homogeneous national culture.[37] Both involve translation, hybridity, transformation, and resistance. The transnational habitus in both senses was significant to the formation of Chinatown opera theaters and the social practices they generated in these North American cities. These contact zones engendered "the imagination of the community in multiplicity of ways, which also mediate the imagination of the nation."[38] In other words, transnationality became a constituent part of these cities' identity. As transnational habitus was tied to locality, the social and political context of these Chinatown theaters affected their forms, opportunities, and institutions.

TRANSNATIONALITY AND LANGUAGE

As the U.S. government continued in the 1920s to fortify the border against Chinese immigrants, Chinatown theaters provided both institutional structure and activities for immigrants within and across national borders. Language plays an important role in a multilayered transnational community. From the linguistic perspective, Chinatown theater as a practice was particularly meaningful in the intersection of the local and the transnational in the 1920s. The language's significance was magnified given the social and political climate, and the expressive and dramatic usage of language on the Chinese opera stage had great impact on the spectators. Chinese functioned both as a language (in the collective sense, because many regional dialects—Cantonese, Taishanese, Hokkien, Teochew, Mandarin Chinese, and so on—coexisted in the North American communities of this time)[39] and as a cultural signifier that crossed national borders. The role of Chinese is complex and dynamic. For example, Chinese was set side by side with English on the theater playbills produced for special occasions such as the staging of the decade's first theatrical troupe[40] (see Chapter 6). At a time when stereotypes of Chinese permeated American popular culture, this tactic was part of the theater's optimistic, if not always successful, effort to establish itself as equal to other theatrical entertainments, glossing over the antagonism toward the language associated with the target of exclusion. The bilingual playbills underscored the transnational context within which the theaters operated. Chinese script, as a cultural signifier and an opaque text, functioned as part of a "bridge discourse" in the form of respectability that mediated between the cultural arenas of Chinatown and mainstream society.

For Chinese Americans, the rhetorical styles, interpretive strategies, and semiotic systems involved in Chinese language gave meaning to the beliefs, practices, and social relationships of their community. It also functioned as a means of perseverance in the face of social constraints. Chinese literacy was crucial in producing social relationships and creating literary, musical, and artistic works. Until 1954 Chinese children attended a segregated public school in San Francisco. According to the scholar Marlon Hom, they typically received inferior education in the English language, and until the 1930s few excelled in creative writing in English.[41] The generally forbidding social environment for Chinese Americans, even the youngsters, was spelled out by an official of Stanford University in the 1920s:

> It is almost impossible to place a Chinese or a Japanese of either the first or second generation in any kind of position, engineering, manufacturing, or business. Many firms have general regulations against employing them; others object to them on the ground that the other men employed by the firms do not care to work with them.[42]

With little chance of advancement in English-speaking America and a fractured sense of belonging to a nation in which they held citizenship, Chinese American youth acquired Chinese literacy in order to succeed and attain positions within the community. Many were ready to pursue extended Chinese education, with tutors and in language schools, or even for schooling in China. They inevitably saw themselves as outside the national image of the United States. As the San Francisco–born architect Philip Choy noted poignantly, "When we were young, because of our isolation and rejection, we would all think we're gonna go back to China . . . [;] that's where we're supposed to be. But, then, it isn't real."[43] It is not surprising that the early literary legacy was not only articulated in the Chinese language but in many cases was dependent on its tradition and genre. Chinese literary utterance is at once a reflection upon society, and action on society.[44] Little wonder, then, that the musical aspirations of Chinese Americans would also be found and articulated in Chinese, for example, Cantonese opera performances. Some second-generation Chinese Americans, as noted by opera fan James Lee, would learn Chinese by following lyrics on the playbills at opera theaters, while others engaged with opera recordings or became amateur singers who might even perform periodically with professionals or make recordings (see Chapter 7).[45] Cantonese opera therefore became part of the communicative means that Chinese American youth leveraged as a resource and used to bridge differences in their transnational habitus.

Rather than considering it as foreign, this transnational viewpoint makes visible the role of multiple languages in daily routines, activities, and institutional affiliations for Chinese Americans. Literacy scholars have developed the term *polycentricity* to describe the connection between multiple-language literacy, and associated values and norms that are mobilized as interpretive frames for social behaviors. In order to comprehend polycentricity in the American musical landscape, acknowledging the significance of Chinese languages is important both in practice and at the symbolic level. It resists the hierarchy of languages in American music historiography by ceasing to consider the Chinese language as opaque and inscrutable, or Chinese materials as inconsequential. Such acknowledgment goes beyond any idea of Chinese as a static source for the Chinese American community and demonstrates the language's ongoing, dynamic, and defining roles. In many ways, the book's focus on the movement of performers, music, and cultural institutions aims to privilege the agency of the figures whose transnational habitus and polycentricity had in the past been considered non-American, and in particular to reverse the earlier exclusion of trans-Pacific influence from American music historiography.[46] It is to consider the nuanced ways of transnationality as a constituent part of American cities.

FINANCIAL AND SOCIAL POWER OF TRANSNATIONAL CHINESE COMMUNITIES

Money and political connections were essential to the establishment of transnational Chinese theaters in the 1920s. This seems paradoxical to some. The popular notion of Chinese immigrants as oppressed and impoverished has prompted many people today to be baffled: How could the Chinese immigrant community have financed such fully staffed, extravagant theaters and performers, many of whom were the best Cantonese opera singers of the day?

Migrants from China were merchants and artisans, on one hand, and rural or menial laborers, on the other. For example, immigrants from the Pearl River delta's Sanyi region were known for engaging in business.[47] In the United States and Canada an organization of businessmen known as the Chinese Consolidated Benevolent Association led various social organizations (established through clans, districts, and fraternal affiliations) and performed a quasi-official role in the community. While laundries, restaurants, and retail or import stores made up the three most common types of businesses owned by Chinese Americans, in the early twentieth century a prominent merchant class emerged—thriving on trans-Pacific commerce and canning businesses, among others—and newer organizations and infrastructures were established within the Chinese American community.[48] In California, prominent merchants including Lew Hing, Ng Poon Chew, and Look Tin Eli represented an elite who endeavored to modernize San Francisco's Chinatown and boost its image, to improve their social lives as well as attract tourists. Their sustained activity generated large amounts of capital from their local and transnational activities.

The success of Lew Hing's Pacific Coast Canning Company (opened in 1904 in Oakland) is a prime example. A prominent employer of Chinese in the area—one thousand at peak seasons—Lew's business included factories in Mexicali. The cannery offered the largest post-earthquake employment opportunity in the Bay Area. Lew also led the founding of the China Mail Steamship Company in 1915, the first Chinese-owned firm to offer trans-Pacific routes.[49] Expanding political connections into the Anglo world of the city, he also became involved with the politically prominent Rolph family, making William Rolph his business partner. When James Rolph Jr. became the longest-running mayor in San Francisco history (1912 to 1930), Lew was considered part of his inner circle and his political savvy was repaid. Furthermore, the infrastructure of the community was also greatly strengthened by the founding of many Chinese-owned businesses and institutions. These included the Canton Bank (1907), the Telephone Exchange (1909), and the Tung Wah Chinese Hospital (1922), as well as organizations such as the Chinese Chamber of Commerce (1908), the Chinese-American Citizens Alliance (1915), the Chinese YMCA (1911), the YWCA (1916), and the Chinatown Public Library (1921).

Chin Lain succeeded Lew Hing as the president of the China Mail Steamship Company in 1918; both also served as directors of the Canton Bank. Between 1910 and 1930 he traveled frequently to China, as well as to his business in Mexicali. In addition, Chin was the president of one of the four prominent Chinese daily newspapers in San Francisco (*Chinese World*), and he headed the Constitutionalist Party, a Chinese political group that was affiliated with his paper. He led the powerful Suey Sing Tong, whose reach extended across the continent. (A *tong* is a type of organized association for support and protection, with the reputation of a secret society or sworn brotherhood tied to criminal activity.) Merchants of Chin's stature were highly regarded in the Chinese American community and by the American government.[50] Though immigration officials at the notorious Angel Island sought to protect the United States by excluding Chinese laborers, they opened their arms for merchants like Lew Hing and Chin Lain.

Merchants and the elite mercantile class were closely tied to Chinatown theaters. Chin Lain was the founder of the Mandarin Theater; Lew Hing's eldest daughter Lew Yung, later Mrs. Quan Yick-sun and a formidable figure in the Chinese community, would become a patroness of a Cantonese opera actress. Sustained by strong financial backing from transnational commerce and the continuing goal of raising respect for the community, Chinese opera theaters were not isolated social and musical spaces. They were the endeavors of prominent merchants and community leaders whose economic and social power and transnational networks commanded respect from people and even government officials on both sides of the Pacific. A contemporary parallel may be found in Southeast Asia, where, as Wing Chung Ng notes, the Singaporean business tycoon Eu Tong Sen was key to the vibrant Cantonese opera scene. Singapore's opera theater benefited greatly from his transnational commerce. His participation made available new capital, business resources, and networks of commerce. With extensive business also in Malaysia and Hong Kong, Eu recruited highly skilled and reputable actors in the 1920s. Through his sponsorship, Singapore saw the expansion of an existing theater and the opening of a new theater, Tianyan Dawutai, in 1927 (or Tianyan Mandarin Theater, later renamed the Dahua Theater).[51]

The United States had a long tradition of immigrant theaters, also often established by elite members of the community. Yet because of the state-sanctioned racial hierarchy, Chinatown theaters faced more challenges and constraints than did their European counterparts and thus required a stronger system and joint endeavors. The interconnectedness of family, business, and cultural networks provided the key mobilizing force for the circuit of performers, troupes, and theaters in North America. For example, when it opened in 1927, the Yong Ni Shang Theater in New York garnered financial investment from businesses, merchants, and even theaters in San Francisco, Vancouver, Montreal, Seattle, and Boston. Chinatown theaters were significant both as business entities and as cultural institutions, the symbols of the considerable economic power and social forces of their communities. From San Francisco to New York, Chicago, Vancouver, and Havana, these theaters worked through legitimacy issues, competitions, and conflicts to bring performances to the community. Chinatown theater deeply entangled with its political, economic, technical, and cultural environment. It registered the layers, textures, and richness that defined this historic space in the American musical landscape.

In summary, Cantonese opera in North America in the 1920s emerged from the intersection of transnational and national histories and was shaped by local cultural and economic forces. Following the large migration from China in the mid-nineteenth century it was established in North America. It had cultural and social significance for the Chinese community and made a unique imprint on the urban histories. The return of the genre in the 1920s continued that tradition with new momentum and constraints, both national and transnational. Not only was the genre steeped in the social milieu of cosmopolitan cities of southern China such as Shanghai and Hong Kong, but also on its arrival in the United States it was greeted by the extraordinarily diverse musical, theatrical, and entertainment scenes of the

Roaring Twenties. The political uproar and instability of China continued to affect the performers' availability and the theaters' political affiliations. As the number of American-born Chinese grew in the 1920s, many were exposed to the genre, so the prosperity of Chinese theaters was all the more important for linguistic, social, educational, and cultural reasons. The performing network was established at an extraordinarily fast pace, connecting major cities in North America. It was helped by capital from transnational commercial and familial networks and prominent local business tycoons, and by new technologies that expedited transportation, on one hand, and on the other created the infrastructure needed to produce and circulate their daily playbills, advertisements, and arresting photographs. Two other significant histories shaped these theaters in fundamental ways: the history of U.S. immigration, to which I turn in the next two chapters, and the development of Cantonese opera up to the 1920s, which is the subject of Part II.

CHAPTER 2

THE CHINESE EXCLUSION ACT AND CHINATOWN THEATERS

The vibrant theater life, and the mobility of performers discussed in Chapter 1 might give an impression of relative freedom for Chinese opera performers entering the United States in the 1920s. Quite the contrary was the case. The early twentieth century started rather unpromisingly as anti-Chinese sentiment grew even more rampant than it had been in the preceding decades. In 1882 Congress passed the Chinese Exclusion Act, the first and only U.S. law to restrict immigration on the basis of race. Its amendments and extensions led to more anti-Chinese laws and regulations. Growing public opinion against the flow of immigrants from Asia, southern and eastern Europe, and elsewhere led to the passage of the 1924 Immigration Act, under which China was given an annual quota of 100 immigrants (compared to the two largest quotas, 51,227 for Germany and 34,007 for the United Kingdom). Furthermore, the act mandated that no alien ineligible to become a citizen could be admitted as an immigrant. Because Chinese were barred by the 1790 naturalization law stipulating that whites only could be naturalized as citizens, the 1924 act in effect completely excluded them from being admitted as immigrants.[1] They could only enter the United States as temporary (non-immigrant) visitors. An important manifestation of anti-Chinese feeling was the restriction of cultural productions such as theaters. This chapter, focusing on immigration policies in the United States, considers how Chinatown opera theaters came to be created, structured, and defined by immigration policies and exclusionary principles and practices.

CHINESE THEATERS OF THE PRE-EXCLUSION ERA

From the 1850s to the 1870s Chinese opera theaters could be established with few constraints; performers were permitted on U.S. soil much as other immigrants at the time. The United States signed the Burlingame Treaty with China in 1868 to establish an open immigration policy. The two countries entered the treaty to increase mutual trade; for the United States, it also held the promise of opening up a vast foreign market. Because of the treaty's granting of privileges to citizens of either country residing in the other, Chinese people were allowed entry into the United States. As music commonly accompanied social activities such as funerals, festival parades, New Year celebrations, and worship of various deities, it soon followed. Nineteenth-century pictures of festive processions for Chinese New Year reveal the important roles of musical instruments. Gongs were ubiquitous in these processions, whether in Denver, Phoenix, Boise, or San Francisco.[2] Given the importance of music, the prosperity of Chinese opera theaters in this period is not surprising. The conditions desirable for their existence were clearly present. These include (1) audience demand from the quickly rising number of Chinese immigrants; (2) the financial resources, Chinese or American, for sponsoring troupes and leasing or erecting theatrical space; (3) the steady stream of Chinese opera performers seeking opportunity; and (4) the growing need for entertainment in frontier towns. In addition, for Chinese businessmen in the United States, access to music and theaters was integral to a higher quality of life. Chinese communities took great pride in their theaters, which were symbolic of prosperity.

For mainstream American society Chinese theaters, particularly their elaborate costumes and tumbling and acrobatic movements, were novel. An advertisement in the *Daily Alta Californian* on December 2, 1856, shows that Chinese theater provided attractions and entertainment much needed at the frontier:

> THE CHINESE DRAMATIC COMPANY have just received from Canton, China, new and beautiful dresses and other theatrical articles, and will commence to play on Tuesday, the 21 inst., and will perform EVERY NIGHT until further notice, at the ADELPHI Theater, Dupont street, between Washington and Clay. The public will find it an excellent place to have their evening amusements. There will be Chinese singing and good performances. Price of admission: Boxes ($1.50) Pit ($1.00)[3]

After their arrival, the earliest Chinese opera troupes were managed by American impresarios or staged at American-owned theaters as entertainment for general audiences. For example, after its premiere at the American Theater in San Francisco, the Hong Fook Tong troupe was contracted by an American impresario to perform at Niblo Garden in New York in 1853. In 1860 a Chinese opera company called Hing Ching Yuen gave performances at the Union Theater on Commercial Street in San Francisco. Although the company intermittently toured the interior of California, it continued to perform at the Union Theater into the next decade.[4] In late 1867 this Chinese theater ranked among the five highest-earning theaters in San Francisco. The monthly receipts of theatrical entertainment published in the *San Francisco Chronicle* shows that the Chinese Theater Company sometimes ranked third highest in the city. It had a monthly average of $5,657.20 in revenue (see table 2.1).[5]

The financial prospects of Chinese theatrical entertainment were attractive enough that American businessmen provided part of the capital for the Royal Chinese Theater, or Yew Hin Look. It opened on the north side of Jackson Street on Chinese New Year in 1868.[6] The new theater had seats for one thousand and offered performances every afternoon and evening. When a second theater on Jackson Street (this time on the south side), Sing Ting Yuen, opened in 1874, the newspaper predicted that its spacious new building would attract even more Americans.[7] The theater, which seated eighteen hundred, would later carry the name Quan Sun Yoke (Gem of Mount Quan).[8] In order to attract general audiences, Chinese theaters advertised in English newspapers' entertainment sections from time to time. For example, the Union Theater placed an advertisement in the *San Francisco Chronicle* to promote the debut of an actor "newly arrived from Canton" in the summer of 1870.[9] Calling attention to another new arrival, the Royal Chinese Theater in September 1874 placed advertisements in the *Daily Evening Bulletin* for "A new Troupe of First-class performers; Just from the Orient."[10] In December 1877 the Royal Chinese Theater and a new theater on Washington Street (Look Sun Fung, or "Peacock"),[11] the third in town, took their competition to the pages of the *San Francisco Chronicle*, placing advertisements next to one another.[12] The abundance of Chinese theaters

Table 2.1. Revenue of theaters in San Francisco, 1867–1868

Theater name	Sept. 1867	Oct. 1867	Nov. 1867	Dec. 1867	Feb. 1868
American (Occasional)	3,094	2,262	2,912	2,635	
Anatomical Museum	1,084	1,032	1,149	893	458
Bella Union	3,489	4,019	3,379	3,079	3,304
Chinese Theater (Union)	5,365	9,102	6,199	4,026	3,594
Maguire's Opera House	19,675	14,746	9,836	8,275	15,773
Metropolitan Theater	12,227	9,913	10,441	21,643	17,146
Olympic					5,165
Piato's Music Hall			5,753		
Temple of Music			12,606	6,470	7,142
Total	44,934	41,074	52,275	47,021	52,582

Source: Data extracted from the *Daily Dramatic Chronicle* (San Francisco), January 25 and February 17, 1868.

caught the media's attention, and many papers reported in 1879 on the fourth to be built. Designed to seat twenty-five hundred people, it was later named the Gee Quen Yung (or Donn Quai Yuen) Theater.[13] By the end of the 1870s, then, with four running concurrently, Chinese theaters were among the city's main attractions. The roster of their famous visitors over the years included the Hungarian violinist Miska Hauser (1853), the British soprano Euphrosyne Parepa-Rosa (1868), the duke of Manchester (1873), and President Rutherford B. Hayes (1880). Though anti-Chinese sentiment was gradually gathering momentum in California, it did not hamper the booming business of Chinese theaters.

Cantonese opera performers arrived in droves to fill the stages. When in 1877 the New Chinese Theater on Washington Street was erected—a four-story structure with three stores on the ground floor and the actors' lodging on the upper levels—the *San Francisco Chronicle* reported that a manager sailed from Hong Kong with a troupe of ninety actors and six cooks.[14] Theaters were prosperous, and many performers and managers were well paid. For example, actor Long Yow of the Royal Chinese Theater received an annual salary of $6,700 (the equivalent of $171,976 in 2015) in 1879, as reported by the Washington, DC, *Evening Star*.[15]

The theaters and performers had by then been adopted as a part of San Francisco's entertainment scene of which citizens could be proud, as the following report shows. When a satirical "Chinese" opera by Jacques Offenbach was successfully staged in London in 1865, a San Franciscan reporter wrote, "They can't get up Chinese opera in the style we do it in San Francisco. Some of the operas performed on Jackson Street would take the shine out of Offenbach's bogus Chinese opera, *Ching-Chow-Hi*."[16]

Like Chinese cigar makers, bookkeepers, cooks, and laborers, opera performers became members of the community. The U.S. census records of 1870 and 1880 reveal a large number of Chinese actors and musicians residing in the United States.[17] Particularly interesting was the fifty-member Sun Heen Lok Theater Company in San Francisco listed on the 1870 census. It comprised a manager, a lead actor, forty-five other actors, and three cooks. The business was lucrative enough that the forty-year-old manager of the theater, its namesake, drew an annual income of $10,000 (the equivalent of $189,152 in 2015).[18] As Yong Chen observes keenly, the theater had its own social hierarchy, with the manager and some musicians in the top tier, other performers in the middle, and at the bottom, laborers providing food and basic services.[19] Ten years later, according to the 1880 U.S. census, the number of actors, musicians, and other theater employees (managers, workers, watchmen, doorkeepers, and cooks) totaled more than two hundred, including in San Francisco the 111 members listed at 818 Washington Street (the newer Grand Chinese Theater) and 65 members at 623 Jackson Street (the Royal Chinese Theater).[20] Some of the managers and actors lived with their wives and children.[21]

Marysville also had registered 11 members working for a theater.[22] These numbers necessarily reflect only a fraction of the population of opera performers.

Unfortunately, at the same time, virulent anti-Chinese sentiment, particularly potent among organized labor in California yet used by politicians as well, made life increasingly difficult for Chinese and would pave the way for Chinese exclusion. A series of discriminatory ordinances and laws were passed in the 1870s.[23] For example, in 1870 the City of San Francisco passed the Sidewalk Ordinance, which prohibited persons from walking on sidewalks with traditional shoulder poles to carry goods. Because most Chinese could not afford a horse and cart, the ordinance in effect took away their only means of transporting goods. The Laundry Ordinance of 1873 required laundries with horse-drawn wagons to pay a license fee of $2 per quarter and laundries without wagons to pay $10 per quarter. Although these ordinances were not written in discriminatory language, they were clearly directed at Chinese.

In similar fashion, many noise ordinances specifically targeted Chinese theaters. In 1880, a superior court judge affirmed a nuisance citation issued to a Chinese theater in Sacramento for which four actors and two performers were arrested, calling the performance unlawful: "Under our civilization a theater is not understood to be an institution so noisy as to disturb the neighborhood."[24] In March 1882 in Portland, an ordinance was in effect which stated that "only string instruments may be played after midnight."[25] When the police arrested musicians of the Chinese theater for violating the ordinance, the audience rioted. In New York, Portland, San Francisco, and Honolulu, nuisance complaints were repeatedly brought against Chinese theaters.[26] The number of such complaints ironically underscores the vitality of the business. At times, the crowded theaters became the targets of police raids, whose numbers increased in the later part of the nineteenth century.

Whereas the Chinese satisfied the urgent need for laborers during the gold rush and railroad construction, from early on they also were blamed for driving down wages and taking jobs away from others. When the Transcontinental Railroad was officially completed at Promontory Point, Utah, in 1869, thousands of Chinese workers were laid off. As California's economy slowed and job opportunities dwindled, white laborers increasingly saw Chinese laborers as the source of their inability to find work. The animosity became politicized by Denis Kearney and the Workingman's Party and by California governor John Bigler. In 1879, California adopted a constitution that allowed legislation to be passed to enforce the exclusion of Chinese from the state. The same article also included a ban on employing Chinese "on any state, county, municipal or other public works."[27] More than 153 anti-Chinese riots swept through the American West during the 1870s and 1880s, and they included arson, property damage, murder, and lynch mobs. Los Angeles suffered a riot in 1871; the one in Denver (1880) prompted requests from the

Chinese consul in San Francisco for reparation, but to no avail.[28] Finally, Congress passed the Chinese Exclusion Act in 1882, thereafter sanctioning the restriction of Chinese immigration. The Exclusion Era put a halt to the free movement of the actors and threatened the very existence of Chinatown theaters.

CHINESE THEATERS IN THE EARLY YEARS OF THE CHINESE EXCLUSION ACT

The impact of the Exclusion Act on Chinese theaters did not seem very great at first. In the 1880s and 1890s, two theaters were operating concurrently in San Francisco: the Royal Theater (renamed Donn Sahn Fung), and the Washington Street theater, renamed the Grand Chinese Theater (or Donn Quai Yuen). In 1890 an advertisement for the Grand Chinese Theater in the *San Francisco Chronicle* noted that it was "the largest Chinese theatrical company in America," offering "first class performances."[29]

Initially, the Chinese exclusion laws were aimed at prohibiting new Chinese laborers from coming to the United States. Describing them as "indentured coolies" and linking them to slavery, anti-Chinese people tactfully lobbied for their exclusion under the pretense of preventing slavery from reoccurring on U.S. soil.[30] During the early years of the Exclusion Era, so long as there was evidence that they were not laborers, Chinese opera performers were generally allowed to enter the country. At the heart of the issue was the definition of *laborer*. It became a subject of uncertain interpretation for immigration offices and courts. *In re Ho King* was a famous case centering on this issue. In January 1883 an immigration inspector in Portland denied entry to Ho King, a Chinese opera performer, pursuant to the Chinese Exclusion Act. Yet Matthew Deady, a federal judge who was known for his fair treatment of the Chinese, sided with the actor, writing: "A Chinese actor engaged in dramatic representations upon the stage of a Chinese theater seems as far removed from such competition [with other laborers] as it is possible to be."[31] *In re Ho King* not only set the precedent that a theatrical performer was not a laborer within the purview of the law, but also was notable for the way it construed exclusion by reference. Judge Deady also explicitly upheld the promise of the 1868 Burlingame Treaty, later amended as the Angell Treaty in 1880, that Chinese should receive "most favored nation" guarantees.

Yet despite such rulings and the stated purpose of the 1882 act many Chinese immigrants were detained upon entry by zealous inspectors at the port and frequently had to resort to appeals at state and federal courts to avoid deportation. Consequently, case files relating to habeas corpus actions flooded circuit and district courts. Certificates of occupation issued by the Chinese government (so-called Section 6 certificates) generally served as proof of their non-laborer status, but other evidence could be used as well.[32] Immigration officials or judges often required that the detainees, in order to prove that they were not menial laborers, demonstrate appropriate skills, physiological traits, or social markers. Luckily, the usually onerous task of proving one's occupational identity was one particularly suited to Chinese opera singers and actors. This irony did not escape a contemporary journalist, who wrote a tongue-in-cheek report in the *New York Times* in 1884 that colorfully captured a meeting of American jurisprudence with Chinese theater:

> Among the Chinese habeas corpus cases that came up for hearing before Judge Hoffman yesterday were those of four Chinese actors, Ah Sie, Long Kwong, Quong Wa, and Lee Tong. The four claimed that they had been employed previous to 1881, when they returned to China, at the Chinese theatre on Jackson street, near Dupont. During the course of their examination some doubts were cast upon their respective abilities as exponents of the Chinese drama, and at the request of Carroll Cook [court clerk] each of the four exerted himself to display his dramatic worth. Long Kwong was a "jumper." . . . He displayed such agility that no one disputed his claim and he was discharged. Quong Wa was a sweet singer, . . . and he commenced a Chinese rendering of the "Babies on our Block," beginning in a low foghorn key and rising suddenly to a shriek that caused the building to shake. Ah Sie was a female impersonator, and went through the performance of a forlorn maiden with an imaginary villain still pursuing her . . . Fearful that the zeal of the [remaining] actor would lead him too far, . . . Judge Hoffman declared himself satisfied and ordered him discharged and bail exonerated.[33]

Judge Hoffman was known for his commitment to legal equality and insistence on applying principles of evidence in adjudicating Chinese petitions.[34] (He wrote Judge Deady to express his agreement with the result of *In re Ho King*.) Despite his view of the Chinese as an inferior race, as reflected in his endorsement of the objectives of the exclusion acts, he was often criticized as too sympathetic with the Chinese in his rulings and in his refusal to follow the California statute that banned testimony by Chinese, and the newspaper report made fun of him as well.[35]

Thus performers at the border might be detained in terrible conditions or go through endless court appearances, but in principle they were classified as nonlaborers and therefore were admitted. From 1883 to 1892, Chinese theaters or troupes continued to be run in Los Angeles, Sacramento, Fresno, and Boston, in addition to San Francisco.[36] The grand opening of Chinese Theater in March 1893—a decade after the Chinese Exclusion Act passed—on Doyer Street at the center of New York's Chinatown serves as another example.[37] Funded by entrepreneur Chu Fong, the opening was reported favorably in the *New York Times*. The obstacle for the theater was not the admission of performers but its frequent brushes with the

Sabbath law.[38] Before the turn of the century, waves of opera performers also arrived from China for world's fairs. For example, four hundred performers came for the Trans-Mississippi Exposition in Omaha in 1898.[39] Hundreds of opera actors were admitted in order to perform in the Chinese theater at the World's Columbian Exposition in Chicago in 1893. In 1897 the SS *China* arrived in San Francisco from Hong Kong, carrying well over 130 theatrical professionals for the Tennessee Centennial and International Exposition.[40]

THE EXCLUSION OF CHINESE OPERA PERFORMERS

The exclusionary laws became increasingly stringent, however. After the 1882 act came the Exclusion Act of 1888 (also known as the Scott Act), which openly abrogated U.S. treaties with China by revoking the right of free travel for Chinese laborers in and out of the United States, and the Geary Act of 1892, with its added requirement of registration and certification.[41] These provisions were extended to the Territory of Hawaii in 1900. The judicially defined class of exemptions from exclusion was under closer scrutiny, too. In his discussion of the loophole, the historian Adam McKeown includes opera performers in his list of ambiguous classes: "The proper categorization of preachers, naval officers, wives of merchants, opera singers, bookkeepers, acrobats, cooks, landowners, and factory owners within the less than all-encompassing categories of laborer, merchant, teacher, student, or traveler was far from obvious."[42]

As noted by Nayan Shah, that Chinese continued to arrive despite of the zeal of immigration inspectors angered vitriolic opponents of Asian immigration.[43] A trend toward tightening of regulation and enforcement culminated in the U.S. Attorney General's 1898 opinion that "the 'true theory' of exclusion was not that only Chinese laborers were barred from entry but that only carefully defined exempt classes were admissible."[44] Soon the official regulation mandated the exclusion of all Chinese except for the five named exempted classes—diplomats, merchants, students, teachers, and travelers—who were required to present a certificate of their identity issued by the Chinese government. In 1904 all immigration laws regarding the Chinese were extended indefinitely. After the Supreme Court's 1905 decision in *United States v. Ju Toy*, the Immigration Bureau had the final say on all Chinese denied entry at the port, and due process was denied to all, regardless of their status as alien or citizen. The Chinese community's resistance was futile. Anti-American boycotts to protest the humiliation of these laws spread in May 1905 from Shanghai to twenty-one cities throughout China and were supported by Chinese communities from Singapore to the United States. Yet after reaching a climax in September, the boycott died out by early 1906.

In San Francisco the most vocal critic was Ng Poon Chew, a prominent community leader and editor of a Chinese newspaper, *Chung Sai Yat Po.* He proclaimed, "It appeared to be their [the immigration bureaucrats'] ambition to deny all Chinese admission, and anyone admitted was regarded as a lost case." He included opera performers in this 1908 statement: "As a result, [Chinese] physicians, proprietors of restaurants and laundries, employers, actors, newspaper editors, and even preachers . . . were excluded from the shores of the United States."[45]

This stringent regulation dealt Chinatown theaters a fatal blow by choking the pipeline of actors. Their demise needed no help from the 1906 earthquake and fire that destroyed San Francisco. But the catastrophic fire ended even the slim possibility of decent Chinatown opera theaters for at least fifteen years. The reconstruction of the city's Chinatown after the fire did not include opera theaters, despite a clear intent to revive the district's tourism industry.[46] Nor did the 1915 Panama-Pacific International Exposition in San Francisco, in sharp contrast with the world's fairs and expositions of the late nineteenth century, with hundreds of opera performers. As one reporter for the *San Francisco Call* wrote in 1913,

> The reason why there is now no Chinatown theater . . . is because there are no Chinese actors left. . . . [After 1892] the actor was barred and Chinese audiences in our local Chinatown were forced thereafter to content themselves, year after year, with the same stock companies, unrelieved by the appearance of new faces. . . . By the time the fire came . . . the Chinese playhouses were already on the point of closing up their doors for lack of patronage, due to scarcity of performers.[47]

The reporter also offered that after the 1906 fire a committee of leading Chinese merchants met to consider the possibility of a new Chinese theater but agreed that even if a class A $150,000 theater could be built (required to conform to the fire law), operas could not be staged properly because of the lack of actors.[48] With their performers inadmissible at any U.S. shore, Chinese opera theaters were wiped out of the cultural landscape in the United States.[49]

In the fifteen years after the fire, occasional performances were staged, mostly by amateurs or lingering professional performers in San Francisco and surrounding areas. The glory days of Chinese opera, however, had vanished. Nostalgic Western journalists lamented the disappearance of the once-lively theaters. Will Irwin, in a 1921 *New York Times* article titled "The Drama That Was Chinatown," wrote, "The Doyers Street Theatre had closed its doors, as the Jackson Street and Washington Street houses in San Francisco had long closed theirs. The Chinese theatre in America is forever gone, and the cinema did the business."[50] Although Irwin attributed the disappearance to the rise of motion pictures, the absence of Chinese theaters during this period was the result of a complex mix of factors, Chinese exclusion significant among them. Indeed, Chinese opera performances were still highly desirable, perhaps more so than ever. As Chinese immigrants became more concentrated in the cities, the demand for entertainment increased. And as the laborers were stranded in the United States because the amended Chinese Exclusion Act from 1888 disallowed their return to the United States once they left, opera theaters became surrogates for familial rapport.

A TURNING POINT

The Chinatown community was not alone in its desire to present Chinese performers on stage. Since their arrival a half-century earlier, Chinese theatrical spectacles had become popular among Westerners. Not only were artists such as the famous English actor Sir Henry Irving, the Polish violinist-composer Ignacy Jan Paderewski, and the American composer Edgar Stillman Kelley known to seek inspiration at Chinese theaters in San Francisco, but visitors also expected to see these key tourist attractions. The *San Francisco Call* explained that they felt cheated when told that the institution no longer existed, and asked, "Why don't the Chinese rebuild their theaters?"[51]

Furthermore, many yellowface performers offered acts that mimicked imagined Chinese behaviors. In the late nineteenth century, for example, Charles Parsloe was particularly famous. Playing the character Wing Lee in the play *My Partner,* he reportedly earned $100,000 over the course of thirteen hundred performances.[52] Also popular at about that time were performers such as Chung Ling Soo, actually the magician William Robinson, whose acts accentuated the exotic characteristics of the Chinese. In the early twentieth century circuses started to use real Chinese performers. Famous presenters such as the Sells Brothers, the Ringling Brothers, and Barnum & Bailey featured Chinese acrobats and vaudeville performers in their shows, with the Ching-Ling-Hee troupe leading the way. At the height of the Chinese Exclusion Era, ironically, the "Chinese act" was ubiquitous in show business.

Vaudeville became the premier amusement of growing urban populations in the United States during the first two decades of the twentieth century.[53] Between 1910 and 1920 more than forty Pantages vaudeville houses were erected across the United States and Canada, and the Keith-Albee and Orpheum theater circuits had been popular since the previous decade, controlling eastern and western regions, respectively. These shows typically comprised a theatrical hodgepodge of routines including fiddle players, barbershop quartets, acrobats, and short plays. Arriving in 1914 from Austria, the Chinese magician Long Tack Sam quickly became a sensation in the vaudeville circuit with his twelve-person company of acrobats and magicians, performing often on the Orpheum circuit (see figure 2.1).[54]

By 1917 the *Atlanta Constitution* noted, "The Long Tack Sam Company, already favored among Atlanta vaudeville lovers, and long recognized as a standard big-time

Fig. 2.1. Long Tack Sam Troupe, ca. 1910 (courtesy of Ann Marie Fleming).

attraction, is the headliner. They present a series of captivating illusions, no small amount of legerdemain, and a number of gymnastic thrills mounted with an impressive scenic display."[55] The *Los Angeles Times* described a typical show: "[Y]ou would witness breath-taking miracles, performed in an atmosphere of embroidered hangings, as romantically oriental as a Chinatown Joss house. There is a small Chinese miss with as many joints in her body as a spider, and a parchment-faced youth who plays American ragtime."[56] One writer was so smitten that he praised the immensely talented Long Tack Sam as "a worthy successor of Ching Ling Soo."[57] The convention of yellowface performance, or "Chinese acts," ironically became a trope that even Chinese vaudeville performers had to follow in order to appease the audience's desire for the Oriental. The appeal of Chinese acts remained strong all through that decade. Exoticism and the notion of "consuming the Orient" played a significant role in the popularity of Chinese performers in vaudeville.[58]

It was, then, the popular demand for Chinese performers that prompted American entrepreneurs to intervene and circumvent the exclusion: theatrical impresarios eagerly sought their admission into the United States. Their well-connected lawyers befriended immigration officials and called on elected officials who could apply political pressure for them. For example, in 1916, Barnum & Bailey Circus applied for the admission of Chinese performers to the New York port. The request was forwarded to Washington, DC.[59] The U.S. Department of Labor wrote tersely to H. R. Sisson, a Chinese Inspector in Charge in New York, "As you are doubtless aware, Chinese persons coming to the United States in the capacity of acrobats or vaudeville performers are not admissible."[60] Yet, since he was friendly with the legal agent of Barnum & Bailey Circus, who urged him to "talk the matter up and arrang[e] their landing,"[61] this inspector pressed ahead. After more correspondence, the department changed its tune, writing, "[Chinese actors] may be considered as admissible, insofar as the Chinese-exclusion law is concerned, on the submission of a bond in the sum of $1,000 for each, stipulating for departure at or before the expiration of one year from date of admission."[62] (Unsurprisingly, Sisson would later begin a private practice as an immigration broker representing Chinese actresses in New York.)[63] The practice of temporary admission had been established between the government and the entertainment industry, but officials agreed to it only under pressure. The terms of the agreements were far from uniform; the duration of maximum stay varied, as did the amount of the bond. In any case, the agreements ensured the temporary nature of these performers' stay and close monitoring of their residency, which kept them out of the formal and legal structures of society. A review of their files from the period between 1910 and 1920 showed that the Barnum & Bailey Circus was able to renew the permits of fourteen Chinese performers for several years at a time. By 1916 the Immigration Bureau had established the practice of approvals for temporary admission of Chinese vaudeville performers at ports on both coasts.

Despite the success in gaining admission for Chinese performers, nothing had actually changed regarding their inadmissibility in principle. Their admission was at the discretion of the immigration bureaucrats—who deemed it a leniency—and every six or twelve months the residency permit needed to be renewed.[64] Crucial to the success of the applications were the entrepreneurs' social standing and attorneys' savvy in handling the bureaucrats, from administrators in Washington, DC, to inspectors at the entry ports. Professional and social connections were crucial: Barnum & Bailey's legal agent, Frank A. Cook, previously had been an investigator for the U.S. Department of Commerce and Labor (which contained the Bureau of Immigration from 1903 to 1913).[65]

The practice of temporarily "admitting Chinese performers to responsible parties under the bond" opened new possibilities for Cantonese opera troupes and theatrical agents; rather than bringing in a handful of Chinese performers, however, they brought in full troupes.[66] Representing the first Chinese theatrical company to bring professional Cantonese opera back to San Francisco was a lawyer named Roger O'Donnell who was based in Washington, DC. By the middle of the 1920s he would become one of the most prominent legal brokers for Chinese theatrical businesses, representing theaters from New York to Honolulu.[67] With American vaudeville charting a path through barriers to immigration, the return of Chinatown opera theaters to the United States was possible.

An ironic turn of the "Chinese fetish" this was. At the turn of the century, the Chinese acts seen in popular entertainment had had phenomenal success by using caricatures and stereotypes.[68] As Judy Tsou's insightful study shows, popular songs were full of stereotypes about Chinese.[69] Many songs such as "Chinatown, My Chinatown," "China Boy," "China Dreams," "China Girls," "Under the Golden China Moon," "Chong: He Come from Hong Kong," and "Chan: Song of China" perpetuated the caricatures. Their wide circulation made an indelible impression on the American popular imagination and affected the public's perception of real Chinese theaters, which was no doubt harmful to their legitimacy. Yet the popularity of the Chinese act created demand for authentic Chinese performers. That the majority of them were acrobats, magicians, and entertainers, most with significantly different training than opera performers had, mattered little in this situation: government officials' incapability of distinguishing between Chinese acrobats or entertainers and opera performers worked to the latters' advantage. In a memo regarding a 1922 Chinese theater application submitted by O'Donnell, the Immigration Bureau's general review board approved unenthusiastically: "Aside from the fact that the application is for the admission of a rather large number of Chinese, the facts are identical with those in a number of cases in the past which the Department authorized."[70] If the difference in the types of performers eluded the officials, then certainly they would also have little understanding that, unlike acrobatic acts, Chinese opera was a deep-rooted, powerful cultural form. In fact, admitting opera troupes conflicted directly with the exclusionist principle of limiting and diminishing the Chinese community.

Following the lead of Barnum & Bailey and various vaudeville circuits, other entities submitted a series of applications for Chinese theaters in the early 1920s. Typically, legal brokers would first lobby government officials and then file petitions with rationales and plans for establishing the theater, on one hand, and proof of their bona fide status, on the other. Then investigations and interviews by inspectors at the local level would follow. Often more negotiation and lobbying behind the scenes would be needed in order for the theaters to obtain a favorable decision from the Department of Labor. Once approved, the theaters would be allowed to sponsor performers. In later years a quota would be set as well. This process could take up to six months or a year, even with well-connected attorneys.

REGULATING MUSICAL SPACES

In January 1921 the Assistant Commissioner General of Immigration, W. W. Sibray, gave the first approval of an application by a Chinese theatrical business, and set the renaissance of Cantonese opera in motion.[71] (The Bureau of Immigration, a branch of the Department of Labor from 1913 to 1940, was headed by the Commissioner General of Immigration.[72] Later, the position of Second Assistant Secretary of Labor was established for the administration of immigration laws.[73]) The theaters were required to put up a $1,000 bond for each of the actors for a permit valid for six months and renewable for up to three years. The bond was cancelled only when the departing actor was checked out at the port. If a performer stayed beyond the expiration of his or her permit, the theaters risked forfeiting the bond. For purposes of the permits, the category "actors" included singers, instrumentalists, stagehands, wardrobe-keepers, scene painters, dramatists, and others. Regardless of their roles, the maximum stay was three years; this resulted in constant turnover.

The bureau's close monitoring of most aspects of the opera theaters—their location, numbers of performers, expiration dates of permits, and the transfers of performers to different theaters—required theaters to seek the government's approval for most business moves. The contingent nature of the actors' status was the tool by which immigration officials exerted control over the theaters. The requirement of renewing admission permits every six months was crucial. If a renewal was denied, the performers would be deported, and the theater would have to close. In order to ensure the government's approval, Chinese businessmen engaged legal brokers, attorneys, political allies, and others. In 1925 the Immigration Bureau repeatedly rejected the expansion of the ambitious Mandarin Theater for what it deemed a transgression—opening a branch in a different city—and for requests for an increase in its quota of performers. Toward the end of a seven-month legal tug-of-war, it looked as though the theater would close. Chapter 3 discusses this case and its various ramifications.

For the bureau, keeping control of such a large number of theatrical companies became increasingly complicated and burdensome. In 1924 the department changed the term of admission permits to twelve months rather than six and allowed theaters to submit their entire cast for renewal on the same date.[74] Even so, administration was a tedious task involving documents concerning many people and organizations: attorneys both at the port and in Washington representing the theaters, surety companies and their lawyers, immigration offices at ports of both entry (Seattle, San Francisco, Calexico, New Orleans, and New York) and departure, the General Board of Review, the Second Assistant Secretary at the Department of Labor, and often the collectors at the steamship companies as well. A routine process involved documents from the Department of Labor and the immigration offices at various ports, including the department's initial authorizations and extensions, bond papers, local arrival and departure records, performer ID cards, transfer requests, bond cancellation authorization, medical records, interviews, theater managers' affidavits, and other forms. More complicated cases might require other filings, petitions, letters, medical reports, investigation reports, rulings, and so on. The increasingly common practice of transferring actors between theaters added to the complexity. All these activities added to the possibility of oversights, errors, confusion, and delayed actions. Furthermore, changes in government policies and court decisions complicated the procedure.

THE INFLUENCE OF REGULATION

The influence of these anti-Chinese constraints was substantial, and it affected the rise and fall of Chinese opera theaters quite apart from the size of the Chinese population, the prosperity of the communities, and competition from other forms of entertainment.

All Chinese actors, on completing the maximum stay of three years, were required to leave the country.[75] This rule gave rise to a type of itinerant theater. Although no laws stipulated whether an actor could reapply for admission, judging from the common use of pseudonyms at reentry and efforts to conceal their previous entry history, it seems likely that returning actors were not treated favorably. Chinatown theaters were less sure of their future because they relied primarily on opera performers arriving from China. The number of local performers was too small to mount or sustain professional productions. So, dealing with the Immigration Bureau was part of the theaters' daily business.

The legal status of the performers defined them as transient figures. Barred by the 1790 naturalization law, Chinese performers were not eligible for citizenship. Since they were also ineligible as immigrants, their admission was dependent on officials' "leniency" (in their words), with bonds to ensure they did not become a public charge. Despite their significant role in the community's cultural activities, the performers lived and worked outside the normative immigration categories and had no formal membership in American society. For example, while the actress Mudan Su, mentioned in the introduction, was an important part of the social memory of Chinese theaters in North America, in legal terms she was a transient figure. Though collectively the itinerant performers were ingrained in social memory and identity, they also were peripheral. Little wonder, then, that the majority of performers vanished into forgotten history soon after their residences. The dramatists and stage directors, who were typically the soul of the theaters, had little chance of establishing a public discourse on opera in the community. A dramatist, Guan Jingxiong, of San Francisco's Great China Theater, began the journal, *Chinese Drama*, to chronicle significant historical and contemporary events, and preview shows. However, it did not survive beyond its first issue.[76] This lack of discourse was one of the reasons the lively Chinatown opera scene of the 1920s left few traces. The literary sections of Chinese newspapers and laudatory poems on theater playbills became the only platforms for public discourse about Cantonese opera in the United States.

Chinese performers, like Chinese immigrants in general, went through interrogations and medical examinations upon arrival. Faulty responses or failed health inspections could result in deportation or lengthy detention and questioning, and some fell ill or died during appeal. It became common to avoid the immigration station notorious for the fiercest enforcement and least fair processes, Angel Island, the main port of entry and exit from the Pacific. Performers instead entered through such ports as Calexico and Seattle. Starting in 1925, Seattle emerged as an important gateway for Chinese performers, many of whom then traveled down to San Francisco. The busy corridor between the two cities added to the already vibrant Pacific Northwest.

Finally, the requirement that the theaters apply for extension of their permits every six months made them vulnerable. In essence, the immigration service extended its power from the ports to the cities. The immigration officers had the ultimate power. The permit could be used as a tool to virtually terminate the existence of a theater. This precariousness reveals the profound tenuousness of the actors' rights: they were only a thin hair's breadth away from becoming illegal immigrants. They were outside the formal legal system and therefore were not protected by the privileges and rights accorded other immigrants or aliens. The situation did not protect the theaters' rights, either. For example, in September 1933, after being denied an extension by the Immigration Bureau, the last Chinatown opera theater in New York was ordered to deport all its actors.[77] Ironically, it was the theater's own attorney, Charles Booth, who clandestinely reported its worsening financial situation and suggested that the bureau deny an extension.[78]

CHAPTER 3

IMMIGRATION

Privilege or Right?

From 1924 to 1925 the Mandarin Theater in San Francisco, the second Chinatown opera theater to open there in that decade, grew from a business initiative to an eighty-five-member ensemble. It was the fastest-growing such theater of the 1920s and the first to erect a purpose-built theater. The path to this status was nonetheless arduous. The immigration struggle that the Mandarin endured was, though not unusual, illustrative of a bureaucratic process with copious restrictions, official suspicions, political pressure, and intimidating procedures.[1]

The Mandarin Theater's eventual success was due to the prudence, financial prowess, and business skill of Chinese merchants, as well as their mobilization of legal professionals. Quite contrary to the common image of a mute, oppressed social group, as the legal historian Christian Fritz points out, "It is clear that [the Chinese] routinely had access to some of the best lawyers in the state ever since the late nineteenth century."[2] The right to run a top-tier Chinese opera theater was earned not only by amassing capital but also by using political and social connections and legal skill.

The Mandarin Theater's battle with immigration officials, which never evolved into a case before a court, was mainly conducted through bureaucracy. The case offers an unusual glimpse of the struggle behind the theater's spectacle. It tells us about not just the abstract—the exclusionist policy—but also about the everyday life of a Chinese opera theater as it dealt with laws and regulations.

OBTAINING PERMISSION

Starting in 1922, Cantonese opera performers were able to enter the United States and professional shows were staged in San Francisco (October 1922), Seattle (February 1923), and Boston (November 1922). By late 1923, when a new application was submitted by the Mandarin Theater to bring opera performers from China, the general procedure for such admission had been more or less stabilized. The process would normally begin with a petition to the Department of Labor requesting permission for a theater to operate and to bring performers from China. The government's scrutiny was often extensive and its approval highly selective. Once authorized, the theater would be granted a quota of performers it could bring to the United States under the terms of temporary admission. Detailed justification was required to obtain the initial permission and quota, and at each extension the theater would again be at the mercy of the officials.

The Mandarin Theater's application was met with resistance from the start. The prominent merchant Chin Lain began in mid-1923 to seek a permit for starting a theater—with a new building and a troupe of fifty members from China—in San Francisco, where a new Cantonese opera company was already very successful.[3] Paperwork alone would not suffice; personal visits were paid to high-level officials of the department by lawyers;[4] in December, photos of the theater being built on Grant Avenue were submitted to legitimize the proposed venture. When nothing transpired, in late December several other applications were made under different names and through different attorneys and immigration brokers, all for the same theater. The duplicate applications could have been attempts by the merchants to maximize the chances of approval. Unfortunately, they complicated the case because they raised suspicions of fraud.[5] After the confusion was clarified by late January, the Department of Labor focused on the petition brought by an Oakland lawyer, Chas A. A. McGee.

In this application the Mandarin distinguished the proposed theater from ordinary and earlier ones. "Unlike many Chinese theatres," it stated, "it is the purpose of your petitioner . . . to have Chinese male actors take the part of the male characters, and Chinese actresses the part of the female characters in the play, and to have expert scene-shifters and stage-hands trained and schooled in their work." By abandoning the conventional practice of using female impersonators, the petition seemed to suggest, the theater would be morally appropriate for American society and thus become "a source of amusement and entertainment to distinguished visitors, not only locally, but more particularly from abroad." In an effort to distance the performers from Chinese laborers, the petition states that the minimum yearly salaries would range from $1,800 to $6,000 (the equivalent of $25,364 to $84,548 in

2014). It also argued that the community could use another Chinese theater, noting that the existing one, owned by the Lun Hop Company, always filled its seven hundred seats, generating an average of $300 per day in revenue.[6]

The skepticism that met the application revealed much about the contemporary social and political climate. As anticipated by the Mandarin Theater's sponsors, immigration officials were concerned that San Francisco already had one Chinese theater and that a second one would be excessive. *Excess* had been repeatedly used since the nineteenth century to negatively characterize the Chinese, as noted by the historian Nayan Shah: "The references to excess and extremes stood in menacing contrast to the presumed norms of the white middle class. The danger of excess lay in its perceived capacity to expand across class and racial differences and spatial boundaries, carrying lethal contagion."[7] Anxiety about excess was high; in interviews with community members, the Immigration Bureau's local inspector expressed a general distrust of the idea of having multiple Chinese theaters.[8]

Meanwhile, missionaries and churches in Chinatown rushed to depict the bad influences of Chinese theaters on society, condemning Chinese actresses as belonging to the lowest class, as well as speculating on the theaters' connection to tongs and criminality. Their letters were forwarded to the Department of Labor for consideration. Reverend Bradley of the Chinatown mission of Old St. Mary's Church protested strongly against the theater in a three-page letter, noting that

> there is now a large show house in Chinatown and its productions are frequently immoral. I have already lost a number of girls, whose moral breakdown has been traced to their frequent attendance at this low theatre. . . . I am convinced that we have too much of the oriental spirit over here now, and that spirit not only retards the work of those especially interested in the moral and spiritual up-building of the Chinese in our country, but it also seriously hurts the morals of our own boys and girls—I mean the whites.[9]

Donaldina Cameron of the Presbyterian Chinese Mission Home, a legendary figure known for her efforts in rescuing Chinese prostitutes, strongly stated her objections as well:

> Our long experience in this community has made us realize the extremely evil influence of the Chinese theater. . . . The class of women who come as actresses are acknowledged by their own race to be the lowest social order, and those who indulge in the most flagrant immorality. The addition of a larger number of this class would inevitably mean an increase in social evils in the Chinese community of San Francisco.[10]

To these religious organizations, one of the theaters' many offenses was their popularity, which posed a threat to their efforts to assimilate and transform the Chinese. Though the missionaries' hostility did not in the end stop the Mandarin Theater, their denigration of the theaters and performers contributed to the attitude of hesitant government officials.

Within the Chinese community, competitors tried to turn the government's hesitation to their advantage: members of the Chinese Consul General and civil organizations, as well as political and business rivals, opposed the new theater privately, citing possible discord between the theaters that could disturb the community. On the other side stood the approving Chinese Chamber of Commerce and Chinese Consolidated Benevolent Association (also known as the Chinese Six Companies). The secretary of the Chamber of Commerce, B. S. Fong, wrote, "The undersigned remembers that some years ago, there were two Chinese theaters in San Francisco up to the time of the 1906 earthquake. Since that time there has been no Chinese theatre here. . . . My opinion in this matter is that the proposed theatre will meet with the approval of the entire Chinese community"[11] (see figure 3.1). As for the theater owner, Chin Lain, the immigration inspector found it easy to confirm his bona fides as an entrepreneur.

He was, in the inspector's eyes, "a man of prominence in Chinatown, and [. . .] has business interests of considerable magnitude in this city."[12] As discussed in Chapter 2, Chin Lain was the president of China Mail Steamship, a director of the Canton Bank of San Francisco, the proprietor of the famous Hang Far Low restaurant, and the president of a local newspaper, *Chinese World* (the official organ of the Constitutionalist Party).[13] In addition, as a community leader, the fifty-four-year-old Chin headed the San Francisco branch of the Constitutionalist Party. For an individual of his prominent social standing, the theater business held much potential.[14] He might have considered the new theater important in countering his political rivals' Lun Hop company, run by the pro–Nationalist Party contingent.

Stating that there could easily be two or three Chinese theaters serving the Chinese population of thirteen thousand in the Bay area (of whom eight thousand were in San Francisco), Chin Lain concluded his interview with the immigrant inspector superciliously. Their exchanges show a confident merchant, often impatient with the pedantic questions.

> Q: Mr. Chin Lain, just what do you propose to do in regard to entering the theatrical business?
> A: My theatre is being erected and I intend to get permission from the Department of Labor to permit the entry of a Chinese troupe, to perform in my theatre.
> Q: Is this a company organized and incorporated under the laws of the State of California, or another State?
> A: The building is entirely financed by me. I have not decided if the company will be incorporated or be owned by myself.
>
> . . .
>
> Q: Do I understand you are constructing the building and financing the entire expense?
> A: Yes. I am financing the entire enterprise, myself.
>
> . . .

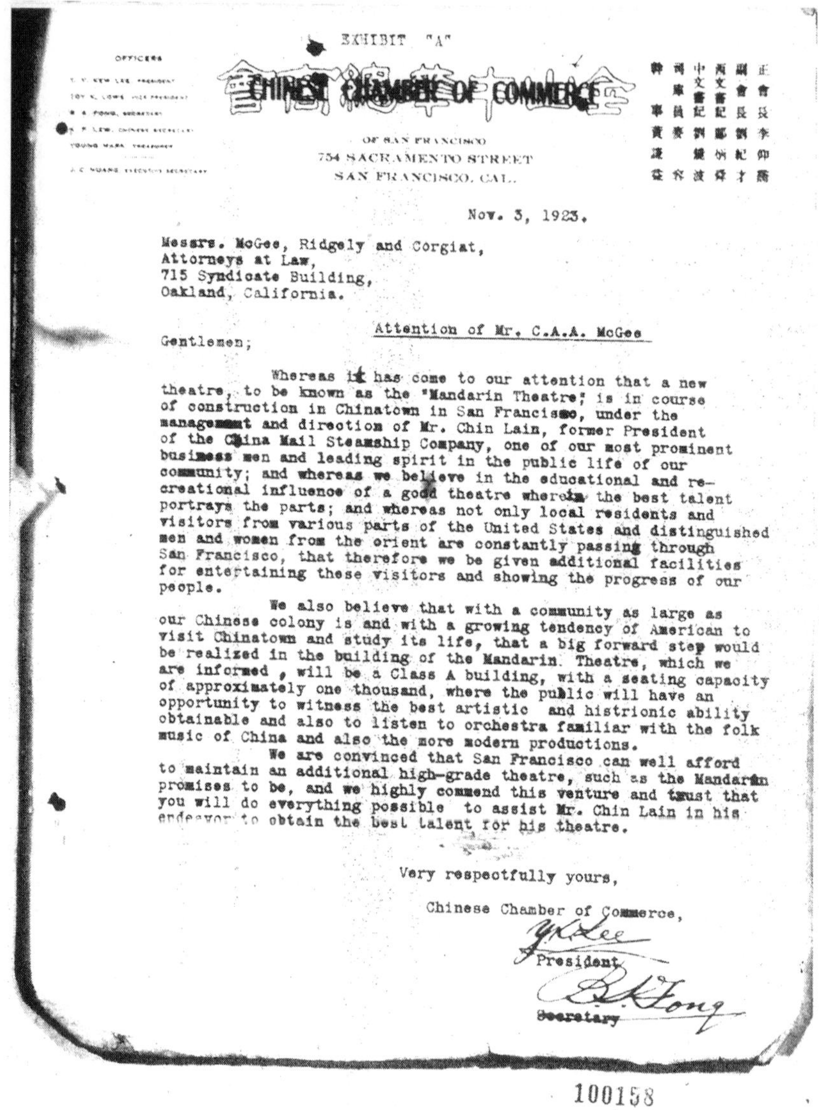

EXHIBIT "A"

CHINESE CHAMBER OF COMMERCE
OF SAN FRANCISCO
754 SACRAMENTO STREET
SAN FRANCISCO, CAL.

Nov. 3, 1923.

Messrs. McGee, Ridgely and Corgiat,
Attorneys at Law,
715 Syndicate Building,
Oakland, California.

Attention of Mr. C.A.A. McGee

Gentlemen;

Whereas it has come to our attention that a new theatre, to be known as the "Mandarin Theatre" is in course of construction in Chinatown in San Francisco, under the management and direction of Mr. Chin Lain, former President of the China Mail Steamship Company, one of our most prominent business men and leading spirit in the public life of our community; and whereas we believe in the educational and recreational influence of a good theatre wherein the best talent portrays the parts; and whereas not only local residents and visitors from various parts of the United States and distinguished men and women from the orient are constantly passing through San Francisco, that therefore we be given additional facilities for entertaining these visitors and showing the progress of our people.

We also believe that with a community as large as our Chinese colony is and with a growing tendency of American to visit Chinatown and study its life, that a big forward step would be realized in the building of the Mandarin Theatre, which we are informed, will be a Class A building, with a seating capacity of approximately one thousand, where the public will have an opportunity to witness the best artistic and histrionic ability obtainable and also to listen to orchestra familiar with the folk music of China and also the more modern productions.

We are convinced that San Francisco can well afford to maintain an additional high-grade theatre, such as the Mandarin promises to be, and we highly commend this venture and trust that you will do everything possible to assist Mr. Chin Lain in his endeavor to obtain the best talent for his theatre.

Very respectfully yours,

Chinese Chamber of Commerce,

Y.K. Lee
President

B.K. Fong
Secretary

100158

Fig. 3.1. Letter from the Chinese Chamber of Commerce of San Francisco (courtesy of the U.S. National Archives and Records Administration).

Q: Do you consider that the opportunity warrants at this time an additional Chinese theatre in this community?

A: Yes. If I did not, I would not spend the sum of $100,000.00 to erect a building.

Q: Have you criticism to make of the present Chinese theatre now operating in San Francisco?

A: No. They are doing business by themselves. So far as I know, they are doing a wonderful business.
Q: What character of plays do you propose to produce in your theatre?
A: High-class, classical plays.

...

Q: Do you have more to add before we end?
A: I have not much to say now. But I am spending a little more than $100,000 and, of course, I expect the Department of Labor will favor my application.[15]

Chin Lain was part of a group of elite merchants who, starting in the second decade of the twentieth century, endeavored to modernize San Francisco's Chinatown and boost its image, in order to improve the lives of its residents and attract tourists. In the first quarter of the century, Chinese Americans' founding of major institutions in the district such as a bank, a hospital, a YMCA and later the first playground (1927) were key steps in accommodating the growing families and rehabilitating the reputation of the community.[16] Understandably, in revitalizing popular entertainment and musical life, Chin Lain wanted Cantonese opera to be presented in a highly reputable and hygienic environment, and to position it as a respectable performing art.

The Department of Labor deliberated for several months. After the attorney Chas A. A. McGee made personal contact with the assistant secretary and commissioner general of the Department of Labor in Washington, DC—the head of the immigration bureau—and San Francisco's commissioner of immigration, John D. Nagle, he finally persuaded them to give a green light for the application. The petition was approved on February 21, 1924, when the building was near completion. The theater was granted a quota of forty-five members, a bit lower than requested.

Upon approval of the permit a troupe of performers was contracted, and it sailed from Hong Kong, arriving at Angel Island on June 25. Three days later, they made their U.S. debut at the new Mandarin Theater.

THE FIRST EXTENSION

The troupe arrived in San Francisco barely two weeks before the enactment of the 1924 Immigration Act, the passing of which on May 26 precipitated a rush of Asian immigration, in anticipation of tighter controls at the port when the act took effect in July. The act basically made inadmissible people who were ineligible for U.S. citizenship (Chinese and Japanese immigrants in particular). Five troupe members were detained for clonorchiasis (liver fluke disease)—considered dangerously contagious then—but thirty-three were successfully admitted. The roster showed many females: ten actresses between the ages of eighteen and twenty-seven. The Mandarin Theater rushed to fill the remaining twelve spaces in its quota of performers. Yet the tightened controls imposed by the new law sent their attorney on a bureaucratic chase, and the lack of a clear policy hindered the admission of actors retained at Angel Island during the later months of 1924.[17] Discrepancies in policy enforcement in various ports caused the Mandarin to quickly change its port of entry to Seattle, despite its distance, because it had less rigorous document requirements.[18]

In November the Mandarin Theater's six-month permit was due to expire, and the first application for renewal was submitted. The renewal subjected the theater to another thorough investigation and reevaluation. The Department of Labor, considering the Mandarin to be on probation, requested a full report from its San Francisco office. The investigation turned up one allegation, made by Donaldina Cameron of the Chinese Mission Home, that eleven or twelve members of the troupe were slaves. This was clearly a recycling of the banal cliché about Chinese coolies, a job for which the theatrical professionals, sponsored with $1,000 bonds, were rather unlikely candidates. An inspector's visit to the living quarters of the actresses followed, and the allegation was dismissed. Unexpectedly, Rev. Bradley of Old St. Mary's came to the aid of the theater this time, though in a back-handed way, saying, "While the reputation of Chinese actresses generally is bad, this particular troupe's conduct while in San Francisco has been above reproach."[19] The Mandarin had gained a good reputation. After nearly fifty days of investigation, the first extension of the permit for another six months was granted.

THE QUOTA INCREASE AND THE LOS ANGELES BRANCH

The Mandarin Theater, however, soon realized that changes were also imperative if it was to sustain its success. Dramatic surges in revenue had always coincided with the arrivals of new performers, especially actresses.[20] (For details about the fluctuation and arrivals of performers, see Chapter 9.) Yet in order to bring in additional new performers regularly, it needed a higher quota. A larger cast would also allow another profitable initiative—opening more branches and rotating performers among different locations—a model used by its competitor Lun Hop, with a quota of sixty-five performers. At that time, Lun Hop's extended operation included regular performances in Portland and Seattle, as well as a new theater in Los Angeles. This arrangement allowed the performers to be fully utilized without being overexposed. The urgency of the Mandarin Theater's need to expand explains why in less than a year after its hard-won initial approval the theater again filed a petition, this time to increase its quota and to support a branch in Los Angeles.

In a petition dated January 16, two attorneys, Chas McGee in San Francisco and Russell Tyler in Los Angeles, laid out the rationale for the quota increase, demonstrating the benefit of a larger Chinese theater to the communities and recounting the theater's law-abiding record. The petition requested a quota of ninety for the Mandarin's two theaters: fifty for San Francisco and forty for Los Angeles. They were promptly handed a rejection. Again the underlying assumption about the vice of excess played a role. One immigration official pointed out that Los Angeles should not have a second Chinese theater. In the next petition, filed in March, the lawyers reduced the requested quota to "65 or 70," giving up the idea of having an advantage over its rival Lun Hop. McGee stated that with twenty-six performers already sent to Los Angeles, the Mandarin Theater in San Francisco was short-staffed. He explained that the request was not new but simply a modification to the theater's initial request of forty-five, which had been insufficient to begin with. And, he noted, "Surely a quota of seventy-five to be divided between San Francisco and Los Angeles cannot be held to be excessive."[21]

While the petition was under review at the Department of Labor in March, the *Young China* reported the departure of a group of Mandarin performers for Los Angeles to establish a branch. It listed nineteen performers (thirteen actors and six actresses) covering nine role types.[22] When the petition was denied again, the attorneys appealed with additional justifications. This seven-page petition, filed on April 9, provided substantial details about the theaters. In order to demonstrate what constituted a sufficient staff for an opera theater, it listed the minimum number of performers needed:

7 musicians
2 electricians
3 wardrobe men
2 stage hands
2 scene hands
4 leading ladies
4 leading men
1 lady comedian
3 men comedians
6 ordinary lady actresses
15 ordinary men actors
49 persons[23]

This list was quite modest if compared to contemporary troupes of 80 to 120 in China. Yet in the United States, such a cast was considered a complete troupe.

Second, the petition argued that the idea of limiting a troupe to one location was impractical for theatrical operations, because "the patronage of said theatre [would] become wearied by reason of having to witness the same actors and actresses perform night after night; that in so doing the entire performance becomes tedious, monotonous and devoid of any interest to the patrons." The lawyers provided details of the monthly receipts of taxes on admissions, and the dues the Mandarin Theater paid to the city, in order to establish that a fluctuation of revenue indeed coincided with the arrival of new performers (see Chapter 9). All nine months' receipts accompanied the petition.

Third, the petition pointed out that the Lun Hop Company had a strong alliance with several Chinese theaters in different cities and alleged that it was in negotiations for a possible merger. If the merger took place, the combined rivals would have an unfair advantage. If it was to be unbiased, the petition argued, the Department of Labor should grant the Mandarin Theater a quota increase. Though the alleged merger talks may not have been real, there were alliances among Chinese theaters during this time. Table 3.1 shows the two main alliances of the theatrical companies, as proposed by the attorneys, and the total quota for each. In response, the Department of Labor ordered an investigation of the alleged merger in May and was able to verify the stated alliances and even one imminent merger. However, while forwarding to the Department of Labor his office's detailed report and endorsement of the theater's expansion, the commissioner of San Francisco's immigration office nevertheless held back his approval, stating, "On the other hand, this office feels that the extension of the business beyond its present limits is not advisable and has to recommend that further applications for additional actors to be landed under bond be denied."[24]

Again the department ruled on the basis of the paranoia of excess. On June 4, the Department of Labor denied the Mandarin Theater's petition, stating that "at this time, two theaters [in Los Angeles] are not warranted." It reiterated that "the Board of Review is of the opinion that the time has come when there should be a limit placed on this privilege [of special permission for Chinese actors]."[25] The annoyed officials also now declared fraudulent the theater's expansion into Los Angeles in March because it was unsanctioned by the immigration office. By the time it reviewed the application for a six-month extension in June, the Department of Labor said that further extension of the permit was now contingent on immedi-

Table 3.1. Alliances of theater companies

Mandarin alliance			Lun Hop alliance		
Theater	City	Quota	Theater	City	Quota
Jock Ming On	New York	40	All-Star	Los Angeles	17
Mandarin	San Francisco	45	Lok Tin Tsau	Boston	40
			Lun Hop	San Francisco	64
			Tai Ping Young	Portland/Seattle	26
Alliance total		85	Alliance total		147

Source: Assistant Commissioner General to Commissioner of Immigration, San Francisco, April 21, 1925, file 55374/227C, INS-SPF.

ate termination of the Mandarin Theater's operations in Los Angeles. On June 10 the Department insisted that, although nothing in the original permit explicitly prohibited the theater's opening of a Los Angeles branch, the original authorization of the Mandarin had "merely intended" for the theater to operate in San Francisco alone. This ruling echoed that of the February rejection letter, in which an official could hardly conceal his disdain:

> In passing upon such a request, the Department set forth that recently an unprecedented number of requests has come before it for permission to bring in more and more Chinese actors and actresses and it was stated that a line must be drawn somewhere. *It should be borne in mind at all times that the admission of Chinese actors to this country is strictly a privilege and, if a line is not drawn somewhere, this privilege, like all privileges, will be abused.*[26]

This rhetoric had reoccurred in the repeated rejections like a constant refrain. Still, the June ultimatum was devastating; the Department of Labor now had ultimate authority over these matters.[27]

Yet closing down the Los Angeles branch would be a major blow. Taken together, the statements of witnesses called during the investigation provided the following sketch of the Mandarin Theater's operation in Los Angeles.[28] The theater had spent $9,500 on renovating a rented theater at 323 Jackson Street (which seated five hundred on the main floor and two hundred in the gallery), and had opened on March 14 that year. It served the Chinese population of six thousand that also included San Diego, Oxnard, San Bernardino, Riverside, Santa Barbara, Ontario, Orange, and Santa Ana.[29] Staffed by fourteen actors and actresses, six musicians, and three wardrobe keepers, the theater had been prosperous: nightly proceeds averaged $250 to $350 on weekdays, $500 to $600 on holidays or weekends, and $800 to $900 with new actresses, yielding $9,954.60 in March, $6,743.70 in April, and $6,293.25 in May. The ticket sales per night ranged between $40 and $909. The theater's supervisor, Lew Kang Poo, noted that in China a troupe would have eighty members; in the United States forty would be needed. He also noted that, on average, three hundred people attended per night, among whom between twenty-eight and sixty were white. Having made a considerable investment in overhauling the theater with proper seats, plumbing, and carpentry, the theater had very good prospects.

Such power was given to the Bureau of Immigration, however, that a contemporary journalist writing in the *Atlantic Monthly* described it as "represent[ing] the epitome of 'bureaucratic tyranny.'"[30] For example, in the same year Chinese merchants were suddenly required, without an official change in regulations, to post $500 bonds when entering the port—to be forfeited if their occupations were changed—even though according to both the Chinese exclusion laws and treaties with China they should be allowed freely into the United States. In any case, hoping to reverse the Department's decision, the Mandarin Theater sent another petition and mobilized its political connections and influence at once.

CHALLENGING THE RULINGS

A lawyer from Washington, DC, M. Walton Hendry, was hired within days. He challenged the Department of Labor on June 18. First, he asked whether, at the federal level, it had the authority to restrict a business from operating at a particular locality, especially when the bond for each performer placed no such constraints on the business. Second, he pointed out that in California, as in all other states, theatrical businesses were licensed by the local government, and the federal government had no role in such decisions. Third, he questioned the government's intent, drawing attention to its unfair targeting of Chinese theater alone for such restrictions. Last, Hendry wrote that its ruling pertaining to the Los Angeles operation of the Mandarin Theater would make "a new policy retro-active and thus cause [the business] a sudden and unfair loss."[31]

Hendry was a frequent litigator before the United States Court of Claims. He routinely challenged the government's rulings, holding it accountable for its actions and their harmful consequences for businesses. He was also involved with Chinese immigration cases and had argued one four years earlier before the U.S. Supreme Court. Earlier in 1925 he joined the prominent immigration attorney George A. McGowan in two famous U.S. Supreme Court cases—*Chang Chan v. Nagle* (268 U.S. 346) and *Cheung Sum Shee v. Nagle* (268 U.S. 336)—both of which would establish important interpretations of the Immigration Act of 1924.

The two cases pertained to the denial of entry to wives of Chinese merchants and wives of Chinese American citizens, respectively. The Chinese community, exasperated by the increasing difficulties at the port, was naturally very concerned with the outcome of these two cases and took them on as a collective effort, underwritten by the San Francisco Chinese Consolidated Benevolent Association.[32] Their outcome would affect in a fundamental way the ability of Chinese to form a family life in the United States. The ratio of females to males in the country's Chinese population was low: according to the United States census of 1920, the number of Chinese was 61,639, of whom 53, 891 were males and 7,748 were females. California was home to 24,230 males and 4,582 females.[33] Yet Chinese-white marriage was forbidden in at least eleven states at the time. So if the Supreme Court ruled against the entry of the wives, the Chinese males would basically be forced to choose between bachelorhood, permanent separation from their family in China, or returning to China. In any case it would cause the Chinese community in the United States to diminish. These cases were reported at length in local Chinese newspapers, and the final argument before the U.S. Supreme Court was published in full in *Chung Sai Yat Po*. In May 1925 the Court ruled that the wives of Chinese merchants would be admitted, whereas the wives of U.S. citizens of the Chinese race would not be admitted.

With the hiring of Hendry, the theater at once put the Department of Labor on the defensive. The racial bias, capriciousness, and arbitrariness at the core of the department's decision to reject the Mandarin Theater's petition could not withstand close scrutiny. Hendry's charge that the department lacked jurisdiction over the local affairs of Chinese theaters, in particular, was significant. It laid bare how far the Department had gone to extend its exclusionist prowess and to prevent the theaters from attaining prominence. In the interest of total surveillance and restriction of Chinese opera performers, the department meddled with local governing. The nineteenth century's anti-Chinese city ordinances—such as the Cubic Air Ordinance, which mandated that living and working quarters had to contain at least five hundred cubic feet of air per inhabitant—notoriously had aimed at restricting the Chinese, but at least city government was acting within its own jurisdiction. (And even then, many were declared unconstitutional by higher courts.) The Department of Labor's order amounted to "grounding" the troupe in San Francisco, while no other performing troupes or business enterprises, immigrants, or visitors were denied free movement once they were in the country.

The recent victory regarding the admission of wives of Chinese merchants and the higher courts' ruling as illegal the arbitrary $500 bond the Immigration office imposed on Chinese merchants, enhanced Hendry's position. Nevertheless, the Department of Labor's response was circuitous; with no direct comments, it immediately ordered its first local investigation to be conducted by the immigration office in Los Angeles to determine whether a permit should be granted to the Mandarin Theater there. The final decision would not become available until nearly two months later.

SIXTEEN ACTORS IN EXCESS

During the course of these petitions and appeals, the Mandarin Theater showed few signs of scaling back. It was too critical a time—its rival Lun Hop had opened its new theater in June, now called the Great China Theater. Aside from seeking a larger quota, the Mandarin also imported the latest stage sets and costumes and brought in a stream of new performers. Because of the small fixed quota, this was always a cumbersome process. In order for the newcomers to be admitted, the theater generally had to have vacancies within its quota, spaces that often had to be created by sending current performers away. Switching performers without disturbing or short-staffing regular productions was nearly impossible. The difficulty was exacerbated by the theater's shift to Seattle as its port of entry at the beginning of 1925. After the outgoing actors departed from San Francisco, their replacements would be admitted. Then it took at least three days for the gate entry and the travel from Seattle to San Francisco.

In January the theater's San Francisco attorney, McGee, had persuaded the Department of Labor to allow for the time lag by admitting new performers before a sufficient vacancy in the quota was made. As a result, by the end of January the Mandarin had eleven more performers than its quota allowed. This latitude, the Commissioner General noted, was justified by a recent amendment to the 1921 Immigration Act that allowed certain aliens arriving in excess of quotas to be temporarily admitted and remain in the United States "to relieve cases of extreme hardship."[34] With similar reasoning, five more performers were admitted in early June, pushing the number in the theater's employment to sixty-one, now sixteen over quota. In light of the competition and the Mandarin's new theater in Los Angeles, this was just what the theater needed. Without it, the Mandarin was unlikely to maintain operations in two cities. Yet the temporary solution did not last long. As the department hardened its stance, the upcoming application for the routine six-month permit extension (which expired on June 24) would force the theater to clear out all the extra performers and return to the original quota of forty-five or else forfeit the bonds posted for them. The theater had hoped to obtain a quota increase before the expiration of the permit. But now it was faced with the worst-case scenario: an order of deportation for the sixteen additional actors, and an order for the immediate closing of the Los Angeles branch. Failing to comply with the latter would result in the denial of the extension of its six-month permit, which would mean the deportation of all of its performers and therefore the shuttering of both its theaters.

It would seem that the theater had three main objectives at that point: a quota increase, needed for the Los Angeles branch; the admission of performers in excess of quota, to cover the travel time of those joining and leaving the troupe; and the routine six-month extension of permission for its operations. They inevitably became linked, with adverse effects on each individual outcome. The theater made a plea for the temporary stay of the sixteen members, pending investigation, on June 23. Unfortunately, this new petition was doomed from the start; the Department of Labor had become increasingly impatient with the various requests. Rather than use its discretion to help the Mandarin Theater avoid hardship, as it had in January, it now held the theater strictly to the letter of the law. The extra actors had to go.

Chin Lain, however, had considerable political and financial capital. Chinese commerce was highly valued by the U.S. government, and Chin Lain and his theater were sure that his important allies and top attorneys would help him "regulate the regulators."[35] He also expected to receive more respectful treatment by the immigration officials, as Chinese merchants of his stature would. Three years earlier, prior to a China trip, he applied to the Angel Island immigration office to depart the United States as a merchant (needed for his return). On the memo of prompt approval was the handwritten message, "Set for any day convenient to Mr. Lain by order Mr. Boyer."[36]

As the Mandarin Theater mobilized its influence, figures of social and political prominence such as senators, representatives, the mayor, businessmen, and city police lieutenants brought pressure to bear on both the local immigration office, the Department of Labor, and others. For example, U.S. Representative Florence Kahn wrote directly to the Commissioner General, and a San Francisco police lieutenant wrote to ask a friend to lobby the Labor Department.[37] A host of letters, phone calls, and telegrams rushed in to the department. A note from Senator Lawrence Flaherty to Commissioner General Husband registered his displeasure: "Exceedingly sorry you cannot see way clear to grant extensions."[38]

Under pressure, the department issued a temporary permit for the Los Angeles branch to continue its operation, pending investigation. The deportation order for the sixteen extra actors, however, remained in effect. This put the Mandarin Theater in a bind. The small victory was a pyrrhic one. Having only forty-five performers to divide between two theaters was ruinous to both. Yet if the theater retained the extra performers, it stood to lose a bond of $1,000 for each. As the expiration date of the six-month permit drew near, the theater, with no other alternatives in sight, began to deport actors. It was slow to comply, however, while it continued the negotiations. By June 29, the theater was still twelve performers in excess of the quota. The local newspaper *Chung Sai Yat Po* reported on July 7 the departure of nine performers for China, two actors, two actresses, four instrumentalists, and one scene shifter, stating that their contract was up.[39] Finally, two weeks past the expiration date, the Secretary of Labor instructed the San Francisco office that the bonds should be forfeit unless all members in excess were deported immediately.

TWENTY-FIVE MORE AT THE PORT

But that was not all. Just as all sixteen extra members were ordered deported, twenty-five new performers arrived from Hong Kong on July 4 at Seattle, where they were detained pending admission. But there was no chance for them to enter the United States. The theater did not risk its precarious relationship with the Department of Immigration by petitioning for their admission. Their arrival meant more hardship for the theater: the new actors incurred daily fees for their detention, for which the theater was liable. By mid-July the theater managed to reduce its roster to forty-four so that one famous actress could be admitted; the others remained in detention.

One common strategy among Chinese merchants during the exclusion was, in the phrase of immigrant historian Erika Lee, "negotiating their way through exclusion."[40] The authorities' repeated rejections did not stop the theater from moving along with its expansion, developing strategies as needed. The stakes were high and the pressure only intensified as the two theaters, Mandarin and the newly opened Great China, run by Lun Hop, raced to be the best in town.

In many ways this was not a typical immigration case. The theater's main claim, although it had a goal of admitting Chinese, was the pursuit of business, and politicians were always mindful of the benefits of Chinese commerce. The astronomical profits earned from the first months of the Mandarin Theater's new operation in San Francisco and Los Angeles gave a clear indication of the community's appetite for Cantonese opera. It had proved already that the department's notion that San Francisco had no need for a second Chinese theater was unfounded, and neither was its fear that community discord would result from the rivalry. The increased competition between the two theaters made the Mandarin Theater's business expansion a necessity. Lun Hop reemerged with its new theater, the Great China Theater, and had been profiting from its new Los Angeles wing since January.[41] Whereas Lun Hop had its request of quota increase to eighty rejected in 1924 by the Department of Labor, it still had the largest quota (sixty-four) and seemed to have control of the majority of the Cantonese opera theaters in the United States (see Chapter 6). In contrast, the Mandarin Theater did not have as much flexibility in its cast. One point repeatedly made by the Mandarin's attorneys and prominent allies was that the department should not appear to be granting a monopoly in Los Angeles to Lun Hop.

Most likely the reason for the Department's rejection of the quota increase went beyond the stated problems. Rather, it probably was the result of the department's disdain and its apprehension that the theater was thriving and expanding. Much to its dismay, the popular Chinese theater was growing more permanent as time went on.

Given the limited number of Chinese opera performers in the United States and the popularity of this entertainment, they were much sought after. Even in detention, the actors of the Mandarin Theater in Seattle were not unnoticed: a Chicago company attempted to offer a contract but failed for lack of any quota (apparently yet to be granted by the department), and in August the Chinese consul in Seattle sponsored the detained performers for a one-week benefit, which raised several thousand dollars.[42] Still, the timing of this troupe's arrival seemed curious: Why did the Mandarin Theater contract twenty-five actors when its pleas with the Department of Labor were met with such frequent rejection? Was the theater not putting itself at risk?

As a transnational operation, the Mandarin Theater had to contend with social, political, and economic factors on both sides of the Pacific. The timing of the twenty-five actors' arrival in Seattle in July could have had much to do with schedules in Hong Kong and China. May was typically the turnover season, when all the Cantonese opera troupes in southern China finished their yearly contracts, and most actors signed new contracts to begin in June. In order to be a serious contender for top singers, the Mandarin booking agent had to sign up its choices during this turnover time. Similarly, in 1924, it was in late June that the Mandarin brought the first group of performers, although approval had been granted in late February. As discussed in Chapter 1, the difficult political and economic situation in China also played a role. In 1925 the huge Hong Kong–Canton strike, which started in late May, left many actors and actresses available during the normal turnover period. Troupes were hesitant to draw up contracts since the strike shut down the theater business altogether. That June, therefore, the agents in China had the opportunity to engage an exceptionally large number of outstanding performers for the Mandarin. The booking agent of the Mandarin always tried to get the best; the theater's attorney once pleaded with the secretary of the Department of Labor, "The [Hong Kong] agent scouring very desirable talent . . . has bound my client both as to salary and cost of voyage, and I hereby respectfully petition you to admit the said individuals . . . [so they may] enter upon their duty at the [Mandarin Theatre]."[43] The group's arrival in early July, though a large financial burden to the theater, also was necessary for the theater's expansion. It was a bold move.

NON-IMMIGRANT ALIENS

None of the rules that the Department of Labor devised to regulate Chinese opera theaters—the quota designation, the permit control, the six-month operating period, or the constraints on the length of their actors' stay—were mandated by immigration laws and regulations. Arbitrary in origin, they were established at the discretion of the Department of Labor, especially its Immigration Bureau, which had full autonomy in devising procedures such as these, which had an immense impact on Chinese American musical space. Many aspects of the designated rules, such as the jurisdiction issues discussed above, were questionable. Just as tricky, however, was a core issue, and a most ambiguous one, concerning the legal status of the performers.

In a July memo Hendry set out to dismiss the notion that there was any "legal obstacle" to admitting Chinese actors to the United States. It was a counter argument to the department's contention that Chinese actors were inadmissible in principle. He reminded the department that *In re Ho King* had established that Chinese performers were non-laborers and therefore not subject to exclusion or deportation under Chinese exclusion laws. Although it was a district court case and not argued before the U.S. Supreme Court, Hendry noted, there was little reason to think that the Supreme Court would rule any differently. Therefore, he suggested, the notion that Chinese actors had "no legal right or standing" was incorrect. In fact, he asserted, they had a clear legal right of admission to the United States.[44]

Hendry might have had in mind one of the two above-mentioned Supreme Court cases that challenged the government's interpretation of the 1924 Immigration Act. Both could have had a bearing on the situation of Chinese actors. In one of them, *Cheung Sum Shee v. Nagle*, the Court determined that wives of Chinese merchants must not be excluded from the United States because they are *non-immigrant aliens*, who are not subject to Chinese exclusion rules. The wives were entitled to enter according to a treaty with China from the late nineteenth century.

Using a similar rationale, Hendry laid out the argument that Chinese actors were in fact legally non-immigrant aliens—aliens who visited the country temporarily to conduct business—and thus were fully entitled to enter:

> In as much as Chinese actors are not laborers, . . . it follows that they have a legal right of admission under bond under the Immigration Act of 1924, and I respectfully refer you to Clause #2, Sec. 3, as well as subdivision c of Sec. 13, wherein specific provision is made for the temporary admission of those asking to enter the US for business purposes. It is inconceivable that anyone would argue that the giving of theatrical performances is not a business. . . . So that I submit that *the application for the admission of actors . . . is not based upon the granting of a mere privilege, but is based upon a clear legal right*, and is clearly within the intent of Congress as manifested by the provisions of the Act of 1924, supra.
>
> A Chinese applying to enter this country for the purpose of transacting some financial business dealing or to purchase goods or what not of a business nature, could demand admission without question under the aforesaid provisions of the Act of 1924. That being the case, I cannot understand why a troupe of actors applying to enter the United States for the purpose of giving theatrical performances, which as stated before, is one of the greatest business enterprises in this country, could not likewise demand temporary admittance under proper bonds.[45]

Hendry's brief of July 21, 1925, was the first document to suggest a legal status for Chinese performers of aliens of visitor, and thus non-immigrant, status, and infer from it the *rights* accorded such persons, which included entry into the United States.[46] This rights-based argument was new.[47] The policy-based approach used far more often by Chinatown theater attorneys, which meant arguing against the immigration policy itself or against regulations underlined by the anti-Chinese principle, was often doomed. In contrast, the rights-based argument concerned fairness to individuals. Chinese performers, as non-immigrant aliens, should be accorded the right of entry into the United States. With this memo Hendry suggested, albeit implicitly, that the department had little ground on which to detain the actors at the port.

Hendry's filing had an indelible impact on the immigration process for Chinese opera performers. Since the beginning of the twentieth century they had been deemed "in principle not admissible," their entrance into the United States at the discretion of immigration officers.[48] Hendry's argument gave Chinese actors a basis to claim the right of free movement into and within the country. The Immigration Bureau would eventually agree with Hendry, and adopt his rationale, so that in subsequent years its official document for Chinese performers stated, "No. 2, Sec. 3, and c of Sec. 13 of Immigration Act 1924." Their entry into the United States was a right from that point on. The decision standardized the legal status of Chinese performers until the repeal of the Chinese Exclusion Act in 1943.

It is instructive, here, to reconsider *Cheung Sum Shee v. Nagle,* whose rationale Hendry used in the case of Mandarin Theater. The U.S. Supreme Court's positive ruling was in large part due to the State Department's insistence that the rights granted Chinese in the United States by the 1880 treaty with China should be preserved and survive subsequent exclusionist immigration laws; they included Chinese merchants' right to bring family members into the country. The decision to comply with the treaty—a policy—led to the Supreme Court ruling based on the merchants' wives' status as non-immigrants. In other words, the government's obligation to an international treaty became the real protector of Chinese in the United States at the height of the harsh exclusionist policy embodied in the Immigration Act of 1924. This protection, however, did not extend to Chinese who were U.S.-born and therefore citizens. (Hence the failure of *Chang Chan v. Nagle*—an appeal for the entry of the wives of Chinese American citizens.) Because the citizens' wives lacked the treaty's protection, the immigration laws prevailed.

Focusing on the status of performers as non-immigrant businesspeople, Hendry skipped the usual argument about the needs of the Chinese American community. Instead he cast them as temporary, transient, and to be protected by the international treaty. In a peculiar way, therefore, this perpetual foreignness was what allowed Chinese opera performers to enter and perform during the Chinese Exclusion Era. It was necessary to camouflage their true significance and influence on the community. Playing up this foreign image also linked Chinese opera to the realm of exotic art (for visitors) and kept it further away from the local community (for undesirable citizens). This result was more palatable to the immigration officials, as it was to the Supreme Court.

HARD-EARNED TRIUMPH

As a rule, immigration officials were generally "reluctant to accept defeat" and would continue to investigate until something could be uncovered.[49] Neither Hendry's skillfully written brief nor an investigative report from a Los Angeles inspector that the city could easily support two Chinese theaters was sufficient to persuade the skeptical Department of Labor. In fact, it merely specified that replacements for departing troupe members not be released from detention in Seattle until the departing members checked out at a port. This created further hardship on the already short-staffed Mandarin Theater, which, while waiting for new performers in transit, had to operate with fewer than the permitted forty-five in two cities. The wait for the replacements would severely impair the performances, and consequently ticket sales. By the end of July attendance at the Los Angeles Mandarin Theater dropped by 90 percent as a result of insufficient staffing. Reporting a loss of $400 per day due to poor ticket sales and detention costs, the theater was in terrible shape.[50]

In the meantime, with a growing distrust of the situation, the Department of Labor decided to conduct its own investigation on "the whole Chinese actor situation throughout the country," claiming that it would "pursue a general review of all the Chinese theaters in the States."[51] The department dispatched a young high-level officer, Assistant Secretary Edward Shaughnessy, a member of the Board of Review, to Los Angeles, as well as to other major cities, to investigate the situation at first hand. The bureaucrat finally stepped out of his office, closing up the distance between Washington, DC, and Chinese theaters.

The Department of Labor, meanwhile, was facing lobbying efforts from U.S. congressmen, some from quite unlikely corners. They paradoxically included Senator Hiram Johnson, a former two-term California governor who was now chairman of the Senate Committee on Immigration and a sponsor of the 1924 Immigration Act (also known as the Johnson-Reed Act). Senator Johnson wrote repeatedly to pressure the Department of Labor on the theater's behalf and kept close tabs on the status of the decisions. This was ironic because as governor Johnson had been outspoken in his support of California's Alien Land Act in 1913, which forbade the ownership of land by aliens "ineligible for citizenship" and so targeted all Asians. Perhaps the promise that "[Chinese actors] in no way interfere[d] with labor in the way of competition," in the words of the San Francisco police lieutenant, helped.[52] But more important, as indicated in Johnson's letter to the Secretary of Labor, the true beneficiary of his lobbying effort was the brother of an appellate court justice: the Mandarin Theater's attorney, Russell Tyler. Johnson's endorsement was a personal favor.[53] As this example shows, opponents of Chinese immigration sometimes privately represented Chinese causes for their own benefit, while "publicly maintaining an aggressive anti-Chinese posture."[54]

Well into August, the department's replies to senators' inquiries were scornful of the Mandarin Theater. Thus it was extraordinary when the tune was suddenly changed and approval for both the increase to eighty-five and a branch in Los Angeles was granted on August 19. The ruling was remarkable for its overwhelmingly positive and empathic tone.

> A representative of the Bureau and Department recently made a personal investigation of the Chinese theatre situation throughout the country. It was found that the

> Mandarin Theatre in San Francisco is one of the leading Chinese theatres in the country. Furthermore, it was also found that the Mandarin Theatre in Los Angeles is also in that class.... The claim was made that it will be impossible for this troupe to continue to successfully operate both theatres on the limited strength. As a matter of fact, it has always been claimed by the various theatrical interests that it is impossible to successfully operate a bona fide Chinese theatre with less than forty or forty-five actors. When a comparison of the personnel of these two theaters was made with that of others when operating in full force, it was plainly evident that both theatres, that is the Mandarin theatres, were undermanned. When visiting these theatres the plays were in operation, which were carefully interpreted and explained to said representative. Certain actors were pointed out under the present limited personnel who were compelled to take as high as five different parts in the course of one evening.... It was plainly evident that both theatres were undermanned. In considering the personnel of a Chinese theatre, it must be borne in mind that the orchestra, which consists of 6 or 10, is classed as actors. Said orchestra is located to the left of the stage and its members have to be thoroughly familiar with the play. A different series is given each night so that it results that practically what might be called a new play is given each night, and this without rehearsal.... The interests cannot recruit talented musicians at random. Furthermore, a number of the stagehands are likely classed as actors, as they too have to be thoroughly familiar with the costumes which must be changed quickly between acts.[55]

Assistant Secretary Shaughnessy had had the opportunity to meet the petitioners and see for himself—the elaborate theaters and their spectacular performers—and to listen to evidence, histories, testimony, and argument in favor of expanding the theaters' operation. In other words, he could make decisions affecting a particular theater, rather than an entire category of Chinese opera theaters, an underclass of the society.

The dignity and wealth of merchants such as Chin Lain might also have played a role. The ruling was written with a kind of compassion rarely exhibited in the bureau's correspondence with Chinese theaters. The positive tone might have been aimed at justifying the department's ultimate reversal or catering to the interested parties listed on the memo: Senators Johnson and Cameron. The report even went so far as to suggest that the bureau could assist the five actors with clonorchiasis in obtaining proper treatment, in order to be admitted. Regardless, it seemed that the Mandarin Theater had managed to negotiate its way through exclusionism.

The performers detained in Seattle since early July were immediately admitted on August 22. In less than a week, the number of performers at the theater increased from forty-five to sixty-six.[56] In subsequent weeks there was a parade of new performers onto the stage of the Mandarin. It also expanded its capability to compete with rival theaters. The Mandarin Theater's rich offering of daily productions in the succeeding years was a direct consequence of this decision.

EVERYDAY LIFE OF THE REGULATIONS

The Mandarin Theater was extraordinary among Chinatown theaters in the 1920s. From the start, it erected its own building and engaged performers directly from China, while others typically took more cautious steps by renting their theater space and by recruiting performers who were already in the Americas. Because immigration policies required the theater to gain approval from the government nearly every step of the way, the Mandarin's troubles with immigration illustrated the kinds of legal battles and dilemmas a Chinese theater faced. Yet with its opportune timing and exceptional resources associated with Chin Lain, whom *Life* magazine dubbed "Chinatown's No. 1 Citizen,"[57] the Mandarin weathered the test when a lesser theater would patently have failed. Immigration restrictions truly put to the test the prowess and perseverance of merchants who supported theaters. The Department of Labor at the end did not intimidate the recalcitrant Mandarin Theater. The Mandarin stands in contrast to the Lun Hop company, which a year earlier did not resist when its request for a quota increase was rejected.[58]

With this victory Chinese performers were formally classified as non-immigrant aliens, a category with rising significance in the coming decades. It would serve to standardize the legal status of Chinese performers until the repeal of the Chinese Exclusion Act in 1943. The Mandarin Theater's perseverance thus succeeded at both the institutional and the symbolic level. Without the victory, San Francisco in the 1920s might have had to succumb to the immigration officer's dictum that the city could only have limited Chinese opera with limited impact on future generations. The case of the Mandarin Theater, fought behind the scenes while elegant and attractive productions went on daily, provides a window into the everyday life of immigration control.

While all theatrical or musical entrepreneurs have to be mindful of audience taste, repertoire, and appropriate singers, for Chinatown theaters there was the added constraint of working around immigration regulations during the Chinese Exclusion Era. As a group they also faced additional economic and political pressures which were quietly fought through administrative channels and remained mostly unnoticed. One could hardly detect from the playbills of the Mandarin Theater in June and July 1924 the immigration-related hardships it was facing.

Today it seems unfathomable that running a top-tier opera theater would require such intense battles with the Department of Labor. Yet given that the Immigration Bureau was charged with implementing Chinese exclusionist principles, this was the daily life of Chinatown theaters. The Mandarin Theater's small victory benefited Chinese theaters across the country. However, immigration constraints continued to plague them until the end of the exclusion era, long after the golden age of the theatrical business was over, after the audience had dwindled, and after new entertainment genres such as movies replaced the once-irresistible lure of nightly Cantonese opera performances.[59]

PART II

PERFORMANCE PRACTICE OF THE 1920S

CHAPTER 4

AESTHETICS, REPERTOIRE, ROLES, AND PLAYBILLS

What was Cantonese opera of the 1920s in North America like? What works were sung and performed on stage and what were the popular role types? Clear answers to these questions are quite elusive. In southern China, Cantonese opera went through significant changes in the twentieth century. Its performances relied heavily on oral tradition and improvisation, and its practices were far from homogeneous. These factors significantly shaped Chinese theaters of North America, whose network of performers linked them closely to southern China. As a whole the practice of the 1920s was very different from Cantonese opera as performed in the 1970s and later. In addition, the documentation is piecemeal, and the period did not receive much scholarly attention until fairly recently. In order to reconstruct the practice in North America, I rely on more than one thousand Chinese playbills of the 1920s from theaters in San Francisco (primarily), New York, Vancouver, Seattle, and Havana that survive in various archives and personal collections. Together the playbills provide a complex picture of these Chinatowns' stage performances. Just as important are seminal works on Cantonese opera history by prominent writers of the 1940s such as Mai Xiaoxia, and memoirs and oral histories by veteran performers such as Chen Tiesheng, Chen Feinong, Liu Guoxing, and Huang Tao.[1] Both types provide valuable accounts about performance practice in the first half of the century in southern China. Also, Bell Yung's important study of Cantonese opera as musical process provides a systematic understanding of the opera's musical elements, and recent studies of the beginning of Cantonese opera as urban theater provides crucial historical context.[2] Drawing from these sources, as well as commentaries found in contemporary Chinese magazines and newspapers, the chapter offers a working knowledge of Cantonese opera as practiced in North America during the 1920s. It begins with a consideration of the general aesthetics of Chinese opera and the earlier history of Cantonese opera, followed by an examination of the significant changes that took place in the period 1910–1920. They were reflected in four areas: staging, female troupes, role types, and opera scripts. I then introduce key elements of Cantonese opera that include its vocal music, instrumental accompaniment, and repertoire. A close examination of the convention of the playbill concludes the chapter.

GENERAL AESTHETICS OF CHINESE OPERA

Cantonese opera, a genre with a distinctive tradition and style, is inextricably connected to the general history of Chinese opera. As spectacle, performance, and sound, Chinese opera is characterized by richly embroidered costumes, colorfully painted faces, choreographed stage movements, powerful singing voices, heightened speech, elaborated melodic types, and classic percussion gestures that punctuate the drama. Its repertoire has persisted through live stage performance for eight centuries, produced in countless renditions in a great variety of regional genres. One of the genres—Peking opera—evolved into a refined performing art between 1910 and 1930, represented by virtuosic stars such as Mei Lanfang. It grew to have immense mass appeal and gained the attention of the nation during the era of the Republic of China. Mei Lanfang, a performer of young female roles, became an iconic figure who was introduced prominently to the American public as early as 1923 in a page-long *New York Times* article titled "The Chinese Stage and the Dark Lady of Its Sonnets."[3]

Throughout its history, Chinese opera consisted of many singing styles that were geographically dispersed and widely circulated.[4] In the mid-Ming Dynasty, singing styles evolved through the involvement of literati and were lauded for their refinement and quality. By the mid-Qing Dynasty, several styles spread into the geographically expansive China of vastly different dialects and ethnicities, facilitating the emergence of many distinctive regional genres. From then on, the regional genres developed their individual characteristics, showing different degrees of dominance by local dialects, colloquial expressions, tonal inflections, vernacular materials, and so on. About three hundred regional genres were recorded by the early twentieth century, many of which became integral to cultural practices and traditions of their respective regions.[5] Whether high art, vernacular music theater, or ritual performances, they have enchanted a broad spectrum of audiences, from elites and merchants to the common folk.

Chinese opera is well known for its symbolic tradition, which is made up of a host of tropes and gestures. A hand gesture can denote gracefulness or role type, a distinctive percussion pattern can create a certain mood, a passage of heightened speech can have the effect of an eloquent soliloquy, and a painted face with specific lines and colors can bring to life even for a young audience particular historical, literary, and legendary characters. Even the costumes' style, colors, and embroidery can reveal the characters' status and predicament. Many symbolic elements shared by various Chinese opera genres are widely understood across Chinese culture.

The aesthetics of Chinese opera are traditionally distinguished by its abstraction. With minimal stage props and a simple backdrop, the performers embody the characters, their movements—pantomime, martial arts, and dance—depicting the locale and the music and dialogues rendering the story. The aesthetic quality of a performance is generally determined by the central attributes of singing, recitation, acting, and martial arts. Together, vocal skills, musical improvisation, acrobatic dexterity, and complex choreography coalesce into the portrayal of a character, be it a significant legendary personage or a stock figure in a historical drama. This focus on performing explains why discourse about Chinese opera often places much emphasis on the execution of particular characters. Writers commenting on virtuosic artists such as Peking opera's Mei Lanfang or Cantonese opera's Li Xuefang tend to focus on their execution of famous arias and characters, down to nuanced and minute musical and performing details. Chinese opera performers were not merely vocalists; singing was never their only talent, and in some situations it was not their primary one.

Audiences focused on the overall expression. Take the young belle role, for example: an opera performer (either male or female) trained for this particular role type wore a spectacularly embroidered gown, sang melodious and expressive arias, enunciated in the heightened speech style, and carried himself or herself with highly stylized movement, or even in choreographed steps, all in a seamless whole. The performing body not only portrayed the role but also animated the world in which he or she resided, making it vividly present to the audience. Such virtuosity could be quite mesmerizing.

This general set of characteristics was shared by many regional genres during this period, and there was much cross-fertilization among them. Whereas Peking opera epitomized the style of northern China, Cantonese opera came to represent the south. Cantonese opera was more spirited, its performance freer with improvisation, and its costumes were more ornate and flashy. Cantonese opera also developed its own variations of accompanying instruments, music, role types, staging, and other characteristics reflective of its region.

THE 1920S: ITINERANT AND URBAN TROUPES, STAGES, GENDER, AND REPERTOIRE

In the late Ming Dynasty (about 1600), when many regional genres of Chinese opera grew to have their distinctive forms, Cantonese opera rose as the most prominent regional style performed in the Guangdong and Guangxi areas. While the early history of Cantonese opera remains the subject of scholarly debates, most agree that it grew out of the work of itinerant troupes. There were the local and indigenous *bendiban* troupes, which performed seasonally in rural areas, and the *waijiangban* troupes, which emigrated with merchants from other provinces to Guangzhou, the center of business and foreign trade. The *waijiangban* troupe brought to the region dominant music styles in Chinese opera: *erhuang*, *kunqiang*, *gaoqiang*, and *bangziqiang*. Indigenous and newly arrived styles melded, and professional troupes absorbed local influences. A performers' guild was formed in the late Ming Dynasty (about 1620), and by the Qing Dynasty (about 1650) an opera genre with a unique Cantonese quality emerged. In order to perform in cities and towns throughout the Pearl River delta, early itinerant Cantonese opera troupes lived on junks and barges called Red Boats, which became synonymous with Cantonese opera. By 1889 the Cantonese opera professionals' organization, Bahe Huiguan (Eight Harmonies Association), was formed, overseeing business regulations, contractual agreements, mutual aid and protection, resources, and dispute arbitration. It regulated, for example, the size of the boats a troupe could have based on its cast.

At the beginning of the twentieth century Cantonese opera went through significant transformations. Changes in four areas were most significant in the decade leading up to the 1920s, and they greatly influenced the renaissance of Chinatown theaters in the United States. I consider each in terms of its historical context and its manifestation in Chinatowns of North America.

Performance Spaces

Starting at the end of the nineteenth century, the performance space of Cantonese opera was indelibly affected by modernity; the changes reflected not only the rise of new types of theaters but also the general cultural surroundings. Previously, because of the peripatetic nature of the troupes, Cantonese opera had been performed on temporary stages consisting of bamboo sheds. Such stages were minimal in terms of facilities and décor, and a simple cloth divided the backstage from the front. The sets and props comprised mainly a table, chairs, and cloth covers for two customary gates (for entry and exit) at the back of the stage, as well as poles and flags representing everything from mountains to bedchambers, and from horses to carriages.

As urban centers formed in southern China and the merchant class grew near trade ports in the late nineteenth century, purpose-built theaters for Cantonese opera appeared in large port cities such as Guangzhou, Hong Kong, Foshan, and Macau. Guangzhou's first theater was built in 1899; in Hong Kong theaters appeared even earlier. The grand three-story Taiping Theater, built in 1904, had one thousand seats offered in three tiers—wood benches, regular seats, and box seats. As the city expanded, more theaters were opened: two on Hong Kong Island and three on the newly developed Kowloon Peninsula. Theater owners were often also the proprietors of the troupes. Modern theatrical architecture was used; the Lee Theater in Hong Kong, for example, completed in 1925, was designed by a French architect and modeled after late nineteenth-century French opera houses.[6]

As the historian Chen Meibao notes, although a regional genre, Cantonese opera had many distinctive features formed by a rich cosmopolitan culture.[7] This included Shanghai, where Cantonese opera troupes had had an active presence since the 1880s and which had its own theaters such as the Shanghai Grand Theater (1917) and the influential Canton Grand Stage (Guang Wutai 1917).[8] The cultural milieu of Shanghai also encouraged significant cross-fertilization between Cantonese opera and forms of entertainment such as dance bands, Western opera and concerts, other Chinese opera genres (especially Peking opera), and contemporary Chinese plain-spoken dramas, as well as motion pictures.

Stages also evolved. The most notable changes were the use of spectacle and the move toward realism. There was plenty of inspiration: the 1908 opening of the New Stage Theater (Xin Wutai) in Shanghai marked the first appearance of Western aesthetics and innovation on Chinese stages. They began to use painted backdrops featuring scenes of gardens, lakes, interiors, and so on, as well as fancy props operated by machine, and stage lighting.[9] In 1920 the Shanghai newspaper *Shen Bao* reported that the Canton Grand Stage spent $5,000 on grandiose new scenery for Cantonese opera star Li Xuefang and her troupe, making it comparable to the glorious stage of Peking opera star Mei Lanfang.[10] When the theater engaged a male troupe called Da Ronghua in 1923, it arrived with 130 performers and more than one hundred hand-painted scenes.[11] Another *Shen Bao* report of the same year noted that a new opera, *Beauty on the Palm*, would include eight scenic backgrounds: wilderness, a snow-covered plum flower meadow, a glittery golden palace, a grand pond in moonlight, a celestial pavilion, a gorgeous royal garden, a royal tomb, and a mobile lotus.[12] The scenes would be accompanied by designs of electric lights that made indistinguishable the real and the staged. By 1928 an enthusiastic report about an elaborate opera not only named the librettist-composer and the dramaturge-producer but also the scene artist and the paper-sculpture master. Cantonese opera theaters incorporated modern trends and innovations that were sweeping urban centers in the Republic of China.[13]

In the United States, the stages of Chinese theaters in the late nineteenth century were simple and bare, adorned with only wooden chairs and a table. But when Chinese theater professionals arrived in the U.S. Chinatowns in the 1920s, they brought with them experiences and visions from the urban centers of their native land. San Francisco's new theaters, the Mandarin Theater and the Great China Theater, were comparable to the modern specialized theaters in southern China. They embraced realism from the start. When the Great China Theater opened in 1925, its stage backdrop was built from sheet metal painted with a colorful garden scene, a realistic painting that could be seen in some photos from its early days and that remains mostly intact today.[14] The theaters' fanciful backdrops depicted perspective paintings of garden scenes, grand palaces, inner chambers, rugged mountains, and more. New scenery (and wardrobes) continued to arrive from China, and many professional scene painters such as Xu Jianbo and Muo Keming came. A Works Progress Administration study carried out in 1936 found in the backstage of the Great China Theater sixteen different painted backdrops labeled with descriptions such as imperial court, judgment hall, prison cell, great ocean, clouds–celestial abodes, Buddhist temple, and stream with boat. The Mandarin Theater had thirty backdrops of the rolled type.[15] The general penchant for onstage realism was also enhanced by the metropolitan cultural milieu in New York, Los Angeles, and San Francisco of the 1920s, when the entertainment industries were in their heydays. In addition, rivalry hastened San Francisco Chinatown theaters' embrace of realism, as the troupes strove to outdo each other with three-dimensional backdrops, multi-tiered sets, and scrim effects or cinematic montage (see Chapter 7). By the end of 1920s props such as coffins, rows of rifles, and large paper sculptures of sea creatures or animals were common. Silhouettes of actresses cast by special lighting would appear in a window high up on the backdrop—typical for a ghost or dream sequence—or characters would enter the stage by descending on a chair or cage from the ceiling. The grandiosity and complexity of the productions were captured in professional photographs of dramatic stage poses, made for playbills to showcase new productions.[16]

Emergence of Female Troupes

During the Qing Dynasty women were not allowed on stage, so all-male troupes dominated the profession of Cantonese opera. Typically troupes engaged performers with contracts starting in mid-June of the lunar calendar (before the birthday of the goddess Guanyin), and disbanded at the end of the following May. In the early twentieth century performers with signature styles emerged, and virtuosity became more important. As a result, bidding wars for top stars intensified. The buzz surrounding the formation of new troupes was reflected in the tradition of issuing a popular trade newsletter, *Zhenlan Bao*, every June, right before the season began, announcing the casts and role types of all thirty-six "new" troupes.[17] Aspiring performers moved up the professional ladder from one contract to the next, angling for the more prestigious troupes and highest salaries.

Although female singers were strictly disallowed on stage, they did perform in venues such as teahouses. (Some of their performances can be heard in the early recordings of Cantonese opera of the beginning of the twentieth century.) However, when the 1911 revolution overthrew the last Chinese dynasty, the Qing, and paved the way for a modern republic, the restriction was eased, and actresses began to appear on the theatrical stage. Female troupes became popular, and two troupes rose to great acclaim in 1919: Qunfang Yanying (Brilliant Reflection of Blossom) and Jinghua Ying (Mirror Flower). The lead actresses for these two troupes, Li Xuefang and Suzhou Mei, respectively, were the top actresses at this time. In its first engagement in Shanghai in 1919, Qunfang Yanying and Li Xuefang enthralled the astute audiences at the Shanghai Grand Theater.[18] When they returned to Shanghai the following October, engaged by the newly opened Guang Wutai theater, the troupe arrived with more than 120 members, 20 more than the male troupe that had performed in April. It was the most talked-about event of the town.[19] According to press reports, the stardom of Li Xuefang was comparable to that of the reigning star of Peking opera, Mei Lanfang. By 1925 the large number of female troupes prompted the patriarchal organization Bahe Huiguan to form a female division.[20] All through this decade, the female troupes performed in parallel with the all-male troupes in southern China, without, however, sharing the stage. Not until 1933 did the Hong Kong government lift the ban on mixed-sex stage performance; the Guangzhou government followed in 1936.

Star actresses as a whole were not given the same regard as were actors by theaters, managers, or critics. In Guangzhou, female troupes' performances tended to be featured at smaller or less prestigious venues such as modern department stores or entertainment parks.[21] Many critics readily dismissed their popularity as merely a fad. Nevertheless, actresses in the 1920s had an indelible impact on the Cantonese opera profession, from vocal style and song types to glamorous wardrobes.

In the United States, Chinatowns benefited immensely from the rise of female Cantonese opera performers. In the nineteenth century Chinatown theaters presented male troupes only, with female roles performed by female impersonators, but by the 1920s many actresses appeared on stage. They did not perform as female troupes, either; rather, actors and actresses shared the stage from the start. Not only did female opera singers take prominent roles, but they were often billed as the main attraction. Famous actresses were given top billing and were well paid, and their signature repertoire was staged with increased frequency. Photographs of the actresses were sold in stores, printed on playbills and in newspapers, and featured in window displays. They contributed significantly to the popularity of the theaters. When traveling across the Pacific, stellar actresses were treated well: like the top star actors, they stayed in first-class cabins and had companions.[22] Mixed-sex performances did not immediately replace the older patriarchal practice. Instead, a wide range of casting possibilities opened up, in conceptual terms or pragmatic terms. One common practice was to feature an actress and a female impersonator taking turns performing the same character in the same evening, in order to benefit from the strength of both. An actress playing multiple roles of both genders was a frequent attraction. Thus Chinatown theaters were at times experimental in terms of gender performance; unmarked gender crossing became marked in expected and unexpected ways.

New Shift in Role Types

The decade of the 1920s was a pivotal period in the transformation of role types as well. Like other Chinese opera genres, Cantonese opera has distinctive role types (*hangdang* or *jiaose*). Performers were trained for particular role types and followed their respective conventions closely. Discussions of early practice usually list ten general role types common to most genres of Chinese opera; these could be further divided into twenty subtypes or more. However, starting in the early twentieth century, the diversity was gradually reduced. This did not happen across the board, but nonetheless, there was a general move toward a system of six role types, the so-called six-pillar system. This change was seen as progress toward modernity as it emulated a newer theatrical form—spoken drama that was introduced to China only at the end of the nineteenth century or, later, cinema. It meant cutting back the complex tradition of role types in Cantonese opera and the characteristics that distinguished those rich role types, and instead focusing on the leading male and female roles. The rise of performing stars also contributed to this trend.

While it is hard to pin down with any certainty the active role types employed during this transitional period, a system of twelve role types seemed to dominate.[23] They routinely appeared on printed cast lists, *hengtou dan*, which were often used for contractual purpose by troupes for hire.[24] They were as follows.

1. *Wusheng* (bearded warrior)
2. *Xiaowu* (young warrior)
3. *Huadan* (young belle)
4. *Xiaosheng* (young scholar)
5. *Nanchou* (male comic role)
6. *Nüchou* (female comic role)
7. *Zhengdan* (decorous middle-aged woman)
8. *Zhengsheng* (dignified middle-aged man)

9. *Zongsheng* (middle-aged scholar)
10. *Gongjiao* (bearded old man)
11. *Da Huamian* (villainous man)
12. *Er Huamian* (tempestuous man)

In addition to hengtou dan of famous troupes, these were also listed in the trade newspaper *Zhenlan Bao*.[25] There were many variations on the list; some had fewer role types, and others had subcategories. This was particularly true of the huadan role, which was frequently divided into warrior huadan, comic huadan, exquisite huadan, and virtuosic huadan. Regardless, the first six role types appeared consistently, though 5 and 6 often were grouped simply as the comic role. The last six were definitely lower in significance for this time period, and roles 7 through 9 were at times simply omitted.

In the twelve-role-type tradition, wusheng was accorded the highest regard, though the statuses of xiaosheng and huadan were on the rise, as were the comic roles. The role type was often reflected in the stage name of the performer, which emphasized the role's attributes and characteristics. Gongye Chuang (Warrior Chuang) was a famous actor of wusheng (half a dozen actors' names began with "Warrior"); Fengqing Qi (Amorous-Feeling Qi) was a respected actor of the xiaosheng type, reflecting the romantic nature of the role type; Daniu Bing (Big Bull Bing) was an actor of *er huamian,* the role type of the forthright, tempestuous man.

These twelve role types were featured regularly on Cantonese opera stages in the 1920s before the move toward the six-pillar system. Three factors contributed to this change: the increased emphasis given to virtuosity, a shift of preference in role types (from warrior types to civic types and from a myriad of roles to principal male and female roles), and the influence of other performing arts, in particular, spoken modern drama and motion pictures. In general, urban audiences had become accustomed to romances featuring young lovers, rather than the different role types of traditional operas.

As a result, role types became less distinctive. In the six-pillar system, which was not formalized until the late 1930s, the great variety of role types was replaced with six primary ones: *wenwusheng* (young civil-martial male), young scholar, *zhenyin huadan* (young belle), *erbang huadan* (secondary young belle), *chousheng* (comedian), and bearded warrior. The new wenwusheng merged several earlier role types.

Chinatown theaters in North America followed the general trend, although the twelve role types remained in use perhaps a bit longer than in urban theaters of southern China. All through the late 1920s, role types that were later dropped in the six-pillar system, such as the two *huamian* types and the *gongjiao* role remained. In San Francisco Daniu Bing was active, and Gongye Chuang was a top-billed actor at the Great China Theater. In addition, a full range of role types averaging twenty to thirty performers was presented in the cast lists in daily theater playbills. Although playbill cast lists could be padded and should not be taken as actual records of the performances, the existence of these actors' names well into the early 1930s suggests that their role types remained active.

Nevertheless, xiaowu, xiaosheng, and huadan grew more prominent. Because actresses were often revered for their young belle roles, or huadan, their sharing the stage with male lead characters gave a certain verisimilitude to romantic repertoire. Overall, a more "contemporary" kind of actress emerged and worked to cement the theaters' move toward modernity. At the same time, because the categories of roles grew less strict, performers became in general capable of a wider range of stage movements and singing skills. Various popular plot lines involving cross-dressing also encouraged the performers to be versatile.

From Tigang xi to Scripted Opera

Traditionally, the performance of Cantonese opera relied heavily on the convention of *paichang*—stock episodes—which had been passed down for generations.[26] The term *paichang* refers to scenarios or episodes with defined patterns or formulas. Familiar examples of paichang are elopement, secret engagement, beauty being rescued, father-daughter reunion, teary farewell, and chasing after the husband. Each is a specific dramatic situation with particular dialogue, arias, percussion accompaniment, wardrobe, stage movement, and scenery. Some were derived from specific operas and named after them. In general, paichang can be divided into those that could be performed by any role type, such as mounting the horse, and those that require certain role types, such as elopement. As many as two hundred paichang existed.[27] They were committed to memory by performers during their early training, and they constituted the foundation of performing knowledge.[28]

The convention of paichang was essential to a practice common in Cantonese opera: *tigang xi*, or a performance stemming from a plot outline (similar to the *canovaccio* of seventeenth-century *commedia dell'arte*). A theater director (*kaixi shiye)* would create an opera by stringing together scenarios (paichang). He would devise scenes with paichang and designated performers in a plot outline, which he laid out on a large sheet of paper with a grid drawn on it. The outline was then posted by the right-hand door of the backstage for reference. Each square designated a scene with names of characters and performers, paichang, tunes, and props written in abbreviated form (some more detailed than others). The paichang tradition and the use of tigang xi allowed itinerant troupes to be very flexible with their performances, adjusting the program to meet local tastes or needs. No *tigang* of this period from San Francisco seem to have survived; however, figure 4.1 reproduces an example from the 1940s. On a large piece of paper, the *tigang* laid out essential

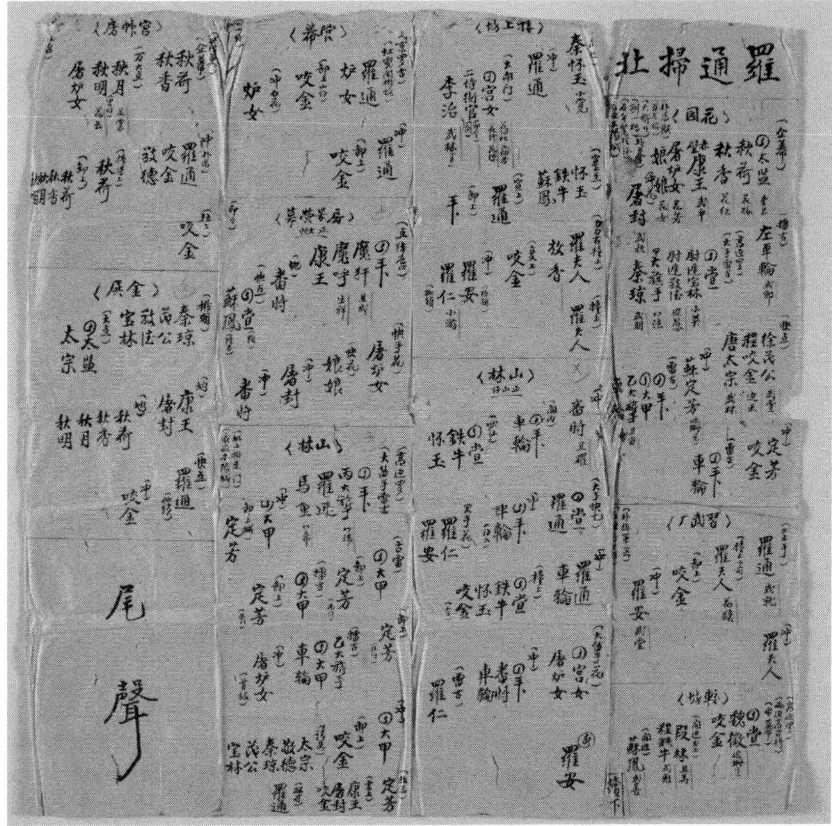

Fig. 4.1. Tigang Poster, *Luo Tong Conquers the North* (courtesy of the Hong Kong Heritage Museum).

information about the performance. At the top right-hand corner is the opera's title, *Luo Tong Conquers the North*, a story based on a Qing-Dynasty semi-fictional tale, the Heroic Legend of Tang. Underneath it are ten scenes listed in separate boxes in four columns reading from right to left: garden, martial art practice field, fighting arena, woods in the mountain, palace chamber, golden palace hall, and so on. Each square contains columns of copious notes about the scenery, setting, characters, performers, props, and music. Such tigang posters served as guides to all aspects of the productions.

All the details were left to the performers. Therefore, they had to be not only very learned in paichang but also endowed with quick wit. The success of the opera depended on their creativity in fleshing out the details of a paichang and providing the bridges to connect paichang. The spotlight could fall on the actors' virtuosity and ex tempore performances. The more elaborate and extended improvisations, which were highly entertaining, had a special name, *baodu*, meaning literally "exploding the belly." Comic roles in particular could enliven the performance with jokes and gags. In the process of improvisation, cues were communicated onstage with fellow performers and accompanying musicians by a set of hand gestures (*shouying*, or hand shadow). As sign language, numerous shouying—as many as twenty-six—were used to signal a change in percussion patterns (to punctuate stage actions and create moods), speech, and musical forms.[29] The need for rehearsal was thus minimal. With tigang xi, the theaters could feature different operas from one evening to the next.

Improvisation was an integral part of Cantonese opera performance. It allowed the performers to adjust the formulaic patterns of paichang to a particular story, connect smoothly to the next scenario, or prolong a scene. It was typical for an opera to include twenty or thirty paichang. Audiences' familiarity with the formulaic episodes also enhanced their theatrical experience and enjoyment of improvisations. Furthermore, because it depended on capable performers and active audience response, successful improvisation helped develop a close rapport through the fourth wall.

The rise of urban theaters precipitated the creation of a new type of opera, however, that changed the common practices of Cantonese opera. The downside of tigang xi was that it could be too loosely structured and have plots lacking originality or novelty. The establishment of urban troupes meant competition to secure a loyal following. Scripted opera arose as a response. More tightly structured, it included new lyrics and story lines and original melodies. Newly scripted operas were created, published, and circulated. This trend meant a greater need for good playwrights, whose responsibilities exceeded those of the traditional kaixi shiye and whose fame rose with their operas' success. They did not compose new operas from scratch. Their task involved devising storylines and scenes, creating new lyrics (with the proper tonal inflection, syllables, and rhyme and metric scheme) for existing aria types and fixed tunes, and composing new melodies according to existing models of musical structures, styles, and cadence patterns. To be sure, some of the new scripts were well-crafted. When the actress Li Xuefang mesmerized Shanghai on her second visit, the newspaper *Shen Bao* reported, "In this visit, she will stage three new operas, enhanced by $5,000 worth of new scenery. The three operas were penned by eminent erudite playwrights with an eye to enlightening and inculcating values."[30] Li Xuefang was thereafter considered to share the Peking opera icon Mei Lanfang's reliance on literati for her signature repertoire.

Many new operas had full scripts, elaborate speeches, and colloquial dialogues, although at times the playwright could opt for shortcuts such as using paichang names for secondary or transitional scenes while composing new material for the key scenes. The new operas also covered a greater variety of topics including historical legends and contemporary stories, traditional and modern characters, mythical and modern fables, and fictitious and true stories. Many erudite singers also wrote new fully scripted operas, which allowed them greater scope for innovation and experimentation. Many of these newly scripted operas would remain in the repertory for decades.

According to a 1924 commentary printed in both San Francisco's *Young China* and in Shanghai's *Shen Bao*, typically the writer of a tigang xi was paid two dollars (in Mexican silver dollars), whereas authors of fully scripted plays received as much as two hundred dollars. Many singers wanted to write operas but found it to be a difficult task: aside from providing the plot, bridges, lyrics, dialogue, and music, they also needed to see to its production—directing singers, coaching musicians, coordinating the timing of scene changes, cueing stage action with appropriate musical passages, and even tracking down lead singers.[31]

It is unsurprising, then, that Chinatown theaters were lagging behind southern Chinese theaters with this new trend. For the most part they continued with tigang xi, which made it easier to adapt to constraints on casting possibilities, to meet varied audience preferences, and to stage a wide array of operas easily. The flexibility and spontaneity of the tigang xi practice also allowed the theaters to accommodate the constant new arrivals, who typically made their debuts immediately.

The new practice did reach the United States, however: in late 1925, many top actors arrived with new scripted operas, followed by veteran playwrights. For several years new operas were written and produced. Names of dramatists began to be noted prominently along with the lead performers on the playbills. Among them were Pang Yifeng, Li Wutian, and Li Renzhou. However, new operas accounted for only a small portion of the programs. Even when new operas were staged, they were most likely given in the flexible tigang xi style. Popular stories could then be staged without the effort of learning the full script. Fluidity and similarity between the new scripted opera and tigang xi-type opera abounded; both drew from familiar performance idioms or stock episodes.

The decade of the 1920s was a transformative era for Cantonese opera. It was a period uniquely rich for the coexistence of the conventional and the new in repertoire, performance practices, role types, and gender balance. Experimental stage productions reflected the newly introduced realism in Cantonese opera, the dominance of actresses was a direct consequence of the rise of all-female troupes, the complexity of gender- and role-crossing performances revealed the theaters' adjustment to changes in role types, and the mixture of classical and new operas and the rise of the playwright showed a theatrical culture relying on tigang xi, while looking ahead to fully scripted opera.

THE MUSIC OF CANTONESE OPERA

Far from being homogeneous, musical practices varied widely. In south China, each troupe's practice was shaped by factors including its location (urban theater or itinerant), gender (male or female), place in the hierarchy of troupes (from a high rank of 120 members to a lower rank of 60), and penchant for novelty. These variations account for the discrepancies found in contemporary sources. Chinatown theaters in the United States, in general, were at the periphery of these new ideas. All these factors further complicate any attempt to understand the musical practice of this period. Below I offer a sense of the musical practices based on a compilation of sources. Its goal is to provide a general understanding, while allowing the possibility of alternatives.

There are four categories of music in Cantonese opera: the percussion ensemble, the melodic instrument ensemble, recitation or dialogue, and arias or songs. Built on an abundance of traditions, the music is characterized by much flexibility and improvisation.

Instrumental Ensemble

Like other forms of Chinese opera, Cantonese opera accompaniment included two sections: *xiansuo* (strings and winds) and *luogu* (percussion).[32] The player of the *erxian*—also known as *toujia*—was considered the leader of the ensemble. A list provided in a 1924 article in the *Young China* includes the instruments shown in table 4.1.[33] The xiansuo ensemble draws from a repertory of tunes called *paizi* to play opening preludes or interludes such as the opening of a scene or the accom-

Table 4.1. Instruments for Cantonese opera accompaniment in the 1920s

Xiansuo Instruments	
Strings	
erxian	two-string bowed instrument (higher voice, bright sound)
zhutouqin	two-string bowed instrument using wood as resonator (a.k.a. bamboo violin)
sanxian	three-string banjo
yueqin	moon guitar
Winds	
hengxiao	transverse flute
xiao	end-blown flute
houguan	double reed instrument
Luogu Instruments (Percussion)	
gu	several drums
ban	woodblock
ba	cymbal
luo	several gongs

paniment for particular paichang scenes. Paizi, which have a long history, came to be shared among many regional genres of Chinese opera. They are generally performed *tutti* and with a fuller sound than accompaniment passages. When the ensemble accompanies the singers, the instruments play the same melody as the vocal line, the instrumentation depending on the particular scene and song type. Figure 4.2 shows seven of these instruments. In the foreground is a *gu* (drum); the instrument closest to the foreground on the table is an *erxian* (bowed instrument); the round brass object on the right is a *luo* (gong); the large round fretted instrument is a *yueqin* (moon guitar); to its left is the *houguan* (a reed instrument); the long-necked fretted instrument is a *sanxian* (banjo); and the instrument suspended in the background is a *xiao* (end-blown flute).

Fig. 4.2. Picture of instruments at the California Historical Society (courtesy of the University of Southern California, on behalf of all USC libraries).

The percussion ensemble had a myriad of dramatic functions. Drawing from a repertory of formulaic patterns (*luogu dianzi*), it accompanied songs or stage movements, revealed the psychological dimensions of the characters, depicted the mood and the surroundings, and punctuated dramatic moments. The length and effect of the percussion patterns ranged widely. For example, a loud stroke on the drum and gong together indicated a sudden revelation or underlined the significance of a speech; a short characteristic rhythmic pattern often accompanied the entrance of characters onto the stage; a long series of percussion patterns could increase the excitement of a combat sequence, depict the complicated interaction between two characters, or serve as an introduction to an aria.

Each player in the instrumental ensemble was in charge of two or more instruments; a well-staffed ensemble included seven players. The musicians were referred to by their position: the drum master, *zhangban*, handled the drum and woodblock; the "upper hand" (*shangshou*), the end-blown and transverse flutes and moon guitar; the "second hand" (*ershou*), the three-string banjo and houguan; the "third hand (*sanshou*)," the two-string bowed instruments and large cymbal.[34] Although Cantonese opera was known for its incorporation of the violin and the saxophone by 1930, and in 1924 Hong Kong opera superstars such as Xue Juexian had already begun hiring personal violinists for accompaniment,[35] the playbills and newspaper advertisements of Chinatown theaters of the 1920s showed no traces of such novelty. The musicians, whose arrivals were sometimes announced in the newspapers, were active in the community, extending their reach into music clubs and forming instrumental ensembles for playing Cantonese music.

In addition, the hammered dulcimer, or *yangqin* (also called the *hudie qin*, butterfly zither) was a popular accompaniment for Cantonese opera singing. Its trapezoidal wooden body is strung with several courses (from seven to eighteen sets) of strings on four or five bridges. In the United States, performance on the yangqin by actresses, a popular attraction, became an opportunity for displaying feminine grace. The actress, gracefully seated, struck the strings with two thin, supple bamboo hammers, one in each hand—a physical gesture reinforcing the young belle's beauty. In Chinatown theaters the use of the yangqin was frequently worked into the operas' plots and noted prominently in theater advertisements.

Speech, Songs, and Arias

Cantonese opera scholar Bell Yung uses the term "oral delivery" for the vocal dimension of the opera, which included both stage dialogue and singing.[36] There was a wide variety of Cantonese stage dialogues, which Yung considers on a spectrum ranging from the ordinary to the stylized. On one end is "stage speech," the plain speech that resembles vernacular Cantonese, and on the other end are "poetic speech" and "rhymed speech," with a rigid verse structure based on either five or seven syllables, following a particular rhyme scheme. In between are many more.

Songs in Cantonese opera were divided into three types: aria types, fixed tunes, and narrative songs. Aria types, or *banghuang qiang*, constituted the most important category of songs: about thirty in number, they were the only songs sung in Cantonese opera until the early twentieth century. They belonged to two different traditions, *bangzi* and *erwang*, which together formed the core of vocal music shared by various Chinese opera genres. Before the 1920s these aria types had long been Cantonized, although they were sung not in Cantonese but in "central dialect," which was borrowed from northern areas and more akin to Mandarin. Each aria type was distinguished by a particular verse structure, metrical pattern, syllable placement, tonal rule, structural ending note, and accompaniment.

In contrast to the flexibility and endless variations within these aria types, the second category, fixed tunes, comprised preexisting songs with few variants and included two types of songs: narrative, popular, or folk songs (*xiaoqu*), and traditional songs (paizi), which came from traditions such as *kunqu* (another genre of Chinese opera). These fixed tunes were associated with particular verse structures and rhyming patterns, to which new lyrics could be composed. The compositional process, referred to as *tianci*, involved the selection of a tune from a vast repertory to fit a particular dramatic situation, and then the writing of a poem to fit.

Narrative songs, which represented the significant influence of southern China, were introduced to Cantonese opera in the early twentieth century. They belonged to the folk ballad genre, characterized by "speaking and singing" (*shuochang*). They were immensely popular, as demonstrated by the large number of printed booklets of song texts widely circulated at the time. These narrative songs included such genres as *nanyin* (*naamyam*, southern tone), *muyu* (*mukyu*, wooden fish), *longzhou* (dragon boat), and *yueou* (Cantonese love song). They have specific lyric structures, similar to those of classical poetry, and flexible melodic shapes, and they are distinguished by formulaic melodic patterns that occur at fixed points of the song. Nanyin expresses tender feelings between romantic couples, characteristically accompanied by instruments of a darker and mellower quality. Muyu expresses loneliness and is known for its free rhythm and lack of accompaniment.

The rise of virtuosity and the appearance of actresses in the 1920s precipitated significant changes in vocal styles and in music. Actress Li Xuefang was credited with establishing a significant female singing style with her signature aria *Shilin Paying Respects at the Pagoda* (see Chapter 5). A new form of male vocal style, *pinghou* (soft voice), also came to replace the high-pitched falsetto vocal style of the young scholar role type. It was a rounder and suppler tone that was not falsetto. Pinghou was spearheaded by two actors who performed in Chinatown theaters at different times: Jin Shanbing and Bai Jurong.

Like other kinds of Cantonese music, opera songs were disseminated via phonograph records. In North America this new medium allowed audiences to enjoy opera in their homes and even in places where no theaters were close by. Cantonese opera recordings were available by mail order through advertisements in Chinese newspapers. At the same time, they were billed as "ethnic records" by major labels such as Victor and served to satisfy the curious in the general market, such as Swiss-born American composer Ernest Bloch, who was the director of San Francisco Conservatory of Music.[37] Amateur singing clubs were formed in San Francisco and other cities in North America with sizable Chinese populations, facilitating the learning and performing of opera songs and music.

REPERTOIRE AT CHINATOWN THEATERS IN THE 1920S

Repertoire ranged widely in style and origins, differently suited for social occasions, community functions, and seasonal holidays. Some operas were carefully produced, while others were hastily put together; some required literary sophistication, while others appealed to sensation or offered comic relief. Generally speaking, the popularity of classical titles at the beginning of the era gradually yielded to productions of contemporary types characterized by adventurous spirits. This section considers the origins of the repertoire in six categories: (1) classic paichang opera, (2) classic civic opera, (3) unscripted opera concerning local legends or famous story, (4) new unscripted opera in tigang xi style, (5) new scripted opera, and (6) ritual opera.[38] Rather than forming a taxonomy, these categories are meant as lenses through which to consider the multifarious nature of 1920s repertoire.[39] They were dynamic and fluid: an opera originating in one category could be remade and circulated in another —a new scripted opera might be performed in tigang xi style, or a classical title might be given a full script with new verses penned by playwrights. The same opera could easily carry different names depending on the emphasis given to the particular episodes of the story. And even under the same name, it could be produced differently depending on the strength of the cast. By considering the categories separately, the following section describes the world of Chinatown opera.[40]

Classic Paichang Opera

Cantonese opera had a core repertoire based on historical legends or the literary canon, which it shared with other regional genres of Chinese opera.[41] Some scenes in these operas were considered established paichang (stock episodes) and were frequently used in tigang xi. From the mid-nineteenth century on, the eighteen grand paichang operas constituted the core traditional repertoire. Their lyrics and sometimes parts of the dialogue, which were in classical Chinese, were passed on from one generation to the next in both oral and written form. Many of the eighteen operas were frequently performed and were required training for all apprentices. These operas lean heavily on conventional role types such as wusheng, gongjiao, and er huamian.[42] The following titles were particularly popular throughout the 1920s: *Thrice Going to Southern Tang, Pinggui Bidding Farewell,* and *Pinggui Returning Home* are famous legends about historical figures, with strong warrior roles; *Pan Jinlian Trifling with Her Brother-in-Law,* derived from a classic novel, features a flirtatious female; *Sanniang Teaching Her Son* is a moral story well known in Chinese society, featuring three role types: the strong or chaste woman, the loyal servant, and the rebellious-turned-filial son.

Classic Civic Operas

Just as prominent as the eighteen grand operas was another group of classical operas characterized by their focus on civic and literary drama: *wenjing xi.* They emphasized classic lyrics and virtuosic singing, and many became repertoire items for leading young belle or young scholar actors. Often about characters entangled in romance, they stood in sharp contrast to the martial operas of the first group. Familiar literature or historical legends formed the basis of these operas, which often focused on one particular episode in an epic novel or complex legend. Volumes of beautiful lyrics for the classic civic operas were learned by generations of singers. Some scenes or arias were so well established and popular that they came to be considered paichang (stock episodes) as well, and were adopted in later operas. Popular titles in this category include *Shilin Paying Respects at the Pagoda* from the legend *Madame White Snake, Daiyu Burying Flower Petals* from the classic novel *Red Chamber,* and *Su Wu Herding Sheep,* about the historical figure who was a symbol of perseverance and integrity.

Unscripted Operas Concerning Legends and Familiar Stories

Cantonese opera also derived its repertoire from many other well-known literary sources, fictional people, and historical legends. These operas were distinguished by their use of colloquial expressions, popular tunes, and traditional or historical plots that generally reinforced the social and moral order. Some were new spinoffs from well-known legends and generic fictional period dramas; others were stories of contemporary society. Many featured figures from well-known local mysteries, folklore, or histories combined with the usual twists of common plots. The famous writer Mai Xiaoxia once summarized the general principles of common plots, revealing the social order or logic of the fictive world: "If a young scholar, he is in dire straits; if a young lady, she is enamored and lovesick; if a civil servant, he schemes deceitfully; if a rich son, he is prurient; if a king, he is ignorant and libidinous; if a courtesan or queen, she is shrewd and exploitive; if a monk, he is salacious; if a bandit, he is chivalrous; if a servant, he is loyal; if an official, he is cunning; if a stepmother, she is wicked."[43] These attributes could make for quite convoluted melodramatic operas. Nonetheless, the stories inevitably conform to the moral world of Cantonese opera—courageous warrior, honorable statesman, virtuous wife, filial sons—ones that constituted the informal though primary education of younger generations. The plots of these traditional operas shared the characteristics of relative optimism, ethical conduct, and moral responsibility. Among the many such titles are *Women Generals of the Yang Family*, *Drunken Concubine*, *Farewell, My Concubine*, and *Thrice-Defeated Zhouyu*.

New Unscripted Opera

The flexibility of tigang xi is especially well suited for the telling of new stories that accord with the social hierarchy described above. The majority of these new titles were on stage merely for a short time and were soon forgotten, and only very few weathered changes in trends and tastes and remained in the program all through the decade. Whether romance, comedy, mystery, or tragedy, these unscripted operas were composed of familiar paichang strung together. Some had many unexpected twists in a melodramatic and complex story line. Others, however, were based on current events or contemporary stories, and modern or Western costumes were worn, rather than period attire. This was where the merging of the traditional and the contemporary could show the most contrast. For example, one opera depicted the experience of China's founding father, Sun Yat-Sen, being seized by a Qing Dynasty operative in London; another told of the reunification of a father and his son in the United States after overcoming many obstacles placed by the government. In the 1930s, even cowboy stories, with appropriate garb, were featured.

New Scripted Opera

This form emerged with urban troupes in the 1920s. Many grew to significance quickly and became the signature operas of famous performers. Not only were the popular titles produced frequently, but their scripts were published, quickly reprinted, and widely circulated. By the middle of the decade the practices of tigang xi were deemed old-fashioned in south China by leading actors such as Xue Juexian. The new scripted operas included many inspired by Cantonese folk legend or popular tunes and were responsive to current trends or topics as well. *Wayfarer's Autumn Lament* was derived from a very popular Cantonese nanyin tune; *Losing the Red Sack* was derived from the story of a Cantonese muyu. Two famous titles from this time are *Nocturnal Mourning of White Lotus* and *Mourning of the Chaste Tree Flower*. One after another, these works were performed in North America.

It is worth noting that many of the scripted new operas were derived from muyushu, chapbooks or songbooks containing popular narratives in the Cantonese vernacular. Widely circulated, muyushu were singing handbooks that used a mixture of classical Chinese and Cantonese colloquial expressions and were supposed to be chanted.[44] Mass-produced at a low price, these prosimetric narratives (in a song-prose form that is formulaic and appears derivative of oral tradition, often with tonal patterning and rhyme schemes) have seven-character rhymed verses that were sung and read by many, especially women at home.[45] The operas' adaptation of muyushu titles not only pointed to narrative songs' strong influence but also brings to light the theaters' role in mediating between the more private and the vernacular. A Chinese writer noted that muyushu mostly "deal with filial sons and loyal servants, chaste wives and virtuous maidens," a description that fit many plots of Cantonese opera as well.[46]

Ritual Opera

An additional type was ritual opera, performed on particular occasions. It consisted of playlets used as a form of worship. These occasions included the celebration of festivals such as New Year, Mid-Autumn, the Rites of Purification for Thanksgiving, the Ghost Festival, and deities' birthdays, the debut of a new troupe or theater, and other such religious or secular communal events. Brief ritual preludes sometimes preceded the performance of the main opera. Because ritual operas were given for very specific purposes or sacred functions, performances followed convention closely. *The Joint Investiture of a Prime Minister of Six Warlords* is a traditional opening play that features a grand parade of the entire cast in their elaborate costumes, and scenes with highly skilled stage movements. Perhaps the most spectacular of all ritual operas, it is also an opportunity for a show of artistic strength, assuring audiences that the troupe has talent and wherewithal. When Cantonese opera was first staged by Hong Fook Tong in the United States in 1852, *Joint Investiture* was featured. The principal function of such auspicious playlets was to secure good fortune for all concerned. Other examples of ritual opera include *Heavenly Maiden Offers a Son* and *A Birthday Greeting from the Eight Immortals,* which served as visual images of fertility and longevity, respectively. These playlets were for the deities' delight and the audiences' pleasure, but more important, they were believed to "have at least a degree of ritual efficacy."[47]

At one end of the spectrum lay paichang operas and classical works, which drew heavily on classical verse; at the other end lay the mostly colloquial, and less literary, unscripted operas, which were a nod to contemporary drama or other modern entertainments. The ubiquitous and popular muyushu was an additional colloquial influence. Between the two extremes lay an increasingly popular hybrid, the new scripted operas, which skillfully combined arias whose texts drew from classical verses, with dialogue and songs in colloquial speech. Adherence to lyrics or scripts was not always expected of the performers, and this flexibility allowed for innumerable variations. With the frequent arrivals of top performers from Hong Kong and Guangzhou and their collaboration with dramatists at the theaters, much new repertoire gradually became the mainstay of Chinatown theaters. The adaptation of new stories was as common as was the reconstruction of familiar ones. In both, there was the theme of a righteous figure fighting against evil, the authorities, or bureaucrats. As scholar Barbara Ward keenly observed, "the structure of [Cantonese] opera in performance explains both the possibility of variation and the process of homogenization."[48] At the end, usually, the protagonist prevailed through chance and perseverance. Sustaining and renewing the familiar social order in the context of North American urban space was an indispensable role for Chinatown theaters.

THE CONVENTION OF PLAYBILLS

Playbills were professionally printed, and starting in 1925 they regularly included pictures. Pictures on the Crescent Theater's playbills in the earlier part of the decade were the work of Jingmei Yingxiangguan, the predecessor of May's Studio, which grew to become one of the most prominent Chinese American photography shops.[49] Later the theater switched to another studio, that of Leguan Yingxiangguan, or Suen's Photo Studio, whose logo appeared on all of the theater's photos of performers. At the beginning, most photographs were close-ups of the prima donna or leading actor, sometimes in costume and sometimes in regular formal dress. Next appeared mid-range photographs of dramatic poses by several main performers on set. By the late 1920s and early 1930s, studio photographs would often be taken of complete scenes. Thus, the visual focus of the theatrical troupes moved from the attractive individual to the skillful display and pose to the imaginary world of a whole stage. Although the content of the opera did not undergo such a dramatic change, the visual display appears to have caught up to the world of modern entertainment with its cinemas, musicals, and contemporary theater.

Playbills, which also told of coming attractions, were posted daily on walls near the theater. They were also distributed widely to nondescript businesses such as tailor shops, an indication of the everyday presence of theaters in all strata of Chinatown communities. In the San Francisco Bay area, it would include Oakland, whose loyal fans rode ferries and cars to go to the theaters across the bay in the era prior to the opening of the Oakland Bay Bridge in 1936. The practice was so common that the playbills typically included a car-service ad. The playbills were expressive of the power of print and the information network it created, which transcended social, economic, ethnic, political, and even urban boundaries. As advertisement, the playbills had immediate impact, supplying the community with information about the theaters' daily productions, forthcoming attractions, prospective new performers, or the final appearances of favorite stars. They were among the things that Chinese residents from the larger vicinity were looking for when they combined trips to Chinatown stores and temples with visits to theaters; a set of playbills from the 1920s is part of the collection of a prominent Chinese merchant family in Oroville, 150 miles north of San Francisco.[50] These visitors might not be able to see all the performances, but the playbills were nevertheless souvenirs of their trips. As memorabilia, they could even be exchanged by opera fans across the country.[51] The format and details—the synopses and cast lists were typically of the same size as the inside text in local Chinese newspapers, and perhaps were read in essentially the same way—appeared to be for close reading.[52] A comparison between the playbills of the 1920s and those of the early 1930s shows that the latter adopted large text sizes, thus giving shorter synopses.

San Francisco's Chinese playbills are the focus of the following section, because the number of playbills from elsewhere is very small. Note, however, that based on what was available for this book, playbills from New York, Honolulu, Havana, and Vancouver differed little in format and content. They even shared pictures from San Francisco. A Chinatown playbill is typically seventeen inches by ten inches or smaller, on newsprint with a white or occasionally tinted background, with central black and white pictures and small text in black ink (sometimes red ink for festive occasions such as Chinese New Year). With text in Chinese but for the English name and address of the theater, the playbills primarily catered to Chinese audiences. Across the top is the theater name and address. Reading from the right to the left are first the date and time, then (inside a decorative box) the title of the play. Below the title are names of lead performers (from one to three), and above the title is an indication of the opera type (tragic, comic, romantic, mythological, classical, patriotic, and so on). This title box is often preceded or followed by a few lines of elaborate text highlighting the attraction's significance. This could consist of a commentary about the opera or its production or laudatory poems and lavish tributes to the lead performers referring to their art, beauty, or critical acclaim. Then typically would come a full-length picture, or several small headshots, of the lead performer or performers in dramatic poses, or of the cast posing with full stage sets. The middle section often offered the most substantial text—synopsis, scene titles, or even a full section of lyrics annotated with aria or tune types. The middle section was often recycled when the same opera was produced. Sometimes, accompanying or in place of synopses could be a list of twenty or thirty scenes or chapter headings similar to those found in muyushu. The listing alone gave a good sense of the production. To its left was the cast list (generally having fifteen to thirty roles), showing the strength of the cast or the complexity of the production: the reader learned of a performer playing multiple roles or a character played by multiple performers. Following the cast was a standard list of ticket prices and sales information. Ticket prices were typically raised for the debut of famous performers. Sometimes extra lines of text would be given alerting the reader to a coming attraction such as a newly scripted opera, new production, new singer, or special performance by instrumentalists. Occasionally, advertisements followed. Playbills of the early 1920s were simpler and the paper smaller, but by 1925, all had a similar format and degree of complexity.

Figure 4.3 reproduces a Mandarin Theater playbill for *Boat Chase of White Peony*, featuring actress Mai Sulan as the lead (see also Chapter 11). To the right of the title box are several laudatory couplets. The actress's picture is sandwiched between highlights of the performing cast and music on one side and the synopsis on the other. The synopsis indicates the opera's use of paichang from *Frolicking with a Maid in the Cantina* and *Su Wu Herding Sheep*. The cast list includes twenty-three performers, more than half of whom were actors of high caliber who could lead a performance. Promotional text indicates the upcoming production of a new romance opera by playwright Li Wutian. The ticket prices ranged from $.50 to $1.50. This is a rather comprehensive playbill from a high point of the theater's history, and it is typical of a full-fledged Chinese opera theater of the 1920s in North America.

Though information was no doubt important, since the text was filled with stock phrases that were familiar to readers, the playbills could also be read for the pure pleasure of their conventions. As texts, the lyrics were literary, and as music

金山 大舞臺最新著名男女班 正埠

十月三號（禮拜日）下午六点半鐘開台

配景 艷情 佳劇

白牡丹追舟

麥素蘭著名首本 全班拍演

內 橋畔遇美 酒店結婚 妖精暗害 舟中戲美

附 大搜洞門 仙妖鬥法 改裝尋夫 夫婦團圓

麥素蘭

注意新劇預聞

多情到極地 不能成妻妾

爲編劇家黎伍田最新編排傑作不日開演了

入場券

賣票處

Fig. 4.3. Playbill, *Boat Chase of White Peony*, Mandarin Theater, October 3, 1926 (courtesy of the Ethnic Studies Library, University of California, Berkeley).

(with the annotation of aria or tune types), they could elicit the memory of melodies heard previously or of a quiet performance. The popular genre of laudatory poems printed on playbills also provided a forum where the literati shared their morsel. Today, these playbills reveal the complexity and varied traditions of the theaters' offerings, which form the basis of the second half of this book.

Although it is tempting to treat the playbills mainly as text, it is perhaps more fruitful to consider them as not the blueprint but the footprint of a theatrical culture and history. When the performers and theater producers devised an opera, infinite possibilities stretched in front of them, suggested rather than limited by existing conventions. Opera performances were shaped not only by the existing materials of the genre they worked with but also experience, which told them what suited the Chinatown community. For their part, the audiences expected to see familiar stories and characters and enjoy the familiar music. Predictability was part of the joy. At the same time, production was actuated in significant ways by the quest for innovation, a constant endeavor to extend the range of theatrical, musical, and performative features. While the theaters and their performers' ability to meet expectations was important, it alone could not sustain a decade's worth of successful opera production. As the anthropologist Karin Barber noted in relation to the Yoruba Theater in Nigeria, "[It] is precisely those features—generated in accordance with the conventions of a specific genre—that enable things to be said and enable the listener to interpret them."[53] A flexible performance practice with a strong component of improvisation allows for an exciting theater experience. Chinatown opera theaters, therefore, increasingly put on operas that drew on traditions yet reshaped them, using characters excavated from various traditions yet infused with cosmopolitan experiences and updated versions of preexisting music and lyrics. As for Chinese audiences, the opera performances depicted subjects they cared about in a genre and language of their choosing.

An example of the role of playbills in Chinese American communities is a San Francisco Chinatown tailor's daughter, Margaret Leung. She read them daily. Every day the tailor shop, like other stores, received playbills, which she and her older sister scoured for opera stories and pictures of top performers to see what was going on at the theater that evening. They usually went with friends of their mother, who was often delayed by housework, staying sometimes until midnight. The sisters learned to play hammered dulcimer like the actresses and kept scrapbooks of their glamorous photos and stage poses clipped from the playbills, with the names meticulously written next to the photos and checks marking off the operas they had seen.[54] The ephemeral playbills became mementos of melodious, fantastic, enjoyable evenings.

CHAPTER 5

AN EXAMINATION OF THE ARIA SONG "SHILIN JITA"

Whether for Margaret Leung and her family or for men doing menial work at laundries, canneries, or stores and passing time at general stores, clubhouses, and community organizations, opera arias were an important form of musical utterance. Few other music genres matched opera songs as expressions of mood, values, and feelings. Recordings of opera songs could be heard everywhere, but they were also common in print form as published anthologies of lyrics, pamphlets that came with recordings, and playbills on which lyrics were printed with their aria types. The last allowed readers to "hear" the new lyrics, because arias were based on a body of existing tune families and types, and experienced listeners could infer from the names of aria types the music to be sung with the text.

As an introduction to this sound world, this chapter examines an immensely popular aria of the 1920s: Li Xuefang's "Shilin Jita" from *Madame White Snake*, an example of the *fanxian erhuang* aria type. Transcriptions of historical recordings are used to consider the basic elements, essential features, and possible performance styles. Although this chapter only focuses on a single aria from a very large repertoire, it highlights many important musical characteristics and aesthetics of Cantonese opera in the 1920s.

MADAME WHITE SNAKE AND "SHILIN JITA"

The legend of Madame White Snake has been adapted into many genres of Chinese opera. It is a story about a young man, Xu Xian, and a white snake spirit who becomes immortal after centuries of training. The white snake spirit is transformed into a young woman, Bai Suzhen, while a green snake turns into her maid, Xiaoqing. They meet Xu Xian at the Broken Bridge in Hangzhou, where he lends them his umbrella because of the rain. Xu Xian and Bai Suzhen become lovers. Meanwhile, a terrapin spirit who assumes human form as a monk called Fahai sets out to separate them. Fahai convinces Xu Xian to make Bai Suzhen drink wine made from realgar (a red mineral) that reveals her true form. Xu Xian dies from the shock. With a magical herb that she steals from a remote mountain, Bai Suzhen restores him to life. Yet he is then abducted by Fahai and brought to Jinshan Temple. Bai Suzhen uses her powers to flood the temple trying to save Xu Xian, but fails—her power is weakened because she is pregnant. She gives birth to their son on the Broken Bridge, before Fahai captures her and imprisons her under the Leifeng Pagoda. Years pass as she remains imprisoned under the pagoda, while the son, Xu Shilin, earns the top honor in the imperial civil service examination. He returns in glory to visit at the pagoda, and eventually frees her. The mother and son reunite.

The adaptations of this legend in most other Chinese opera genres focus on earlier episodes of the story such as meeting on the Broken Bridge, Xu Xian lending his umbrella, and flooding the golden mountain, but the Cantonese adaptation of the 1920s uniquely dwells on the son's return to the pagoda. It prominently features filial affection, the reminiscence of sorrow and suffering, and redemption. In particular, it highlights the aesthetic ideal of a virtuous woman. The episode, named "Shilin Jita" (Shilin Paying Respects at the Pagoda), tells of Xu Shilin's return to pay his respects. The climax is the scene of Bai Suzhan's expressing her feelings on seeing her son after twenty years of separation. In a famous long aria, the subject of this chapter, Bai Suzhan tells the tumultuous history of romance and sacrifice, lamentation and joy.

LI XUEFANG'S "SHILIN JITA"

Li Xuefang's performance style is representative of the 1920s and was particularly famous for this aria, which was said to be co-written with Lü Wencheng, a famous Cantonese composer.[1] She made at least two recordings of this aria song.[2] A version collected by the Chinese University of Hong Kong, recorded on three disks, was issued by the Da Changcheng (Big Great Wall) record label.[3] The total length of the three disks is 22:30. The following discussion of the aria song is based primarily on this version (version A). Another version comprises four disks, as noted in an advertisement in New York's *Chinese Nationalist Daily* in 1929 in which four titles by Li Xuefang, each taking up from one to four disks, were promoted on the Pathé label.[4] It likely is the version that was the basis for a transcription into cipher notation (a numerical notation whose digits represent steps in the major scale) in *A Dictionary of Cantonese Opera (Yue ju da ci dian)*.[5] This version (B) is used for comparison below.

Example 5.1 presents the author's transcription of version A—the five couplets included on the first two of the three disks. The total duration of these two disks (four sides) is 14:36. This transcription shows the vocal line sung at the tempo of *adagio* (quarter note = M.M. 60). A few notes in parentheses indicate the accompaniment, which is otherwise not transcribed. The accompaniment plays the vocal line nearly note for note, as well as the bridges (*guomen*) between phrases, reflected here by the rests in the vocal line. This transcription does not attempt to notate all the finer points and graceful slides of Li Xuefang's performance. It transcribes primarily the basic melodic line.[6] The following is the translation of the lyrics of "Shilin Jita."

LYRICS OF "SHILIN JITA"

I-1 Before any words could be uttered,
I no longer could control
tears rushing down my face,
and I drowned in sorrow.

I-2 Calling out to you,
Shilin my son.
Now listen carefully
to your mother's words:

II-1 Hei Fengxian
was once a fellow ascetic
just like your mother;

II-2 He encouraged me
to strive for virtue
to pave the road to final enlightenment.

III-1 On top of the Ehmei Mountain,
we learned and practiced,
hoping to gain eternity.

III-2 Ah, how I regret now
that I was lured by the world of mortals
and came down the mountain
to wander.

IV-1 At the West Lake,
with your father,
I shared a boat,
sailing together.

IV-2 Ah, how I regret now
that I borrowed his umbrella,

and to him
I became betrothed.
V-1 At Zhenjian,
we opened a drugstore,
and prospered
with good fortune.
V-2 Yet on that fifth of May,
I drank the realgar wine,
and it fatefully initiated
all the tribulation.

CHARACTERISTICS OF COUPLET FORM IN THE *JITA* ARIA

"Shilin Jita" is known as the *jita* aria. It belongs to the *banghuang* family of aria types, commonly sung in an older official dialect in the early twentieth century, before other types of tunes, vernacular music, and narrative songs using the Cantonese dialect were introduced in the 1920s. Each aria type in the banghuang family has certain structural features (mode, verse structure, pitch hierarchy, melodic patterns, tempo, and voice type, the last of which dictates the register and hence the ending tones and tuning). Musicians create arias by setting new texts to existing aria types according to a melodic model.[7] The jita aria belongs to the *fanxian erhuang manban* type, which uses a seven-note scale and 4/4 meter and has *re* as the ending note of the couplet. Being a *fanxian* (a type of mode and tuning of the accompanying instruments to be a fifth lower than normal), it has a "minorish" sound and several 3/4 tones (three-quarters of a whole step).[8] This aria type is generally known for being "slow and melismatic, induc[ing] a mood of melancholy."[9] In his study of this aria type, Chow Sze Sum notes that because of the lower range of *fanxian* mode, it has a wider tonal range and tends to linger in the lower register, expressing sorrow and bitterness. The jita aria became so popular that it was later set to different texts and reused in other operas, sung by various characters with different voice types.[10]

As in most genres of Chinese opera, rhymed couplets provide the basis for the structure of the arias, whose formal features include the number of words or syllables in a line (line length), the grouping of words (*dun*, literally, "pause," hereinafter represented by "phrase"), and patterns of linguistic tone and rhyme. The line length of the lyric for the *fanxian erhuang manban* aria type is ten words.[11] Each couplet comprises an upper and a lower line whose last words rhyme. The aria in couplet form can comprise as many rhymed couplets as dramatically necessary. Each ten-word line is broken into four phrases. Frequently, extra words are inserted

Ex. 5.1. Version A of "Shilin Jita" as sung by Li Xuefang

27
31
34
2
I-2
Jiao yi
叫 一
38
sheng
聲
41
shi lin er ni yao
仕 林 兒 你 要
43
ting niang
聽 娘
47
yan
言

(*continued*)

Ex. 5.1. (*continued*)

81
84
87
2
II-2
Ta quan niang
他 勸 娘
91
ku xiu xing ze you
苦 修 行 自 有
95
chu tou
出 頭
99
103
2
III-1
Er mei shan
峨 眉 山

(*continued*)

Ex. 5.1. (*continued*)

137
2
IV-1
Zai
在
141
xi hu
西 湖
144
yu ru fu
與 汝 父
148
3
tong zhou gong
同 舟 共
154
ji
渡
IV-2
Hui bu gai
悔 不 該
158
jie yu san yu ta gong
借 雨 傘 與他 共
162
jie luan
結 鸞

(*continued*)

Ex. 5.1. (*continued*)

as padding syllables to add interest or to complete the idea, and do not interfere with the basic ten-word line length (see table 5.1).

Musically, the four phrases are separated by caesuras. Because of the word grouping (3 / 3 / 2 / 2) and the lengthy melismas, the phrase lengths are irregular. Phrases 3 and 4 generally complement each other: phrase 3 is often the shortest, while phrase 4 is the longest and most melismatic, starting on the third beat of the bar. The close relation of the two last phrases is also underscored by a regular break between phrases 2 and 3, where a short instrumental bridge appears. Lines I-1 (mm. 1–34) and II-1 (mm. 55–86) are clear examples. Yet this general characteristic could be negated by the expressive needs of the lyrics. In I-2, phrase 1, "Jiao yi sheng," means "calling out [to the son]," an exclamation expanded on by a melismatic passage and an interlude to prolong the effect. A short phrase 2 follows, stating the son's name and continuing directly to phrase 3 with no break.

Underneath the melodic flourishes, the couplets follow a certain rhythmic pattern. I summarize the rhythm-duration prototype of the couplet, as an eighteen-bar basic structure, seen in example 5.2, which I explain below. (Cumulative numerals substitute for each syllable in the lyric. The prototype depicts the couplet, generally considered as a complete structural unit.) In his study of the syllable placement in various ten-syllable arias from the later part of the century, Bell Yung observes "a peculiar rhythmic characteristic in that . . . phrase 3 is delayed so that the resultant durational proportion of the last 4 syllables (in terms of the number of beats) [is]

Table 5.1. Verse structure of "Shilin Jita"

	Phrase 1			Phrase 2			Phrase 3		Phrase 4	
Syllables/words	1	2	3	4	5	6	7	8	9	10
Line I-1 (upper)	Wei	kai	yan /	bu	you	ren (na) /	zhu	lei /	fang	bei
	未	開	言	不	由	人 (哪)	珠	淚	放	悲
Line I-2 (lower)	Jiao	yi	sheng /	shi	lin	er /	ni (yao)	ting /	niang	yan
	叫	一	聲	仕	林	兒	你 (要)	聽	娘	言
Line II-1 (upper)	Hei	feng	xian /	ta	ben	shi /	niang	de /	dao	you
	黑	風	仙	他	本	是	娘	的	道	友
Line II-2 (lower)	Ta	quan	niang /	ku	xiu	xing /	zi	you /	chu	tou
	他	勸	娘	苦	修	行	自	有	出	頭

4 + 6 + 6 + 4."[12] This rhythmic characteristic is found in the jita aria as well. The pattern is illustrated with brackets underneath phrase 3 and phrase 4 in example 5.2. Yet because of the long melisma associated with the last syllable, the duration pattern we observe in example 5.1 might be better described as (4 + 6 + 6 + x). The durational pattern prototype explains why it is typical for phrase 4 to start on beat 3. (In this aria, all but two lines follow this durational proportion closely.) Furthermore, I propose, a basic rhythmic prototype is at play with phrases 1 and 2 as well, and it serves to distinguish a couplet's upper and lower lines. The difference is shown in example 5.2. In the upper line phrase 1 and phrase 2 both start on the downbeat, rendering the same duration proportion pattern (2 + 2 + 4). In the lower line, however, the duration patterns of phrases 1 and 2 are (2 + 2 + 6) and (2 + 1 + 3) respectively, whereby phrase 2 starts on the third beat rather than a downbeat. As such, the two lines of a couplet have different rhythmic profiles, and the syncopated figure in the lower line provides interesting rhythmic fluctuation. While this prototype can be expanded with elaborate ornamentation, the metrical positions of the beginning syllables in all eight phrases remain mostly the same.

The pitch organization of the couplet form includes the line-ending pitches and the phrase-ending pitches. The line-ending pitches in the first two couplets follow the pattern of D (upper line) and C (lower line), or mi–re; the next two couplets are B♭–C, or do–re; the fifth couplet is F–C, or sol–re (see table 5.2).

The four phrases follow a complex pattern of linguistic tones, and musically the phrase-ending pitches show recurring patterns as well. The second line of all five couplets here shares the same pattern of phrase-ending pitches: D–G–D–C, or mi–la–mi–re. For example, in I-2, the ending pitches of its four phrases appear as follows: D(m.40)-G(m.42)–D(m.45)–C(m.52). With shared durational proportion

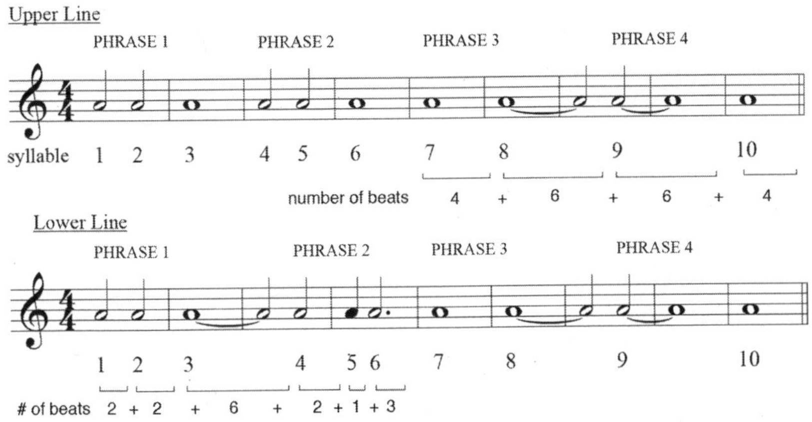

Ex.5.2. Proportional duration of upper and lower lines

Table 5.2. Patterns of line-ending pitches in "Shilin Jita"

Couplet	Verse	Measures	Line-ending pitch	Scale tone
I	1	mm. 1–34	D	mi
	2	mm. 37–52	C	re
II	1	mm. 55–86	D	mi
	2	mm. 89–102	C	re
III	1	mm. 105–119	B♭	do
	2	mm. 121–136	C	re
IV	1	mm. 139–155	B♭	do
	2	mm. 157–169	C	re
V	1	mm. 171–190	F	sol
	2	mm. 191–204	C	re

and pitch endings, the melodic contours of these lower lines have a high degree of resemblance. In addition, despite their different linguistic tones, texts, and even ending pitches, many couplets have very similar melodies: couplets II and V are identical except for the ending pitch of their first lines. At the same time, in some highly varied and melismatic lines, few vestiges of resemblance to the couplet form of other verses are left.[13] The opening couplet is a prime example: the singer's expressiveness and virtuosity, as well as the intense emotion of the lyrics, nearly conceal the basic prototype. The dramatic and melismatic melodies are emotionally charged. The remaining couplets mostly retell the life story of Bai Suzhen and therefore are less emotive. As a result, the duration of the lines varies greatly. The same line length (ten words) is sung in thirty-one bars in I-1 and in twelve bars in III-1. Yet even in highly elaborated passages, because experienced listeners understood the four-phrase structure convention, a lengthy improvisation is easily perceived as the melodic expansion of a single phrase unit, because metrical placement is retained.

Two features also obscure normal divisions in the couplet structure. First, the aria incorporates a large number of winding lines with small intervals and twisting melodic figuration, a characteristic that music scholar Alan Thrasher also observed in the melodies of the Sizhu ensemble of Shanghai, which he notes as an ideal of Chinese musical aesthetics.[14] They result in a certain sense of coherence between different phrases. Moreover, a musical phrase often comprises many recurring melodic fragments or patterns (or what Peking opera scholar Nancy Guy calls "melodic formulae") in an overlapping, nesting, or crisscrossing manner.[15] These melodic fragments create mosaic patterns that undermine the subdivisions suggested by the formal structure.[16] Example 5.3 illustrates one such melodic cell and its repetition in various couplets. The model of the melodic cell has five notes, but its recurrences appear in various expanded and contracted forms in all couplets of the aria. In couplet IV-2 the variant of this cell is, unusually, repeated in succession (mm. 164–66 in example 5.1), creating text painting; it corresponds to the lyrics referring to the two lovers and their eternal love affair.

Ex. 5.3. A melodic cell and its variants

COMPARISON OF TWO VERSIONS: BALANCING THE EMBELLISHMENT

The length of each musical phrase in the aria varies with the degree of elaboration. Li Xuefang's jita aria is known for the length of its first line, which spans nineteen measures. Example 5.4 is a transnotation of a version from cipher notation (version B, upper stave) that fits this description (not counting the two-bar accompaniment), lined up with version A (lower stave).[17] Although version B and version A use different note values for transcription, it is clear that their melodies are similar, sharing skeletal tones throughout. A comparison of Li's two renditions makes clear the invariable features of this opening line, in particular, the skeletal tones, and sheds light on the use of their embellishment and elaboration as expressive means.

Ex. 5.4. Comparison of versions A and B of "Shilin Jita" as sung by Li Xuefang

B
A
由 人
you ren
由 人
you ren
PHRASE 3
珠 淚
zhu lei
珠 淚
zhu lei
PHRASE 4
雙
shuang
放
fang

(*continued*)

Ex. 5.4. (*continued*)

In version A, the length of phrases 1 and 2 varies only a little (8 bars + 7 bars), while in version B they are asymmetrical (4 bars + 7 bars) (see table 5.3). The difference is suggestive: version B is more improvisatory than version A. Generally, one bar of version B corresponds to two bars of version A, showing a 1-to-2 augmentation that retains the metrical placement. For example, measures 1–2 in version B correspond to mm. 1–4 of version A. Though the recording of version B is not available in order to verify its tempo, it is likely that version B is the "slower" version of the two. To quote Bell Yung on the topic of tempo comparison in arias, "tempo difference is defined as a change in the real-time density of the same set of musical events."[18] In other words, when a tune is performed at a slower tempo, more embellishment can be inserted so that the real-time density of musical events is the same or increases compared to the "fast" version. Calculating by the 1-to-2 augmentation in the beginning of phrases 1 and 3, version B was likely performed twice as slowly as version A, and with higher density of musical events. This also means that phrases 2 and 4 in version B are more expanded and of longer duration than their counterparts in version A.[19] In other words, version B takes longer to perform. (This conclusion supports the hypothesis that version B could be a transcription of the four-disk Pathé recording.) It is generally more complex, and its winding melodies with their wide range (particularly in phrases 2 and 4) depict well the psychological intensity, the subtlety of mixed feelings, and the emotional turmoil.

While skeletal tones can be deduced from comparing the two melodic lines, Li's ornamentation at times yields melodic contours that vary greatly in the two versions. This is most obvious in phrase 2 here. The metrical positions of the skeletal tones (F–G–F–D–C–A–F–G–A–C–B♭) are quite different in the two versions. One is not simply a variation of the other; rather, they are two improvisations, each with its own elaborate melodic trajectory that incorporates the skeletal notes. In interesting ways, these two passages also subtly change how phrase 2 can be positioned within the first line. The more melismatic phrase 2 of version B hovers over the high G and moves up to B♭ several times, creating a clearer arch that connects to phrase 3 with its similar range. In contrast, the less melismatic version A merely skirts an escape tone to B♭, creating a lyrical line with a clearer descent to rest on A and therefore providing a registral contrast to the subsequent climb to the arch in phrase 3.

Table 5.3. Comparison of the setting of the first verse in versions A and B of "Shilin Jita"

	Phrase 1				Phrase 2	Phrase 3	Phrase 4	
Measure no. (version A)	*1 2*	*3 4*	*5 6 7 8*	*9 10 11*	*12 13 14 15*	*16 17*	*18 19*	*20–31*
Measure no. (version B)	*1*	*2*	*3 4*	*5 6*	*7 8 9 10*	11	*12*	*13–19*
Line 1	Wei		kai yan	bu	you ren	zhu lei	Fang bei (shuang piao)	

While some melodic embellishments are idiomatic, others are specific to the aria, reflecting Li Xuefang's improvisation skills, creativity, and virtuosity. Example 5.5 is a comparison of the simple (upper staff) and embellished (lower staff) figures found in the two versions. As Jonathan Stock pointed out, in such melodic elaborations, many "ornamental pitches are themselves decorated, the result being that secondary and tertiary clusters of embellishments form around each primary structural note and its original decorations."[20] Examples 5.5a–5e show melodic figurations that embellish the intervals of a third, fourth, or fifth. Example 5.5f presents two versions of ornamentation on G. They are idiomatic variations, akin to the turn in Baroque music. Example 5.5g shows an augmentation that provides a new rhythmic interest with the dotted quarter note. Examples 5.5h–5i are both flourish ornamentations in which the skeletal notes are given a different metrical placement. Ornamentation often creates more density in the lines, as well as a melodic expansion that stretches out the placement of skeletal notes. The continuous thirty-second notes in the middle

Ex. 5.5. Comparison of embellishment in versions A and B of "Shilin Jita"

to upper registers shown in this example express the emotional intensity of the lyrics. Examples 5.5h and 5.5i, last two examples, are individual in nature and are passages that may be performed differently each time, according to the performer's mood and to the interaction with instrumentalists, other singers, and the audience. They are what Alan Thrasher describes as the "interpretive" and "creative" type of variation, that is, the more individualized inventing of "variant forms of melodic motifs or phrases, following certain 'inner rules' regarding modal structure, metric structure and proper melodic style."[21] And as noted above, the main thrust of creativity occurred at the ending of phrases 2 and 4, where the impassioned words are expanded upon by the elaborate yet not showy, complex yet subtle, embellishment. The twisting and turning runs express not an animated mood but, rather, the affective state and the spirit of the aria, the complicated emotional turmoil. In version B, Li Xuefang takes more liberty in her invention.

The idiomatic embellishment echoes variation patterns discussed in a treatise of 1916 by Qiu Hechou titled *Xiange Bidu* (Essential String and Vocal Music). Qiu was a famous contemporary of Li Xuefang who also performed in the United States in the 1920s. This treatise was widely available in North America and constantly advertised in Chinese newspapers. It contains a section with the heading "Rules on Ornamentation" that offers a list of standard ornamentation with melodic figurations. Figure 5.1 reproduces his complete set of melodic patterns as transnotated by Yung from their original notation (*gongche*).[22]

Fig. 5.1. Excerpt from "Rules on Ornamentation" by Qiu Hechou, transcribed by Bell Yung (courtesy of Bell Yung).

The climactic fourth phrase in both versions shares a melodic background structure comprised of three basic descending motions (B♭–G–F–D, B♭–G–F–D, and G–F–E♭–D), and two ascending motions (G–C–B♭ and G–B♭–C–D). (See the reductive analysis in the upper stave of each system in example 5.6. The two versions occupy the central and lower staves.) These basic melodic structures underlie both long phrases, with similar general motion centering on D as the final note. Note that the different ways they are realized in the two performances create different affects.[23] In version B the patterns animating the skeletal notes are much more melismatic, whose intertwined ornamentations betray the sense of panic and agitation. In contrast, version A has sustained notes, but they are sung with a variety of portamento, wave note, and gentle sliding effects to express the weighty sentiment.

PERFORMANCE AND EXPRESSION THROUGH SLIDING TONES

The first line of the lyrics expresses speechlessness and joy mixed with sadness. Phrase 1 of version A comprises three simple yet weighty words, "without uttering words," sung over the course of eight bars. The expressive line is full of nuanced and eloquent slides. As in most singing styles in Chinese music, Cantonese arias were sung with various slides and wave notes. These vocal slides were rarely discussed in the opera literature because it was the general practice, familiar to all and, as such, unnecessary to mention or think about. These sliding effects and ornamentations are not only central to the articulation of the vocal line but also are imitated by the two-string fiddle, the *erhu*, in the accompaniment to enhance the effect. For example, Li Xuefang's opening line is preceded by a soft sliding dyad C–A on the erhu played with a striking resemblance to the human voice. The instrumental "vocal slide" returns later in the aria, for example, for the two notes in parentheses in m. 28 (see example 5.1). Indeed, the erhu is particularly well suited for this form of expression. The vocal slides are rather similar to the sliding and wave notes of erhu in Jiangnan silk-bamboo music as discussed by music scholar John Lawrence Witzleben.[24] He lists many sliding effects, four of which can be directly applied to vocal style (see figure 5.2).

Although Witzleben uses these examples to discuss the fingering and bowing techniques applied in order to create these sliding effects, here I focus on the sound represented by these figures. They include (a) a slide of a third from above, (b) a rapid and narrow ascending slide from an indefinite pitch, (c) a slow and narrow slide downward and then back to a note, and (d) a dipping slide downward and back with the effect of subdividing the beat. These slides are ubiquitous in this aria. In addition, several other sliding effects are observed in this performance: (e) a quick slide from a previous pitch that begins only on the beat, much like grace

Ex. 5.6. Primary pitch motion of phrase 4 in versions A and B, "I drown in sorrow"

Fig. 5.2. Witzleben's analysis of slides (courtesy of John Lawrence Witzleben).

notes, creating a delayed effect; (f) the wave tone that spans the interval of a minor third, creating an undulating effect, or strong vibrato, on sustained notes; (g) a slide downward or upward to an indefinite ending pitch at moderate speed with beginning accentuation; (h) a slide downward or upward to an indefinite ending pitch at moderate speed with accentuation midway; and (i) a sliding tone in the melody followed by similar sliding effects in the accompaniment. Finally, note that all these slides are curved, often with beginning or ending emphasis, and with a slight acceleration in ascending and a slight deceleration in descending.[25] So the opening phrase in fact sounds like example 5.7.

Li's silky voice carries these complex, supple, and subtly different slides with incredible grace, molding the melody into a sophisticated, expressive whole. Her delivery is mellifluous and lyrical, soulful at times, and witty at other times, elevating the dramatic scene and complex sentiments to an exquisite musical nar-

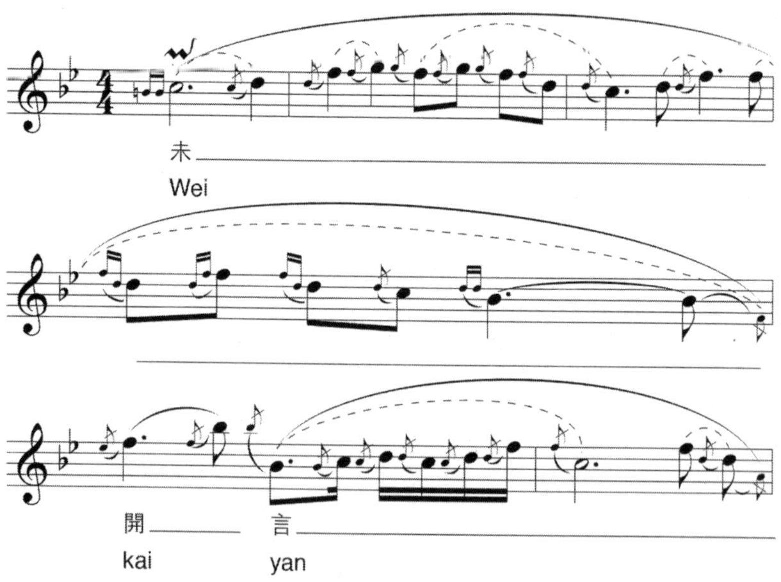

Ex. 5.7. Opening phrase with the sliding effect notated

rative. There were numerous accounts about how audiences were mesmerized by her virtuosic performance of the famously extensive aria, itself a richly creative process that could extend the aria still longer. The extra repetition in m. 166 provides a glimpse of the artistic license: on the recording one can hear the otherwise seamless accompaniment adjusting adeptly to catch up with Li leading into the unusual additional repetition of the melodic figure (a third time).

Despite the great flexibility shown in different renditions, the basic features of an aria were shared among the four participants in the creative process: listeners, who aurally identified these conventional cues and therefore the aria types and associated dramatic mood; composers, who wrote verses to fulfill the textual and musical requirements of the aria types prescribed by convention; singers, who improvised on the basis of the conventional structural features; and the accompanying musicians, who followed the cues given in the hand gestures of the singers to provide appropriate accompaniment.

The jita aria is one among many popular types of Cantonese opera arias and songs from the 1920s whose essential features and creative variants were closely connected to the web of aria song types. And since characteristics of aria types were part of musical literacy and identifiable to experienced listeners, when the name jita was annotated next to new lyrics, the listeners would deduce how the new lyrics would be sung and even know the appropriate mode of ornamentation. The elaborate style of aria performance Li was known for would later be considered to unfold too slowly and would be replaced by more moderate ornamentation and shorter melismas. Nevertheless, her rendition on the recordings, as well as many other virtuosic recordings of this era, attests to the beauty and creativity of aria performances during this time.

PART III

BRITISH COLUMBIA AND REMAKING OPERA IN SAN FRANCISCO

CHAPTER 6

POWDER AND ROUGE

Theaters in British Columbia

If Li Xuefang's jita aria could be considered to show audible traces of the expressive power of performers on the theater stage, face makeup could be regarded as its quintessential visual trace—opera powder and rouge were indispensable to Cantonese opera. A box of powder wrapped in the cloth of its Guangzhou maker (figure 6.1) was uncovered in a 1989 renovation at an old Vancouver building—the Wing Sang Company, owned by one of the city's most powerful Chinese merchants, Yip Sang (1845–1927). On its covering the crisp red Chinese characters named the brand, Yin Qiantai, detailing its quality and listing a full range of available powder types. Also uncovered were rectangular palettes of rouge by the same maker, each folding accordion-style into a small rectangle, with vibrant red foil on the inside leaves.[1] These powders were manufactured specifically for Cantonese opera performances. (The white powder was applied as a foundation, then rouge in different shades was applied to the cheeks and eyelids.[2] Then, eyebrows were drawn at an upward angle from the nose, making the eyes looked more engaged.) As crucial theatrical supplies, these remnants are symbolic of one of the liveliest periods of Cantonese opera in Canada. This chapter tells this important history, from 1910 to early 1920.

CHINESE THEATERS AND EXCLUSION MEASURES

In Canada the anti-Chinese reaction took a different course than it did in the United States, where the 1882 Chinese Exclusion Act and its restrictive measures became roadblocks for Cantonese opera performers and theaters. As noted in Chapter 1, the

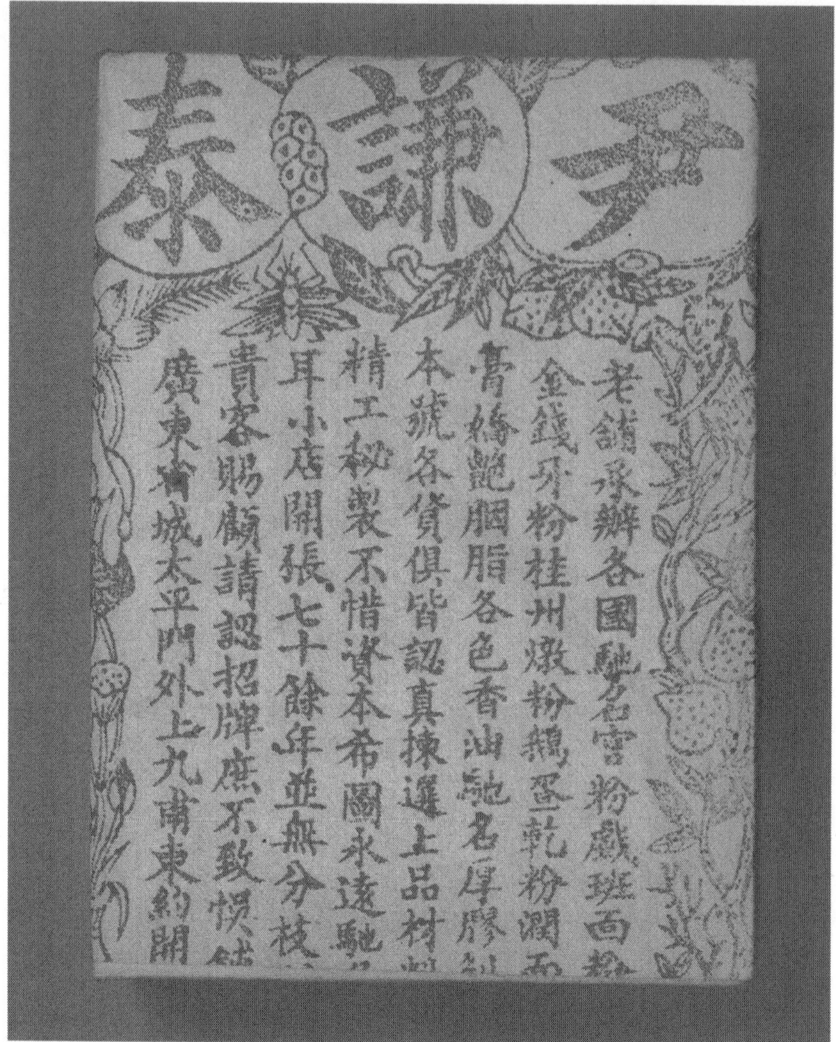

Fig. 6.1. Chinese opera powder makeup, Wing Sang Company (courtesy of the Museum of Vancouver).

first large influx of Chinese immigrants began with gold rush of 1858. Then, in the 1880s, the construction of the Canadian Pacific Railway brought many more. On the completion of the railroad, Canada imposed a head tax on Chinese workers in 1885 to discourage further immigration. The head tax did not stop the influx, and in 1923 the Chinese Immigration Act would replace the fees with a ban on most Chinese immigration to Canada.[3] Chinese opera performers were admitted into Canada with regularity. In the early twentieth century, Chinese theaters continued to thrive despite anti-Chinese initiatives. Their performers were exempted from the head taxes; they were admitted under the sponsorship of a local business with a bond of $500, refundable on their departure.[4] In fact, the discrepancy between the two countries' exclusionist policies made Canada particularly attractive. British Columbia became the new Gold Mountain; Victoria and Vancouver had a lively Cantonese opera culture after 1910.

OPERA IN VICTORIA

Chinese opera appeared in Victoria as early as the 1880s; the capacities of the five theaters that existed between 1882 and 1885 ranged from 250 to 800 seats. Money from the construction of the CPR allowed many Chinese merchants and contractors to finance theaters. The enjoyment was not for the Chinese alone, however. In 1885 a Chinese theater run by Wo Lock and Company hired white actors to join Chinese actors onstage in order to attract white customers.[5] The erection of theater buildings was also often a public affair: English-language newspapers announced the architects contracted, reported on the costs and progress of construction, publicized their openings, and printed Chinese theater advertisements along with those for other entertainment such as the Theatre Comique or John Robinson's circus.[6]

During this time, mobility within the Pacific Northwest allowed Canada to benefit from the active opera scene in the United States. Like the manual laborers in the region, performers in Seattle or San Francisco also traveled to British Columbia. In 1901 the *Daily British Colonist* reported that a new troupe called Shu Foon Neue had opened with great fanfare in Victoria, featuring performers from China and San Francisco.[7] In 1907 it noted that a troupe coming from Vancouver would begin a run in Victoria, to be followed by performers from Seattle. The reporter mused that "the Chinese population seem to have great pleasure in it for they flock to the theatre night after night and the players seldom have to perform without a full house."[8]

In British Columbia the Chinese community was thriving, as reflected by the emergence of the second-generation Chinese Canadian and the establishment of a musical performing group for youth. A surviving picture from 1913 shows a seventeen-member marching band formed by Chinese students of a Victoria middle school attending its first competition.[9] March 1915 was considered a milestone in Chinese Canadian history: the community celebrated the first graduating class at Victoria's Chinese public school.[10]

The busy scene sustained several Cantonese opera troupes—Qing Fengnian, Guo Taiping, Jock Ming On, and Zhu Huanian—during 1915 and 1916. Some merchants who owned businesses in both Vancouver and Victoria sponsored performances in both cities, the troupes taking residence in one or the other for several weeks or months at a time. Occasional references to them in Vancouver's Chinese paper, the *Chinese Times*, provided glimpses of an active opera scene. A female impersonator debuted to an enthusiastic audience in June 1916, and when the admired actor Jing Fu of Zhu Huanian finished his engagement and departed for China, colleagues sent him off at the dock with gifts.[11] Immigration control remained mostly in the background, but people were occasionally reminded of it: the Victoria office arrested two actresses for failing to stage performances regularly as they were required to do in order to maintain their status. They were bailed out by colleagues and returned to the stage.[12]

OPERA IN VANCOUVER

Demand for theaters increased in Vancouver when it supplanted Victoria as the leading commercial center on Canada's west coast. After 1910 Vancouver had three Chinese theaters. Three prominent merchants, Yip Sang, Chang Toy, and Loo Gee Wing, were involved in the opera business, from constructing buildings and managing the theaters to hiring performers in China and organizing their tours. A former CPR contractor, Yip Sang built a five-hundred-seat theater in 1898 adjacent to his family's building near Shanghai Alley and the Wing Sang Company on Pender Street. In late 1913 Chang Toy (and his Sam Kee Company) built a new theater on Keefer and Columbia Streets at a cost of $25,000 that eventually was named the Sheng Ping Theater.[13] Loo Gee Wing, who already owned a theater in Victoria, built the Gao Sheng Theater on 124 East Pender Street in late 1914 and hired a troupe from China to perform in January 1915.[14] In that year, the two latter theaters were busy: the Qing Fengnian troupe was featured at the Gao Sheng and the Guo Taiping troupe was at the Sheng Ping. The community relied increasingly on theaters for public initiatives such as meetings and fund-raisers; occasionally, the two troupes, despite their rivalry, came together for operas concerning moral drama (with specially designed scenery) as a fundraiser. The *Chinese Times* reported that a production in February—staged at the Sheng Ping Theater—attracted audiences of six hundred to seven hundred people.[15] Another benefit performance at the Sheng Ping in July included sixteen actors for male roles, three female impersonators, and three actresses, together with nine musicians and seven staff members for wardrobe and staging.[16]

Vancouver's Chinatown theaters already employed many performance practices characteristic of North American Chinese theaters in the next decade: actors and actresses sharing the stage, repertoire drawn from classical titles, the portrayal of a character by several performers in the same evening, and improvisation and paichang—performances based on plot outlines rather than scripts. Also prominent was a penchant for certain elements and styles from Peking opera, which hinted at a certain degree of sophistication or aesthetics. These characteristics can be found in the three 1916 playbills surviving from the Guo Taiping Troupe at the Sheng Ping Theater, perhaps the oldest surviving playbills in Canada. The information included on them—the synopses, the roster of performers, and the ticket prices—provides a glimpse of the theater stage.[17]

Figure 6.2 reproduces the playbill of June 23, 1916, which featured the classic opera *Pinggui Returning Home*. Half of the text reviews the key plot points of the opera. The other half is a promotion for the casting choices. It goes through the strengths and weaknesses of Peking opera as opposed to Cantonese and describes how the theater's adaptation of Peking opera styles suited its performers' strengths. The casting and plotlines showed much flexibility. Two actors played the protagonist General Pinggui, while three actresses played his wife in three different scenarios: one of the young couple from engagement to farewell and the heart-breaking scene on the news of his death in battle, another of a mock tryst preceding their happy reunion after the general has returned from the battle, and the last of the wife chasing after her departing husband on board his boat. The last scenario, however, did not belong to the original tale of General Pinggui; it was a popular episode from a

加拿大 昇平戲院國太平班 雲高華

民國五年六月廿三號
舊歷丙辰五月廿四日
星期五晚七時開演

新成私下三關
套平貴回窰

俗傳王允三女寶釧。二月二日。彩樓招親。繡毬墜落平貴
花郎之手。允嫌貴貧。致父女擊掌。逃貴破窰。平貴功服宗
(从彭)馬。奉征西涼。。戴宮贅壻。爲西涼王十有八載。。訛
言平貴已死。寶釧在窰聞耗。江邊祭奠。平貴忽接雁書。
偸令出關。既抵五家坡。與寶釧會面。復僞稱平貴之友。故
意調戲。以試寶釧節操。誰知寶釧詞意嚴正。不涉於邪。乃
歷悉眞情。夫妻相會。然已鬢髮蒼蒼。。非復當年張緒矣。。
惟同是劇也。有京戲粵戲之別。粵戲有搆桑一場。京戲無
之。但京戲則唱工冗長。又非粵戲可及。本班今仿京戲之
唱工。不演搆桑之浮夫。。仍以武生祥、女蘇妹、演回窰。女
金好、演追夫。女霞犀、演祭奠寫書。角色配置。各擅所長。
況回窰是蘇妹心得之手本。曾經初演。已蒙同胞稱善。。今
者、別埠歸來。再点演之。觸景生情。不啻現身說法。。其善
舞善歌。應知分外傳神也。

內附
三打平貴 被擒招親 江邊祭奠 鴻雁傳書
偸令出關 戴女追夫 坡前試妻 會妻團圓

薛平貴 武榮 武祥 何芳 小柏 蘇龍 式秋
戴戰女 金好 李江 邊法 魏虎 肥元
王寶釧 花犀 花妹 王允 小杞 宮女 花華
戴麻王 邊生 甘后 花奇

價目
樓下對號每貳毫五 對號房位每弍毫五
樓上對號每二毛正 弍號椅位每壹毛正
至尾

Fig. 6.2. Playbill, Guo Taiping Troupe at the Sheng Ping Theater, Vancouver, June 23, 1916 (courtesy of the Chinese Opera Information Centre, Chinese University of Hong Kong).

different opera, *Wenji Returning to Han.* In other words, it was a paichang known for its display of sophisticated acrobatic skills and theatricality (see Chapter 8). Adding popular paichang to the plotline of the original story no doubt enhanced the theatrical excitement. The practice continued in the next decade and was shared by many Chinatown theaters.

EASTWARD EXPANSION

Merchants who brought Cantonese opera troupes to Victoria and Vancouver sought additional opportunities for them in British Columbia and beyond. Chinatowns in cities such as Cumberland and Nanaimo periodically hosted performances.[18] The Chinese population of British Columbia was nearly three-quarters of the total Chinese population of Canada, but opera troupes still looked elsewhere for bookings. Not long after the date of the playbill discussed above the Guo Taiping troupe disbanded, and some of its performers joined a performing tour put together by the Guomin Zhong Theatrical Association. In April 1916 the association announced plans to embark on a tour of eastern cities. Starting with Calgary, Winnipeg, and then Toronto, the troupe would visit more cities until it reached Montreal.[19] The public pledge the company made noted that people in those regions had been deprived of the enjoyment of opera, or, if they had seen any, it had been of the "wrong" kinds (namely, Chinese acts in vaudeville or burlesque shows; see Chapter 2). The cause was worthy of the high cost of transporting the troupe. The eastward expansion also provided an alternative opportunity to the many performers who exhausted their opportunities in British Columbia.

Montreal, which would have the third-largest Chinese community in Canada (after Vancouver and Toronto) by 1921, embraced opera. The flyer of the troupe Guo Fengnian noted that it performed at the Monument National on St. Lawrence Boulevard, a theater close to the Chinatown of the time. (Figure 6.3 shows a playbill for this troupe.) The *Chinese Times* of Vancouver reported in January 1917 that Guo Fengnian had done a flourishing business in Montreal for several months and generated handsome revenues.[20] The surviving flyer shows a professional operation, complete with elaborate wardrobe and full orchestra.[21] It highlighted the theater's convenient location. In the style of *hengtoudan* (the cast list used for contracting purposes in southern China), the flyer shows a cast of eleven role types with sixteen actors and two actresses, as well as five musicians and two costume and property men. It covers most of the role types except for the less important ones (nos. 6, 7, 8, and 12; see Chapter 4). Five performers are listed for the young belle role type, three of whom were female impersonators. The cast was essentially a male troupe with two actresses. A comparison between the flyer and the 1916 playbill (figure 6.2) reveals that actress Jin Hao, and a few others also listed with Guo Taiping, had traveled three thousand miles east to Montreal.

Today little is known about these performers. Yet at the time they were clearly part of the Vancouver Chinese community's cultural fabric, having previously been associated with the Guo Taiping troupe; three of the actors' names appeared periodically in the *Chinese Times*.[22] An article from March 1917 shows that Jin Hao and another actress, Suzhou Mei, still had fans in Vancouver who fondly remembered their performances in previous years.[23] Beyond Montreal, however, the Guo Fengnian troupe did not leave much of a trace. Taking a troupe of this size across the U.S. border would not have been likely. They might have continued to other destinations with active Chinese theaters such as Havana and other cities in Cuba, Tampico, Mexico or Lima, but this matter will have to await future research.

An opera tour required capital and sponsorships at the start and along the way. This tour across Canada suggests a growing Chinese business network beyond British Columbia and a demand for Cantonese opera in the prairies and in eastern Canada. The path of the trailblazing Guo Fengnian troupe was a model for the performing network of the next decade.

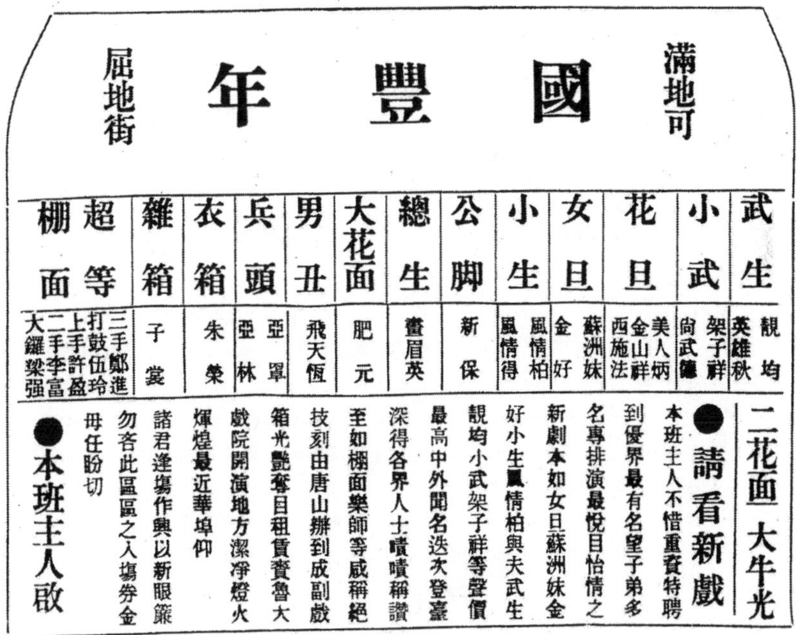

Fig. 6.3. Flyer, Guo Fengnian Troupe, Montreal, 1917 (courtesy of the Chinese Opera Information Centre, Chinese University of Hong Kong).

VANCOUVER, 1915–1920

Back in Vancouver, Cantonese opera continued to grow with the arrival of the new wave of virtuosic female performers after the profession underwent significant changes in southern China. The three theaters had their own troupe. Chang Toy and other merchants founded a theatrical firm called the Yongkang Nian Company, which imported a troupe of twenty-nine members to perform in the newly vacated Sheng Ping Theater.[24] The troupe performed for seven months (November 1916 to May 1917). It was an immediate success, taking in more than C$2,000 in the first ten days (C$38,000 in 2014) alone.[25] By contrast, the Gao Sheng Theater was doing so poorly that owner Loo Gee Wing delayed paying his staff at the end of 1916, citing the recession resulting from World War I as the cause.[26] When Yongkang Nian's troupe completed its engagement, a second troupe was hired to perform for another eight months (October 1917 to May 1918). The highlight of its second season was a four-week stretch (December 8, 1917, to January 5, 1918) during which it made over C$4,600. It was an astounding success, considering the presence of a new rival troupe. In September 1917, Puruyi, a new troupe run by the Lian An Company, opened at the theater on Shanghai Alley. It employed as many as fifty-two members.[27] The troupe was managed by Ma Dachun and Li Shizhang, and it had at least thirty actors, three actresses—including a star, Zhang Shuqin—and nineteen acrobats.[28] This troupe was significantly larger than the previous ones, if not extraordinary by the standards of southern China. Together these theaters offered the community a large number of opera performers and lively musical entertainment.

The growth of the recording industry kept pace. In early 1918 the Eng Chow Company of Vancouver began advertising record catalogs in the *Chinese Times*; within six months, the initial twenty-one titles grew to ninety-seven.[29] An increasing number of general stores included Cantonese opera records in their merchandise; one advertiser noted that it would ship to any deliverable address by mail. Through recordings, Cantonese opera reached rural and remote locations and brought the music to non-Chinese communities.

Leading actresses Zhang Shuqin of the Puruyi troupe and Huang Xiaofeng of the Yongkang Nian Company were already well regarded in southern China. Zhang commanded an annual salary of $6,000 according to the *Chinese Times*; by comparison, the salary of the highest-paid actress in 1915 was $1,000.[30] On January 21, 1918, the *Chinese Times* printed a long note, with laudatory poems, written by a fan marveling at her beautiful voice, graceful dancing, and artistic interpretation of classical heroines of legend: the astute and charming maid of *The Romance of the West Chamber,* the brilliant young lady of letters Xie Daohui, the quintessential melancholy woman in *The Great Wall Story of Meng Jiangnu's Bitter Weeping*, and the outstanding heroine in *Lady Liang Fending off Insurgent Attack*. This praise foreshadowed the critical acclaim she would receive in Shanghai a few years later in the city's largest newspaper, *Shen Bao*.[31]

Zhang Shuqin was the first actress to receive this level of attention—promotional newspaper articles, laudatory poems and announcements, and (later) pictures—from fans and promotion from the theater. This type of representational discourse concerning star performers, particularly actresses, would appear regularly all through the 1920s. The poems, and the star's gracious responses, were important ways in which stars and opera fans expressed their mutual admiration and appreciation. The adulatory poems crystallized attributes of the star for her fans, idealizing her not only in terms of singing and acting but also as a model of womanhood.[32] Some of the poems were gathered in pamphlets or poetry collections; Chinese classical poetry has a long tradition of such occasional pieces. Such poetry was both an ephemeral tribute and a durable promotional tool.[33] Photographs also enhanced and extended the stardom of opera singers. Long after Zhang's departure, her photographs were still popular enough that pirated copies circulated, prompting the photographer Zhou Yaochu to issue repeated warnings against piracy.[34] At the time of her later departure for China, in June 1919, Zhang expressed her gratitude in a public forum as well—notices of appreciation (probably written by the theater) in the newspaper extended her graceful gestures from the stage to the public arena.[35]

No such public praises have been found for Huang Xiaofeng, who was junior to Zhang and likely not as famous. Nevertheless, an incident at the theater aptly revealed her popularity. On March 19, 1918, the newspaper reported a tumultuous evening at the Sheng Ping Theater, where the classic opera *Golden Leaf Chrysanthemum* was interrupted when audience members in the balcony threw apples at the lead actor, hitting his head as well as the stage's electric and oil lights, sending broken glass flying. One audience member bled profusely, while others jumped on stage, brawling with the actor and stopping him from performing. The cause, as it turned out, was his behavior on the previous evening toward Huang Xiaofeng. The instigators felt that Huang had been disgraced by the actor's lewd movement.[36] The company later dismissed the actor for his questionable conduct.[37] Furthermore, Huang was made an officer of the Actors' Alliance. The alliance by early 1919 had ninety-three members and a thirty-two-person administration; of the three female members, Zhang was an assistant vice president, and Huang was a vice council chair.[38] The positions accorded the two popular actresses were remarkable. In comparison to southern China, where actresses were not yet allowed to take part in the professional organizations of Cantonese opera (Chapter 4), here they were glamorous, wielding influence and having higher social status.

Zhang and Huang would both reemerge in San Francisco in 1925, embraced by an even more exuberant community and playing in finer theaters. They were the respective prima donnas of the rival Mandarin and Great China theaters.[39] In Vancouver, however, they seemed to be quite collegial. Their popularity was enshrined in playbills (the Yongkang Nian Company daily ordered seven hundred to twelve hundred copies)[40] and local Chinese newspapers.

Innovative programming was one way of enlivening Cantonese opera culture. Adapting a play by Shakespeare would perhaps be the last thing one would expect of a Chinese theater in Vancouver during this time. Yet several Chinese translations of stories of Shakespeare's plays were popular in southern China at the turn of the century. The drive to do unorthodox plays and to be on a par with the best theaters, or perhaps a desire to highlight its affinity for modernity, might explain the Puruyi troupe's adaptation of an unspecified Shakespeare play into an opera titled *Family Education*, which was enthusiastically reported on by the *Chinese Times*.[41] With the stated purpose of following the modern trend of enlightening society with uplifting new plays, Ziyaba, known in China as an erudite actor of the gongjiao type—a bearded, middle-aged character associated with filial piety, loyalty, and honesty—led the production. He even incorporated a speech about modern society and various Chinese cultural customs into the middle of the opera. The merging of such a quintessential Chinese archetype with a Shakespearean character (albeit an unidentified one) pointed to the theater's aspirations: using Shakespeare as a portal to modern identity and using the association in a bid to universalize Chinese values.

NEW TROUPE AND CULTURAL PRACTICES BEYOND THE CITIES

Whether because of the negative effect of rivalry or the wearing out of novelty, the fortunes of the Yongkang Nian Company gradually ebbed, and eventually it made way for newer initiatives. Its decline is evident from the following figures: the revenue of the company's best two-week run (December 9–22, 1917), C$2,532.58, contrasted sharply with that of the last two-week run (April 14–27, 1918): C$277.15. Following the end of its second season, the company dissolved in May.

In the following years, the Sheng Ping Theater had a series of short-lived troupes. The first was named the Zhu Sheng Ping troupe (*Zhu* means "best wish") and began operations sometime between May and September 1918.[42] It engaged Huang Xiaofeng.[43] The new troupe raised its visibility in the community by publishing daily playbill advertisements in the *Chinese Times*, a practice that would be adopted by all Chinatown theaters in North America. At this beginning stage, there were two main types. The first type listed the most essential information: date, repertoire, lead performers (the famous Huang Xiaofeng would perform on the zither, for example), theater address, and phone number. The second type included more text promoting the opera with laudatory prose about the lead actress and reflections on the predicament of the protagonist or related matters.

These advertisements brought theater culture to a wider public. Newspaper subscriptions often extended beyond the community, reaching cities without their own papers. Now with a mere glance at the playbills, people from the vicinity could learn of theater attractions, sometimes with detailed descriptions of arias, synopses, or cast members. Their use shows the increased significance of opera in the lives of Chinese immigrants during this time. Recorded music was reaching the same readers: the Eng Chow Company's advertisements for phonograph records grew in size from a portion of a column to a quarter of a newspaper page by 1925 and to half of the page by 1928.[44]

In his study of Chinese entering Canada between 1885 and 1923, Henry Yu reveals that, despite the preconception that they lived in Chinatowns, many in fact spread quickly into rural areas, often with just one or two running a restaurant or general store in a small town.[45] Print media in general were especially important for this group—the *Chinese Times* grew from four pages in 1915 to twelve pages by 1919—and its literary page often published brief pieces about Cantonese opera: satires and musings about the profession, innuendo about performers, new song lyrics, or laudatory poems by opera fans. Thus, Chinese across Canada maintained a certain interest in news of the opera world or musing about it, helped by mail-order phonograph records.

From the start the Zhu Sheng Ping troupe was a tentative endeavor. During its first month of operation, September 1918, it printed public notices inviting interested parties to take over the theater. By April 12 the following year it folded, citing the Spanish influenza epidemic and an insufficient number of performers with unexpired immigration permits. It would be merged with the Puruyi troupe. The merger gave rise to a new theatrical company, Lian An, which would wield great influence the following decade. The Lian An Company managed the newly merged troupe called Puruyi at the Sheng Ping Theater.[46] It was not an easy merger; in June Puruyi went to Victoria, not returning to Vancouver until the following year.[47] Both prima donnas left Vancouver by the end of the year. Huang Xiaofeng reemerged in Shanghai in 1920, and Zhang Shuqin departed for China in June 1919. As the decade drew to an end, the vibrant Cantonese opera scene in Vancouver had quieted down. It was in need of a new stimulant.

Nevertheless, its contribution was unmistakable. One indication was the establishment of the Actors' Alliance (Youjie Huiguan or Youjie Tongzhishe). It played a role in providing discipline and maintaining order within the profession, as well as supporting actors and performing social functions. As a 1915 notice by the alliance put it, "Since our inception, the association has been keen on participating in public welfare undertakings. We have provided assistance in adversity, and facilitated opera performances in both of our homes in the East and West. We value pacifism."[48] Occasional newspaper reports reflect that mission. For example, in August 1915 the alliance publicly expelled a member who had violated its regulations four times, warning its members against working with him.[49] A month later, nearly twenty members of the alliance performed at a festive occasion in Victoria celebrating the birthday of Five Elders of Shaolin in honor of a powerful fraternal organization called Hongmen.[50] In April 1916 it held a benefit performance for an actor in dire medical need, for which the theater waived utility and other fees.[51] The alliance was frequently listed among the contributors to and participants in various community initiatives and regularly appeared at occasions such as the birthdays, anniversaries, or funerals of prominent figures. At the same time, it was an important counterforce to the theaters. When in January 1917 the theater owner Loo Gee Wing finally caught up on paying back wages to his actors, the alliance printed a note of appreciation in the newspaper.[52] As evidence of its effectiveness in this regard, the Yongkang Nian Company included in its actor's contract a clause forbidding any membership in such organizations.[53] Nonetheless, the alliance had grown substantially by 1920.

On February 11, 1919, the *Chinese Times* reported that the Actors' Alliance was celebrating its fifth anniversary. On the same page was the alliance's own announcement listing sixty-three members and thirty elected officials, including not only performers but also community dignitaries in the organization's key positions. The list incorporated prominent members of both troupes then active in Vancouver. Its inclusion of the two prima donnas from the rival companies reflected its all-encompassing nature. In this quickly evolving community, with three theaters, itinerant performers, and ever-reconfiguring troupes, such an organization could provide continuity.[54]

Vancouver experienced a high rate of turnover among its theater troupes and companies, and the complexity surrounding their naming practices is indicative of the fluid nature of troupe names, casts, theaters, or even itineraries. Troupes' names are unreliable indications of their origins, since they changed identities often, adopting freely the names of prominent troupes in southern China. While some performers continued with the troupes that initially engaged them, others moved among different troupes. Performers' affiliations could change of their own accord or as a result of a merger or a change of owners. Even when the name of a troupe can be traced, the performers might be altogether different. For example, troupes called Guo Fengnian appearing in 1917 in Montreal and in 1923 in Honolulu (the latter troupe owned by the Kue Hing company; see Chapter 12) had few artists in common. But they were both run by Vancouver merchants. The same can be said of troupes named Jock Ming On that appeared in 1913 and in 1923, both of which performed in Victoria and Vancouver. (See the discussion of Jock Ming On in Chapter 11.) On the other hand, troupes with different names—for example, Guo Taiping (figure 6.2) and Guo Fengnian (figure 6.3)—shared many performers. Finally, in Vancouver, troupes and theaters, despite being distinct entities, could be owned by the same proprietor or be mentioned interchangeably in advertisements and news reports.

LEADING THE 1920S OPERA RENAISSANCE IN NORTH AMERICA

Important changes in Vancouver's Chinese theaters were imminent, even if it did not seem so at the start of the 1920s. It was clear that the theaters continued to do poorly. The troupe at that Sheng Ping Theater, run by the Lian An Company, had a quiet year from 1920 to mid-1921; its top ticket price slipped from $0.65 to $0.55 in December 1920, then to $0.45 (January 1921) and to $.35 (June 1921).[55] Playbill advertisements still appeared regularly in the newspaper but contained only basic information.

In southern China, however, Cantonese opera had recently witnessed rapid growth involving female troupes, virtuosic performers, urban theaters, new operas, and modern stages. This new energy came to shape its presence in Canada. A series of virtuosic performers began to arrive at the Sheng Ping Theater in 1921. The announcement in April of the engagement of two renowned actresses, Gui Huatang for young belle roles and Huang Mengjue for the young scholar roles, began to invigorate the otherwise nondescript offerings.[56] In the fall more performers came. Fengqing Qi was an actor of the young scholar type whose work would be remembered as representative of that role type in the 1920s.[57] (His photo is shown in figure 12.1.) His stage counterpart was a female impersonator, Xian Huada, also known for his excellent voice. The newspaper reported in October the successful debut of a significant actor of the bearded warrior role type, Jiazi Ren, praising his magisterial posture, powerful voice, and elegant dancing. His art was acclaimed as providing "timely exhortations to virtue and purity in the New World"![58] Many other performers, such as Zhou Yulin, a warrior role–type actor known for the quintessential warrior Guan Gong, and Doupi Qing, a comic actor from a top all-male troupe, were of similar caliber. Finally, in November the actress Li Xuemei arrived.[59] Li's appearance in Vancouver even warranted a notice in *Chung Sai Yat Po* in San Francisco. She contributed to that city's initiative for a Chinese hospital with a $100 donation, and in turn was revered as a model figure in its newspaper.[60] In Vancouver her $100 donation to local causes was at the level of top merchants in the community.[61] With many performers of similar stature arriving, by the end of 1921 the Sheng Ping Theater hosted ten good performers of a wide variety of role types. It would need them in order to compete with a new rival.

On September 1, 1921, readers of the *Chinese Times* opened the paper to an unusual advertisement: the announcement of a new troupe, Le Wannian, arriving in the New

World (figure 6.4). This ad signaled the renaissance of Cantonese opera in North America. The former Imperial Theatre on 720 Main Street was bought to house it. The announcement, which took up the bottom row of a newspaper page, listed full details about the new troupe.[62] At the center was a cast of twelve different role types in large boldface print, a list similar in format to those found in the contemporary trade paper *Zhenlan Bao* in Guangzhou, which printed the cast lists of top troupes every June. In addition, detailed commentary on key performers was given on the sides, highlighting their special repertoire and prior success. Of the four actresses listed, Mai Sulan would become an active performer on the opera circuit in this decade. (Her photo appears on the 1926 playbill shown in figure 4.3.) This fully equipped professional troupe, complete with new repertoire and theatrical techniques, grew from Vancouver's opera culture, however. Le Wannian was sponsored by the eminent merchant and owner of the former Chinese theater on Shanghai Alley, Yip Sang, and his successful Wing Sang Company; among its cast was an elite actor formerly of the Puruyi troupe, Ziyaba, whose ambition was evident in his 1918 adaptation of a Shakespeare play for Cantonese opera. This venture put the level of professionalism in Vancouver on par with that of the top theaters on the other side of the Pacific.

Le Wannian was a trailblazer for several reasons. It was the first theater troupe to organize and advertise a full cast with known performers for each role type. In addition, the unprecedented public announcement of the management team showed clear organization and structure: two managers, two accountants, a secretary, a bookkeeper, a public relations person, an administrative assistant, and a supervisor. The cast showed a more even gender balance than had any previous troupe, including

▼○▲新大舞臺發現

▲樂萬年班角式名列

武生 靚金玉　小武 靚少保　女旦 李秋文
女旦 黃麗卿　女旦 麥素蘭　女旦 何桂棠
女旦 鄺聯芳　正旦 黃鮮　正生 三多
總生 畫眉八　小生 孤寒奕　公腳 子牙八
大花面 大牛權　二花面 馮仁　男丑 指天指
女丑 阿九

樂萬年戲院同事人列左
總理 李世瑋 馬大治
書記 馬心平 交際 李鵝
財政 黃昂湛 庶務 黃節章
監督 曾瑞 馬恒兆 管班 林南

▼○▲洪門代表團公議催收捐歀章程

Fig. 6.4. Advertisement of the Le Wannian Theater in the *Chinese Times*, September 1, 1921 (courtesy of the Simon Fraser University Library, www.chinesetimes.lib.sfu.ca/ctimes-26650/chinese-times).

four actresses of the young belle type, with no female impersonators. The troupe also advertised its use of realistic scenery paintings, common in Hong Kong since 1910, as backdrops. (One fan praised their beauty in the *Chinese Times*.)[63] The Chinatown theater stage now matched the most recent developments in Cantonese opera and suited the norms of Western spoken drama. Le Wannian was presented as the most ambitious Cantonese opera venture on this side of the Pacific Ocean.

Furthermore, the troupe broke with Vancouver convention by moving Cantonese opera out of Chinatown. Built in 1912 at a cost of $60,000, the Imperial Theatre was designed by George B. Purvis, a Seattle architect of many theater buildings in the Pacific Northwest, and was managed by the Sullivan-Considine vaudeville circuit. It opened in October 1912 with a production of Verdi's *Il Trovatore* by the Sheehan English Opera Company on tour; since then the theater, with its grand entrance arch, had been part of popular vaudeville circuits. Le Wannian's contemporary image went hand in hand with the modern facility and its reputation as a place for mainstream entertainment.

Opening on September 7, 1921, Le Wannian brought a fresh energy to the opera scene. Then the troupe reached its greatest prominence when it featured the actress Guan Yinglian in November; she inspired enormous enthusiasm that foreshadowed her future success in the United States. For her debut the price of the best ticket jumped from $0.60 back to $1, the same as it was in the theater's opening week. A photo in the Chung Collection at the University of British Columbia is likely the earliest picture of this actress. In it she was about twenty-five years old (figure 6.5).[64]

Fig. 6.5. Guan Ying-lian, Vancouver, 1921 (courtesy of the Chung Collection, University of British Columbia Archive).

Guan Yinglian immediately became an idol. On the day of her debut, November 2, both the Le Wannian Theater and the Sheng Ping Theater opened productions of a popular opera featuring a young belle, *Daiyu Burying Flower Petals*. Gender was the difference: the opera's willowy beauty, Lin Daiyu, was played by Guan Yinglian at the Le Wannian and by the female impersonator Xian Huada at the Sheng Ping. On one hand was Guan Yinglian's youthful beauty and command as a prima donna and on the other was the mastery and established performance style of a female impersonator. If ticket price was a reflection of their relative popularity, Guan was the bigger attraction. Later, several poems were published in the *Chinese Times* praising her graceful heroines as melancholy, wistful, sensitive, and fragile.[65] One passionate prose work was nearly seven hundred words long.[66]

As the new sensation, Guan became a focal point of the theater's offerings. A photo taken by C. B. Wand shows the pride of the theater owner in having a high-class Cantonese opera troupe (figure 6.6).[67] The careful staging of the troupe with the splendid wardrobe and set captures its aspirations. Guan Yinglian appears in full splendor. The embroidered characters of her name are embedded in the elaborate circles of the center banner directly above the symmetrical pattern on the backdrop, framed by two tall, ornate lanterns. She appears as a female aristocrat with a regal bearing at the rear center. This photo marked the landmark presence of the extraordinary troupe in Vancouver.

Fig. 6.6. Cantonese opera troupe in Vancouver, 1922, photographed by Cecil B. Wand (courtesy of the Chung Collection, University of British Columbia Archive).

The prosperity of the Chinese community was reflected well in such a spectacle full of talented actors and exquisite costumes with sophisticated embroidery. The photo might have been taken on the occasion of the ritual grand opera *The Investiture* as an auspicious sign. The troupe charged higher ticket prices than did its rival at Sheng Ping. At first, their daily playbills were tactfully placed on different pages of the newspaper, but after a short time they were placed side by side every day. As would be expected, each tried to lure audiences with grand productions, fanciful titles, new casts, or elaborate props. Even from such advertisements one can sense the intensity of the competition, as well as the richness of their productions, the best the city had ever seen.

SETTING OUT FOR THE UNITED STATES

Not even the best troupe, however, can retain its allure without fresh faces. The price for the top ticket at the Le Wannian theater again decreased. The occasional debut might bump up the ticket price, but only briefly. The need for new venues and audiences was urgent. Both theaters' newspaper advertising abruptly stopped after February 6, 1922, although we learn from news reports that more actresses were active or had joined the troupes: Mai Sulan was increasingly active, and Yangzhou Mei arrived in November.[68] Vancouver's theatrical entrepreneurs began to broaden their circuit in North America by bringing their star performers across the border. The success at the Imperial Theater might have given them the incentive to create the same in the even larger Chinese community in the United States.

The Lian An theatrical company, a group of twelve merchants from Vancouver and Victoria using the name "Lun On Co." in its application to the U.S. Immigration Bureau, leased the Crescent Theater, a vaudeville house, in San Francisco (see Chapter 7). Le Wannian's success at the Imperial Theatre might have been the reason for the choice of venue. The Imperial Theatre was known to theatrical and vaudeville syndicates from coast to coast, and such circuits could serve as a network for Cantonese opera troupes. The Lun On Company took the name Renshou Nian after a top male troupe in southern China. The plan was for the troupe of thirty-eight members (most from the Sheng Ping Theater) to enter the United States at Seattle.

Although it met with outright rejection initially, after careful negotiation with the American government, Lun On entered the United States, and on October 5, 1922, a professional Chinese theater opened its doors in San Francisco for the first time since 1906. The showing was successful enough that three months later Lun On recruited Vancouver's other troupe, Le Wannian, to perform at the Orpheum Theatre in Seattle, also a prominent vaudeville theater, before joining the Renshou Nian troupe at the Crescent. This venture served to explore Cantonese opera's potential in the United States. Promoted as part of a general entertainment circuit, the troupe's Seattle debut was noted in the mainstream English news media from Seattle to Chicago and New York.[69]

Back in Vancouver, the news of Le Wannian's successful debut on February 26 was reported immediately.[70] The good news suggested a lucrative future for Cantonese opera in the United States. The troupe had been admitted only after days of detention at the port and purchase of a bond of $31,000, but backers were encouraged by the prospect, and shares of Le Wannian became a hot commodity. For the following month a brief advertisement in large bold-face print ("Share of

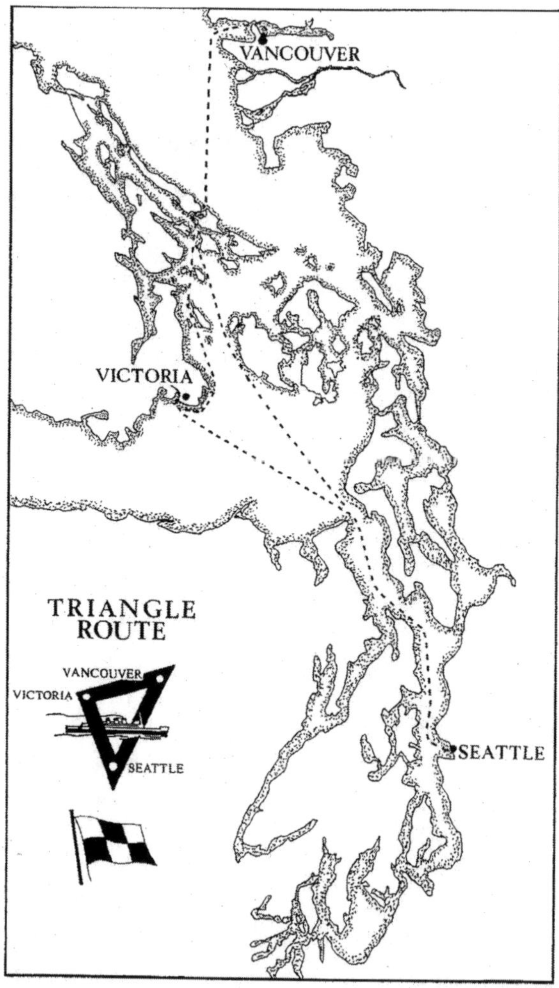

Fig. 6.7. Map of the Triangle Route. Robert Turner, *The Pacific Princesses: An Illustrated History of Canadian Pacific Railway's Princess Fleet on the Northwest Coast* (courtesy of Robert Turner).

Le Wannian troupe wanted!") appeared daily in the *Chinese Times*. The ad's constant appearance reminded the community how profitable the theatrical troupes could be. Within the year, several similar ventures were formed in Vancouver with the aim of going to Boston, New York, or Honolulu. Le Wannian's success symbolized not only the revival of regional commerce for Chinese merchants but also the restoration of professional opera troupes to the Chinese community in the United States.

Convenient transportation within the Pacific Northwest played a key role. In subsequent years, the mobility of opera troupes would continue to be helped by the popular Triangle Route of Canadian Pacific Railroad steamships (using the lighter steamships of the CPR Coast Service), which provided short-distance travel to the United States (see figure 6.7).[71] It was, after all, the SS *Princess Adelaide* that brought the first troupe of Cantonese opera performers of the decade to the United States on September 29, 1922.[72] The proximity of the three cities to one another greatly facilitated movement on the performance circuit. The movement would continue in both directions, in fact.

CHAPTER 7

FROM LUN ON AND LUN HOP TO THE GREAT CHINA THEATER, 1922–1925

San Francisco was a logical first destination for the Cantonese opera troupe. Not only was its Chinese population the largest in North America, but it also had not had professional Cantonese opera since the earthquake of 1906. Yet since then the Chinese community had developed a stronger social, political, and economical standing within the city, despite anti-Chinese sentiment. The Lun On Company, which was led by Canadian merchant Chen Yiyao (Chin Yee You), assembled thirty-eight performers, secured half of the proposed capital of $40,000, and leased the Crescent Theater at 649 Broadway.

When applying to the Department of Labor for the troupe's entry, its legal broker, J. Fred Sanders in Vancouver, astutely pointed as precedent to recent admissions of Chinese actors joining vaudeville circuits and circuses. But Lun On was, of course, different from these in size, intended audience, genre, and sponsorship. The Commissioner General of the Bureau of Immigration, W. W. Husband, denied the application, noting that unlike previous applicants, these performers were not "billed to appear at different theaters or with circuses in the United States. The Bureau is not inclined to look with favor upon a request of this kind involving such a large number of Chinese."[1] The bureau, without approving the establishment of the theater, eventually consented to review the performers' eligibility for admission at the port of Seattle when they arrived. With no other choice, the troupe sailed from Vancouver to Seattle. Its broker's persistent effort and connections paid off: on arrival on September 28, Lun On's troupe, Renshou Nian, was admitted.

On October 7, 1922, Renshou Nian made its debut at the Crescent Theater in San Francisco.[2] Its daily playbill advertisements soon appeared in a prominent local newspaper, the *Young China*, which was affiliated with China's Nationalist Party. It is clear from the repertoire of the first week that classic operas such as *Thrice Going to Southern Tang* (October 10) and *Pan Jinlian Trifling with Her Brother-in-Law* (October 16) were favorites. The troupe's immense popularity was reflected in the amazement of a reporter from the *San Francisco Chronicle,* who wrote in a full-length article: "THEY SELL TICKETS—The S. R. O. [Standing Room Only] sign hangs out nightly. While the performance starts at 7 o'clock and lasts until midnight, there is not a vacant seat in the house after 8 o'clock. Some gate receipts!"[3] The prominent article, which featured photographs of the performers, was followed the next day by another major piece as shown in figures 7.1a and 7.1b.

Although billed as a mixed troupe, Renshou Nian was really more like a male troupe with three female performers; four female impersonators still had prominent roles. The sixteen-year-old actress Li Xuemei (whose debut in Vancouver the previous year raised ticket prices; her photo is featured in figure 7.1b) and the venerable female impersonator Xian Huada were featured in the same role in the same performance, an arrangement that tapped into the strengths of both. We have observed the casting of three actresses playing the same role as early as 1916 in Canada (see figure 6.2). Here the strong voice and traditional skills of a female impersonator and the youthful voice of a teenaged actress showed the different phases of the female protagonist's life. The featured operas, *Pinggui Bidding Farewell* and *Pinggui Returning Home*—which tell the story of the protagonist's journey through life—benefited from the double casting, which showed both the tender youth and prudent adulthood of the leading female character. Throughout the decade such double casting would be common in the United States but not in Hong Kong or southern China, where mixed-sex performance was not allowed until the 1930s.

Renshou Nian worked in many different genres. For example, as shown in figure 7.2, a playbill printed by the *Young China* promises an evening filled with acrobatic spectacle: a bearded warrior lifting a stone lion, a young warrior scooping up a prized pearl, and the slaughtering of a fox-turned-belle played by a female impersonator. They were spirited spectacles featuring lead actors who had received critical acclaim in Vancouver, Victoria, and Southeast Asia. On the surface these displays of extraordinary feats of balance, agility, and martial arts seem to come from the familiar mold of Chinese acrobatic performances widespread in American popular entertainment, such as the famous Long Tack Sam. But they were actually derived from existing scenarios, or paichang, and were rooted in traditional Cantonese opera.

The theater also featured romantic operas and actresses. In November the company recruited, among others, the eighteen-year-old actress Tan Huizhuang. The initial response to Tan's performances was so overwhelming that the theater put a cap of eight on the number of tickets a person could purchase at a time.[4] The *San Francisco Chronicle* reported that the long line for her debut at the theater's box office, formed four hours prior to the show, required the supervision of the police

SAN FRANCISCO CHRONICLE, SUNDAY, OCTOBER 29, 1922

San Francisco's Chinese Theater Gives Occident New Slant on Drama
The Ten-Hour Play's the Thing Since Thespians From Orient Arrived

Bit of Cathay Transplanted To Former Home of Picture Thrillers by Art Pilgrims

Women in Company Include "Mary Pickford of Celestial Kingdom;" Ancient Dramas Given for Chinatown

By HERB B. GEE

WHETHER the Sunday editor of The Chronicle, because of my last name, was under the impression that I am of Chinese descent, or if he thought I understood and spoke Chinese when he suggested that I go over to the Crescent Theater on Broadway—former home of Carusoed opera and later given over to Bill Hart thrillers—to find out all about a Chinese play there, with real Chinese men and women actors and actresses from China, and what it was all about, I don't know. He little dreamed that in carrying out his plans it would become necessary to put myself at the mercy of a small army of interpreters.

Actors From Cathay Star in Own Theater

Gee Tai Yuen

Members of the Chinese company playing native drama here, showing some of their gorgeous costumes. Note the makeups of Gee Tai Yuen, the "villain," and Moo Sang Yun as "the emperor." Also the Chinese actresses.

Mysteries of Art Field Are Exploded

By RAY BOYNTON

Plans Made to Organize New Hebrew Players' Club Here

Y. M. I. Plans Its Thanksgiving Dance

Fig. 7.1a. Article about Chinese opera in the *San Francisco Chronicle*, October 29, 1922. (Courtesy of the University of California, Berkeley library.)

squad.[5] Adulatory tributes to Tan soon appeared in the pages of the *Young China*. The theater was also successful with patriotic repertoire, which it staged in three benefit performances to raise funds for the local Chinese school.[6] Chinatown theaters occupied a different place in the Chinese community than Western ones did for Americans: fundraising was a significant function for them, and a prosperous Chinese theater was a powerhouse for creating a collective spirit in the community. They all carried out such a social responsibility seriously.

Having secured its business in San Francisco, Lun On started to recruit more performers. From October to December 1922, thirty-one performers came to the Crescent Theater from Vancouver. Although it admitted them, the Immigration Bureau was not pleased. An unenthusiastic approval noted: "the venture had proven a far greater financial success than anticipated . . . [though] the advisability of admit-

SECOND SECTION
Miscellaneous and Classified Advertisements

San Francisco Chronicle

SECOND SECTION
PAGES 9 TO 18

FOUNDED 1865 — SAN FRANCISCO, CAL., MONDAY, OCTOBER 30, 1922 — VOL. CXXI, NO. 107

13,000 VISIT PARK MUSEUM DURING WEEK

Great Memorial Institution Draws Throng of Nearly 11,000 Yesterday

NOTABLES LAUD EXHIBITS

Many New Treasures Being Donated at Marvelous Art Collections

A "Chinese Mary Pickford"

Lee Shut Moy, ingenue from Hongkong, who holds much the same place in the hearts of San Francisco's Chinatown as "America's Sweetheart" does in the U. S. A.

Oriental Actress Has All Chinatown at Her Feet

Pretty, Dainty and Only 16, World's Youngest 'Leading Woman' Here for Long Engagement

By HERB B. GEE

RED VICTORY IN MANCHURIA PROVES COSTLY

Leaders Admit Suffering Heavy Losses at Hands of White Army

VLADIVOSTOK CLEARED

Chita Forces Express Desire to Co-operate With the Natives

VLADIVOSTOK MADE CAPITAL OF PROVINCE

'Rah! Maud's Here!

Ralph Mule Rides From Ukiah

Mayor Pays Fare

Won at Barbecue by S. F. Chieftain Declines to Trek With Big Auto May Become Kiddies' Pet in Park

Manslaughter Laid To Steamer Clerk

Ship Barber Dies After Scuffle on Deck

Autoist Flees on Foot After Crash

Runs Down Man and Woman; Held for Quiz

S. F. Naval Airplanes Headed for Home

Bandits Hold Up Soft Drink Place

RECTOR'S WIFE CHALLENGED BY HER ACCUSER

Insists She Saw Mrs. Hall at Scene on Night of New Jersey Tragedy

THREATENED SHE SAYS

Mrs. Gibson Tells of Efforts to Buy Her Silence; Moon Story Disputed

"Lightnin'" Star Sees His Play From Box

Fig. 7.1b. Article about Chinese opera, featuring Li Xuemei, in the *San Francisco Chronicle*, October 30, 1922. (Courtesy of the University of California, Berkeley library.)

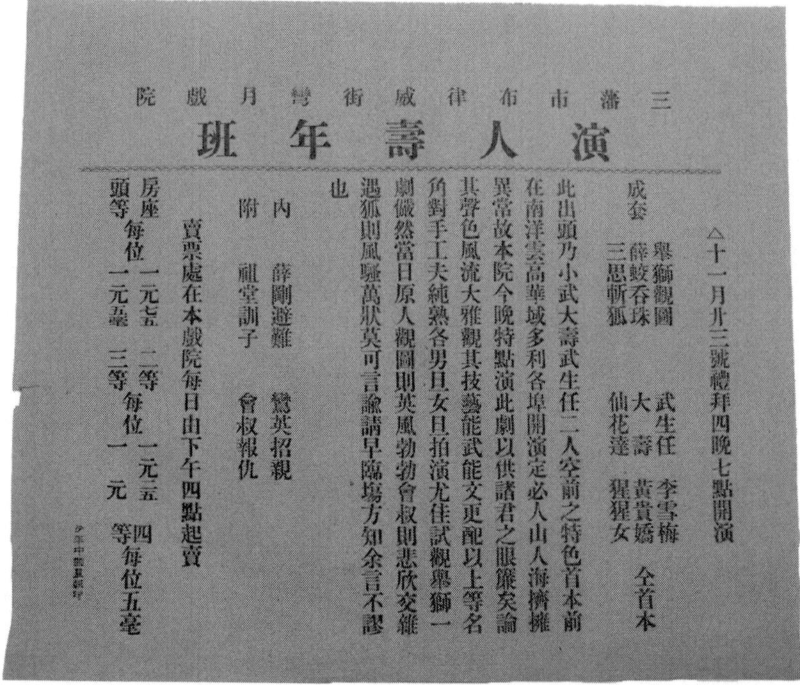
三藩市布律威街彎月戲院

演人壽年班

△十一月廿三號禮拜四晚七點開演

成套 舉獅觀圖
薛蛟吞珠
三思斬狐

武生任 李雪梅
大壽 黃貴嬌 全首本
仙花達 猩猩女

此出頭乃小武大壽武生任二人空前之特色首本前在南洋雲高華域多利各埠開演定必人山人海擠擁異常故本院今晚特點演此劇以供諸君之眼簾矣論其聲色風流大雅觀其技藝能武能文更配以上等名角對手工夫純熟各男旦女旦拍演尤佳試觀舉獅一劇儼然當日原人觀圖則英風勃勃會叔則悲欣交雜遇狐則風騷萬狀莫可言諭請早臨場方知余言不謬也

內 薛剛避難 鸞英招親
附 祖堂訓子 會叔報仇

賣票處在本戲院每日由下午四點起賣

房座每位一元七五 二等每位一元二五 四等每位五毫
頭等每位一元五毫 三等每位一元

Fig. 7.2. Playbill, Renshou Nian Troupe, Crescent Theater, November 23, 1922 (courtesy of Ren Fan).

ting a large number of Chinese actors might be doubted, nothing has happened to call into question the good faith of this particular theater company."[7] In January 1923 Lun On received approval to import an entire second troupe from Vancouver. This was a good time for Chinese theaters. During the Thanksgiving holiday in 1922, a twenty-six-member troupe named Lok Tin Tsau arrived in Boston from Montreal and started regular performances. At about the same time, a Guo Fengnian troupe was performing in Los Angeles, according to playbills printed in the *Young China*.[8] From this point on, Cantonese opera grew quickly, and its network stretched from Vancouver to Havana, Mexico City, Mexicali, and Lima.[9]

THE LUN HOP COMPANY

According to its application, Lun On initially planned on continuing on to New York and other American cities. But after a very short time in San Francisco the troupe had already exceeded all expectations. In January 1923 the theater held a week-long benefit for the local Tungwah Hospital. This event raised more than $7,000 (equivalent to $99,309.58 in 2014).[10] The sum shows not only that there was support for Chinatown's only hospital but also that the theater could really mobilize the community. Therefore the Canadian theatrical company was bought by local merchants even before its second troupe arrived. The revenue for the Lun On Company over the course of three months was $147,554 (equivalent of $2 million in 2015).[11] The Department of Labor was notified in late January 1923 of the new ownership of Ying Mee Lun Hop, a San Francisco company (hereafter Lun Hop).[12] The new acquisition made it more certain that the troupe would stay in San Francisco.

The Chinese New Year, which fell on February 16 in 1923, is important for theaters, particularly in Chinatowns. At the Crescent Theater the troupe held two daily performances for five days, including New Year's Eve, when traditionally there were no performances. Many festive opera productions, such as *Monkey's Journey to the West*, were chosen to suit the celebratory occasion. Inevitably, the theater also included ritual operas such as *The Heavenly Maiden Offers a Son* and *A Birthday Greeting from the Eight Immortals*. Performance of these playlets (lasting about eighteen minutes) was also a form of worship. They were the theater's offerings to various deities showing gratitude for prosperity and praying for a blissful new year.[13]

Fig. 7.3. Entrance to the Orpheum Theatre at 3rd Avenue and Madison Street, Seattle, 1920 (courtesy of the Pemco Webster and Steven Collection, Museum of History and Industry, Seattle).

Meanwhile, newcomers arrived to strengthen the company. On February 24 the Le Wannian troupe entered the United States via Seattle and made its U.S. debut at the city's Orpheum Theatre (figure 7.3).[14] It retained much of its strong cast from Vancouver. It billed two top actresses—Guan Yinglian and Yangzhou Mei. With her prior success in Vancouver, Guan Yinglian was made the troupe's new focus and received special attention in the English-language press. The *Seattle Post-Intelligencer*'s report on the troupe's premiere and her debut was soon reprinted in news outlets around the country, from Chicago and New York to El Paso.[15] In *Time* magazine, Guan's debut was reported on the same page as that of Meyerbeer's *L'Africaine* at the Metropolitan Opera House (with Beniamino Gigli in the title role) and Massenet's *Cleopatra* by the Opera Company of Chicago:

> The Ying Mee Lun Hop Opera Company gave a performance in Seattle, presenting Mook Kwee Ying Ha San, or The Mountain Queen. Most of the audience was Chinese. The prima donna, Kwung Ying-Lin, is called the best-known woman on the Chinese stage. Cymbals played a prominent part in the music. The settings were somewhat sketchy. A table and two chairs represented impenetrable mountain fortresses. Whole armies were frequently on the stage, but they were invisible except to the hard-working imaginations of the spectators.[16]

Like the other opera news, this report was aimed at the magazine's middle-class readers. Though an ordinary notice by the standards of Western opera, it was an extraordinary public relations coup for a Chinese theater. The *Chicago Daily Tribune* compared the performance to an evening of Wagner's *Götterdämmerung* uncut.[17] These reports presented Cantonese opera as a legitimate genre and received attention from the English-speaking audience, which might have been interested in the popular representation of Chinese theater in the recent revival of *The Yellow Jacket*.[18]

The Seattle playbills, too, were clearly meant for the general public, rather than the Chinese community only. Figure 7.4b shows the English side of the well-designed bilingual playbill, one far fancier than those used at the Crescent Theater, for *The Butterfly Cup*, whose high drama wove together conflict, romance, and revenge. Yangzhou Mei was the lead actress and Jing Runcai was the lead actor. (The English side of the playbill is much simpler; for example, it lists a cast of seven rather than eighteen, and shows only the characters and their names in the opera.) The Chinese side of the playbill (see figure 7.4a) has additional details about the theater, such as the names of eighteen performers, ticket prices (from $.50 to $2), and performance time (7 P.M. to 12 A.M.). It may not be a surprise that, like the troupe, the playbills were from Vancouver. They underscored the fluidity with which cultural practices were shared in the Pacific Northwest. Seattle and Vancouver used the same erudite theater professionals necessary for the production of these playbills. Seattle did have its own Chinese printing facility with the newspaper the *Chinese Star*, which would later take over the printing of the playbills.[19]

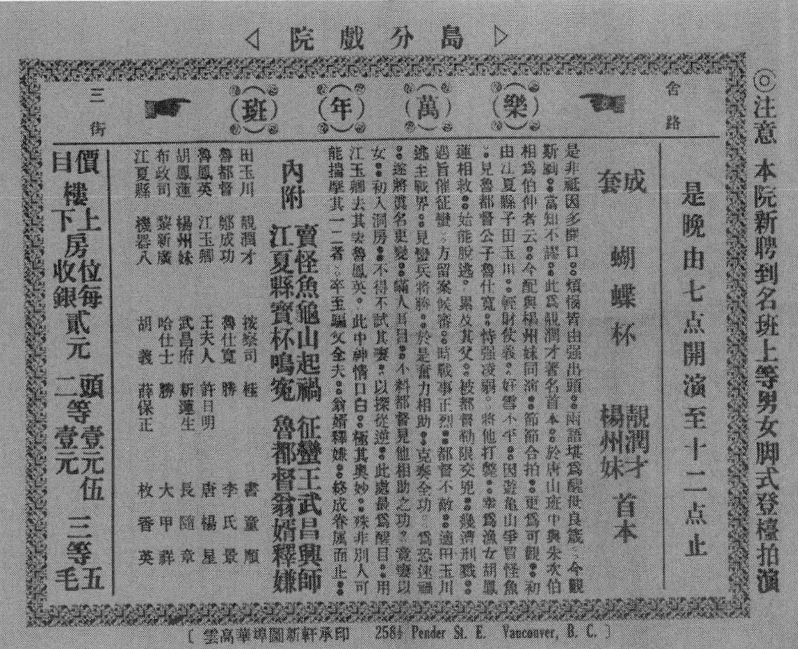

◁ 島分戲院 ▷

舍路 （樂）（萬）（年）（班） 三街

◎注意 本院新聘到名班上等男女脚式登檯拍演

是晚由七点開演至十二点止

成套 蝴蝶杯 靚潤才 楊州妹 首本

是非祗因多拼口。。煩惱皆由强出頭。。兩語堪爲醒世良箴。。今觀斯劇。。當知不謬。。此爲靚潤才著名首本。。於唐山班中與朱次伯相爲伯仲者云。。今配與楊州妹同演。。節節合拍。。更爲可觀。。初由江夏縣子田玉川。。輕財仗義。。好雪不平。。因遊龜山爭買怪魚。。見魯都督公子魯仕寬。。恃强凌弱。。將他打斃。。幸爲漁女胡鳳蓮相救。。始能脫逃。。累及其父。。被都督勒限交兇。。幾遭刑戮。。過旨催征蠻。。方留案候審。。時戰事正烈。。都督不敵。。適田玉川逃主戰界。。見蠻兵將勝。。於是奮力相助。。克奏全功。。爲恐洩漏。。遂將眞名更變。。瞞人耳目。。不料都督見他相助之功。。竟妻以女。。初入洞房。。不得不試其妻。。以探從逆。。此處最爲醒目。。用江玉卿去其妾魯鳳英。。此中神情口白。。極其奧妙。。殊非別人可能描摹其一二者。。卒至騙父全夫。。翁婿釋嫌。。終成眷屬而止。。

內附 寶怪魚龜山起禍 征蠻王武昌興師 江夏縣寶杯鳴冤 魯都督翁婿釋嫌

田玉川 靚潤才　按察司 桂　書童 順
魯都督 鄒成功　魯仕寬 勝　李氏 景
魯鳳英 江玉卿　王夫人 許日明　唐楊 星
胡鳳蓮 楊州妹　武昌府 新蓮生　長隨 章
布政司 黎新廣　哈仕士 勝　大甲 薛
江夏縣 機器入　胡義 薛保正　枚香 英

價目 樓上房位每位貳元 樓下收銀 頭等壹元伍 二等壹元 三等五毛

〔雲高華埠新圖軒承印 258½ Pender St. E. Vancouver, B. C.〕

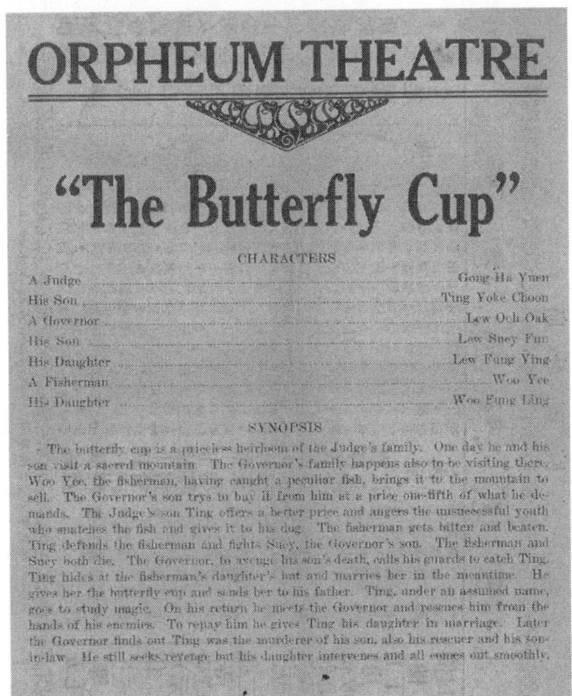

ORPHEUM THEATRE

"The Butterfly Cup"

CHARACTERS

A Judge .... Gong Ha Yuen
His Son .... Ting Yoke Choon
A Governor .... Lew Och Oak
His Son .... Lew Suey Fun
His Daughter .... Lew Fung Ying
A Fisherman .... Woo Yee
His Daughter .... Woo Fung Ling

SYNOPSIS

The butterfly cup is a priceless heirloom of the Judge's family. One day he and his son visit a sacred mountain. The Governor's family happens also to be visiting there. Woo Yee, the fisherman, having caught a peculiar fish, brings it to the mountain to sell. The Governor's son trys to buy it from him at a price one-fifth of what he demands. The Judge's son Ting offers a better price and angers the unsuccessful youth who snatches the fish and gives it to his dog. The fisherman gets bitten and beaten. Ting defends the fisherman and fights Suey, the Governor's son. The fisherman and Suey both die. The Governor, to avenge his son's death, calls his guards to catch Ting. Ting hides at the fisherman's daughter's hut and marries her in the meantime. He gives her the butterfly cup and sends her to his father. Ting, under an assumed name, goes to study magic. On his return he meets the Governor and rescues him from the hands of his enemies. To repay him he gives Ting his daughter in marriage. Later the Governor finds out Ting was the murderer of his son, also his rescuer and his son-in-law. He still seeks revenge but his daughter intervenes and all comes out smoothly.

Figs. 7.4a and 7.4b. Bilingual playbill, *The Butterfly Cup*, Orpheum Theatre, Seattle (courtesy of the Wing Luke Museum, Seattle).

Lun Hop's two troupes finally joined forces. The union, marked by Yangzhou Mei's San Francisco debut on March 31, formed the largest troupe in the United States for the next two years, with a total cast of sixty-four members. The large number allowed it to expand its reach to cities and towns along the Pacific coast, as well as inland to mining towns. Within its first year the company had sub-troupes going to Portland, Fresno, Sacramento, Los Angeles, and even Mexicali, where a substantial Chinese community had arisen. By the end of 1923, when the Department of Labor formalized its admission procedure by setting a quota for each Chinese theater, sixty-four became the allotted quota for Lun Hop. The combined cast now featured several prima donnas, as well as a score of other actors for leading and comic roles.[20] They continued to perform at the Crescent Theater, whose playbill bore both troupes' names, until the company opened its new theater in 1925.

GUAN YINGLIAN AND YANGZHOU MEI

One example of Lun Hop's strength after the merger was its cast of actresses. Guan Yinglian and Yangzhou Mei were accomplished performers with different strengths. The former made her debut in San Francisco on March 3.[21] Within weeks, laudatory poems were hung on the curtain at the Crescent Theater during her performances.[22] The theater also published a promotional piece in the *Young China* on March 31, 1923, accompanied by her photo. It read:

> The eminent actress Guan Yinglian is an unusually superb performer from Guangdong, where she led performances of a renowned all-female troupe, Qunfang Yanying, with Li Xuefeng. Guan, whose fame paralleled that of Li's, is known among Cantonese opera fans. Her singing is ethereally melodious, her beauty is sublime, and her acting is excellent. She is equally graceful in amorous and melancholy expressions, and equally excellent in both warrior and chivalric repertoire. Truly unique among her peers.[23]

The photo of Guan (in regular attire) was the first to appear in Chinatown theaters' newspaper advertisements. It also reflected the trend in Cantonese opera of talent, charisma, and beauty becoming ever more important. In any case, placing photos in newspapers quickly became a regular publicity tool.

Guan's advanced vocal skill was the focal point. The twenty-seven-year-old former lead performer of an all-female troupe soon became the chief of the three prima donnas.[24] A commentator for the *Young China* noted that, along with a highly polished supporting cast including actresses such as Tan Huizhuang, Guan sang the leading role with power and nuance. Her skillful performance, noted the writer, was hampered only by the bulky set (for the scene of lotus gathering), which blocked one of the two normal backstage doors, making the usual exit awkward. She made an indelible impression that led to the patronage of a community matriarch, Mrs. Quan Yick-Sun, who shared the (fairly common) family name. (*Quan* is the Cantonese pronunciation of *Guan*.) She was the eldest daughter of tycoon Lew Hing, owner of the Pacific Coast Cannery, and she acted as his liaison to the community. She became Guan's patroness (or according to Chinese custom, a godmother). That December she hosted the wedding of Guan and Ou Runcai, a fellow actor who was featured on the Orpheum Theatre playbill shown in figure 7.4.[25] The prominent patronage lent Guan support in both stage life and personal life, forming a strong tie that would continue until the death of Mrs. Quan.[26] Their extended relationship was an exceptional case (see the epilogue), although in general, patronage of a performer by the Family Association of the same name was typical.

For Guan's performance of *Pavilion Peony* on August 5, the playbill lauded her talent and singled out her unique interpretation of the classic romantic role, her newly designed tunes, and her extraordinarily delicate performances. Her work in the opera of moral drama *Twilight Scarlet Tears* occasioned further praise for her virtue: "Opera singers have a significant role in the society because of their ability to promulgate moral excellence and to rectify flaws in social culture, as well as the beauty of their graceful performances and musical talent. Guan's elegance and beautiful voice made her extraordinarily suitable."[27]

Yangzhou Mei, on the other hand, brought a different interpretation to the young belle role. She was a versatile performer playing complicated, changing roles, and she reveled in the challenge of using different vocal styles and personas. For example, in a new production on August 12, the playbill extolled her transformation through seven role types from young belle to young warrior, young scholar, male clown, female clown, scholar-warrior, and white-bearded warrior. It made for exciting theater. Furthermore, while these seven roles demonstrated Yang's versatility as an actress, they also anticipated Cantonese opera's six-pillar system, which came to prominence in the 1930s. The initiative to modernize the opera genre was clear as the theater proudly noted that the significance of her role shifting went beyond mere novelty to signal "the progressive style" of the theater. The playbill underscored the point in a somewhat sententious tone:

> Her singing of the young male vocal type has wonderful resonance. Her capable voice easily managed all these parts; meanwhile it is her improvisations [bridging main arias] that make the performance so compelling. To understand the world's modernization, we need to follow trends of recent progress. With Yang's residence in San Francisco, we can see the rare and skillful singing of multifarious vocal types in [seven] role types.[28]

Dynamism was reflected in Yang's private life as well. Lun Hop cancelled her bond in October, before her contract ended, and tried to have her deported, though the reason was not clear. Having already earned thousands of dollars, Yang procured her own bondsmen and secured a bond.[29] She then went to Mexicali, where there was a lively opera scene with two theaters, only to return to San Francisco a year later to play at the rival Mandarin Theater. It should not be overlooked, however, that this was an example of a Chinatown actress gaining financial and professional independence. For the Lun Hop Company, nevertheless, such independence could be a sign of trouble.

Despite signs of occasional internal discord, Lun Hop maintained a pipeline of top performers. After ten months of relying on the talent from British Columbia, it finally began to hire performers directly from China. Twenty-nine-year-old Xin Baiguo, notable as the first prominent actress to play martial roles, was the first to arrive; she made her debut on August 21. Although nothing in the advertisement suggested her star status, many signs such as her traveling with a companion, and the elaborate costumes and sets that accompanied her on her Pacific voyage, revealed her stature. Her expertise in warrior roles prompted a spate of operas featuring martial, acrobatic, and gymnastic acts with weaponry in the following weeks; the theater's abundant offerings of romantic operas with young belles began to be spiced up that week with spirited titles such as *Riot in the Nengren Temple* and *Double Rapier Female Warrior*.

COMMUNITY, SLAVERY CHARGES, AND IMMIGRATION

The first sign of Lun Hop's meeting resistance from the mainstream community was a public allegation of slavery. In late September the Presbyterian Missionary of Chinatown claimed that it took in two girls, aged nine and eleven, who escaped from enslavement at the theater.[30] Founded by Donaldina Cameron, the Presbyterian Missionary had been known for its rescue efforts since the beginning of the century. Cameron had built her reputation on dramatic rescues of Chinese slave girls, including a large raid in Marysville two years earlier.[31] She associated Chinese theaters with prostitutes and immoral activities and would continue in later years to be vocal about their adverse impact on the community. The theater, for its part, asserted that the girls were children of the actor Taizi Hui and had arrived with him the previous November and participated in performances. A long legal battle ensued between the theater and Cameron over the destiny of the girls.[32] Eventually, the Juvenile Court ruled Cameron the girls' guardian and arranged for them to be returned to China.[33] The incident was reported in the newspapers, and whether false or not, it renewed the stigma of theater as immoral.[34] Whether Lun Hop's Chinese identity served as a stigma or an attraction, it was not an identity that it could escape. In this case, it was unfortunate that the theater's integration into the community required being subjected to the cultural power of narratives and stereotypes of "yellow slavery," a phrase used as a heading for the report in the *San Francisco Chronicle*.[35]

With a growing reputation on both sides of the Pacific, Lun Hop had its own agent recruiting performers in southern China, and new actors arrived in San Francisco on steamships of the President Line directly from China.[36] Because the theater had a quota of sixty-four performers, however, a large number of new arrivals in effect created a need to send current opera performers to neighboring countries, thus creating vacancies in the quota. Through this type of maneuver, Lun Hop was able to accommodate new arrivals. Those who went to neighboring countries to perform would often join other troupes on returning. In September 1923 the twenty-five-member All-Star troupe in Los Angeles employed ten performers who had entered under the sponsorship of Lun On in 1922, including the actress Li Xuemei.[37] They were transferred to the All-Star troupe with new bonds.[38] Directly and indirectly, therefore, Lun Hop contributed to the circulation of performers across borders and helped supply performers to other theaters.

As Lun Hop's roster, with subsidiary troupes across the continent, grew more complicated, it ran into various difficulties with immigration authorities. In late April the company recruited three performers from Cuba who were arriving at Key West en route to China. Yet the engagement would last for merely ten days.[39] The actors applied to the Immigration Bureau for a change of in-transit status in order to continue performing, but the bureau denied the request, saying no leniency would be given this time. Such rejections did not stop performers from making similar attempts, however, especially if they were already in North America. Many were arriving from all directions in addition to China, and Lun Hop routinely charged higher ticket prices for debut performances—the top ticket price being raised from $1.50 to $2—for two to five days with new lead performers, regardless of their rank or fame.

The theater responded to these obstacles by hiring a new legal team to handle the at times thorny immigration issues and mountainous paperwork. It retained a veteran attorney of the entertainment business in Washington, DC, Roger O'Donnell, and a Seattle attorney, Hugh Todd. The two worked together to make sure that routine immigration matters could go through smoothly.[40] In order to expedite the process telegrams were often used, the expense paid by the theater. In addition, the lawyers often dealt with the renewal of permits. Upon the expiration of its one-year permit in October 1923, the company successfully received extended permission to continue its performances in San Francisco.

Lun Hop's monopoly on the city's theater business faced an imminent threat, however. By the beginning of 1924 a new Chinese theater building was going up on Grant Avenue. The new theater was sponsored by the political contingent of China's Constitutional Party, which opposed the Chinese Nationalist Party, to which Lun Hop belonged. Both parties had their own Chinese newspapers in San Francisco and maintained ties with their constituency, and theaters aided their standing within the community. Hoping to stay in the lead, Lun Hop's attorneys made an application to the Immigration Bureau in March 1924 for a quota increase from sixty-four to eighty members, with thirty-five in Portland and Seattle and forty-five in San Francisco. The attorneys' explanation revealed a lot about the theater's business situation:

> It is a big help to be able to transfer the actors between the show towns, as in this way the patrons of the shows get a change of actors. The company informs me that after certain leading actors play for a certain time, the patrons begin to stop coming and as soon as a new actor is brought on or returns from an absence, the old patrons come to see the show again. . . . Every 12 days the Admiral Line boat arrives [from China] and on each such boat we have from one to four actors coming to take the places of actors who are checking out.[41]

Variety and novelty were among the most reliable means for theaters to attract audiences. Lun Hop found having only sixty-four performers limiting. With the increase, it would be able to have a full-size troupe similar in size to a top-tier troupe in China.

Yet Chinese theater continued to be stigmatized, and Lun Hop's success was taken as a problem of excess. The Department of Labor rejected the request for a quota increase, writing, "The department has already taken about as lenient an attitude as is consistent with good administration. Recently an unprecedented number of requests has come before it for permission to bring Chinese actors, the line must be drawn somewhere. It cannot go on indefinitely permitting Chinese actors to come here in ever-increasing numbers."[42] The attorneys did not press further. Perhaps they did not want to antagonize the officials. Conflict of interest may have also played a role; Roger O'Donnell was by then also representing other theatrical companies. In any case, the attorneys' good relations with immigration officials meant that frequently the troupe could temporarily exceed its quota. So it simply continued to send performers on the road to make space for newcomers. During the first half of 1924 alone, thirty-five new performers were brought in, and a sizable subgroup was sent to Portland in late January; another went to Mexicali. From July to October the company brought in sixteen more performers. Connections within the Pacific Northwest were also evident as Guan and her husband formed part of the subgroup in Portland, joined by four actresses and six actors arriving from Vancouver.[43]

CHINESE NEW YEAR AND PROMINENT WARRIOR ROLES

With the large number of new arrivals, the theater's second Chinese New Year celebration was augmented by an abundance of new actors in warrior roles, the animated performance of which enhanced the festive and jovial mood. The celebration began three days prior to the New Year. Productions were on a grander scale than they had been in the previous year. There were four playlets each evening.[44] A matinee and an evening performance were offered daily for the first three days of the celebration. The playlets on the first evening included three popular operas: *Pinggui Returning Home*, *Pan Jinlian Trifling with Her Brother-in-Law*, and *Lament of Jia Baoyu*.[45]

The warrior operas continued into mid-April, interrupted only by comic operas. For the warrior theme the theater branched out from the traditional repertory to more contemporary and political events. The patriotic opera *Bu Qing Tian*, performed on March 16, was interesting in this regard. The title was a reference to the government official Bao Zheng of the Song Dynasty, a cultural symbol of justice and integrity. *Bu Qing Tian*, which featured two leading martial actors, wove a typically melodramatic reunion of long-lost lovers into a plot including three contemporary events: Sun Yat-sen's victory over the Qing Dynasty, the warrior lord Yuan Shikai's abduction of the child emperor Pu Yi, and the establishment of the temporary Nanking government for the Republic of China. It enacted political stories that were crucial to the population's historical consciousness, albeit in the lighter form of operatic entertainment. The traditional warrior roles took a contemporary twist.

The theater's production of warrior opera received another boost with the arrival of the renowned actor of the bearded-warrior type, Dongpo An. A *Young China* report of the critical acclaim he received in Portland at his debut raised anticipation for his arrival in San Francisco on March 31.[46] He played an important part that required sophisticated martial arts techniques as well as an awe-inspiring appearance and dramatic singing skills. On arrival he performed nine consecutive evenings as the lead. Dongpo An ignited the audiences' interest in sophisticated old warrior roles in the classic repertoire.

Many statesmen of courage and wisdom in Chinese legends were performed by actors of this role type in Cantonese opera. Dongpo An's signature role Su Shi (also known as Su Dongpo) was an eleventh-century statesman who was unjustly banished and exiled many times for his opposition to radical reform. Su, one of the Song Dynasty's most famous poets, demonstrated optimism and lack of bitterness in the face of long exile. The opera of April 5, *Su Dongpo Encounters Red Cliff*, evoked Su's famous poem "Red Cliff Rhapsody," about a Han Dynasty grand naval battle in Red Cliff, Hubei.[47] Another great role for Dongpo An was in *Su Wu Herding Sheep*, which is about the Han Dynasty general Su Wu, who was captured in 100 B.C. while on a diplomatic mission to the Xiongnu, a Turkic clan in central Asia. Su Wu, who could not be forced to surrender, was tortured and then exiled, and he herded sheep for twenty years before he could return to Han. In Chinese culture Su Wu was regarded as the epitome of perseverance in the face of great odds and trials. In the subsequent weeks Dongpo An played many of the inspiring, majestic figures of Chinese legend.

In the second quarter of 1924 many more actors arrived, and the Crescent Theater staged a dazzling range of operas for various male role types. The leading actresses at the theater, however, were of the second rank since Guan had left with a sub-troupe for Portland in January. One actress from China, Chin Siuying, arrived at Seattle, but she fell ill and died at the port.[48] The situation changed somewhat when, on May 30, Ziyou Hua arrived with her two younger sisters from Portland, where her graceful performances had won the approval of Portland audiences.[49] Figure 7.5 reproduces a portrait of Ziyou Hua in costume. She led nine consecutive

Fig. 7.5. Ziyou Hua. May's Photo Studio (courtesy of the Wylie Wong Collection at the Museum of Performance and Design, San Francisco).

evenings of opera and was clearly a versatile actress because on the second day she had already cross-dressed as a male character, singing in a masculine vocal style. She played female warrior roles on other evenings. The twenty-year-old Singapore native was already popular in Southeast Asia, as well as in southern China; an enthusiastic Shanghai critic had eagerly anticipated her the previous year, noting that her skill compared favorably to that of the two leading prima donnas of the era.[50] Ziyou Hua brought to the fore the significance of Southeast Asia, whose opera circuit, together with that of southern China, extended to North America, as well as elsewhere in the Cantonese Pacific. All through the 1920s adulatory descriptions of opera performers made frequent reference to their popularity in Southeast Asia.

On June 22, 1924, the *Young China* reported that Lun Hop's troupe opened in Seattle at a theater built by the company.[51] Having performers stay in the north allowed the theater in San Francisco to make the best of the performers' novelty, by introducing them one at a time. And a favorable response in Portland or Seattle created high expectations for the debut in San Francisco. The new theaters in the north enhanced the circulation of artists within the Pacific Northwest corridor.

RESPONSE TO A NEW RIVALRY

The same newspaper page that announced Ziyou Hua's arrival on May 30 also informed the city of the completion of a building to be named the Mandarin Theater, for which a troupe of thirty-eight would arrive on June 13, along with new scenery. It even included a lengthy list of twenty-five performers' names and role types. With the opening of the Mandarin Theater, Lun Hop's monopoly ended. Because no other entertainment at the time made money the way opera did, it was only a matter of time. By the end of June, key Chinese newspapers such as the *Young China* and *Chung Sai Yat Po* printed the theaters' daily playbills side by side. The Mandarin's advertisements boasted a stage filled with advanced technology: chairs decorated with light bulbs, electrically lit lotus and temple towers, paper sea creatures, and a mechanical device that could elevate singers into mid-air. As far as spectacle was concerned, Lun Hop paled by comparison. Yet the veteran company's superior cast was hard to beat. The new Mandarin Theater had a much smaller quota and needed to recruit more top performers. Five days after the new theater's opening, Lun Hop ran an advertisement that might be read as a veiled criticism: "Fancy programming alone is not enough. Talented actors with excellent skills are also necessary. Our world-class cast includes the actress Yu Baiguo with superb vocal and acting skills, the actor Dongpo An who has received the highest acclaim in the profession, and also the actor Xi Qi, who can cross-dress for female roles."[52]

The rivals sometimes featured identical repertoire on the same evening in order to outshine one another. And the tigang xi practice allowed each to tailor the opera to its strengths, whether a virtuosic singer, an actor of impressive skill, or one with great dexterity or graceful movement. On July 15 both theaters programmed *Shilin Paying Respects at the Pagoda*. The adroit, agile actress Yu Baiguo at the Crescent played the lead, competing with the graceful, willowy Xin Guifei at the Mandarin. Two days later both theaters put on *Sanniang Teaching Her Son*. Lun Hop played up the loyal servant in the story, a typical gongjiao role, by featuring a new actor, Zeya Yu. In contrast, the Mandarin Theater put the spotlight on the virtuous lady in the story and featured the popular actress Yangzhou Mei. Lun Hop's approach was somewhat old-fashioned, while the Mandarin's strategy reflected the newly emerging practice favoring female virtuosity. Cantonese opera was dynamic and flexible enough to be adapted to theaters' constraints and strengths, and the same operas could offer audiences different types of enjoyment.

Lun Hop also responded to the new rivalry by promoting its cast more aggressively: the performers' photos now regularly graced the pages of the *Young China*, accompanied by lengthy commentaries on their attributes and signature repertoire. When their pictures had first appeared in the newspapers in the previous year, they were little more than pictorial records. Even when in costume, the performers did little more than look into the camera. In contrast, photos from the second half of 1924, expertly photographed by May's Studio, showed them in elaborate costumes and dramatic poses. The picture of the young-warrior type Dayan Shun in the *Young China* on October 12 is a clear example. Our attention is drawn to the elaborate armor, headpiece, flags, and the prop in his right hand. His feet and left hand convey muscular tension and virility. The steadiness of his gaze suggests a fearlessness that fits with the patriotic opera described below the picture.

The debut in mid-October of the sister pair Jin Hudie and Yin Hudie (Golden Butterfly and Silver Butterfly) was acknowledged by another photo. Golden Butterfly played the role of the woman warrior Mu Guiyin. In her picture, the elaborate headpiece, armor, robe, and flags appear animated and impressive. Her face, framed by a sophisticated ornament and a silk bow, shows resolution. Silver Butterfly is on one knee, with the effect of accentuating the upright pose of her sister.[53] The portraits alone afforded sheer pleasure to their viewers and brought some of the magic of opera into the home. In fact, most newspaper photos of Lun Hop's casts showed performers in their costumes. The convention was that the wardrobe's elaborateness corresponded to the actors' mastery and the theater's professionalism and wealth. They were among the theaters' most valuable assets. Although the profession of photography in Chinatown was young, as reflected by the homespun inscription of the studio name at the photos' corners, they captured the dramatic presence of the actors. The steady flow of portraits contributed to the dissemination of opera culture as the papers were posted on bulletin boards and circulated to home or businesses. The photos brought daily opera performances to every part of social life in San Francisco's Chinatown.

In this context, the plain photo of the female impersonator Xiao Likang in a Western suit was curious. Xiao was an actor of high caliber who, arriving directly from China, continued after his debut in August for nine consecutive performances.[54] His photo in Western attire had an aura of modern professionalism rather than the elaborate conventions of the opera world, and it showed no trace of his female role. It highlighted his other professional role, that of an erudite playwright, instead. (As a playwright he assumed the name Lei Junqi; the caption, however, identified him as Xiao Likang.)

Finally the rivalry was such that the two theaters could no longer use the same photography studio. Toward the end of the year, Lun Hop switched from May's Studio to Suen's Photo Studio. The new studio would soon have its work featured in playbills and would faithfully record the theater's penchant for stage novelty for years to come.

THE JOINT INVESTITURE AND OTHER ATTRACTIONS

Perhaps the most public step that Lun Hop took to showcase its superior cast was the staging of a grand ritual opera. For most of August and September the company augmented its cast in earnest. Most of the new arrivals were stellar actors including Zheng Xinbei, a young scholar type, and Shezi An, a male comedian, both from top male troupes in China. It also sent for a new set of scene paintings to be imported from China. By mid-September the theater offered a special staging of the grand ritual opera *The Joint Investiture of a Prime Minister of Six Warlords*, with a particular spotlight on the bearded warrior. The company also printed a special flier, listing the cast of twenty-nine actors and actresses, to be distributed with the playbill.[55] The flyer emulated a *hengtou dan*, a paper with a cast list commonly used in southern China for promotion and contractual purposes. It included fourteen categories of role types, with the performers' names listed under each category (see table 7.1). It has all of the twelve types discussed in Chapter 4, except for no. 8, zhengsheng. The two additional categories are a newer role type of the 1920s, *wenwu xiaosheng*, which earlier would have been listed under *xiaosheng*, and an old-fashioned category, *sibuzheng*, which meant utility men or actors playing a bit part. This 1924 cast list of Lun Hop's shows that Cantonese opera in North America had prospered greatly, especially when compared to the playbill featuring Guo Fengnian in Montreal in 1917 (figure 6.3). Lun Hop's hengtou dan no doubt greatly impressed the community, making the new theater's roster pale by comparison.

Table 7.1. Hengtou dan of the Renshou Nian and Le Wannian Troupes at Lun Hop Company, September 1924

Role type	Characteristics	Names of performers
1. Wusheng	bearded warrior	Dongpo An
2. Wenwu Xiaosheng	young scholar-warrior	Zheng Xiqi
3. Xiaowu	young warrior	Dayan Shun, Yingxiong Jin, Lian Ren, Zhou Yurei
4. Male huadan	young belle	Xiao Likang
5. Huadan	young belle	Yu Baiguo, Lin Caiyu, Xin Baiguo, Chen Jinglian, Ziyou Hua, Liang Zhuzi (all female)
6. Zhengdan	graceful young belle	Huang-niang Xi, Chang'er Yue (female)
7. Zongsheng	middle-aged scholar	Bai Linggui
8. Xiaoshen	young scholar	Zheng Xinbei
9. Gongjiao	bearded old male	Zi Yayu
10. Da Huamian	villainous man	Gao Laochun
11. Er Huamian	tempestuous man	Da Niubao
12. Nüchou	female comic role	Lin Boxiang
13. Nanchou	male comic role	She Ziyi, Ziyou Zhou, Shezi An, Fei Nan
14. Sibuzheng	miscellaneous	Zhou Hua, Ya Sheng, Da Kuahuo, Yabao

The hengtou dan was remarkable also because Chinatown theaters could not always maintain a full cast such as this. So it was an occasion for celebration, and the specially printed list was produced as a flyer for distribution and posting. Then with the arrival of an actress of young belle roles, Xiyang Nü, the Crescent Theater could really claim to have a prominent actress who matched its actors and was comparable to those of its rival the Mandarin. According to the *Young China*'s report on December 12, Xiyang Nü performed in Boston with the Guo Min An troupe before coming to San Francisco with a dozen of her own scene paintings. Her debut was in a recent opera, *The Garden of the Peaches of Immortality*, the four episodes of which she staged on four consecutive evenings. Her debut also prompted the theater to print her photograph on the playbill, the first instance of this practice.[56]

Another important production of Lun Hop's was a newly scripted opera in multiple episodes by Lei Junqi. It was based on a popular Chinese translation of the French detective novel *Monsieur Lecoq* and featured all of the troupe's prominent performers.[57] The opera was performed on five Saturdays. After an enthusiastic response, it was extended to a sixth performance. The success of Lei Junqi's opera was a harbinger of the rising significance of professional dramatists in Chinatown opera.

GROWING AND PUTTING DOWN ROOTS

The improved playbills were not the only sign of the theaters' prosperity. Every year, Lun Hop brought in a sizable number of new performers, reaching a peak in 1925. Table 7.2 shows the numbers of new arrivals of the Lun On and Lun Hop Companies over a six-year span, based on immigration records. These figures are likely to be lower than the actual numbers, since they do not take into consideration those who appeared without being on the theater's official immigration record; they nevertheless provide a sense of the theater's prosperity. The 269 new arrivals not only sustained the opera but also made it a bustling place. Note that the number of newcomers for 1925 almost equals the company's quota of 65.

Performers typically arrived in waves brought in for specific occasions. The numbers surged for the Chinese New Year; the dramatic escalation of 1925 was due to the rivalry with the Mandarin Theater. Between December 1924 and the Chinese New Year of 1925 (January 24), fourteen performers arrived from China and two from New Orleans. Among them a new sister pair, Xiao Caiji and Xiao Caichan, and an actress named Xiao Susu were of high caliber.

Lun Hop produced a playbill with a full-length studio portrait of Xiao Susu in an elaborate costume on January 4, 1925. (A former lead with the female troupe Xunfang Yanying, she revealed her varied skills at her debut—changing roles from young belle to young scholar to young warrior—and on the third evening, she performed the male role against the young belle, performed by the comedic actor Shezi Yi.) It used photographs with increasing frequency, and by mid-year the Mandarin started to do the same. Among the earliest playbill photos, the images of the Xiao sisters showed their gentle grace—they were the most popular sister pair to appear in the U.S. Cantonese opera circuit, and they could later be traced to Mexico, Havana, New York, and Vancouver—while the image of a male impersonator of scholar-warrior type role, Zhu Jianshang, was handsome. Xiyang Nü's photos also reappeared frequently. This new focus on visual representation might have been prompted as much by advances in photographic technology, lower costs, and the growing number of Chinese American photographers as by the increase in actresses; their images, widely disseminated, inevitably helped ticket sales.

As mentioned above, the Chinese New Year celebrations included a lot of opera-going. Lun Hop's attorney once remarked on the importance of the festive occasion:

Table 7.2. Numbers of new arrivals of performers at the Lun On and Lun Hop companies

Year	1922	1923	1924	1925	1926	1927
Number of new arrivals	31	45	56	66	29	42

"[At the time of Chinese New Year] thousands of Chinese from California come to San Francisco for a holiday, which in many cases extends over a month. The full strength of the company is essential to play the repertoire needed for the entertainment of such a large number of patrons."[58] Capitalizing on the lucrative festival meant extending performances beyond San Francisco. The *Young China* reported on January 19, 1925, that a group of seventeen Lun Hop performers (in ten role types) was to depart for Los Angeles the following day to take the place of the recently dissolved Yong Tai Ping Company, just in time for the Chinese New Year on January 24.[59] It is not surprising that they had arrived the previous year and now were being rotated out to make space for new arrivals. The Mandarin Theater soon made a similar move, sending a seventeen-member troupe there in March.[60] The Cantonese opera scene in Los Angeles would become as lively as San Francisco's.

The rivalry in San Francisco had an impact on New Year's programming. For the thirteen-day celebration, held from January 22 to February 1 (one day before New Year's Eve to the ninth of the first month in the lunar calendar), both theaters featured matinee and evening performances on most days, including New Year's Eve. (According to tradition, performers would have a break on New Year's Eve and on the next day would honor deities with ritual playlets, but beginning in 1925 Chinese theaters in the United States held performances on the eve to enhance the festive mood.) Every aspect of the productions was part of the competition. For the matinee on New Year's Eve the same three classic playlets were featured in both theaters: *Lihua Punishing Her Son*, *Shilin Paying Respects at the Pagoda*, and *Pan Jinlian Trifling with Her Brother-in-Law*. The program followed a common crowd-pleasing sequence from an action-filled, warrior-type opera to a melancholy, tuneful, and lyrical opera, and finally to a comic opera filled with innuendos. Over the course of the holidays Lun Hop arranged for three debuts: one actor of comic roles, one actress of young belle roles, and one actress of young warrior roles.

On March 24 Lun Hop brought to its stage a new opera set in the Ming Dynasty, *Menacing Waves Daunting Beauty*, by the well-known Cantonese playwright Luo Jianhong (Law Kim-Hung), a founder of the Association of Drama Studies in Guangzhou. The theater's staging of such a famous dramatist's opera despite the extra work involved was an effort to move away from the conventional tigang xi to be on a par with the newest trends in Cantonese opera, a fact proudly proclaimed in the playbill. On April 19 a special Sunday matinee was offered in honor of the birthday of a pair of guardian deities of Cantonese opera, Generals Tian Dou. With ritual opera playlets the performers presented the special offerings in the hope of ensuring the continuing prosperity of the troupe (see figure 7.6). This opportunity must have been much appreciated by the performers, as they collectively placed a

Fig. 7.6. Altar for two deities, Generals Tian Dou. Brooks Photo Studio (courtesy of the Lois Rather Papers at the Museum of Performance and Design, San Francisco).

notice in the newspaper expressing their gratitude for the theater owner's assistance in the production. A shrine with Tian Dou's statues was a constant presence in Cantonese opera theaters.

Paying tribute to theater deities served to reassure opera performers who were uncertain in a new country. As their numbers increased, so did their call for ritual offerings. Lun Hop had dramatically increased its hiring of performers. In addition to the sixteen who arrived in the weeks leading to the Chinese New Year, eight to fourteen came every month from February to May, most directly from China but a few from Cuba, Mexico, and Canada as well. Occasionally the total number of performers would exceed the quota of sixty-four, but immigration officials gave Lun Hop a little latitude, assuming extra performers would depart in due course.[61] As Lun Hop readied for the opening of its own new theater building in June it welcomed two outstanding performers: Huang Xiaofeng (Wong Sieu Fong) and Xin Zhu.

HUANG XIAOFENG, PRINT CULTURE, AND AN ANTHOLOGY

The arrival of the actress Huang Xiaofeng on May 4, 1925, was a coup for Lun Hop. After she left Canada in 1918 (see Chapter 6), Huang returned to China, where her fame continued to grow; she had been praised by a Shanghai critic with *Shen Bao* as recently as 1924.[62] Embarking on a tour of the Americas again, she had a successful residency in Havana before entering the United States at New York. The *Young China* reported that she earned an annual salary of $15,000, with an additional allowance in the thousands of dollars for transportation, companions, and luggage. Arriving from Cuba, she was accompanied by her mother and a maid, as well as more than 4,500 pounds of luggage that included elaborate costumes, stage props, and scenic backdrops.[63] On reaching San Francisco, she first made a round of visits to the community, including the Huang Family Association. Her United States debut featured her signature repertoire, an opera titled *The Romance of Two Lotuses*. Adapted from a popular vernacular ballad (muyushu), the opera was known for its lyrical tone. Included in her first week of performances was an opera in three episodes (*Tale of Lovesick Woe*), performed on three consecutive evenings. For the following four weeks the theater featured her as the lead in order to showcase her finesse in a series of romantic lyrical classics. In lengthy advertisements, Lun Hop noted the uniqueness of Huang's portrayals of these favorite and familiar roles.[64] As a star, Huang had a remarkable combination of vocal skills, performing talent, and beauty.

Huang's performance on the yangqin (a Chinese hammered dulcimer) was praised in verse by an anonymous author on the playbill of May 12. "In her technique," the fan wrote, "she is gentle, charming and feminine; in her performing, she is mellifluous, dulcet, and musical." On May 18, Huang's performance of *The Goddess Scattering Flowers*, a story adapted from a recent Peking opera by Mei Lanfang, drew comparisons to the great star. The set was decorated with two hundred light bulbs, with a special colorful light directed on the front stage. That the Mandarin Theater quickly recalled its distinguished prima donna Zhang Shuqin from Los Angeles to perform on May 20 underscored Huang's immense success. From the day of Huang's debut, Lun Hop included photos on its playbills almost daily.

Opera culture was so active now in San Francisco that the publication of an anthology of Cantonese opera arias and songs was advertised in May 1924. Compiled by a local amateur group called Log Quon Shear, the anthology *Essence of Cantonese Arias and Songs* was published by the *Young China.* On the cover was Lun Hop's new actor, Xin Zhu, as the legendary Guan Gong, flanked by two actors from Vancouver (see figure 7.7).[65] It begins with more than twenty pages of pictures of opera singers from both theaters, followed by the lyrics of over a hundred songs, many of which were the signature arias of these singers. While the lyrics were assembled from opera recordings made in southern China, the pictures recorded the top twenty performers in the first two-and-a-half years of opera's return to San Francisco. Four performers highlighted in the anthology's newspaper advertisements could be regarded as the most popular in San Francisco at the time of its publication. They are Lun Hop's Dongpo An and Huang Xiaofeng and the Mandarin's Gongye Chuang and Zhang Shuqin (in both cases, bearded warrior and young belle, respectively).[66] The anthology was available for the rest of the year and was even sold in other large Chinese communities such as Vancouver that hosted the same performers.

The publication of *Essence of Cantonese Arias and Songs* also reflected the active life of opera amateurs and connoisseurs in San Francisco and elsewhere in North America. Their sponsorship of and admiration for the performers were evident from the laudatory poems that appeared in the anthology, in playbills, and in newspapers. Although the fans' performing activities might not be reported in the newspaper, the opera books regularly on sale at the general stores give a clue. Two popular and authoritative books on Cantonese opera arias and music by Qiu Hechou, *Xiange Bidu* (Essential String and Vocal Music) and *Qin Xue xinbian* (A New Edition of the Study of Qin), appeared often in the advertisements, which noted that they could further readers' appreciation for Cantonese opera by letting them practice along with recordings (since the books compiled lyrics from popular recordings).[67] In 1929 *Essence of Cantonese Arias and Songs* would be advertised as a bonus to boost sales of phonograph records in Vancouver.[68]

Fig. 7.7. *Essence of Cantonese Arias and Songs* (courtesy of the Ethnic Studies Library, University of California, Berkeley).

A GRAND OPENING AND THE CANTON–HONG KONG STRIKE

A month and half after Huang Xiaofeng's debut, San Francisco witnessed the opening of Lun Hop's new theater. For the previous two and a half years the company had leased the Crescent Theater for its performances. It was far from ideal. Soon after the Mandarin's opening, rumors about Lun Hop's scouting locations for its own theater gained such currency that the company had to publicly deny it. Yet by October 1924 it purchased a lot at 630 Jackson Street to build a theater with a capacity of 950 seats, at a cost of more than $100,000. All through the first half of 1925, scene painters, wardrobe personnel, musicians, and dramatists were being hired from China to prepare for the opening of the new theater; new costumes and scenery were imported as well. Even recruiting top actresses such as Huang Xiaofeng might well have been part of the preparation for the grand opening. Finally, the Great China Theater opened on June 19, 1925 (figure 7.8).

Fig. 7.8. The Great China Theater on Jackson Street in San Francisco's Chinatown, 1925. May's Photo Studio (courtesy of the Wylie Wong Collection at the Museum of Performance and Design, San Francisco).

The building has an imposing entrance with an elaborate Chinese archway (*pailou*). Above it is a Western awning with ornamental trim and curved diagonal ornaments at the corners, and above that are two eaves, both with similar ornaments. It has a front wall extending to the third floor. Inside, the stage was slightly narrower than the Mandarin's but significantly greater in height and depth. Overall it is an impressive purpose-built theater.[69] Though the Great China Theater's opening did not receive as much notice from the mainstream English-language media as Lun Hop had in February 1923, it quickly became a landmark and was applauded in other Chinese communities in North America. The opening ceremony at 11 A.M. was attended by leaders of community organizations, whose speeches were followed by group photos and lion dances. In the evening, a ritual playlet celebrated the momentous occasion and showcased the theater's large cast. The next day Chinese newspapers detailed the large crowd of people, as well as the banquet hosted by its president Chen Jiantai. Two days later, the Great China Theater advertised in the *Young China* its cast of thirty-four actors and actresses in residence, plus one dramatist and one scene painter.[70] The list included two famous actors who arrived shortly before the opening: Xin Zhu, a warrior role type, and Guima Yuan, a veteran and versatile comedian. The opening drew good wishes from Chinese theaters elsewhere such as Lun Hop's own branches (the Renshou Nian troupe in Portland and the New China troupe in Los Angeles), the New Republic Theater in Mexicali, and the China Theater in Havana.[71] The enthusiasm from Chinese theaters of the transnational network showed that all had a stake in the Great China Theater's prosperity.

Meanwhile, the Chinese newspapers were filled with somber news about major turmoil in China. The incident involved Sikh police under British command opening fire on a crowd of anti-imperial Chinese protesters in Shanghai's foreign territory on May 23, killing nine. Subsequently, an anti-imperial coalition was mobilized all over China, and it called for labor strikes to paralyze the economy in Hong Kong, a British colony at the time. The Canton–Hong Kong strike lasted from June 1925 to October 1926. Urban Cantonese opera theaters closed, leaving most of their performers without work. Mid-June was typically the time of year in which professional troupes and performers signed yearly contracts, yet with the strike few contracts were signed. With no prospect of acting work in China, even the best performers found themselves looking for alternatives. The Cantonese opera song recording industry in southern China mushroomed as a result. Many famous performers also accepted engagements outside China, including the Great China Theater.

All through July and August the San Francisco Chinese community was busy raising funds for the strikers. Both theaters were heavily involved with benefit performances; each raised about five thousand dollars. Actresses such as Huang

Table 7.3. Donation for Canton–Hong Kong Strike by Individual Performers at the Two Theaters

Great China Theater		Mandarin Theater	
Huang Xiaofeng	$125	Zhang Shuqin	$200
Xin Zhu	$50	Xin Baicai	$30
		Xin Yi	$20
Zheng Xinbei	$50	Chen Feifeng	$10
Xiyang Nü	$50	Guan Yingxue	$10
Dayan Shun	$50	Tan Yaoshen	$10
Xin Guima Yuan	$50	Deng Shaohuai	$5
Gongzheng Lian	$50	Liang Susu	$5
Xiao Caiji and Xiao Caichan	$50	Jin Shanbing	$5
Lin Qian	$20	5 members, each @	$2
Zhu Jianshang	$20	Zhang De	$1.50
6 members, each @	$10	Liang Do	$1
5 members, each @	$5	Xie Lin	$1
He Zhu	$3	Mandarin Theater Total	$308.50
Daniu Lo	$2		
Ziya Yu	$1		
Great China Theater Total	$606		

Xiaofeng and Zhang Shuqin led the way in pledging funds. Lists of the performers' personal donations, published in the *Young China* in late June, are reproduced in table 7.3.[72] The donations provide a window into the theaters' and performers' relative wealth and status, as well as their rivalry. The Great China had a larger cast, and its performers donated more, with eight of them pledging $50 or more. The top donor in each theater was its leading actress. (The meeting of Huang and Zhang in Vancouver in 1917–1918 was discussed in Chapter 6.) The financial strength of the Great China's cast was apparent: it collected nearly twice as much from its performers as did the Mandarin.

These triumphant months for the Great China Theater were greatly enhanced by the appearance of the young actor Xin Zhu, a warrior type who arrived shortly before the new theater's opening, just in time to be featured prominently at the new theater. Famous in China and Southeast Asia for his performance of the quintessential warrior—the legendary figure Guan Gong (Guan Yu)—from the historical novel *Romance of the Three Kingdoms*, Xin Zhu acquired the nickname "living Guan Gong." His signature opera, based on the legend *Guan Yu Floods Seven Armies*, had been a box office hit everywhere in southern China. In San Francisco the opera was such a success that it returned to the stage of the Great China only ten days after its first performance on May 27. By popular demand, the theater repeated the opera in each of the subsequent four months. It became the theater's favorite opera. Xin Zhu also led six other operas featuring the same legendary warrior.

In a memoir, his wife Xiyang Nü recalled his successful performing career in the United States:

> Xin Zhu's reputation as a "living Guan Gong" spread, even across the ocean to the other side of the Pacific. An agent of the U.S. theaters came to present him with an invitation. Since he had somewhat of a "Gold Mountain itch" then, and wanted to travel, he went to the United States in 1924. When the Chinese audiences saw the heroic character he performed on the opera stage, they were just thrilled. He first performed in New York, then was eagerly recruited to San Francisco, where he performed for two years. His enormous popularity soon prompted a raise in his annual salary, from $9000 to $12000. It was also in San Francisco where he ran into a former fellow trainee, Cun Dulian, who introduced us, and we became a couple. He collaborated with several famous stars there, and made many recordings. Though he performed in Chinatown, a lot of non-Chinese audiences were attracted to the theater by his reputation; they took many stage photographs of him and gave them to us as mementos. In 1927, we returned to China, despite numerous invitations for us to perform, even in Chicago.[73]

In Chinese culture, Guan Gong was seen as the epitome of loyalty and righteousness. Though a real historical figure, he was worshiped in temples as a deity of strength and courage. Given China's weakening international status and Chinese exclusion laws in the United States, as well as the society's strong anti-imperialist sentiment, Xin Zhu's superheroic figure was particularly timely as Chinese Americans sought an outlet for their patriotic urges. Xin Zhu's iconic Chinese warrior character was one that the youth in Chinatowns could emulate.

The Great China's advantage over the Mandarin ended with the quota increase granted to the latter in August. The Mandarin now had eighty-five members, twenty-one more than the Great China. And its new performers, already in Seattle, were immediately brought to San Francisco. Its subsequent parade of new performers over the course of three weeks was dazzling. The Great China Theater could only respond with programming calling for the collaboration of its top performers, as well as the return of its most popular repertory, such as Xin Zhu's *Guan Yu Floods Seven Armies*.

BAI JURONG AND OTHER STARS

The effect of the strike on Cantonese opera, though tremendous in China, was positive for the Great China. In November 1925, six months after the strike started, a wave of extraordinary opera professionals arrived in San Francisco. If the voyage, contract, or unfamiliarity with and uncertainty about Chinatown theaters had deterred them previously from such ventures, the strike changed that. The Great China's agents in Hong Kong engaged some of the best actors. First came two actors formerly associated with renowned male troupes, Zihou Qi (Tsi-Hau Tsat) and Xin Shezi Qiu; their annual salaries were more than $10,000 each, according to the *Young China*.[74] Zihou Qi was considered the "king of comedians."[75] He was a versatile actor, performing with ease everything from young belle and warrior to male and female comic roles. Advanced ticket sales for his debut in *Pranks on the Bridal Chamber of Ugly Girl Zihou Qi*, full of his humorous dramatics and skillful singing, were unusually successful.[76] The Wo Kee & Company general store was quick to respond, making available his recording of the same title four days after his debut.[77] Xin Shezi Qiu was a comedian particularly well known for his musical versatility.[78] The debut performances of all the new actors in trendy repertoire went on for weeks, interrupted only by a brief appearance of the actress Zhou Shaoying, who had arrived from Cuba, performing trouser roles. The spotlight was on Zihou Qi and Xin Shezi Qiu, such that their handsome photographs in costume, taken by Suen's Photo Studio, were printed in the *Young China* on November 22.

Then, the strike brought the arrival of one of the very best actors in Cantonese opera, Bai Jurong (figure 7.9). It did not merely add grandeur to the Great China Theater but signaled its status as the leading theater in North America. It was clearly the theater's most significant event of the decade. As Bai noted in his memoir,

> The unexpected invitation [from the United States] made me pause. I thought, though there was a large Chinese community in San Francisco, I had not performed there, and was not familiar with its audience. Would I be able to establish myself there? On the other hand, if I didn't go, the uncommitted Guangzhou troupes could not solve the difficulty of unemployment. So I decided to accept the agent's contract and try it out in San Francisco.[79]

As famous as he was, Bai did not assume his popularity in southern China would necessarily carry over to the United States, yet he turned out to be a celebrity just the same on this side of the Pacific.

Bai brought a companion and an elaborate wardrobe to Seattle, as well as new repertoire and his signature operas. The *Young China* wrote enthusiastically on the day of his arrival, "Bai is undoubtedly the best actor of xiaosheng roles in Cantonese opera today. Critics would say that with the engagement of Bai, the Great China Theater's cast has now surpassed that of the theaters in China."[80] Following his debut at the beginning of the Thanksgiving holidays, Bai performed six consecutive evenings of new operas, mostly written in the 1920s, such as *A Scholar Meets His Girlfriend in Disguise*, *Tear of Plum Flower*, *Mourning of the Chaste Tree Flower*, and *Amorous Emperor*. These were works for which Bai had gained critical acclaim, and

Fig. 7.9. Bai Jurong (courtesy of the Ethnic Studies Library, University of California, Berkeley).

were immensely popular in southern China. They were, however, novel to San Francisco audiences. Therefore, the theater distributed the lyrics at the performance, as noted in the advertisements for the first week.[81]

Performing in the new setting required some adjustments, however, for a star accustomed to a perfect cast and conditions. In his memoir, Bai described frustration in his endeavor to change Chinatown's practices.[82] Not only were his operas new to the local performers but they came with through-composed lyrics, melodies, and scripts, written for a cast used to producing newer operas. It was quite different from the looser and more traditional tigang xi style. A compromise must have been at work: at the beginning of his residence, Bai's signature operas were likely performed in the tigang xi style because of the lack of time between his arrival and his debut. It was the only way the new opera could be promptly staged to sate the public's appetite for novelty. Only later, with the help of several other recently arrived actors, could the whole cast learn new operas more fully. Indeed, it took much effort to produce newly scripted operas. During his residency, on average Bai led only three or four opera performances per month. For the premieres of the new productions, the lyrics booklets were typically distributed to the audiences, calling attention to the beautifully written lyrics. Over time, many of Bai's representative operas became regulars of the repertoire. Of the thirty titles he staged, ten returned to the stage four or more times within the year and a half of Bai's residence. Among them, the most popular (*Mourning of the Chaste Tree Flower*) was staged nine times.

As a star singer in a Chinatown theater, Bai had a rather complex task. He had a direct hand in broadening the theater's offerings by educating both its performers and its audiences. Unlike other opera stars, Bai staged mostly new operas, rather than the classic repertoire. In addition, he played an important role collaborating with dramatists to create the new productions and with other leading performers in the new operas. For example, a new dramatist, Pang Yifeng, would arrive at the Great China the following year, and the two would produce many new works. Bai also made adjustments to his star status for his residence at the Chinatown theater. Most notably, sometimes he appeared in minor roles.[83] In the strict hierarchical structure of the opera profession in China, playing supporting roles was unthinkable for actors such as Bai. However, in the United States it was necessary in order for him to fulfill the required number of performances in his contract.

This second wave of newcomers in 1925 generated much excitement, as summed up by a commentary published in the *Young China* near Thanksgiving. That its anonymous author was not previously a regular opera-goer made this all the more impressive.

> Allured by the frequent reports of Cantonese opera performers' arrivals in the newspapers, I was taken over by a desire to see the opera yesterday and went by car to San Francisco. However, because Bai is so famous, the tickets for the night were already sold out the previous day, and I nearly left without seeing the opera. . . . Recently, many famous actors in Guangdong have come to San Francisco, such as Bai Jurong, Zihou Qi etc. . . . And if other equally famous performers such as Xue Juexian, Ma Shizeng, Chen Feinong, Xiao Dingxiang . . . would also come, then fans in Guangdong would certainly be left deprived, while in San Francisco many new fans for Cantonese opera would appear. . . . What do I listen for? First, I like to listen to the aria sung with clear enunciation and accompanied by expert musicians. Second, I enjoy the visual extravaganza of the elaborate costumes. Whether they are for historical operas or contemporary ones, the costumes are always in gorgeous colors. Sometimes the characters would change costumes simply for the sake of it, while going on a trip or preparing for imprisonment. It's hard to decipher the reasons for such excess sometimes, but they are a feast for the eye, nevertheless. Third, I enjoy watching a large cast. Even though I was often confused by multiple performers who take turns portraying the same character, it is still fascinating to watch. . . . Finally, the mixed troupe not only makes sense but is also more pleasurable to watch than the all-male troupe. And it will be even better if the actresses

> would be less constrained in their formal manners, and do less to mimic the vocal style of the female impersonators imitating women.[84]

The commentary reflects the way a performer such as Bai really changed the way the community viewed its theaters. A new crop of audiences emerged, and opera culture became more and more an integral part of popular entertainment and, indeed, an everyday part of general Chinatown culture. The anonymous writer's hypothetical musings about more famous performers coming to the United States quickly became reality. The arrival of one of the stars he named, Xiao Dingxiang, was merely months away, and Ma Shizeng came later. The theater would be filled with even more famous performers the following year. In addition to anthologies of arias and booklets of new lyrics, the increasing use of the gramophone also helped inspire listeners and educate amateurs. Over the years there were more advertisements for gramophone machines and opera records in the newspaper, often on the same page as the playbill advertisement.

Lun Hop had been building a theatrical empire, and by the beginning of 1925 it had established a wide-ranging influence beyond San Francisco. The company extended its reach to cities such as Seattle, Portland, Honolulu, Los Angeles, New York, and Mexicali, helped by frequent importation of new performers. The establishment of its own theater in mid-1925 stabilized its residence in San Francisco. And the engagement of top-notch performers in 1925 such as Dongpo An, Xin Zhu, Huang Xiaofeng, Zihou Qi, and Bai Jurong sealed the theater's reputation. The changes to its name from Lun On to Lun Hop to the Great China Theater reflect its transformation from a performing troupe to a resident theater and finally to a professionally managed theater.

CHAPTER 8

THE AFFLUENT YEARS

The Great China Theater, 1926–1928

The Great China Theater by 1926 had firmly established itself as a prominent cultural institution in San Francisco. Its cast of performers from the top tier of the Cantonese opera profession put on different operas daily all year long with no breaks. The lively scene attracted more professionals such as playwrights, musicians, and scene painters to play key roles at the theater and in the community. The stage designs and theatrical spectacle grew bolder and more grand, showing influences from other forms of entertainment; a record label of Cantonese opera was started. The theater had greater impact on the public culture. Furthermore, the opera culture engendered by the theater also bore fruit in the increased participation of native-born Chinese Americans.

A FAMOUS FEMALE IMPERSONATOR

The contribution of the female impersonator Xiao Dingxiang was important and unique. While Bai Jurong's residency was a boost to the theater's reputation, his fellow actors had an important role in both helping his transition to Chinatown's performing culture and facilitating the production of his signature repertoire. In his memoir Bai noted appreciatively the collaborative efforts of actors Zihou Qi, Xin Zhu, and especially Xiao Dingxiang. The son of an accomplished female impersonator, Xiao Dingxiang was known for his extraordinary voice. Cantonese opera's increasing attention to virtuosity in the 1920s resulted in elaborate vocal and performing skills, especially for the young belle role type; Xiao Dingxiang was considered one of the era's best female impersonators of that type. He specialized in melancholy, lyrical roles with demanding passages. The Chinese community eagerly anticipated his arrival.

Xiao Dingxiang was originally to have had a limited engagement. According to the *Young China,* he was to follow a stint in Seattle with only two weeks of performance at the Great China Theater and then move on to other cities.[1] But apparently plans changed once he performed at the Great China. His debut prompted the Mandarin Theater to present Mudan Su in the work she had performed just four days earlier, the hit *Nocturnal Mourning of White Lotus*. The stiff competition pitted a famed female impersonator against a critically acclaimed actress in a trouser role. Xiao Dingxiang had a graceful stage presence, as reflected in the portraits printed on numerous playbills (see the photo reproduced in figure 11.6). Two days after the debut, a reviewer in the *Young China* raved about his performance:

> In the debut opera—*Swords on the Red Cliff*—his vocal virtuosity and performing skills were delicate and profound. He received three rounds of applause from the audience. For years, Cantonese opera enthusiasts here had grown increasingly indifferent to performances by actresses, yet their excitement was apparent again with Xiao Dingxiang's performance. Many fans opined that his extraordinary talent and skill were absolutely unobtainable by actresses. Tickets for all three types of premium seats on the second evening were all sold out well before the performance yesterday.[2]

Despite the quick rise of talented actresses, then, some of the social elites might have favored the traditional female impersonator. These fans were also more likely to be opera connoisseurs and intelligentsia, most of whom were politically and culturally prominent in the community. They thus led the public discourse about taste.

Because of the enthusiastic reception, Xiao Dingxiang extended his engagement with the theater well beyond two weeks. Before the end of 1926 he was billed as the lead for fifty-three performances, more than any actress at the theater at the time. His success even prompted the theater to increase its use of female impersonators, keeping it more closely aligned with the practice in China, where the mixed troupe was still banned. Judging from the theaters' programs, it seemed that there co-existed within the community a fascination for both actresses and female impersonators. Xiao Dingxiang alternated with actresses in playing the female leads, although he was clearly the favored one, since the playbills frequently used promotional text to highlight elements of his performance.

Just as Bai expanded the theater's repertoire in operas of the young scholar type, Xiao Dingxiang brought new operas of the young belle type, many of which became staples. *Wayfarer's Autumn Lament* was one. The title came from a well-known Cantonese ballad, a *nanyin*, which was made into an opera in the 1920s. It tells of the romance of a scholar and a courtesan-songstress. Alone under the cool autumn moon, the scholar sings nostalgically of his lover's beauty and talent, the memorable times they shared, and his worries about the dangers that presently surround her. Despite her loved one's lack of wealth, the courtesan, unlike others, chooses to remain faithful to him. It was a romantic old tale that audiences could easily connect to their own experience. And the ballad was melodious and beautiful. The opera's June 18 premiere was advertised days in advance; fans were urged to get their tickets early because they were sure to go fast. The overwhelming response brought the opera back on stage in only eight days. *Wayfarer's Autumn Lament* was so popular that it was made into a movie in 1930, and the song even emerged in the 1990s in Cantonese pop music by Hong Kong singers.[3] In 1926, however, Xiao was the first to bring the piece to San Francisco's Chinatown, and it renewed the audiences' interest in tuneful narrative.

Even in China Xiao Dingxiang had received the level of regard reserved for only a handful of performers. With him and Bai Jurong, the Great China could now be considered a leading theater of Cantonese opera, not only in the United States but all through the Cantonese Pacific. The theater's ability to engage a top female impersonator added to its reputation in the eyes of those who considered themselves arbiters of Cantonese opera, people who might have sneered at the attention some actresses received.

This is not to say that actresses were no longer in the spotlight; theaters need versatile performers, and they remained high in demand. The prima donna Huang Xiaofeng was still a favorite, and her signature operas had become staples for the theater. Toward the end of 1926 another star actress, Xiyang Nü, returned to the theater from a long tour in Chicago and New York. Her arrival was prominently announced on the playbills and by her own gracious note in the newspaper expressing "gratitude for the community's previous support and for the opportunity to engage the audience again with her songs and dances."[4] (She was to become the wife of the warrior actor Xin Zhou, whom she met in the United States.) The actresses had claimed their place in the fabric of the intricate community life, despite the patriarchal tradition of the profession.

Other fresh talent had also arrived at the theater during the year, and the new blood created excitement. The twenty-one-year-old Zhang Qiaohua, who arrived before Xiao Dingxiang, had a successful debut week featuring many roles involving cross-dressing situations.[5] She would have a successful career on both coasts during her stay in the United States. An actress trained for the male warrior role type, the twenty-year-old Chen Xiahun arrived from Cuba and frequently led performances.[6] In the second half of the year, as many as six young actresses of the young belle role type made their debuts on the stage of the Great China Theater. Although they were not top-tier talents, much of their repertoire was recently written and fashionable, if ephemeral. And with classic repertoire they added a novel flair.[7] For example, the theater often drew attention to the physical adroitness of the young Chen Xiahun. On one playbill for *Twilight Scarlet Tears*, an opera made famous by Li Xuefang, the theater emphasized how Chen's unique interpretation of the role distinguished her from Li: "Although the famous performances of this opera by celebrity actresses such as Li Xuefang had long been a favorite of audiences and were generally considered truly brilliant interpretations, they still had not reached the level of perfection. . . . Chen brings to this role a special dexterity that makes it truly perfect."[8] But as their numbers increased, these praises began to sound obligatory and hollow. When the actress Ma Yanfang debuted on August 17, a tribute of eleven-line verses in boldface print, praising everything from her melodious and bright voice, innocent beauty, and brilliant acting to her gentle temperament, took up one-third of the playbill.[9] As it turned out, she was not remarkable and played only supporting roles after her debut. Such lavish praises blurred the distinction between top actresses and second-tier actresses, giving validity to the skepticism of opera fans who had a bias against actresses.

Although the mixed-sex stage in San Francisco was by now the norm, the traditional male hierarchy in Cantonese opera could still be seen at work if one looked more closely. When Bai played the lead, typically Xiao Dingxiang was the leading lady, just as in an all-male troupe (indeed, the two leading actors would continue to co-star with the top male troupe after their return to China). Very infrequently did actresses play a leading role opposite Bai. And if they did, they were famous ones such as Huang Xiaofeng and Xiyang Nü. Considering that Bai played even supporting roles in some productions, which his stature would not allow in China, it seems he might still have had either the conventional prejudices toward actresses' capabilities or hesitation in working with them.

PLAYWRIGHTS, INSTRUMENTALISTS, AND SCENE PAINTERS

By recruiting renowned dramatists, leading musicians, and scene painters from top all-male troupes in China, the theater took an important step in increasing its professionalism. Whereas in the past the theater had been quite low-key about their arrival, now the newspapers and playbills prominently reported the famous names of playwrights and instrumentalists. Thus began an era of higher-caliber theater professionals in San Francisco, as well as a more integral role for them in production and in community life. Not only did they bring theatrical productions to a spectacular level and provide singers with more support, but they also engaged with the musical life of the community in more important, visible, and diverse ways.

The dramatist Pang Yifeng was the first significant new professional at the Great China Theater. The purview of Cantonese opera dramatists included scripts as well as music and required considerable skill in both areas. They also crafted traditional arias to allow a star singer's talent to shine. Pang's engagement was an important development. Two days before the premiere of his first new work, the *Young China* reported on June 11:

> The Great China Theater has engaged the dramatist Pang Yifeng to be in charge of arranging operas and authoring new opera titles. He is now working on a new drama, *The Danger of Thunder*, scheduled to be produced this coming Sunday. Mr. Pang was formerly a writer and arranger for famous Cantonese troupes such as Song Taiping and Guo Fengnian. He has been known in particular for composing new operas. His work includes such famous titles as *Amorous Emperor* and *The Piteous Girl*. With Mr. Pang on the staff of the Great China Theater, we can anticipate a variety of new operas for the enjoyment of the community.[10]

The audiences were familiar with the operas. As early as April 1923 *Amorous Emperor* was produced at the Crescent Theater by Yangzhou Mei, and it had since been brought to the stage many more times. *The Piteous Girl* was first staged there during Bai's debut week in 1925.

In order to introduce the playwright to the community, two notices were printed side-by-side in the *Young China* on the same day as the report quoted above. One was an advertisement from the Great China Theater. It announced the arrival of Pang, calling him a major figure in Cantonese opera dramaturgy and promising an upcoming feast of beautiful melodies, profound stories, and expressive lyrics. In the other notice, Pang himself offered a literary salute.[11] Its showiness foretold the erudite playwright's significant role in this community. Pang would become the spokesperson for the theater and a leading advocate for community causes.

By the end of the year Pang had produced thirteen new operas in San Francisco, many of which featured Bai Jurong prominently. He also brought many new practices to the theater. To familiarize the audiences with the new lyrics and tunes, they were printed and distributed at performances. The playbills, in addition to or instead of a synopsis, devoted half of their space to new lyrics. They were accompanied by indications of aria types, allowing repeated enjoyment: reading beforehand, following along at the performance, remembering afterward, or pasting into scrapbooks. The playbill for *A Pair of Mandarin Ducks under Water* of August 14 is one such example; the playwright's name is given a prominent place underneath the opera title, a space that more typically listed the leading performer (see figure 8.1). The nine leading performers are listed in three lines next to the title box. The lyrics take up half of the space in the left middle section, fourteen vertical lines of small text with tune types marked in parentheses. The lyrics, concerning a broken

Fig. 8.1. Playbill, *A Pair of Mandarin Ducks under Water*, Great China Theater, August 14, 1926 (courtesy of the Ethnic Studies Library, University of California, Berkeley).

romance, shift from narrating to lamenting and imitating sensuous longing. The twenty-seven-member character list on the left shows the extraordinarily strong cast. Such playbills replaced visual appeal with literary interest and reinforced the impact of new operas in the community.

That there were not more operas under Pang's name was perhaps due to the longer preparation time that new operas required. Rather than the more loosely structured tigang xi–style performances, these productions were individually scripted, composed, and choreographed to achieve a tighter structure. They at times required new backdrop paintings or props as well. Also, Pang had to collaborate with leading actors to enhance classic repertoire with new tunes or lyrics. Playwrights such as Pang now had more significant roles than had their predecessors.

Also emerging from anonymity were the musicians of the orchestra, who now enjoyed recognition previously reserved for singers. In February 1926 the engagement of Zhu Hong, a master of the *er xian*, was made into a major event. (The instrument is pictured in figure 4.2.) The newspaper report and the theater's playbill highlighted his association with the top male troupe in China, Renshou Nian, with which Bai Jurong also performed from 1922 to 1925.[12] (As noted above, this famous troupe's name was adopted by the Lun On Company for its first troupe and remained on the playbills of the Crescent Theater.) In September, the newly arrived Ou Lai was hailed as the master of *hou guan*, the double-reed instrument known for its forceful and bright timbre, playing the main melodies in the orchestra.

As Cantonese opera grew to be an integral part of the social life of Chinatown, the number of amateur performers grew as well, increasing demand for advanced musical expertise in the community. The theaters' instrumentalists played routinely with amateur music ensembles and took on the roles of coaching and accompanying amateur opera singers. An interesting example during this period was a Fresno amateur group called the Tian Zhong Drama Club whose Cantonese opera performances were reported in *Young China*.[13] The paper noted that the group staged three evenings of popular opera playlets with virtuosic arias, including *Shilin Paying Respects at the Pagoda*, to a packed hall.[14] A week later the paper announced new training sessions at an amateur school of Cantonese opera in Fresno.[15] The school turned out to be the Tian Zhong Drama Club, which already had thirty members. It now offered three-month courses in which the members would be coached by singers and instrumentalists.[16]

The theater professionals became involved in other community events such as benefits and festive occasions. For a benefit concert held on September 19, 1926, to raise funds for a political cause, the *Young China* noted, Huang and the er xian master Zhu Hong were featured as distinguished guest performers. The report stressed especially that Zhu Hong, the best string player among Cantonese opera troupes in Guangzhou, would be performing on the yangqin, a Chinese hammered dulcimer, and singing new songs. As a result, pledges for a ticket to the performance reached $100.[17] A fundraising initiative for the local Chinese school involved the generous donation of a large-scale painting by the Great China Theater's scene painter, Xu Fengbo. He was also noted for donating a painting to St. Mary's School on September 1.[18]

As noted above, there had been a steady increase in elaborate, naturalistic paintings as backdrops in Cantonese opera since the early twentieth century. In San Francisco, this new trend was further enhanced by the city's rich and varied artistic influences, especially the highly popular form of stage naturalism led by producers such as David Belasco. At the Great China Theater, stage sets included different hard (wood or sheet metal) or soft (cloth) backdrops representing typical operatic scenes. As such backdrops grew more creative, elaborate, and even daring, the painters also gained recognition. Linear perspective—providing the illusion of a deeper and broader stage—soon became ubiquitous in their designs, as was the use of real, rather than symbolic, props. For example, in figure 8.2, the backdrop depicts a typical room in a palace, with centered perspective and curtains and windows to emphasize the effect. The stage design also turned the two traditional unadorned backstage doors for entering and exiting the stage into elaborate doorframes with panels containing painting and calligraphy, connoting a higher social class. The props—tables and chairs with embroidered covering—remained similar to the kind traditionally used, however. The colorful and elaborate valences covering the tables also typically bore the names of the star performers. A still more creative stage set of the type shown in figure 8.3 was common. The backdrop of a garden scene uses linear perspective with the temple positioned at an angle to one side, while the trees and ivy, with a floral lattice arch, smartly disguise the two conventional backstage doors. Moreover, the

Fig. 8.2. A scene from the Great China Theater. May's Photo Studio (courtesy of the Wylie Wong Collection at the Museum of Performance and Design, San Francisco).

use of a garden table and chairs, as well as the real plaques, departed further from the traditional sparse, symbolic set.

In fact, from its start, the Great China Theater valued realism so highly that it had a scenic painting of a colorful blooming garden as the original permanent stage backdrop. Painted on a full wall (12 feet × 15 feet) of sheet metal by Xu Fengbo, it was framed by painted marble columns and real doorways on both sides leading backstage. Xu also painted a firewall backdrop on a heavy cloth: the famous West Lake, where the legend of Madame White Snake took place.[19] It is likely that this semi-permanent backdrop was made for the popular opera *Shilin Paying Respects at the Pagoda*.

Fig. 8.3. A scene from the Great China Theater. May's Photo Studio (courtesy of the Wylie Wong Collection at the Museum of Performance and Design, San Francisco).

The popular depictions of Chinese theaters in burlesques, vaudeville, plays, and operas in San Francisco's bustling entertainment scene would also have an impact on Chinatown theaters themselves. *The Yellow Jacket* by George Hazelton and Harry Benrimo, for example, was a partly amusing and entertaining, and partly experimental take on Chinese opera theater that had many revivals in the 1920s in San Francisco, Oakland, Palo Alto, and elsewhere.[20] It was, as scholar Jo Yun Kim notes, "a realistic representation of Chinese drama . . . [with] the double framing of" imaginative dramatic structure and realistic reproduction of "quaint, strange" ethnic culture.[21] The opera *Fay Yen Fah* by San Francisco's own Joseph Redding also had its U.S. premiere in that city in January 1926, to which "S.F. society gave royal welcome," noted the *San Francisco Chronicle*. Their fictional portrayals of Chinese theater stages became the standard in American theatrical culture that Chinatown theaters also contended with. Surrounded by the various types of fanciful representations of itself, the Great China Theater seemed to have taken creating elaborate spectacles as its response.

The stage designs of the Great China already were fostered in a complex cultural milieu of theatrical conventions and novelty. Pioneered by innovative theaters in Shanghai, many elaborate or even electrically lit props were used in Cantonese opera performances of the 1920s. The rise of urban theaters in southern China hastened the move to spectacles of light, color, and mechanical sophistication. The realism favored by Chinese spoken drama that quickly rose after 1910 was another influence. At the Great China Theater, objects such as the grandfather clock shown in figure 8.4 were commonly seen on stage. In the image, the clock and the Western-style brick wall together with singers in period costume depict a

Fig. 8.4. A scene from the Great China Theater. May's Photo Studio (courtesy of the Wylie Wong Collection at the Museum of Performance and Design, San Francisco).

juxtaposition of old and new in a strikingly contemporary dialogue. These stage sets demonstrate the dualist strategy to lay claim on aesthetic experimentation and modernity, on one hand, and classic tradition and cultural knowledge, on the other. And more playwrights and artists would arrive to join the endeavor. By the end of the decade, the scene painters at the Great China would include Mo Keming, Wu Changting, and Xu Fengbo. Their work would reflect in interesting ways the sense of space and time.

POPULAR REPERTOIRE

Innovative settings were in high demand due to the wide range of topics covered in Cantonese opera at this time. In 1926 the programming included many different genres, though it leaned toward young belle repertoire. Ten new actresses arrived at the theater, bringing young belle operas on contemporary topics or inventive and unorthodox performances. Together these actresses led about one-third of the year's overall production. Meanwhile, the number of young scholar operas increased due to Bai's residence. Another small yet crucial part of the repertoire was the warrior opera. The warrior Xin Zhu, though injured earlier in the year, was mostly responsible for them, and his popularity outweighed that of any other new actors of the warrior types.

Comic opera always had a special role in Chinatown opera. That year, two top comedic actors, Zihou Qi and Shezi Ying—the former a leading actor in the famous Renshou Nian troupe in China—led more than fifty productions of comic-themed opera during his time at the Great China. Zihou Qi played both female and male comic roles and performed in a wide range of repertoire. A representative opera was the theater's October 31 program, *Stealing Chicken to Offer up to Mother* by Shezi Ying. An elaborate advertisement in the newspaper provided the highlights:

> (1) the scene of chicken stealing includes many vivacious and adroit stage movements, and the scene of proposing marriage where Xiao Dingxiang played a clever maid is especially witty and charming; (2) the scene of fighting for the girl provokes many chivalrous displays; (3) the scene of "Dressing up as Ah Jin" involves much unconventional, entertaining, and outlandish action, with humorous dialogue; and (4) the performance of Shezi Ying in the lead promises a quintessential experience of this popular opera.[22]

Comic operas such as this were lighthearted affairs with amusing subjects, ridiculous characters, farcical tangles of events, and happy endings. No Cantonese opera theater could do without them. In 1926 the number of comic operas equaled that of young scholar type operas (Bai's specialty).

Table 8.1. Two weeks' programing at the Great China Theater, 1926

Date	Opera	Principal performer	Role type	Performer information
Oct. 28	*Ugly Girl and Bridal Chamber*	Zihou Qi	Comic female	Star male comedian
Oct. 29	*Duel of Fox and Plantain*	Zheng Jinsi Mao	Young belle	Young actress
Oct. 30	*Wife Emperor 1*	Xiao Dingxiang	Young belle	Star female impersonator
Oct. 31	*Stealing Chicken to Offer up to Mother**	Shezi Ying	Comic	Famous male comedian
Nov. 1	*Qianchun Emperor*	Bai Jurong	Young scholar	Star actor
Nov. 2	*Guan Yu Floods Seven Armies**	Xin Zhu	Young warrior	Star actor
Nov. 3	*Wife Emperor 2*	Xiao Dingxiang	Young belle	Star female impersonator
Dec. 7	*A Perfect Match**	Shezi Ying	Comic female	Famous male comedian
Dec. 8	*Peony Demoted to Jianan*	Zheng Jinsi Mao	Young belle	Young actress
Dec. 9	*Wife and Concubine Through a Knife*	Bai Jurong	Young scholar	Star actor
Dec. 10	*Hibiscus Remorse*	Liang Shaoying	Young warrior	Young actor
Dec. 11	*Bird Cage Phoenix*	Xiyang Nü	Young belle	Prima donna
Dec. 12	*Wayfarer's Autumn Lament**	Xiao Dingxiang	Young belle	Star female impersonator
Dec. 13	*A Pitiable Wife**	Xin Zhu	Young warrior	Star actor

Note: The two weeks represented here were not consecutive.
* These operas were later made into movies, and the English translations are in common use.

By 1926, therefore, the Great China Theater had an array of operas and leading performers of every genre and was at the level of the finest Cantonese opera houses. Table 8.1 presents two snapshots of a typical week's program at the theater. The programming of classical repertoire as well as contemporary plays worked to pique the interest of audiences of a wide range. From classical operas such as those featuring either warrior Xin Zhu in heavy armor and weaponry or emperor Bai Jurong in a royal gown, to contemporary melancholic operas with courtesan Xiao Dingxiang and the folk-style comic drama featuring local simpleton Shezi Ying, the theater offered a full range of topics and the musical numbers associated with them. At the same time, these operas address many popular and common themes reflecting the everyday sentiments, aspirations, and difficulties of existence within the Chinese community of the United States. These themes included enduring hardships before achieving triumph, romantic love and longing, the injustice of biased or corrupted officials, and overcoming all obstacles despite the odds. Often a moral message was involved. Though presented as entertainment, they often had a didactic character as well, even the most outlandish comedy.

FAREWELL NOTICES AND THE LASTING IMPACT OF CELEBRITY SINGERS

The very public farewells and returns of the theater's prima donnas reflected the close ties they established with the community. After one and a half years of residence at the Great China Theater, Huang Xiaofeng was to perform in other American cities, starting with the Lok Tin Tsau Theater in New York. After the departure was announced, she began a series of farewell performances. Laudatory poems, many of which expressed sadness at her departure, appeared in the newspapers. Huang responded in the newspaper with gracious and lyrical words expressing her gratitude and reluctance to part. Still in San Francisco a month later, she performed in a benefit concert sponsored by members of the Great China Theater.[23] She did eventually appear in New York in 1927, though her San Francisco fans were not completely left out of her journey: a short film of her East Coast tour appeared before movie showings in 1928.[24] Public letters printed in the newspaper became a popular means for performers to exhibit or even rekindle ties with the community.

Most of the performers who arrived in the aftermath of the Hong Kong–Canton Strike had left the United States by the first quarter of 1927, marking the end of an era of extraordinarily strong casts. The Great China Theater had to bring in forty-eight new performers that year to fill the void created by the departure of celebrity singers. The farewell of Bai Jurong was the most significant and symbolic. By the end of his residence at the theater, Bai had played the lead in 114 performances and supporting roles in numerous others. Bai, who was at the peak of his career, had been the most frequently staged leading singer at the theater. During the last three months of his residence, Bai played the leading role in twenty-six operas and shared the lead in eleven others.

Perhaps the most impressive opera Bai brought to the community was *Mourning of the Chaste Tree Flower.* It filled the house nine times during his time in San Francisco, three of them during his last month.[25] The opera had a well-known scene at a monastery in which Bai portrayed a scholar-monk in the aria "Meditation." It conveyed a moment of spiritual epiphany: the realization that emptiness was the ultimate truth of all things. Bai incorporated various tunes with religious themes, spiritual contemplation, or music resembling Buddhist chanting to cultivate a serene spirituality in this aria, thus creating a new style. No record is found of the aria being performed after Bai left, however. His famous rendering of this aria was preserved in a recording on the Odeon label and made into a movie in 1934.

On February 7 Bai staged an important opera of this era, *Tibet Lama Monk,* which the previous November had drawn very enthusiastic audiences. The dramatist Pang helped refine this production and even joined Bai on stage. In March the superstar Li Xuefang arrived at the Mandarin Theater. Marking the height of the two theaters' rivalry was Li's debut on March 7. Two superb performances on one evening—Bai's signature opera *A Scholar Meets His Girlfriend in Disguise* at the Great China and Li's signature opera *Shilin Paying Respects at the Pagoda* at the Mandarin—marked a considerable feat for the Chinatown community. That recordings of their singing of key arias in the two operas became legendary reflects the high level of performing events in San Francisco's Chinatown that evening.

Bai's grand farewell began on March 20. His leading performances of fourteen operas in two weeks amounted to a feast of contemporary Cantonese opera repertoire, much of which he himself had made familiar to the audience. He also performed an opera curiously omitted from his earlier performances, *Wayfarer's Autumn Lament*, in one of the last two evenings. The female impersonator Xiao Dingxiang had staged this much-loved opera four times in the previous year, but Bai had yet to perform it at this theater. His performance of its signature aria—also recorded in the late 1920s—is now a time-honored rendition of this famous song.

On March 21 Bai's public farewell note appeared prominently on the theater's playbill, where he expressed his gratitude in a stately manner, quoting a famous farewell couplet by the Tang poet Qian Qi.

> There is no endless banquet in the world; there is no unceasing drama in history. All good things must come to an end. Ruminating on the poem "The song has ended, no one is in sight / Above the river the peaks stand green" my heart is heavy with sadness. Time flies, and it has been more than a year since I arrived here to share my art. How time and tide wait for no one! I am beholden to you for your graciousness all through this time.[26]

Bai boarded the SS *Taiyo Maru* at San Francisco on April 26 for China. He left behind a legacy at the Great China Theater and for generations of Cantonese opera lovers in San Francisco's Chinese community.

By this time few of Bai's peers remained. The comedian Zihou Qi had left for China the previous November. The female impersonator Xiao Dingxiang also departed, emerging in March in New York, where Huang Xiaofeng was also performing, though at a rival theater. The star actress Xiyang Nü had her formal farewell performance on February 19. The last of the group, the young warrior Xin Zhu, reemerged in May before departing for China. Bai returned to the center of the profession in southern China, where the strike was over, and he and his fellow performers were engaged by top troupes, bringing in notable innovations such as the *pinghou* singing style.

YOUNG LEADS AND A UNIQUE NEW YEAR

A great star's farewell performance might be used as a boost to the theater's audience base. Jinsi Mao represented the new young performers who rose to replace the departing stars. Quite a transnational performer herself, she had already established her fame in Southeast Asia, and in 1924 a critic for the Shanghai newspaper *Shen Bao* praised her portrayal of the empress Yang Guifei in *Drunken Empress* and the talented courtesan Qiuxi, comparing her to the best actress to play these roles.[27] During her week of debut performances at the Great China Theater in October 1926, however, she probably was overshadowed by the male stars.[28] Once they left, she became the leading singer, adored by audiences and billed as the lead in nearly thirty shows and co-lead in twelve in the remainder of the year. Although Jinsi Mao did not become a prominent figure in Cantonese opera history, superb performers like her sustained the theater and its lasting impact on San Francisco.

From a lengthy ode to Jinsi Mao on the playbill, we can get a glimpse of her appeal. The commentator, noting that tragedy is the ultimate art form, reviews several legendary performances by two Peking opera actresses and by the famous female impersonator Mei Lanfang in China. Then he continues:

> [Those famous Peking opera singers'] brilliant performances evoked such profound sadness and bitter tears, as many audiences were moved to tears, or lowered their heads while listening intently. It taught me the deep melancholy of tragedy as a genre. Since then, my itinerary had taken me to Tianjin, Shanghai, Japan, and finally the United States, where I have seen hundreds of both Chinese and Western dramatic performances. In the past I was occasionally moved to tears, or felt deeply touched, yet no other performances that cast a spell on me were comparable to Jinsi Mao's *Sanniang Teaching Her Son* [at the Great China].[29]

Aside from comparing her to the top opera singers of the day, the first line is a nod to descriptions in classical Chinese literature of the profound effect of a moving musical performance, and thus an endorsement of the aesthetic level of her work. Jinsi Mao sang this well-known opera three times at the theater. Like classics such as *The Piteous Girl* and *Farewell on a Winter Night*, it features a virtuous woman who unwaveringly holds to her principles to fulfill her familial duty against all odds. In the case of *Sanniang Teaching Her Son*, the heroine brings up a son despite extremely difficult circumstances. Her self-sacrifice and struggle in defiance of strenuous circumstances are eventually rewarded. The heroine's enduring hardships and her aspirations for her son make them a showcase for touching, skillful performances of the young belle role types. Jinsi Mao excelled in her interpretation of such an emotionally charged role.

As a rising star of the newer generation, Jinsi Mao was also known for an innovative singing style that used a more natural voice, a deviation from the traditional high nasal tone used by veteran female impersonators and most actresses. In October a playbill noted, "Receiving the most critical acclaim recently was Jinsi Mao's expressive singing and nuanced performance. Especially, her 'open throat' singing style gives melodious sound, clear diction all around, and an even quality of natural voice. The falsely or artificially produced voices simply cannot compare."[30] Her popularity is also seen in theater playbills' frequent previews of her upcoming productions, noting the tunes and aria types she would perform, sometimes naming up to ten titles.[31] Below we will see how the theater featured her recordings when it co-founded a new record label.

The year 1928 marked the Great China Theater's fourth year of residence in its own building. For Chinese New Year, San Francisco's Chinese Consolidated Benevolent Association secured in advance permission from the city for a one-week period of fireworks (symbolizing a plentitude of bliss) to be lit all through the Chinese community and for street vendors to set up their stands for special holiday goods three days prior to New Year's Day.[32] These special permits encouraged a large crowd to descend on Chinatown for the holiday season.

The theater also made an unusual announcement in the pages of the *Young China*. It would relieve its entire staff of all duties for the two days leading to New Year's Day (January 22).[33] Instead, the staff would use the two days to mount their own productions, and all of the proceeds would go directly to the performers. It might have been a year-end bonus. The two evenings' programs featured the entire cast in popular excerpts from famous repertoire for the festive occasion. The second evening began with a new production set in a grand palace, followed by three playlets performed by the Great China Theater's most popular actors of the moment. The shows were also clever ways to compete with the Mandarin Theater, which offered two playlets that evening, one featuring Li Xuefang and the other the famous comedian Doupi Yuan (discussed in Chapter 9). This was New Year's Eve, when the biggest celebration of the holiday falls, and the annual family reunion dinner was served.

The shrewd tactic gave an incentive for the performers to put on their best shows and for the audiences, undoubtedly rooting for their favorite performers, to come to the theater. And the theater rivalry was put on hold. Perhaps the intensity of competition between the two theaters had diminished, as they later held a joint celebration and performance on the birthday of Sun Yat-Sen in March led by the dramatist Pang, who had become a public figure heading community initiatives at large. The numerous such benefits were both reflections of the theater's prosperity and occasions to show their altruism. During the late 1920s the Great China Theater, together with the Mandarin Theater, also mounted a campaign for the building of a library in Guangzhou, a fundraising initiative led by a delegate from that city on tour in the United States.

NEW CHARACTERISTICS

With the arrival of many actresses of a high caliber, actor-actress pairs arose as a new form of attraction at the theater. When an actor and an actress frequently co-starred as the leading couple, they came to be regarded as a stage couple. They included actresses Jinsi Mao, Lin Liqing, Yin Feiyan, Pixiu Su, and Xinxin Qun and actors Wei Zhongjue, Huang Shaoqiu, and Jing Baolin. Famous American film couples such as Douglas Fairbanks and Mary Pickford might have provided inspiration for this new trend. It ensured more balanced performances, unlike the pairing of, for example, a virtuoso actress and an ordinary actor. The emphasis on stage couples was part of a subtle shift away from the single-virtuoso performance to a more fully fledged drama. In China, a similar shift was launched by the actor Xue Juexian who in the mid-1920s altered the name of *Madame White Snake* to *White Snake Story* in order to reflect the equal significance of the leading couple, rather than simply the eponymous heroine. In North America, the pairing of performers was particularly convenient when the pairs traveled widely to play in other cities, and of course many of them became spouses as well.

Another trend in theater production was using novelty to bring new excitement and surprises. This deviated from conventional Cantonese opera. Like other theaters in the United States, the Great China Theater was influenced both by the extreme realism of producer David Belasco and by motion pictures, which included many convincing details, lighting effects, and pastiche. For example, a new opera titled *Moonlight Sieved Through Sparse Cloud*, performed by the stage couple Lin Liqing and Wei Zhongjue, used a new backdrop by Xu Fengbo and cinema-like montage or scrim effects (see figure 8.5). In a scene with a pensive monologue, the protagonist sat in the middle of the night, longing for her husband, whose silhouette was projected in a window screen high up on the painted wall of the backdrop. The montage added another layer of dramatic action and a new theatrical attraction. The playbill for the production, which was twice the usual size, underscores prominently the modern cinematic effect. The move was timely; after all, the Los Angeles native Anna May Wong had by then achieved stardom and become a Hollywood icon. Aside from receiving critical acclaim for her role in the popular Douglas Fairbanks film *The Thief of Baghdad*, she had starred in more than two dozen films including *The Silk Bouquet*, financed in part by Chinese merchants. The Great China Theater's adoption of montage effects in opera reflected the close-knit culture of entertainment. With its nod to modernity, the scrim effect also gave the opera actresses a more modern image. It is not surprising that during the Chinese New Year in 1928, the actress Lin Liqing was invited to perform at a banquet hosted by an organization advocating equality for Chinese organized by San Francisco dignitaries.[34]

The theater's stagecraft included not only painted backdrops but also panels painted to resemble a three-dimensional surface or vista and even mechanized sets. Paper replicas of horses, cows, and lions or stage props such as bridges and caves were used to enhance the realism of the opera. At the same time, real objects such as guns and coffins were incorporated. Particularly interesting were the multi-tiered sets and backdrops. Figure 8.6 shows a combination of props

Fig. 8.5. *Moonlight Sieved through Sparse Clouds*, Great China Theater, October 8, 1927, showing the montage effect. May's Photo Studio (courtesy of the Wylie Wong Collection at the Museum of Performance and Design, San Francisco).

and hard and soft scenery backdrops allowing one actor to appear to be riding on the back of an elephant, with the other actor held on top of the animal's long trunk, holding a scimitar. In this scene the performers poked their heads through the holes of the set, making them nearly part of the backdrop. The actor in dark clothing on the right was the leading scholar-type actor, Huang Shaoqiu, and the actress shying away from the threat is Jinsi Mao. Although little could be found about the opera for which this set was designed, it was one with a novel setting.

Fig. 8.6. A scene from the Great China Theater (three-dimensional design). May's Photo Studio (courtesy of the Wylie Wong Collection at the Museum of Performance and Design, San Francisco).

Neither the elephant nor the palm trees normally appeared in Cantonese opera. It was no doubt a form of cultural novelty for the theater, possibly linked to the opera's Southeast Asian source. In any case, these were merely two examples from the many that juxtaposed characteristics of different cultures.

With novel stage designs to boost its offerings, the theater still mainly relied on star performers to sustain interest. It is interesting that the residencies of stars in leading female roles seldom overlapped. The year 1928 was dominated by three successive leads: Jinsi Mao, Suzhou Li, and Xiao Dingxiang, who were also busy on the performing network across North America. Their travels show the increasing interdependence of Chinatown theaters.

After appearing in thirty shows since January, Jinsi Mao left in March for Boston's New China Theater and later moved to the Yong Ni Shang Theater in New York.[35] Days after her departure, Xiao Dingxiang returned to the stage of the Great China. During the year he was away, he first appeared in New York and then with the Tai Kwan Company in Chicago. The community's response to his return on March 26 was enthusiastic. As a countermeasure, the Mandarin Theater presented Li Xuefang in her signature young belle repertoire. This remarkable occasion was the first time these two legendary singers of the young belle role in the 1920s competed directly with each other in San Francisco, for four days of performances (March 26, 27, and 31 and April 1).[36] Both were at the very top tier of their respective field. This turned out to be the beginning of Xiao Dingxiang's long farewell. For the next three months the theater would showcase him playing a delicate young maid, showing his acrobatic skills, singing florid new tunes, giving premieres, and performing time-honored classics.[37] The highly versatile Xiao Dingxiang played the lead in thirty-eight shows in these months, of which only four were repeated repertoire. His last performance was on June 20. For the penultimate evening, he sang the highly popular signature opera *Wayfarer's Autumn Lament.*[38]

Suzhou Li, having made her debut on June 25, 1928, would play the leading roles at the Great China Theater for the next six months, until Jinsi Mao's return. Her appearance was newsworthy largely because of the stardom of her sister Suzhou Mei, the only actress of the 1920s whose fame came close to, or perhaps even matched, that of Li Xuefang at the Mandarin. Two days after her debut the *Young China* reported its great success, and during her first month she was featured as a lead for twenty-five performances.[39] Before the end of the year she had staged more than fifty leading roles, the largest number for any actor that year.

THE ORIENTAL RECORD COMPANY

An important step for the Great China Theater in 1927 was its collaboration with a record label, resulting in many recordings over the next few years. Between 1903 and 1930, major labels from Europe and the United States expanded the recording industry to Asia. Many gramophone companies produced recordings of Cantonese opera songs in Hong Kong, and by the late 1920s they shipped the manufacturing equipment to China to expedite the production process, the market being not only southern China but also overseas Chinese.[40] Among non-Chinese listeners was Ernest Bloch, a composer born in Geneva who apparently had owned such recordings prior to his tenure as director of the San Francisco Conservatory of Music from 1925 to 1930.[41] Cantonese opera record production surged with the 1925 Canton–Hong Kong labor strike, when producing records became one of the few employment options available to opera singers.

In the United States, major recording companies turned to immigrant groups for so-called foreign and ethnic music.[42] As early as 1903, Edison Records had dispatched a team to San Francisco to record Cantonese opera singers and then had released a catalogue of eighteen titles claimed to be "the best Chinese Records yet made for any talking machine,"[43] marketed enthusiastically to general audiences. The company magazine, *Edison Phonograph Monthly*, noted that the records were sold to Chinese immigrants from San Francisco to Worcester, Massachusetts, and to Rangoon. In 1910 the company had recorded Chinese actors in New York, producing fifteen titles on Amberol cylinders (early cylinder recordings made of a brittle, waxlike compound) that played for four minutes and eventually were replaced by 78 r.p.m. disks in the early 1920s.[44] Aside from providing singers and musicians for recording sessions, however, the Chinese community did not appear to have had influence over production. This situation changed with the prosperity of the 1920s. In mid-1927 a new company, Oriental Record, was founded (see figure 8.7). It was billed as the first Chinese-owned phonograph record company in the United States as well as Hong Kong.[45] A collaboration of San Francisco merchants, the Great China Theater, Hong Kong merchants, and prominent opera performers such as Bai Jurong, it featured singers in both cities. A September report in the *Young China* portrayed the monumental step in an anti-imperialist light:

> The current recordings [of Cantonese opera were] produced by Western companies, who therefore owned all the rights and profited from them. This situation had prompted Hong Kong Oriental Record Company to call for Chinese merchants in the United States and the Cantonese opera profession in Hong Kong to form a company in order to advance domestic products, and to regain the rights and resist the invasion of imperial capitalism. The first record, to be released shortly, is full of novel songs and new tunes. Its superb sound quality and durability can withstand numerous replays. This is a truly first-rate entertainment. The staff of the company includes Bai Jurong, Qian Liju, Ma Shizeng and Jing Rong, who are hard at work on the production. The records will be of a high quality paralleling that of the Beka Record Label.[46]

The company released its first catalogue on December 16, 1927, as an advertisement in the *Young China*. It included twenty-nine titles, sung by ten singers. Five of them (all top male singers such as Bai Jurong) recorded most of the titles. The first catalogue catered especially to the Chinatown community, and audiences of the Great China Theater in particular. Bai was featured in eight popular opera arias familiar to those who frequented his performances in San Francisco. And although the first catalogue favored male singers, as did nearly all the Cantonese opera recordings at this time, it included one title sung by Jinsi Mao. Aside from her piece, Oriental Record's first catalogue was rather similar to those of other labels, with the same popular arias and singers. A major source of its appeal was its Chinese proprietorship. By December 28 the full catalogue started appearing in the daily advertisements of the Kee Chong Company, one of the two large Chinese stores in New York, in the city's *Chinese Nationalist Daily*. And by January 17, 1928, the largest counterpart in Vancouver, Eng Chow Company's advertisement in the *Chinese Times* followed suit.

Catering to Chinatown audiences' tastes with familiar names helped the record company ensure sales. Meanwhile, releasing newly composed arias on record validated the new work and enhanced the theater's reputation; they were also good publicity. And being featured on recordings enhanced the performers' stardom, especially in San Francisco. Highlighted on an October playbill of the Great China Theater was a reference to Jinsi Mao's recording of *Lovelorn Couple* by Pang:

> As this opera has many well-liked new arias, the Oriental Record Company in Hong Kong and the recording crew in San Francisco considered it an opera of choice today and have already made a recording of it. The record's worldwide release is imminent, so we have recently taken the step to produce the opera on stage at the theaters to satisfy the wish of our audiences. It is complete now and will be staged this Saturday.[47]

One playbill noted that Wei Zhongjue, a comedian, would perform several popular arias already featured on his recordings.[48] The venture into the recording industry thus allowed the Great China Theater to chart new territory of business.

Fig. 8.7. Recording by Bai Jurong, Oriental Record Co., no. 5055-A (courtesy of the Archives of Traditional Music, Indiana University).

Precipitated by the rise of Oriental Record, newspaper advertisements for gramophones and records increased substantially in 1928. Many more stores carried advertisements for recordings. They were not cheap, but they were affordable. At the time, Cantonese records were made on ten-inch disks, each holding four to five minutes per side. Depending on the aria, a title generally took up two to four disks. The price per disk ranged from $0.75 to $1.25 (the equivalent of $10 to $17 in 2014), depending on the label and how recently it was issued. The tickets at the Great China Theater ran from $0.50 to $1.25 (for comparison, an annual subscription to the *Young China* ranged from $10 to $13 depending on one's location).[49] For approximately the same cost as the highest-priced ticket, opera fans with gramophones could enjoy one disk's worth of opera at home.[50]

The Oriental Record Company was one of the latecomers to the long list of labels that produced Cantonese opera records to sell in Chinatowns in the mid-1920s. It was advertised prominently. The existing labels included Beka Records and Odeon Records (Germany), Victor Phonograph Company (United States), New Moon Records (China), and China Records (issued in Shanghai by a Japanese sponsor). Perhaps due to its novelty, the new label was more expensive. According to the advertisements, a disk on the issued Oriental label cost up to $1.25 whereas others were mostly $1. In most record ads the Great China Theater's Jinsi Mao was the only female singer featured.[51]

Remarkably, Oriental Record's second catalogue showed an even closer connection between the Great China and the company. Issued on April 4, 1928, it was devoted exclusively to four actresses, four actors, one instrumentalist (Zhu Hong), and one amateur singer, all from the Great China.[52] Jinsi Mao sang six of the seventeen titles. Also prominent in this catalogue were duets by the famous stage couples discussed above. Furthermore, the theater's involvement was made more apparent when individual headshots, with names, of ten recorded performers were featured in the advertisement that ran for the month of May in the *Young China*. The ad enhanced the appeal of the recordings with the familiar faces seen on the playbills. In contrast, the usual record advertisements used text, listing the arias followed by the performers' names, and only occasionally included an image such as the photograph of a famous singer. The May advertisement's images of the performers were emphasized, while relegating all aria titles to one side. This novel advertisement no doubt helped customers make an immediate connection to the theater.

In fact, it blurred the boundary between record and theater advertisements. To the right of the advertisement, a standing female is saying "No. 1 in the world," while her counterpart on the opposite side says "Entranced listening." The modern images of the performers with contemporary dress and close-cropped or permed hair also suggested that Cantonese opera, much like the modern phonograph technology which carried their voice, embodied the spirit of contemporary society.

Key figures of the Great China Theater such as the actor Bai Jurong or the actresses Jinsi Mao and Huang Xiaofeng all appeared regularly in the Oriental Record catalogues. Their performances, through the convenience of this medium, could now be repeated indefinitely. The wide circulation of the Chinese newspapers also ensured that their photos or, at least, their names would reach far beyond the San Francisco community. In late October another catalogue from Oriental Record titled "Supplement to the Second Catalogue" featured two actresses and two actors of the Great China Theater in residence (Jinsi Mao, Yin Feiyan, Zihou Hai, and Wei Zhongjue), as well as four titles by Bai Jurong. Most remarkable were the three titles sung by the theater's playwright, Pang Yifeng,[53] a recognition of his talent beyond writing scripts. The connection between the label and the theater was apparent in subsequent releases as well. The third catalogue, issued in January 1929, featured arias by Huang Xiaofeng. The newspaper advertisement simulated a stage monologue in colloquial Cantonese with the voice of the adored star actress who had returned to China the previous year:

> [monologue] Your little sister is always reticent with words, yet melodious in singing. So let me then sing a song for you: [switch to song of the *manzhongban* melody type] Ever since our parting and my return to Hong Kong, I've thought of you often. On occasions of morning blossom and evening moon especially, my heart flits so very anxiously. Dear sisters and brothers overseas, have you forgotten me? Sadly I do not know when we will meet again. . . . I look forward to our reunion wholeheartedly, though my wish may simply be futile. Luckily we can now count on the "machine" for our reunion. Sending you my voice through the "machine" is like being face to face with you again. If you want to hear my new song, come buy my recordings. [monologue] Okay, first let me sing several songs. The first piece will be sung in the style of Qian Liju's aria "Serenade at Guan Yin Temple." I have also learned a few new songs since I returned. If you don't believe me, try buying my duet with Jing Rong.[54]

Pitched in this playful manner, the record advertisement intended to evoke the audiences' fond memories of their beloved star. However intangible, this voice linked Chinatown audiences to the experience of memorable performances and reinforced their bond with the singer.

The third catalogue was the result of a second recording trip, in which an engineer from New York brought the newest equipment to Hong Kong to record twelve top opera singers. It was noteworthy enough for the *Young China* to report the engineer's departure for Hong Kong on September 1, 1928, and his return to the United States on December 13.[55] The popularity of stage couples at the Great China Theater also had an impact on the project. The recording effort in Hong Kong had focused, the report noted, on thirteen duets between leading male and female characters. After this catalogue the Oriental Record Company continued to release more recordings.[56] Its preference for the performers of the Great China Theater spurred the Mandarin Theater to form its own association with a record company, Xin Yuefeng, but without any apparent result.[57] As the Cantonese opera record business surged, the advertisements in the newspapers expanded to as much as two-thirds of a page. The frequent release of new catalogues and quick increase in advertisement suggest a robust local listening culture. Even general stores such as Wo Kee, whose newspaper advertisements in this area had previously included merely the words *phonograph records*, began to advertise full-column-sized comprehensive catalogues.[58]

Nineteen twenty-eight could be called the year of the phonograph for the Great China Theater. And the expansion of the Oriental Record Company's advertisements reflected the transformation of the community's listening culture. The company's complete catalogues were printed regularly in Chinese daily newspapers across North America, keeping these performers' names and signature arias constantly in people's minds. Oriental Record became one of the largest companies to have its own representatives in various North American cities, following the touring routes of Cantonese opera. A half-page ad in the *Chinese Times* (Vancouver) on January 25, 1928, announced the city's exclusive agent for the record company, Eng Chow Pharmacy. It advertised new catalogues as soon as they were released. Shipping costs were waived for orders of six or more disks. In September, advertisements of the second catalogue (devoted to performers of the Great China Theater) had just one photograph—of Jinsi Mao—at the top.

The advertiser also made the business a nationalist concern for the Chinese community. In January the half-page advertisement that had listed the first catalogue began with a plea from Oriental Record: "This company is a collaboration of exclusively Chinese merchants and contemporary star performers. In order to preserve and support our own national culture, we record Cantonese opera songs, with a fine selection of new tunes, innovative melodies, and original music."[59] The company continued to produce records into the 1930s, targeting audiences in both Hong Kong and the Americas. A 1933 advertisement in the *Chinese Times* listed Oriental Record catalogues 2 through 6.[60]

CHINESE AMERICAN YOUTH AND OPERA

The younger generation not only found their cultural expression in opera but on special occasions were able to perform alongside the professionals. One example was a recent graduate of Oakland High School, Guan Yundi. In a regular staging on March 11 he performed at the Great China Theater. The highly publicized event was indicative of the community's increasing participation in the opera culture.

On this evening the theater prepared a special program for the teenager's debut. The program began, as the *Young China* reported three days in advance, with the ritual opera *The Joint Investiture of a Prime Minister of Six Warlords* in a novel and unconventional production. Though a spectacular ritual opera was typically performed on celebratory occasions and showcased the complete cast of the theater, this evening's production was unique—a full reversal of the role types. The whole cast cross-dressed. Actresses of young belle roles played old statesmen or young warriors, actors of leading young scholar or warrior role types played young belles or comedians, old male comedians played young belles, and even the female impersonator of young belle roles cross-dressed to play the young warrior. The playbill printed a diagram to list the cross-dressing of all twenty-one performers. The unorthodox casting choice promised an exciting evening of wicked fun.

Following *The Joint Investiture* was the main performance, *Mourning of the Chaste Tree Flower*, in which Guan Yundi co-starred with Jinsi Mao. The biography of Guan on the playbill describes a handsome, graceful, intelligent, and kind young man who loved and studied opera with the theater's top actor:

> Last year, Guan Yundi sang successfully in a benefit performance raising funds for the Chinese school. He studied with Bai Jurong during the famous actor's residence at the theater, and his talent was considered exceptional even by professional standards. The theater specially invited him to perform his signature aria with Jinsi Mao, on the occasion of Jin's imminent departure from the theater. In addition, the Oriental Record Company has made a record of his singing, which will soon be released.[61]

The biography referred to Oriental Record's second catalogue. Guan was one of the four actors in this catalogue. A week later he was featured again in a complicated program: a grand opening number was followed by three opera excerpts. This time, he performed an aria from the popular *Wayfarer's Autumn Lament*.

Guan was from an affluent family, as shown by the report in the *Young China* that he donated the thirty-dollar honorarium to the theater's fundraising for a hospital. He was likely the son of a stout supporter of the theater. For merchants, the opera satisfied their craving for the edifying study of historical and moral legends and enhanced their status in the community. For the theaters, merchants' patronage was very important, and showcasing a talented young man from Chinatown's elite class strengthened this connection, even if he might not be a box-office magnet. Backing him with a fancy production allowed the theater to indulge its major patrons without losing money.

More importantly, such stories showed how theatrical culture had been passed on to a younger generation. Cantonese opera was no longer just for immigrants, and this was perhaps a key aspect of the 1920s renaissance of the art form in American Chinatowns. It constituted the community's thriving musical life so that the youth were acculturated in the aesthetics of the opera tradition. Some performers, quite young themselves, joined the young Chinese Americans. For example, according to one report, aforementioned actress Suzhou Li attended and graduated from high school in San Francisco.[62]

Opera culture took root with youngsters in extracurricular activities at the Chinese schools. Xie He School, also known as Hip Wo Chinese School or the Chinese Union Christian Academy, was one of the largest Chinese-language schools in San Francisco. It was founded in 1925 by the Chinese Congregational, Presbyterian, Methodist Episcopal, and Baptist churches.[63] It offered a Chinese curriculum from elementary to high school, and its classes ran from 5 P.M. to 8 P.M. on weekdays and from 9 A.M. to noon on Saturdays.[64] In January 1928, Hip Wo Chinese School planned a major fundraising event featuring two Cantonese opera excerpts. According to an advertisement for the event, the cast of the first opera included nine young girls and eleven young boys. Nine roles were listed with the names of the young performers, one of whom was characterized as "the second Bai Jurong." The second opera playlet would be performed by twenty-four young women (according to the *Young China*, the school's enrollment of girls outnumbered that of boys).[65] The lyrics of more than ten songs would accompany the performance. The benefit appealed to the community's support for dual-language education, and the listing of more than forty young students in its cast aimed to portray the school's uniqueness and impress on readers the importance of continuing to support such a cultural and educational institution. Xie He Chinese School would continue to use Cantonese opera in its cultural curriculum.

That the youngsters were trained to perform opera in public showed that it was considered a significant, positive piece of cultural identity, connected to the knowledge of historical tales and legends. This phenomenon might be unique to the Chinatown community and its desire to engage with living art and music. Traditionally, in Chinese society, musicians and opera performers occupied the lower strata, and children of well-heeled families or at prestigious schools would hardly be encouraged to participate in public performances of opera. Yet the situation was markedly different for Chinatown communities in North America. These performances symbolized the cultivation of cultural aesthetics, more urgent in this community. Furthermore, the widespread distribution of phonograph records contributed to the validation of Cantonese opera as artistic expression and a part of middle-class leisure. Staging the community's youngsters in operatic performance now signaled a kind of cultural sophistication.

THE RISING SIGNIFICANCE OF CINEMA

Even as the Great China Theater finally established itself as a significant cultural presence, the end of the decade was also indisputably the time when opera theaters would begin to lose their unique place in Chinatown. The advent of sound in films in 1927 had enormous repercussions for live performance in general. Just as Al Jolson brought his musical talent to the soundtrack of *The Jazz Singer* (1927), many Cantonese opera stars brought their musical talent to the soundtracks of Chinese feature films. The years from 1925 to 1929 in China were remarkable for the number of new film studios established and feature films produced. Of the more than sixty new studios, seventeen were successful and prolific, producing Keystone Cops–style comedy, romance, historical drama, contemporary satire, myths, and of course opera. There were more than a hundred releases each year from 1926 to 1929.

In the San Francisco Chinese community in 1928, people could see films in many different ways. In January, for instance, when Chinese New Year was approaching, they were shown by day as matinees at the Mandarin Theater and in the evening at the Chinese American Citizens' Alliance. Or they were shown at smaller public spaces such as Catholic churches in the community.[66] The showings extended occasionally to nearby Stockton and Sacramento. For example, the latter responded enthusiastically to the film *The Date of Ne Zha's Birth*, claiming it was the greatest of Chinese films.[67] Early Cantonese cinema was largely based on Cantonese opera, and one short film, as noted above, followed actress Huang Xiaofeng's tour across America.[68]

One news report about the attraction of a motion picture titled *Mr. Wife*, a comedy made in Shanghai by the Happy Film Studio, is an example of the novelty films offered to the community. The report underscored the following: the film's production cost of 10,000 Chinese dollars, the joint efforts of the best in the movie business and the social elites, and the featuring of Shanghai's scenic places and vistas.[69] Without question, some of these attractions were novel to the audiences and could not be found in opera performances.

In addition to providing novelty, motion pictures were cheaper to show. Given the minimal expense, screening movies was highly profitable for businesses such as the Chinese Film Exchange (New York) and the Xianshi Motion Picture Company (San Francisco), which received movies from China. Compared to opera tickets, which ranged from $0.25 to $2, film tickets were either $0.25 or $0.50.[70] Very soon, Chinese movies also began to be shown in cinemas. On May 3, an advertisement appeared in the *Young China* for the movie *The Night of a Full Moon*, showing at the Verdi Theatre at 644 Broadway.[71] It was issued by the Shenzhou (Wonderful Continent) Film Company, one of the most prominent film studios in Shanghai.

While the opera performances at the Great China Theater continued, the community was introduced to what would become the most popular form of entertainment of the next decade. For the time being, however, cinema and opera would coexist for quite a while. The end of the year saw the Great China filled with newly arrived performers; in September alone, seven well-known actors came including the bearded warrior actor Shao Baicai, several warrior and scholar types, and a dignified middle-aged male.[72] However, a company shareholder meeting was called in early 1929. A follow-up public announcement noted that, although the profits had been very good in the past two years, the company had resolved to stop paying dividends and instead return the profits to capital investment to expand the business. Meanwhile, each stockholder would receive two tickets at the box office for every $100 of company stock.[73] Such signs of compromise continued throughout the year, signaling the end of the golden era of Cantonese opera and the seemingly unlimited prosperity of the Great China Theater. Nevertheless, Cantonese opera still had immense appeal. In 1931 the superstar Ma Shizeng would join the theater for a year. For the next decade or two the Great China would continue to thrive on the path that it had paved, but it would no longer enjoy the same prominence. Other forms of entertainment had arrived.

PART IV

SAN FRANCISCO'S NEW THEATER AND RIVALRY

CHAPTER 9

A SUCCESSFUL, MAJESTIC STAGE

The Mandarin Theater, 1924–1926

The Mandarin Theater played an immense part in the renaissance of Cantonese opera in San Francisco. Led by local tycoon Chin Lain, it had, from its inception, planned to be a prominent theater that gestured to the city's long tradition of Chinese theaters by remaking itself as a post-1906 institution of the Roaring Twenties. Its history, therefore, offers us another perspective on that prosperous decade for Chinatown theater in North America. In particular, the large number of performers it engaged directly from southern China allowed several clear themes to emerge over the years.

A BRAND NEW BUILDING

Though it was the second Chinese theater in San Francisco, the Mandarin Theater was the first to establish itself as an architectural landmark. An upscale building in the heart of Chinatown, it was designed by civil engineer Clarence K. Chan and architect A. A. Austin. It has a pronounced lower eave with a gable end in the middle, curved ridge ornaments at the corners, and bright color tracing the outline.[1] An image of it was featured prominently in the *San Francisco Chronicle*, and it was praised as "absolutely modern in perfect accord with Chinese ideas of decorative art" (see figure 9.1).[2] It was "a Class-A structure, built of concrete and steel," conforming to the post-1906 fire law.[3] On June 26, 1924, the Mandarin Theater at 1021 Grant Avenue opened its doors to the community. Local dignitaries and prominent community organization leaders, among others, were invited to a large opening ceremony filled

Fig. 9.1. Postcard showing the Mandarin Theater building (courtesy of Ren Fan).

with speeches, instrumental music, and spoken-drama performances. It was the first purpose-built theater for Cantonese opera since the 1906 earthquake and fire. The construction of this theater was an important step in resurrecting the physical spaces for opera performance. The building, with artistic front entry, spacious seats, and ornate stage, remade the glory days of Chinese theater in new neon lighting.

The ceremony began at noon; at four o'clock all the guests and performers were invited to a multi-course banquet at Chin Lain's upscale restaurant Hang Far Low Cafe; at six o'clock all returned to the theater for the inaugural performance. For the invited guests, synopses in both English and Chinese were delivered to their private boxes. *The Joint Investiture of a Prime Minister of Six Warlords* commenced the performance. To accommodate the large audiences, matinee performances were offered on Sundays throughout the month. The spectacular scenes and props were emphasized in the advertisements in Chinese newspapers such as the *Young China* and *Chung Sai Yat Po.* Among the scenes described were a Buddhist shrine, a prison cell, a Western-style stone grave, a snow-covered straw hut, a private garden, and a bushy woodland. Among the props were chairs and lotus flowers decorated with light bulbs, and a papier-mâché tower and sea creatures. Special effects included electric lighting to create the effect of an exploding stone grave.[4] The Mandarin was the grandest Chinese theater in North America.

Quite unlike its rival theater's premiere only eighteen months earlier, which featured a male troupe with the addition of three actresses, the Mandarin Theater brought a true mixed-sex troupe with prominent young actresses. On average the performers were in their twenties, according to immigration records.[5] This group included singers of all eight major role types, as well as musicians and a dramatist. Following the opening week's large production, leading actors took turns staging individual debuts in their signature operas. Toward the end of July the activity quieted down and the stage was taken over by three actresses of the young belle role type: Zhang Shuqin, Chen Feifeng, and Xin Guifei.

Just as in 1917–1918, when she performed with Vancouver's Puruyi troupe, Zhang Shuqin was the prima donna at the Mandarin Theater (see figure 9.2). That the twenty-seven-year-old Zhang was the most famous of the Mandarin's initial group of thirty-three members is reflected by the number of her leading performances. From July 23 to September 2, she was billed as the lead in twenty-seven shows. Xin Guifei and Chen Feifeng, both in their early twenties, played the lead in classic young belle type repertoire (*Shilin Paying Respects at the Pagoda* and *Nocturnal Mourning of White Lotus*), although just as often they performed supporting roles while Zhang played the lead. This focus on young belle type operas, the Mandarin's strength, meant the theater was mostly staging melodramatic, melancholy, and romantic drama. The two above-mentioned operas and *Deranged Mother Seeking Son* (Zhang Shuqin's signature opera) were all presented three times.[6] Performances of comic opera or operas of young scholar and warrior types became sparser.

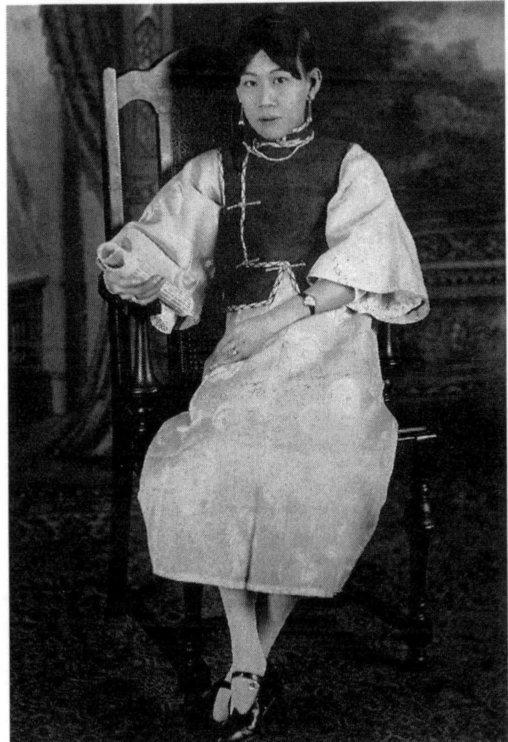

Fig. 9.2. Zhang Shuqin (courtesy of Ren Fan).

A photo taken two months after the opening shows the cast of the new Mandarin Theater in formal attire (see figure 9.3). The occasion was a fundraising event, the significance of which is discussed below. The two long embroidered drapes hung in front of the symmetrical back-stage doors carry Zhang Shuqin's name in the center, signaling her status as a prima donna. (Such decorated textiles proclaimed the status of opera performers, and stars typically had a canopy, valance, or banner bearing their names on stage while they acted.) Zhang (in a light-colored dress) is also the dedicatee of the top left banner, while the top right banner is dedicated to Xin Guifei (in a dark skirt). These banners were made in San Francisco. The two actresses are in the center of the front row.[7]

The cast was quickly enhanced by additional performers from all over North America. Two caused problems, however. In mid-July an actress formerly employed by Lun Hop named Yangzhou Mei arrived from Mexico. She was not new to San Francisco audiences, having been one of the two leading actresses with Lun Hop in 1923, as discussed in Chapter 7. Her return to San Francisco to perform with the Mandarin Theater annoyed the Lun Hop Company. It immediately apprised the immigration office of her status—"in transit"—which did not give her permission to perform at theaters for long.[8] Her time at the Mandarin was thus shortened abruptly. In October, the theater brought in an eighteen-year-old actress from Cuba, Shao Dingxiang, who had been touring the Americas with her father.

Fig. 9.3. The Mandarin Theater's initial troupe, August 10, 1924 (courtesy of Ren Fan).

Despite her success in Havana, however, she had little luck in San Francisco and quickly disappeared. She might not have been on a par with the rest of the cast.

BALANCE IN A MIXED TROUPE

Given that gender segregation in Cantonese opera was still in effect in China and Hong Kong, mixed troupes in this period still featured female impersonators. Although the Mandarin Theater's proposal declared that it would "straighten up" the genders on stage—letting actors play men and actresses play women—it was not very easily done. Many aspects of the profession were changing quickly, but matching the genders of the performers with role types was not yet a primary concern. As it had pledged, the Mandarin included no female or male impersonators initially. Instead, the troupe leaned heavily on actresses, such that its actors primarily performed minor roles, and even the leading actors were eclipsed by the actresses. At times it seemed more like a female troupe with a male cast playing the secondary roles. The imbalance tilted further when in early November an actress, Wu Weijun, of the young scholar role type, arrived from China. Although she helped alleviate the theater's shortage of leading male characters, the flavor of an all-female performance was reinforced. Nonetheless, the Mandarin had enough actors to stage a wide variety of operas, and in any case the audiences were quite well adapted to a fluid sense of gender-bending.

The theater's cast of actors only improved when a male comedian, Guijiu Sheng, joined in November, bringing with him the comic repertoire that was always crucial to Cantonese opera. Then, the addition of Jinshan Bing (Chan Hing), an actor of the young scholar role type, finally provided the theater with the proper cast for balanced mixed-troupe performances. The first actor from the top tier of the profession to perform at the Mandarin, Jinshan Bing arrived in San Francisco on November 29, 1924. On the playbill of December 3, the theater proudly noted,

> The opera *Three Heroes Combating Lü Bu* was masterfully done by the famous actor Jinshan Bing. Known for his clear and resonant voice, superbly sophisticated technique, suave hand gestures and stage motions, expressive and captivating eyes, Jinshan Bing has long gained high praise from theater critics. Here he will be supported by top performers. . . . At the warrior scene, as intense as a battling dragon and tiger, his skill is unique; at the farewell scene, so beautiful and perfect, his singing is hardly matched by others.

In addition, the playbill noted that Jinshan Bing penned several of the opera's lyrics, tunes, and bridge passages; he was an actor-singer with significant literary talent. The twenty-six-year-old actor would contribute notably to the Mandarin Theater in the next two years. However, the timing of his arrival, three weeks before the expiration of the theater's first permit, placed him in an awkward situation.

He was notified by the Immigration Bureau, together with the performers whose six-month permits were expiring on December 25, that he needed to prepare for departure. In a letter to the bureau the lawyer Chas McGee implored,

> Mr. Chan Hing [Jinshan Bing] is a very famous actor who was brought here at great expense... His departure before the 25th would mean he would be here less than a month. No theater on earth could operate under such terms and I am satisfied that it is not the purpose of the Department to work any such hardship in a business which requires new blood from time to time in order to satisfy the demands of the theater-going public.[9]

This hiccup was symptomatic of the Mandarin Theater's somewhat strained relationship with the immigration office at this time (see Chapter 3). Luckily the matter was quickly solved.

Jinshan Bing's presence turned the focus of December's shows to repertoire for the young scholar type. He was the sole lead in eight performances and co-starred with actresses in seven. The shift in emphasis—nineteen operas with principal male roles versus four with female role types—may have contributed to a sharp increase in revenue. Jinshan Bing's young warrior operas brought to the stage fearless, heroic figures, a very welcome genre that reminded people of courage, patriotism, and uplifting thoughts. At the same time, his youthful heroic characters had flings with romance, producing love scenes with the leading actresses. Soon, the new focus on actors was helped further by another actor of the young scholar role type, the veteran Zheng Xinyi, long in residence with theaters in Vancouver, and Sheng Zhangfei, an actor for er huamian role type, playing peevish and petulant characters. For the Christmas holiday, a new opera, *Tale of the Golden Butterfly,* led by Jinshan Bing, Zhang Shuqin, and Zheng Xinyi took three days to complete. The Mandarin still had many more star actresses than star actors, but at least a balanced performance was now possible.

EXPANSIONS: QUOTA AND TERRITORY

Overall the Mandarin Theater did well for its first nine months. Yet its revenue fluctuated greatly, as reflected in the theater's city tax records (table 9.1).[10] According to the newly implemented Revenue Act of the time, the city tax was 10 percent on all tickets priced \$.50 and above. (Regular tickets ranged from \$ 0.50 to \$1.75, though matinees and after-hour entry could be lower.) On the basis of the amounts of city tax paid, one can estimate that the monthly revenue fluctuated between at least \$8,000 and \$30,000 (ca. \$111,000 to \$415,000 in 2014).[11] The oscillation was such that after the first month's extraordinary success, the revenues twice dropped by half in two consecutive months. The rebound in November, December, and Janu-

Table 9.1. Amounts of city tax paid by the Mandarin Theater from July 1924 to March 1925

Date	City tax	Comments	Names of new performers
July 1924	$3,176.73	grand opening	
Aug. 1924	$1,595.16		
Sept. 1924	$873.11		
Oct. 1924	$854.21	1 minor new actress	Shao Dingxiang
Nov. 1924	$1,452.48	2 new performers, including 1 male impersonator and 1 famous comic actor	Wu Weijun, Guijiu Sheng
Dec. 1924	$1,200.61	1 new star actor	Jinshan Bing
Jan. 1925	$1,893.23	several famous new performers	Zheng Xinyi, Sheng Zhangfei, Gongye Chuang, et al.
Feb. 1925	$1091.36	12 new performers arriving on Jan. 3	Guan Yingxue, Guan Xing, Wen Xi, et al.
Mar. 1925	$801.53	no new performers arriving from February to May	

ary coincided with the above-mentioned arrivals of significant performers, but income never rose back to the astronomical figures of the first month.

In early January the government granted the renewal of the Mandarin's first six-month permit. The theater promptly petitioned for its quota to be doubled to ninety, probably as a result of the lesson learned from its fluctuating revenue: that audiences wanted to see new talent. This was also necessitated by the activity of its rival company. Lun Hop, in response to the challenge posed by the Mandarin Theater, had brought in twenty-one new performers in the second half of 1924 alone. Ever since the Mandarin had come on the scene, Lun Hop had kept its cast at the limit of its quota and continually rotated new performers in, regularly sending the overflow to Mexicali. It also showed off with a full display of its sixty-four members in a production of *The Joint Investiture* in the fall.

Another reflection of Lun Hop's strong standing within the community was a benefit performance on August 17 for the rescue effort after a flood in Canton (also the cause of the fundraiser by the Mandarin documented in figure 9.3). In this matinee performance led by Lun Hop's top warrior actor, Dongpo An, $1,307 were raised. The *Young China* raved about Dongpo An's significant contribution.[12]

The Mandarin was confident enough in its request for a quota increase that it did not wait to extend its size. In January 1925 alone, twenty performers were brought from China.[13] The most famous among them was the veteran actor Gongye Chuang. The fifty-five-year-old, part of a famous family of theater performers, was an important actor of the early twentieth century of the bearded warrior type. He created a unique vocal technique that inspired later singers. He was the Mandarin's answer to Lun Hop's veteran warrior actor, Dongpo An, who was equally well regarded. The playbill for Gongye Chuang's debut touted his significance:

> Mr. Tan Yetian [Gongye Chuang] is a star among the bearded warrior role type actors. In China, no matter whether on the local stages of touring troupes or the stages of city theater troupes, his performances gathered enormous crowds and all the seats were fully packed. Anyone who had experienced his staging considered his remarkable performances most extraordinary and memorable. In the past, those of us overseas or born in the United States could only hear of the name while lamenting the lack of a chance to listen to his performance. Until recently, we could do little other than envy those who could hear his singing, or appreciate his beautiful melody.[14]

Gongye Chuang was famous for playing characters of high moral standing, virility, or patriotism. He was undoubtedly a source of pride for this new theater seeking to build the image of the new China.

Because the theater raised the ticket prices for debuts, they generated higher yields than did other shows. Given the theaters' limited quota, even lesser-known newcomers were given the spotlight, at times upstaging more significant performers who had been at the theater for a while. For example, arriving with Gongye Chuang were an actress and two other young warrior actors. Though relatively unknown, they were given leading roles and much fanfare for their debuts. The theater next celebrated the nineteen-year-old Guan Yingxue, another actress joining the theater from New Orleans.

When the Chinese New Year celebration started on January 22, the two rival theaters staged several of the same operas on the same evenings, which must have added excitement to the holiday. At other times the theaters distinguished themselves by different approaches to programming: the Mandarin tended to stage an opera for one evening, while Lun Hop favored the newer practice of staging groups of famous playlets. The latter approach was quite common among the theaters in Shanghai, and it would be the tactic adopted by Peking opera star Mei Lanfang when he visited the United States in 1930. It is interesting, then, that while the Mandarin Theater sought to remake the image of Chinese theater, it valued the more orthodox and classic practice of opera production.

Soon the rivalry moved from San Francisco to Los Angeles. With its large number of performers, Lun Hop's Chinese New Year programming in San Francisco fared well, although it had just dispatched seventeen performers to Los Angeles.[15] It offered the only opera performances in that city during the holiday. Little wonder that on March 12 the Mandarin Theater also sent a group of seventeen performers to Los Angeles.[16] The division of its limited number of performers probably put a strain on its casting capability. The Los Angeles troupe (which made its debut on March 16) included top members of the original cast such as Zhang Shuqin. Dispatching subgroups to other cities was merely the first step to expansion, however. Before their departure, the farewell of Zhang Shuqin included *The Joint Investiture*, showcasing again the full strength of the theater, as well as new scenery and costumes just arrived from China. The scenery included mountains, rivers, towers, forests, and elegant rooms. The new wardrobe was such a significant investment that it received a half-page write-up on the playbill.

The Mandarin's branch in Los Angeles carried the same name, establishing it as a brand. It opened on March 14, 1925, and was described in the *Los Angeles Times* as being more modern and Westernized than the Chinese theater at 114 Court Street. The *Times* underscored the theater's dapper image: "Chinese Theater Is Jazzed Up: Wailing of Native Instruments on Bare Stage Gives Way to Scenery and Real Orchestra at Jackson-Street Playhouse." Noting its popularity, the article reported, "the crowds begin to gather at the Mandarin early in the evening and are seated by 7 o'clock, when the performance begins."[17]

THREE KEY PERFORMERS AT TIMES OF CRISIS AND CHALLENGE

After its Los Angeles troupe departed in late March, the Mandarin Theater had other new actresses join its cast from China, but none were as famous as Zhang Shuqin. Judging from its daily playbills, the cast consisted of only fifteen or nineteen performers, compared to the former twenty-seven. Jinshan Bing emerged as a prominent lyricist. The playbill for March 22 announced a new opera named *Camellia Rewarded by the King*: "Brilliantly written by Jinshan Bing, the new work reflects a cosmopolitan perspective, and conveys the mind and spirit of the contemporary society. It contains expertly written bridges and expresses melancholy beautifully."[18] In addition, the theater boasted of its stars' portrayals of roles in classic operas, as opposed to the contemporary operas being staged by Lun Hop, the novelty of which apparently compelled the Mandarin to defend its programming. One playbill noted:

> When it comes to opera script, new or old matters little. It is far more significant that the performances are poignant and meaningful. Failing that, the performances would lose hold of the audiences' interest rapidly. Skill and craftsmanship are the true determinant of an opera's success. So an old script could be performed afresh. This opera, *Shan Bo Fang You*, is an old script, yet with its newly written bridge passages, it is full of wonder and beauty.[19]

The Mandarin's commentary took a jab at the apparently trendy series of new operas offered up by Lun Hop, especially those by the dramatist and female impersonator Lei. Yet especially at modern urban theaters, new titles were greeted by much enthusiasm during the 1920s.

Several additions to the Mandarin Theater's playbills revealed the direction of the changes it made in response to the threat of appearing old-fashioned. In March the playbills began to carry advertisements for pharmacies and restaurants. On April 20 it began to include photographs of performers, following the lead of the Lun Hop Company. Xin Guifei's photo appeared in the first such playbill (see figure 9.4). A month later, the playbills began to include photos daily. After her return from Los Angeles on May 20, pictures of Zhang Shuqin were frequently featured as well. With the headline "Famous performers arriving in succession," a report in the newspaper *Chung Sai Yat Po* commented on theater's higher purpose as well: "Drama is a kind of art, which has the potential for transmitting culture and improving society. In recent years, the community is more desirous of this quality than before." The report went on to note Zhang's return to San Francisco, Lun Hop's engagement of three performers from Seattle, and the arrival of two performers en route to Havana.[20] Enlivened by the competition between two spectacular theaters, the community had found a new focus in its musical and cultural life.

Zhang's return to the Mandarin was embraced by audiences. "Two months was a long time for such a prima donna to be away," the playbill of May 20, 1925, sighed. Just as her departure in March had been marked by a grand staging of *The Joint*

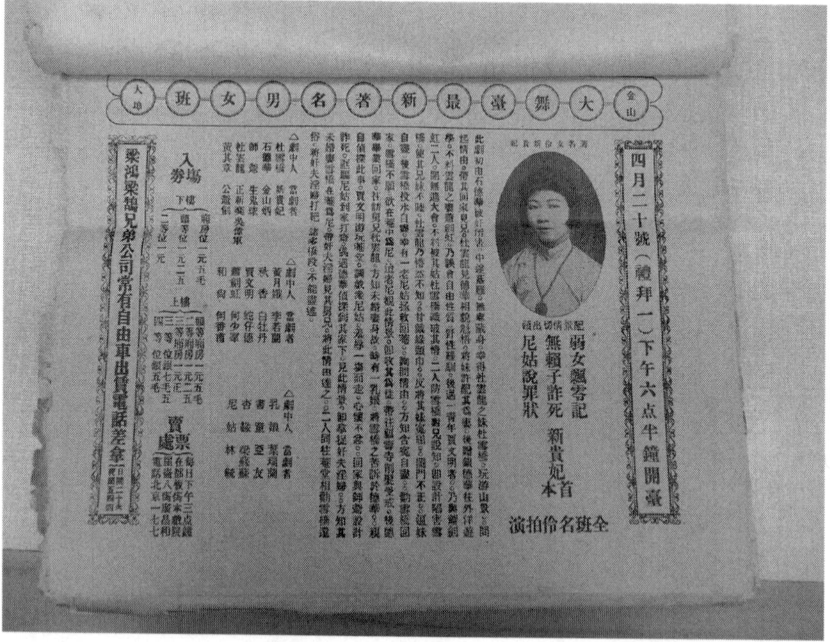

Fig. 9.4. Playbill of the Mandarin Theater featuring Xin Guifei, April 20, 1925 (courtesy of the Ethnic Studies Library, University of California, Berkeley).

Investiture, Zhang's return in May was celebrated with the same ritual and special features. It involved highly challenging dance and acrobatic moves. Zhang's great versatility was detailed on the playbills with descriptions of her in such roles as the young belle, male or female warrior, and young scholar. Her cross-dressing in young male warrior roles was particularly popular. The focus on her was interrupted only by the arrival of Xin Baicai.

All the excitement concealed the immigration crisis facing the theater. The government's repeated rejections of its petition for a higher quota exacerbated its situation (detailed in chapter 3). This struggle, however, or bad news in general, was not made public by the theater. Perhaps for the theater or for the Chinese community at large, immigration hurdles were simply part of daily living. The theater continued to offer new daily productions. In early June more new performers were admitted from Seattle. This might seem odd, considering that the theater had already exceeded its quota by six. Apparently their lawyer's shrewdly worded request camouflaged the situation and raised no red flag with the immigration officials.[21] This small victory was significant because of the fame of the new arrivals.

Xin Baicai was a veteran actor of the bearded warrior type (*wusheng*) known for his singing. At this time the wusheng was often considered the anchor of the cast, as shown by the popular response to Gongye Chuang, another warrior type. Arriving with his fourteen-year-old daughter, the fifty-two-year-old Xin Baicai made his debut on June 11. His mastery immediately drew audiences. On June 14 the playbill noted, "Since Xin Baicai's debut, there has not been one empty seat at his performances." The full cast supported him in spectacular performances such as that of *Returning Home on Autumn Lake* on June 17:

> Because of Xin Baicai's brilliant skills, all eyes are on him. He is superb in the bearded warrior roles, yet his performance of young warrior roles is absolutely eye-pleasing as well. Tonight's performance features him first as young warrior . . . when he and Jinshan Bin duel and then join together in solidarity, it is a quintessential display of heroism and valor. Then, with Zhang Shuqin playing the role of his mother throughout the opera, there is plenty of expressive and emotive singing and acting. Toward the end, Xin Baicai resumes his usual bearded warrior role, and He Xiaoqing and Xin Guifei play his mistress and wife. At the scene where he tests his wife's faithfulness, each act and movement is so genuine and convincing that the suspense leaves the audiences on tenterhooks throughout. This performance is a feast for the eye and ear; the audiences would have no choice but to sigh with gratification.[22]

On June 20 Xin Baicai devised an opera titled *Saving Daughter*, featuring the acrobatic skills of his daughter He Xiaoqing in a novel spectacle, as shown in the playbill photo of He Xiaoqing suspended in mid-air. This photo is unique in capturing a live act, rather than choreographed poses simulating action. It captured the excitement of a moment full of motion, and its novelty had shock value.

Xin Baicai had arrived on the eve of a new challenge for the Mandarin. The community was eagerly anticipating the Lun Hop Company's new 950-seat Great China Theater, scheduled to open on June 19. Construction was already complete, and they were waiting only for new backdrops and costumes.[23] Only a year earlier, the Mandarin's own grand opening had made more than $30,000 in profit in its first month, hurting Lun Hop's bottom line. Now it was its rival's turn. When the Great China Theater opened, the Mandarin challenged Lun Hop by featuring its two best performers, Zhang Shuqin and Xin Baicai, and announcing its own renovation, albeit on a small scale.[24]

Despite the money spent on buildings and scenery, the most significant part of the theatrical business was the cast. Though the Mandarin Theater could pride itself on a stellar cast of key performers in main role types or even unusual talent, it had to keep using them for the following two months before any new performers could be admitted. In the world of Chinatown theaters, repetition was stagnancy. As a reporter wryly noted, one of the "elements most insistently demanded by Chinese audiences" was new faces.[25] A lack of newcomers meant a drop in ticket sales. No doubt these were trying months for the Mandarin Theater.

INCREASED VISIBILITY AND FUNDRAISING ACTIVITY

Nevertheless, it was a special time. Cantonese opera performance took on an increasingly significant and visible role in North American life generally. Reports of the activities of Cantonese theaters on the continent appeared frequently in the newspapers. On June 25 an item in the *Los Angeles Times* gave a sense of the modern appearance of the Chinese theater there:

> The Chinese theater in this city's Chinatown used to play all Chinese music. Today, however, it even includes dancing music of the West. Its stage was once very plain with nothing, leaving people imagining or guessing; now it is equipped with paintings of mountains and lakes, as well as real pictures. Furthermore, all female roles are now played by actresses, unlike previously when the female impersonators filled those roles on stage. A question about the reasons for these new changes was brought up to the owner of the theater, who said that this trend is in vogue with young people of our contemporary society. It has been important for the theatrical profession to progress in the direction of more current and popular trends.[26]

The changes described here reflected a new face of Cantonese opera. The updated aesthetics also pointed to modernized means of couching the traditional art in ways that would be more on a par with other contemporary entertainment presented in the city of Los Angeles. Why not enjoy the Cantonese opera as a new vogue? The news that Chinese opera theaters were incorporating elements of modern life was printed even in places where there were no theaters of this type, such as Washington, DC.[27]

The opera theater's eagerness to connect to the modern notwithstanding, it was inseparable from the community's more traditional function, as was perhaps best reflected in benefit performances. These were among the most frequently reported events regarding theaters. When there was a common cause, the community turned to opera. For example, when a troupe in Portland had a benefit performance on the day a San Francisco community leader visited, aiming to raise money for Chinese schools, local Chinese merchants closed stores to attend the significant occasion.[28]

After tragedies or other dire situations in China, news about theaters' fundraising activities across North America increased significantly. Chinese communities in the United States responded to the brutal May 1925 incident in the foreign territory of Shanghai (see Chapter 7) with numerous benefit performances. Many cities, with or without Cantonese opera theaters or troupes of their own, scheduled benefit performances and raised remarkable sums to help victims of the crime and people who suffered from the general strike. A June 27 report regarding Chicago noted that three opera singers en route from New York to Seattle for a voyage back to China stopped to pay respects to local dignitaries and were invited to offer benefit performances there to help the relief fund for Chinese laborers.[29] Opera performance, the report noted, was more effective for fundraising than door-to-door efforts. On July 3 a report about Los Angeles noted the scheduling of a benefit performance in the Mandarin Theater branch there by Gongye Chuang, featuring the famous story *Courtesan Wang Zhaojun Leaves for the Frontier*; the Renshou Nian troupe in Portland was reported to have raised $3,600 after expenses from two performances and a flower sale on July 1.[30] On July 6, an article reported the remarkable success of a June 26 benefit performance at the Jock Ming On Theater in New York:

> Patriotic banners were hung across the top and the sides of the stage, with flags of China and the United States in the middle. In the theater, two thousand dollars were raised from the flower sale by the American-born Chinese girls, as well as actresses and female foreign students. The actor Xin Jinbiao made the biggest contribution of 50 dollars. Two thousand dollars were raised from the sale of snacks. A Mr. Wu Tai sipped from a bottle of water for which he paid 50 dollars. The ticket and snack sales of the performance combined to raise more than ten thousand dollars. This showed people's high spirit and that the country [China] still has a bright future.[31]

A comparison of the amounts raised in the different cities shows New York's great strength (see table 9.2). This fundraising success resulted from a combination of factors. First, much to the envy of their West Coast counterpart, New York's Chinatown theaters had always been able to charge higher ticket prices and were therefore able to raise more money. Second, the despicably gruesome event, the reports of which were accompanied by horrifying pictures, prompted a strong patriotic fervor. And on the East Coast there were fewer fundraising activities and joint community efforts, so a large part of the community contributed to this initiative. Finally, there were many more Chinese elites in New York holding politically, financially, or intellectually influential positions. The raising of $10,000 in one evening was unparalleled. Even with a smaller population of Chinese that San Francisco had, New York's Chinatown had an active and wealthy community base.[32]

Fundraising was also a front in the rivalry between the theaters in San Francisco, with a rather clear winner. In a June initiative for opera performers to make contributions to the relief fund, the sum raised from performers at the Mandarin ($306) was half of that raised at the Great China. These figures reveal the lean cast of and uncertainty at the Mandarin Theater at that time, as detailed in Chapter 7.[33] Meanwhile, the gravity of China's situation compelled the Chinatowns to continue fundraising. More benefit performances were planned, typically as Sunday matinees. Table 9.2 compiles from newspaper reports the fundraising events of several prominent Chinatown theaters within the span of two months and the amounts raised. The performances at the Los Angeles branches of the Mandarin and the Great China show a continuing gap in their fundraising capabilities. In San Francisco, the Great China Theater, led by Xiyang Nü, also staged a benefit performance on July 12. The performance befittingly featured a contemporary opera based on the Shanghai incident. The leading actress, Huang Xiaofeng, gave a patriotic speech at the intermission. The enthusiastic response was among the largest sums in this theater's fundraising history. Meanwhile, gruesome pictures of the Japanese brutality in Shanghai, and updates of the strike on Chinese newspapers, kept communities across the United States briefed about the difficult situation in China.

Table 9.2. Fundraising performances held for labor strikes in 1925

Date	Theater/troupe	Location	Amount
June 26	Jock Ming On Theater	New York	$10,000+
July 1	Renshou Nian Troupe	Portland	$3,600
July 5	Mandarin Theater	Los Angeles	$1,860
July 12	Great China Theater	Los Angeles	$2,400
July 12	Great China Theater	San Francisco	$3,565
August 16	Mandarin Theater	San Francisco	$4,000+
Total			$25,425+

The Cantonese opera business in China was greatly affected by the general strike. A brief note appearing in July about the Cantonese opera actress Mei Lanfang (not the Peking opera star of the same name) gave a glimpse of its impact on an individual singer.

> Mei Lanfang was very popular for her staging. Previously she could perform four episodes in an evening and earned as much as 70 dollars, which meant 40 dollars net for herself. But since the staged performance was banned in Hong Kong, she could now only appear as a singer at the tea house. Now unable to showcase her performing skills and beauty—leaving her voice to stand alone—her earnings were reduced dramatically. It is said that she had been gathering several other beautiful and talented performers together to leave for San Francisco to perform.[34]

The article gives some sense of the bleak situation in Hong Kong and the increased incentive for actresses to work in the United States, where they could be greeted with enthusiasm and often obtain gifts, large salaries, and high social status. The turmoil at home only intensified their desire to leave. Mei would have her debut in the Mandarin Theater only two months later.[35]

Principal actresses were often featured in fundraisers, either as the leads for performances or as leading contributors. On July 19 a notice in the *Young China* indicated that Xiyang Nü of the Great China Theater alone sold $1,739 worth of tickets, almost one-half of the funds raised by that time. The actresses' charisma, strong ties to the community, and high status, as well as their fan bases, all worked together to increase ticket sales.[36]

An August 9 event, a memorial service for anonymous heroes of the Shanghai killing, brought the theaters together. Staged at the Mandarin Theater, the service featured four moral speeches delivered by the leading actresses—Zhang Shuqin and Huang Xiaofeng—from the two theaters. (The eminence the community accorded the two actresses recalls their high-ranking positions in the Actors' Alliance of Vancouver in 1919.) The newspaper reported that the theater, the final destination of a long memorial parade, was packed, leaving a large crowd waiting outside. On August 16 another benefit was scheduled at the Mandarin, for which Zhang was reported to have personally sold $1,200 worth of tickets, and even the newly arrived Li Zhifang raised $700. The program was to have been a contemporary patriotic title. At the last minute, the patriotic title was paired with a melodramatic opera in order to maintain the entertainment aspect of the program.[37] This was a good move on the theater's part, as the show raised more than $4,000.[38] The status and prowess of these Chinese theaters in the community should not be underestimated; it is hard to imagine such a communal collaboration without their significant draw.[39]

A CAST DOUBLED IN SIZE

As for the Mandarin Theater's immigration battle, positive signs started to appear at the end of July. *Chung Sai Yat Po* on July 24, 1925, noted that the performers had arrived in Seattle and would travel by railroad to San Francisco. Actually, the group had been detained outside Seattle, since negotiations with the Immigration Bureau were still ongoing. The theater was sending away performers to create space within its quota in order to accommodate newcomers. It was in this manner that Li Zhifang, the most famous actress in this group, was granted admission and traveled to San Francisco on July 16. Her debut on July 30 was the first on the Mandarin's stage in nearly two months, an unusually long interval.

A well-established singer, Li Zhifang presented both classic and new repertoire in her nine consecutive days of debut performances. The new opera Li Zhifang performed, her signature *Flower Agony,* was so popular that it returned in just a little over a month. While she shone in the newer repertoire, Li was also well-versed in the classics. On August 5 she sang a classic opera—*Shilin Paying Respects at the Pagoda*—against the rival theater's staging of the same title with its prima donna, Huang Xiaofeng. One can only imagine the difficulty that die-hard opera fans had in choosing between them. Huang was famous, but Li was new and talented. Two other newly arrived performers of the young belle role type were significant as well. The female impersonator Wuxing Deng was a leading actor for a male troupe in China; the Cantonese actress Mei Lanfang was a leading actress in a female troupe in China. In September and October the three dominated the stage, each playing from ten to thirteen shows, while most other newcomers were featured in only two or three leading performances. As the only female impersonator recruited by the Mandarin Theater to that point, Wuxing Deng had to be versatile: he collaborated with an actress of the young belle type, with a male comedian, and with multiple principal singers in an assortment of role types. His appearance created many more gender-bending performances.

As discussed in Chapter 3, the Mandarin's requested increase from forty-five to eighty-five was finally approved in August. Immediately the remaining twenty-one performers in Seattle, mostly actors, were admitted. For the government, the Mandarin Theater's forceful legal stance caused its regulation of Chinese troupes to be more formalized, and their official legal status to be redefined as that of visitors with basic rights. The general dissemination of Cantonese opera in North America also stood to benefit from this decision. Indeed, in Seattle the Chinese Consolidated Benevolent Association had already made arrangements with the Mandarin Theater to borrow the new group of performers for several benefit performances before they traveled to San Francisco.[40] At the Mandarin, August saw only three evenings led by the original prima donna, Zhang Shuqin. The rest of the performances were by the new talents. And in September and October, aside from the most significant appearances of the three new leads and Gongye Chuang, the theater featured a string of two- to four-day debuts.

DIAMOND JUBILEE PARADE

In September 1925, San Francisco's two Chinese opera theaters participated in the spectacular Diamond Jubilee Parade celebrating the seventy-fifth anniversary of California's statehood. An estimated fifty-five thousand people took part in the seventeen-mile parade while more than three hundred thousand people watched. Chinatown offered five decorated floats, three depicting the history of the Chinese in America and two from the world of Chinese opera.[41] The first float, from the Chinese Consolidated Benevolent Association, comprised a locomotive engine coming out of a tunnel with a figure representing railroad tycoon Leland Stanford standing in the middle with two Chinese by his side. It paid tribute to Chinese laborers' contribution to the construction of the central railroad and at the same time alluded to the ironic injustice of the Chinese Exclusion Act. The second float, from the Chinese Chamber of Commerce, depicted a sailboat commemorating the arrival of Chinese in 1848 in the United States. On the float stood Chinese men in classic Chinese attire and *tong gu* hats.

Acknowledging the hardship facing their ancestors, the Chinese Chamber of Commerce celebrated their perseverance and eventual prosperity. The third float, from the organization of Native Sons of the Golden State (created by Chinese who had been born and raised in the United States and later renamed the Chinese American Citizens Alliance), portrayed a gold mine, paying homage to the pioneering Chinese immigrants of the nineteenth century. The fourth was produced by the Great China Theater. Titled "History of Creation as Based on Chinese Legends," the float depicted a legend regarding the goddess Nüwa Shi patching up the sky. This mythic story was made into a popular Cantonese opera as well, and would later be performed in its theater. The final float, by the Mandarin Theater, presented a theatrical piece called *Son to Be Killed at Outer Gate*, one of the eighteen grand classic operas based on the romance between the woman warrior Mu Guiyin and a rival general's son that angered the general. It required a large number of soldiers and generals, and hence was a showy piece with warriors in elaborate costumes. In addition to the decorated floats, spectacular stage props, such as giant lanterns, palace umbrellas, and fans were part of the parade. There was also a dragon parade performed by nineteen men and a Chinese music ensemble of thirty-one members. It was likely the largest event of its kind in years.[42]

Although the parade displayed the theaters' props and wardrobes rather than their musical performances, it nevertheless marked the re-entry of Cantonese opera into San Francisco's public space in the 1920s. The parade's Executive Committee acknowledged the impressive designs, displays, and significance by awarding to the Chinese the first prize in the category of Best Units of Nationals, followed by Russia and France. The honor underscored another landmark event in the 1925 parade: the installation of forty streetlamps of bronze sculpted as golden dragons, designed by the influential lighting engineer W. D'Arcy Ryan, on Grant Avenue in Chinatown.[43] The new streetlamps graced the front of the Mandarin Theater, where it still stands today. At the parade's very public self-presentation of the Chinese community, the presence of two spectacular Chinese theaters reflected the prosperity of the community in San Francisco and the glamour of the theatrical troupes. The floats allowed the theaters to be seen by all, and the streetlamps even led tourists to the Mandarin Theater. The parade might have attracted interested visitors to the theater and dispelled erroneous assumptions about odd, poor, or hideous entertainment.

A NEW ERA

With its increased quota, the Mandarin Theater quickly became a full-fledged troupe. The total number of performers on September 12, 1925, was sixty-six, and by March 26, 1926, it had risen to eighty-four. Between September 1925 and the

Fig. 9.5. Tan Xiufang. May's Photo Studio (courtesy of the Wylie Wong Collection at the Museum of Performance and Design, San Francisco).

end of June 1926 when another six-month permit was up for renewal, fifty-five new performers were brought in.[44] The timing of the quota increase was fortunate because there were many performers available in China.

Tan Xiufang was the first of the wave of famous performers to arrive after the quota increase was approved (see figure 9.5). A fine female singer of the young belle type, she debuted on November 12, 1925, and performed for a full week. On November 27 the actress Nü Muzhen made her debut and also played the lead for seven evenings straight. Though only nineteen years old, Nü must have been quite remarkable: her debut was set against the second performance of the rival theater's most famous new star, Bai Jurong, in his signature opera, *A Scholar Meets His Girlfriend in Disguise*.[45] Like the veteran actor Bai, Nü had also arrived with a case of elaborate costumes of her own, in accordance with tradition and reflecting her status as a highly regarded performer. Being presented against Bai Jurong would be a true test for any performer, a task that even in China, only a handful of performers would be deemed suitable for. Nü Muzhen staged two evenings of newer operas and then performed classic operas such as *Daiyu Burying Flower Petals* and *Shilin Paying Respects at the Pagoda*. Unfortunately, today there is little information about this actress.

Now, only performers of very high caliber would be given leading roles. As the competition between the two theaters intensified, the Mandarin's leading actors were scheduled against those of the Great China Theater. December at the Mandarin saw the arrival of three actors: a young scholar type, a young warrior type, and a comedian type. Still, for this particular month, the Great China Theater seems to have fared better: Bai Jurong triumphed, and he was helped by several other top-tier performers. And Bai, Huang Xiaofeng, and Zihou Qi, all employed by the Great China Theater now, were of the top class in the profession at this time.

The Mandarin adopted a strategy of offering full-cast, spectacular productions and operas that spanned more than one day. For example, on December 10, 1925, the classic opera *Eight Belle Spectacle* starred eight young actresses competing in a talent show. In the same week five more large-scale productions of all types were staged. Unlike the repertoire at the Great China Theater, which celebrated virtuoso performances, the Mandarin Theater leaned toward sheer entertainment, glamour, and crowd-pleasers.

A lengthy opera titled *Ten Belle Spectacle* was staged over the course of seven evenings from December 18 to 27. It was based on a famous folk legend, *Crown Prince Qian Long*, a story from the classic *Romance of Three Kingdoms.* It begins with a coup in which the king of Jin is assassinated and the villain Wang Dun takes his place, forcing the prince to flee into exile. The struggle for power, however, continues, until the prince of Jin returns and takes his rightful place. Intricate story lines make for a lengthy and complicated plot calling for many characters in each of the seven episodes and culminating in a finale with ten leading performers.

Encouraged by the result, in January 1926 the theater produced another famously long historical story, *Losing Red Sack,* in six episodes spread over ten days. The popular story circulated widely as the vernacular muyushu. A comic opera of contemporary affairs, *The Imperial Appeal of Liang Tianlai*, was staged on four consecutive days from January 21 to 24. These grand productions must have been successful, if its rival's immediate imitation was any indication: from January 20 to February 10 the Great China Theater programmed five episodes of *Princess Fox*, a new opera named after the famous character in *Journey to the West* but based on a mystery set in Hong Kong.

Thus began a trend of grand stage productions and multi-episode operas only possible because of the increased quota. The audience's response was not unanimously positive. An article in the *Young China* published in six installments took the theater to task. The critique was that the length of multi-episode grand opera compromised the dramatic effect, filling the opera with superfluous plots or scenes. Instead, it would be preferable to program multiple playlets on one evening.[46] Although such a commentary may reflect only one author's opinion about the subject, its publication immediately after the change in strategy reflected the responsiveness of the audience, showing lively dialogue about opera, and its ultimate relevance to the community's cultural life.

DEPARTURES, SEQUEL OPERAS, AND TICKET PRICES

According to immigration records, nine new performers arrived at the Mandarin in November 1925 and nine more in January 1926. Still more remarkable was the month of February 1926, when twenty-three new performers arrived in Seattle in three groups. This was the largest entry of performers in a single month since the previous August. It made for a spectacular New Year's celebration, with fresh programs every evening. There were daily matinees as well. During the New Year holidays the young scholar actor Chen Shaohua and the young warrior actor Zhou Yurong made their debuts, as did the unusual staging of the playwright Li Wutian, who normally remained behind the scenes. Eleven members of the theater's original troupe departed on the same day, February 20, making space in the quota for the new arrivals. Among them, the couple Jinshan Bing and Xin Guifei were the two most important lead performers; they had led most of the performances the previous April and June when Zhang had gone to Los Angeles.[47] Their departure at the height of the theater's activity was an indication of the quality of the new talent. After a successful performing career in the United States, they would continue to travel between China and North America. By September 1927 they would reemerge in Vancouver, as discussed in Chapter 10.

At the same time, however, the theater's treatment of another couple, Chen Feifeng and Deng Shaohuai, reflected a darker side of its business. Chen was an actress and Deng was a stage manager. After the couple had already boarded the steamship *President Lincoln* for China in February, they were stopped and returned to the port by court order. Conflicting reports about this incident paint an ambiguous picture. One report noted that an unresolved financial problem required their further stay. Another stated that the actress's advanced pregnancy was the cause for what amounted to a medical delay.[48] Later, the Chinese Consolidated Benevolent Association requested Deng's release for the purpose of staging a benefit performance.[49] The bottom line, however, might have been that while Chen was unable to perform, the theater wanted to send the pair away to make room in its quota. Later, the theater's attorney requested that they stay but not be counted toward the quota. In the end, the child was born in early March, although the mother's condition required them to remain in the United States until October. The incident showed, however, the reality for performers who lacked legal status: they were dependent for their legitimacy on the theater.

With the abundance of new talent, the large productions continued at the Mandarin Theater, whose casting choices often included at least four and sometimes up to nine leading performers for one opera. The growing number of large productions, as opposed to operas centering on a few virtuoso performers, increased the need for dramatists at the theater; the arrival of the playwright Li Renzhou in mid-February was timely. Increasingly, even operas centering on one or two virtuoso performers began to be produced in episodes. Many operas were produced in three episodes including the popular new comic opera *Steal the Shadow and Imitate the Shape* (February 21–23), the historical drama *Yingyang Mountain* (March 3–5), and the new actress Chen Xiufang's debut, *Beauty's Tear* (March 9–11). The dramatist Li himself joined the actors on stage for the March 3 opening of *Yingyang Mountain*. There was a rush to recruit even stage dramatists. As the Great China Theater engaged the top-notch Pang Yifeng in June, the Mandarin Theater brought in an additional dramatist, Wu Jingchi, in November. The Mandarin now had three playwrights.

The intense competition between the two theaters could have led to a price war. But with the expense of lavish new productions, it was in both theaters' interests to stabilize ticket prices. Chinatown theaters routinely sold discount tickets for late admission, making opera more affordable to those in the lower stratum of the economy; now, this practice would be regulated.[50] On March 8 the *Young China* published a joint notice by the two theaters announcing the unifying of different tiers of discount ticket prices for multiple parts of the evening, as summarized in figure 9.6. The notice also pointed out that the unified price for discount tickets would ensure that the shareholders' interest remained intact.[51] The two theaters in New York made a similar move after their competition led to a severe reduction of ticket prices.

JOINT NOTICE FROM THE GREAT CHINA AND MANDARIN THEATERS

Regarding Time and Prices of Discount Ticket, effective 7 p.m. March 6

- Door opening at 7 pm
- At 9:15 pm

  Box seat $1 Special seat $.75 First-class seat $.75 Second-class seat $.75
  Third-class seat $.50 Fourth-class seat $.25
- At 10:30 pm

  Box seat $.50 Special seat $.35 First-class seat $.35 Second-class seat $.25
  Third-class seat $.25 Fourth-class seat $.25

Fig. 9.6. A translation of the joint notice of theater ticket prices, March 8, 1926.

A THEATER OF ACTRESSES, AND THE VOGUE OF CROSS-DRESSING PERFORMANCES

With February's arrival of new performers, the Mandarin Theater's repertoire emphasized actresses even more, often jointly featuring three newly arrived females in grand productions. The most significant addition to the Mandarin's cast in 1926 was the actress Mudan Su (figure 9.7), whom we encountered in the introduction of this book through Wayson Choy's memoir. In China the twenty-nine-year-old Mudan Su was recognized as a leading performer of one of the most famous female troupes. After her debut in San Francisco on April 19, 1926, she would become a favorite actress in the Chinatown theaters of North America for years to come, finally settling in New York. Mudan Su was adored by the audience as soon as she arrived. After a three-evening production of *Gathering at Zhu-Ai*, her debut continued for fourteen consecutive evenings, the repertoire showing a multitude of talents and special skills. At the Great China Theater, two evenings with its top performer Bai Jurong, several evenings of the programming of famous excerpts, and the debut performances of the star female impersonator Xiao Dingxiang were all part of a frenzied effort to counter the popularity of Mudan Su.

That year, Mudan Su was featured as the sole leading performer in forty-eight shows and as one of the two leading actresses in seventeen other. Only the actress Nü Muzhen came close to that level of exposure. Also, the programming generally shifted after her success. For weeks following Mudan Su's debut, no actors were staged as the lead; instead, the young belle roles largely reigned, and when there were large productions, actresses were typically featured as the leads as well. The Mandarin Theater refashioned itself as a theater of actresses.

Fig. 9.7. Actress Mudan Su, cross-dressed as a young scholar. May's Photo Studio (courtesy of the Wylie Wong Collection at the Museum of Performance and Design, San Francisco).

The large productions were made still more interesting by Mudan Su's frequent performance of cross-dressing roles. She and Nü Muzhen were often featured as the leading couple, with Mu playing the male and Nü the female. Yet Mu was unlike the usual male impersonator in all-female troupes such as Zheng Huikui. Photos of her in male costume appeared in the playbills, and her singing in the style of *daho*, a natural voice used instead of the higher and nasal voice of female roles, was often noted. In fact, with the theater's general shortage of actors for young male roles—principal actor Jinshan Bing having departed in February and other actors not being of the same caliber—the theater came to rely on actresses for some trouser roles. All through May the pairing of Mudan Su and Nü Muzhen appeared in the program. The regular staging of the cross-dressed Mudan Su underscored the rise of the trend.

Gender-bending on stage was indeed in vogue and was an important source of theatrical excitement, as seen in the September programming. When both theaters staged the classic opera *Daiyu Burying Flower Petals* on the same evening—actress Nü Muzhen at the Mandarin and female impersonator Xiao Dingxiang at the Great China—it might seem a straightforward comparison of actress and female impersonator.[52] Nü was a virtuosic actress of young belle roles, never cross-dressing to play a man, but the Mandarin spiced up the romantic tragedy with the cross-dressing of a renowned actor, Qiansui He, as a comical maid. And though Xiao Dingxiang, playing the melancholy female protagonist, most certainly would not "cross-dress" to play male roles, the Great China cast a beautiful young actress as the protagonist for part of the evening, pairing with the male lead. After the female protagonist died, Xiao Dingxiang reemerged to play another prominent female role in the opera. Gender-bending was incorporated somewhere on the Great China's stage, but at least both leads played strictly female roles. However, when the opera *Amorous Emperor* was staged at both theaters, with actress Mudan Su at the Mandarin and actor Bai Jurong at the Great China, matters were more complicated.[53] Whereas the Great China touted Bai's portrayal of this famously romantic emperor from the Tang Dynasty, the point of attraction for the Mandarin was Mudan Su in a cross-dressing performance, flirtatiously courting fellow actresses. Mudan Su already claimed the young male role as one of her specialties, and the theater constructed an elaborate Chinese bed with embroidered drapery for a chamber scene to underscore the intimacy with realism. And since Bai Jurong was a star of the young scholar type, winning audiences by traditional means, *Amorous Emperor* was a good opera for this rivalry because these very different performers would have otherwise defied close comparison.

When Fengqing Yao, a new actor of the young scholar role type, arrived, the Mandarin Theater finally took a break from the eight-week spell of featuring mainly actresses. A week later, Chen Yinglin, of the same role type, made his debut against the staging of a newly arrived actress at the Great China. Yet that evening's programs vividly reflected the fad of cross-dressing (see the advertisement in the *Young China* reproduced in figure 9.8). The next evening's program at the Great China followed suit, the playbill stating, "Bai Jurong will cross-dress as a young female and sing with female voice."[54] In a flurry of similar casting choices, the aesthetics

Great China Theater	**Mandarin Theater**
Debut! Famous actress of young belle type: Xue Juefei Opera: *Tale of One Enmity and Three Grudges* —led by Xue Juefei	Debut! Renowned actor of young scholar type: Chen Yinglin Opera: *Ying Hua Yan Ying* —led by Chen Yinglin
Notice! Xue Juefei will cross-dress performing the male role	Notice! Mudan Su will cross-dress performing the male role and sing in the dahou style; Chen Pimei will cross-dress performing as the nanny

Fig. 9.8. Translation of playbills of the Mandarin and Great China theaters, June 14, 1926.

of gender-crossing had captured the fancy of both theaters. Even regular debuts or performances of top stars such as Bai Jurong now had to be spiced up with some cross-dressing.

Comic acting was the theaters' next major attraction. Though the Mandarin had many stellar performers, the actor Qiansui He, who arrived at the end of August 1926, was a top-tier performer of comic roles. Regarding his performance with the highly regarded troupe Da Ronghua, the Shanghai newspaper *Shen Bao* noted in 1924, "He has a masculine strong voice, a clear reciting style, and his clever and humorous words cracked up the audience. A truly top choice for comic roles."[55] Two of his fellow performers from Da Ronghua, Xiao Likang, the female impersonator and playwright, and Zhou Yulin, were now associated with the Great China. Skill in improvisation was the key to such role types. A week later a commentary noted, "Qiansui He is funny and talented, exceptionally humorous, yet always in a tasteful rather than ostentatious manner. What is special is when he performed, no matter the characters or roles, his lyrics or words were filled with satire and an uplifting message, offering a critical view of the society. His utterance was refined and relevant, his words humorous, all skills of veteran performers. An extraordinary performer."[56]

The Mandarin Theater had not seen an actor of comic roles of such caliber until now, two years after its opening. Upon arriving Qiansui He led the programming for a week, bringing a great deal of recent popular repertoire to the Chinatown stage. His signature opera *Steal the Shadow and Imitate the Shape*, a hit since it first appeared shortly before 1920, was staged for three non-consecutive evenings in the first week, a triumph that could not be matched by the comic actor of the rival theater, Shezi Ying. That week, the Great China stayed away from the comic repertoire. The Mandarin escalated its recruitment of top comic performers.

A MONTH OF COMIC OPERA REPERTOIRE

In November a group of sixteen performers from the Mandarin Theater arrived in Seattle.[57] The largest group to travel there since February, it was remarkable for its inclusion of nearly all role types: bearded warrior, young scholar, elderly scholar, young belle, young warrior, and cross-dressing comedians for both female and male roles. Responding to the popular demand for comic repertoire, the theater brought in two top-notch cross-dressing comic performers—actor Zihou Sen for female roles and actress Zheng Huikui for male and comic roles—for a month at the Mandarin.

Figure 9.9 reproduces one scene from the famous opera *The Humiliation of the Rickshaw Man,* popular as early as 1910.[58] The opera tells the story of an heir of a wealthy family who depletes the fortune by gambling and ends up a rickshaw man. His wife hides some of the family fortune away, and after seeing that he is truly contrite and transformed, helps him regain a dignified life. The scenery integrated painted backdrops with a replica of an elaborate pavilion and tree trunks, adding naturalism to the staging. Real objects such as the rickshaw (popular in the early twentieth century in China), as well as conical bamboo hat and straw sandals, were incorporated to invoke a vivid sense of drama. The Belasco-esque staging juxtaposed traditional period costumes with a real vehicle for public transportation in modern urban China to comic effect.[59] Zheng Huikui, a male impersonator, plays the cross-dressed scholar role type, shown at center stage. Next to her is the wife, whose wisdom and virtue saved the family, played by the stellar actress Nü Muzhen.

In China, Zheng Huikui had been known for her versatility, particularly in comic roles. She was the first actress of such role types to appear in North America. Among her comic roles were caricatures such as the lowly male character with torn or patched clothes, or the middle-class male character with a pompous look; others were regular characters experiencing colorful encounters and events. For the subsequent months at the Mandarin Theater, she would be joining the leading actresses of young belle roles in many productions, approximating a female-troupe type of performance.

The multifaceted performance of comic roles had become popular in Cantonese opera. Zheng Huikui's work was much in keeping with that of the famous stars of this type in southern China such as Ma Shizeng, who would perform at the Mandarin in 1931 (see chapter 10). One of Zheng Huikui's debut performances at the Mandarin was the first episode of *Fighting Bride*, a signature opera of Ma in Hong Kong. The plot allowed Zheng, playing the prince, to be a multi-faceted character.

She was prominent in a scene of faking madness, a scene of military preparation, a scene in which she was disguised as an old lady, and, of course, a romantic scene. In addition to superb acting required for such a convoluted plot, many scenes

Fig. 9.9. Scene from *The Humiliation of the Rickshaw Man* with Zheng Huikui (center) and Nü Muzhen (to her right). May's Photo Studio (courtesy of the Wylie Wong Collection at the Museum of Performance and Design, San Francisco).

involved extensive singing as well, for which she was highly praised. The playbill noted her singing in the style of Ma Shizeng, but better. Unlike Mudan Su, Zheng had not been trained for young belle roles. There was always an anticipation of surprise and transgressions of all sorts, as well as a comical effect instead. Her "rebellious" performance was part of her persona as an actress, and audiences loved it.

The new comic actor Zihou Sen, a female impersonator, also debuted in early December. The forty-five-year-old actor was at the height of his career, having always been engaged with top troupes in China. Zihou Sen was advertised in San Francisco as a comedian who played both female warrior and young belle types, an interesting hybrid that had recently risen to prominence. Such comic roles required both good vocal skills and martial arts techniques. Zihou Sen's stage name already referred to his special skills in falsetto singing (*Zihou* literally means "young vocal cord").

The opera in which he made his debut, *Duo-Nanny and Fortune Telling*, featured him as a young belle, a free-thinking young woman, and Zheng Huikui as the male lead. The opera raises many interesting issues of gender on the stage. First, Zihou Sen played a young belle type, beautiful yet unconventional. As reflected by the stage picture on the playbill, it was an eccentric and nonconformist yet positive female image. Second, Zheng Huikui's role, the typical goof-off, featured comic acts—such as liking gambling, using vulgar language, and flirting improperly with young women—that one expects of a comic actor. Third, a female impersonator and a male impersonator portray a married couple, for which the reversed performers' genders resulted in double cross-dressing. Fourth, this comic opera actually does not have many humorous characters. It is the encounters and situations that bring about comic moments. Operas with such complicated twists were very common during this time, as they helped create frantic and sentimental moments.

In mid-December another famous comic actor, Doupi Mei, came. He and Qiansui He, who arrived in September, were two of the most prominent comic actors in the Cantonese opera profession at the time. Doupi Mei's annual salary was more than $10,000, according to one playbill. The opera of his December 16 debut, titled *Reform through Pragmatism/Detective Seeking the Truth,* showed another style of comic plot (see figure 9.10). A young scholar named Zhang urges his cousin's recent widow Chen to remarry, but she declines, holding steadfast to society's moral standard for women. Meanwhile, another scholar, Huang (played by Doupi Mei), and his friend discuss their ambitions for studying abroad. Later the widow Chen invites monks to chant prayers for her deceased husband, but gets murdered and beheaded by the lecherous head monk (played by actress Zheng Huikui). Zhang is immediately a suspect because he once urged her to remarry. The idiotic judge orders him to produce the missing head. By this time, the young scholar Huang, and a lady named Kong (played by Mudan Su) have both finished their studies abroad and returned home. At an inn, they are drawn toward each other, though they are too shy to express their affection. So instead they start a flirtatious contest of new

金山 大舞臺最新著名男女班 正埠

The Mandarin Theatre, 1021 Grant Ave., San Francisco, Cal.

◉十二月十六號（禮拜四）下午六点半鐘開台

○粵省唯一男丑生豆皮梅即晚登台

聽名 醒世 良劇 （維新求實學）（偵探究真情） 男丑生 豆皮梅 唯一首本 全班拍演

豆皮梅

○大注意豆皮梅化裝扮僕夫訪案

豆皮梅

Fig. 9.10. Playbill, *Reform through Pragmatism/Detective Seeking the Truth*, Mandarin Theater, featuring two views of Doupi Mei, December 16, 1926 (courtesy of the Ethnic Studies Library, University of California, Berkeley).

tunes. (This scene allowed Doupi Mei and Mudan Su to show off their singing skills.) Kong's uncle, after learning of Huang's talent, arranges their marriage and makes Huang a governor. When the murder suspect Zhang is brought before him, Huang suspects his innocence. After consulting with his wife Kong, he disguises himself as a servant to investigate and ends up correcting the wrong by punishing the judge and the villainous monk.

This opera required Doupi Mei to play a young scholar, a governor, and a servant. The playbill shows him in the plain clothes of a servant on the right and in the formal attire of a governor on the left in order to highlight disguise as a central plot line and point of interest. The vicious monk was played by Zheng Huikui, bringing comical twists to the opera. Though the plot allowed various comic moments to be elaborated, the idea of modernity and progress also played an important role: practical knowledge learned overseas was positively pitted against the less desirable tradition, associated with women and superstition. The drama reflected a general wish for social reform shared by contemporary Chinese both in China and overseas since the May Fourth movement of 1919, while at the same time producing many opportunities for satire and funny moments. Convoluted plots such as this provided much-needed comic relief for the audience. For weeks Doupi Mei's photos appeared on the playbills, signaling the high demand for his performances of comedies and satires.

CHAPTER 10

A THEATER OF ACTRESSES

The Mandarin Theater, 1927–1928

So busy was the Mandarin in gaining a foothold in the San Francisco opera scene that it might not have considered as competition a "Chinese opera" presentation in the city in 1926. The opera *Fay-Yen-Fah,* written by San Francisco's own Joseph Redding and Charles Templeton Crocker, was given its U.S. premiere by Gaetano Merola, founding director of the San Francisco Grand Opera Company at the city's Columbia Theater. Most likely, though, both Chinese theaters took note of the great spectacle that had attracted the high society and news media. With choreography by a youthful George Balanchine and with Sergei Diaghilev's Ballets Russes (the latter having danced in the opera's world premiere in Monte Carlo on February 26, 1925), and opulent costumes and scenery, the extravagant work was considered a great success. Chinese opera proved to have immense potential, and the Mandarin Theater would step out of its boundaries and move in the direction of grand spectacle as well.

And the time was just right for a bold move. After a triumphant first year, a tumultuous second year, and a quick but cautious expansion in the third year, the Mandarin had an established relationship with the immigration officials and had grown to be a significant cultural institution. By the beginning of 1927 it operated a branch in Los Angeles, had troupes in Mexicali and elsewhere, and had built a close relationship for the exchange of performers with the Jock Ming On Theater in New York. This year's offerings would be the most substantial, both for the quality of its stars and for the scale of its productions, since it opened its doors.

The first day of 1927 was celebrated with a matinee performance of episodes of a farcical comic opera and a spirited warrior opera. The evening performance featured the debut of a young actress, Xue Feifei, and programs were printed on the playbills in red ink as auspicious sign for the New Year. On January 3 the Mandarin featured the debut of its first star actress of the year, the eighteen-year-old Tan Lanqing, who had arrived in Seattle from China only a week earlier.[1] Her photos, in modern Chinese dress, brightened the daily playbills for the full week of her debut. Delicate and beautiful, she had a grace and fresh talent that immediately captured the audiences' attention. From an early age, Tan had worked hard at her métier as an opera singer, traveling to Havana's Chinese theater with her actress sisters at the tender age of fourteen. Now she was on the ascent. Figure 10.1 reproduces the playbill for the second day of her debut, featuring *Yielding to the Empress*. The new opera was the story of a young woman becoming honored as the emperor's concubine by virtue of her curing his mother, only to be forced to become a nun by the empress accidentally. Through her wit and perseverance, she overcomes the obstacle and is awarded the title of Lady. The interesting production had convoluted plot twists to add interest and included Tan's special version of the popular *fanxian erhuang* aria (the style discussed in Chapter 5) and new songs. This was her second trip to the Americas.[2] Tan would later become one of the most innovative actresses of the 1930s, noted for incorporating vernacular songs into Cantonese opera. When the ban on mixed troupes was lifted in Hong Kong in 1933, she became the first actress to co-star with the famous actor Ma Shizeng.

金山 大舞臺最新著名男女班 正埠

正月四號（禮拜二）下午六点半鐘開台

讓昭陽

譚蘭卿

Fig. 10.1. Playbill, *Yielding to the Empress*, Mandarin Theater, with Tan Lanqing, January 4, 1927 (courtesy of the Ethnic Studies Library, University of California, Berkeley).

After the first week, Tan shared the stage regularly with Mudan Su, who was still a leading prima donna. Featured often in romantic repertoire, the two frequently played young belles and also played a stage couple with Mudan Su taking the role of a young scholar, for example, in *Nocturnal Mourning of White Lotus* (January 11). They dominated the stage until the end of January, when another popular young belle actress, Nü Muzhen, returned from a six-week residence with the Mandarin's Los Angeles branch. With her return, the Mandarin now had three top-tier actresses. It was increasingly distinguishing itself as a theater of actresses. At the same time, faced with intense competition from the Great China Theater, the Mandarin also expanded the scale of its productions with larger casts.

GRAND PRODUCTIONS FROM NEW PLAYWRIGHTS

The first step to creating a grand production was tighter control, which needed the expert hand of a good playwright. As noted in Chapter 9, the dramatist Wu Jingchi arrived in November 1926. By December, Wu had produced his first opera in San Francisco, *Wrenched Dragon and Harrowing Phoenix*, which showcased star performers. He took two novel approaches. First, whereas the program usually heeded the tradition of having the most famous performer sing the signature aria to conclude the evening, Wu took things a step further in planning who would sing when. The playbill's description served both as a tight control on the length of each episode and a detailed guide so audiences would not miss their favorite scenes and performers.

> At 8 P.M. Mudan Su sings a song of fraternal bonds; 9:30 P.M. Fengqing Jian sings a romantic song of nuptial consummation; 10 P.M. Fengqing Yao and Nü Muzhen join in a duet reminiscing about a beautiful lady and languishing in lovesick melancholy; 11 P.M. Zheng Huikui sings a lament by the tomb; then Mudan Su sings the *fanxian* aria.[3]

Such an unusually precise program might have proven difficult to follow, considering the improvisational nature of Cantonese opera. The idea was never repeated. Nevertheless, it reflects the control that the young dramatist sought over his creation, as well as his effort to formalize the practice. According to Eva Chan, who lived above the theater for quite a while, significant actresses generally began singing at 10 P.M. and could sometimes sing for half an hour.[4] Although fans might be pleased with performers' extended virtuosity, a playwright like Wu wanted no more drawn-out playlets early in the evening to force later ones to be compressed and rushed, a pitfall about which a critic had complained just months earlier. This new mode of programming, though not very realistic, was clearly a corrective.

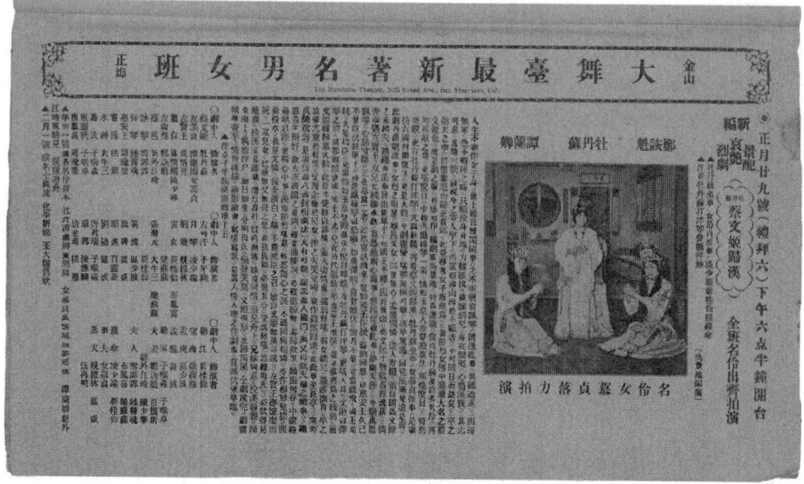

金山 大舞臺最新著名男女班 正印

正月廿九號（禮拜六）下午六点半鐘開台

新編 景配 哀艷烈劇 蔡文姬歸漢

全班名伶出齊拍演

Fig. 10.2. Playbill, *Lady Cai Returning to Han,* Mandarin Theater, with Tan Lan-qing (*left*), Mudan Su (*center*), and Mei Lanfang (*right*) (courtesy of the Ethnic Studies Library, University of California, Berkeley).

Second, Wu planned an elaborate production of great complexity given on January 15 and 29 (see figure 10.2).[5] The playbill for Wu's new grand opera *Lady Cai Returning to Han* listed a cast of fifty-two roles, exceeding the usual number by twenty. The new opera was based on a familiar historical episode, which allowed ample opportunity for sentimental and emotional moments. Actress Mudan Su took the complex eponymous role, beginning as a young maiden of the Han nation abducted by the foreign Hu nation, becoming its king's beloved wife, and then a mother to a son and a daughter. Yet Lady Cai longs for the home of her youth, and her desire to return to Han does not diminish with time. Finally the king grants her wish, the outcome of a convoluted contest on the yangqin (Chinese hammered dulcimer). After sadly bidding farewell, she leaves on a boat. Her dispirited children follow on another boat, trying to change her mind. (The boat-chasing scene here was a famous paichang in Cantonese opera adopted in another opera discussed in relation to Figure 6.2). Lady Cai, desolate and forlorn from having severed ties to her family, throws herself into the river and drowns.

Though the melodrama did not necessarily require grand spectacle, Wu filled the production with spectacular scenes: the yangqin competition at the king's palace, a procession of the full cast (when Lady Cai and the king bid farewell to each other), a cart-pushing and -riding routine, an elaborate boat-chasing scene, and a ghost scene (when the children come upon Lady Cai's body in the water). The elaborate production was embraced by audiences and returned to the stage only two weeks later. The latter production also included the newly returned Nü Muzhen doubling Tan's role as the daughter, presumably displaying her renowned acrobatic skill.

Another opera of Wu's creation, *Victory and Defeat of Reviving the Han Dynasty* incorporated elements from Peking opera and trendy Shanghai drama. The opera, based on familiar characters from the famous historical novel *Romance of the Three Kingdoms*, featured Mudan Su in the leading trouser role as Han Xian, a young warrior.[6] However, Wu created thirty-six roles to be played by thirteen performers. The theater provided the audiences with a detailed diagram of the roles and performers on the playbill to navigate the complexity. This was necessary because many primary performers crossed over to play other role types. While theaters often featured a performer playing two or more minor roles in the same opera, seldom was this practice applied to multiple performers. One might imagine that most audiences were familiar with the story on which the opera was based, so it was probably not too confusing. However, the playbill's meticulously cross-referenced list of the cast remains unique and is not found in any other surviving playbills. The scheme probably proved to be too complicated to have a good dramatic effect.

A visionary and innovative playwright, Wu made significant contributions to the theater, as the frequent advance announcements of his grand productions suggest. The Chinese New Year (January 23) featured a festive production with four leading actresses.[7] Increasingly, the playbills used photos of scenery or poses particular to the evening's productions instead of portraits.

Wu's grand dramatic creations might not have generated such enthusiasm had it not been for the immensely popular and talented actresses at the theater, especially the omnipresent and versatile Mudan Su. Most of the announcements of Wu's new dramas specified Mu's particular roles in them. Occasionally, grand productions conceived and performed by Mudan Su herself, such as *Mudan Su Laments the Dead Spirit,* similarly were announced weeks in advance. Except for one night featuring actor Fengqing Jian in an acrobatic display using two swords, the month of January almost exclusively featured female leads, whether in young belle roles, young scholar roles, or comic roles. It quickly became a recognizable way in which the Mandarin Theater distinguished itself from the Great China Theater.

SUPERSTAR LI XUEFANG

The cast of actresses was further buttressed by the February arrival of the ultimate actress of the era, Li Xuefang. She was preceded by her younger sister, the eighteen-year-old Li Xuefei, who had already issued multiple recordings on the Victor Record label, having sailed from China to San Francisco via Honolulu.[8] Billed as an actress of a newer role type combining female warrior and young belle, Li Xuefei made her debut at the Mandarin Theater on February 7. Though it had been delayed for a week due to the flu, it lasted for nearly two weeks, interrupted on only one evening by a returning grand opera featuring Mudan Su. With a nice singing voice, she was one of the few actresses whose recordings were widely available in U.S. Chinatowns. She brought to the stage a kind of repertoire that the Mandarin had not seen. These operas (both new and old) either featured female warriors in challenging acrobatic scenes or young belles in highly choreographed, complex dances influenced by the newer trends in Peking opera. Her successful debut prompted the Great China Theater to feature, one after the other, signature repertoire by its top performers: Xin Zhu, Bai Jurong, and Xiyang Nü. Li Xuefei's appearances heightened the community's anticipation for her older sister. In order to sate that appetite, toward the end of her debut she staged two of her sister's signature operas, which would appear on the same stage just a month later: *Shilin Paying Respects at the Pagoda* and *Twilight Scarlet Tears*.

At the end of February, newspapers reported Li Xuefang's itinerary and imminent arrival with increasing frequency.[9] The publicity reflected the high expectations of both the community and the theater. As was usual for a celebrity, Li's voyage was leisurely. Having sailed from China on the ocean liner *Empress of Canada* on January 27, Li and her companion arrived at Vancouver, and then took the coastal steamship *Princess Charlotte*, reaching Seattle on February 13. Finally admitted at the port on February 16, they arrived in San Francisco three days later.[10] The twenty-four-day voyage exceeded the time necessary for this journey, which was about a week. It is highly probable that she gave performances on the way, yet no evidence has surfaced thus far. In any case, her sponsor in the United States was the Mandarin Theater, as recorded in immigration documents. Her bond was put up by the theater, and her

Fig. 10.3. Li Xuefang, photograph from pamphlets printed at the Mandarin Theater (courtesy of Ren Fan).

salary was $36,000. The twenty-seven-year-old Li claimed to have retired from the stage, and her U.S. visit was, typically, reported in China as personal travel, her staging being mostly serendipity for the community.[11] This might explain why Li's presentation at the Mandarin was comfortably spaced. In general, singers rushed to their debut performances almost as soon they arrived and continued for a week or two as the leads. They were seldom given time to rest after the trans-Pacific journey. Li, on the other hand, was not subjected to such a rush. And the confidence and glamour evident in her various pictures showed that she came as a star.

On March 7, two weeks after her arrival in San Francisco, Li Xuefang debuted at the Mandarin Theater. Special pamphlets were printed to commemorate the occasion. That evening, Li was heard in her signature opera, *Shilin Paying Respects at the Pagoda*, with which she had become famous ten years earlier.[12] It contains the famous jita aria discussed in Chapter 5. Her singing was generally considered an example of the highest distinction since the late 1910s. Captured on numerous recordings, it remains significant in the history of Cantonese opera. Co-starring with Mudan Su in the leading male role, Li received roaring applause from the full house.[13] In the rival theater, Bai Jurong's staging of his signature opera that evening was an attempt to counter Li's long-awaited debut. On her second evening Li featured *Daiyu Burying Flower Petals*, another classic young belle opera, again with Mudan Su playing the male lead.[14] The next two evenings saw her in two other signature operas, *Cao Dajia* and *Misery Love*. For every opera, *Chung Sai Yat Po* reported in detail the performances, highlights, and audience responses.[15] The original plan was for Li, after four performances, to leave for the East Coast. Yet that was clearly not enough to accommodate the audience's enthusiasm; the theater extended the engagement, and Li ended up staging three more performances: *Shadow of Lady Mei*, *Birth and Departure of Green Jade*, and *Twilight Scarlet Tears*.[16] Altogether, Li gave seven performances during this appearance in San Francisco.

Exquisite pamphlets with heavy glossy paper were devoted to each of the seven operas Li performed at the theater. Each pamphlet begins with a brief, mythologizing biography, describing her modest yet virtuous origin and linking her diligence and devotion for the opera profession to her patriotism and loyalty. The biography is followed by many fine photographs, both in stage wardrobe and modern clothes, and then by pages of laudatory poems or prose (see figure 10.3). In several, the lyrics and melody types were included. These booklets, crafted with care and evident admiration for the prima donna, were offered to the theater's most prized patrons. A brief essay in one of the pamphlets revealed the high regard for her artistic accomplishments:

> While in Canton, I went to Li Xuefang's performances at the theaters frequently. Attending her performance of the same repertoire multiple times does not diminish the

> enjoyment of seeing her art each time; it is never something the audience could be tired of. Her excellent singing is unparalleled in Cantonese opera. In *Twilight Scarlet Tear*, at the scene where her character learned of the assassination of her parents, she expressed such genuine dismay and loneliness, a heart-wrenching performance; at the scene of paying respect at the tomb, she appeared in plain clothes with barely any make-up, as ethereal as if she were descending from the sky, and she sang with visceral sorrow in her famous *fanxian*-style aria. In *Cao Dajia*, she conveyed the beauty of the aristocrat lady with utter grace, and her singing of a *fanxian* aria lasted over an hour. The performance of *fanxian* arias is her special strength; the clarity and roundness of her tone, and the crisp and full diction of her voice are extraordinary. As for the audiences, a fraction was social dignitaries and literati, who could always be seen at her performances. In my view, even polished up with refinement—Li Xuefang had perfectly executed make up, with excellent pearl necklace and fine scenery—she would not have attracted such a loyal following, if not for her truly extraordinary skills and talent.[17]

As noted by Yong Chen in his study of the significance of the performance, an opera such as *Twilight Scarlet Tears* had additional meaning for the community. In it Li Xuefang would depict the scenario of a Chinese American returning home too late to find parents already deceased.[18] Li's voice was pure, elegant, and capable of sweetness as well as melancholy; she put its expressive quality at the service of sentiments so close to the heart. Her success signaled a beauty of cultural expression beyond the aural or visual aspects alone. This made her so famous that Peking opera star Mei Lanfang made a point of attending her critically acclaimed performance in Shanghai.[19]

Li Xuefang's performance of seven operas over ten days demonstrated a wide range of skills. An actress who was famous for virtuosic vocal skills typically stayed away from complex acrobatic movement on stage. It was somewhat surprising, then, that, as a newspaper noted, in the fifth performance, *Shadow of Lady Mei*, she featured a special dance.[20] Li Xuefang, as part of the first generation of female virtuosi, had a unique place, one that emphasized feminine beauty, vocal skills, and singing styles, as well as certain role types. Her successors never surpassed her legacy of pure femininity.

As we will see, this was merely the beginning of Li's prolonged stay in North America. She moved in the transnational performing network with much fluidity. After appearing at the Mandarin Theater Li departed for the East Coast, and on April 22 re-emerged on the stage at the Yong Ni Shang Theater in New York.[21] Her itinerary would take her to Cuba and Mexico in subsequent years. Later in 1927, after appearing in New York and Havana in April and May, she would return to the stage of the Mandarin as the main attraction for the Thanksgiving and New Year's holidays, between which she made a brief trip to Los Angeles and Mexicali as well.

Li's time on Chinatown stage deepened the influence of opera on the community. Actresses like her became idols for many Chinese American girls, as evidenced by the collection of their pictures in scrapbooks. Still, few commanded the extraordinary respect that Li Xuefang did. Even in her absence, she resonated in powerful ways with the audience by means of references, nostalgic notes, recordings, and news reports of her whereabouts.

RESIDENCY OF GUAN YINGLIAN

Because the community adored opera actresses, the Mandarin continued to engage more. Some of them could be characterized as the second generation of top-tier actresses whose age was typically between seventeen and twenty. Li Xuefang, twenty-seven years old, had been the prima donna of a top all-female troupe, taking it to great fame in the early 1920s; the second generation of prima donnas at the theater included her sister Li Xuefei and Huang Xuemei. Li Xuefei, having made her debut in February, continued performing throughout the year there. In her debut on July 21, Huang Xuemei, arriving from Seattle, was billed as the most important successor to the famed Li Xuefang. Her week-long debut performance featured several works never heard on this stage such as *Breaking Lingzhi Mushroom*. The seventeen-year-old actress was already well regarded and had performed at trendy Shanghai theaters. For her debut week the playbills were printed in red ink to highlight the occasion.[22]

Having a stronger cast also made Mandarin Theater a more powerful advocate for community causes. As Christianity became an important influence on the second-generation Chinese—through parochial schools or the associated Chinese-language schools—Chinese theater came to represent an important cultural link valued by missionaries. It was no small irony, because Christian missionaries had previously tried to banish Chinese theaters from the community. In February 1927 the Chinese Catholic mission St. Mary's School (a parochial school with a Chinese after-school program) organized a ten-day lantern festival that drew over six thousand spectators.[23] Chinese theaters had an important role in this event. It began with a parade at which dignitaries gave speeches, and San Francisco mayor James Rolph Jr. crowned the Lantern Queen elected by the community. Lantern floats followed, divided into ten different categories. Each of the theaters offered a decorated float (*Chang'Er Flying to the Moon* by the Mandarin Theater and *A Fairy Maiden Scatters Flowers* for the Great China). Both portrayed ethereal goddess or fairy figures in some sort of celestial sphere, such as the moon. The scene painter Xu Fengbo from the Great China Theater designed and constructed the showpiece Lantern Queen's float. In addition, on every evening of the lantern festival the students put on a presentation of Chinese costumes, showcasing clothes borrowed from the wardrobes of the theaters. The event also drew assistance from Catholic youth and women's associations, the Native Sons of the Golden State, Chinatown Boy Scouts, the Nam Cham Chinese school ensemble, and others.[24] Both theaters, as well as Xu, received gold or silver plaques as tokens of appreciation.[25]

This harmonious relation was a remarkable turn, considering that only three years earlier Father Bradley of Old St. Mary's Church had strongly opposed the opening of the Mandarin Theater.[26] Now the teachers at St. Mary's School not only had the students don opera costumes in order to emulate the period drama of Cantonese opera, but also drew on the resources and influences of the theaters to support the school. The lively and auspicious presence of the Mandarin Theater, as well as patronage from leading Chinese merchants, contributed to this change of general attitude. Community dignitaries such as Lew Hing and his daughters built spacious homes on Lakeshore Avenue in Oakland. They would have regular opera performances in the houses, and their children—Chinese Americans of the second or third generation—would also learn to sing opera.[27]

In October 1927 another actress of the second generation, Lin Baoqing, arrived at the Mandarin Theater. She was a sister of the famous actress Lin Qimei (Suzhou Mei), who was considered the only actress parallel to Li Xuefang in fame and accomplishment during this decade. These two prima donnas were often compared as they each had led a troupe that came to fame in the early 1920s. Their distinctive styles became models for later actresses. On one hand was Li Xuefang, whose extraordinary voice, musical skill, and expressive singing of the melancholy of young belle characters symbolized the quintessential feminine ideal; on the other was Lin Qimei, whose brilliant interpretation and acting and extraordinary physical dexterity including acrobatic movements and warrior fighting scenes greatly expanded the image of the feminine on stage. Lin's sister Lin Baoqing's staging was said to emanate from that tradition, reflected in her choice of repertoire.

The year's end brought the return of a familiar name: Guan Yinglian, formerly of the Le Wannian troupe in Vancouver (1921–1923) and the Lun Hop Company (1923–1924). Guan had last appeared in San Francisco at the Crescent Theater as its leading actress and then married. In early 1925 she returned to China after performing in Los Angeles, Mexico, and Honolulu. Her second trip to the United States was sponsored by the Jock Ming On Theater in New York, where she had been performing since early 1927. This time, she returned to San Francisco to perform on the stage of the Mandarin Theater.

The opera scene had changed, and not only because she switched theaters. Now the city had two prosperous theaters, and she was just one among a dozen star actresses and a similar number of stellar actors of various role types. For example, her performances began on November 30, following a full week of performances by the superb Li Xuefang, although the *Young China* raved about Guan's beauty, voice, and acting.[28] What is more important, Guan also returned to a more elaborate and realistic trend in staging. Theatricality and spectacle had been made more central to the productions at both the Mandarin and the Great China. Figure 10.4 shows Guan with a real coffin in a scene from the classic opera *Pan Jinlian Trifling with Her Brother-in-Law*, with Guan in a black dress being led away and Nü Muzhen as the woman in a white dress on the right. Guan played the widow Pan Jinlian, the suspect in her husband's death. The vivid outdoor scenery of the backdrop, the small elevated bridge at the center, and the full-size coffin were much more realistic than the scenery and props of earlier productions. Although they perhaps had been unthinkable four years earlier, now such real stage props were necessary in both theaters.

The busy comings and goings of top-tier actresses at the Mandarin Theater in 1927 was part of the increasingly active performing network in North America. More and more actors traveled among cities along the Pacific Coast, as well as further away, especially Boston, Chicago, and New York. In these months, New York's Yong Ni Shang Theater (which seems to have had an active performer-exchange arrangement with the Mandarin) was the destination of three top actresses whose farewells to San Francisco were made quite public and eventful. Tan Lanqing bade farewell in early August and, after first performing in Boston, began at the Yong Ni Shang Theater on November 23 and ruled the stage for the Thanksgiving holidays. At the beginning of December, Nü Muzhen appeared at the Yong Ni Shang as well. Mudan Su, last seen on the Mandarin's playbill on December 14, emerged on the

Fig. 10.4. Scene from *Pan Jinlian Trifling with Her Brother-in-Law* with Guan Yinglian and Nü Muzhen. May's Photo Studio (courtesy of the Wylie Wong collection at the Museum of Performance and Design, San Francisco).

Yong Ni Shang stage on December 21, and led for weeks. All three actresses would stay in New York through 1928.

A stage picture from the Mandarin Theater provides a snapshot of the "theater of actresses" about this time: the crowned Li Xuefang enshrined at the rear center like a goddess, Mudan Su in white standing close by in a trouser role, Huang Xuemei (third from the right) and Li Xuefei (second from the left). (See figure 10.5.) The drapery over the doorway has Li Xuefang's name embroidered at the center, showing her prominence. This picture recalls that of the Le Wannian troupe in Vancouver from 1922 (figure 6.7), in which the prima donna was similarly placed at the rear center in a grand formal display. The difference between these two troupe photos attests to the shift over the six or seven years that separated them. Whereas the 1922 picture shows uniformity among the period costumes and the traditional lamps and banners, the wardrobe of the 1928 stage is eclectic. The variety ranges from the newer dresses of the early Republic of China, or cheongsams (the two women on the left) and fanciful faux-Chinese costumes (Li Xuefang and Mudan Su) to traditional period costumes. The picture's inclusion of quirky poses also reflected the increased significance of comic performers (third from the left, and the man to the right of Mudan Su). They appeared with more frequency now on the playbills. The lack of uniformity in this

Fig. 10.5. Troupe photo, Mandarin Theater, with Li Xuefang at rear center. May's Photo Studio (courtesy of the Wylie Wong collection at the Museum of Performance and Design, San Francisco).

photo, however, underscores the situation of the theater: after being a revolving door for years, it had become more eclectic and uneven in quality. It is also more genuinely a mixed troupe: roughly half of the performers on stage are female, in contrast to only one-third in the Vancouver picture. The sense of informality also reflected the "ordinariness" of such a theatrical group as part of the community, where the stage could be realistic and eclectic, as was the case with other forms of entertainment in the community.

Another stage photo reflects the type of scenery and props commonly used at the theater (figure 10.6). The backdrop is a perspective drawing of a valley in the wilderness. An apparent confrontation is marked by the flags signaling victory and the post of the female warrior (played by Guan Yinglian). The weaponry included on stage is plentiful and likely consists of the combat weapons used in martial arts, rather than merely decorative ones. The single- and double-edged swords, knives, long-range sabers, sticks, spears, and round shields suggest an energetic scene with fencing and duels. Such real props became commonplace at both the Mandarin and the Great China Theater. Many other striking scenes printed in playbills throughout the year including the Chinese goddess of creation, Nüwa shi, with her companions, who smelts together five-colored stones to patch up the azure sky; a frozen lake and large papier-mâché fish for a battle between a goldfish-spirit-turned-young belle, underwater creatures, and human; a courtroom with a judge presiding and other characters pulling swords; a scene with brick steps in

Fig. 10.6. Stage photo of the cast of *Valley of the Red Butterfly*, December 17, 1927. May's Photo Studio (courtesy of the Wylie Wong collection at the Museum of Performance and Design, San Francisco).

a back garden where a man appeared to be pulled down by a dog (an actor with a head cover); and an actress dressed in a colorful butterfly costume with full wings spread four feet on each side. Most of these stage photos are characterized by bold composition, exaggerated expressions, sharp contrasts, and striking poses, which mirror the theatrical and striking effects of silent film images.

GROWTH, PAINS, AND ADJUSTMENTS

Another sign of prosperity for the theater was its enlarged management team. At the beginning of 1927, it sponsored the admission of a general secretary, Wong Tsze Hong; a treasurer, Woo Yueng; and an assistant manager, M. Q. Fong.[29] They all belonged to the merchant class, and therefore did not take up any of the places in the quota of performers. The addition to management was necessary because by this point there were a large number of loans and exchanges of performers between the Mandarin and other theaters. For example, according to immigration files, three performers were transferred to the Chinese theater (the Lau Tau Seck Company) in Boston, while seven performers were loaned less officially to the Tai Wing Wah Theater in Chicago in a short span.[30] The transfer to Boston of the Mandarin troupe was stalled for a while because the Boston company did not have enough room in its quota at first. Then, the Department of Labor was irate that the Mandarin Theater had made exchanges with a Chicago theater without first seeking its approval. The officer wrote, "Actors may not be transferred from one company to another without permission of the Department."[31] Although the government intended to maintain close control of Chinese performers, given the fluid situation, as well as the prosperity of the theaters, the voluminous and tedious paperwork proved too challenging. Yet, with new performers constantly arriving and the total number of cast members always near the quota, the theater had to continue sending performers to other cities, loaning them to other theaters, or taking them to neighboring countries whenever possible.

Between June and December the theater brought in at least seven comic actors, all quite famous in China. The first of these, Xin-shuishe Rong, was hailed as one of the best in southern China, his satire earning critical acclaim. After his successful debut, unfortunately he fell ill and died only three months into his residence at the Mandarin Theater. Next a famous actor of the new scholar-warrior comic type, Xin-shuishe Qiu, arrived in September with his apprentice and a group of four comic actors, the most famous of whom was Doupi Yuan (Liu Guoxing). Doupi Yuan would later write a significant memoir about the lives of Cantonese opera singers in the performing circuits from Southeast Asia to North America. Judging from his frequent leading performances, he was the top comedian at the theater. According to his memoir, he was offered the annual salary of $8,500, which was paid half in U.S. dollars and half in Chinese dollars, as was the customary arrangement for actors' contracts then.[32]

According to Doupi Yuan, there was a hierarchy among various locations: San Francisco remained the best environment for performance, with New York and Vancouver very close behind; Seattle, Boston, Los Angeles, and Chicago were certainly on the second tier.[33] Small towns such as Mexicali, on the other hand, were far less desirable. He noted that the performing space in Mexicali was considered dismal, really more of a casino, and thus hardly qualified as a theater. The theater sometimes had to pay $300 extra to convince reluctant actors to perform there. But as we will see, sometimes, even that was not enough to ensure success.

At the end of January 1927, the Los Angeles Mandarin Theater, after daily performances for nearly a year, decided to move its troupe to Mexicali for ninety days (the Chinese community there comprised roughly six thousand people). After careful negotiation with the Immigration Bureau, twenty-two performers made the trip freeing up much space in the U.S. quota of eighty-five.[34] This endeavor seemed promising at first, as the star actress Tan Lanqing joined the Mexicali troupe on March 9, scheduled to perform for three weeks. Yet before the end of the month, the whole troupe returned.[35] One reason given was that heightened anti-Chinese sentiment in Mexico had left many Chinese workers unemployed, and the performances could no longer be supported. The details of the situation remain unclear and await further study.[36] Nonetheless, this incidence shows the volatile situation of the Cantonese opera enterprise in North America, and its vulnerability within a nation-state with different means of expulsion.

In any case, eighteen members regained admission to the United States. And for the remainder of 1927, there was no further large exodus of performers to neighboring countries. It is not surprising that in October it exceeded its quota, necessitating transfers of performers. The attorney was busy dealing with the situation.[37] In the last three months of the year, over thirty letters went back and forth between the immigration service and the theater's attorney concerning matters of transfer, admissions, and bond.[38]

A felicitous start for a new year always boded well for the theater. Just as 1927 had commenced promisingly with the debut of Tan Lanqing, 1928 began with four performances by Li Xuefang, who would be in residence at the Mandarin Theater for most of the year, eventually staging as many as seventy-seven leading performances, not including various benefit appearances. Led by Li, the Mandarin Theater continued as a theater of actresses. Even though several prominent actresses, such as Tan Lanqing and Li Xuefei, went to Vancouver in April, many returning and new actresses kept the stage lively.[39]

The Mandarin Theater grew in significance for the Cantonese opera circuit.[40] As the performing network in North America grew, the transnational movement became busier as well. For example, Tan Xiufang, who was a star at the Mandarin Theater in December 1925, had been performing in New York's Yong Ni Shang Theater, Boston's New China Theater, and Chicago's Tai Wing Wah (Grandview Theater), accompanied on her travels by her bearded warrior father, Xianrong.[41] Another actress, Li Zhifang, also performed at the Tai Wing Wah, where she was briefly joined by Tan Xiufang. Li's return to the Mandarin's stage was celebrated by her signature opera *Flower Agony*. She took on more leading roles, including co-starring with Li Xuefang on October 1 in a famous supporting role—the witty and clever maid, Hong Niang—to the lovelorn young lady Cui Yingying in *The Romance of the West Chamber*. In October she, too, departed for China.[42] Groups of performers passed through often, staging performances en route. At the beginning of February, for instance, thirty-two actors from the Los Angeles Mandarin Theater traveled by car to San Francisco and, joined by several local performers, took the South Pacific Train line for Seattle, where they performed.[43]

LI XUEFANG'S LONG RESIDENCY AT THE MANDARIN

The year's residency (from Thanksgiving 1927 to the end of 1928) gave Li Xuefang the chance to offer a fuller presentation of her performing skills and musical talents. Although in 1927 she had been featured primarily in lyrical roles, this year saw her in operas with more warrior or battle scenes as well. Some performances were collaborations with other top actresses such as week-long stints with both Mudan Su and Nü Muzhen. However, most popular with the audiences was still her signature operas, which had become staples of the theater's programming. They established her prominence as an artist and were widely available on recordings.

Li also contributed to the year-end bonus of her fellow performers. The prosperity of the Mandarin Theater was now reflected in its established norm of turning the ticket sales from the two evenings leading up to the New Year over to the performers as their year-end bonus. On January 21 and 22, Li Xuefang led these two performances with her signature repertoire *Shilin Paying Respects at the Pagoda*, co-starring with actor Bai Yutang.[44] As a celebrity, Li was naturally made the public face of benefit performances and was their greatest attraction. February and March 1928 were very busy for fundraising initiatives in San Francisco's Chinatown. The Chinese Consolidated Benevolent Association held a benefit for the construction of the association's Chinese school building and also urged the community to support a fundraiser led by a prominent doctor from Guangzhou for the construction of Sun Yat-Sen Library there. On February 23, a report in *Chung Sai Yat Po* calling for support of the library initiative put the spotlight on Li from the start:

> It is a precious sign of true devotion that Li Xuefang, who has completed her residence and is ready to leave for China, extended her departure date in order to volunteer her performance for the fund-raising event. And Li will collaborate with her fellow famous performers with the topmost brilliant skills and artistry to stage an extraordinary performance. The level will no doubt be of the same excellence as the music culture of ancient instruments *qin* and string, just as choreographically pleasing and literarily graceful. The stage would be like the palace and the script like the order of the world.[45]

Li was to leave for the East Coast, to return in August. No doubt this imminent departure increased the appeal of the benefit performance. Tickets were distributed to various contingents of the community that were responsible for their sale. On February 19, Li staged a matinee for a Chinese school fundraiser; her *Twilight Scarlet Tears* was preceded by three other classic playlets performed by three pairs of leading performers from the Mandarin Theater. The matinee event raised a total of $2,796.[46] On February 26, for the library fundraiser, Li led the classic *Daiyu Burying Flower Petals*, preceded by Doupi Yuan's comic opera and Guan Yinglian's classic *Sanniang Teaching Her Son*. At the beginning, a speech was given by the representative from Guangzhou.[47] The evening raised only $1,200.[48] Three weeks later Li led a benefit for Chinatown's Tung Wah Hospital on March 18, which mobilized the community so successfully that it raised nearly $3,000.[49] The community, in turn, expressed its appreciation; the Li Family Association presented her with a golden plate worth several hundred dollars on March 30, on the occasion of her performance of a new opera titled *Yanzi House*.[50] Throughout her stay in San Francisco, Li was esteemed more than all other performers at both theaters. Her fame was such that when she finally left San Francisco to sail for China, the English-language press paid some attention. A small newspaper on the East Coast printed a picture of Li in wrap-over coat and scarf with a nicely decorated flapper-style cloche hat and noted, "Miss Lee Sue Fong, Cantonese actress, said by Chinese critics to have a voice second to none on the native stage, sails for home from San Francisco, after 'conquering' Chinese theater-goers there."[51]

THE MANDARIN IN VANCOUVER AND ELSEWHERE

The Mandarin Theater prospered in a way unlike any other Cantonese opera theater in North America. It had by the end of 1928 established itself as not only a key player in the performing network, but also as a troupe and a brand. In Vancouver, where the last opera troupe had folded years earlier, merchants in late 1926 had explored the possibility of recruiting performers from U.S. Cantonese opera theaters. When negotiations with the Great China Theater failed, they had decided to recruit actors from the Mandarin instead. The merchants had then formed the Tong Li Company and worked out an agreement to bring in performers from the Mandarin and from the Jock Ming On Theater in New York. Tong Li had named the group the Mandarin Theater Troupe and offered daily performances in the existing Sheng Ping Theater. The theater had been doing well for two full years in 1928, and many of its performers were familiar names from the cast of San Francisco's Mandarin Theater.

As noted above, performers changed affiliation from time to time, so a troupe existed primarily in name only. Typically, a recognizable name was used to give it legitimacy, and such was the case in Vancouver. The naming of the Mandarin Theater Troupe reflected the prosperity of the theater in San Francisco. A playbill from July 1927 shows the connection (see figure 10.7). Aside from the Chinese characters for "Mandarin Theater Troupe" and Tong Li Company, the playbill also included English wording to underscore the troupe affiliation: "THE MANDARIN THEATRE CO., LTD."[52] So far as we know, San Francisco's Mandarin was not a financial sponsor of the Vancouver theater. (Chapter 12 discusses this Vancouver theater further.) Other Cantonese opera theaters' adoption of the Mandarin Theater's name reflects the significance of the San Francisco theater. Incidentally, it was also in 1927 that Singapore's most prominent Chinese merchant, Eu Tong

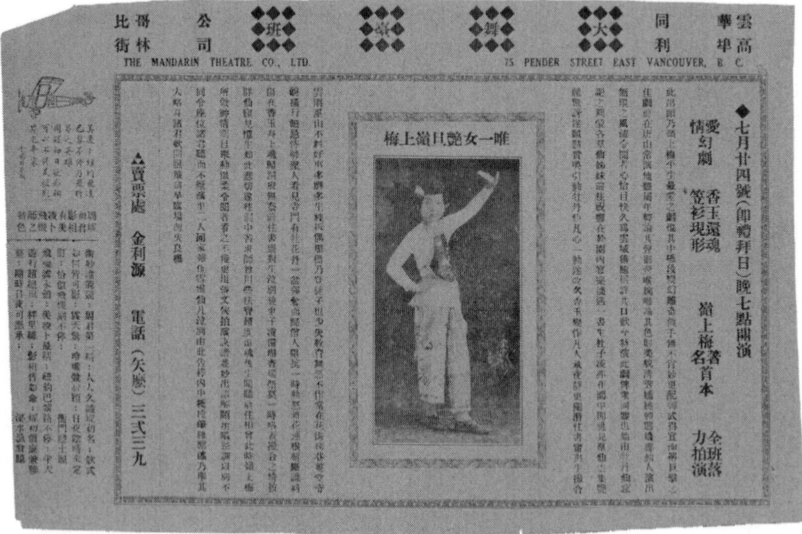

Fig. 10.7. Playbill, Mandarin Theater/Troupe in Vancouver, July 24, 1927 (courtesy of the Hong Kong Heritage Museum).

Sen, established a purpose-built Cantonese opera theater and called it Tianyan Dawutai (Heaven Performing Mandarin Theater). By this time, San Francisco's Mandarin Theater had its own agent in Hong Kong to scout talent.[53] Eu Tong Sen did the same for his Mandarin Theater in Singapore, recruiting top talent in Hong Kong to fill its stage. The transnational network of North America was linked back to that of Southeast Asia.[54]

Back in San Francisco the Mandarin continued to thrive as a theater of actresses. For example, the last month of 1928 saw only three performances led by actors alone. Also, the theater was clearly enthusiastic about producing novel operas, as can be seen by the playwrights it engaged that year: Liu Zixuan (April), Luo Jianhong (May), and Gu Bokeng (November).[55] Luo was one of the leading Cantonese opera playwrights of the 1920s. His operas had became really popular, and his presence in the city stirred up excitement. He not only wrote operas but also published lyrics in newspapers reflecting on contemporary politics and spoke eloquently at community events. A report in *Chung Sai Yat Po* noted that he would not only be composing the lyrics and music and directing but also coaching the performers. Basically he would be in charge of the production.[56] Even the names for his operas were quite novel for this community. They reflected a new middlebrow fiction style popular among Chinese city-dwellers, the so-called Mandarin Ducks and Butterflies literature that favored love stories of ordinary people, tales of knights-errant, or urban scandal stories. It was also the favorite source material for Chinese filmmakers. The novelty was received well. Ten playbills printed in June and July featured Luo Jianhong, the playwright, as the main attraction. This unprecedented attention reflected the way the playwright's role was now so important to the production that his name alone could entice audiences. The trend was now to present large productions of newer operas, crafted and designed by professional playwrights.

Besides fundraisers, the theater participated in other public events. In June the Mandarin organized a committee called "Fighting and Boycotting Japan." A recent Japanese-Chinese military confrontation in Jinan quickly escalated into imminent threats to China's sovereignty, and Chinese communities in North America responded strongly. A movement to break economic relations with Japan began as a result. The Mandarin formed one of the first such committees in San Francisco (the Great China soon followed). In its first meeting, on June 3, the theater enlisted seventeen members to offer speeches, songs, comic skits, and acrobatic shows, with the printed lyrics supplied to the audience.[57] Luo Jianhong led the way in giving the first speech, on the topic of striving.[58] He followed the speech with a long lyric on patriotic themes in the literary supplement of the *Young China*.[59] The Great China Theater followed with a parade demonstrating against Japanese imperialism and an opera production.[60]

The theater became visible in various public venues as well and developed a special rapport with mainstream society in San Francisco. From May 6 to May 13 the city held its eighth annual Music Week. The Mandarin Theater was invited to participate, and it sent actress Hudie Ying, who sang and performed on hammered dulcimer.[61] Earlier in the year, the performers were invited by the Berkeley Women's Club to perform at its annual meeting at the Claremont Hotel.[62] In an effort to accentuate the city's unique characteristics, Mayor James Rolph invited the Mandarin Theater to be part of the reception for New York mayor Jimmy Walker in July.[63] When the American Pharmaceutical Association held its annual meeting in San Francisco that year, the delegates went to the Mandarin Theater for a special evening of performances.[64] The theater featured its best: the first opera playlet was with Mudan Su and Huang Xuemei, the second playlet was with Li Xuefang, and the concluding warrior opera was with actor Zhou Shaobao. Numerous such formal visits to the theaters were reported by *San Francisco Chronicle*, though not in as much detail.

Opera performances were often held at school events. At the June commencement of the Xie He Chinese School, the awards and speeches were followed by performances from four Cantonese operas adapted to various moral and contemporary stories.[65] In November, to commemorate the anniversary of the end of World War I, the school staged *Lone Tomb in the Wilderness*.[66] When a Chinese-language school in Oakland was short of funding due to increased enrollment, the youths arranged and staged a comic opera, *Emperor's Dream*, to raise funds.[67] And advertisements of instruments for opera troupes now appeared prominently in the newspaper. One by Shing Shun & Company read "New arrival: Troupe's fashionable bowed and plucked instruments, as well as percussion," next to its advertisements of opera recordings.[68]

The end of 1928 was marked by a sign of change for the Mandarin Theater—an unusual public announcement in the *Young China* calling for a stockholder meeting on the last day of the year to plan for its future.[69] At the meeting the theater decided to increase its capital, expand the business, and purchase the theater building, which was leased.[70] In 1929 and beyond, the theater continued to be active.[71] A surviving unsigned stock certificate for San Francisco's Mandarin Theatrical Company dated October 16, 1932, shows a share value of $10 at 2,500 shares, for total capital of $250,000.[72]

Many playbills and photos survive from performances in the 1920s and 1930s, the study of which could reveal more detail about their programs, trends, popular signers, and operas, as well as practices. In particular, the 1936 Works Progress Administration study included a list of repertoire for daily performance between January and April of that year.[73] In 1934 a *San Francisco Chronicle* report on the weeklong Chinese New Year performances noted that seven actresses and fifteen actors were stock performers at the Mandarin Theater with the occasional visiting star.[74] Judging from the annual New Year greeting cards that the theater issued between 1929 and 1941, the Mandarin Theater's cast and personnel numbered between twenty-seven and forty-two.[75] The theater continued to offer opera performances, adjusting to coexist with growing competition from other types of entertainment, and later it alternated live opera with cinema presentations.

Nevertheless, in years to come, many more celebrity performers would become part of the Mandarin's cast. It would include the superstar Ma Shizeng, whose arrival in 1931 marked a new high point for the theater. A household name in Hong Kong and Guangzhou, he remains one of the most famous Cantonese opera actors in history. Ma was the only Cantonese opera performer aside from Li Xuefang whose performing in San Francisco warranted the publication of a special pamphlet to commemorate the event. But in 1931, it was a different time: Ma Shizeng produced and printed this pamphlet in China and brought it with him on this ambitious trip to disseminate the art of Cantonese opera.[76]

PART V

IN NEW YORK AND THE TRANSNATIONAL ARENA

CHAPTER 11

TWO THEATERS AND A MERGER IN NEW YORK

When a Cantonese opera theater was established in lower Manhattan in July 1924, it was the sixth new professional troupe founded in the United States since October 1922. The Department of Labor's approval for its admission, however, dated to January 1921. During the intervening years Cantonese opera theaters had opened and thrived in San Francisco, Los Angeles, and elsewhere in the United States. The theaters in New York would soon become nodes of the performing network and share many of its talented performers. Chinese theater would take its place in a city with a long and prestigious tradition of theatrical and performing arts.[1]

Such troupes were not new to New York. As early as 1853 the Hong Fook Tong troupe, the first to appear in San Francisco, performed at Niblo's Garden, creating a sensation.[2] In the late nineteenth century a series of Cantonese opera theaters appeared in New York. Wong Chin Foo was an early advocate. Founder of the first Chinese newspapers in the United States (1881 and 1883), he lectured widely and began the effort of establishing Chinese theater in New York as early as the 1880s, along with newspapers and language schools.[3] Through his introduction and a local sponsor, in June 1889 the Swin-tien Lok Royal Chinese theatrical company performed for two weeks at the Windsor Theater. According to a report in the *New York Times*, prior to the premiere, every box and all eight hundred seats for the opening performance were taken.[4] With the headline "Joy Reigns in Chinatown," the *New York Tribune* reported that the leading actor, Moo Sung Jee, confidently noted that "a regular Chinese theater can be established and maintained in the city."[5]

Fig. 11.1. Chinese Theater on Doyer Street, New York, 1908, with playbills posted by the doors (courtesy of the Bain Collection, Library of Congress).

Chu Fong, a merchant who was of the same mind, opened the Chinese Theater in 1893 on Doyer Street. It soon served as a stopping point for Chinese performers who came from Havana heading to Chicago for the World's Columbian Exposition.[6] The theatrical company's fortunes rose and fell in the next fifteen years, gradually declining by the first decade of the twentieth century.[7] Figure 11.1 shows the theater in 1908. One can see that it offered professional troupes and performances. On the wall near the entryways are old playbills featuring an opera based on the classic Chinese novel *Red Chamber Story*, listing eleven characters and their performers.

Several factors contributed to the decline of the theater on Doyer Street. Aside from the tightening of immigration controls that limited the availability of opera professionals, high-profile tong wars took place.[8] In 1910 the Rescue Society of New York bought the theater and made it the Chinese Rescue Mission. After that, the city was without a Chinese theater, a fact that did not go unnoticed by the mainstream public. Diane Rice of the *New York Times*, in a report on the changes in Chinatown, noted, "Gone, too, is the Chinese Theater."[9] Will Irwin expressed a similar nostalgia in a 1921 *New York Times* article, writing, "The Doyer Street Theatre had closed its doors, as the Washington Street and Jackson Street [in San Francisco] did. . . . The Chinese Theater in America is forever gone."[10] However, the presence of Chinese theater in New York was not forgotten.

JOCK MING ON THEATER (1924–1927)

The 1921 approval from the Department of Labor was obtained by the veteran Washington, DC, attorney Roger O'Donnell. He applied on behalf of a young San Francisco businessman, B. S. Fong, for permission to bring "a Chinese theatrical troupe of 50 to 60 via San Francisco to stay for one year, including actors, musicians, jugglers and acrobats: a high-class organization. Perhaps in two divisions, one for Chinese audiences and the other for the American vaudeville stage."[11] Fong was the English secretary of the Chinese Consolidated Benevolent Association in San Francisco. With his long experience as the attorney for Barnum & Bailey, O'Donnell had a certain authority on the matter. "Aside from circus performers who have been brought here from China by Barnum & Bailey and other showmen, there has been no high-class Chinese magician since the time of Ching Ling Foo."[12] The application was paradoxically helped by the mainstream society's fascination with Chinese acts as discussed in Chapter 2. Just one day after making the request, on January 19, 1921, O'Donnell was granted approval for the admission of a Chinese troupe of no more than sixty members.

This approval was not put to use for some reason, but it came in handy for O'Donnell, who used it in April 1924 to request permission for the forty-member Jock Ming On troupe to establish a theater in New York. In the metropolis the entertainment business was extraordinarily lively. On Broadway, as many as seventy theaters were active in the 1920s.[13] Cantonese opera had returned to North America in 1922, but none had yet successfully reached New York. O'Donnell noted that the troupe would arrive from Canada, where it had performed in Vancouver and Victoria from March 1923 to May 1924.[14] He reasoned that the twenty-five thousand Chinese in greater New York would be sufficient to support a troupe of first-class performers, and the local inspector concurred. To underscore New York's need for a Chinese theater, O'Donnell pointed to the desire of the Kue Hing Company in Honolulu to bring its Chinese troupe to New York, though it did not succeed.[15] (He represented the Kue Hing Company as well.) Following a satisfactory local investigation the request was approved with a quota of forty-four, similar to that of the Mandarin Theater.

Right after receiving the approval, the Jock Ming On troupe in Vancouver was sold. A planned benefit performance in Victoria was cancelled. Members of Vancouver's Chinese community were notified by newspaper announcements to finalize all transactions with the troupe.[16] The thirty-two performers left Vancouver and on a CPR steamship sailed to Seattle, where they performed for two weeks before heading east by train. They arrived in New York in July 1924. In San Francisco, the *Young China* reported on the July 9 premiere in New York City featuring *Joint Hearing of Empress Lun*, led by actress Chen Huifang.[17]

Jock Ming On's premiere at Miner's Bowery Theater, a venue for burlesque and light opera, reminded New Yorkers that the city was once familiar with Chinese opera. A report of its success, "Bowery Resonant with Chinese Opera," in the *New York Times* noted that the house was standing room only. It included several details about the operation:

> The company consists of thirty principals and an orchestra of six. Night after night every seat in the theatre is filled at admission prices ranging from $1 to $5, the audience coming from New York's Chinatown and from Chinese settlements in several near-by states. The highest and the lowest in the Chinese social scale are to be found occupying seats long before the time set for the rise of the curtain. Weber and Fields and other Miner's stars never in their heyday played to more enthusiastic audiences than do the members of the Chinese Grand Opera company.[18]

At this time the new Jock Ming On troupe had raised only part of the targeted sum of $75,000, though it had enough to run a full-scale theater in New York City for an extended period. It planned to move to an uptown theater after a month. The renaissance of Chinese opera in the city was in the mode common in the 1920s, featuring novelty, professionalism, spectacle, new scripts and tunes, and virtuosity.

The initial troupe's thirty-two members were predominantly male; only three were female. Half of the troupe was over forty years old.[19] Not much information about the troupe's repertoire or performing activity can be found. It was so successful that it quickly enhanced its cast with performers from Vancouver and Cuba, from the Lun Hop Company in San Francisco, or directly from China. By the end of 1924 the theater had reached its quota of forty-four.[20] In January 1925, when its permit was due for renewal, the theater had exceeded its quota by one.

After just nine weeks at Miner's Bowery Theater, the troupe, as planned, moved north two blocks to the Old London Theater at 235 Bowery. At this theater, which seated eight hundred, tickets ranged from $1.50 to $2.50 for performances that started nightly at 6:00 and ended at about 10:00. In February 1925, when its manager, Chan Wing, applied for a return certificate before leaving for Hong Kong to recruit actors, he was interviewed by the New York office of the Immigration Service. He provided details about the company's finances. While it had capital of $60,000, it had already made about $45,000 in its first eight months of operation, making it a rather lucrative business. It had an average daily audience of three to four hundred. Estimating on the basis of figures provided by Chan Wing—$3,000 weekly payroll and $1,250 monthly rent—the company's monthly revenue was likely about $19,000. Its success prompted Chan Wing's fellow Brooklyn businessman, Philip Kee, to bring a second Cantonese opera troupe to New York. As Kee noted years later, "When the business was going well, you make money really quick."[21]

The sponsorship of the Jock Ming On troupe involved multiple communities. In Vancouver the troupe was sold to Chin Nom of New York.[22] Yet the financial backing also included the Yee Chung Company of Seattle, Wallace Mah of Salem and Allston, Massachusetts, and Chin Yee You, the prominent Vancouver merchant first encountered in Chapter 7. Chin Yee You, now the treasurer, previously led the Lun On company from Vancouver to San Francisco.[23] He brought both expertise in the theatrical business and connections in the Chinese community of the Pacific Northwest. The manager, Chan Wing, who had worked in Montreal and Vancouver for six years before coming to New York as a merchant, also frequently went to Victoria to hire performers.

New York Chinatown magnate Chin Nom was the only local business partner, and his political connections proved crucial to the success of the theater. The profitability of Chinese theaters in New York depended on two important conditions: first, a stream of new performers, and second, a peaceful environment for daily productions. The latter was not easily achieved during this period of fierce rivalry among tongs within the Chinese communities on the East Coast. It was the largest public space in the Chinese community, and the bustling crowds might conceal assassins. The theater's image suffered because of potential tong wars, police raids, and reluctant audiences. One of the wealthiest and most influential merchants in Chinatown, Chin Nom was well-respected for his role as a mediator between the two largest rival tongs, On Leong and Hop Sing. His success in resolving tong warfare won him the title "peacemaker and sage of New York's Chinatown" in the *New York Times*.[24] Only three months after Jock Ming On's opening in lower Manhattan, a major tong war broke out on the East Coast and lasted for nearly five months. While tong murders and gunfights in the community were reported regularly, Jock Ming On Theater remained peaceful, a miracle that could be attributed to Chin Nom's reputation. Nevertheless, the police raided the theater several times, claiming to be searching for assassins. During the worst period of the tong war in Jock Ming On's first year, the daily attendance dropped from 800 to 150.

The raids revealed the precarious situation facing the Chinese community at the time. Raids had been part of the reality of Chinese theaters since the nineteenth century, but the exclusion laws made them even more dangerous. In September 1925 a *New York Times* report described a raid that resulted in the arrests of 450 Chinese, noting the absurdity of "performances keep[ing] on"—the singers and musicians on stage continuing to perform to empty seats after much of the audience had been arrested.[25] Arrest might easily have led to imprisonment, deportation, or other forms of humiliation, yet the actors, vouched for by managers, avoided that fate. Singing to empty seats was an obligation or privilege, not a choice or hardship. Even in the exclusionist society being a performer could have its advantages.

A fundraising event in June 1925 for the Canton–Hong Kong strike showed how the Jock Ming On Theater mobilized the community for social causes. The curtain was decorated with Chinese and American flags at the center, banners on the sides, and couplets commemorating the victims across the top.[26] Young

Chinese women, either American-born or students from China, raised $2,000 by selling flowers to the audience. Another $2,000 was generated from concessions and the sale of memorabilia. Together with the ticket sales and other donations, the theater raised over $10,000, more than other theaters in North America. Soon fundraising events were organized with some regularity; for instance, a benefit performance in October for a Chinese school raised $2,000.[27]

From the beginning of 1927, when the *Chinese Nationalist Daily* (New York) began publishing, Jock Ming On placed regular playbill advertisements. The surviving forty playbills (published between January 27 and March 16, 1927) show that the programs were on a par with those of the San Francisco theaters, with similar operas. As a mixed troupe Jock Ming On generally had actors playing the leading male roles, and actresses playing the lead female roles, while leading comic roles were cast more often with actors than actresses. Among the leading male actors was Fengqing Qi, first encountered in this book with his appearance at Vancouver's Sheng Ping Theater in 1921. He was a well-respected actor of xiaosheng roles in the 1920s.[28] As was typical of actors on the North American performing circuit, he would later appear in Honolulu as well. A majority of the performers were also active in San Francisco's Mandarin Theater. This would include actor of the scholar type, Jing Yulin. Shengjia Tong was a warrior type who was outstanding enough to be included in the anthology noted in Chapter 7. The renowned comic actors Guima Zhao, Chen Pimei, and Doupi Mei appeared with Jock Ming On as well. The latter's engagement in New York followed his successful performances at the Mandarin Theater. The title of his performance of February 10, *Reform through Pragmatism/Detective Seeking the Truth*, shows how the repertoire of different Chinatown theaters had become homogenized, as this unique opera had been featured only eight weeks earlier in San Francisco (see figure 9.8).

Many familiar actresses were shown in the playbills, including the ubiquitous Guan Yinglian. By far the most popular performer on the North American circuit since her 1921 debut in Vancouver, she was sponsored by Jock Ming On. As its prima donna, she led nearly half of the forty performances given in 1927. This was the beginning of the second of many more trips for her to North America. Principal actresses Tan Xiufang and Li Zhifang were also familiar to the Mandarin Theater's stage all through 1926.[29] Both were in the second year of their U.S. residency. Their journey to New York benefited both theaters—the engagement at Jock Ming On freed up space in the Mandarin's quota, and the New York theater could, at a fraction of the usual cost, enjoy the brilliant performances of top actresses. They would also find that their fame preceded their appearances on the New York stage, as all three actresses' pictures were featured prominently in *Essence of Cantonese Opera and Songs* (San Francisco, 1925) which was widely circulated in North America.

One Jock Ming On playbill reflects the cast of early 1927 discussed above (see figure 11.2). With its well-written synopsis, it demonstrates the professional level of the staff at the theater. Its cast of fifteen, though small, had as many stellar performers as would be found in one performance in San Francisco—two leading young belles, Guan Yinglian and Li Zhifang, four young scholars, a warrior, a comedian, and others. The troupe was engaged for a special performance commemorating the birthday of Wu Zixu, a respected symbol of the powerful Wu Family Association. It featured the common story of a couple forced apart by a slew of unfortunate circumstances, misunderstandings, and evil forces. Yet helped by several chivalrous and virtuous acts, coincidences, and the honorable female protagonist's perseverance, they reunite in a happy ending. Staging this opera allowed the leading actress, Guan, to perform a great range of familiar scenarios in different moods and expressions: defiant and righteous, romantic, vulnerable, sorrowful, grateful, and happy. It is a good showpiece, as well as an uplifting story appropriate for the occasion. The playbill makes the moral of the story clear: when a couple is destined to be together, no hardship can stop them. Since the family associations were important anchors for Chinese communities in North America, the significance of such opera performances for their annual celebrations cannot be underestimated. Every year, it seemed, this family association bought an opera performance for the

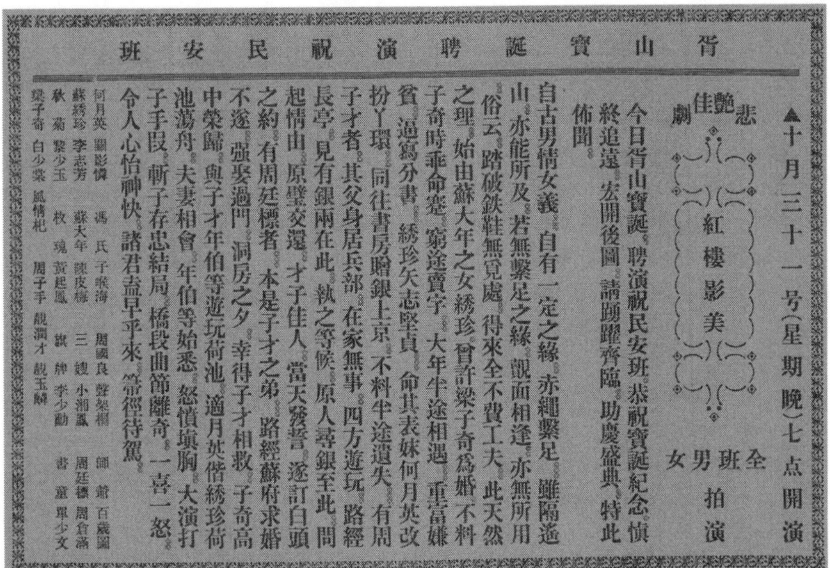

背山寶誕聘演祝民安班

▲十月三十一号(星期晚)七点開演

悲艷佳劇 紅樓影美 全班男女拍演

今日背山寶誕。聘演祝民安班。恭祝寶誕紀念。慎終追遠。宏開後圖。請踴躍齊臨。助慶盛典。特此佈聞。

自古男情女義。自有一定之緣。赤繩繫足。雖隔遙山。亦能所及。若無繫足之緣。覿面相逢。亦無所用。俗云。踏破鉄鞋無覓處。得來全不費工夫。此天然之理。始由蘇大年之女綉珍。曾許梁子奇為婚。不料子奇時乖命蹇。窮途賣字。大年半途相遇。重富嫌貧。逼寫分書。綉珍矢志堅貞。命其表妹何月英改扮丫環。同往書房贈銀上京。不料半途遺失。有周子才者。其父身居兵部。在家無事。四方遊玩。路經長亭。見有銀兩在此。執之等候。原人尋銀至此。問起情由。原璧交還。才子佳人。當天發誓。遂訂白頭之約。有周廷標者。本是子才之弟。路經蘇府求婚不遂。强娶過門。洞房之夕。幸得子才相救。子奇高中榮歸。與子才年伯等遊玩荷池。適月英偕綉珍荷池蕩舟。夫妻相會。年伯等始悉。怒憤填胸。大演打子手段。斬子存忠結局。橋段曲節離奇。一喜一怒。令人心怡神快。諸君盍早乎來。竚徑待駕。

何月英 關影憐 馮氏 子喉海 周國良 聲架桐 師爺 百歲圖

蘇綉珍 李志芳 蘇大年 陳皮梅 三嫂 小湘瓜 周廷標 周倉滿

秋菊 黎少玉 枚瑰 黃起鳳 旗牌 李少勳 書童 畢少文

梁子奇 白少棠 風情杞 周子才 靚潤才 靚玉麟

Fig. 11.2. Playbill, *Beautiful Silhouette at the Red House*, Jock Ming On, October 31, 1926 (courtesy of the Wing Luke Museum, Seattle).

occasion of the birthday of Wu Zixu, according to the news reports in the *Chinese Nationalist Daily*.

From the playbills we can see that the Jock Ming On's repertoire followed conventional practices, as illustrated in the program for Chinese New Year. For symbolizing a blessed commencement of the New Year, the program began, as was typical, with the ritual operas *A Birthday Greeting from Eight Immortals* and *Heavenly Maiden Offers a Son*. The former reenacts a gala scene celebrating the birthday of a deity, and the latter is about a goddess bringing a son back to her mortal husband. These performances were a formal gesture of gratitude to both the audience and the deity. Classical repertoire such as *The Romance of the West Chamber* and *Farewell on a Winter Night* were the norm, and trendier operas such as *Ill-Fated Lady of Thirty Years* and *My Wife, My Wife* were often seen as well.

At the same time, the theater's program on Chinese New Year's Eve, February 2, 1927, showed the mutual reliance of performers and audiences. On this day the Jock Ming On Theater's playbill featured scenes from five opera playlets, with ten different actors and actresses in the leading roles. The long evening program was more elaborate than those at the San Francisco theaters. Neither the program nor performing on the eve of the Lunar New Year was a Cantonese opera tradition. In China, this day typically offered no performances, for it was of paramount significance as an occasion for the reunion of the entire family. The New York theaters' decision to perform on this day was a response to the reality that reuniting with family was made impossible for many by the exclusion laws, and the situation was further exacerbated by the large number of Chinese scattered in the vicinity of New York. Those who desired a conventional, warm, festive evening in the chill of winter would find the spirited opera theater of Chinatown a sort of substitute for a family reunion. The extended program on New Year's Eve, therefore, was a response to a need of the community. This practice was adopted by many Chinatown theaters, but Jock Ming On's elaborate programming showed its particular significance in New York.

Featuring five playlets, the evening started with scenes from the classic opera *Pan Jinlian Trifling with Her Brother-in-Law*. Guan Yinglian, famous for this opera, played the flirtatious, attractive woman attempting to convince a reluctant lover, a handsome brother-in-law. Then a stage couple, the young scholar Fengqing Qi and the young belle Tan Xiufang, led a classic romantic opera scene, likely featuring amorous duets. A comic affair, *Madame Black and White*, followed, played by Zhihou Hai, a scholar-style comedian, and Sheng Jiatong, a warrior-clown type comedian. It was followed by another classic opera from the Tang Dynasty, *Luo Chen's Patriotic Appeal*, featuring Jing Yulin as the loyal young official who saved a doomed battle with a letter written in blood. The protagonist's eventual triumph provided an uplifting spirit for the evening. The program concluded with the comic playlet *Yalan*

Trades Pigs, about a buffoon whose frivolous quarrels and misunderstandings have such twists that the play could last until the early hours of the morning. It was an urbanized version of a practice called *tianguang xi* (daylight drama), in which the final performance of the evening is stretched out until dawn. The practice was common in rural China so that the audience would not have to return to remote villages after town gates were closed or transportation had stopped. Operas chosen for such an occasion were often so loosely constructed that the audience or even the performers would fall asleep! The choice of *Yalan Trades Pigs* was typical for this occasion. In Chinatown, however, tianguang xi might substitute for the New Year custom of *shousui*—staying up to witness the old year crossing over to the new, a moment conventionally cheered by the roar of firecrackers set off throughout the community. That *Yalan Trades Pigs* cannot be found in the playbills of other Chinatown theaters during the New Year's Eve celebration underscores the unique situation in New York for the special holiday. The New Year's Day program that year featured five conventional ritual or festive opera playlets as an auspicious sign for the coming year.

In the two subsequent months, every evening had a different opera, alternating between romantic, comic, melodramatic, and suspense themes and led by one of the ten star performers. There seems to have been no sign that the fate of the theater would soon take a sharp turn. Yet after the performance led by actress Tan Xiufang on March 16, the theater was closed. It was acquired by the He Xing (Woh Hing) theater company in a merger with the Lok Tin Tsau troupe, Jock Ming On's rival of two years. A week later, Jock Ming On joined the rival troupe. Although it may not be clear what prompted this merger, it might have been inevitable, as discussed below.

Traces of the Jock Ming On troupe still exist. The wardrobe and costumes that carried the troupe's name, after a long journey from Canada to Manhattan, are now in the collection of the Museum of Chinese in America.

LOK TIN TSAU THEATER (1925–1927)

At the time of Jock Ming On's Manhattan opening in July 1924, Lok Tin Tsau in Boston was the only other Cantonese opera theater on the East Coast.[30] Prior to arriving in Boston, the Lok Tin Tsau troupe performed in cities across Canada, following the 1918 route of the troupe Guo Zhongxing (see Chapter 6). Its performances in Toronto caught the attention of the mainstream media, as evident in feature articles from the *Christian Science Monitor* and the *Toronto Daily Star* in July 1922, six months before the troupe's arrival in Boston.[31]

The *Christian Science Monitor* included a Chinese playbill of June 23, 1922, in the half-page article "Chinese Company Presenting Series of Operas in Toronto." The troupe, owned by the Lin Yick Company, featured the opera *Maid Qingwen Stitching at Her Sickbed,* based on the classic story *Red Chamber.* (The same opera episode was featured in the 1908 playbill of the Chinese Theater on Doyer Street; see figure 11.1.) Reporting the success of the troupe's series of shows, the writer noted that the music and stage performance were so beautiful that the language barrier was no obstacle to its appreciation. According to the report, the location, the National Theatre on Terauley Street, had been a Yiddish theater, and some scenery remained on the stage, contrasting sharply with the troupe's own staging: "The contrast between the priceless fabrics used as drapes, and in the gorgeous costumes of the characters, with the crude canvas drops and wings proved as incongruous as anything one has ever seen in a theater." This incongruity did not lessen the effect of the spectacular production, noted the reporter, who was impressed that "the impersonator of the hero had a certain quality of distinction that any 'leading juvenile' of the Occidental might envy."[32]

The 1922 playbill, printed in Toronto by the China Printing Company, resembles Sheng Ping Theater playbills from Vancouver from 1916 (see fig. 6.2).[33] As shown in figure 11.3, the troupe's name is enclosed in a box across the top; the date, time, and location are noted in the boxed column on the far right, followed by two short lines on the troupe's significance, and the main opera title with the names of three

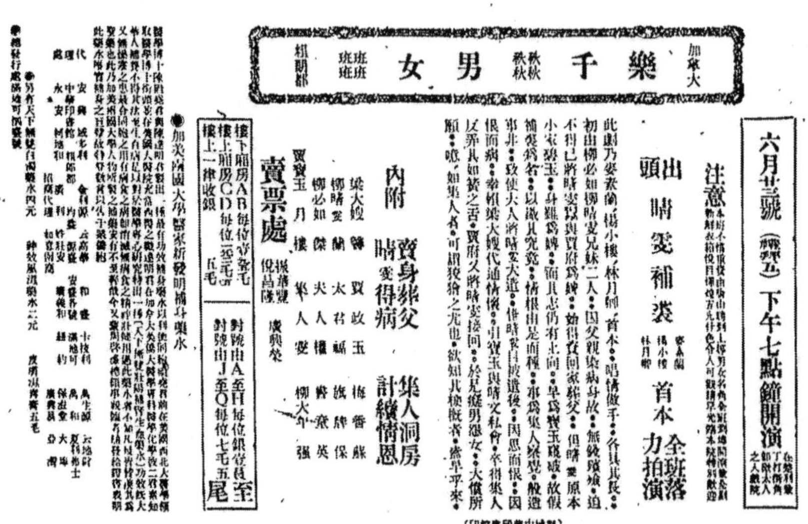

Fig. 11.3. Playbill, *Maid Qingwen Stitching at Her Sickbed,* Lok Tin Tsau, Boston, printed in the *Christian Science Monitor.* June 23, 1922.

leading performers underneath. The center block of text presents a brief synopsis of the famous story, with larger-print characters depicting four scenes: the sorrowful, the melancholy, the sentimental, and the romantic. A small cast of twelve roles is listed in the next few columns, followed by the lists of ticket agents and ticket prices in the box. The remaining space is taken up by copious notes about various medicines, their prices, and retailers in twelve cities from Canada to Cuba. These medicine ads poignantly reflect the connection between the Chinese business network and opera performances.

The *Monitor* article was filled with information likely provided by theater managers, noting the troupe's ambition to perform in "New York, the Mecca of all actors." Several days later, the *Toronto Star* published a shorter story about the troupe with a picture of the leading actress, Mai Sulan, in a modern Chinese two-piece outfit. In this full-length portrait taken by the popular photographer Frederick William Lyonde, the slender and beautiful Mai Sulan exerted the confident aura of a fashionable lady (see also figure 4.3). Both articles show the Lok Tin Tsau troupe's savvy in dealing with the media in its aim to appeal to audiences beyond the Chinese community. The troupe ensured good communication with the mainstream press.

On the eve of Thanksgiving in 1922 the troupe arrived in Boston, where it would perform for about two and a half years. According to its immigration records, the troupe now comprised twenty-six members, including two actresses listed on the Toronto playbill, Lin Yueqing and Mai Sulan. That the performers were domiciled in Canada might have been the reason for the ease with which the troupe acquired approval and entered the United States by train at Richford, Vermont.[34] The convenience of rail travel would be suspended in April 1923, when the Department of Labor informed the immigration service in Boston that Chinese performers had to enter via the water route, like European immigrants at the time.[35]

In Boston, the Lok Tin Tsau troupe was closely connected to other parts of the performing network, especially Cuba and Canada. For example, in December 1924 alone, ten members left for Cuba.[36] The regularity of such exchanges reveals the extent of Havana's Cantonese opera activity. Many Lok Tin Tsau troupe members also routinely returned to Canada for registration in order to maintain their domicile there. By departing the U.S. for Montreal or Vancouver and reentering, they effectively circumvented the three-year rule that constrained other Chinese performers. The border-crossing routine allowed them to extend their overall stay in North America. According to immigration files, Lem Gat Cheang, an actor with Canadian domicile status in the original cast, remained on the troupe's roster from November 21, 1922 (with Lok Tin Tsau) to May 28, 1933, returning to Canada intermittently and visiting Cuba often. This length of stay was highly unusual among Chinese performers, and reflected a savvy actor's creative response to the U.S. government's iron-clad immigration control.

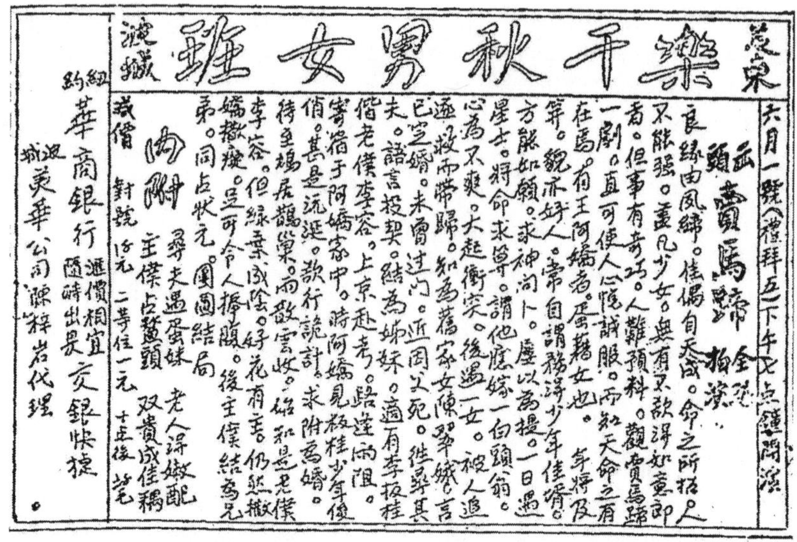

樂千秋男女班 演戲

六月一號（禮拜五）下午七点鐘開演

賣馬蹄 全班拍演

戲價 對號 1.50元 二等位一元 十点後 35仙

紐約華商銀行 匯價相宜 隨時出票 交銀快捷

波城美華公司陳梓岩代理

PROGRAM OF BEDROOM FARCE AT CHINESE THEATRE

Fig. 11.4. Playbill, *Horseshoe Sale*, Lok Tin Tsau, Boston, printed in the *Boston Daily Globe*, June 17, 1923.

In Boston, the troupe seems to have made a different impression than it did in Toronto. In a 1923 article in the *Boston Daily Globe* accompanied by the theater's Chinese playbill, the reporter described a limited performance in which dust covers were draped over backdrops with gorgeous embroidery, and stage hands interrupted the performance with their casual milling about. One of the most prominent elements of the American popular trope of Chinese opera was "property men," so this reference was not surprising. The reporter complained that the theater was unwilling to provide information and appeared unwelcoming. The accompanying Chinese playbill of June 1, 1923, printed as a mimeograph rather than offset, uses a colloquial style of Chinese and provides scant information (see figure 11.4). This plain playbill indicates merely the troupe name and a brief synopsis but gives no information about the actors. The date (June 1, Friday, at 7 P.M.) reflects a certain regularity in the troupe's performances, while the modesty of the playbill itself reveals its informal operation. It also indicates a new discount in the ticket price, \$1.50, \$1.00 and \$0.35 after 10 P.M. A recently discovered letter written by a Montreal merchant, Huang Yusheng, provides a glance at the situation during this period. The letter was sent from Boston to Havana.

> During the 21-month operation in Boston, the revenue totaled 168,000. Now the company assets are sold for 10,000, together with the advance payment 16,800, deposit 11,000 and surety 10,800, the profit is about one hundred dollars for each hundred dollars. The transaction is set for May 9, after which I will return.[37]

Although very little context is provided for this calculation, it would seem that the theater troupe was making a good profit. (More on this set of letters and circumstances is found in Chapter 12.) Still owned by the Lin Yick Company, it was performing at 23 Edinboro Street in Chinatown, according to a 1924 report.[38] A notable event was a benefit performance on March 27, 1925, reported in *Chung Sai Yat Po*, that raised $3,000 for a legal fund set up to challenge new laws that further tightened Chinese immigration.[39] (The 1924 Immigration Act barred the wives of U.S. citizens of Chinese ancestry from entry, and Chinese communities all over the United States had reacted by gathering support for a major Supreme Court challenge.)[40] Over a period of two and a half years (1922–1925), however, the modest theater declined. Many of its cast members stayed in Havana from six months to a year, and its exchanges of performers with other theaters did not seem frequent. The problem of the troupe's management became most obvious when in January 1925 its immigration permit for five performers expired and the troupe was in danger of forfeiting the sizable bond posted for them.[41] The troupe finally renewed permits for only nine members.

Seven months later, the decline of the Boston theater became an opportunity for the Brooklyn businessman Philip Kee. A former interpreter for the Immigration Service, he led the Lok Tin Tsau troupe to request several changes with the Department of Labor, such as an increase in its quota to forty-five, and a move to New York. This request was made on the eve of the Department of Labor's re-evaluation of all the Chinatown theaters around July 1925, prompted by the Mandarin Theater's persistent requests for a quota increase. The internal correspondence of August 19 noted the following:

> re: Troupe of Chinese theater controlled by Philip Kee
> Edward Shaughnessy, chairman of the Chinese Board of Review in the Office of the Secretary of Labor, has been conducting a comprehensive investigation regarding the actor situation through the U.S. Although favorable action was determined some time ago, due to miscomprehension it was not sent out before Shaughnessy started the trip, now it has to wait till he comes back.[42]

Historian Mae Ngai has brought attention to the increased prominence of Chinese interpreters at the beginning of the twentieth century.[43] Kee's involvement in the business represents the engagement of this emerging class of Chinese Americans with the Cantonese opera venture, which was previously run by merchants. Because he could operate in both the Chinese and English worlds, he could act as an intermediary. Fortunately for Kee, this 1925 proposal met with no resistance from the Department of Labor, whereas the Mandarin Theater still struggled.

In the end, however, the Lok Tin Tsau troupe was likely also a beneficiary of the Mandarin Theater's persistent pursuit, which prompted the Department of Labor to take a different approach in its dealings with Chinatown theaters. It may explain why, rather than being rejected for months, like the Mandarin, for practically the same request Lok Tin Tsau was given a green light with very little effort. As discussed in Chapter 3, the victory of Mandarin in increasing its quota and clarifying the immigration status of Chinese actors improved the situation for the whole Chinese community, and Lok Tin Tsau was the first to benefit from it. By the end of August, less than two weeks after the Mandarin Theater's victory and merely five weeks after its initial application, Lok Tin Tsau was also approved for both a quota increase and its move. The following month, September 1925, Lok Tin Tsau completed the move and staged its first performance at the Thalia Theater in New York, an established immigrant theater. This was a turning point for the troupe: less than a year later it grew to a healthy size of forty-four members and put on daily shows.[44] Its earlier dream of performing at "the Mecca of all actors" had finally come true.

The Thalia Theater, also named the Old Bowery Theater, had for more than a hundred years been home to a host of performers including Irish, Yiddish, German, and Russian players, as well as various vaudeville groups. However, its staging of Chinese opera raised some eyebrows. The title of a *New York Times* article said: "Chinese Players Revamp Our Oldest Theatre—The Thalia in the Bowery, having exhausted the repertory of the Occident, turns to Oriental drama."[45] The impression given by this article in the *Times*'s Sunday magazine is one of amusement. It included a drawing of the busy stage and the packed house, as well as three drawings of the performers "Gom Woo Deep, Mon Gah Yin, and Jeong Gow Yer," noting the overwhelmingly enthusiastic responses of Chinese audiences.

Though no newspaper advertisements or theater playbills for the Thalia seem to have survived, the *Chinese Nationalist Daily* reported its activities often. And the troupe's immigration records indicate successful growth. Among the forty-three members it had in 1926, fourteen entered from the port of New York, likely the result of increased interaction with Havana. And Lok Tin Tsau seemed to have a formal exchange of performers with San Francisco's Great China Theater, which loaned famous actresses such as Huang Xiaofeng to them. The two rival theaters in San Francisco now had New York extensions.

Thus from September 1925 to March 1927, New York had two theaters with full-scale Cantonese opera performances: Jock Ming On at the London Theater and Lok Tin Tsau at the Thalia. Their main sources of performers remained different. Jock Ming On used Seattle as the main port of entry for its performers, while Lok Tin Tsau maintained its close links with Canada. Because members with Canadian registration exited the United States so regularly, they constituted a unique and highly mobile group shuttling among the cities of United States, Canada, and Cuba. New York's lively Cantonese opera scene also encouraged a regular flow of performers from Cuba via the popular New York and Cuba Mail steamship. A large number of Chinese performers would enter the United States at Ellis Island in the next few years. Meanwhile, according to the *Chinese Nationalist Daily*, Boston gained another Chinese theater, Da Guanyuan, and Chicago also had Da Ronghua (established in 1925).[46]

Nevertheless, the many types of entertainment in New York, as well as its reputation as a major cultural center provided a different social milieu for Chinese theaters than other cities offered. Established organizations such as Metropolitan Opera House, the abundance of theaters and revues, and educational institutions such as Columbia University and the New School of Social Research provided an interesting context for Chinese opera, as reflected in a series of commentaries in the *Chinese Nationalist Daily* in February 1927. An author of a series of five essays discussed the difference between opera and drama. He used the Western term *opera* (or literally *song drama* in Chinese) to describe Cantonese opera, whose Chinese name is in fact "big drama," with no reference to the musical component. Such a distinction was timely because of the quick rise of spoken drama in the Chinese community of New York, for example, at the newly established Minzhi Dramatic Club and the drama association of Chinese students at Columbia University. In that same month, Lok Tin Tsau participated in a fundraising event for the Minzhi Dramatic Club.[47] Operatic arias were offered as interludes in a patriotic spoken drama, while several opera singers took speaking roles in this special drama, which was scripted by Lok Tin Tsau's producer. For example, on February 14, Minzhi Dramatic Club's three-act play featured actress Bailing Xian in an English-speaking role as the wife of an English man, while Yu Baiguo and Kuang Jinye both played female warrior roles in a timely story about the 1925 Northern Expedition in China, fending off foreign power and instituting reforms.[48] Juxtaposing Cantonese opera arias with modern Chinese drama became a common approach to theatrical presentations in New York during this time, reflecting the community's conscious endeavor to forge its identity. In addition, several news reports in the *Chinese Nationalist Daily* brought attention to, and condemned, vaudeville acts or plays that denigrated Chinese.[49] As a part of a cosmopolitan city with a great reputation for theater and an appreciation of fine art and music, the Chinese community showed much self-awareness regarding its dramatic presentations.

YONG NI SHANG THEATER (1927–1929)

In March 1927 Jock Ming On and Lok Tin Tsau were merged by the He Xing Company, forming the Yong Ni Shang troupe at the Thalia Theater. The premiere of the newly merged troupe on March 17 began with the conventional *Joint Investiture*, symbolizing an affluent future for the new endeavor. While the details of the merger remain unknown, its goal undoubtedly was to strengthen the theater business and avoid competition. New York was a valuable location for Cantonese opera on the East Coast, as exemplified by its support of two troupes. Yet fierce competition might eventually have hurt the well-being of the opera business. A merger meant a monopoly and more resources: higher ticket prices, larger wardrobes, more stage properties, and a higher caliber of performers. It also allowed the New York stage to bring together the strengths of two San Francisco theaters. The June 21 report in the *Chinese Nationalist Daily* on the merger conveyed a sense of collective effort: "He Xing Company summoned leaders of various organizations and associations in the community, as well as affluent merchants and companies, to discuss the continuing call for shareholders. It urged everyone to assist and share the responsibility of maintaining the theater. The attendees approved the resolution unanimously."[50] The He Xing Company encouraged the general public to purchase the company stock at the price of $20 per share. The community's cooperation was also important in maintaining safety in the theater, keeping at bay the possibility of tong fights. All the leaders present agreed to share the responsibility of peacekeeping.

Soon afterward the *Chinese Nationalist Daily* printed a series of lists of the theater's shareholders' pledge. The largest amount, $7,800, came from Chin Yee You, the impresario and sponsor of Lun On (1922) and Jock Ming On (1924), followed by $6,000 from Montreal's Huang Liangzi (see Chapter 12). The Mandarin and Great China theaters in San Francisco each held shares totaling $5,000. Other large shareholders were from Seattle, Vancouver, Boston, Montreal, and New York.[51] Clearly this was an important cultural institution for New York and all Chinese communities in North America, and its prosperity was important to the opera network. The total pledged amount from three available lists published in the *Chinese Nationalist Daily* is $85,180.[52] The number of individuals and companies exceeded 130, showing the great promise of this theatrical venture.

The new financial sponsorship meant the engagement of more top performers. The billing of the lead for the opening performance was somewhat tricky. *The Joint Investiture* features the role of "Push Cart" to showcase the stars of the new company, a part traditionally given to the performer of the principal roles. The prima donnas of the two troupes that merged—Huang Xiaofeng and Guan Yinglian—were both featured for the Push Cart routine.[53] A week later Huang would disappear from the playbill, emerging briefly in July at the Great China Theater in San Francisco, en route to China. Huang's departure made Guan the leading female performer, but not for long. She was soon joined by new arrivals, including the famous female impersonator Xiao Dingxiang, whose first performances included the new opera *Wife Emperor*.[54] And by June 21 her farewell notice appeared in the *Chinese Nationalist Daily*, expressing her deep gratitude for the community's hospitality.

There were many exciting performances during the opening months of the Yong Ni Shang Theater. The most celebrated event was the debut on April 22, 1927, of

Li Xuefang, who had arrived in the United States only two months earlier and was adored by San Francisco. The *Chinese Nationalist Daily* gave a special commentary with the highest possible, if clichéd, praise: "So perfect a sound that it should only exist within the ethereal realm of Heaven, rarely could we hope to hear such a beautiful tone in this earthly life."[55] This piece also compared her to the famous Peking opera star Mei Langfang with the phrase "North-Mei-South-Li," coined by the prominent political thinker Kang Youwei and circulated in Shanghai and Hong Kong since 1920.[56] Soon the newspaper reported that tickets to Li's performances were sold out. Li stopped to perform in New York on April 22, 23, and 25 and May 3, 4, and 6. For the East Coast debut she performed her signature opera, *Shilin Paying Respects at the Pagoda*, followed by such other favorites as *Misery Love*, *Cao Dajia*, and *Daiyu Burying Flower Petals*. Her portrayal of the famous maiden Daiyu was spellbinding, as a fan had reflected the prior month in San Francisco, writing, "She was mannered, graceful and refined, as if the delicate maiden Daiyu was reborn. From the scenes of burying the flower petals, to dying and then to a reunification in heaven, she sang with such a pure voice that makes one forget oneself. Her portrayal of the fragile and willowy maiden was perfect, down to every mesmerizing look. Truly commendable."[57] Her reputation in China had preceded her. According to the *World Journal*, "In Guangzhou, she was most popular for her jita performance, in Shanghai, it was Daiyu and Cao Dajia. When she performed jita, the fans cheered at the sight of her, and when she got to the scene of meeting with the son, it would evoke such tumultuous applause that the roof would shake. . . . She was one of the four topmost prima donnas today, together with Li Qimei, Zhang Shuqin and Huang Xiaofeng, but really she was the lead."[58] Following these performances, Li sailed for Havana. After two months, she returned to perform at the theater again starting at the end of July. New York was a meeting point of two important pathways—the one along the Atlantic coast and the one across the continent. As a result the theater was often graced by the best performers in North America.

Although Li performed all of her signature operas on the Yong Ni Shang stage, she also sang the less-well-known *Tears in the Bleak Palace*. Its playbill is one of the only two for her U.S. performances that survive (see figure 11.5). She played a commoner whom a king meets and falls in love with during an outing in disguise. The king makes her a concubine, turning a deaf ear to his generals' objections. He soon indulges himself in pleasure and neglects his kingly duty; an official intervenes, sending her to the palace's most deserted part (Bleak Palace). She falls ill and dies in misery. The strength of her love, however, allows her one last meeting, during which she is happily reunited with the king. Li excelled in roles such as this, one that personifies the conventional female ideal.

The appearance of Xiao Dingxiang, who made his debut at the Great China Theater in 1926, at the Yong Ni Shang Theater also highlighted its unique place in

Fig. 11.5. Playbill, *Tears in the Bleak Palace*, Yong Ni Shang Theater, August 6, 1927, featuring Li Xuefang (courtesy of the Hong Kong Heritage Museum).

the performing circuit. Whereas in San Francisco, Xiao Dingxiang and Li Xuefang were rivals belonging to different theaters, here they appeared successively on the same stage, less than three weeks apart. With distance, New York's stage obscured the antagonism of the West Coast. The playbill reproduced in figure 11.6 features Xiao Dingxiang in a new work that he produced which strung together twenty-six scenes to make an opera with a moral story, a loosely structured clichéd story quite typical of the period. It shows a full supporting cast of sixteen, including the rather famous Dayan Shun and Shezi Ying. This cast was, however, quite unusual, for it was nearly all male; the only female was the stellar Chen Xiufang, playing a supporting role. The East Coast location evidently made the cast even less predictable, and a balanced mix-gender staging still less tangible.

Also, the theater made the most of Xiao Dingxiang's performing on the mixed-gender stage by toying with gender-crossing casting. Whereas his co-starring with the leading actor Bai Jurong in San Francisco for the most part adhered to the conventions of male troupe, in New York he co-starred with actresses, creating baffling situations. In the opera presented on October 17, *Plum Blowing in the Wind*, Xiao played a melancholy woman, a young wife.[59] Actress Zheng Huikui, known for comic male roles, played half of the stage couple with reversed genders, and the actress Zhou Shaoying played the male judge.[60] The drama wove in themes of arranged marriage, modern divorce, and a modern Chinese woman who had studied in Europe and America. If one of the reasons for mixed-gender perfor-

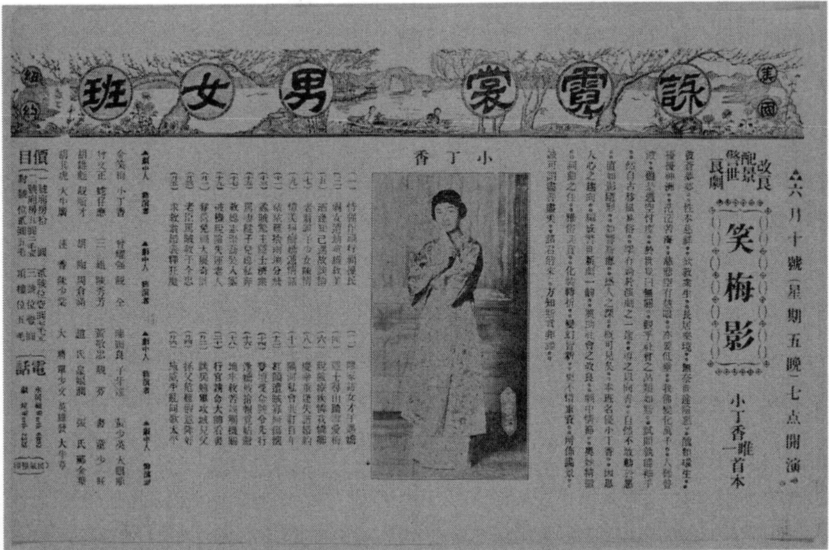

Fig. 11.6. Playbill, *Smile at the Shadow of Plum Flower*, Yong Ni Shang Theater, June 10, 1927, featuring Xiao Dingxiang (courtesy of the Hong Kong Heritage Museum).

mance was realism, then this New York theater's casting choice seemed quite the opposite—it used a double measure of gender crossing, and it was intentionally playful and funny.

The 1920s were famous for cultural advancement and theatrical novelty; many theatrical, musical, and dance productions were looking boldly ahead. So Chinese theaters' gender-bending did not escape the critics who looked to leave behind aesthetics rooted in the older Victorian ideal. The portrayals of men by Cantonese opera actresses had caught the attention of the mainstream press, who used the example to support women's liberation. In 1927 a report in the *New York Times* noted, "Breaking down the custom of centuries, Chinese women have been acting of late in the Chinese Theatre on New York's Bowery. Where once only the male actor appeared, now black-eyed maidens entertain the Westernized Chinese audience. Indeed, they have outdone the West, for recently the women portrayed, very excellently, the parts of men, in their ancient scenes of folklore and presentations of past heroes." In contrast, the author lamented, "the Occidental stage has not seen fit to entrust serious male roles to women."[61] Though it was a misreading derived from lack of awareness of the history of male impersonators on the Chinese stage, the report nonetheless painted a positive and modern image of the theater. And it also showed how the Chinese theater fared against the robust performing culture in Manhattan at this time.

Likely a result of having a monopoly and performers of the highest rank, the ticket prices for the newly merged theater were remarkably high. Judging from the surviving playbills, in mid-1927 the highest ticket price was $2.50 in general, with tickets for Li Xuefang's debut week ranging from $1.00 to $4.00. By November of that year evening performances were $0.50, $1.00, $1.75, $2.50, $5.25, and $10.00. Those led by either famous singers, such as Xiao Dingxiang, Li Xuefang, or later Tan Lanqing, or second-tier singers such as actresses Ling Shaorui and Zhang Qiaohua had the same ticket prices. The top ticket price was five times what Jock Ming On had charged in 1925, when $2.00 was the highest price. On the West Coast, San Francisco theaters were still charging only $2.00 for the highest-priced ticket even when famous performers made debuts. Yong Ni Shang Theater's ticket prices were even higher than Broadway's, where the ticket prices were as high as $3.50.[62]

Forty full-size theater playbills from Yong Ni Shang, dating from April 24, 1927, to January 15, 1928, provide a glimpse of this prolific and vibrant opera theater. That they mostly reside in the archive of the Tai-Ping Theater Collection in Hong Kong further indicates the transnational nature of the opera business. These playbills were similar in every aspect to those in San Francisco theaters, including format, content, and identical studio pictures. However, a picture by a New York photograph studio on a June 16 playbill shows that the theater also began to establish itself locally. The Natural Photo Studio, one of three regularly advertised in the *Chinese Nationalist Daily*, had existed since 1920.[63] Many of these playbills advertised traditional and familiar titles or their derivatives. One dated October 30, however, lists a contemporary opera reflecting the predicament of Chinese immigrants in the United States: *In Search of Father in the United States, Lament at the Immigration Office* (figure 11.7). In this opera, the conventional storyline—a son overcoming all obstacles to be united with his long-lost father—was set against the backdrop of U.S. immigration. Making satire of the bleak reality, the opera was produced and led by the famous comic actress Zheng Huikui, who played the son. It wove in common themes for immigrants: the glorious moment of returning to the village as a successful immigrant, the hardship of separation from family members, loyal and disloyal wives at home, detention at a U.S. port, and love affairs in bachelor society. The question of infidelity was omnipresent: early in the story, the women who betrayed their absent husbands all meet their demise. In the final twist the father himself succumbs to the charms of a young lady who is in fact his son, who approached his father in the United States in the disguise of a young maiden to test his father's loyalty to his mother. (It was also a reversal of the classic opera *Pinggui Returning Home*, in which the waiting loyal wife was tested by the skeptical returning husband.) Even in lighter moments the opera has scenes of interrogation at the immigration office as well as ill-treatment at the detention center. Yet all is resolved happily at the end, and the father and son have their long-sought reunion.

詠霓裳男女班
十月三十日(禮拜晚)六点半開演
金山尋親父
移民局自嘆
鄭詠魁著名首本

Fig. 11.7. Playbill, *In Search of Father in the United States, Lament at the Immigration Office*, Yong Ni Shang Theater, October 30, 1927, featuring Zheng Huikui (courtesy of the Hong Kong Heritage Museum).

The virtuoso actress Tan Lanqing arrived for the Thanksgiving holidays of 1927, having performed earlier in San Francisco and Boston to critical acclaim. Her two-week engagement in New York reflected her popularity on this performing circuit. Advance reports and advertisements show that her appearance was a significant event. On November 21, the day of her debut in New York, an unusually long report in the *Chinese Nationalist Daily* praised her in the most superlative terms:

> Tan is an outstanding performer who emerged recently in Canton. Her voice is as pleasing to the ear as that of the nightingale, so ringing that its resonance can encircle a pillar three times and still continue. Her stage movement is as graceful and willowy as it can be, so much so that it recalls the Tang royal lady Zhao Feiyan. Her beauty, as delicate as flowers of pear trees after a spring rain, surely surpasses that of the Tang royal lady, Yang Gui-fei. She is indeed outstanding among the existing prima donnas of Cantonese opera.[64]

Tan possessed the wonderful blend of beauty, superb musical skills, and the delicate acting and graceful body movement required of Cantonese opera stars, as reflected by the reference to the two quintessential beauties of the Tang Dynasty. Her repertoire included popular classics as well as contemporary operas. For her debut she performed a contemporary opera, *Female Lawyer Rebuke*, playing a statesman's clever daughter, who succeeds in adjudicating a case full of multifarious cover-ups, sending the real villain to jail and uniting a pair of lovers. Tan would become the first actress to co-star with an actor on stage in Hong Kong when the ban was lifted there in 1933. There she would later become a household name for witty comic roles.

The actress Mudan Su, who arrived in the second half of December, dominated the stage for the length of her residency. Creative, talented, and resourceful, in New York she scripted new productions, created more trouser roles, and demonstrated her virtuosity in multiple role types frequently. On loan from the Mandarin Theater, she would appear on the Yong Ni Shang stage for the next year as well. From the day of her debut, December 21, 1927, she led the performance for nine consecutive evenings. In the available playbills from the following months, the theater featured her as the sole lead in fifty-two performances. As a popular star, she received constant praises and reports in the *Chinese Nationalist Daily*. She brought several productions of longer classics that lasted many evenings, such as the four consecutive nights of the new popular opera *Gathering at Zhu Ai* and three nights of the traditional legend *Mulan*. Her signature trouser roles such as *Nocturnal Mourning of White Lotus* were greatly anticipated, and the recordings were readily available in stores.

An important lesson could be learned from a comparison of the playbills of *Nocturnal Mourning of White Lotus* from the Mandarin Theater on January 11, 1927, and the Yong Ni Shang Theater on January 15, 1928. It raises larger questions about the performing circuit. Pictures and promotional text from San Francisco's playbill were used in New York. The synopses were similar but there were some minor variations. Yong Ni Shang had a smaller cast, sixteen rather than nineteen, and a streamlined plot with fewer secondary young scholar and warrior roles. Its synopsis was also not as polished in style as San Francisco's, though the plotline remained intact. Both theaters, however, had the same performers playing the four main characters: actresses Mudan Su (the young scholar), Tan Lanqing (the young belle), and Zheng Huikui (the villain), and actor Zihou Sen (the mother).

This similarity was remarkable since the two performances were a year apart on opposite coasts, and the performers did not have the same itinerary. Performers arrived in New York at different times, and sometimes they came by different routes, so they were probably not dispatched by the Mandarin Theater as a group. Yet the identity of the leading players was not just coincidental, either. The Cantonese opera network of North America had greatly enhanced the mobility of performers, such that the opera stages in different cities not only had similar repertoire but often also the same scenes with the same performers. The actors brought all the key elements—including previous experiences of performing together—for a popular opera such as *Nocturnal Mourning.* In conceptual terms, therefore, one can say the formulaic nature of tigang xi was manifested at the level of performers as well. Their shared appearances could be considered the established paichang for the large North American Cantonese opera culture, from which individual cities drew to put together their productions. These shared scenes contributed to a certain homogeneity of this culture in communities from San Francisco to New York, Vancouver, Boston, or Havana as collective social memory. The transnational cultural influence that the theaters exerted on these Chinese communities of the 1920s came from not only Cantonese opera convention but also its practice.

In March and April 1928, the *Chinese Nationalist Daily* published commentaries on two performances of trouser roles by Mudan Su, both of which were well received. These accounts likely refer to roles in operas such as *Mulan*, in which female cross-dressing was part of the plot. (The heroine's disguising herself as a man in order to take her elderly father's place in the army was the basis of the Disney film.) Several reports in April of 1928 also promoted her new opera, *Two Stars with Fine Dew*, which she produced and led in a trouser role. Mudan Su remained active throughout her stay in New York. With the versatility of her performances and the breadth of her repertoire, Mudan Su was likely the most influential Chinese opera performer in Manhattan. Her success in North America was such that she returned frequently in the 1930s and 1940s before finally settling in New York.

Stage couples were also fashionable there. From the beginning of March to June 1928, Xin Guifei led twenty-three performances, many together with Jinshan Bing, a leading actor. We encountered the couple, who had important roles in the Mandarin Theater's opening month, in Chapter 9. This New York performance was likely part of their second visit to the United States, after stopping in Vancouver. Like Chinatown theaters in other cities, Yong Ni Shang was active in the community, offering performances at holiday gatherings of family associations, fundraising events, and more.

Famous performers whose tours took them to engagements in Canada or Cuba, or on the West Coast often stopped in New York. The city's Chinese community was keenly aware of its role as an important nodal point on the transnational network. News reports of star performers' arrivals were usually peppered with information about the cities they came from and the cities they were headed to. The route of actress Xiao Caiji was representative of New York's pivotal position. Initially arriving from China in January 1925, she performed in San Francisco for a year and left for Mexicali in March 1926. Thereafter she went to perform in Havana's Teatro Cina until she was engaged in late 1927 by the newly formed Mandarin Theater in Vancouver. En route, she stopped at the end of 1927 to perform in New York, where the theater asked her to stay longer in order to perform with Mudan Su.[65] A common itinerary it must have been, because the actor Chen Cunjin, appearing in New York in July, also reemerged in Vancouver in December that year.

Despite the regular appearance of Yong Ni Shang Theater's playbills and news reports in the *Chinese Nationalist Daily*, the advertisements ended abruptly on June 19, 1928, and therefore little about its later programming is known today. From occasional reports in the *Chinese Nationalist Daily* about the arrivals of well-known actresses from San Francisco at the theater, we know that the performances seemed to have continued with the same high quality. A playbill for May 22, 1929, featuring Li Feifeng showed a prosperous theater.[66] Tragically, on June 6, 1929, the Thalia Theater burned to the ground, ending not only the most glorious era of Cantonese opera theater in Manhattan, but also the long history of a Bowery landmark that had served as a home to theater groups since October 1826.[67] There were conflicting reports about the significant loss to the Yong Ni Shang Company. The *New York Times* stated that the costumes were preserved intact in dressing rooms behind the stage, and so was most of the scenery, valued at $10,000. The *Chinese Nationalist Daily* estimated the theater's losses at $40,000 in addition to the scenery.[68]

Whatever the damage, the community expressed a strong desire for the restoration of Cantonese opera. Four days after the fire, the *Chinese Nationalist Daily* reported that the theater fire deprived numerous Chinese immigrants of their favorite entertainment.[69] The owner of the theater, Charles King, president of the He Xing Theatre Company, quickly found a new location at the Grand Street Theater at 255–261 Grand Street.[70] Nevertheless, considering the property loss, it was difficult to resume full operations or retain its strongest cast members. Before long, the leading actress, Mudan Su, reemerged at San Francisco's Mandarin Theater, and by the end of 1930 the He Xing Company officially declared bankruptcy.[71] Afterward, some of its cast members continued to act in the community, offering a small number of regular performances. They would continue in this reduced way until they were all forced to leave the country by immigration officials in 1934 as a result of dwindling performance opportunities.[72] This situation was revealed, ironically, by the theater's own attorney during a routine request for renewal of permits for its performers.[73]

PAVING THE WAY FOR MEI LANFANG'S U.S. VISIT

That New York was the first destination for public performance of the Peking opera star Mei Lanfang indicates the city's unique significance. As early as 1927 the *Chinese Nationalist Daily* reported the star's planned tour of the United States.[74] This complicated plan would weather many difficulties, including turmoil in China and the Great Depression in the United States, before finally materializing in early 1930. The New York Chinese community contributed in important ways to its success.

In the pages of the *Chinese Nationalist Daily* one could easily find the community's admiration for the Peking opera star, with commentaries about his activities, repertoire, and new roles or performance plans, or reports of his interaction with foreign artists or diplomats in China. New York's non-Cantonese Chinese placed

Chinese opera in a different light, one that showed a certain affinity for Peking opera. The newspaper in general printed more literary musing about Peking opera than about Cantonese opera (the reverse of the case in San Francisco's and Vancouver's Chinese newspapers). The Chinese population in New York included many diplomats, tycoons, and intellectuals from different parts of China. Chinese students at Columbia University were quite active in theatrical presentations, featuring primarily Peking opera or spoken drama. They sometimes borrowed inspirations and expertise from Chinatown theaters that featured Cantonese opera exclusively, however. Guan Yinglian and Ou Runcai were reported to be featured in an event held by the Columbia Chinese Student Association in the spring of 1927, together with the Minzhi Dramatic Club and a female student's Peking opera performance.[75]

New York's Chinese actively contributed to the success of Mei's tour. Sage journalists such as Brooklyn-born Ernest K. Moy wrote several pamphlets in English and toured with him.[76] Eloquent speakers such as Columbia alumnus P. C. Chang served as consultant, interpreter, and spokesperson, as well as a lecturer on opera. A student, Yang Soo, served as commentator at every performance. The trip was arranged under the auspices of the China Institute of America, founded in 1926 by a group of Chinese and American elites including Columbia professors John Dewey and Paul Monroe and alumni Hu Shih and Kuo Pingwen.[77] In order to present Mei the institute undertook a campaign to accrue a long list of dignitaries to act as sponsors. Differences in dialect were no hindrance to the appreciation of Mei's virtuosity in Peking opera; many in the Chinese community admired his art all the same, as did the audiences in Shanghai or Guangzhou.[78] And Chinatown was rallied to support Mei's visit with a welcoming ceremony upon his arrival. New York Chinese, keenly aware of the trope of Chinese opera in American popular imagination, however, also steered Mei to Francis Charles Coppicus, general secretary of the Metropolitan Opera and manager of many opera singers including Enrico Caruso. His performance thus treaded the fine line between presenting the high art of Chinese opera and meeting the preconceptions of the American public. When he finally performed in New York, Mei's virtuosity and extravagant staging at Broadway theaters became a must-see for all the social elite. Mei was "adopted by Park Avenue," as the *New York Times* claimed, and his art was set apart from the Cantonese opera then performed in Chinatown.[79] The latter was featuring the newly arrived actress Huang Xuemei, a famed disciple of Li Xuefang, who went from San Francisco to Havana to New York. Mei and Huang were thus both performing in New York in 1930,[80] underscoring the cultural complexity of Chinese community there.

In general, Chinese theaters and communities in the United States smoothed the way for Mei Lanfang's visit with their political influence, audience base, and even performer quota. For example, when Mei and his performers first arrived, the immigration authorities in Seattle detained them until the Great China Theater used the vacancy left in its quota of eighty-four to sponsor their entry into the United States.[81] The theatrical communities also played host to Mei's visit in all things except as venues. The locations for his performance include the 49th Street Theater and the National Theater (New York), the Princess Theater (Chicago), the Tivoli Theater, the Liberty Theater, and the Capital Theater (San Francisco), and Philharmonic Auditorium (Los Angeles). That he generally performed in larger venues and away from Chinatown underscores both the popular demand in mainstream society and the Mei Lanfang group's conscientious efforts to avoid being associated with the stereotypical image of Chinatown. Paradoxically, as the incident at Seattle immigration office showed, Mei's U.S. tour was made possible by the theaters. But the American public wanted to keep the two as separate as possible, even, as the *New York Times* reporter Grace Lynn did, using Mei's artistic status to cast aspersions on the city's Chinatown theater.[82]

RECORD COMPANIES AND ADVERTISEMENTS

As the capital of the recording industry in the United States, New York was the home of many major record labels during this time, such as Victor, Columbia, and Brunswick. They soon noticed the popularity of opera in the city's Chinese community. The case of Li Feifeng provides an interesting example of the Chinese connection to the local record industry. In a Yong Ni Shang playbill of May 1929, she was featured as the lead of *Snowy Plum Flower in the Wind*, whose cast included twenty actors for this performance of twenty-six scenes. The elaborate couplets devised for each scene depict a plotline filled with twists and turns, as well as the common themes of disrupted romance, separated lovers, and a lovelorn young belle. It also promised characters in disguises, scenes of battling warriors, and majestic generals. Li Feifeng appeared in traditional Chinese costume on the playbill, showing her prominent role in this traditional drama.[83]

While performing in New York, Li also began her recording career, through an introduction by Lee Eng, a fan and the owner of a prominent general store, to agents at the Victor Talking Machine Company. The company had begun to sell the new electrical recordings (using technology that captured sound using microphones instead of singing into horns) just four years earlier, in 1925. Li became a Victor artist (as "Lee Fee Fun") and recorded three titles that became instant hits in the Chinese community. Their success led to the recording of two more titles soon afterward.[84] The record company had an impetus to invest in "ethnic recording." Altogether, Li recorded three titles on six double-faced discs in March 1929 and two more titles on six discs in October.[85] In New York's Chinatown these recordings were promoted prominently, with her photos appearing in the Lee Eng Store's general advertisements in the *Chinese Nationalist Daily* (see figure 11.8). Unlike the

Fig. 11.8. Advertisement for a recording by Li Feifeng by the Lee Eng Company, *Chinese Nationalist Daily*, December 13, 1929 (courtesy of the New York Public Library).

playbill photo, in which Li wore a Chinese dress, the record advertisement shows her in a fanciful modern dress that did not resemble the conventional wardrobe for the Cantonese opera stage. The costume is part traditional and part fanciful, in general unorthodox and modern. It was suitable for a city that prided itself on cultural innovation and where the milieu was such that this faux oriental style had particular appeal.

Benefiting from its proximity to the headquarters of the major recording studios and factories, the New York Chinese community became a conduit between Cantonese opera and this new technology. Li's recordings were widely available where she toured in North America. The advertisements for these recordings remained in the newspapers for months, often with her photos. Later in 1930, when Li Feifeng returned to Hong Kong, she brought them to be manufactured there. Her fame must have been helped by the recordings, which were in wide circulation: when she performed for several evenings in San Francisco, en route to China, she was presented with a gold plaque worth between $700 and $800.[86] It was customary for the community to present a plaque to famous performers as a tribute and to show its admiration, so this honor was an affirmation of her status. Later a similar recording deal would be offered to the Cantonese music master Qiu Hechou while in New York, also by the Lee Eng Company, which made recordings for four titles.[87] And when Peking opera star Mei Lanfang visited in early 1930, he also went to the Victor studio to record several arias.[88] These recordings with the Victor label, similar to those on the Oriental Record label made by the Great China Theater, paralleled the performing network and marked the start of Chinese opera's local engagement with the city's fast-growing recording industry.

The liveliness of Cantonese opera culture in New York is also suggested by the detailed advertisements for recordings that frequently appeared in the *Chinese Nationalist Daily*. And that three prominent general stores—Kwong Sun Chong Company (30 Mott Street), Lee Eng and Company (42 Mott Street), and Kee Chong and Company (51 Mott Street)—almost next to each other regularly displayed large record advertisements showed the high demand for opera records. A fourth, the Lawson Company, could be found at 22 Pell Street. They supplied these opera recordings to the city-wide Chinese community connected to Chinatown through the convenient public transportation system. Furthermore, amateur singing groups made use of the recordings to learn operatic songs, and they sang for community events from Chinese school fundraisers to family association banquets.

In addition, these companies' advertisements were seen in Chinese communities outside New York. For instance, correspondence from 1926 between the merchant Zhou Fayin in Toronto and the Lee Eng Company discussed the payment arrangements for a purchase of recordings. The customer, after having received eight disks ordered from the store, requested that the balance be applied to other purchases.[89] The Lee Eng Company was the largest advertiser in the *Chinese Nationalist Daily*, and in 1928 its advertisements could easily be distinguished by photographs of stars such as Li Xuefang and Li Feifeng. Catalogues of various record labels were available on demand, and pamphlets of lyrics often accompanied the recordings. Through the print media and the quickly rising modes of listening, Cantonese opera culture thus reached well beyond the paths and nodes of the performance network.

Two advertisements for recordings in the *Chinese Nationalist Daily* illustrate the role of operatic songs and phonographs in the larger Chinese community, in particular, the connection to notions of modernity. The first features a modern middle-class woman posing with a book of operatic songs in her hand and a phonograph nearby (figure 11.9a). While the focus of the image is clearly on musical enjoyment, it takes place in a comfortable drawing room rather than the bustling theater. A sense of exclusive enjoyment is subtly implied. The stylish female persona is epitomized by the book she holds in her delicate hand whose cover means literally "Collection of Songs." In the upper part of the advertisement, along with mention of clothes, fabric, brands of phonographs, and other miscellaneous items, appears the clichéd praise, "So perfect a melody that it should only exist within the ethereal realm of Heaven; rarely could we hope to hear such a beautiful sound in this earthly life." The second, by the Kwong Sun Chong Company, shows two women in the act of playing a phonograph (figure 11.9b). Compared with the previous advertisement, these two women are less modern, with flatter shoes, less

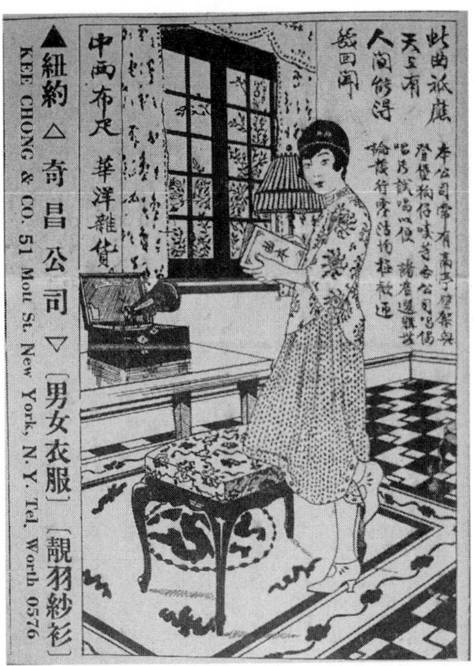

Figs. 11.9a and 11.9b. Advertisement by Kee Chong & Company, *Chinese Nationalist Daily*, July 4, 1928 (*left*); advertisement by the Kwong Sun Chong Company, *Chinese Nationalist Daily*, October 10, 1928 (*right*) (courtesy of the New York Public Library).

makeup, and traditional hairstyles. The bottom of the advertisement announces new recordings, teas from famous regions, and miscellaneous items such as embroidery, shoes, silk, and ceramics. Together, these two advertisements point to the popularity of operatic songs as part of the image of both the new glamorous lifestyle and the traditional one. The observation of American ethnographer Stewart Culin, reported by the *New York Times* in 1925, also shows the increasing popularity of phonographs: "While strolling through one of the narrow streets [of Chinatown], he was surprised to hear some excellent Chinese music. Entering a building from which the strains emanated he discovered it was a phonograph. He was amazed and purchased several records."[90]

Unlike their counterparts sans photos in newspapers of other Chinatowns, the advertisements of Cantonese opera recordings in the East Coast newspaper had a compelling visual effect and cultural significance. The confident poses in the images, together with the popular operatic song collections and instrumental accompaniment manuals, all suggest the active enjoyment of Cantonese opera. In New York's Chinatown in the 1920s, opera was an art form that united spectacle, drama, local and visiting talents, regional musical tastes, and musical tradition into a vibrant whole. And with the advent of the phonograph, Cantonese opera became part of modern life. An American curator's observation on attending the theater was rather telling:

> I visited the Chinese theatre with a Chinese friend. The play which we attended was in one of the old Bowery theatres on the east side. I was the only white man in the audience, which was composed of some 600 Orientals. Most of them were young men, wearing straw hats, silk shirts and modish attire. They might have been so many college boys. The scene and the atmosphere were modern, the electric lights were glaring.[91]

What was presented on the New York stages in the 1920s was at the same time local and transnational. And the performances, while rooted in the Cantonese opera tradition, were also adapted in different ways to reflect life in New York, one that was full of theatrical and musical excitement. Chinese theaters had an aura of contemporary life in the cosmopolitan city.

CHAPTER 12

FROM HONOLULU TO HAVANA

Though the Cantonese opera network spanned the continent, its manifestation in any particular place varied according to local conditions. This chapter considers three Chinese theaters (in Honolulu, Vancouver, and Havana) of the 1920s to offer further perspectives on the renaissance of Cantonese opera during that decade. In doing so, we gain a fuller appreciation of how their theaters were linked to, steered by, and shaped by the transnational performing network, and in turn, how the network was affected by them. As we will see, the national borders, national legislation, and geopolitics were still important parts of the picture, but something else comes into focus as well: the transnational network.

THE KUE HING COMPANY

After the Lun On Company's San Francisco success in 1922, merchants in British Columbia responded with enthusiasm to the new business possibility, taking advantage of new border-crossing opportunities and Vancouver's position as a major port on the Pacific Coast near Seattle. The Kue Hing Company was a particularly intrepid venture.[1] Sponsored by the most prominent Chinese merchants in Vancouver and Victoria, Kue Hing registered in Vancouver as a private company with capital of C$20,000 in early 1923. Among its twenty-two directors and forty-five shareholders were both Chinese-born established merchants and up-and-coming Canadian-born ones. The bilingual Lim Bang, a manager of the Gim Fook Yuen

Company in Victoria and of the Chinese Victoria branch of the Bank of Vancouver, was the president. Yip Sang's fifth son, Yip Kew Him, served as a director, and his family's famous store (the Wing Sang Company) often hosted meetings of its directors.[2] The company engaged the troupe Guo Fengnian from China (with the same name as the 1917 troupe, but likely no relation), and opened in the Sheng Ping Theater on April 9, 1923. After three months, it left for Seattle to perform in the United States.

The company ran into its first obstacle at the U.S. Immigration office, which rejected their landing at Seattle with a list of reasons: the results of medical examinations (hook worm and liver flukes), an invalid merchant certificate (Lim Bang), an overabundance of similar applications by Chinese theaters, and opposition by rivals. After mobilizing the help of the Chinese Embassy and Roger O'Donnell in Washington, DC, and the consulate in Vancouver, as well as engaging the services of Seattle lawyer Paul Houser, and changing its application—now going directly to Honolulu, with no performances on the continent—the application was approved. The Department of Labor authorized a quota of thirty members for the Honolulu operation. The endorsement of two prominent bankers at Liberty Bank, a Chinese-owned bank in Honolulu, helped the Kue Hing Company receive a one-year waiver of the cash bond requirement for performers.[3] On August 2, 1923, the troupe successfully made its debut at the Asahi Theater in Honolulu. The nightly ticket sales for the opening few days totaled about $1,000.[4]

Honolulu was a nexus in the trans-Pacific crossing and a gateway into the United States. The location made this endeavor unique. The performers traveled in both directions. At Honolulu the company conveniently recruited performers passing through the port on the way to other theaters in North America or on the way to China. There were three company members stationed in Honolulu to manage the theater's operation, while the head office in Vancouver supervised from a distance.[5] The latter retained control of most decisions and received daily reports of ticket sales. Inevitably, running such a transnational operation with the awkward arrangement had its challenges; the company at times struggled to adapt swiftly to unpredictable or spontaneous events.

The theater's playbills of October 11 to 16, 1923, show a cast including actresses Meiren Su and Huozhuan Zi, and the actor Fengqing Qi, along with elaborate sets and modern props. Fengqing Qi had performed at Vancouver's Sheng Ping Theater starting in mid-1920 and joined the Jock Ming On troupe there in March 1923. After his stint with Kue Hing, he would return to China.[6] A famous actor, his costumes and props were valued at $450 for customs purposes (luckily, the duty was waived after a prominent Honolulu merchant intervened). The initial troupe only had two actresses, one of whom was Wenwu Hao. Then Kue Hing recruited Meiren Su for the Honolulu run in September right after her popular performance in Victoria.

Fig. 12.1. Meiren Su (*left*) and Fengqing Qi (*right*), Kue Hing Company, October 1923, File 55007/18, INS-SPF.

One manager proudly reported that her fellow passengers were enchanted by her performances at sea and that her imminent appearance at Honolulu was much to fellow passengers' envy.[7] The hiring of Huozhuan Zi was even more impromptu. She was en route from Havana to China. The theater managers, taking advantage of the few hours when her ship was docked for refueling, went on board to offer her and her father a contract and rushed her immigration paper to the Department of Labor for approval.[8] The ticket sales always surged for new arrivals, so the theater excelled at such prompt responses to opportunities.

Several surviving playbills from around this time provide examples of the theater's grand productions. A playbill for October 16, 1923 for the classic opera *Shilin Paying Respects at the Pagoda* promised a chair decorated with light bulbs (a fashion of the time), an electrically lit pagoda, and a papier-mâché sea creature. The ample use of electric decoration in props echoed the type of sensation then in vogue in southern China. The theater's lively description of the scenes underscored the intriguing and fantastic ethereal and moral worlds of this legendary romance and alluded to the beautiful arias. It points to the popularity of Huozhuan Zi in Havana, Southeast Asia, and elsewhere and highlights her virtuosity in singing the famous jita aria. Three days earlier, a new opera had been put together to showcase the excellent Fengqing Qi with three other actors and the actresses Meiren Su and Wenwu Hao. Titled *Female Warrior Saving the Country,* the cosmopolitan opera was a newly created story of patriotism incorporating the Soviet invasion of Poland.[9] The plot celebrates bravery and underscores the importance of standing up for a country's sovereignty in the face of hegemonic military force, a clear commentary on the imminent Japanese invasion of China. The European backdrop of the story was reflected in the characters' Western names, as well as such roles as consul general, rather than traditional Chinese officials. It provided a glimpse of the worldliness of Cantonese opera production and awareness of geopolitical contexts. The Kue Hing Company's playbills had a professional appearance on a par with the theaters on the continent. Two local Chinese newspapers, the *Liberty News* and *New China Daily*, took turns acting as the printing facility for the troupe. The collaboration of these two rival papers of opposing political affiliations reveals the significance of this new troupe to the community.

An inevitable consequence of such a long-distance operation was its unpredictability, especially when it came to personnel. The theater manager reported that after his first performance, actor Fengqing Qi refused to perform on account of insufficient numbers of actresses in leading roles and background actors to support his performance. Although he had seemed agreeable in Vancouver, the letter noted, Fengqing Qi turned out to be difficult for the manager at Honolulu. And although initially signed up to take charge of opera production, the veteran actor Shezi Yao refused to take the responsibility of *kaixi shiye* (lead producer), a skill other actors apparently did not have. It created very touchy situations at the theater and eroded the company's trust in the local management. The head office in Vancouver, skeptical of the staff, the fluctuation of ticket sales, and the pricing policy, hired private detectives to understand the local situation. Replacements for the theater managers were sent by the end of October.

There were also local problems. The manager of the Asahi Theater reported disruption by neighborhood thugs, incompetent personnel, and a rival theater.[10] By early 1924 the Kue Hing company had moved to the 1,300-seat Liberty Theater. The distance between the theater in Honolulu and the company in Vancouver also meant that the local managers could not rein in misbehaving performers when their contracts and terms were kept at the headquarters or when impromptu hires were not firmed up by clear contracts. The immigration process became more onerous, as the theater encountered numerous denials of entry of its performers, including Guan Yinglian and her husband in August, until attorneys and officials from Vancouver, Washington, DC, and Honolulu intervened.[11] This inefficiency also meant that though Kue Hing Company received permission for a tour on the continent as early as January 1924, it never moved to materialize the plan. Competition soon sprang up both locally and from other theatrical companies on the continent. Lun Hop sought financial backing from the Canton Bank in San Francisco to buy part of Kue Hing, but did not succeed.[12] An application by an All-Star troupe in Los Angeles later in 1924 sought to establish a second theater in Honolulu, but it was turned down.[13] In the spring, fifteen actors defected to form a rival troupe sponsored by L. Ah Leong, a wealthy and prominent Chinese merchant in Honolulu. The Kue Hing was affected badly and could barely continue. At a point when the fate of the theater was in the balance, merchants and residents stepped up with financial support and wrote a petition to the commissioner general of immigration, W. W. Husband in Washington, DC, in support of the continuation of the theater:

> For the first time in almost twenty years a regular company of players has come to our city of Honolulu with performances of the ancient plays of China, and while in thought and daily life, we are Americans, the old ancient characters of Chinese history and mythology as portrayed in these plays and performances are an education to most of us. The show now playing in Honolulu is financed and operated by the undersigned who have come forward voluntarily and assumed the expenses incidental to its operation at our own costs. And as now conducted, the performances are a great benefit to us and to those who still understand the Chinese plays and languages. We beg to vouch for the character of the actors and actresses who have remained with the Kue Hing Company since their arrival at Honolulu, they being men and women of refinement and have contributed much to the recreational and education side of our isolated existence here in Hawaii during their short sojourn in our midst. We most respectfully beg that their efforts in our behalf be recognized as being in the utmost good faith, and that our request is not founded on any desire to abuse the first privilege, or to evade the immigration laws.[14]

The letter reveals the unique situation of the Chinatown community in Honolulu in the early part of the twentieth century. The historian Adam McKeown notes that whereas in the nineteenth century most Chinese in Honolulu were born in China, by 1930 as many as half of them were locally born. A wide spectrum of Chinese consisted of respectable merchants engaging in small-scale or large business. And although they maintained a strong connection with the Chinese government, they "increasingly defined themselves in terms of Hawaii as a coherent ethnic group in a multicultural society."[15] The proportion of Chinese residing in Honolulu increased from 35 percent to 71 percent between 1900 and 1930.[16] This led the Chinese community to promote its culture as an ethnic heritage, and Chinese theater was deemed an important part of that heritage.

Finally the company's headquarters authorized new company shares totaling $10,000 to be made available to Honolulu merchants. The owner of the rival Chinese theater, L. Ah Leong, bought the new shares, and his financial backing ensured the continuation of Kue Hing's performances.[17] And by July 1924, it received permission to continue. Later in 1926 after Vancouver ceded still more control to local investors, the theater was reorganized with new capital and with thirty members (five musicians, eight actresses, and seventeen actors, two of whom were also the stage director and property man, respectively). It then obtained an increase in its quota to forty members and staged performances all through the 1920s.[18] The theater was, as its new attorney Charles Dwight noted, highly "beneficial to Chinese community. It is the only form of entertainment enjoyed by them."[19]

At least two hundred of Kue Hing's performers arrived at Honolulu between 1923 and 1929, most of whom also performed in the theaters of San Francisco and New York.[20] Kue Hing benefited from the convenience of recruiting star performers to Honolulu either before or after their residency in San Francisco. Performers, on the other hand, benefited from the theater as a possible additional venue on their trans-Pacific voyages. For example, while Yangzhou Mei was still performing with Lun Hop at the Crescent Theater in San Francisco, she was also negotiating with Kue Hing for a Honolulu engagement, in addition to entertaining offers from two other theatrical companies.[21] The troupe cast its net wide: the managers would write to their contacts regularly, asking for information on performers returning to China from San Francisco, Havana, and Peru. Notices of performers' availability and inquiries about possible employment were also treated promptly. They frequently fielded inquiries from Los Angeles and even Sydney about performance possibilities for those en route to China.[22]

Geographically speaking, Honolulu was an ideal stop for the performers on the trans-Pacific journey, not only providing an additional performing opportunity, but also letting them circumvent the three-year limit on their stays. Performers checked out by immigration officials at ports such as Seattle or San Francisco could apply for admission anew from the Territory of Honolulu. While performing in Honolulu en route to China, some actors would receive a new contract from the United States and turn around. As examples of the sort of activity of which Honolulu was the center, records show that Guan Yinglian and her husband arrived on September 13, 1924, and the Singaporean actress Ziyou Hua on March 3, 1925, all after performing at the Crescent Theater.[23] In June 1927 Huang Shaoqiu arrived on his way to the Great China Theater, while in the opposite direction, Huang Xiaofeng arrived en route to China, after Havana, New York, and San Francisco.[24] The divas disembarking in the autumn of 1929 stood out: Li Xuefang arrived on August 6 from the Mandarin, and Mudan Su in November from the Great China.[25] Each actress performed in Honolulu for a month. The theater was bustling with top actors traveling in both directions. Although, as attorney Roger O'Donnell once noted, "The high rates of compensation now demanded by and paid to first class talent" might not always translate to profit, the first-rate performances shaped the opera culture in Honolulu in important ways.[26] After conceding some control to the local sponsors (one-third of the total company shares in 1924, and likely more later), Kue Hing continued operating the vibrant theater in Honolulu. The company's immigration file at the U.S. National Archives ends with December 1929, however; the company's business papers in Vancouver stopped in 1924, when the troupe began to be sponsored by local merchants.

The few surviving playbills, stage photos, and advertisements provide limited information about the repertoire and performers. This lack is remedied, however, by the voluminous immigration documents. Two splendid headshots from the Kue Hing Company bond papers in 1929 captured the star actresses Li Xuefang and Mudan Su at the end of the decade, departing for China. With the flapper's finger wave hairstyle, they had acquired modern Western metropolitan glamour. On her silk dress Mudan Su also wore the gold plate that was customarily an honor presented to opera performers by adoring audiences.

The combination of Western sophistication and traditional marks of prestige seen in these photos is suggestive. Marking the end of the decade they encapsulated the fashionable female icon, an image richly imbued with the traditional aesthetics of Cantonese opera yet symbolizing the figure of modern womanhood. In these pictures they exuded confidence and the glow of success.

THE MANDARIN THEATER COMPANY

If, as discussed in earlier chapters, the arrival of the Le Wannian troupe in Vancouver in 1921 marked the beginning of the modern era of Cantonese opera in North America, then its departure for the United States in early 1923 signaled the end of Vancouver as the prime destination in North America for opera performers. The establishment of its Mandarin Theater Company in 1927 reflected the change in Vancouver's role in interesting ways.

Only a month after the Le Wannian troupe left Vancouver, the Jock Ming On troupe opened in March 1923 at the Chinese theater on Shanghai Alley.[27] Within a month, another troupe, the Guo Fengnian troupe, sponsored by the Kue Hing Company, opened at the Sheng Ping Theater. Vancouver became a springboard for performers who would then travel in the North American circuit. For example, Guo Fengnian's female warrior Wen Wuhao, who dominated the Vancouver stage in her opening month, went to San Francisco and debuted with Lun Hop at the Crescent Theater in July 1923. The three-month rivalry of Vancouver's two troupes ended when Guo Fengnian left for Honolulu. Jock Ming On continued until June 1924, when it departed for the United States.

After Canada passed the Chinese Exclusion Act in 1923, the Vancouver community was devastated. The shrinking Chinese community and stringent immigration regulation combined to hurt the theater business. It was unsurprising that Vancouver had only one active troupe, Guo Zhongxing, run by the Tong Yi Company, from late 1924 to 1926. Guo Zhongxing, direct from China, made its debut at the Sheng Ping Theater in November 1924.[28] In its cast were many actresses and female impersonators, as well as other actors, showing an increasingly gender-balanced stage. The troupe was short-lived, however. At the end of May 1926 it put out its final notice, listing two difficulties: (1) some of its performers were ordered by the government to leave immediately; and (2) the financial situation of the troupe was no longer sustainable. The company sold off all its musical instruments and props in both Vancouver and Victoria, as well as any remaining portions of its performers' contracts.[29] Several Chinese theaters from the 1920s to the 1940s were terminated in similar ways.

Still hoping to reenergize their opera scene, Vancouver merchants turned to the successful theaters in American cities. A new company named Tong Li, which bought the equipment from the defunct Guo Zhongxing troupe, tried soliciting help from the Mandarin Theater in San Francisco and the Jock Ming On Theater in New York.[30] Its proposal of collaboration was turned down by the Mandarin, which instead promised to send performers, whom Tong Li would supplement with actors from China. Under this plan, Tong Li began to work with its counterparts in other cities.

On February 1, 1927, the Tong Li Company presented its troupe—the "Mandarin Theater Troupe Co."—at the Sheng Ping Theater. Instead of a name that referenced famous troupes in southern China, it adopted the name associated with the modern image of San Francisco's theater. Most performers, nevertheless, came directly from southern China, including seventeen actors and actresses, and five musicians and other professionals. A youthful Huang Yulian was the leading actress.[31] One top actor came from the Great China Theater—Xin Shezi Qiu, who had performed there with the star Bai Jurong since November 1925. When Bai finished in San Francisco and left for China, Xin Shezi Qiu left for Vancouver. In order to raise anticipation, the *Chinese Times* praised his portrayal of the dignified general Yang Yanzhou as having poised movement, skillful singing, and wit.[32] The paper similarly raved about Jinshan Bing and Xin Guifei, who had performed with San Francisco's Mandarin Theater since 1924, in anticipation of their arrival in Vancouver in August. The community's enthusiasm for them was also expressed in monetary terms through giving the actors silver plaques. An opinion piece in the *Chinese Times* detailed the individual strengths and signature operas of these two performers.[33] Another popular comic actor, Shezi Ying, arrived in late 1927 after successful performances at the Great China, Jock Ming On, and Yong Ni Shang theaters. While the establishment of the Mandarin Theater Company in Vancouver met the demand of the community's opera fans, it also made Vancouver more central to the larger performing network.

Cantonese opera was shown to connect closely to the community's self-image and creativity, as revealed by two poignant examples. The first is the design of theater playbills. Whereas San Francisco's studio photographs of performers were

雲高華埠 同利 大舞台班 公司 哥比林街

△新曆二月六號(即禮拜一)晚七点開演

新編艷情佳劇 茶薇恨 蕭彩姬一唯首本 全班拍演

戲劇所以令人動目怡情。不外一類一。所以引人凝神悅耳。不外一唱一和。超等文武名伶蕭彩。描寫無不善體人意。按合劇情。茶薇恨一劇。誠該伶得意之傑作也。其中悲歡離合。大演唱情。諸君公餘遣興。仰早光臨爲盼。

女旦蕭彩姬

詠該伶詩

Fig. 12.2. Playbill, *Regret of Chawei*, Mandarin Theater (Vancouver), February 6, 1928 (courtesy of the Hong Kong Heritage Museum).

also used on playbills in cities such as New York and Havana, they have not been found in Vancouver theater playbills. Photographs on the playbills of Vancouver's Mandarin Theater were supplied by C. B. Wand (discussed in Chapter 6). At the beginning the subjects were shown with basic postures and dramatic, but stiff, gestures in front of typical scenic paintings, with a basic border (see the playbill for August 24, 1927, in figure 10.7). A playbill from February 1928 is drastically different (see figure 12.2). It almost shows a need on the photographer's part for creative reinvention. There is much more artistic and creative flair in this playbill than in figure 10.7. The portrait, which is of actress Xiao Caiji, resembles the aesthetic effect of an oil painting. The actress is seen at full length in a three-quarter view, draped in a stylish gown. The photographer seemed to revel in the subtlety of her facial expression: a subdued smile expressing dignity, and an engaging gaze expressing intelligence. Her delicate hands are folded elegantly, and her pointed feet suggest a long, graceful line with the legs. The dark, rather than scenic, backdrop made the pose of the actress stand out. The adulatory verses surrounding the picture, as well as a detailed floral border, produce a memorable whole. No photo credit was provided for this playbill, yet this portrait of the actress no doubt pointed to Western aesthetics. It is almost painterly; the pointed foot recalls ballet dancers; the gown flows in the style of a Western dress. The portrait reflects a public identity linked to the community's aspiration and self-image, that of the second-generation Chinese Canadian. Such aestheticized images of actresses reflected the inspiration of the photography studios to move beyond realism or functionality.[34] The creativity went hand-in-hand with the theater's forward-looking image.

The second example of the theater's interaction with the community is a Chinese school event in 1927. The school produced a performance to celebrate the birthday of Confucius and to raise funds. It was a modern play by a large number of students and community members. The three-act play was billed as a modern dialogue drama, yet the convoluted story used many improbable twists, characteristic of Cantonese opera. It was a medley of different styles: Western-style chorus, duet and ensemble, Chinese folk songs, crosstalk skit (comic dialogue between two performers in a bantering style, rich in puns and allusions), and Cantonese opera arias. One of the highlights of the play was an eight-year-old girl singing the famous aria from the popular opera *Nocturnal Mourning of White Lotus* discussed in the introduction.[35] The hybrid performance used Cantonese opera to add local color and to aid the community's acculturation to other forms of musical entertainment. The opera was evidently part of the youngsters' daily practice and musical identity. The same community had by now established soccer and rugby teams. It also had Chinese brass bands, as did Portland and San Francisco, as part of their extracurricular activities.[36] Nevertheless, the local theater and opera performing culture remained an important part of social life.

Vancouver's Mandarin Theater remained active through the end of the decade, featuring actresses Liang Lizhu, Xue Yingluan, and Lu Xuehong, all of whom would become prominent performers at the Mandarin Theater in San Francisco well into the 1930s.[37] Gradually, Vancouver became a conduit for the performing network, serving as a stop for stars who were either destined for San Francisco or leaving North America.[38] By the end of the decade, activity on the performing network from high-traffic destinations such as New York and San Francisco theaters to the periphery were still going strong. For example, a troupe named Tai Ping Young, which maintained a theater in Los Angeles, brought in twenty-seven performers in 1929; Tai Wing Wah (Choy Ding Quay), operating in Chicago, brought in twenty-eight performers in 1928.

A FAMILY AND BUSINESS NETWORK: CIENFUEGOS–MONTREAL–HAVANA–BOSTON

The year 1923 was a vibrant one for new theatrical endeavors in North America. As we have seen, during that year no fewer than six troupes were sponsored by merchants across North America. A folder at the Library and Archives of Canada contains correspondence exchanged among businessmen in Cuba, Canada, and the United States between the months of April and October 1923, with various references to Cantonese opera performers, troupes, supplies, and theaters.[39] While they are no more than a snapshot of business concerns, they still provide a glimpse of the interconnections among the nodes of the network.

The correspondence places the opera business in the context of family networks and general import businesses. The letter writers were shareholders of the company Wan Shenglong, which included theater among its business. Located in Cienfuegos, Cuba, the import company had twenty-nine shareholders owning shares in amounts ranging from $500 to $2000, with the capital totaling $30,000 (likely Mexican silver dollars). Many letters were addressed to "Teatro Chung Wah, Calle Zanja No. 35, Habana Cuba," a prominent Chinese theater in Havana, and to La Mariposa de Yau Yee Shun, an import business in Havana. The letter senders represented High River, Alberta, Montreal and Sherbrooke, Quebec, Boston, and of course Havana and Cienfuegos. The geographical distances, however, do not disguise the kinship ties around which the business was built. The elder of two Lin brothers (Lin Shounan) lived on Tyler Street in Boston, and the younger (Lin Zhuonan) was in Havana, at the Teatro Chung Wah. References are made to theatrical business, but the letters are personal in tone, informal, and mixed with family news such as the birth of a baby and contributions of money for relatives. It seems that three families were involved; in addition to the Lin brothers there was the Huang family, associated with the prominent Montreal merchant Huang Liangzi (owner of the city's largest Chinese importer, Si Shengfa), and another Lin family, linked to Mariposa, another import business in Havana. Both Huang Liangzi and Lin Shounan also invested in the Yong Ni Shang Theater (see Chapter 11).[40]

One letter from a staff member of Cienfuegos's Wan Shenglong Company to Lin at the Havana theater revealed the state of its affairs. The writer noted that the business had been doing very well.[41] The latest internal audit concluded its finances were in good standing, though it recommended that special attention be given to its venture in the theater business. The latter was evidently a recurring theme in letters to the same addressee, although the connection among the theaters was unclear. The older brother wrote from Boston about immigration matters for performers, citing constraints imposed at the New York port, and suggested solutions. From Montreal, Huang Yusheng wrote to report the staging of three performers over whom he did not have full control because they were engaged by the Lok Tin Tsau troupe.

Opera theaters also became convenient channels for merchandise. Herbal medicine was transnational by nature as well.[42] Chen Daming was a well-known Montreal herbalist whose medicine advertisements appeared frequently in Chinese newspapers across North America throughout this decade (see figure 11.3). One document shows that the herbalist had supplied the mold disk for the printing of his advertisement on the playbill of the Havana theater, and was requesting sample playbills with the herb advertisement. Chen Daming's letterhead listed agents in fourteen cities—nine in Canada, four in the United States, and one in Cuba. The herbalist, part of the artisan class and a learned man, was also an opera connoisseur: the letter expressed appreciation for the theater manager's gracious acceptance of lyrics he had recently composed.[43]

The letters' references to Cantonese opera also reflected Cuba's long tradition of hosting Chinese theaters. By 1873 Havana had its first, built on Zanja Street with capital investment of 15,000 pesos, although it could have been a puppet theater.[44] Two years later a theater called Sum Yen was built on Lealtad Street, presenting Chinese performers arriving from California. Cantonese opera theaters, educational societies, and performances then proliferated across the island. A company of ninety-four performed at a spacious three-story theater in Sagua La Grande in 1876. At a Cienfuegos theater set up in 1875, a fifteen-day performance of the full book of the classic operas *Pinggui Bidding Farewell* and *Pinggui Returning Home* reportedly attracted Chinese from the neighboring towns of Ranchuelo, Cruces, Lajas, Palmira, Rodas, and Abreues.[45] In 1883 Cienfuegos opened a second Chinese theater. In addition to staging performances, theaters were also associated with schools or societies, teaching Cantonese opera to both Chinese and non-Chinese Cubans. Kathleen López identifies eight educational societies dedicated to Cantonese opera in the 1880s, two for Chinese, three for whites, and three for people of color.[46] Cienfuegos's operatic activities reached beyond the confines of theaters and beyond Chinese communities. The theater tradition grew even stronger during the 1920s, when the Chinese population increased quickly. Whereas 6,258 Chinese arrived in Cuba from 1903 to 1916, the number nearly tripled in the years 1917 to 1924.[47] However, immigration matters made the theater business more difficult. For example, the *Chinese Times* (Vancouver) reported in February 1923 that due to a new immigration law in Cuba, three Chinese actors arriving at Havana were detained on their arrival from New York.[48] Such obstacles clearly made the intervention of merchants crucial for the theater's success.

This exchange among five shareholders in three locations suggests that family connections might themselves form the basis of transnational operations. And there were good reasons to do so; judging from the figures discussed, the theater business could be very profitable, and it opened up the sale of other related merchandise as well. A key shareholder (with shares worth $2,000) of Wan Shenglong from the Huang clan in Montreal, Huang Yusheng, reported that after performing in Boston for twenty-one months, the troupe (unnamed, but likely Lok Tin Tsau; see Chapter 11) generated $168,000.[49] The letter reported the selling of the opera business, and after calculating bonds and sales, Huang concluded the profit for the shareholder would be a hundred dollars for each hundred dollars of investment.

Now he was finishing the deal in Boston and would return home. Back in Montreal, he was a bookkeeper for the Huang family's import company Si Shengfa, where he managed the import of theatrical supplies and musical instruments. Several purchase orders were made for opera costumes and props from the Tongqing Company and for Chinese oboes (*suona*). One order for a set of opera costumes cost $761.19.[50] The invoices gave no indication of the identities of the buyers, but they might have been from Cuba, given the large purchases of Chinese oboes. The instrument was known as *trompeta china* or *corneta china*, and since the late nineteenth century it had become an essential element of congas during Carnival in Santiago.[51]

Though sparse and often little noticed, signs and traces in the United States and Canada point to Havana as a prominent post in the North American performing circuit in the 1920s. Later in the decade, theaters in Cuba were prosperous enough to entice stars such as Li Xuefang and Huang Xiaofeng to perform. A surviving playbill of Teatro Chung Wah for April 13, 1930, nicely summarized the prosperity of the 1920s (see figure 12.3). A troupe called Renshou Nian was performing at the theater. It had the same name as the troupe that Lun On brought from Vancouver to San Francisco in 1922. It could have been a subgroup of that troupe that went to Havana, though no document has surfaced to support this hypothesis. In any case, the Havana playbill includes the usual adulatory verses, the titles of twenty scenes, and a list of performers and their roles. The lead actor, Zhou Shaobao (Chow Siu Po), had a prior tie with the Mandarin Theater in San Francisco. He started performing there in May 1928 and went briefly to Mexicali before coming to Havana in January 1930. According to the playbill advertisements in *Chung Sai Yat Po* in 1928, he stood out as one of the most popular actors in the Mandarin

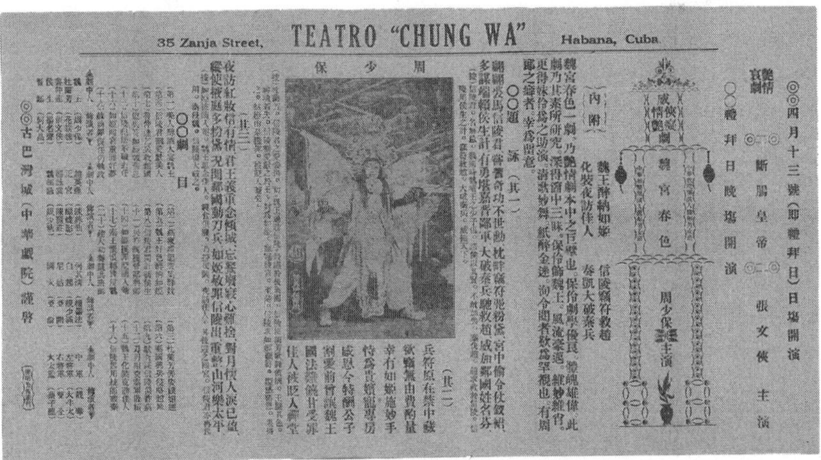
35 Zanja Street, TEATRO "CHUNG WA" Habana, Cuba
◎◎四月十三號(即禮拜日)日場開演
艷情宮劇 斷腸皇帝 張文俠主演
〇〇禮拜日晚場開演
魏宮春色
周少保主演
周少保
◎◎古巴河城(中華戲院)謹啓

Fig. 12.3. Playbill, *Heartbroken Emperor, Spring of Wei Palace*, Teatro Chung Wa, Havana, April 13, 1930 (courtesy of the Department of Special Collections, Stanford University Libraries).

Theater. His photo on this playbill—by May's Studio in San Francisco—attested to this connection. The performers on the roster were also mostly familiar names on the North American circuit.

A TRANSNATIONAL NETWORK

From the perspective of musical practice, Cantonese opera performance connected different Chinese communities in North America. Chinatowns from Mexicali to New York, and from Portland to Havana, were connected by shared performers and repertoires. The same record labels and catalogues were advertised and sold across the continent.

Just as important, however, was another perspective: the sprawling network of kinship and family in North America upon which the musical practice came to flourish. The Cantonese opera performing network was built on and sustained by the efforts of prominent financial players as well as the connections of people in different economic tiers and geographical locations, who could be vocationally diverse as well. The transnational orbit of Chinese labor and commerce followed these networks, as did Cantonese opera. This meant that, just as the network expanded the prominence of hubs such as Honolulu and reinforced the importance of popular regions or routes such as the Pacific Northwest, it also made less central places such as Cienfuegos important for Chinese opera. Their success relied on the tenacity and assiduity of family networks. The dissemination of opera performance and cultural products coincided with the circulation of other general merchandise such as Chinese herbal medicine.

Cantonese opera performances provided cultural spaces and resources through which to foster social memories, cultural identities, and musical imagination. To trace these activities is in many ways to bring to life the social memories and narratives surrounding the once-prominent cultural form, rescuing it from silence. The transnational network of performers and theater professionals, which penetrated different layers of the Chinese community in distinctive ways, confirms the immensity of opera's influence. The busy trans-Pacific network also ensured that opera culture in North America was not just a transplant from an unchanging past but, rather, a dynamic movement back and forth among different locations in North America, China, and other parts of the Cantonese Pacific.

EPILOGUE

Born and raised in Taiwan, I grew up watching Taiwanese opera divas on television with my younger sister and our nanny at noon on weekdays, switching to more formal Peking opera on Saturday afternoons with my mother, who, as a native of Chaozhou (a region of eastern Guangdong Province), also listened to a treasured stash of Chaozhou opera cassette tapes given to her by relatives. When asked why she indiscriminately enjoyed these different genres of Chinese opera, my mother replied, "Oh, they are all actually the same." What did she mean? Were these different regional genres legible to her because she identified common musical elements? Did she find pleasure in the dramatic world or the tuneful and expressive singing voice associated with Chinese operas? Did the operas evoke for her a sense of desire, longing, and identity? Was opera malleable as a means of negotiating her complex personal history? Later I would learn that she, as the ninth and youngest child, spent most of her childhood not in Guangdong, as I had always thought, but in Bangkok, where her father and eldest brothers ran a successful jewelry trade and often traveled between the two "home" cities. The operas accompanied her transnational childhood in southern China and Bangkok, as well as her later moves to Guangzhou for school, Shanghai for university, and finally Taiwan to teach and stay. Her fondness for operatic songs, together with our nanny's loyalty to her Taiwanese opera divas, kept the sonority a regular presence in our household. Chinese operas not only accompanied Mother's crossing of various national, linguistic, and geographical borders but also continued on to lodge in the imagination and sonic world of her offspring (some more tangentially than others), a process not unlike the cultural circulation described in this book.

During its heyday Cantonese opera was woven into multiple facets of Chinese community life in North America, as evidenced in ample detail by the playbills and arresting stage photos studied in previous chapters. Today, collected in archives, their materiality still conveys the significance and the intense endeavors of the theaters. The spirit of professionalism, innovative energy, and urgency is captured well in a biographical sketch of actress Guan Yinglian written by her grandmother Kitty Tsui.

> Both the Great China Theater and the Mandarin were producing the classical operas in the best style they could; neither could allow itself to fall behind the other. But in addition the Great China was animated by a radical urge that could only be satisfied by the bold production of modern operas, not only in themes but in modern dress. They even put leading personalities of the day on the stage. . . . Other modern operas followed this. They dared to break all precedents by putting contemporary and even living characters on the stage. The performers lived with the rigors of presenting a different show every night.[1]

This fervor for maintaining the highest level of performance made these theaters, and it continued well into the 1930s, as shown by the increased sizes of playbills and annual holiday greeting from the full casts of the theaters in that decade. Guan, a veteran of nearly every theater discussed in this book, had a distinguished career that bears witness to multiple facets and phases of this performing history. Her career on North American stages started in 1921 in Vancouver, then progressed to Seattle, San Francisco, New York, and other cities all through this and subsequent decades. Stellar actresses like her and Mudan Su were household names in many Chinese communities, even fabled—legend has it that Guan's voice was once so electrifying as to cause a light bulb to burst on stage.

As it enjoyed a new golden age in North America, Cantonese opera was entwined in the urban scenes of the Roaring Twenties. With nine theaters established in seven cities, the total quota of performers grew to 355 by the end of 1925.[2] The frequent rotations facilitated by savvy managers, agents, and attorneys ensured that an extraordinary number of opera performers would arrive regularly on these shores in these two decades. Once the border crossing was standardized in mid-1925, the theaters preprinted the immigration status "temporary visitor for business" on applications submitted to the U.S. Department of Labor. Photo identification cards issued to performers included troupe name, port, steamer name, and date of arrival.[3] Aside from performing at the theater productions, they also fulfilled many social functions within their communities. The theaters became an apparatus through which transnational businesses and kinship networks operated and allowed opera performance to permeate many parts of North America. The two purpose-built theaters erected in San Francisco were not only the physical space for performing but also landmarks of distinctive modern style with novel Chinese ornaments; they were major attractions and entertainment centers of the city for decades to come.[4] At the start the Mandarin Theater was distinguished by its strong cast of actresses and novel plays, and the Great China Theater made its mark by attracting top actors specializing in traditional repertoire, yet their rivalry was so intense that both theaters learned from each other's success and certain programming traits became the norm. Their ability to engage performers of high caliber and to boost their offerings with novel stories and fancy backdrops made live performance flourish, enticing audiences of all social classes and ages. Erudite audiences found their muses in the ethereal operatic world. The theaters also offered numerous conventional narratives whereby spectators' emotions were mediated: feeling exultant and powerful watching victorious warriors and martial arts in battle scenes; drowning in the ecstasy of emotion and melancholy in scenes of love or separation in romantic drama, finding delight and hearty laughter in humorous or even vulgar comic drama, or getting lost in the fantasy world of mystical scenes. The affect accumulated over time and became connected to the theaters and associated with the performers. The boom in Cantonese opera phonograph records in the 1920s helped expand the devoted fandom of opera beyond connoisseurs. Chinatown theaters' music scene became more volatile as time went on.

Virtuosic opera singers had great appeal everywhere they performed. Their transnational experience and artistic sophistication gave them a certain sense of superiority and integrity. They won the community's admiration and devotion. Many were regularly recruited for private performances by patrons not only for enjoyment but also as symbols of ethos, culture, wealth, and status. When the actress Li Xuemei arrived in 1922, the community was so enthusiastic that *San Francisco Chronicle* called her "China's Mary Pickford."[5] In 1925 the newspaper reported the nomination of the Mandarin Theater's Sai Yung Nui (discussed as Xiyang Nü in Chapter 7) as queen of the carnival held for the opening of a new Chinese hospital, Tung Wah.[6] Such an honorary title was typically given to young women from families of wealth and influence in the community, and thus the nomination reflected the blurring of the line between opera actress and Chinese American socialite. Actress Li Xuefang was not only an idol of the community, heralded as a moral figure spearheading the community's important causes, but also a role model for young Chinese American females. Across the Pacific, performers' reputations grew. Virtuosic singers such as Guan were revered by the North American Chinese community while remaining active in southern China; Bai Jurong and Ma Shizeng were both much anticipated on both sides of the Pacific.[7] Their superb performances, popular recordings, and, later, opera films cultivated an audience in the next generation. As cultural icons and role models, they were inseparable from the cultural identity to which young Chinese Americans and Canadians found various forms of attachment.

Opera culture permeated different social classes and was felt in communities near and far. Two brief stories and a photo, collected in interviews, reflect the influence of the genre. While growing up in Mississippi, Bonnie Lew, a grocer's daughter, learned to enjoy opera songs listening to the recordings of her opera-loving mother, who played them constantly in the back of the store where they lived.[8] The recordings became the music of the Lew sisters, who grew up in the segregated South, and they also made their visits to San Francisco's Chinatown like going home. That sonic literacy could underpin her feeling of cultural belonging and trigger a sense of social identity. And H. Robert Lee, the son of an owner of a San Francisco laundry in Pacific Heights, 1.5 miles from Chinatown, began his fascination with the opera when his father's workers took him to the Mandarin Theater periodically. Thrilled by the pounding of the drums and crashing of cymbals in the staged battles, as well as the costumes and scenery, he said he never

Fig. E.1. Photo of actress Guan Yinglian with her godmother and family, the late 1940s. Guan is in the center with a boy on her lap (courtesy of Bruce Quan Jr.).

lost his fondness for Cantonese opera.[9] The sonic encounter was clearly formative for him as a Chinese American. For the more affluent, the connection could run even deeper, as reflected in figure ep.1, which shows Guan Yinglian and the family of her godmother, the matriarch Mrs. Quan Yick-Sun. Next to them are Mrs. Quan's husband, sons, and, on Guan's lap, the oldest grandson, Bruce Quan Jr. The actress and the family were kin in the broadest sense; Quan and Guan are actually the same character in Chinese as well.

The intimate family portrait of the elite and highly influential Chinese merchant, from the late 1940s, reveals not only Guan Yinglian's exalted status within the community but also the way opera patronage had a part in the family's leisure life.[10] Outfitted in formal attire—men in three-piece suits and women in silk Chinese dresses with heavy gold bracelets and multiple rings with jewels and accessories—they posed for a special occasion—a birthday? Chinese New Year? a parting? Regardless, we can feel the ease and warmth of their mutual bond, and the photo is a deposit and expression of that relationship. This picture recalls the 1921 portrait of Guan discussed in Chapter 6. Together, the photos show the trajectory from the beginning of the golden era to the tail end of regular live performance of Cantonese opera, reflecting a singer's evolving roles in the complex, shifting social context of three decades' duration.

Skilled and versatile, performers shone on Chinatown theater stages of North America, developing new ideas and advancing opera production. They responded to many of the decade's ideas and trends. Among other things, Anna May Wong's famous performance in the silent film *The Thief of Baghdad* (1924) established the popularity of the "Chinese flapper" and provided inspiration for integrating fantastic staging and even risqué attire in Chinatown theaters. Cinematic effects such as montage, special lighting, and mechanical props were also used on the opera stage. The theaters experimented with a mixture of styles such as characters in European costumes, contemporary three-piece suits, bathing suits, or cowboy outfits and bullwhips.[11] Despite the challenges of the Great Depression, competition from new forms of entertainment and the social turmoil of World War II, these fantastic productions carried on into the next two decades, fostering local amateur clubs, and re-created the genre in the new medium of cinema. Indeed, the creative energy of opera performers and layers of complexity on theater stages became the main forces behind the burgeoning Chinese American film industry. Even the theater itself became the subject of a movie.

White Powder and Neon Lights (1946) is a Chinese American film about Chinatown theater life produced by the Grandview Film Company in San Francisco.[12] Its storyline echoes the spirit of professionalism expressed by Kitty Tsui above. Determined to reignite the opera scene, a group of young Chinese actors in San Francisco hires an opera diva from China and opens the theater door to enthusiastic audiences. The collaborative spirit is high, the theater vibrant. However, as she grows distracted by courtship and relinquishes her professional responsibility, the theater suffers, loses its audiences, and closes. She eventually comes to her senses and together with other actors revives the theater. The film's juxtaposition of actors appearing on stage in opera costumes with their donning chic 1940s fashions and going about San Francisco as typical Chinese Americans reveals vividly opera performers' complex roles in the transnational community.

With its candid camera, the film literally located Chinese theaters within the San Francisco community and provided an alternative to the imagined space of Hollywood cinematic logic whereby Chinese theater or Chinatown constituted a symbol of incomprehensibility and danger, as in Orson Welles's *The Lady from Shanghai*. The cast and crew of *White Powder and Neon Lights* drew from Cantonese opera theater and took the spectators backstage to portray lovingly the complex though seamless process of theater production, as well as the symbolic significance of its success for the community. The plotline of the comeback, rebuilding, and triumph of a Chinese theater is an allegory of the transnational community's perennial efforts to strengthen solidarity among the Chinese in the face of difficult reality. Its cinematic narratives and cameras show the opera world through the eyes of many various groups of participants and spectators, as well as operatic practices within the urban community.

As the literary scholar Shumei Shih notes, the fluidity, complexity, and logistics of various transnational moments were consequential, while "[t]he intention to stay and the duration of the stay are neither absolute nor useful markers of national, cultural and individual 'identity,' whether for Chinese gold diggers and laborers of the nineteenth century or for Chinese women in the late twentieth century."[13] This point is particularly poignant with regard to Chinese opera singers. If the limitations of their legal status—as alien and visitor—as well as the transnational nature of the business made individual performers seem transient figures in the community, their influence was anything but transient. Through their theater work they kept the circulation of opera cultural icons and music going, thus contributing significantly to the establishment of the cultural memory and identity of Chinatown. These Cantonese opera theaters and their much-adored performers were the most important public face of Chinese communities all through the 1920s, and their memorable performances constituted social memory unconstrained by geography.

This book, therefore, joins the historian Lisa Rose Mar in challenging "conceptions that transnational migrants [were] 'no where' in national history."[14] As transnational beings, these performers' presence and artistry defined the operatic culture of multiple local communities, and in one production after another they maintained and re-created the vitality of this musical genre in North America. As historical actors, their constant movement between cities led to the emergence of a homogenous Cantonese opera culture in terms of repertoire choices, performance practice, and even casts. The complex modes of cultural embodiment that accompanied opera performers made opera going such a mesmerizing experience that audiences were not just entertained but also empowered and transformed. Opera singers captured the imagination of theater audiences and the communities, as reflected in Wayson Choy's reconstruction of the viewing experience in his memoir and in the glamorous playbill photos that fill the scrapbooks of San Francisco natives Margaret Leung and Raymond Fong.[15] Generations of Cantonese opera amateurs were also inspired to learn and sustain opera performance in various musical spaces and groups.

The unmistakable presence of Chinese theaters in American urban life attests to their place in American music history. Collected at the Museum of the City of New York is one loose page from the scrapbook of an anonymous New Yorker. On one side is a 1929 playbill of the Yong Ni Shang troupe (performing at the Thalia Theater) with a full-length picture of the popular actress Li Feifeng, featuring the classic opera *Snowy Plum Flower in the Wind*. On the reverse are playbills and photos from two Broadway comedies, *Merry Andrew* at the Henry Miller Theater on 43rd Street with Walter Connolly and *Jonesy* at the Bijou Theater on 45th Street. Together these playbills reflect the suppressed racial divisions within the city's leisure culture of the late 1920s.[16] From the Lower East Side to Midtown, a convenient transit system connected these theaters. The city's transportation infrastructure enabled the crossing of cultural and ethnic categories that encouraged "the formation of a heterogeneous collective ethnic identity in which people of diverse affiliations could participate."[17] Performance culture as represented by these theaters was shaped by the city and its infrastructure of mobility, and Chinatown theaters in turn were constituent parts of the musical and racial terrain of urban space.

The influence of Cantonese opera as a theatrical form is especially profound for Chinese American writers and musicians, even as they undoubtedly were also attracted by or became fluent in a wide variety of other forms of music and theatrical genres. The legends, myths, and characters portrayed vividly in the opera, infused with cultural beliefs, were not only passed on from generation to generation but also given rebirth at each new hand. Many works by the Chinese American writer Maxine Hong Kingston resonate with the richness of the opera world. In her memoir *Woman Warrior*, she uses Chinese opera to depict elegantly the dichotomies of opaque blackness and colorful fantasy, oppression and freedom, and silence and sound.

The closed stage curtains, symbolized by layers of black paint covering over a child's painting, conceal the opera world behind them, whose colorful characters and dance existed in the imagination of this young school girl. For Kingston, therefore, operas stand in for the imaginary connected to the young girl's self-expression and artistic identity. The beautiful allegorical account elucidates the extent to which Cantonese opera constituted a kind of social memory and aesthetic realm for young Chinese Americans. In her third book, *Tripmaster Monkey: His Fake Book,* Kingston depicts another search for identity and freedom of self-representation through Chinese theaters. The protagonist, Wittman, undertakes a personal crusade to start a new type of theater as an ideal form of self-representation. He points to the long history of Chinese theaters in the United States when he underscores the significance of his favorite story of legendary warriors: "Every matinee or evening for a hundred years, somewhere in America, some acting company was performing *The Oath in the Peach Orchard.*"[18] At one point, Wittman thinks, "[W]haddayaknow, I've written one of those plays that leave room for actors to do improv, a process as ancient as Chinese opera and as far-out as the theatre of spontaneity." The fake book of the novel's subtitle therefore is a nod to both the jazz term for compilation of tunes, melodies and chords, and the Cantonese opera term *tigang xi*, a plot outline with spaces provided for the singer to improvise and insert his own imaginative segments and bridges. (See Chapter 4.) For this Chinese American figure, the theater stage symbolized artistic autonomy. Cantonese opera culture belongs to a core of social memory with which many artists engaged and found their own modes of attachment in personal and widely varied ways. Other notable yet divergent examples include Frank Chin's novel *Donald Duk,* David Wong Louie's *The Barbarians Are Coming,* David Henry Hwang's play *The Dance and the Railroad,* Jason Hwang's opera *The Floating Box: A Story in Chinatown,* and Fred Ho's bilingual opera *A Chinaman's Chance*, and his jazz opera *Monkey Trilogy*.[19] In different forms, opera sonorities, characters and legends remain in the creative psyche of generations of Chinese American writers and artists. Furthermore, in a pragmatic way, the opera's musical and performance practice are continued by amateur groups. For instance, in her study of New York in the 1990s Su Zheng listed twelve Cantonese opera clubs, and Daphne Lei studied a second-generation Chinese American Red Bean Opera production in the Bay Area of California.[20]

Chinatown theaters had many lasting influences on the broader American culture and music as well. At the surface level, they were a subject of mimicry in mainstream theaters and in quick-rising cultural forms such as parties, revues, plays, musicals, films, and radio, culminating in the 1927 grand opening of Grauman's Chinese Theatre in Los Angeles.[21] In the Hollywood orientalist style, the mise-en-scène of Chinese theater offered up a series of illusions, from beckoning usherettes in Chinese theatrical gowns and wax mannequins of Chinese people to faux pagoda façades, such that "original and simulacrum are enfolded within one another."[22] It offered the thrill of a fetishistic style of entertainment. Plays purporting to be Chinese were produced as well. By claiming "authenticity," the play *The Yellow Jacket* (1912) was revived in New York at the Coburn Theater and returned to

San Francisco in 1929, making use of a prescribed and restricted "Chinese opera" vocabulary. Its authors evidently learned of the practices from a lengthy article on San Francisco's Chinese theaters published in 1884 in *Century* magazine.[23] Its eventual success was built on adopting the trope of Chinese opera to "explore [an] anti-realistic, alternative approach to theater making."[24]

In a more profound way, at the same time, the presence of Chinatown theaters contributed to the sonic memory of many American composers and played an interesting role in American music, especially modern music. From popular songwriters Lee Johnson and William Furst, who composed music for *The First Born* (an 1897 yellowface play by Francis Powers), to classical composers Edgar Stillman Kelley and Henry Eichheim (both known for their study of or immersion in Chinatown music), composers incorporated music they heard in Chinatown theaters.[25] Jazz scholars have also documented the influence of Chinese theaters on the early development of the jazz drum set, which included Chinese woodblocks and cymbals and tom-toms based on Chinese designs.[26] By 1930 these instruments were part of the standard drum set.[27] They can be heard throughout the recorded history of ragtime and jazz. For example, Chinese tom-toms are heard in Jelly Roll Morton's "My Little Dixie Home" (1929) and Benny Goodman's "Sing, Sing, Sing" (1937), and cymbals and woodblocks are used in Tommy Dorsey's "Stop, Look and Listen" (1938). Modern composers such as Henry Cowell and Lou Harrison long counted Chinatown among their main musical influences, and John Cage and Harry Partch linked aspects of their compositions to it as well. For Cowell, however, the sonority was also astutely transformed into an abstract musical concept that became part of his music legacy. Through earlier analyses I have shown that his notion of sliding tone is associated with Chinese operatic singing and string instruments which he heard in childhood while living near Chinatown. The intricate and subtle use of vocal slides in Cantonese opera is discussed briefly in Chapter 5 of this book, especially Example 5.7. In his composition treatise, Cowell sketches a music example and connects what he calls Chinese sliding tone to the appoggiatura, "except that it comes after instead of before the tone, the slide thus ending in mid-air, so to speak."[28] Originating from slides in pitch, the core concept was extended by him and other modernist composers to other music parameters such as tempo and dynamics. The sliding concept formed a new basis for a music system in his prodigious and influential book *New Musical Resources* (1919, 1929), and gave rise to the novelty of sonority of piano works such as his *Banshee* (1925), with its different layers and timbres of tonal slides; it also formed the colossal design of the string section in Symphony no. 11 (1953). The sliding concept, one of Cowell's most original ideas, would later become the basis of more innovative sounds and aesthetics in American modern music, employed in landmark works such as Ruth Crawford's *String Quartet 1931*, John Cage's *Music of Changes*, and Conlon

Nancarrow's *Studies for Player Piano*.[29] To the extent that this American ultramodern aesthetic is inextricably linked to a musical concept that originated with Chinese opera, it serves as an apt example of how the interiority of the racial terrain was molded by the transnational contacts where negotiation, mimicry, and transformation brought forth new musical languages. Whether intentional or not, whether an inborn or a chosen identity, the use of the sonority, the memory, and the expression of Chinese theaters facilitated the crossing of racial lines and cultural boundaries, created affiliations, and called for our attentiveness in new ways.

The history of Chinatown opera theaters is intertwined with the evolution of a variety of literature and performing arts enjoyed throughout the twentieth century. To chronicle the history of Chinatown theaters is to recognize the complex history of many of these creative expressions today, and to recover the voiceless from its suppressed silence. In particular, to do so is to challenge the invisibility of opera performers, to hear and watch them through the words left by its fans, to reimagine it in its full richness and complexity, to relocate Chinese opera theater in both local communities and transnational circuits, to reconstruct its image, and to build a bridge between the past and the present. To make it an interlocutor of American music history is to enlarge the Atlantic frame of genealogical reference in American music historiography to include the Pacific. In this way we can begin to see and hear the nuanced contours of the racial terrain in American music.

APPENDIX

LIST OF CHINESE NAMES AND TERMS

Personal Names, Company Names, and Other Terms

For terms that are better known or are documented in their non-pinyin form, the pinyin is given in parentheses. For terms transcribed in pinyin form that are also well known in non-pinyin, the latter is provided in square brackets.

Romanized Form	Chinese
B. S. Fong	鄺炳舜
Bahe Huiguan	八和會館
Bai Jurong / Chen Shaobo [Pak Kui Wing; Bak Kui Wing; a.k.a. Chin Shu Bo]	白駒榮/陳少波
Bai Lingxian	白菱仙
Baisui Tu	百歲圖
ban	板
banghuang qiang	梆黃腔
bangziqiang	梆子腔
Bao Zheng	包拯
baodu	爆肚
bendiban	本地班
bo	鈸
C. B. Wand Studio	黃寶泉映相館
Chang Toy (Chen Cai)	陳才
Chang'e	嫦娥
Chee Chong Co.	奇昌公司
Chen Cunjin	陳村錦
Chen Daming	陳達明

Chen Feifeng [Chan Fai Fung]	陳飛鳳
Chen Feinong	陳非儂
Chen Huifang	陳慧芳
Chen Jiantai	陳健泰
Chen Pimei	陳皮梅
Chen Shaohua	陳少華
Chen Tiesheng	陳鐵生
Chen Xiahun	陳俠魂
Chen Xiufang	陳秀芳
Chen Yinglin	陳應鱗
Chin Lain (Chen Lian; a.k.a. Chen Dunpu)	陳連/陳敦樸
Chin Nom (Chen Xugun)	陳緒袞
Chin Yee You (Chen Yiyao)	陳宜耀
Chinese Consolidated Benevolent Association (Zhonghua Huiguan)	中華會館
chou	丑
chousheng	丑生
Cui Yingying	崔鶯鶯
Da Changcheng	大長城
Da Guanyuan	大觀園
Da Huamian	大花面
Da Paichang Shiba Ben	大排場十八本
Da Ronghua	大榮華
dahou	大喉
dan	旦
Daniu Bing	大牛炳
Dayan Shun	大眼順
Deng Shaohuai [Dung Sui Wai]	鄧少懷
Dongpo An	東坡安
Doupi Mei	豆皮梅
Doupi Qing	豆皮慶
Eighteen Grand Paichang Operas	江湖十八本
Eng Chow & Co.	五洲大藥房
er huamian	二花面
erbang huadan	二幫花旦
erhuang	二黃
ershou	二手
erxian	二絃
Essence of Cantonese Arias and Songs	粵調歌曲精華
Eu Tong Sen (Yu Dongxuan)	余東旋
fanxian	反線
fanxian erhuang manban	反線二黃慢板
Fengqing Jian	風情見
Fengqing Qi	風情杞
Fengqing Yao	風情耀
Gao Sheng Theater	高陞戲院
gaoqiang	高腔
gongchi pu	工尺譜
gongjiao	公腳
Gongye Chuang [a.k.a. Tan Yeh Tian / Tan Yetian]	公爺創/譚業田
Great China Theater (Dazhonghua Theater)	大中華戲院
gu	鼓

Guo Bokeng	古伯鏗
Guan Gong	關公
Guan Jingxiong	關景雄
Guan Yin	觀音
Guan Yinglian [Kwan Ying Lin; Kwung Ying-Lin]	關影憐
Guan Yingxue	關影雪
Guan Yundi	關雲迪
Guang Wutai	廣舞台
Guihua Tang	桂花棠
Guijiu Sheng	鬼九生
Guima Yuan	鬼馬元
Guima Zhao	鬼馬昭
Guo Fengnian	國豐年
Guo Min An	國民安
Guo Taiping	國太平
Guo Zhongxing	國中興
guomen	過門
Guomin Zhong	國民鐘
Hai Nan	海南
Haizhu Theater	海珠戲院
Hang Far Low (Xinghua Lou)	杏花樓
hangdang	行當
He Xiaoqing	何小青
hengtou dan	橫頭單
hengxiao	橫簫
Hip Wo School (Xie He School)	協和中文學校
Hong Fook Tong (Hongfu Tang)	鴻福堂
Hong Niang	紅娘
Hongmen	洪門
Hop Hing (Hexing)	和興
Hop Sing Tong (Hesheng Tang)	合勝堂
houguan	喉管
huadan	花旦
Huang Liangzi	黃良滋
Huang Mengjue	黃夢覺
Huang Shaoqiu	黃少秋
Huang Tao	黃滔
Huang Xiaofeng [Wong Sieu Fong]	黃小鳳
Huang Xuemei [Wong Suet Mui]	黃雪梅
Huang Yusheng	黃雨生
hudie qin	蝴蝶琴
Hudie Ying	蝴蝶影
huiguan	會館
Huozuan Zi	火鑽子
Jiazi Ren	架子仁
Jin Hao	金好
Jin Hudie	金蝴蝶
Jing Baolin	靚寶林
Jing Fu	靚福
Jing Rong	靚榮
Jing Yulin	靚玉麟
Jinghua Ying [Flower's Shadow on the Mirror]	鏡花影

Jingmei Yingxiangguan [May's Studio]	精美映相館
Jinshan [San Francisco]	金山
Jinshan Bing	金山炳
Jinsi Mao	金絲貓
Jinzhi Ye	金枝葉
jita	祭塔
Jock Ming On (Zhu Min An; a.k.a. Jok Man On)	祝民安
juese	角色
kaixi shiye	開戲師爺
Kang Youwei	康有為
Ko Sing (Gao Sheng) Theater	高陞戲院
Kue Hing (Qiaoqing)	僑慶
kunqiang	崑腔
Kwong Sun Chong	廣信昌公司
Lao Ba	勞八
Le Shan Theater	樂善戲院
Le Wannian	樂萬年
Lee Eng & Co.	李典公司
Lee Theater (Liwutai)	利舞台
Leguan Yingxiangguan [Suen's Photo Studio]	樂觀映相館
Lei Junji	雷君殛
Leqianqiu [Lok Tin Tsau]	樂千秋
Lew Hing (Liu Xin)	劉興
Lew Yuet-yung (Liu Xingshang)	劉杏裳
Li Feifeng [Lee Fee Fun]	李飛鳳
Li Renzhou	黎仁州
Li Shizhang	李世璋
Li Wutian	黎伍田
Li Xuefang [Lee Sue Fong; Lee Suet-Fong]	李雪芳
Li Xuemei [Lee Suet-Moy; Lee Shut Moy]	李雪梅
Li Zhifang	李志芳
Liang Lizhu	梁麗珠
Lim Bang (Lin Bin)	林彬
Lin Baoqing	林寶卿
Lin Daiyu	林黛玉
Lin Liqing	林麗卿
Lin Qimei [So Chow Mui; a.k.a. Suzhou Mei]	林綺梅 (蘇州妹)
Lin Shounan	林壽男
Lin Yick (Lin Yi) Company	林益公司
Lin Zhuonan	林灼男
Ling Shaorui	凌少瑞
Liu Guoxing	劉國興
Liu Zixuan	劉子軒
liuzhuzhi	六柱制
Log Quon Shear (Lequn She)	(金門)樂群社
Lok Tin Tsau (Leqianqiu; a.k.a. Lau Tau Seck)	樂千秋
Long Tack Sam (Lang Deshan)	朗德山
longzhou	龍舟
Loo Gee Wing (Lu Zirong)	盧梓榮
Look Tin Eli (Lu Runqing)	陸潤卿
Lü Wencheng	呂文成
Lu Xuehong	盧雪鴻
Lun On (Lian An)	聯安

luo	鑼
Luo Jianhong [Law Kim Hung]	羅劍虹
luogu dianzi	鑼鼓點子
Ma Dachun	馬大諄
Ma Shizeng [Ma Sze Tsang]	馬師曾
Ma Yanfang	馬豔芳
Mai Sulan	麥素蘭
Mai Xiaoxia	麥嘯霞
Mandarin Theater (Dawutai Theater)	大舞臺
Mandarin Theater Troupe	大舞臺班
manzhongban [slow moderato]	慢中版
May's Studio	精美映相館
Mei Lanfang	梅蘭芳
Meiren Su	美人蘇
Minzhi Dramatic Club	民智劇社
Mo Keming [Mok Pak Ming]	莫克明
Mu Guiying	穆桂英
Mudan Su [Mah Dang Soh; Mow Dan So]	牡丹蘇
muyu [*mukyu*]	木魚
muyushu	木魚書
nanchou	男丑
nanyin [*naamyam*]	南音
Natural Photo Studio (Tianran Yingxiangguan)	天然映相館
New World Troupe (Xin Shijie Ban)	新世界班
Ng Poon Chew	伍盤照
Nü Muzhen	女慕貞
nüban	女班
nüchou	女丑
nüdan	女旦
Nüwa shi	女媧氏
On Leong Tong (Anliang Tang)	安良堂
Oriental Record Co	遠東唱片公司
Ou Runcai [a.k.a. Jing Runcai]	區潤才/靚潤才
Ouyang Yuqian	歐陽予倩
P. C. Chang (Peng Chun Chang; Zhang Pengchun)	張彭春
paichang	排場
paizi	牌子
Pang Yifeng	龐一鳳
Pavilion Peony	牡丹亭
pihuang	皮黃
pinghou	平喉
pipa	琵琶
Pixiu Su	貔貅蘇
Pu Yi	溥儀
Puruyi	普如意
Qian Qi	錢起
Qianli Ju	千里駒
Qiansui He	千歲鶴
Qing Fengnian	慶豐年
Qinxue xinbian	琴學新編
Qionghua Huiguan	瓊花會館
Qiu Hechou	丘鶴儔

Qiu Xi	秋喜
Quan Yicksang (Guan Yisheng; a.k.a. Quan Yick-sun)	關翼生
Qunfang Yanying [Brilliant Reflection of Blossom]	群芳艷影
Red Cliff Rhapsody	赤壁賦
Renshou Nian	人壽年
Romance of the Three Kingdoms	三國演義
sanshou	三手
Sanyi [Sam Yip]	三邑
Shanghai Mei [Sheung Hoi-Mui]	上海妹
shangshou	上手
Shao Baicai	少白菜
Shao Dingxiang	少丁香
Shaolin	少林
sheng	生
Sheng Gangban	省港班
Sheng Ping Theater [Sing Ping Theater]	昇平戲院
Sheng Zhangfei	生張飛
Shengjia Tong	聲架桐
Shezi An	蛇仔安
Shezi Li	蛇仔利
Shezi Qiu	蛇仔秋
Shezi Yi	蛇仔逸
Shezi Ying	蛇仔應
Shezi Yao	蛇仔耀
Shilin Jita	仕林祭塔
shousui	守歲
shouying	手影
Shu Foon Neue (Shou Fengnian)	壽豐年
shuochang	說唱
Si Shengfa	泗盛發
Siyi [Sze Yap]	四邑
Sizhu	絲竹
Song Taiping	頌太平
Su Xingqun	蘇醒群
Suen's Studio	樂觀映相館
Suzhou Li [So Chow Lai]	蘇州麗
Suzhou Mei [So Chow Mui]	蘇洲妹
Suzhou Nü	蘇州女
Swin-tien Lok (Shuntian Le)	順天樂
Tai Ping Theater	太平戲院
Tai Ping Young (Taiping Yang) Company	太平洋
Tai Wing Wah Theater [Da Ronghua; a.k.a. Choy Ding Quay]	大榮華戲院
Taishan	台山
Tan Huizhuang [Hom Fee Jong; Tam Wai Jon]	譚慧莊
Tan Lanqing [Tam Lan-Hing]	譚蘭卿
Tan Xiufang	譚秀芳
Teochew (Chaozhou)	潮州
Tian Dou Er Shi	田竇二師
Tian Zhong Drama Club	天鐘劇社
tianci	填詞
tianguang xi	天光戲

Tianyan Dawutai [Tianyan Mandarin Theater]	天演大舞台
tigang	提綱
tigang xi	提綱戲
Tong Li	同利
Tong Yi	同益
Tongqing	同慶
toujia	頭架
Tung Wah (Donghua) Hospital	東華醫院
waijiangban	外江班
Wan Shenglong	萬盛隆
Wei Zhongjue	衛仲覺
wenjing xi	文靜戲
Wenwu Hao	文武好
wenwusheng	文武生
Wing Hong Lin (Yongkangnian)	永康年
Woh Hing Company (He Xing Company)	和興公司
Wong Chin Foo	王清福
Wu Changting	吳暢亭
Wu Jingchi	吳景池
Wu Weijun	吳偉軍
Wu Zixu	伍子胥
wusheng	武生
Wuxing Deng	五星燈
Xi Qi	細杞
Xiange Bidu	弦歌必讀
Xianhua Da	仙花達
Xianrong	顯榮
xiansuo	絃索
xiao	簫
Xiao Caichan	蕭彩嬋
Xiao Caiji	蕭彩姬
Xiao Dingxiang	小丁香
Xiao Susu	小蘇蘇
Xiaoli Kang	肖麗康
xiaoqu	小曲
xiaosheng	小生
xiaowu	小武
xiban gongsi	戲班公司
xidan	戲單
Xie Daohui	謝道輼
xiju dajia	戲劇大家
Xin Baicai	新白菜
Xin Baiguo	新白果
Xin Guifei	新貴妃
Xin Jinbiao	新錦標
Xin Shezi Qiu	新蛇仔秋
Xin Yuefei	新岳飛
Xin Zhu [Sun Chu]	新珠
Xinshui Sheqiu	新水蛇秋
Xinshui Sherong	新水蛇容
Xinxin Qun	醒醒群
Xiongnu	匈奴

xipi	西皮
Xiyang Nü [Sai Yung Nui]	西洋女
Xu Jianbo	許鍵伯
Xue Feifei	雪霏霏
Xue Juefei	薛覺非
Xue Juexian [Sit Gok Sing]	薛覺先
Xue Yingluan	雪影鸞
Yang Guifei	楊貴妃
Yang Yanzhao	楊延昭
yangqin	揚琴
Yangzhou Mei [Yong Chow Moy]	楊州妹
Yaotianle	堯天樂
Yin Feiyan	銀飛燕
Yin Hudie	銀蝴蝶
Yin Qiantai	尹謙泰
Ying Mei Lun Hop (Yingmei Lianhe)	英美聯合公司
Yip Sang (Ye Sheng)	葉生
Yong Ni Shang	詠霓裳
Youjie Huiguan	優界會館
Youjie Tongzhishe	優界同志社
Yü Baiguo	余白果
Yuan Shikai	袁世凱
Yucho Chow Studio (Zhou Yaochu Studio)	周耀初映相館
yue'ou	粵謳
yueqin	月琴
Zhajiao Sheng	扎腳勝
Zhang Qiaohua	張巧華
Zhang Shuqin [Jung Sok-kan]	張淑勤
Zheng Huikui	鄭詼魁
zhengdan	正旦
zhengsheng	正生
Zhengxin Bei	正新北
Zhengxin Yi	正新亦
Zhenlan Bao	真欄報
zhenyin huadan	正印花旦
Zhou Shaobao	周少保
Zhou Shaobo	周少波
Zhou Shaoying	周少英
Zhou Yulin	周榆林
Zhou Yurong	周榆榮
Zhu Hong	朱洪
Zhu Huanian	祝華年
Zhu Jianshang	朱劍裳
Zhu Shengping	祝昇平
Zhu Taiping	祝太平
zhutouqin	竹頭琴
Zihou Hai	子喉海
Zihou Qi (Tsi-Hau Tsat)	子喉七
Zihou Sen	子喉森
Ziya Yu	子牙玉
Ziyaba	子牙八
Ziyou Hua	自由花
zongsheng	總生

Opera Titles

English Title (Romanized Form)	Chinese Title
Amorous Emperor	風流天子
Beauty on the Palm	掌中美人
Beauty's Tear	熊之淚
Bird Cage Phoenix	樊籬彩鳳
Birth and Departure of Green Jade	碧玉離生
A Birthday Greeting from the Eight Immortals	八仙賀壽
Boat Chase of White Peony	白牡丹追舟
Breaking Lingzhi Mushroom	碎拗靈芝
Camellia Rewarded by the King	御賜茶薇花
Cao Dajia	曹大家
Chang'Er Flying to the Moon	嫦娥奔月
Clandestine Meeting with the Xiaozhou Empress	幽會小周后
Courtesan Wang Zhaojun Leaves for the Frontier	昭君出塞
Crown Prince Qian Long	潛龍太子
Daiyu Burying Flower Petals	黛玉葬花
The Danger of Thunder Xian	響雷一聲鴛鴦
Deranged Mother Seeking Son	顛婆尋子
Double Rapier Female Warrior	雙劍女俠
Drunken Concubine (Drunken Empress)	貴妃醉酒
Duel of Fox and Plantain	狐鬥芭蕉
Duo-Nanny and Fortune Telling	雙奶媽看相
Eight Belle Spectacle	八美圖
A Fairy Maiden Scatters Flowers	天女散花
Farewell, My Concubine	霸王別姬
Farewell on a Winter Night	夜送寒衣
Female Lawyer Turning the Verdict	女律師反案
Female Warrior Saving the Country	女俠士救國轟炸賣國奴
Fighting Bride	冤孽新娘
Flower Agony	花愁
Frolicking with a Maid in the Cantina	酒樓戲鳳
Gao Ping Decapitated/Farewell to My Lady	高平取級/夜送京娘
The Garden of the Peaches of Immortality	桃花源
Gathering at Zhu-Ai	聚珠崖
Golden Leaf Chrysanthemum	金葉菊
The Great Wall Story of Meng Jiangnü's Bitter Weeping	孟姜女哭倒長城
Guan Yu Floods Seven Armies	水淹七軍
The Heavenly Maiden Offers a Son	天姬送子
Hibiscus Remorse	芙蓉恨
Ill-Fated Lady of Thirty Years	三十年之苦命女郎
The Imperial Appeal of Liang Tian-lai	梁天來告御狀
In Search of Father in the United States/Lament at the Immigration Office	金山尋親父移民局自嘆
Joint Hearing of Empress Lun	三公會審斬倫妃
The Joint Investiture of a Prime Minister of Six Warlords	六國大封相
Lady Cai Returning to Han	文姬歸漢
Lament of Jia Bao-yu	寶玉哭靈
Li Hua Punishing Her Son	梨花罪子
Losing the Red Sack	背解紅羅

Lovelorn Couple	癡情眷屬
Luo Chen's Patriotic Appeal	羅成寫書
Luo Tong Conquers the North	羅通掃北
Madame Black and White	黑白夫人
Madame White Snake	白蛇傳
Maid Qingwen Stitching at Her Sickbed	晴雯補裘
Menacing Waves Daunting Beauty	猛浪驚鴻
Misery Love	苦中緣
Moonlight Sieved through Sparse Clouds	殘霞漏月
Mourning of the Chaste Tree Flower	泣荊花
Mudan Su Laments the Dead Spirit	牡丹蘇哭靈
Mulan	花木蘭
My Wife, My Wife	余之妻
Nocturnal Mourning of Qiu Xi	夜吊秋喜
Nocturnal Mourning of White Lotus	夜吊白芙蓉
A Pair of Mandarin Ducks under the Water	水底鴛鴦
Pan Jinlian Trifling with Her Brother-in-Law	金蓮戲叔
Peony Demoted to Jiangnan	牡丹被貶江南
A Perfect Match	佳偶兵戎
Pinggui Bidding Farewell	平貴別窯
Pinggui Returning Home	平貴回窯
The Piteous Girl	可憐女
Plum Blowing in the Wind	風飄梅李
Pranks on the Bridal Chamber of the Ugly Girl	醜女鬧洞房
Princess Fox	玉面狐狸
Qianchun Emperor	咸醇皇
Rectifying Injustice	補青天
Reform through Pragmatism/Detective Seeking the Truth	維新求實學偵探究真情
Returning Home on Autumn Lake	秋湖歸家
Riot in the Nengren Temple	十三妹打鬧能仁寺
The Romance of the West Chamber	西廂記
The Romance of Two Lotuses	二荷情史
Sanniang Teaching Her Son	三娘教子
Saving the Daughter	救女
A Scholar Meets His Girlfriend in Disguise	金生挑盒
Shadow of Lady Mei	宓妃影
Shan Bo Visiting a Friend	山伯訪友
Shengsheng Man	聲聲慢
Shilin Paying Respects at the Pagoda	仕林祭塔
Smile at the Shadow of Plum Flower	笑梅影
Son to Be Killed at Outer Gate	轅門罪子
Steal the Shadow and Imitate the Shape	偷影摹形
Stealing Chicken to Offer up to Mother	偷雞奉母
Su Dongpo Encounters Red Cliff	蘇東坡遊赤壁點化釋琴操
Su Wu Herding Sheep	蘇武牧羊
Swords on the Red Cliff	朱崖劍影
Tale of Lovesick Woe	癡情恨
Tale of One Enmity and Three Grudges	一仇三怨
Tale of the Golden Butterfly	金絲蝴蝶傳
Tear of Plum Flower	梅之淚
Tears in the Bleak Palace	淚洒寒宮

Ten Belle Spectacle	十美圖
Three Heroes Combatting Lü Bu	三英戰呂布
Thrice-Defeated Zhouyu	三氣周瑜
Thrice Going to Southern Tang	三下南唐
Tibet Lama Monk	西藏喇嘛僧
Twilight Scarlet Tears	夕陽紅淚
Two Stars with Fine Dew	露洒雙星
Victory and Defeat of Reviving Hang Dynasty	興漢雌雄
Wayfarer's Autumn Lament	客途秋恨
Wenji Returning to Han	文姬歸漢
Wife and Concubine Through a Knife	一刀成妻妾
Wife Emperor	老婆皇帝
Women Generals of the Yang Family	女楊家將
Wretched Dragon and Harrowing Phoenix	悲龍苦鳳
Yalan Trades Pigs	亞蘭賣豬
Yanzi House	燕子樓
Yielding to the Empress	讓昭陽
Yingyang Mountain	陰陽山

NOTES

Introduction. Everyday Practice and the Imaginary

1. Wong Leung Doo Collection (106-020000-7), National Libraries and Archives of Canada, Ottawa.

2. For further discussion, see Adam McKeown, "Conceptualizing Chinese Diasporas, 1842 to 1949," *Journal of Asian Studies* 58/2 (1999): 306–337.

3. The box contains items most likely possessed by men; in addition to letters with mailing addresses, there are primary documents with clear gender identification such as school IDs, driver's licenses, proofs of citizenship, and head tax certificates.

4. Michel de Certeau, *The Practice of Everyday Life* (Berkeley: University of California Press, 1984), 21.

5. Ben Highmore, *Everyday Life and Cultural Theory: An Introduction* (London: Routledge, 2002), 174.

6. Author's interview with Clara Chan, San Francisco, January 7, 2012.

7. Marlon Hom, *Songs of Gold Mountain: Cantonese Rhymes from San Francisco Chinatown* (Berkeley: University of California Press, 1987), 29.

8. Joan Scott, "The Evidence of Experience," *Critical Inquiry* 17/4 (1991): 792.

9. Wayson Choy, *Paper Shadows: A Memory of a Past Lost and Found* (New York: Picador, 2000), 43–44, 51 ("guarded").

10. Arnie Cox, "Hearing, Feeling, Grasping Gestures," in *Music and Gesture*, ed. Anthony Gritten and Elaine King (Aldershot: Ashgate, 2006), 45–60.

11. Diane Taylor, *The Archive and the Repertoire: Performing Cultural Memory in the Americas* (Durham: Duke University Press, 2003), 143.

12. See Suzanne Cusick, "Feminist Theory, Music Theory, and the Mind/Body Problem," *Perspectives of New Music* 32/1 (1994): 8–27.

13. Choy, *Paper Shadows*, 56.

14. Author's interviews with Lillian Jew, James Lee, and Margaret Leung, San Francisco, January 7–10, 2012.

15. See Daphne Lei, "The Production and Consumption of Chinese Theatre in Nineteenth-Century California," *Theatre Research International* 28/3 (October 2003): 289–302.

16. Choy, *Paper Shadows*, 46, 52 ("It was many years").

17. The city was incorporated in 1886, and its population grew to more than twenty thousand by the turn of the century.

18. Guy Beiner, *Remembering the Year of the French: Irish Folk History and Social Memory* (Madison: University of Wisconsin Press, 2007), 28.

19. See, for example, scrapbooks by Raymond Fung (private collection) and Margaret Leung (private collection).

20. Interview with Margaret Leung.

21. Interview with Lillian Jew; author's interview with Judy Yung, San Francisco, August 2011.

22. Pierre Bourdieu, *The Logic of Practice*, trans. Richard Nice (Stanford: Stanford University Press, 1990), 74. Bourdieu further explains, "Body hexis speaks directly to the motor function, in the form of a pattern of postures that is both individual and systematic, being bound up with a whole system of objects" (ibid.).

23. Ibid., 73.

24. Greg Urban, *Metaculture: How Culture Moves through the World* (Minneapolis: University of Minnesota Press, 2001). Choy's description inevitably fused recollection with his desire to reclaim his lost history and childhood common to the genre of memoir.

25. Maxine Hong Kingston's mother was an opera fan. For the influence of opera and folklore on her work, see Sau-ling Cynthia Wong, "Autobiography as Guided Chinatown Tour? Maxine Hong Kingston's *The Woman Warrior* and the Chinese-American Autobiographical Controversy," in *Critical Essays on Maxine Hong Kingston*, ed. Laura E. Skandera-Trombley (New York: Hall, 1998), 146–167.

26. Chinatown theaters in North America had always been the public spaces for political events, and various types of town hall meetings.

27. Michael Broyles, "Immigrant, Folk and Regional Musics in the Nineteenth Century," in *The Cambridge History of American Music*, ed. David Nicholls (Cambridge: Cambridge University Press, 1998), 152.

28. See, for example, Daphne Lei, "The Production and Consumption of Chinese Theatre in Nineteenth-Century California," *Theatre Research International* 28/3 (October 2003): 289–302; Judy Tsou, "Gendering Race: Stereotypes of Chinese Americans in Popular Sheet Music," *Repercussions* 6 (fall 1997): 25–62; Charles Hiroshi Garrett, "Chinatown, Whose Chinatown? Defining America's Borders with Musical Orientalism," *Journal of the American Musicological Society* 57/1 (2004): 119–174.

29. Edward Said, "Orientalism Reconsidered," *Cultural Critique* 1 (autumn 1985): 91.

30. Sara Ahmed, "Affective Economies," *Social Text* 79 22/2 (2004): 117–139, esp. 119.

31. For example, Arthur Dong, author of *Forbidden City, USA: Chinese American Nightclubs*, noted that some Chinese American insisted, "I'm not all about Chinese opera, or kung fu. I'm about this [American popular culture], because this is the culture I was born into." See Robert Ito, "East Meets West, over Cocktails," *New York Times*, April 11, 2014.

32. Peter Chu et al., eds., *Chinese Theaters in America* (Washington, DC: Bureau of Research and Publications, Federal Theater Project, Works Project Administration, 1936), 83.

33. Urban, *Metaculture*, 6, 42.

34. See, for example, Arthur Bonner, *Alas! What Brought Thee Hither? The Chinese in New York, 1800–1950* (Madison, NJ: Fairleigh Dickinson University Press, 1997); Ronald Riddle, *Flying Dragons, Flowing Streams: Music in the Life of San Francisco's Chinese* (Westport, CT: Greenwood, 1983). The quotation is from Daphne Lei, *Operatic China: Staging Chinese Identity Across the Pacific* (London: Palgrave, 2006), 29–30.

35. David Palumbo-Liu, *Asian/American: Historical Crossings of a Racial Frontier* (Stanford: Stanford University Press, 1999), 17.

36. Daphne Lei, *Alternative Chinese Opera in the Age of Globalization: Performing Zero* (London: Palgrave, 2011), 118–119.

37. In his study of Vancouver during the 1918–1919 season, Wing Chung Ng notes that the theater company ordered between seven hundred and twelve hundred copies of daily playbills. See "Chinatown Theatre as Transnational Business: New Evidence from Vancouver during the Exclusion Era," *BC Studies* 148 (winter 2005–2006): 25–54.

38. See Gordon H. Chang, Mark Johnson, and Paul Karlstrom, eds., *Asian American Art: A History, 1850–1970* (Palo Alto: Stanford University Press, 2008).

39. See *Chinese Nationalist Daily*, 1928–1929. The other two regular advertisers of recordings are Kee Chung (Qi Chang), and Kwong Sun Chong (Guang Xin Chang). However, these two companies used only graphics or artistic designs for their advertisements.

40. Oriental Records issued six catalogues of recordings. Their advertisements can be found in the *Chinese Times* from 1927 to 1932.

41. Tong Soon Lee, *Chinese Street Opera in Singapore* (Urbana: University of Illinois Press, 2009), 9.

42. Yong Chen, *Chinese San Francisco, 1850–1943: A Transpacific Community* (Stanford: Stanford University Press, 2000), 225.

43. Alison Marshall, *Cultivating Connections: The Making of Chinese Prairie Canada* (Vancouver: University of British Columbia, 2014), 71.

44. Adam McKeown, "Review of Shehong Chen, Being Chinese, Becoming Chinese American," *American Historical Review* 108/2 (2003): 537–538.

45. Wing Chung Ng, *The Rise of Cantonese Opera* (Urbana: University of Illinois Press, 2015), 191.

46. Sabine Haenni, *The Immigrant Scene: Ethnic Amusements in New York, 1880–1920* (Minneapolis: University of Minnesota Press, 2008), 143–144.

47. Ibid., 55.

48. Decades later, the composer Lou Harrison would plead for a Chinatown theater in financial trouble, adamant that American opera in all its forms should be supported. Ethan Lechner, "Composers as Ethnographers: Difference in the Imaginations of Colin

McPhee, Henry Cowell, and Lou Harrison," Diss., University of North Carolina, Chapel Hill, 2008, 21.

Chapter 1. Shaping Forces, Networks, and Local Influences

1. Adam McKeown, "A World Made Many: Integration and Segregation in Global Migration, 1840–1940," in *Connecting Seas and Connected Ocean Rims*, ed. Donna R. Gabaccia and Dirk Hoerder (Leiden: Brill, 2011), 47.

2. Judy Yung, Gordon Chang, and Him Mark Lai, eds., *Chinese American Voices from the Gold Rush to the Present* (Berkeley: University of California Press, 2006), 1.

3. Najia Aarim-Heriot, *Chinese Immigrants, African Americans, and Racial Anxiety in the United States* (Urbana: University of Illinois Press, 2003), 80.

4. Map of San Francisco Chinatown, compiled by J. P. Wong [or Huang Huape] ([San Francisco]: J. P. Wong, 1929), Bancroft Library, University of California, Berkeley. I appreciate Judy Yung's help in reconstructing this estimate.

5. On the Hong Fook Tong, see Jack K. W. Tchen, *New York before Chinatown: Orientalism and the Shaping of American Cultures* (Baltimore: Johns Hopkins University Press, 1999); Sylvia Sun Minnick, *Samfow: The San Joaquin Chinese Legacy* (Keene, CA: Heritage West, 1987), 17, 20.

6. *Sacramento Daily Record-Union*, January 9 and February 5, 1880. Even today, traces of opera theaters still remain in Oroville and Marysville, California, both historic mining towns once hosting significant Chinese populations. Jeff Gillenkirk and James Motlow, *Bitter Melon: Inside America's Last Rural Chinese Town* (San Francisco: Heyday, 1987), 10.

7. See Ronald Riddle, *Flying Dragons, Flowing Streams: Music in the Life of San Francisco's Chinatown* (Westport, CT: Greenwood, 1983); Arthur Bonner, *Alas! What Brought Thee Hither? The Chinese in New York, 1800–1950* (Madison, NJ: Fairleigh Dickinson University Press, 1996).

8. "Chinese Theatricals," *Sacramento Daily Union*, May 7, 1855; Marie Rose Wong, *Sweet Cakes, Long Journey: The Chinatowns of Portland, Oregon* (Seattle: University of Washington Press, 2004), 223, 253, 306.

9. Lee Chew noted the following for the early 1880s: "I dressed well and lived well and had pleasure, going quite often to the Chinese theater and to dinner parties in Chinatown, I saved $50 in the first six months." Lee Chew, "The Life Story of a Chinaman," *Independent* 55 (February 19, 1903): 417–423. See also Wendy Rouse Jorae, *The Children of Chinatown: Growing up Chinese American in San Francisco* (Chapel Hill: University of North Carolina Press, 2009), 85. Ma Seung noted, "Each month I spent an average of fifty dollars in tickets to the theatre and Chinese operas, together with after theatre snacks usually with several fellow theatre lovers." Alison Marshall, *Cultivating Connections: The Making of Chinese Prairie Canada* (Vancouver: University of British Columbia Press, 2014), 43–44.

10. The 1874 opening was reported widely, from the *San Francisco Chronicle* to the *New York Times*. The theater was recorded as Su Yuan Tong in Pennsylvania's *Juniata Sentinel and Republican*, August 5, 1874, and as Sin Ting Yuen in Louisiana's *Ouachita Telegraph*, August 21, 1874.

11. A nineteenth-century English novelist and traveler, Lady Duffus Hardy gave a complete chapter of San Francisco's Chinatown theaters, noting, "In a space of half a mile, there are no less than four theatres," and portraying vividly a theater "crowded from floor to rafter." Lady Duffus Hardy, *Through Cities and Prairie Lands: Sketches of an American Tour* (New York: R. Worthington, 1881), 195, 198.

12. Krystyn R. Moon, *Yellowface: Creating the Chinese in American Popular Music and Performance* (New Brunswick: Rutgers University Press, 2004), 95.

13. Krystyn Moon, "On a *Temporary Basis*: Immigration, Labor Unions, and the American Entertainment Industry, 1880s–1930s," *Journal of American History* 99/3 (2012): 783.

14. In "The Dilemma of American Music," Daniel Gregory Mason wrote, "Since 1914 musicians of every country on earth have flowed in upon us in an unending stream. . . . Alas, the confusion of traditions among us is disastrously bewildering. . . . Where shall we recapture our native tongue?" Daniel Gregory Mason, *The Dilemma of American Music and Other Essays* (New York: Macmillan, 1928), 11, 13. This was originally published in *American Mercury* 7 (January 1926): 55–61.

15. In order to cut costs, Macdonald insisted on employing the Chinese. In Parliament in 1882, he put it pragmatically: "It is simply a question of alternatives: either you must have this labor or you can't have the railway." Kwok Bun Chan, *Smoke and Fire: The Chinese in Montreal* (Hong Kong: Chinese University of Hong Kong, 1991), 17.

16. David Chuenyan Lai, "From Downtown Slums to Suburban Malls," in *The Chinese Diaspora: Space, Place, Mobility, and Identity*, ed. Laurence J. C. Ma and Carolyn Lee Cartier (New York: Rowman & Littlefield, 2002), 314.

17. *Canada Year Book 1915*, 117. https://archive.org/details/canadabook191500casouoft.

18. Wing Chung Ng, "Chinatown Theatre as Transnational Business: New Evidence from Vancouver during the Exclusion Era," *BC Studies* 148 (2005–2006): 25–54.

19. Margarita Cervantes-Rodríguez and Alejandro Portes, *International Migration in Cuba: Accumulation, Imperial Designs, and Transnational Social Fields* (College Park: Pennsylvania State University Press, 2011), 123–125.

20. Mauro Garcia Triana and Pedro Eng Herrera, "The Chinese in Cuba, 1847–Now," 114–117, and Maria Teresa Linares, "Chinese in Cuba," in *Music in Latin America and the Caribbean: Performing the Caribbean Experience*, ed. Malena Kuss (Austin: University of Texas Press, 2008), 109–11.

21. The total Chinese population of California, Washington, and Oregon was 83,806. U.S. Census Bureau, *Eleventh Census of the United States* (Washington, DC: Government Printing Office, [1895–1897]).

22. U.S. Census Bureau, *Chinese and Japanese in the United States 1910*, Bulletin 127 (Washington, DC: Government Printing Office, 1914), 7. The figures include the United States mainland, Alaska (1,209) and Hawaii (21,674).

23. U.S. Census Bureau, *Fifteenth Census of the United States*, Population (Washington, DC: Government Printing Office, 1930), 34.

24. Even if the practice of "paper sons" makes this number not fully reliable, it is still quite sizeable. The phrase refers to a deceptive method devised to counter the anti-Chinese immigration laws established since 1882. Young Chinese males entered the

United States with purchased identity papers. The papers were established by American citizens of Chinese descent who left the United States to travel back to China. On returning, they would claim a marriage and the birth of several sons. Then the young Chinese males would appear, claiming to be the sons of these citizens. These boys were sons on paper only, hence the term "paper son."

25. See E. Mowbray Tate, *Transpacific Steam: The Story of Steam Navigation from the Pacific Coast of North America to the Far East and the Antipodes, 1867–1941* (New York: Cornwall, 1986); Gordon R. Newell, ed., *The H. W. McCurdy Maritime History of the Pacific Northwest* (Seattle: Superior, 1966).

26. Isabelle Lausent-Herrera, "The Chinatown in Peru and the Changing Peruvian Chinese Community(ies)," *Journal of Chinese Overseas* 7 (2011): 73.

27. For example, at Kam Wah Chung and Co. in John Day, the herbalist and general store owner had a listening room for the community. Jeffrey Barlow and Christine Richardson, *China Doctor of John Day* (Portland, OR: Binford, 1979); Oregon Experience: Kam Wah Chung, http://oregonstateparks.org/index.cfm?do=parkPage.dsp_parkPage&parkId=5.

28. See Kornel Chang, "Enforcing Transnational White Solidarity: Asian Migration and the Formation of the U.S.-Canadian Boundary," *American Quarterly* 60/3 (2008): 671–696.

29. See Burton W. Peretti, *The Creation of Jazz: Music, Race, and Culture in Urban America* (Urbana: University of Illinois Press, 1994), chap. 3.

30. See, for example, Leta E. Miller, *Music and Politics in San Francisco: From the 1906 Quake to the Second World War* (Berkeley: University of California Press, 2011).

31. Harriette Ashbrooke, "Chinese Players Revamp Our Oldest Theater," *New York Times*, September 20, 1925.

32. Nancy Yunhwa Rao, "The Color of Music Heritage: Chinese America in American Ultra-Modern Music," *Journal of Asian American Studies* 12 (2009): 100–101.

33. Anthony W. Lee, *Picturing Chinatown: Art and Orientalism in San Francisco* (Berkeley: University of California Press, 2001), 68. See also Nick Pearce, "Directness, Quaintness and Squalor: Aspects of Translation and Transformation in Franco Leoni's Opera *L'Oracolo*," in *Travels and Translations: Anglo-Italian Cultural Transactions*, ed. A. Yarrington, S. Villani, and J. Kelly (Amsterdam: Rodopi, 2013), 337–352.

34. Martin Banham, *The Cambridge Guide to Theatre* (Cambridge: Cambridge University Press, 1995), 773.

35. Luis Eduardo Guarnizo, "The Emergence of a Transnational Social Formation and the Mirage of Return Migration among Dominican Transmigrants," *Identities* 4/2 (1997): 281–322.

36. The discussion here is much influenced by Keith H. Basso, *Wisdom Sits in Places: Landscape and Language among the Western Apache* (Albuquerque: University of New Mexico Press, 1996).

37. Arif Dirlik, "Transnationalism, the Press, and the National Imaginary in Twentieth Century China," *China Review* 4/1 (2004): 14–15.

38. Ibid.

39. *Cantonese* generally refers to the dialect of Guangzhou. There are many Cantonese dialects used outside the city in regions such as Si Yi (Sze Yap), San Yi (Sam Yip), and

Hai Nan. Taishanese is a prominent and distinctively different dialect. Hokkien and Teochew are used as well. Mandarin Chinese, though the official language of China since 1913, was not generally spoken among emigrants from southern China. Cantonese opera was comprised of the vernacular Cantonese and a somewhat official dialect closer to Mandarin Chinese (used in most traditional arias).

40. At the same time, this featuring of Chinese and English on the same playbill can be read as a tacit nod to respectability. Evelyn Higginbotham, *Righteous Discontent: The Women's Movement in the Black Baptist Church, 1880–1920* (Cambridge: Harvard University Press, 1993), 185–197.

41. Marlon Hom, *Songs of Gold Mountain* (Berkeley: University of California Press, 1992), 29.

42. Eliot Grinnell Mears, *Residential Orientals on the Pacific Coast* (Chicago: University of Chicago Press, 1927), 200.

43. Christine Cushing, interview with Philip Choy, interviewed by Christine Cushing, https://www.youtube.com/watch?t=90&v=j7hbFhV4keY.

44. This expression is borrowed from the anthropologist Karin Barber. See *The Anthropology of Texts, Persons and Publics* (Cambridge: Cambridge University Press, 2007), chap. 1.

45. Author interview with James Lee, San Francisco, January 7–10, 2012.

46. Patricia Clavin, "Defining Transnationalism," *Contemporary European History* 14/4 (2005): 422.

47. Hom, *Songs of Gold Mountain*, 5–8.

48. See Him Mark Lai, *From Overseas Chinese to Chinese American: History of the Development of Chinese American Society during the Twentieth Century* (Hong Kong: Joint Publishing, 1992).

49. Kenneth J. Blume, *Historical Dictionary of the U.S. Maritime Industry* (Metuchen, NJ: Scarecrow, 2011), 104.

50. Tate, *Transpacific Steam*, 73; See also Record group 85, box 1760, file 21703/14–30, Chin Lain, National Archives, San Francisco; "San Francisco's Chinatown Buries Its No. 1 Citizen," *Life*, August 15, 1938, 14.

51. Ng, *Rise of Cantonese Opera*, 142.

Chapter 2. The Chinese Exclusion Act and Chinatown Theaters

1. Lisa Lowe, *Immigrant Acts: On Asian American Cultural Politics* (Durham, NC: Duke University Press, 1996), 180–181, n. 14.

2. See "The Music of Barbarian Bands—The Nerves of the Municipality Agitated—Gongs, Cymbals, Castanets and Tomtoms," *Daily Evening Bulletin*, August 5, 1869; picture X-18263, Denver Public Library digital collection.

3. *Daily Alta Californian*, December 2, 1856.

4. "A Chinese Feast," *Chicago Press and Tribune*, June 2, 1860; advertisement, *San Francisco Chronicle*, July 14, 1870.

5. *Daily Dramatic Chronicle* (San Francisco), January 25 and February 17, 1868.

6. "Chinese Capital," *Daily Dramatic Chronicle*, February 3, 1868; "The Chinese Theatre in San Francisco—Grand Banquet a la Chinois," *Chicago Tribune*, February 22, 1868.

7. "The Celestial Drama: A Glimpse at John Behind the Footlights—Grand Opening of the New Chinese Theater," *San Francisco Chronicle*, June 22, 1874; "Roscius with a Pigtail: A Midnight Hour among the Chinese Actors," *San Francisco Chronicle*, August 30, 1874.

8. *San Francisco Chronicle*, September 25, 1879.

9. *San Francisco Chronicle*, July 15, 1870.

10. *Daily Evening Bulletin* (San Francisco), September 8, 1874.

11. *San Francisco Chronicle*, September 25, 1879.

12. *San Francisco Chronicle*, December 13, 1877.

13. *San Francisco Chronicle*, September 25, 1879; "A New Chinese Theater," *New York Times*, October 27, 1879; "A Chinese Theater," *Detroit Press*, December 28, 1879.

14. "New Chinese Theater: A Grand Star Company of Heathen Artists on the Way," *San Francisco Chronicle*, October 13, 1877.

15. *Evening Star* (Washington, DC), March 13, 1879.

16. *Daily Dramatic Chronicle* (San Francisco), December 2, 1865.

17. These numbers below were taken from the census data of 1870 and 1880 provided by ancestry.com, a most comprehensive database of U.S. censuses I used at the San Francisco office of NARA in 2005, and tallied using the occupational and address search available through the database in 2005. Unfortunately, ancestry.com has since removed "occupation" as a search option.

18. 1870 U.S. census, San Francisco Ward 6, p. 25. NARA, manuscript schedules of the 1870 population census for San Francisco.

19. Yong Chen, *Chinese San Francisco, 1850–1943: A Transpacific Community* (Stanford: Stanford University Press, 2000), 91.

20. This number only accounts for those in the same residence. The actual number for each theater was likely larger, as actors and managers with families tended to reside on separate premises. Various census data of 1870 and 1880, ancestry.com.

21. For example, according to the 1880 U.S. federal census for San Francisco, a manager named Lee Sam and his wife, son, and daughter lived at 66 Dupont Street, Enumeration District 48, Supervisor's District 1, p. 6; an actor named Yung Hing and his wife, son, and daughter lived at 113-166 Washington Street, Enumeration District 34, Supervisor's District 1, p. 12. Various census data of 1880, ancestry.com.

22. Enumeration District 166, Supervisor's District 3, p. 30, Marysville 3rd Ward. Various census data of 1880, ancestry.com.

23. These included in particular ordinances directed at Chinese such as the Cubic Air Ordinance (1870), the Sidewalk Ordinance (1870), the Queue Ordinance (1873), and the Laundry Ordinance (1873).

24. *People vs. Ah Tim and Ah Luck*, *Sacramento Daily Record-Union*, August 5, 1880; *Sacramento Daily Record*, July 1, 1880.

25. *Daily Cairo Bulletin*, March 5, 1882.

26. *J. C. Cluney v. Lee Wai*, 10 Haw. 319 (1896); *Hawaiian Gazette*, October 4, 1882; *Daily Bulletin* (Honolulu), December 2, 1882.

27. Statutes of the State of California (1880), art. XIX, sec. 3.

28. John R. Wunder, "Anti-Chinese Violence in the American West, 1850–1910," in *Law for the Elephant, Law for the Beaver: Essays in the Legal History of the North American West*, ed. John McLaren (Pasadena: Ninth Judicial Circuit Historical Society, 1992), 212–236.

29. *New York Times*, March 28, 1860; *Daily Dramatic Chronicle* (San Francisco), February 8, 1868; *San Francisco Chronicle*, July 14–16, 1870 and September 9, 1890.

30. Moon-Ho Jung, *Coolies and Cane: Race, Labor, and Sugar in the Age of Emancipation* (Maryland: Johns Hopkins University Press, 2006), 13.

31. *In re Ho King*, 14 F. 724, 727 (D.C. Or. 1883), http://ark.cdlib.org/ark:/13030/ft22900486/. For further discussion, see David C. Frederick, *Rugged Justice: The Ninth Circuit Court of Appeals and the American West, 1891–1941* (Berkeley: University of California Press, 1994), 61; Ralph James Mooney, "Matthew Deady and the Federal Judicial Response to Racism in the Early West," *Oregon Law Review* 63 (1985): 615–616. Though pro-slavery and hostile to Chinese in his earlier career, Deady had a remarkable turnaround the mid-1870s toward beleaguered minorities, culminating in a move in 1886 to convene a grand jury to examine charging anti-Chinese crowds with criminal acts.

32. What is generally referred to as a "Section 6 certificate" was issued by U.S. consulates. According to a stipulation of Section 6 of the Chinese Exclusion Act, which has a category for occupation, a Chinese immigrant had to obtain proof of admissibility from a U.S. consulate's office in China.

33. "A Circus in Court: Four Chinese Actors Display Their Ability before Judge Hoffman," *New York Times*, August 23, 1884.

34. Christian G. Fritz, *Federal Justice in California: The Court of Ogden Hoffman, 1851–1891* (Lincoln: University of Nebraska Press, 1991), 210–249.

35. Christian G. Fritz, "A Nineteenth Century 'Habeas Corpus Mill': The Chinese before the Federal Courts in California," *American Journal of Legal History* 32/4 (October 1988): 347–372, esp. 350. For his support of exclusion acts, see Fritz, *Federal Justice in California*, 231, 211.

36. *San Francisco Chronicle*, October 28, 1891; "Chinese Orchestra," *Atchison Daily Globe*, December 1, 1890; *Los Angeles Times*, August 27, 1891; *Saturday Evening Post*, October 13, 1883.

37. *New York Times*, March 27, 1893.

38. *New York Times*, August 4, July 28, 1893. See "A Chinese 'Sacred Concert,'" *New York Times*, March 27, 1893.

39. "Chinese Actors for Omaha," *San Francisco Chronicle*, March 23, 1898.

40. "SS *China*, Hong Kong to San Francisco, May 10 1897," National Archives and Records Administration, film M1414, reel 6, sec. 2, vols. 36, 37, manifest 9579, as transcribed in Immigrant Ships Transcribers Guild, vol. 7, http://www.immigrantships.net/v8/1800v8/ch_china18970510_02.html. They included actors, musicians, stage porters, decorators, and carpenters.

41. Beth Lew-Williams, "Before Restriction Became Exclusion: America's Experiment in Diplomatic Immigration Control," *Pacific Historical Review* 83/1 (2014): 24–56.

42. Adam McKeown, "Ritualization of Regulation: The Enforcement of Chinese Exclusion in the United States and China," *American Historical Review* 108/2 (April 2003): 385.

43. Nayan Shah, *Stranger Intimacy: Contesting Race, Sexuality and the Law in the North American West* (Berkeley: University of California Press, 2014), 43.

44. McKeown, "Ritualization of Regulation," 385.

45. Lucy E. Salyer, *Laws Harsh as Tigers: Chinese Immigrants and the Shaping of Modern Immigration Law* (Chapel Hill: University of North Carolina Press, 1995), 154–155; Poon Chew Ng, "The Treatment of Exempted Classes of the Chinese in the U.S. (1908)," in *Chinese American Voices: From the Gold Rush to the Present*, ed. Judy Yung, Gordon H. Chang, and H. Mark Lai (Berkeley: University of California Press, 2006), 111–112.

46. In addition, perhaps it was considered a vice more than a cultural institution. Some even considered the fire fortunate because it "purified" San Francisco. See "Chinatown Purified," *Pacific Medical Journal* 29/5–6 (May–June 1906): 271; Nayan Shah, *Contagious Divides: Epidemics and Race in San Francisco's Chinatown* (Berkeley: University of California Press, 2001), 152.

47. Walter Anthony, "The Passing of the Chinese Theater," *San Francisco Call*, July 27, 1913.

48. Ibid. According to San Francisco's 1906 building classification, steel-frame structures were designated as Class A. It was reported after the earthquake that no fundamental damage was observed in buildings of this class. Stephen Tobriner, *Bracing for Disaster: Earthquake Resistant Architecture and Engineering in San Francisco, 1838–1933* (Berkeley: Heyday, 2006), 155.

49. Although a small number of Chinese opera performers continued occasional and small-scale performances, the San Francisco earthquake ended the existence of professional theaters.

50. Will Irwin, "The Drama That Was Chinatown," *New York Times*, April 20, 1921.

51. Anthony, "Passing of the Chinese Theater."

52. Obituary of Charles Thomas Parsloe, *New York Times*, January 23, 1898.

53. Andrew Erdman, *Queen of Vaudeville: The Story of Eva Tanguay* (Ithaca, NY: Cornell University Press, 2012), 7.

54. "Will Give 'Food' at the Orpheum," *San Francisco Chronicle*, October 28, 1914; Anthony Walter, "Orpheum's Funsters Help Reconcile You to Life! Long Tack Sam Is Headliner," *San Francisco Chronicle*, October 30, 1916. See Ann Marie Fleming, *The Magical Life of Long Tack Sam* (Toronto: Riverhead, 2007).

55. *Atlanta Constitution*, May 22, 1917.

56. "General Review: Pantages," *Los Angeles Times*, November 14, 1916. "Joss house" is an old name in English for Chinese traditional temples, places of worship where people revere gods and ancestors. They were commonly considered a characteristic part of Chinatowns in America prior to the mid-twentieth century.

57. "Long Tack Sam at Carlton Theatre: An Excellent Performance by Very Clever Troupe," *North-China Herald and Supreme Court and Consular Gazette*, February 11, 1928.

58. Daniella Trimboli, "Memory Magic: Cosmopolitanism and the Magical Life of Long Tack Sam," *Continuum* 29/3 (2015): 479–489.

59. Krystyn Moon traced the way the Chinese acrobat Ching Ling Foo became the catalyst for the creation of a special policy for Chinese performers under which he and his troupe were able to perform in the United States from 1912 to 1915. "'On a Temporary Basis': Immigration and the American Entertainment Industry, 1880s–1930s," *Journal of American History* 99 (2012): 775–776.

60. Assistant Commissioner General of Department of Labor to Chinese Inspector in Charge, New York, January 29, 1916, Bureau file 52854/100D, file 29/417, IACE, NY. Throughout this book the document titles are reprinted as they appear in the files themselves.

61. Frank Cook to H. R. Sisson, Jan 25, 1916, Bureau file 52854/100D, file 29/417, IACE, NY.

62. H. R. Sisson was the Inspector in Charge in New York at the time. Assistant Commissioner General of Department of Labor to Chinese Inspector in Charge, New York, February 12, 1916, Barnum & Bailey File, Bureau file 52854/100D), file 29/417, IACE, NY.

63. Neil Parsons, *Clicko: The Wild Dancing Bushman* (Chicago: University of Chicago Press, 2010), 87–89; "Fong Shum," file 166/22.2, IACE, NY.

64. Memo of General Board of Review, February 26, 1925, file 55374/227B, INS-SPF.

65. Obituary of Frank A. Cook, *New York Sun*, January 12, 1937.

66. Assistant Commissioner General, New York, N.Y., to Chinese Inspector in Charge, New York, N.Y., Jan. 29, 1916, File 29/417, IACE, NY.

67. Roger O'Donnell for Barnum & Bailey, Bureau file 20727/417, IACE, NY.

68. Judy Tsou, "Gendering Race: Stereotypes of Chinese Americans in Popular Sheet Music," *Repercussions* 6/2 (1997): 25–62.

69. See excellent discussions by Tsou, "Gendering Race," and Garrett, "Chinatown, Whose Chinatown."

70. Memo of General Board of Review, January 20, 1921, file 55007/1, INS-SPF.

71. Assistant Commissioner General to O'Donnell, January 31, 1921, file 55007/1, INS-SPF.

72. William Husband (1921–1925), Harry Hull (1925–1933) were the first commissioners of the Bureau of Immigration.

73. This position was established on June 30, 1922. http://www.dol.gov/oasam/programs/history/dpt-changes-old.htm.

74. The procedure was simplified by the use of a common expiration date for all troupe members regardless of their arrival dates. This way, the department only needed to review once or twice a year the company's requests for extension for the whole troupe. So if an actor arrived, say, three weeks before the common expiration date of the troupe's permission, his admission would be valid only until the common date, rather than six months from the date of entry.

75. Cantonese opera performers saw China, Southeast Asia, and North America as a unified field of opportunity, but they were under different constraints in the United States.

76. The Chinese name for the journal *Chinese Drama* was *Drama in America*, whose inaugural issue was published in November 1941.

77. Bryon Uhl, Immigration NYC to Commercial Casualty, September 23, 1933, box 225 56/53.3, IACE, NY.

78. Charles Booth to Immigration DC, July 17, 1933, box 225 56/53.3, IACE, NY.

Chapter 3. Immigration: Privilege or Right?

1. Congress created the Bureau of Immigration in 1891 and placed it in the Department of Commerce and Labor; when that department was divided in 1913, the bureau remained in the Department of Labor. The position of Second Assistant Secretary of Labor was responsible for overseeing the enforcement of immigration. The highest position of the bureau is the Commissioner General of Immigration. In 1922 the Secretary of Labor created an addition to the Immigration Service, the Secretary's Board of Review, or the Board of Review, with four members, chaired by the Second Assistant Secretary of Labor. In practice, it is a court of appeal for the hearing and settlement of exceptional cases. See James J. Davis, "How the Immigration Laws Are Working Now," *Review of Reviews* 65 (1922): 509–516.

2. Christian G. Fritz, *Federal Justice in California: The Court of Ogden Hoffman, 1851–1891* (Lincoln: University of Nebraska Press, 1991), 212.

3. Petition from Chin Lain, December 27, 1923, file 55374/227, INS-SPF.

4. Attorney C. A. A. McGee visited the highest officials including Robe Carl White, the Assistant Secretary of Labor, E. J. Henning, the Second Assistant Secretary of Labor, William Husband, the Commissioner General of Immigration, and a Mr. Booth from the Board of Review. Letter from McGee to White, December 26, 1923, file 55374/227, INS-SPF.

5. There were at least two other simultaneous applications for the Mandarin Theater: one by Chin Lain through the attorney C. A. A. McGee, the other by Chin Ling and Chan Kung Woo through the attorney William Wylie, who previously worked in McGee's firm. Another application was filed by the firm of Stewart and Murphy. One attorney withdrew his petition, noting that several simultaneous efforts were being made, and partnership agreements were entered, upon assurances of special influence in securing the permit. William Wylie to John D. Nagle, Commissioner of Immigration Service, San Francisco, February 7, 1924, file 55374/227, INS-SPF.

6. Petition from Chin Lain, December 27, 1923, file 55374/227, INS-SPF.

7. Nayan Shah, *Contagious Divides: Epidemics and Race in San Francisco's Chinatown* (Berkeley: University of California Press, 2001), 22.

8. For examples, see Interview of Chin Lain by J. W. Howell, February 2, 1924, p. 4, file 55374/227, INS-SPF.

9. Reverend Bradley of the Chinatown Mission of Old St. Mary's Church to John Nagle, Commissioner of Immigration, San Francisco, February 2, 1924, file 55374/227, INS-SPF.

10. Donaldina Cameron of the Presbyterian Chinese Mission to John Nagle, Commissioner of Immigration, San Francisco, February 1, 1924, file 55374/227, INS-SPF.

11. M. S. Fung of the Chinese Consolidated Benevolent Association to McGee, January 31, 1924, file 55374/227, INS-SPF.

12. Interview of Chin Lain by Inspector Howell, February 2, 1924, file 55374/227, INS-SPF.

13. See, for example, Clarence E. Edwards, *The Art of Elegant Dining—Bohemian San Francisco: Its Restaurants and Their Most Famous Recipes* (San Francisco: Paul Elder & Company, 1917).

14. Report by Inspector Howell, February 4, 1924, file 55374/227, INS-SPF.

15. Interview of Chin Lain by Howell, p. 5.

16. Shah, *Contagious Divides*, 211.

17. Angel Island officials insisted that both the so-called Section 6 certificate, issued by the Chinese government to verify an exempt class, and the immigrant visa, to be issued by the U.S. Consulate in Hong Kong, were required before the performers could board the ship to sail west. C. A. A. McGee to John Nagle, February 7, 1924, file 55374/227, INS-SPF.

18. By early 1925 the Mandarin Theater would routinely use Seattle as its primary port of entry for performers coming directly from China. The three actors and the actress who arrived on January 5 were perhaps the last group to arrive at Angel Island.

19. Report from Griffin to Immigration Service, San Francisco, December 16, 1924, file 55374/227A, INS-SPF.

20. The records of tax paid to the city by the Mandarin Theater during the first season show that the revenue fluctuated, surging dramatically with the arrivals of new performers. McGee to James Davis, Secretary of Labor, April 9, 1925, file 55374/227C, INS-SPF.

21. Petition from McGee, March 13, 1925, file 55374/227C, INS-SPF.

22. *Young China*, March 11, 14, 1925.

23. C. A. A. McGee to James Davis, April 9, 1925, file 55374/227C, INS-SPF.

24. E. L. Haff, Acting Commissioner of Immigration, San Francisco, to Commission General, DC, May 22, 1925, file 55374/227C, INS-SPF.

25. Memo from General Board of Review, DC, June 4, 1925, file 55374/227C, INS-SPF.

26. Memo from General Board of Review, DC, February 7, 1925, file 55374/227B, INS-SPF (emphasis added).

27. The writ of habeas corpus allowed a prisoner the chance to challenge his or her confinement, and Chinese exclusion cases in the late nineteenth century became a large source of habeas corpus litigation. By 1905 the decisions of immigration officials were final and generally not appealable in court. http://www.fjc.gov/history/home.nsf/page/jurisdiction_habeas.html.

28. Statements of Witnesses, July 8, 1925. Included are the Los Angeles Mandarin Theater's fireman, manager, general supervisor, and secretary and the president of the Chinese Chamber of Commerce. File 55374/227D, INS-SPF.

29. This information is according to the witness statement of Lee Thing, secretary of the Chinese Chamber of Commerce and English secretary of the Mandarin Theater. July 8, 1925, file 55374/227D, INS-SPF.

30. John W. Foster, "The Chinese Boycott," *Atlantic Monthly* (January 1906), 118–127, quoted in Lucy E. Salyer, *Laws Harsh as Tigers: Chinese Immigrants and the Shaping of Modern Immigration Law* (Chapel Hill: University of North Carolina Press, 1995), 152.

31. M. Walton Hendry to Secretary of Labor, June 18 and 19, 1925, file 55374/227, INS-SPF.

32. *Young China*, March 22, 1925.

33. U.S. Census, *Fourteenth Census of the United States* (Washington, DC: Bureau of the Census, 1920), 3:131.

34. The amendment was passed on June 7, 1924. See General Review Board to C. A. A. McGee, January 23, 1925, file 55374/227B, INS-SPF. The same sentiment about avoiding unnecessary hardship was also expressed by the Secretary of Labor, James Davis, in 1922, See Davis, "How the Immigration Laws are Working Now," 510.

35. Over the years, as Salyer notes, "while Chinese and other immigrant groups resorted to a variety of tactics—economic sanctions, publicity, lobbying—to exert pressure on the Bureau of Immigration, their lawyers simultaneously turned to the courts in the effort to 'regulate the regulators.'" Salyer, *Laws Harsh as Tigers*, 169.

36. From Immigrant Inspector G. W. Kenny to Commissioner of Immigration, Angel Island, August 16, 1922, file no. 21713/151, IACE, SF.

37. Letter from City and County of San Francisco Police Court L. T. Jacks to Frank Monahan, June 18, 1925, file 55374/227D, INS-SPF; Telegram from Representative Florence Kahn to Harry Hull, Commissioner General of Immigration, July 29, 1925, file 55374/227D, INS-SPF.

38. Telegram from Senator Lawrence Flaherty to Acting Secretary of Labor William Husband, June 24, 1925, file 55374/227D, INS-SPF.

39. *Chung Sai Yat Po*, July 7, 1924.

40. Erika Lee, "Defying Exclusion: Chinese Immigrants and Their Strategies during the Exclusion Era," *Chinese American Transnationalism: The Flow of People, Resources, and Ideas between China and America during the Exclusion Era*, ed. Sucheng Chan (Philadelphia: Temple University Press, 2005), 14.

41. Furthermore, Lun Hop also operated Tai Ping Young in Seattle and All Star in Los Angeles and had a working agreement with Lok Tin Tsau of Boston for exchanging actors.

42. Goon Dip, Consulate of Republic of China, Seattle to Luther Weedin, Commissioner of Immigration, Seattle, August 21, 1925, file 55374/227D, INS-SPF.

43. McGee to James Davis, Secretary of Labor, January 16, 1925, file 55374/227B, INS-SPF.

44. Hendry to Commissioner General of Immigration William Husband, July 21, 1925, File 55374/227D, INS-SPF.

45. Hendry to Commissioner General of Immigration William Husband, July 21, 1925, File 55374/227D, INS-SPF. The other case is *Chang Chan, Wong Hung Kay, Yee Sin Jung et al. v. Nagle*, 268 U.S. 346. The emphasis is mine.

46. DEFINITION OF "IMMIGRANT." Sec. 3. When used in this Act the term "immigrant" means any alien departing from any place outside the United States destined for the United States, except . . . (2) an alien visiting the United States temporarily as a tourist or temporarily for business or pleasure . . . and (6) an alien entitled to enter the United States solely to carry on trade under and in pursuance of the provisions of a present existing treaty of commerce and navigation.

EXCLUSION FROM UNITED STATES. Sec. 13 . . . (c) No alien ineligible to [*sic*] citizenship shall be admitted to the US unless such alien . . . (3) is not an immigrant as defined in section 3. Immigration Act of 1924, Pub. L. 68–139, 43 Stat. 153.

47. For a discussion of the rights-based argument see Lea Brilmayer, "Rights, Fairness, and Choice of Law," *Yale Law Review* 98/7 (1989): 1277–1319.

48. In the ensuing years the non-immigrant status established in the Immigration Act of 1924 would become a recurring argument in the court cases brought by Chinese immigrants, citing *Cheung Sum Shee v. Nagle* as precedent.

49. See Erika Lee, *At America's Gates: Chinese Immigration during the Exclusion Era, 1882–1943* (Chapel Hill: University of North Carolina Press, 2003), 210.

50. Attorney Russell Tyler to Robe Carl White, Acting Secretary of Labor, July 31, 1925, file 55374/227D, INS-SPF.

51. Robe Carl White, Acting Secretary of Labor, to Hiram Johnson, US Senate Committee on Immigration, August 10, 1925, file 55374/227D, INS-SPF.

52. City and County of San Francisco Police Court L. T. Jacks to Frank Monahan, June 18, 1925, file 55374/227D, INS-SPF.

53. Hiram Johnson to James Davis, June 13, 1925, file 55374/227C, INS-SPF. Also see Mae Ngai, *Impossible Subject: Illegal Aliens and the Making of Modern America* (Princeton: Princeton University Press, 2004), 47. Johnson was part of the California Joint Immigration Committee, which mounted an aggressive campaign to push the concept of ineligibility for citizenship. For his role in the Alien Land Act, see Greg Robinson, *By Order of the President: FDR and the Internment of Japanese Americans* (Cambridge: Harvard University Press, 2001), 23.

54. Fritz, *Federal Justice in California*, 212. For example, the prominent San Francisco lawyer John Henry Boalt quietly represented Chinese in civil litigation, though he was a strong advocate of Chinese exclusion.

55. Memo from Chairman, General Board of Review August 19, 1925, file 55374/227D, INS-SPF.

56. For the next few years, the number varied between seventy-five and eighty-five.

57. "San Francisco's Chinatown Buries Its No. 1 Citizen," *Life*, August 15, 1938, 14.

58. General Review Board (Robe Carl White, Second Assistant Secretary of Labor) to Immigration Office, Seattle, March 26, 1924, file 55197/81c, INS-SPF.

59. The *New York Times* reported in 1948 on the deportation of Mandarin Theater actors whose final extension of stay was denied and who were to lose their bond. These twelve actors entered in 1939 and 1940, and their three-year limit was temporarily suspended due to the war, but because the war was over, any further extension was denied on June 30, 1947. "12 Chinese Actors Face Deportation in California," *New York Times*, April 3, 1948.

Chapter 4. Aesthetics, Repertoire, Roles, and Playbills

1. See Mai Xiaoxia, "Guangdong Xiju Shilue" (A Brief History of Opera Theater in Guangdong), in *Guangdong Wenwu* (Art and Heritage in Guangdong), ed. Guangdong

Wenwu Zhanlanhui (Hong Kong: Zhongguo Wenhua Xiejinhui, 1942), 3:791–835. It has been reprinted as a book and widely circulated. Chen Feinong, *Yueju Liushinian* (Sixty Years of Cantonese Opera: Chan Feinong's Memoir), ed. Wing Chung Ng and Chan Chak Lui (Hong Kong: Cantonese Opera Research Programme, Chinese University of Hong Kong, 2007); Guoxing Liu, "Yueju Yiren Zai Haiwaide Shenghuo Ji Huodong" (The Lives and Activities of Cantonese Opera Actors Abroad), *Guangdong Wenshi Ziliao* 21 (1965): 172–188; Huang Tao, *Yueju Huibian* (Cantonese Cultural Promotion Association), http://www.cantoneseculture.com/page_CantoneseOpera/index.aspx.

2. See Bell Yung, *Cantonese Opera: Performance as Creative Process* (New York: Cambridge University Press, 1989); Sai-shing Yung, *From Opera Boat to Silver Screen: Visual and Sonic Culture of Cantonese Opera* (Hong Kong: Oxford University Press, 2012); Chen Meibao, "The Trans-regional nature of Local Cultures in recent time: Cantonese Opera, Cantonese Music, and Cantonese opera Songs in Shanghai, 1920s–1930s," *Modern Chinese History* no. 158 (2007): 1–17; Wing Chung Ng, *The Rise of Cantonese Opera* (Urbana: University of Illinois Press, 2015).

3. "The Chinese Stage and the Dark Lady of Its Sonnets," *New York Times*, January 21, 1923.

4. Chinese opera became a synthesis of art, classic literature, song, music, dance and drama through a complicated and long historical process. Early Chinese opera of the Qin (221–206 BCE) and Han (206–220 CE) Dynasties involved dancing, singing, farce, and the "hundred-entertainment," while in the Tang Dynasty (617–907) performances included music played at court feasts and temple fairs. In the Song Dynasty (960–1279) performance activities reached a critical mass in urban centers, where royal music and dance, folk music and dance, and secular balladry were brought together and gave birth to the distinctive art form of Chinese opera. This history comprises a series of important music traditions—from the Tang Dynasty's adjutant plays and song and dance suites to the Song Dynasty's *nanxi* drama and variety plays, the Yuan Dynasty's (1279–1368) *zaju* drama, the Jin dynasty's "all-keys-and-modes," and the *chuanqi* drama of the Ming and Qing Dynasties—all of which are illustrious literary traditions as well.

5. Barbara Ward, "Regional Operas and Their Audiences: Evidence from Hong Kong," in *Popular Culture in Late Imperial China*, ed. David Johnson, Andrew J. Nathan, and Evelyn S. Rawski (Berkeley: University of California Press, 1989), 173.

6. See S. Yung, *From Opera Boat to Silver Screen*; Sai-shing Yung, "'Entering the City and Its Bright Light': A study of Cantonese Opera in the 1920s," in *Qingxun zuji erbainian: Yueju guoji yantaohui lunwenji*, ed. Chow Sze Sum and Cheng Lin Yan (Hong Kong: Cantonese Opera Research Programme, Chinese University of Hong Kong, 2008), 73–97.

7. See M. Chen, "Trans-locality of Local Cultures"; "*A Preliminary Study of the Theatres Built by Cantonese Merchants in the Late Qing*," *Frontiers of Chinese History* 5/2 (2010): 253–278.

8. Huang Wei and Shen Youzhu, *Shanghai yueju yanchu shigao* (Cantonese Opera Performed in Shanghai: A draft history) (Beijing: Zhongguo xiju chubanshe, 2007).

9. See Xie Yinghua, "Shanghai's New Stage: 1908–1927" (Master's thesis, Fudan University, 2005).

10. *Shen Bao*, October 29, 1920.

11. *Shen Bao*, May 7, 1923.

12. *Shen Bao*, October 24, 1923.

13. *Shen Bao*, September 21, 1928.

14. This backdrop was uncovered in 2011 during my visit to the Great China Theater.

15. Peter Chu et al., eds., *Chinese Theaters in America* (Washington, DC: Bureau of Research and Publications, Federal Theater Project, Works Progress Administration, 1936), 126, 134.

16. See playbills at the Ethnic Studies Library, University of California, Berkeley, as well as the May's Studio Collection in the San Francisco Performing Arts Library and Museum.

17. This newsletter began publishing in 1917.

18. *Shen Bao*, October 23, 1919.

19. *Shen Bao*, October 21, 1920.

20. Huang Deshe, "Yueju Nubande Xingqi, Fazhanhe Shuailuo" (The Rise, Development and Decline of Cantonese Opera All-Female Troupe). *Guangzhou Wenshi Ziliao*, no. 6. http://www.gzzxws.gov.cn/gzws../cg/cgml/cg6/200808/t20080826_4224.htm.

21. This conclusion is based on my survey of *Yuehua Bao* from August 1, 1927, to September 30, 1928. See also Huang Chun, "A New Exploration of Cantonese Opera All-Female Troupes in the Early Republican Period," *Journal of the Graduates of Sun Yat-Sen University* 33/11 (2012): 7–18.

22. My research result is contrary to the common belief that all-female troupes were engaged by Chinatown theaters of North America.

23. Li Jian also noted the popularity of the twelve-role-type systems. Li Jian, *Xianggang Yueju Xulun* (Discourse on Cantonese Opera in Hong Kong) (Hong Kong: Sanlian, 2010), 47, 103. See also a contemporary article on this topic: Zheng Luofu, "Yueju Congtan," *Youxi Shijie* 10 (1922): 13–16.

24. See, for example, hengtou dan for the famous troupes Yong Taiping and Song Taiping from 1910 to 1930. Yu Yong, *Mingqing Shiqi Yuejudeqiyuan, xingcheng he fazhang* (The Origin, Formation, and Development of Cantonese Opera in the Ming and Qing Dynasties) (Beijing: Zhongguo Xiju Chuban She, 2009). See also hengtou dan in the Hong Kong Cultural Heritage Museum, item no. 1995.114.323, Taiping Theater Collection.

25. One particularly elaborate hengtou dan of the Song Taiping Troupe (one of the top male troupes) from 1925 listed one additional type of comedian and two additional types of female characters, as well as scholar-warrior, or wusheng. Hong Kong Cultural Heritage Museum, item no. 1995.59.1082.

26. Today many anthologies of lyrics of paichang opera exist in various archives.

27. Lai Bojiang and Huang Jingping, *Yueju Shi* (History of Cantonese Opera) (Beijing: Zhongguo Xiqu Chubanshe, 1988), 228.

28. According to a contemporary star performer, Chen Feinong, the protracted training of an opera singer began with the basic skills: vocal technique (which included particular types of vocalization using proper support, clear diction, combining good placement of voice and enunciation of consonants and vowels, and proper breathing) and physical training (which included basic acrobatic skills, martial arts techniques, and various movements of great dexterity and agility). After establishing these basic skills, the next step was for the

students to be introduced to the basic stock of paichang, which they would need to master. See Feinon, *Yueju Liushinian* (Sixty Years of Cantonese Opera), 48–50.

29. Sau Yan Chan, "Exploding the Belly: Improvisation in Cantonese Opera," in *In the Course of Performance: Studies in the World of Musical Improvisation*, ed. Bruno Nettl and Melinda Russell (London: University of Chicago Press, 1998), 199–218 . For shoying, see Sau Yan Chan, *Introduction to Cantonese Opera in Hong Kong* (Hong Kong: Cantonese Opera Research Programme, The Chinese University of Hong Kong, 1999), 176–181.

30. *Shen Bao*, October 21, 1920.

31. *Shen Bao*, August 2, 1924, and *Young China*, July 4–7, 1924. The two articles were likely by the same author.

32. The accompanying instruments for Cantonese opera have undergone many changes, from a three-piece ensemble to a five-piece ensemble to a much larger ensemble that includes both violin and saxophone. I have used the literature from about the 1920s to reconstruct the ensemble as listed in this table. See, for example, Qiu Shuang, "Duiyu Yuejulide Yinyuede Yanjiu" (Study of Music in Cantonese Opera), *Xiju* 1/1 (1929): 92–110.

33. *Young China*, July 4–7, 1924.

34. Huang Jingming, "Shitan Yueju Changqiang yinyuede xingchenghe gaibian" (The Formation and Change of Cantonese Opera Vocal Music), *Yueju Yishuziliao* (Resources on Cantonese Opera Arts) 2 (1979): 97.

35. See Li Jian, *Discourse on Cantonese Opera*, 259.

36. Yung, *Cantonese Opera*, 148. Cantonese, like other Chinese dialects, is a tonal language; it has six tones.

37. Leta Miller, *Music and Politics in San Francisco: From the 1906 Quake to the Second World War* (Berkeley: University of California Press, 2011), 84.

38. These categories are based in part on the classifications generally discussed in Cantonese opera literature, and in part on the author's study of playbills in North America.

39. Because Cantonese opera underwent major changes from the 1920s to 1940s, much of the repertoire that was highly popular in the 1920s was no longer performed after the 1940s.

40. Synopses for each opera vary significantly in different sources, at times having only the most basic skeletons of the stories in common. Even the characters' names differ. Further complicating the matter is that multiple names were used to refer to the same opera, singling out different episodes of the story. This reflects a very elastic practice in the performance history of Cantonese opera. Whenever possible this book considers primarily the synopses published on the playbills but also compares several sources to generate a common version of the story. Anthologies and memoirs have also been consulted. See, for example, *Yueju Jumu Gangyao* (A Catalogue of Cantonese Opera Titles and Plots) (Hong Kong: Zhongguo xijujia xiehui Guangdong fenhui, 1982).

41. For example, the earliest known core repertoire, "Eighteen New Itinerant Operas," includes Ming dynasty classical play that was made into Peking opera as well.

42. They are wusheng (nos. 5 and 7), gongjiao (nos. 1, 2, 10, and 17), er huamian (nos. 6, 13, 15, and 16), and xiaowu (nos. 11, 12, 14, and 18). Mai Xiaoxia, "Guangdong Xiju Shilue," 22.

43. Ibid., 28.

44. Chen Meibao, "'What Alternative Do You Have, Sixth Aunt?' Women and Marriage in Cantonese Ballads," in *Merchants' Daughters: Women, Commerce, and Regional Culture in South China*, ed. Helen F. Siu (Hong Kong: Hong Kong University Press, 2011), 59–76; Wilt L. Idema, "Prosimetric and Verse Narrative," in *The Cambridge History of Chinese Literature: From 1375*, ed. Kang-i Sun Chang and Stephen Owen (Cambridge: Cambridge University Press, 2010), 389–394; Chen Yongxin, "Muyu and Cantonese Opera," in *Foshancang Muyushu Mulu Yu Yanjiu*, ed. Zeng Yimin (Guangzhou: Guangzhou, 2009), 265–268. This article lists forty opera titles derived from muyushu. See also Sai-shing Yung, "Mu-yushu and the Cantonese Popular Singing Arts," *Gest Library Journal* 2/1 (1987): 16–30; Bell Yung, "Muk'yu: Voices of the People," in *Uncle Ng Comes to America: Chinese Narrative Songs of Immigration and Love* (Hong Kong: MCCM Creations, 2014).

45. Anne McLaren, "The Oral Formulaic Tradition," *The Columbia History of Chinese Literature, ed. Victor H. Mair* (New York: Columbia University Press, 2002), 989–1014.

46. Guangdong native Qu Dajun (1630–1696) gives this description in *New Words from Guangdong (Guangdong xinyu)*, quoted in Idema, "Prosimetric and Verse Narrative," 289–290.

47. Ward, "Regional Operas and Their Audiences," 167.

48. Ibid., 172.

49. Gordon Chang, Mark Johnson, and Paul Karlstrom, eds., *Asian American Art: A History, 1850–1970* (Stanford: Stanford University Press, 2008), 385–386.

50. Eight playbills from San Francisco Cantonese opera theaters of the 1920s were found in the Oroville Chinese Temple and Museum, Oroville, California.

51. A dozen playbills from the New China Theater in New York were mailed by D. F. Chin of New York to an opera fan named Ray Fong in San Francisco in the 1940s. Private collection of David Lei.

52. Gillian Russell, *The Playbill and Its People: Australia's Earliest Printed Document* (Canberra: National Library of Australia, 2012), 80.

53. Karin Barber, *The Generation of Plays: Yorùbá Popular Life in Theater* (Bloomington: Indiana University Press, 2000), 11.

54. Though Margaret Leung was born in 1923, she had heard many of the singers and operas discussed in this book. Author's interview with Margaret Leung, San Francisco, January 7–12, 2012.

Chapter 5. An Examination of the Aria Song "Shilin Jita"

1. Wen, Zhi Peng, "Yueju Nuban Zhi Chutan" (A Preliminary Study of Female Troupes), in *Yue Ju Yan Yao Hui Lun Wen Ji* (Papers and Proceedings of the International Seminar on Cantonese Opera), ed. Ching-Chih Liu and Elizabeth Sinn (Hong Kong: Hong Kong University Centre of Asian Studies, 1995), 375.

2. In Cantonese opera studies, the aria and the aria song are considered different. Whereas *aria* refers to what is sung in the opera, *aria song* refers to what is performed as a solo piece outside the opera production. As a solo piece, a Cantonese aria song tends to incorporate more context about the opera's story, so it is not exactly the same as the

aria performed on stage. Historical recordings are by nature aria songs, performed in the studio, away from the stage production.

3. It was likely a reissue of an earlier recording, since the record company came into existence only in the late 1940s. Li Xuefang, "Shilin Jita" (C-3514, C-3515, C-3516 Great Wall Records, 3 disks).

4. See *Chinese Nationalist Daily*, July 9, 1928.

5. *A Dictionary of Cantonese Opera* (Yue ju da ci dian), ed. Bian Zuan Wei Yuan (Guangzhou Shi: Guangzhou chu ban she, 2008), 433–434.

6. The downbeats are unmarked by voice or accompanying instruments. A different transcription of this recording (the first phrase only) can be found in Chow Sze Sum, "The Evolution of *fanxian erhuang manban* in Hong Kong Cantonese Opera of the Past Hundred Years (Part I)," *Journey to Chinese Opera and Drama* 53 (2006): 68–69. At the tempo of M.M. 30 per quarter note, one bar in Chow's transcription equals two bars in mine. Chow's transcription reflects the current practice used by Cantonese opera scholars in Hong Kong today, both for analysis and for composition. My transcription, on the other hand, renders certain structural features more clearly, as shown later in the chapter. There are many versions of jita that show different variations. See, for example, a version in *Yueju Changqiang Yinyue Gailun* (General Discussion of the Style of Vocal Music of Cantonese Opera), ed. and comp. Guangdongsheng Xiju Yanjiushe (Center for Operatic Research of Guangdong Province) (Beijing: Renmin Yinyue Chubanshe, 1984), 419–420.

7. The term *aria type* was first translated by Rulan Chao Pian from the Chinese term *banghuang*. Rulan Chao Pian, "Aria Structural Patterns in the Peking Opera," in *Chinese and Japanese Music Dramas*, ed. J. I. Crump and William Malm (Ann Arbor: Center for Chinese Studies, University of Michigan, 1975), 65–89. For further discussion of aria types and tune families see Bell Yung, *Cantonese Opera: Performance as Creative Process* (Cambridge: Cambridge University Press, 1989), 67–81. Sau Yan Chan suggests the term *melo-rhythmic type* to reflect the significance of both rhythmic and melodic features in the structure of these songs. See Sau Yan Chan, "Exploding the Belly: Improvisation in Cantonese Opera," in *In the Course of Performance: Studies in the World of Musical Improvisation*, ed. Bruno Nettl and Melinda Russell (London: University of Chicago Press, 1998), 199–218. Jonathan Stock, on the other hand, suggests *mode* rather than *tune* or *aria* to describe the "crosscultural resonances of pitch hierarchy, set melodic patterns, and characteristic ornamental devices that this term implies." See Jonathan P. J. Stock, *Huju: Traditional Opera in Modern Shanghai* (New York: Oxford University Press, 2003), 89. See also his "A Reassessment of the Relationship between Text, Speech Tone, Melody, and Aria Structure in Beijing Opera," *Journal of Musicological Research* 18/3 (1999): 183–206.

8. Yung, *Cantonese Opera*, 15.

9. Ibid., 68.

10. For a close study of the aria type of *fangxian erhuang manban*, see Chow Sze Sum, "Analysis of Fang Yen-feng's *fangxian erhuang manban* and *fangxian bangzi zhongban*," in *Xin Yanyang Chuanqi*, ed. Yue Qing (Hong Kong: Yueqing Chuanbo, 2008), 179–189. The jita aria was used later in operas such as *Youhui Xiaozhouhou* and *Shengsheng Man*.

11. The two most common line lengths are ten words and seven words.

12. Email correspondence with the author, May 14, 2015. I am indebted to Bell Yung for sharing his rhythmic studies.

13. These passages sound as if they are through-composed rather than following a couplet form. Schubert scholar Brian Newbould also notes that the progressive and highly modified strophic form used in some lieder could nearly be read as through-composed. See Brian Newbould, *Schubert: The Music and the Man* (Berkeley: University of California Press, 1997), 144–145.

14. Alan Thrasher, *Sizhu Instrumental Music of South China: Ethos, Theory and Practice* (Leiden: Brill, 2008), 75.

15. See discussion in Nancy Guy, *Peking Opera and Politics in Taiwan* (Urbana: University of Illinois Press, 2005), 172.

16. Ying-fen Wang, "The 'Mosaic Structure' of Nanguan Songs: An Application of Semiotic Analysis," *Yearbook for Traditional Music* 24 (1992): 24–51. Jonathan Stock also notes the appearance of similar structure in huju; see Jonathan P. J. Stock, *Huju: Traditional Opera in Modern Shanghai* (New York: Oxford University Press, 2003), 182.

17. *Dictionary of Cantonese Opera,* 433–434.

18. Yung, *Cantonese Opera: Performance as Creative Process,* 154–155.

19. This is discussed by Yung as the third level of creative process. See *Cantonese Opera: Performance as Creative Process,* 153–157.

20. Jonathan P. J. Stock, "The Application of Schenkerian Analysis to Ethnomusicology: Problems and Possibilities," *Music Analysis* 12/2 (1993): 215–240, esp. 228, 230.

21. Thrasher, *Sizhu Instrumental Music,* 160.

22. Qiu Hechou, *Xiange Bidu* (Obligatory Reading for Singing), Hong Kong: n.p., 1916; reprint, 1921), transcribed in Yung, *Cantonese Opera,* 156; also discussed and partially transnotated in Thrasher, *Sizhu Instrumental Music,* 152–155.

23. The melodic structure discussed here does not represent the performer's view or practice. Nevertheless it provides a framework for understanding and comparing the expressive effects of ornamentation in the aria songs. For different perspectives on such analytical approaches, see Stock, "Application of Schenkerian Analysis," 221–223.

24. John Lawarence Witzleben, *"Silk and Bamboo" Music in Shanghai: The Jiangnan Sizhu Instrumental Tradition* (Kent, OH: Kent State University Press, 1995), 44–45.

25. For more on the notion of acceleration and deceleration of sliding tones in Chinese music, see Li Henbing and Marc Leman, "A Gesture-Based Typology of Sliding-Tones in Guqin Music," *Journal of New Music Research* 36 (2007): 61–82.

Chapter 6. Powder and Rouge: Theaters in British Columbia

1. Cantonese opera powder, Museum of Vancouver, H990.277.160 through H990.277.168.

2. Loretta Siuling Yeung, "Red Boat Troupes and Cantonese Opera" (Master's thesis, University of Georgia, 2010), 55–56.

3. The exceptions were merchants, diplomats, students, and cases involving "special circumstances."

4. Wing Chung Ng, "Chinatown Theater as Transnational Business: New Evidence from Vancouver during the Exclusion Era," *British Columbia Studies* 148 (2005–2006), 25–54, esp. 34. Each permit was valid for six months and could be extended for up to three years.

5. *Daily British Colonist*, August 13, 1885. See also advertisement in the *Daily British Colonist*, August 9, 1885.

6. *Daily British Colonist*, August 11, 1885.

7. *Daily British Colonist*, November 29, 1901.

8. *Daily British Colonist*, October 2, 1907.

9. The photo is labeled EX-5.4-4, UBC CC.

10. *Chinese Times*, March 20, 1915.

11. *Chinese Times*, March 25, June 26, 1916.

12. *Chinese Times*, March 25, July 22, 1916.

13. *Daily Building Record*, September 30, 1913.

14. *Chinese Times*, October 12, 1928.

15. *Chinese Times*, February 16, 1915.

16. *Chinese Times*, July 24, 1915.

17. The playbill is housed at the Opera Information Center, Chinese University of Hong Kong.

18. *Chinese Times*, July 13, 1915. The report mentions a theater in Nanaimo.

19. *Chinese Times*, April 27, 1916.

20. It seemed the only obstacle to the well-being of the troupe was an internal one: discord among members of the troupe led to fights and injuries. *Chinese Times*, January 25, 1917.

21. The name *Guo Fengnian* seems to be a combination of the two aforementioned Vancouver troupes (Guo Taiping and Qing Fengnian). The flyer can also be found at the Hong Kong University Archive.

22. For an example, see *Chinese Times*, July 24, 1915. The three actors' names are Feitian Heng, Fei Yuan, and Jing Jun.

23. *Chinese Times*, March 14, 1917.

24. Wing Chung Ng made a comprehensive study of the business papers at the City of Vancouver Archive; see Ng, "Chinatown Theatre as Transnational Business."

25. This figure is derived from the inflation calculator of the Bank of Canada. http://www.bankofcanada.ca/rates/related/inflation-calculator/.

26. *Chinese Times*, January 24, 1917.

27. *Chinese Times*, September 10, 1917.

28. *Chinese Times*, December 19, 1917.

29. *Chinese Times*, December 10, 1918.

30. *Chinese Times*, January 21, 1918.

31. Ibid.; *Shen Bao*, January 25, 1921.

32. Sai-Shing Yung offers an insightful discussion of a similar phenomenon for another famous actress. See his *From Opera Boat to Silver Screen: Visual and Sonic Culture of Cantonese*

Opera (Hong Kong: Oxford University Press, 2012). Similar practices can be found among prima donnas of nineteenth-century European opera; see Francesco Izzo, "Divas and Sonnets: Poetry for Female Singers in Teatri Arti e Letteratura," in *The Arts of the Prima Donna in the Long Nineteenth Century* ed. Rachel Cowgill and Hilary Poris (Oxford: Oxford University Press, 2012), 3–20.

33. Izzo, "Divas and Sonnets."

34. See a professional photographer's notice warning against plagiarism, *Chinese Times*, April 13, 15, 1921.

35. *Chinese Times*, June 11, 1919.

36. *Chinese Times*, March 9, 1918.

37. This account is according to Ng, "Chinatown Theater as Transnational Business," 37.

38. The notice was printed daily for a week; see *Chinese Times*, February 11–18, 1919.

39. See Nancy Yunhwa Rao, "The Public Face of Chinatown: Actresses, Actors, Playwrights, and Audiences of Chinatown Theaters in San Francisco of the 1920s," *Journal of the Society for American Music* 5/2 (2011): 235–270.

40. This account comes from Ng, "Chinatown Theater as Transnational Business," 37.

41. *Chinese Times*, January 11, 1918.

42. Its advertisements began to appear in the *Chinese Times* on September 3, 1918.

43. *Chinese Times*, September 24, 1918; April 11, 1919.

44. For example, *Chinese Times*, February 11–18, 1925; January 28, 1928.

45. Henry Yu, "Intermittent Rhythms of the Cantonese Pacific," in *Connecting Sites and Connected Oceans: Indian, Atlantic and Pacific Oceans and China Seas Migrations from the 1830s to the 1930s*, ed. Donna R. Garbaccia and Dirk Hoerder (Leiden: Brill, 2011), 393–414, esp. 401.

46. *Chinese Times*, April 10, May 9, 1919.

47. *Chinese Times*, June 24, 1919.

48. *Chinese Times*, August 19, 1915.

49. *Chinese Times*, August 19–23, 1915.

50. *Chinese Times*, September 7, 1915.

51. *Chinese Times*, April 28, 1916.

52. *Chinese Times*, January 24, 1917.

53. Ng, "Chinatown Theater as Transnational Business," 36.

54. For example, the actors' guild was represented by an obituary notice, a delegate, and a vehicle for the funeral procession for a prominent community figure. See the *Chinese Times*, March 1, 1938. It also gathered to celebrate the birthday of a deity at the Mandarin Theater in Vancouver. *Chinese Times*, October 30, 1929.

55. See various issues of the *Chinese Times* for 1920 and 1921.

56. *Chinese Times*, April 19, 1921.

57. *Chinese Times*, December 9, 1921.

58. *Chinese Times*, October 6, 1921.

59. Li Xuemei was featured significantly that year. See *Chinese Times*, November 26 and 29, 1921.

60. Letter from Li Xuemei, *Chung Sai Yat Po*, November 15, 1922.

61. *Chinese Times*, April 24, 1922.

62. *Chinese Times*, September 1, 1921.

63. *Chinese Times*, December 6, 1921.

64. Her immigration file indicates that her age was twenty-seven in 1923. February 21, 1923 file 55197/81a, INS-SPF.

65. *Chinese Times*, December 6, 1921, and January 19, February 28, April 12, April 20, and December 23, 1922, to name only a few examples.

66. *Chinese Times*, December 6, 1921.

67. Two years later, to celebrate the occasion of Yip Sang's eightieth birthday, C. B. Wand prepared a photo collage with portraits of seventy-one Yip Sang family members spanning three generations, arranged to form the Chinese character meaning "longevity."

68. *Chinese Times*, February 6, November 22, and December 5, 1923.

69. *Seattle Post-Intelligencer* quoted in the *Chicago Daily Tribune* (March 23, 1923), *New York Times* (March 18, 1923), and *Time* (March 24, 1923).

70. *Chinese Times*, March 1, 1923.

71. Robert D. Turner, *The Pacific Princesses: An Illustrated History of the Canadian Pacific Railway's Princess Fleet on the Northwest Coast* (Victoria, BC: Sono Nis, 1977), 83.

72. Thereafter, artists traveled to Seattle on other vessels of the Princess fleets. Performers were regularly brought to the port by SS Princesses *Charlotte, Alice, Marguerite,* and *Kathleen*. The compact geographical area covered by the Victoria-Vancouver-Seattle triangle facilitated the live performance network and crystallized the region's significant role in the renaissance of Cantonese opera in North America.

Chapter 7. From Lun On and Lun Hop to the Great China Theater, 1922–1925

1. Memo from Commissioner General Husband, August 24, 1922, file 55197/81, INS-SPF.

2. The Crescent Theater opened in 1909 as the California Theater and was then named the Liberty Theater until 1922, when it was rented by Lun On. It went back to the name Liberty in 1925. The theater underwent many changes of name, closed in 1953, and was torn down. See Jack Tillmany, *Theatres of San Francisco* (Charleston, NC: Arcadia, 2005), 59.

3. Herb B. Gee, "San Francisco's Chinese Theater Gives Occident New Slant on Drama," *San Francisco Chronicle*, October 29, 1922.

4. *Young China*, December 9, 1922.

5. *San Francisco Chronicle*, December 15, 1922.

6. Chin Yeeyou and Lee Gar were listed as owners of the troupe in the news reports. *Chung Sai Yat Po*, December 29, 1922; January 19 to February 2, 1923.

7. Acting Commissioner in Seattle to the Commissioner General in DC, November 6, 1922, file 55197/81, INS-SPF.

8. *Young China*, November 25–28, 1922. Two actors are listed in both Guo Fengnian's playbill of November 28 and Lun On's cast in San Francisco.

9. Indications of a prominent Chinese theater in Lima could be found in a report about a benefit performance by actress Xiao Juan Juan in *Young China*, April 23, 1923. Report of two theaters in Mexicali can be found in Michael Jenkins, "Mexicali Blues: Community Organizations among the Baja California Chinese" (Master's thesis, 2011, University of North Carolina Wilmington).

10. *Chung Sai Yat Po*, January 20–27, 1923; *Chung Sai Yat Po*, February 2, 1923.

11. *Chung Sai Yat Po*, June 3, 1925; *Chinese Times*, June 3, 1925. This figure surfaces in a report on the dispute regarding profit sharing between Lun On's two investors, Lee Gar and Chin Yee You.

12. Correspondence from Shep and Chanto to Immigration Service, San Francisco, January 23, 1923, file 55197/81, INS-SPF.

13. Sou Yan Chan, *Improvisation in a Ritual Context: The Music of Cantonese Opera* (Hong Kong: Chinese University of Hong Kong, 1992), 57.

14. Commissioner of Immigration in Seattle, Luther Weedin, to Immigration Bureau, Washington, DC, February 19, 1923, file 55197/81, INS-SPF.

15. *Seattle Post-Intelligencer*, reprinted in *Chicago Defender*, March 25, 1923; *Time*, March 24, 1923, *New York Times*, March 18, 1923; *El Paso Herald*, April 14, 1923.

16. "Old Favorite," *Time*, March 24, 1923, 17.

17. *Chicago Daily Tribune*, March 25, 1923. "Uncut" refers to the length of the opera.

18. *The Yellow Jacket* is a drama by George C. Hazelton emulating Chinese opera theaters. Premiered in 1912, its revivals in New York (1921), Detroit (1922), San Francisco (1920), and Stanford (1921), received favorable reviews.

19. UBC DD, ID. 100-28-1.

20. The leading male actors included Ou Runcai, Guan's husband.

21. Her debut in Vancouver was on November 2, 1921.

22. *Young China*, March 25, 1923.

23. *Young China*, March 31, 1923.

24. See the sixteenth edition of *Zhenlan Bao* (1920) for female troupes and Singapore troupes, Opera Information Center, Chinese University of Hong Kong.

25. *Young China*, December 4, 1923.

26. Personal correspondence with Bruce Quan Jr., January 18, 2012.

27. Playbill of September 8, 1923, for the opera *Twilight Scarlet Tears*. Cantonese opera playbills, box 8, ESL.

28. Playbill, Crescent Theater, August 12, 1924. Cantonese opera playbills, box 8, ESL.

29. Walton Hendry to Commissioner General of Immigration, October 3, 1923, file 55197/81, INS-SPF.

30. *Young China*, September 25, 1923.

31. Brian Donovan, *White Slave Crusades: Race, Gender, and Anti-Vice Activism, 1887–1917* (Urbana: University of Illinois Press, 2006), 119; "Chinese Slave Girl Is Freed at Marysville: San Francisco Woman Aids Authorities," *San Francisco Chronicle*, February 13, 1921.

32. *Young China*, October 4, 1923; "Chinese Slave Girls Rescued: Souls Salvaged from Substrata of Chinatowns," *Los Angeles Times*, February 26, 1922.

33. Cameron to Immigration Bureau, May 24, 1924, file 55197/81c, INS-SPF.

34. No doubt, however, taking charge of such rescues served also to increase the missionary's moral authority. Gary Y. Okihiro, *Common Ground: Reimagining American History* (Berkeley: University of California Press, 2001), 69.

35. Louis Stallmann, "Donaldina Cameron vs. Yellow Slavery," *San Francisco Chronicle*, June 14, 1914.

36. Roger O'Donnell to Secretary of Labor, August 16, 1923, file 55197/81, INS-SPF.

37. Caminetti and Trabucco to Immigration Service in Seattle, September 20, 1923, file 55197/81b, INS-SPF.

38. Because there is little information about the All-Star troupe, we know only that it began in early 1923 and was active well into 1926, moving mainly between Los Angeles and Mexicali.

39. *Young China*, April 20, 29, 1923.

40. Previously the company's legal representation in Washington, DC, was Bouve and Parker. Starting in August 1923, Roger O'Donnell was in charge of the correspondence.

41. From Roger O'Donnell to Immigration Bureau, DC, March 25, 1924, file 55197/81c, INS-SPF.

42. Chair of General Board of Review White to Immigration SEA, March 26, 1924, file 55197/81c, INS-SPF.

43. *Young China*, January 28, 1924.

44. The festive mood was dampened by the ransacking of the performers' flat during the show on the third evening of the New Year.

45. *Young China*, February 2, 1924.

46. *Young China*, March 23, 30, 1924.

47. *Young China*, April 5, 1924.

48. Weedin to Immigration DC, April 23, 1924, file 55197/81c, INS-SPF.

49. *Young China*, May 30, 1924.

50. *Shen Bao*, February 8, 1923.

51. *Young China*, June 22, 1924.

52. *Young China*, July 3, 1924.

53. *Young China*, October 19, 1924.

54. *Young China*, August 4, 1924.

55. The list was sandwiched between the playbills for September 13 and 14. Cantonese opera playbills, box 8, ESL.

56. Playbill of December 14, 1924, ESL.

57. Émile Gaboriau, *Monsieur Lecoq* (1869), trans. Lu Shanxiang and Qiu Shuyuan (Shanghai: Shang wu yin shu guan, 1912). Whereas a star performer could sometimes be said to have written an opera when it was really a story line being strung together to showcase his or her virtuosity, this was a different matter.

58. Roger O'Donnell to Immigration Bureau, DC, January 30, 1924, file 55197/81b, INS-SPF.

59. *Young China*, January 19, 1925.

60. *Young China*, March 11, 1925.

61. General Board of Review to Immigration Service in Seattle, March 6, 1925, file 55197/81e, INS-SPF.

62. *Shen Bao*, August 20, 1924. The reviewer praised Huang Xiaofeng's performance of a famous character, Pan Jinlian.

63. *Young China*, May 1, 1925.

64. *Young China*, May 18, 1925.

65. See the advertisement in *Young China*, May 21, 1925. Currently only a reprint of *Essence of Cantonese Arias and Songs* edited by Zhu Bingtan (San Francisco: Tai Lok, 1927) is available. The reprint contains all the songs mentioned in the 1925 advertisement.

66. *Young China*, June 2, 1925.

67. *Young China*, May 21, 1925.

68. *Chinese Times*, October 29 to December 30, 1929.

69. The dimensions (in feet) of the stages were 32 wide × 25 deep × 25 high for the Great China and 36 × 16 × 20 for the Mandarin. Peter Chu et al., eds. *Chinese Theaters in America* (Washington, DC: Federal Theater Project, Public Works Administration, 1936), 125, 133. I am indebted to Andrew Li for the architectural observation.

70. *Young China*, June 21, 1925.

71. *Young China*, June 28, 1925.

72. *Young China*, June 27–28, 1925.

73. Xiyang Nü, "Xin Zhou Xiao Zhuan" (Biography of Xin Zhou: The Wife's Memoir), *Guangzhou Wenshi ziliao* 42 (1990): 254–255.

74. *Young China*, November 4, 1925.

75. See *Jade Unicorn*, performed by Zihou Qi , Brunswick Records 49033 (LP, n.d.). The recording was made in November 1929. See Ross Laird, *Brunswick Records: A Discography of Recordings, 1916–1931*, vol. 3: *Chicago and Regional Sessions* (Westport, CT: Greenwood, 2011), 1251.

76. *Young China*, November 6, 1925.

77. *Young China*, November 10, 1925.

78. *Young China*, November 15, 1925.

79. Bai Jurong, *Yihai Fuchen: Bai Jurong Wutai Shenghuo Wushi Nian* (Fifty Years of Stage Life).

80. *Young China*, November 20, 1925.

81. *Young China*, November 25–29, 1925.

82. Bai Jurong, *Fifty Years of Stage Life*.

83. Bai's residence at the Great China Theater encompassed the dates November 13, 1925, to April 27, 1927; file 55197/81K, INS-SPF.

84. *Young China*, November 29, 1925.

Chapter 8. The Affluent Years: The Great China Theater, 1926–1928

1. It is likely that he did enter the United States, possibly under the radar, with the theater's sponsorship. This possibility is supported by the immigration records of the Great China Theater, which do not show the arrival of a new actor at about this time.

2. *Young China*, April 26, 1926.

3. Rey Chow, *Ethics after Idealism: Theory, Culture, Ethnicity, Reading* (Bloomington: Indiana University Press, 1998), 145.

4. *Young China*, November 20–26, 1926.

5. Bond paper of Zhang Qiaohua (Chung Chiu Wah), March 25, 1926, file 55197/81H INS-SPF.

6. Bond paper of Chen Xiahuen (Chang Yoe Wan), July 19, 1926, file 55197/81I INS-SPF.

7. After the novelty wore off, very few of these recently written pieces remained in circulation much after this period, and the unique interpretations of classic opera were also of little importance outside their context.

8. Playbill, Great China Theater, August 21, 1926, ESL.

9. She arrived from New York, having performed previously at the Lok Tian Tsau Theater. *Young China*, August 15, 1926.

10. *Young China*, June 11, 1926.

11. Ibid.

12. *Young China*, February 23, 1926.

13. Ibid.

14. *Young China*, February 22, 1926.

15. *Young China*, March 1, 1926.

16. The growing significance of instrumentalists reached a new high in 1928, when three musicians (Li Xing, Ye Hong, and Jiang Jun) were billed as the producers of the new opera *Zhenjia Huanggu*. See *Young China*, February 26, 1928.

17. *Young China*, September 14, 1926.

18. *Young China*, September 1, 1926.

19. I am grateful to David Lei for not only bringing me to the Great China Theater to examine the stage but also for uncovering the firewall backdrop painting and sending me pictures of it.

20. *Stanford Daily*, March 2, 1921.

21. Ju Yong Kim, *The Racial Mundane: Asian American Performance and the Embodied Everyday* (New York: New York University Press, 2015), 53.

22. *Young China*, October 31, 1926.

23. The residence of Xiao Dingxiang and the continuous arrivals of actresses kept the impact of Huang's departure on the theater's programming to a minimum; fans of young belle role types could find the virtuoso musical performance in the veteran Xiao Dingxiang and feminine beauty in many young actresses.

24. *Young China*, January 21, 1928.

25. *Young China*, October 10, 1926.

26. Playbill, Great China Theater, March 21, 1927, ESL. The poem was Qian Qi, "Examination Poem: Drum and Zither of the Xiang River Spirits." The translation is by Patrick Hanan, *The Sea of Regret: Two Turn-of-the Century Chinese Romantic Novels* (Honolulu: University of Hawaii Press, 1995), 38.

27. *Shen Bao*, July 15 and July 22, 1924.

28. Before she arrived the Mandarin had an actress with the same name, which prompted the Great China to present her debut as the "Zhen" Jinsi Mao—meaning the

"genuine" star with the catchy stage name "Persian Cat." The less authentic star soon vanished from the Mandarin's roster.

29. Playbill, Great China Theater, October 9, 1927, ESL.

30. Playbill, Great China Theater, October 17, 1927, ESL.

31. Playbills, Great China Theater, November 16, 19, 1927, ESL.

32. *Young China*, January 15, February 20, 1928.

33. *Young China*, January 18, 1927.

34. *Young China*, February 2, 1928. This was a banquet held in order to enhance relations between Chinese and Americans, as noted by the newspaper. The organization was mentioned in the *Chinese Times* in Vancouver, May 12, 1928.

35. Letter from local attorney Todd for Lau Tau Seck to immigration service in Seattle, Oct 31, 1927, Immigration file 55197/81L, INS-SPF; *Young China*, March 5, 1928.

36. Playbills, Great China Theater, March 26, 27, 31 and April 1, 1927, ESL.

37. Playbill, Great China Theater, April 7, 1927, ESL.

38. Playbill, Great China Theater, June 11, 1928, ESL.

39. *Young China*, June 27, 1928.

40. Andrew Jones, "The Gramophone in China," in *Tokens of Exchange: The Problem of Translation in Global Circulations*, ed. Lydia H. Liu (Durham: Duke University Press, 2000), 222.

41. Leta Miller, *Music and Politics in San Francisco: From the 1906 Quake to the Second World War* (Berkeley: University of California Press, 2011), 84.

42. See Richard Spottswood, *Ethnic Music on Records*, vol. 5 (Urbana: University of Illinois Press, 1991).

43. "Chinese Moulded Records," *Edison Phonograph Monthly* 1/1 (March 1903): 6.

44. "New Chinese Amberols," *Edison Phonograph Monthly* 8/3 (March 1910): 15; "Chinese Records," *Edison Phonograph Monthly* 8/9 (September 1910): 4. Sai-Shing Yung provided the most comprehensive research and analysis of the early phonograph industry and Cantonese opera recordings. See *Cantonese Opera from the Gramophone: A Cultural History, 1903–1953* (Hong Kong: Institute for the Research of Humanities, Chinese University of Hong Kong, Cosmos Press, 2006).

45. Great China Records was established in 1917 in China in collaboration with an unidentified Japanese company.

46. *Young China*, September 1, 1927.

47. Playbill, Great China Theater, October 17, 1927, ESL.

48. Playbill, Great China Theater, September 27, 1927, ESL.

49. This was comparable to the situation in Hong Kong, as discussed by S. Yung, *Cantonese Opera from the Gramophone*, 115.

50. Ibid.

51. The only other phonograph records of female singers available in Chinatown at this time came from the Victor Phonograph Company. Victor offered several titles by Mandarin Theater actresses Li Xuefei and Mudan Su.

52. An advertisement for the second catalogue appeared in *Young China*, May 16, 1928.

53. *Young China*, November 3, 1928.

54. *Young China*, January 31, 1929.

55. Richard Spottswood lists an Oriental label associated with Turkish and Armenian music in his important study. It seems to have no relation to the Cantonese opera label. See *Ethnic Music on Records*, 5:2515, 5:2525. I am grateful for Tim Brook for pointing this out to me.

56. The fourth was released in December 1929.

57. The founding of Xin Yue Fong was noted in *Young China*, January 11, 1929.

58. *Young China*, January 11, 1928.

59. *Chinese Times*, January 28, 1928.

60. *Chinese Times*, May 11, 1933.

61. Great China Theater playbill, March 11, 1928. Also see *Young China*, March 17, 1928.

62. Interview of Eva Chan by Genny Lim, San Francisco, August 8, 1982, Chinese Women of America Research Project. Eva Chan was the daughter-in-law of Chin Lain, owner of the Mandarin Theater.

63. Him Mark Lai, *Becoming Chinese American: A History of Communities and Institutions* (Walnut Creek, CA: Alta Mira, 2004), 283–284.

64. William W. Lee, *San Francisco Son* (Bloomington: Xlibris, 2011), 45.

65. *Young China*, January 22, 1928.

66. *Young China*, January 21, 1928.

67. *Young China*, February 5, 1928.

68. *Young China*, January 21, 1928. At the Catholic church, a film based on Pan Jinlian was shown together with documentary of Huang's tour.

69. *Young China*, January 20, 1928.

70. The arrival of a new film was noted in the newspaper along with ticket prices. *Young China*, April 7, 1928.

71. *Young China*, May 3, 1928.

72. *Young China*, September 20, 1928.

73. *Young China*, January 17, 1929.

Chapter 9. A Successful, Majestic Stage: The Mandarin Theater, 1924–1926

1. According to the WPA study Clarence Chan was a graduate in civil engineering from Stanford, and the theater was built to his specifications by the architect. Peter Chu et al., eds., *Chinese Theaters in America* (Washington, DC: Federal Theater Project, Works Progress Administration, 1936), 151. The official record and news account lists only Austin.

2. Philip Choy, *San Francisco Chinatown: A Guide to Its History and Architecture* (San Francisco: City Light, 2014), 153.

3. Petition from Chin Lain, December 27, 1923, file 55374/227, INS-SPF.

4. *Chung Sai Yat Po*, June 30, 1924.

5. Petition from Chin Lain, December 27, 1923.

6. *Shilin Paying Respects at the Pagoda* was performed three times (July 15 and 21 and September 16), as were *Deranged Mother Seeking Son* (August 4 and 6 and September 11) and *Nocturnal Mourning of White Lotus* (July 5 and 7 and September 15).

7. Such a stage and curtain were already common in Shanghai and Hong Kong.

8. McGee to Immigration Service, DC, July 19, 1924, file 55197/81d, INS-SPF.

9. Chas McGee to E. G. Henning, Secretary of Department of Labor, December 6, 1924, file 55374/227A, INS-SPF.

10. City tax records, file 55374/227B, INS-SPF.

11. Revenue Act of 1924, Pub. L. No. 68-176, 43 Stat. 320, pp. 320–322. However, in the Revenue Act of 1921, the section on admissions tax indicates a 10 percent tax on any tickets priced more than $.10; the Revenue Act of 1924 changed the level to 10 percent tax on any tickets priced above $.50, and the Revenue Act of 1928 changed it to 10 percent of any tickets priced above $3. I am grateful for the help provided on this topic by Tom Glynn, the reference librarian at Rutgers University.

12. *Young China*, August 18, 1924.

13. Bond papers, file 55374/227B, INS-SPF.

14. Playbills, Mandarin Theater, January 5–8, 1925, ESL.

15. A public announcement about the Zhu huanian and Yong taiping troupes in Los Angeles indicated that the joint venture of four merchants would now be assumed by only two; see *Young China*, January 5, 1925. The change was mediated by Chinese Concolidated Benevolent Association; *Young China*, December 28, 1924.

16. *Young China*, March 11, 1925.

17. "Chinese Stage Is Jazzed Up," *Los Angeles Times*, May 31, 1925. The Sung Jung Wah company is identified as the rival to the Mandarin. However, Jok Wah Ning is identified as the rival theater in *Los Angeles Times*, March 1, 1925.

18. Playbill, Mandarin Theater, March 22, 1925, ESL.

19. Playbill, Mandarin Theater, April 14, 1925, ESL.

20. *Chung Sai Yat Po*, May 20, 1925.

21. McGee to Department of Labor, May 28, 1925 and positive response from Department of Labor, June 5, 1925, file 55374/227C, INS-SPF.

22. Playbills, Mandarin Theater, June 14, 17, 1925, ESL.

23. *Chung Sai Yat Po*, June 8, 1925.

24. *Chung Sai Yat Po*, June 19, 1925. The newspaper used the heading "The Grand Stage of the Mandarin Theater" to introduce the expansion of its backstage: "Because the original stage was narrow, the theater rented adjacent stores and basement, and connected the rooms to become dressing rooms, vacating the original [dressing room] space to expand the stage. The expansion is completed today and ready for use."

25. Walter Anthony, "The Passing of the Chinese Theater," *San Francisco Call*, July 27, 1913.

26. *Los Angeles Times*, June 25, 1925.

27. "Old Chinese Stage Growing up to Date: Younger Orientals Insist on Scenery, Jazz Music and Girl Actors," *Washington Post*, June 29, 1925.

28. *Chung Sai Yat Po*, June 24, 1925.

29. *Chung Sai Yat Po*, June 27, 1925.

30. *Chung Sai Yat Po*, July 3, 1925.

31. *Chung Sai Yat Po*, July 6, 1925.

32. Four months later, in October, when the same theater held a benefit performance for Chinese schools, it easily raised $2,000 in one evening.

33. Yet this was not the case for long, perhaps, because on July 7 the newspaper noted the theater's engagement of twenty-two new performers and anticipated their imminent arrival. While no mention was made of their detention at the port of Seattle pending further vacancy in Mandarin Theater's quota, a separate report on that date noted the departure of nine performers from the theater, four of whom were musicians and one of whom was a scene shifter.

34. *Young China*, July 13, 1925.

35. *Young China*, September 1, 1925.

36. Later Xiyang Nü advocated earnestly for a high school in the Cantonese region of Tai Shan, and she contributed $500 (the equivalent of about $6,803 in 2016). *Young China*, July 20, 1925.

37. *Young China*, August 14, 1925; *Chung Sai Yat Po*, August 14, 1925.

38. *Young China*, August 17, 1925.

39. The figure is compiled from accounts in *Young China* and *Chung Sai Yat Po* of San Francisco and *Chinese Nationalist Daily* of New York.

40. *Young China*, August 17, 1925.

41. Robert W. Bowen and Brenda Young Bowen, eds., *San Francisco's Chinatown (Postcard History: California)* (Charleston, NC: Arcadia, 2008), 76; *Chung Sai Yat Po*, September 11–12, 1925.

42. Michael F. Crowe and Robert W. Bowen, *San Francisco Art Deco* (Charleston, NC: Arcadia, 2007), 11; *Young China*, September 12, 13, 1925.

43. *California's Diamond Jubilee: Celebrated at San Francisco, September 5 to 12, 1925* (San Francisco: E. C. Brown, 1925).

44. These figures are based on the bond papers of performers at the Mandarin Theater during that ten-month period, files 55374/227D to 55374/227G, INS-SPF.

45. The previous day, when Bai made his debut at the Great China Theater, the Mandarin featured Gongye Chuang in his famous older bearded warrior opera. Yet the theater featured Nü Muzhen against Bai Jurong for seven consecutive evenings.

46. *Young China*, May 23, 1926. It states that the purpose of the theaters was manifold: social and moral education (like newspapers and magazines), enhancement of the mind (like fiction and poetry), and entertainment (the most basic purpose). It therefore advocated for any comments, whether constructive or denigrating, about the opera itself, the performers, and the audiences.

47. *Young China*, February 21, 1926.

48. McGee to Department of Labor, March 2, 1926, file 55374/227F, INS-SPF.

49. Chinese Consolidated Benevolent Association to Department of labor, March 4, 1926, file 55374/227F, INS-SPF.

50. The practice of allowing people to arrive late and pay less was common for some U.S. theaters in the nineteenth century. It would be interesting to know whether Chinese theaters did as well, but such information is not currently available.

51. *Young China*, March 8, 1926.

52. It was staged on September 10, 1926.

53. It was staged on September 21, 1926.

54. Playbill, Great China Theater, June 15, 1926, ESL.

55. *Shen Bao*, February 27, 1924.

56. *Shen Bao*, March 4, 1924.

57. Bond Papers for the month, Mandarin Theater, file 55374/227H, INS-SPF.

58. The opera is listed in an advertisement for a fundraising event at the Jiu-ru Fang Theatre; *Hong Kong Huazi Ribao (Chinese Mail)*, July 7, 1916. This popular opera was later made into a movie in 1938.

59. David Belasco was known for his realistic exactitude. For example, he brought on stage the entire interior of a boarding house in *The Easiest Way* (1909) and an exact replica of a famous restaurant in *The Governor's Lady* (1912). He also had a popular yellowface drama called *Son-Daughter* (1919) that depicted San Francisco's Chinatown.

Chapter 10. A Theater of Actresses: The Mandarin Theater, 1927–1928

1. Bond paper, December 28, 1926, file 55374/227I, INS-SPF.

2. Playbill, Yong Ni Shang Theater, November 21, 1927, HKHM.

3. Playbill, Mandarin Theater, December 11, 1926, ESL.

4. Interview with Eva Chan by Genny Lim, San Francisco, August 8, 1982, Chinese Women of America Research Project.

5. Playbill, Mandarin Theater, January 15, 1927, ESL.

6. Playbill, Mandarin Theater, January 26, 1927, ESL.

7. Playbill, Mandarin Theater, January 23, 1927, ESL.

8. See advertisement of Victor Records, *Chinese Times*, February 8, 1927. She was featured in four titles, while Mudan Su was featured in five.

9. *Young China*, February 18, 20, March 2, 7, 1927.

10. Letter indicating the departure dates from Hong Kong, January 19, 1927, file 55374/227H, INS-SPF; Bond paper, February 16, 1927, file 55374/227H, INS-SPF. Her name was listed as Li Yuen Fan or Lee Wan Fan.

11. The news that Li Xuefang was getting married, retiring from the stage, and planning a future U.S. tour was reported in *Shen Bao*, April 10, 1923. See also *Young China*, February 18, 1927.

12. *Young China*, March 7, 1927.

13. *Chung Sai Yat Po*, March 8, 1927.

14. *Chung Sai Yat Po*, March 9, 1927.

15. *Chung Sai Yat Po*, March 8, 9, 12, 14, 1927.

16. *Chung Sai Yat Po*, March 14, 15, 16, 17, 1927.

17. *Li Xuefang Dingmao Youmei Liuhen* (San Francisco: Mandarin Theater, 1927), UCB-HML, 2000/26 ctn 10:17.

18. Yong Chen, *Chinese San Francisco, 1850–1943: A Trans-Pacific Community* (Stanford: Stanford University Press, 2000), 225.

19. *Shen Bao* reported the interaction between Li Xuefang and Mei Lanfang, June 15, 19, 24, 29, 1922.

20. *Chung Sai Yat Po*, March 17, 1927.

21. *Chinese Nationalist Daily*, April 22, 1927.

22. For the remainder of the year, however, Huang did not seem to be as popular as Li Xuefei. Though she and her signature operas returned to the stage, she did not lead performances as frequently as did Li Xuefei.

23. *Young China*, February 20, 1927.

24. *Young China*, February 24, 1927; *Chung Sai Yat Po*, February 19, 22, 24, 28, 1927.

25. *Young China*, March 9, 1927.

26. Letter from Father Bradley of Old St. Mary's Church, February 2, 1924, file 55374/227B, INS-SPF.

27. Interview with Rose Moon by Genny Lim, San Francisco, April 12, 1982, Chinese Women of America Research Project.

28. *Young China*, November 30, 1927.

29. Telegraph from Chas McGee to Department of Labor, January 27, 1927, file 55374/227H, INS-SPF.

30. Telegram from CG Hull to McGee, October 21, 1927, file 55374/227K; letter from McGee to Department of Labor, December 14, 1927, file 55374/227K, INS-SPF.

31. Commissioner General Hull to McGee, December 22, 1927, file 55374/227K, INS-SPF.

32. Liu Guoxing, "Yueju Yiren Zai Haiwaide Shenghuo Ji Huodong" (The Lives and Activities of Cantonese Opera Actors Abroad), *Guangdong wenshi ziliao* 21 (1965): 172–188.

33. Ibid.

34. McGee to Department of Labor, December 29, 1926, file 55374/227I, INS-SPF.

35. McGee to Department of Labor, March 21, 1927, file 55374/227I, INS-SPF. McGee indicated that the law in Mexico made it difficult for the troupe to survive. The following year, the *Young China* ran a long report on a secret alliance between the labor unions of Mexico and the United States whereby enforcing Chinese exclusion in Mexico was a result of negotiations allowing some Mexican laborers in the United States. *Young China*, January 12, 1928.

36. Doupi Yuan's account gives a different picture. He claimed that the theater at Mexicali was never anything close to a legitimate theater like those in San Francisco. Rather, it was simply a modest show place for the entertainment of clients of the gambling houses. See Liu, "The Lives and Activities."

37. For the exceeded quota, see McGee to Department of Labor, October 27, 1927, file 55374/227K, INS-SPF.

38. See the correspondences in file 55374/227K, INS-SPF.

39. Tan Lanqing left on April 26, 1928. She was admitted to Calexico on April 7, 1927, and her bond was cancelled on June 24, 1927. She was admitted again on January 23, 1928, with a permit set to expire on June 24, 1928; she departed Seattle and sailed for Vancouver on April 25, 1928, on the *Princess Charlotte*. Department of Labor to Immigration Service Seattle, May 24, 1928, 55374/227M, INS-SPF.

40. Although they tended to avoid arriving in San Francisco due to the notoriety of Angel Island as a port of entry, the departure posed no particular challenge. Many performers were in San Francisco en route to China.

41. *Chung Sai Yat Po*, May 5, 1928.

42. Memo from San Francisco Immigration Service to Department of Labor, Washington, DC, September 27, 1928, file 55374/227L, INS-SPF.

43. *Young China*, February 1, 1928.

44. *Chung Sai Yat Po*, January 21, 1928.

45. *Chung Sai Yat Po*, February 23, 1928.

46. *Chung Sai Yat Po*, February 20, 1928.

47. *Chung Sai Yat Po*, February 25, 1928; *Young China*, February 26, 1928.

48. *Young China*, February 27, 1928.

49. *Chung Sai Yat Po*, March 10, 16, 17, 19, 1928.

50. *Chinese Times*, March 30, 1928.

51. *Plattsburgh Daily Republican*, August 24, 1929.

52. Playbill, Vancouver Mandarin Theater, July 27, 2917, HKHM.

53. Interview of Eva Chan by Genny Lim, San Francisco, August 8, 1982, Chinese Women of America Research Project.

54. For more on the Mandarin Theater in Singapore, see Wing Chung Ng, *The Rise of Cantonese Opera: From Village Art Form to Global Phenomenon* (Urbana: University of Illinois Press. 2015), 143–144.

55. *Young China*, April 3, May 26, November 26, 1928.

56. *Chung Sai Yat Po*, May 26, 1928.

57. *Chung Sai Yat Po*, June 2, 4, 1928.

58. *Chung Sai Yat Po*, June 2, 1928.

59. *Chung Sai Yat Po*, June 19, 1928.

60. *Chung Sai Yat Po*, June 6, 1928.

61. *Chung Sai Yat Po*, May 8, 1928.

62. *Chung Sai Yat Po*, February 10, 1928.

63. *Chung Sai Yat Po*, July 17, 1928.

64. *Chung Sai Yat Po*, September 13, 1928.

65. *Chung Sai Yat Po*, June 30, 1928.

66. *Young China*, November 11, 1928.

67. *Chung Sai Yat Po*, September 22, 1928.

68. *Young China*, October 30, 1928.

69. *Young China*, December 26, 1928.

70. *Young China*, January 3, 1929. Interview with Eva Chan by Genny Lim, San Francisco, August 8, 1982, Chinese Women of America Research Project.

71. See files 55374/227P to 55374/227X, INS-SPF.

72. Blank stock certificate, Mandarin Theatrical Company, San Francisco; October 16, 1932; share value $10; 25,000 shares; total capital $250,000. Private collection.

73. Peter Chu et al., eds., *Chinese Theaters in America* (Washington, DC: Federal Theater Project, Public Works Administration, 1936), appendix, xxi–xxiv.

74. Katherine Hill, "Putting on Chinese Play at Mandarin," *San Francisco Chronicle*, February 25, 1934.

75. David Lei, private collection.

76. Ma Shizeng, *Voyage of a Thousand Miles* (Qianli Zhangyouji) (Hong Kong: Tongya, 1931).

Chapter 11. Two Theaters and a Merger in New York

1. For example, earlier in 1924 the city had paid tribute to the famous Italian baritone Antonio Scotti on the occasion of his twenty-fifth season at the Metropolitan Opera House. His signature role was the villain Chim Fen in *L'Oracolo*, an opera in Italian about San Francisco's Chinatown. "New Chinese Opera at Metropolitan: Scene of 'L'Oracolo,' by Franco Leoni, Is Laid in San Francisco's Chinese Quarter," *New York Times*, January 31, 1915. And there was much hype in the news about another "Chinese opera"—Puccini's *Turandot*—completed in May 1924. "Puccini's New Opera," *New York Times*, May 14, 1924.

2. "Dramatic and Musical," *New York Daily Times*, May 18, 1853.

3. Scott D. Seligman, *The First Chinese American: The Remarkable Life of Wong Chin Foo* (Hong Kong: Hong Kong University Press, 2013), 127–128.

4. Ibid., 184. *New York Times*, June 20, 23, 24, 25, 1889.

5. "Joy Reigns in Chinatown: Welcoming a Troupe of Native Actors," *New York Tribune*, June 24, 1889.

6. "Got a Good Start Last Night," *New York Times*, March 26, 1893.

7. "Hitchcock's Chinese Actors: Comedian Said to Have Leased Tong Theatre in Doyer Street," *New York Times*, February 20, 1910.

8. Tongs were organizations of Chinese gangs in the United States. They served as a protective force for some, but frequently engaged in criminal activities. Tongs were particularly powerful from 1880 to 1921 in San Francisco and between 1910 and 1940 in New York. Tong wars were violent disputes fought among rival tong factions, often triggered by inter-gang grievances.

9. Diana Rice, "'Left Their Pigtails Behind Them': Common Report Has It Only One Queue Is Left in All Chinatown," *New York Times*, March 30, 1924.

10. Will Irwin, "The Drama That Was in Chinatown," *New York Times*, April 10, 1921.

11. B. S. Fong to Department of Labor, January 10, 1921; O'Donnell to Department of Labor, January 19, 1921; Assistant Commissioner General to Roger O'Donnell, 1.31.1921, all in file 55007/1, INS-SPF.

12. O'Donnell to Department of Labor, January 19, 1921, file 55007/1, INS-SPF; Memo from Acting Commissioner General, January 20, 1921, file 55007/1, INS-SPF.

13. Corinne J. Naden, *The Golden Age of American Musical Theatre: 1943–1965* (Metuchen, NJ: Scarecrow, 2011), 14.

14. Wing Chung Ng, "Chinatown Theatre as Transnational Business: New Evidence from Vancouver during the Exclusion Era," *BC Studies* no. 148 (Winter 2005–2006): 40.

15. O'Donnell to Department of Labor, April 16, 1924, file 55007/1, INS-SPF.

16. The notice by the company Tienli He announced that the troupe was sold to a Mr. Chen Xugun in New York, a.k.a. Chin Nom. *Chinese Times*, May 30, July 18, 1924.

17. The report notes that the Heyi Company in New York rented a theater and hired the troupe from Vancouver. *Young China*, July 17, 1924.

18. "Bowery Resonant with Chinese opera," *New York Times*, July 21, 1924.

19. Bond papers, June 18, 1924, file 55007/1, INS-SPF.

20. The changes to the cast during the first six months included two departing via Seattle, two transferring over to the Mandarin Theater, and eleven arriving from China. File 55007/1, INS-SPF.

21. Interview of Philip Kee with Zucker, Chinese Immigration Service, New York City, May 20, 1933, box 225, file 56/53.2, IACE, NY.

22. *Chinese Times*, July 21, 1924.

23. Sanders to Immigration Bureau DC, July 17, 1922, file 55197/81, INS-SPF.

24. As an indication of his stature, Chin's passing in March 1925 prompted the following: "Chinatown Guarded as Leader Lies Dead," *New York Times*, March 9, 1925; "Pagan Gongs Peal at Christian Burial," *New York Times*, March 10, 1925; "Waif Now an Heir to Chinese Estate," *New York Times*, March 11, 1925.

25. "450 Chinese Seized: Tong Peace Signed," *New York Times*, September 15, 1925.

26. *Chung Sai Yat Po*, June 26, 1925.

27. *Chung Sai Yat Po*, July 6, 1925, October 31, 1925.

28. See Chen Feinong, *Yueju Liushinian (Sixty Years of Cantonese Opera: Chen Feinong's Memoir)*, ed. Ng Wing Chung and Chan Chak Lui (Hong Kong: Cantonese Opera Research Programme, Chinese University of Hong Kong, 2007).

29. Other actresses were Mei Zhiqing and Liang Lizhu.

30. The troupe is also known by the names Lau Tau Seck, Lock Tin Chow, and Lok Tin Chou.

31. "Chinese Company Presenting Series of Operas in Toronto," *Christian Science Monitor*, July 1, 1922; "This Chinese Actress Says She'll Never Wed: Soo Lum Mark, at 18, Is Rather Young Leading Lady, but she's clever," *Toronto Daily Star*, July 17, 1922.

32. "Chinese Company Presenting Series of Operas." The troupe was then run by the Lin Yick Company and managed by Wong Yee Sang and Lim Shew Kam.

33. Playbills of the Guo Taiping troupe at the Sheng Ping Theater, May 8, June 23, July 24, 1916, Chinese Opera Information Centre, Chinese University of Hong Kong.

34. The application, accompanied by the Canadian certificates, was approved on the same day. The bond was $1,000, and the permit was valid for a year. Four days later, on the day of the billed performance, the troupe arrived in Boston by rail. (The ease of the Lok Tin Tsau troupe's admission to Boston was in sharp contrast with that of the Lun On Company, represented by the same attorney, whose petitions to bring in a troupe were repeatedly and sternly rejected for many months.)

35. Telegram from Immigration Service in Washington, DC, to Immigration Service in Boston, April 10, 1923, file 55007/16, INS-SPF.

36. Letter from Department of Labor to Immigration Service Boston, December 23, 1924, box 255 56/53.1, IACE, NY.

37. Wong Leung Doo collection, boxes 01835 and 04203, Library and Archives of Canada, Ottawa.

38. In this newspaper report, the writer suggested that the theater was not meant for Americans. "An Occidental at a Chinese Play," *Christian Science Monitor*, January 14, 1924.

39. *Chung Sai Yat Po*, April 6, 1925.

40. Section 13 of the 1924 act mandates the exclusion of the wives of United States citizens of the Chinese race if such wives are of a race of persons ineligible for citizenship. *Chang Chan v. Nagle*, 268 U.S. 346 (1925).

41. Department of Labor to Immigration Boston, Jan 30, 1925; Department of Labor to National Surety, February 7, 1925, box 255 56/53.1, both in IACE, NY.

42. Correspondence between National Surety and A. Warner Parker, August 19, 1926, box 255 56/53.3, IACE, NY.

43. Mae Ngai writes about what she calls the Chinese American "interpreter class" in fascinating ways; see *The Lucky Ones: One Family and the Extraordinary Invention of Chinese America* (New York: Houghton Mifflin Harcourt, 2010).

44. W. F. Watkins, Inspector in Charge, Immigration Service, New York City to Immigration Service, Washington, DC, August 20, 1926, box 255 56/53.3, IACE, NY.

45. Harriette Ashbrooke, "Chinese Players Revamp," *New York Times*, September 20, 1925.

46. *Chinese Nationalist Daily*, February 9, 1927.

47. *Chinese Nationalist Daily*, January 29, 1927.

48. *Chinese Nationalist Daily*, February 14, 1927.

49. *Chinese Nationalist Daily*, December 17, 1928, April 4, 26, 1929.

50. *Chinese Nationalist Daily*, June 21, 1927.

51. *Chinese Nationalist Daily*, June 30, 1927.

52. *Chinese Nationalist Daily*, June 30, July 2, July 18, 1927. There should be two more lists between July 2 and 18.

53. Indeed, convention allowed as many roles for the push-cart routine as there were prima donnas.

54. Between March 30 and May 18 Xiao Dingxiang played the leading lady in seventeen performances, while Guan Yinglian was featured in eight.

55. *Chinese Nationalist Daily*, April 22, 1927.

56. *Shen Bao*, January 7, 1922.

57. *World Journal* (San Francisco), March 10, 1927.

58. *World Journal* (San Francisco), March 5, 1927.

59. Yong Ni Shang playbill, 1995.52.21, HKHM.

60. *Shen Bao*, various issues. From November 1, 1920, to September 30, 1925, there were many references to her success in a comic male role.

61. "Chinese Women's New Freedom Leads Them into Male Roles," *New York Times*, May 15, 1927.

62. Naden, *Golden Age*, 14.

63. A wedding picture by the Natural Photo Studio (47 Mott Street) dated August 1920 can be found in the Museum of Chinese in America, P2010.007.041. The other two were the Junyoon Studio (14 Bowery) and the Lawson Company (22 Pell Street).

64. *Chinese Nationalist Daily*, November 21, 1927.

65. *Chinese Nationalist Daily*, December 26, 1927.

66. See the playbill collected at the Museum of the City of New York.

67. "Drama of Fire Ends Old Thalia Theatre: Bowery Landmark Wrecked as Roof Drops into Pit Where Crinolines Once Swished." *New York Times*, June 6, 1929.

68. *Chinese Nationalist Daily*, June 6, 1929.

69. *Chinese Nationalist Daily*, June 10, 1929.

70. "Leasehold Deals," *New York Times*, August 8, 1929.

71. *Chinese Nationalist Daily*, December 10, 1930.

72. Letter from Henry Hazard to Chas Booth ("Immediate departure of the members is required in view of the fact that the operation of the troupe has ceased."), May 3, 1934, box 225, 56/53.3, IACE, NY.

73. Letter from Charles Booth to Immigration DC, July 17, 1933, box 225 56/53.3, IACE, NY.

74. *Chinese Nationalist Daily*, April 7, 1927.

75. *Chinese Nationalist Daily*, March 24, April 12, 1927.

76. Ernest K. Moy was a citizen and the editor of the *Chinese Review*. See Ernest Moy, ed., *Mei Lanfang: Chinese Drama* (New York: China Institute in America, 1929); Ernest Moy, ed., *The Pacific Coast Tour of Mei Lan-Fang* (San Francisco: n.p., 1930).

77. It was funded with Boxer Rebellion indemnity money (paid by China to the United States), and Kuo Ping-Wen was its first director.

78. Mei Lanfang performed in various cities in China, including many with their own regional genre of Chinese opera, such as Guangzhou and Shanghai. The series of performances featured in the famous Haizhu theater in Guangzhou from November 28 to December 5, 1928, indicated his appeal to audiences. It was billed as his farewell performance before his U.S. tour. *Yuehua Bao*, November 28, 1928.

79. *Chinese Nationalist Daily*, February 21, 1930.

80. See Nancy Rao, "Racial Essence and Historical Invisibility: Chinese Opera in New York, 1930," *Cambridge Opera Journal* 12/2 (2000): 135–162. Huang Xuemei arrived in New York and made her debut with the Chinatown theater called New World Troupe on February 21, four days after Mei Lanfang's debut at the 49th Street Theater. *Chinese Nationalist Daily*, February 21, 1930. On the same page as that announcement are advertisements by three different ticket services of tickets for Mei Lanfang's performance.

81. A. C. Scott, *Mei Lan-fang: The Life and Times of a Peking Actor* (Hong Kong: Hong Kong University Press, 1971), 107.

82. Grace Lynn, "Mr. Mei and the Local Chinese Drama," *New York Times*, April 6, 1930.

83. The playbill was included in Su Zheng, *Claiming Diaspora: Music, Transnationalism, and Cultural Politics in Asian Chinese America* (New York: Oxford University Press, 2010), 96.

84. *Chinese Nationalist Daily* reported the first release on July 13, 1929, and the second release on October 28, 1929.

85. *Chinese Nationalist Daily*, October 28, 1929, and May 24, 1930. Richard Spottswood lists all these recordings based on information from the Victor ledgers. See *Ethnic Music on Records*, 5:2536. According to the numerical catalog Victor provided to dealers for ordering purposes, the March discs were released in July 1929 and the October discs on December 13, 1929. I am grateful to Tim Brook for this source.

86. *Chinese Nationalist Daily*, May 24, 1930.
87. *Chinese Nationalist Daily*, May 23 and March 24, 1930.
88. *Chinese Nationalist Daily*, March 28, 1930.
89. Zhao Fayi (Chu Bros., 1672 St. Clair Ave. West, Toronto, Ont. Can.) to Lee Eng (42 Mott Street, New York) correspondence, March 18, 1926, http://www.chinesecol.com/covers.html.
90. "Glamour Gone from Chinatown," *New York Times*, September 13, 1925.
91. Ibid.

Chapter 12. From Honolulu to Havana

1. The rise of the theatrical company is detailed in a study by Wing Chung Ng based on a study of its business records from 1923 to mid-1924. Wing Chung Ng, "Chinatown Theatre as Transnational Business: New Evidence from Vancouver during the Exclusion Era," *BC Studies* 148 (winter 2005–2006): 25–54.
2. Frances Hern, *Yip Sang and the First Chinese Canadians* (Victoria, BC: Heritage House, 2011), 89; Letters, September 19, 1923, Kue Hing Company file 0018-03 CC-Folder 0503, UBC-CC.
3. Correspondence, October 10, 1923, UBC-CC.
4. Letter from Tang to the headquarters of Hue King in Vancouver, August 6, 1923, UBC-CC. The printing of the playbills was done first by the *Chinese News* and then by *Liberty News* (*Xin Zhongguo Bao* and *Ziyou Xinbao*).
5. O'Donnell to Assistant Secretary of Department of Labor, January 31, 1924. He indicates corporate capital of $20,000 and cash of $30,000 from investors for actor bonds. File 55007/18, INS-SPF.
6. Letter from District Director to Department of Labor, February 27, 1925, file 55007/18b, INS-SPF (noting his return).
7. Correspondence, September 27, 1923, UBC-CC.
8. Correspondence, October 2, 1923, UBC-CC.
9. Playbill, Guo Fengnian Troupe, October 13, 1923, UBC-CC.
10. Correspondence, October 10, 1923, UBC-CC.
11. Correspondence, August 22 to October 23, 1924, UBC-CC.
12. Telegram from Yip Mow to Wing Sang Company, March 12, 1924, UBC-CC.
13. Letter from Department of Labor, Shaughnessy to Henning, September 18, 1924, file 55007/18, INS-SPF.
14. A Plea from 14 merchants to commissioner general of immigration to endorse Kue Hing's continuing existence, Resident to Husband, Commissioner General of Immigration, June 24, 1924, file 55007/18, INS-SPF.
15. Adam McKeown, *Chinese Migrant Networks and Cultural Change: Peru, Chicago and Hawaii, 1900–1936* (Chicago: University of Chicago Press, 2001), 224.
16. Ibid., 235.
17. O'Donnell to Secretary of Labor, July 12, 1924, file 55007/18, INS-SPF. Also see a letter from Liam Bem to Lee Chuck Sam on March 1, 1924, UBC-CC.

18. Memo of General Board of Review, June 14, 1926, file 55007/18d, INS-SPF.

19. Charles Dwight to A. E. Bernett, District Director of Immigration, Honolulu, May 19, 1926, 55007/18b, INS-SPF.

20. This figure is derived from documents contained in file 55007/18–8h, INS-SPF.

21. Telegram from San Francisco to Wong Ow, Vancouver, Sep 14, 1923, UBC-CC.

22. Correspondence, October 10, 1923, UBC-CC.

23. Bond paper and District Director of Honolulu to Department of Labor September 20, 1924, files 55007/18 and 55007/18b, INS-SPF.

24. Bond paper, June 2, 1927, file 55007/18e, INS-SPF.

25. Letter from Roger to Immigration Bureau, DC, regarding Huang Xiaofeng, June 24, 1927, file 55007/18e; bond paper of Li Xuefang, August 6, 1929, arrived on *Korea Maru* (age 31), file 55007/18g, and checked out for China November 1, 1929, file 55007/18g ; Mudan Su arrived on *Taiyo Maru* (age 27) November 26, 1929, file 55007/18g, INS-SPF. (Document annotations are transcribed verbatim from the files for the sake of clarity.)

26. Letter from Roger O'Donnell to Department of Labor, October 2, 1925, file 55007/18c, INS-SPF.

27. *Chinese Times*, March 23, 1923.

28. *Chinese Times*, November 8, 10, 1924.

29. *Chinese Times*, June 3, 1925.

30. *Chinese Times*, November 13, 1926.

31. *Chinese Times*, February 1, 1927.

32. *Chinese Times*, March 3, 1927.

33. *Chinese Times*, January 28, 1928, September 20, 1927.

34. It is little wonder that photography studios' newspaper ads often included stern warnings against pirated copies of their photos of actresses.

35. *Chinese Times*, September 26, 1927.

36. See various pictures of Portland and San Francisco Chinese bands, as well as Chinese sports teams, in the UBC-CC.

37. These performers appeared in the newspaper advertisements of theater playbills: Liang Lizhu (*Chinese Times*, July 24, 1928), Xue Yingluan (*Chinese Times*, August 26, 1929), and Lu Xuehong (*Chinese Times*, March 7, 1928). They were also familiar names in many theater playbills of San Francisco.

38. A clear example of the latter was Xiao Caiji, whose itinerary began at San Francisco (January 1925–1926) and continued to Mexicali (March 1926–?), Havana (?–December 1927), New York (December 1927 to January 1928), and finally Vancouver (January 1928–?).

39. Teatro Chung Wah, Leung Doo Wong fonds (106-020000-7), Library and Archives of Canada, Ottawa.

40. Huang Liangzi pledged $6,000 and Lin Shounan pledged $1,000. *Chinese Nationalist Daily*, June 30, 1927.

41. As a general store, it was spared losses from a fire at the customs warehouse that burnt merchandise worth $400,000 to $500,000, since the company did not have dutiable goods stored there at the time.

42. Haiming Liu, *The Transnational History of a Chinese Family: Immigrant Letters, Family Business, and Reverse Migration* (New Brunswick: Rutgers University Press, 2009), 47.

43. Teatro Chung Wah, Leung Doo Wong fonds (106-020000-7), Library and Archives of Canada, Ottawa.

44. The following information is derived from Kathleen López, *Chinese Cubans: A Transnational History* (Chapel Hill: University of North Carolina Press, 2013), 207–208; and Yuan Yan, "Historical Transition of Chinese Theaters in Cuba" (in Chinese), *Journal of Latin American Studies* 33/6 (2011): 37–42.

45. Ibid.

46. Ibid.

47. From 1917 to 1924, 17,473 Chinese entered. Adrian Hearn, "Chinatown Havana: One Hundred and Sixty Years Below the Surface," *Chinatowns around the World: Gilded Ghetto, Ethnopolis, and Cultural Diaspora*, ed. Bernard P. Wong and Chee-Beng Tan (Leiden: Brill, 2013), 170.

48. *Chinese Times*, February 6, 1923.

49. Letter from Huang Yüsheng, April 22, 1923, Wong Leung Doo collection, box 01835, box 04203, Library and Archives of Canada, Ottawa.

50. Invoice of Si Shengfa, n.d., Wong Leung Doo collection, box 01835, box 04203, Library and Archives of Canada, Ottawa.

51. Mauro García Triana and Pedro Eng Herrera, *The Chinese in Cuba, 1847–Now*, ed. and trans. Gregor Benton (Lanham, MD: Lexington, 2009), 105.

Epilogue

1. Kitty Tsui, *Kwan Ying Lin, Mao Dan So & Co.: Stars of the Chinatown Stage*. University of California, Santa Cruz, Asian Pacific Islander Lesbian Collection, 1980–2001, box-folder 29:5.

2. This figure was derived by tallying information from numerous immigration files for this period in INS-SPF.

3. Examples of performers' photo IDs can be found in the immigration file for the Mandarin Theater. February 11, 1926, file 55374/227I, INS-SPF. The ID card also included immigration serial number and bond information.

4. *San Francisco Chronicle*, May 15, August 30, 1925.

5. *San Francisco Chronicle*, October 30, 1922.

6. "Chinatown Upset by Trifle Over Queen," *San Francisco Chronicle*, April 11, 1925.

7. For example, Guan's return to Guangzhou from the United States in 1947 was reported in a feature article in a local newspaper, *Gong Ping Bao*, April 27, 1947. The advertisements in *Huazi Ribao* also show her active roles on stage at Gao Sheng Theater in Hong Kong. Clipping, Chinese Opera Information Centre, Chinese University of Hong Kong.

8. Interview with Bonnie Lew by Judy Yung, Stockton, CA, March 26, 1982, Chinese Women of America Research Project.

9. H. Robert Lee and Judy Yung, "Boyhood Memories of the Wing Chun Laundry," *Argonaut* 27/1 (summer 2016): 6–19. He was "fascinated by the staging and costumes,

and thrilled to hear the pounding of the drums and crashing of cymbals in those staged battles . . . [and] never lost his fondness for Cantonese opera."

10. For more on the family history and its significance see Bruce Quan Jr., "In the Shadows of History: Life and Times of Lew Hing, An Extraordinary Life in Extraordinary Times," manuscript.

11. See photographs of Guan Dexing in a cowboy outfit in the Chinese Theater collection, San Francisco Museum of Performance and Design.

12. *White Powder and Neon Lights*, dir. Wong Hok-Sing, produced by Joseph Sunn Jue (San Francisco: Grandview Film Company, 1946).

13. Shumei Shi, *Minority Transnationalism*, ed. Françoise Lionnet and Shumei Shi (Durham: Duke University Press, 2005), 74.

14. Lisa Rose Mar, *Brokering Belonging: Chinese in Canada's Exclusion Era, 1885–1945* (Oxford: Oxford University Press, 2010), 13.

15. Wayson Choy, *The Paper Shadows: A Memory of Past Lost and Found* (New York: Picador, 2000); Margaret Leung, private collection; David Lei, private collection, scrapbook of Raymond Fong.

16. Scrapbook pages in the Theater Collections, Museum of the City of New York. The playbill is for May 29, 1929.

17. Sabine Haenni, *The Immigrant Scene: Ethnic Amusements in New York, 1880–1920* (Minneapolis: University of Minnesota Press, 2008), 97.

18. Maxine Hong Kingston, *Tripmaster Monkey: His Fake Book* (New York: Vintage, 1989), 141.

19. In particular, Fred Ho has written several essays both acknowledging the influence and telling how he navigated the influence of Chinese opera. See Fred Ho, "Bamboo That Snaps Back! Resistance and Revolution in Asian Pacific American Working-Class and Left-Wing Expressive Culture," in *Wicked Theory, Naked Practice: A Fred Ho Reader*, ed. Diane C. Fujino (Minneapolis: University of Minnesota Press, 2009), 247–269.

20. The roles and scopes of Cantonese opera clubs in the United States evolved over time and varied greatly. Sai-Shing Yung and Sau Yan Chan documented a period similar to that of Su Zheng. Daphne Lei deals with slightly more recent practices. Su Zheng, *Claiming Diaspora: Music, Transnationalism, and Cultural Politics in Asian/Chinese America* (New York: Oxford University Press, 2010), 119–125; Sau Yan Chan and Sai-Shing Yung, "Cantonese Operatic Clubs in New York Chinatown: A Fieldwork Report." In *Red Boat on the Canal: Cantonese Opera in New York Chinatown*, ed. Isabelle Duchesne (New York: Museum of Chinese in the Americas, 2000), 70–91; Daphne Lei, *Operatic China: Staging Chinese Identity across the Pacific* (New York: Palgrave Macmillan, 2006), 156–172.

21. Haenni, *Immigrant Scene*, 143–144.

22. Homay King, *Lost in Translation: Orientalism, Cinema, and the Enigmatic Signifier* (Chapel Hill: Duke University Press, 2010), 46.

23. *San Francisco Chronicle*, June 28, 1929; Henry Burden McDowell, "The Chinese Theater," *Century Illustrated Monthly Magazine* 29/1 (1884): 27–44.

24. Dongshin Chang, *Representing China on the Historical London Stage: From Orientalism to Intercultural Performance* (New York: Routledge, 2015), 152–155.

25. Krystyn R. Moon, *Yellowface: Creating the Chinese in American Popular Music and Performance* (New Brunswick: Rutgers University Press, 2005), 95–96, 152–153.

26. For Chinese tom-toms and its American modifications, as well as Chinese cymbals and woodblocks, see detailed discussions, transcriptions, and analyses in Theodore Dennis Brown, "A History and Analysis of Jazz Drumming to 1942," Ph.D. diss., University of Michigan, 1976, especially 112–116. In this influential study, Brown linked the influence directly to Chinese opera in the United States. See also Ben Reimer, "Defining the Role of Drumset Performance in Contemporary Music," Ph.D. diss., McGill University, 2013, esp. 20–21, 41–42.

27. Brown, "History and Analysis," 125.

28. Henry Cowell, "The Nature of Melody," manuscript. See Nancy Rao, "American Compositional Theory in the 1930s: Scale and Exoticism in 'The Nature of Melody' by Henry Cowell." *Musical Quarterly* 85/4 (2001): 595–640.

29. Most specifically, I am referring to the dynamic slide in Ruth Crawford's *String Quartet 1931*, the tempo slide in John Cage's *Music of Changes*, the juxtaposition of tempo slides in Conlon Nancarrow's *Studies for Player Piano*, the tempo slide in Elliott Carter's *Variations for Orchestra*, and the juxtaposition of dynamic and rhythmic slides in Johanna Beyer's String Quartet, James Tenney's *Having Never Written a Note for Percussion*, and Morton Feldman's *Neither*. See Nancy Rao, "Cowell's Sliding Tone and American Ultra-Modernist Tradition," *American Music* 23/3 (2005): 281–323.

BIBLIOGRAPHY

The following abbreviations are used in the endnotes to this book.

ESL	Ethnic Studies Library, University of California, Berkeley
INS-SPF	Subject and Policy Files, 1906–1957, Entry 9, Records of the U.S. Immigration and Naturalization Service, RG 85, National Archives, Washington, DC
HKHM	Hong Kong Heritage Museum
IACE, NY	Investigation Arrival Case Files, Records of the U.S. Immigration and Naturalization Service, RG 85, National Archives, New York City, NY
IACE, SEA	Investigation Arrival Case Files, Records of the U.S. Immigration and Naturalization Service, RG 85, National Archives, Pacific Alaska Region, Seattle, WA
IACE, SF	Investigation Arrival Case Files, Records of the U.S. Immigration and Naturalization Service, RG 85, National Archives, Pacific Region, San Bruno, CA
UBC-CC	University of British Columbia, Chung Collection
UCB-HML	University of California, Berkeley, Him Mark Lai Papers
SFPALM	San Francisco Performing Arts Library and Museum, renamed the Museum of Performance and Design, San Francisco, Collection of Chinese Theater Images

Archives and Individual Collections

American Folklife Center, Library of Congress, Washington, DC.
Amien Lau, private collection of playbills.

Asian Pacific Islander Lesbian Collection, 1980–2001, Special Collection, University of California, Santa Cruz.

Chinatown Theater playbills, Ethnic Studies Library, University of California, Berkeley.

Chinese Opera Collection, National China Art Research Institute, Beijing.

Chinese Opera Information Centre, Department of Music, Chinese University of Hong Kong.

Chinese Theater Collection, Museum of Performance and Design, San Francisco.

Ching Young Tse (son of actor Tse Fook Pui), private collection of playbills.

Collection of Chinese Theater playbills, Chinese Historical Society of America, San Francisco.

David Lei, private collection of playbills and scrapbooks.

Department of Records, New York City Municipal Archives.

"Kue Hing Company File regarding a Chinese Acting Troupe," in Yip Sang Family Series, fol. 0018, file 3, Chung Collection, Rare Books and Special Collections, University of British Columbia Library.

Leung Doo Wong fonds, National Libraries and Archives of Canada, Ottawa.

Margaret Leung, private scrapbooks.

New York Public Library Research Collection, Main Branch.

Prints and Photograph Division, Library of Congress, Washington, DC.

Ren Fan, private collection.

Special Collection, Hong Kong University.

Taiping Theater Collection, Hong Kong Heritage Museum.

Theater Collections, Museum of the City of New York.

Theater Collections, New York Historical Society.

United States National Archives and Records Administration, Records of the Immigration and Naturalization Service, RG 85. Chinese Exclusion Case Files, 1895–1943, New York Branch.

——. Investigation Arrival Case Files, 1884–1944, Pacific Regional Branch.

——. Subject Correspondence Files, Washington, DC.

Wing Luke Museum, Seattle, WA.

Wong Leung Doo Collection (106-020000-7), National Libraries and Archives of Canada, Ottawa.

Wylie Wong collection of May's Studio photographs and San Francisco Chinatown ephemera, Special Collection, Stanford University.

Newspapers

The Chinese Nationalist Daily (New York)	民氣日報	1927–1931
The Chinese Times (Vancouver)	大漢公報	1913–1937
The Chinese World (San Francisco)	世界日報	1922–1932
Chung Sai Yat Po (San Francisco)	中西日報	1922–1932
Shen Bao (Shanghai)	申報	1917–1932
The Young China (San Francisco)	少年中國晨報	1922–1932
Yuehua Bao (Guangzhou)	越華報	1927–1928

Books and Articles

"450 Chinese Seized: Tong Peace Signed." *New York Times*, September 15, 1925.

Aarim-Heriot, Najia. *Chinese Immigrants, African Americans, and Racial Anxiety in the United States*. Urbana: University of Illinois Press, 2003.

Ahmed, Sara. "Affective Economies." *Social Text*, 79 22/2 (2004): 117–139.

Anthony, Walter. "Orpheum's Funsters Help Reconcile You to Life! Long Tack Sam Is Headliner." *San Francisco Chronicle*, October 30, 1916.

———. "The Passing of the Chinese Theater." *San Francisco Call*, July 27, 1913.

Ashbrooke, Harriette. "Chinese Players Revamp Our Oldest Theater." *New York Times*, September 20, 1925.

Bai, Jurong 白駒榮. "Yihai fuchen: Bai Jurong wutai shenghuo wushi nian" 藝海浮沈：舞台生活五十年 (Fifty Years of Stage Life). In *Yueju yishu dashi Bai Jurong*, ed. Li Men, 1–83. Guangzhou: Guangdong Zhongguo Xijujia Xiehui, 1990.

Banham, Martin. *The Cambridge Guide to Theatre*. Cambridge, UK: Cambridge University Press, 1995.

Barber, Karin. *The Anthropology of Texts, Persons, and Publics*. Cambridge: Cambridge University Press, 2007.

———. *The Generation of Plays: Yorùbá Popular Life in Theater*. Bloomington: Indiana University Press, 2000.

Barlow, Jeffrey, and Christine Richardson. *China Doctor of John Day*. Portland, OR: Binford, 1979.

Basso, Keith H. *Wisdom Sits in Places: Landscape and Language among the Western Apache*. Albuquerque: University of New Mexico Press, 1996.

Beiner, Guy. *Remembering the Year of the French: Irish Folk History and Social Memory*. Madison: University of Wisconsin Press, 2007.

Bhabha, Homi. *The Location of Culture*. New York: Routledge, 1991.

Blume, Kenneth J. *Historical Dictionary of the U.S. Maritime Industry*. Metuchen: Scarecrow, 2011.

Bonner, Arthur. *Alas! What Brought Thee Hither? The Chinese in New York, 1800–1950*. Madison, NJ: Fairleigh-Dickinson University Press, 1997.

Bonnie Lew, interview by Judy Yung, Stockton, CA, March 26, 1982, Chinese Women of America Research Project.

Bourdieu, Pierre. *The Logic of Practice*, trans. Richard Nice. Stanford: Stanford University Press, 1990.

Bowen, Robert W., and Brenda Young Bowen, eds. *San Francisco's Chinatown*. Postcard History: California. Charleston, NC: Arcadia, 2008.

Brilmayer, Lea. "Rights, Fairness, and Choice of Law." *Yale Law Review* 98/7 (1989): 1277–1319.

Broyles, Michael. "Immigrant, Folk and Regional Musics in the Nineteenth Century." In *The Cambridge History of American Music*, ed. David Nicholls, 135–157. Cambridge, UK: Cambridge University Press, 1998.

California's Diamond Jubilee: Celebrated at San Francisco, September 5 to 12, 1925. San Francisco: E. C. Brown, 1925.

Canada Year Book 1915. http://creativecommons.org/licenses/publicdomain/.

Cavarero, Adriana. *For More than One Voice: Toward a Philosophy of Vocal Expression*. Stanford: Stanford University Press, 2005.

Chan, Annette Ke-Lee. "A Performance History of Cantonese Opera in San Francisco from Gold Rush to the Earthquake." Ph.D. diss., University of California, Davis, 1993.

Chan, Kwok Bun. *Smoke and Fire: The Chinese in Montreal*. Hong Kong: Chinese University of Hong Kong Press, 1991.

Chan, Marjorie K. M. "Cantonese Opera and the Growth and Spread of Vernacular Written Cantonese in the Twentieth Century." *Proceedings of the Seventeenth North American Conference on Chinese Linguistics*, ed. Qian Gao, 1–18. Los Angeles: GSIL Publications, University of Southern California, 2005.

Chan, Sau Yan. "Exploding the Belly: Improvisation in Cantonese Opera." In *In the Course of Performance: Studies in the World of Musical Improvisation*, ed. Bruno Nettl and Melinda Russell, 199–218. London: University of Chicago Press, 1998.

——. *Improvisation in a Ritual Context: The Music of Cantonese Opera*. Hong Kong: Chinese University of Hong Kong Press, 1992.

Chan, Sau Yan, and Sai-Shing Yung. "Cantonese Operatic Clubs in New York Chinatown: A Fieldwork Report." In *Red Boat on the Canal: Cantonese Opera in New York Chinatown*, ed. Isabelle Duchesne, 70–99. New York: Museum of Chinese in the Americas, 2000.

Chan, Sucheng, ed. *Transnationalism: The Flow of People, Resources, and Ideas between China and America during the Exclusion Era*. Philadelphia: Temple University Press, 2005.

Chang, Dongshin. *Representing China on the Historical London Stage: From Orientalism to Intercultural Performance*. New York: Routledge, 2015.

Chang, Gordon, Mark Johnson, and Paul Karlstrom, eds. *Asian American Art: A History, 1850–1970*. Stanford: Stanford University Press, 2008.

Chang, Kornel. "Enforcing Transnational White Solidarity: Asian Migration and the Formation of the U.S.–Canadian Boundary." *American Quarterly* 60/3 (2008): 671–696.

——. *Pacific Connections: The Making of the U.S.-Canadian Borderlands*. Berkeley: University of California Press, 2012.

Chen, Feinong 陳非儂. *Yueju liushinian* 粵劇六十年 (Sixty Years of Cantonese Opera: Chan Feinong's Memoir), ed. Ng Wing Chung and Chan Chak Lui. Hong Kong: Cantonese Opera Research Programme, Chinese University of Hong Kong, 2007.

Chen, Jack. "Pear Garden in the West; America's Chinese Theatre 1852–1993." Manuscript, SFPALM.

Chen, Yong. *Chinese San Francisco, 1850–1943: A Trans-Pacific Community*. Palo Alto: Stanford University Press, 2000.

Chen, Yongxin 陳勇新. "Muyu yu yueju" 木魚與粵劇 (Muyu and Cantonese Opera). In *Foshancang muyushu mulu yu yanjiu*, ed. Zeng Yimin, 265–268. Guangzhou: Guangzhou Publishing House, 2009.

Cheng, Meibao 程美寶. "Jindai difang wenhuade kuadiyuxing" 近代地方文化的跨地域性：20世紀二、三十年代粵劇、粵樂和粵曲在上海 (The Trans-locality of Local Cultures in Modern China: Cantonese Opera, Music, and Songs in Shanghai, 1920s–1930s). *Journal of Modern Chinese History* 2/2 (2007): 1–17.

Chew, Lee. "The Life Story of a Chinaman." *Independent*, February 19, 1903, 417–423.

Chin, Frank. *Donald Duk*. Minneapolis: Coffee House, 1991.

"Chinatown Purified." *Pacific Medical Journal* 29/5–6 (May–June 1906): 271.

"Chinatown Upset by Trifle over Queen." *San Francisco Chronicle*, April 11, 1925.

"Chinese Actors for Omaha." *San Francisco Chronicle*, March 23, 1898.

"Chinese Company Presenting Series of Operas in Toronto." *Christian Science Monitor*, July 1, 1922.

"A Chinese Feast." *Chicago Press and Tribune*, June 2, 1860.

"Chinese Orchestra." *Atchison Daily Globe*, December 1, 1890.

"A Chinese 'Sacred Concert.'" *New York Times*, March 27, 1893.

"Chinese Stage Is Jazzed Up." *Los Angeles Times*, May 31, 1925.

"Chinese Theater." *Daily Dramatic Chronicle*, February 8, 1868.

"Chinese Women's New Freedom Leads Them into Male Roles." *New York Times*, May 15, 1927.

Ching, May-bo. "Literary, Ethnic or Territorial Definitions of Guangdong Culture in the Late Qing and the Early Republic." In *Unity and Diversity: Local Cultures and Identities in China*, ed. Tao Tao Liu and Faure David, 51–66. Hong Kong: Hong Kong University Press, 1996.

——. "A Preliminary Study of the Theatres Built by Cantonese Merchants in the Late Qing." *Frontiers of Chinese History* 5/2 (2010): 253–278.

——. "'What Alternative Do You Have, Sixth Aunt?' Women and Marriage in Cantonese Ballads." In *Merchants' Daughters: Women, Commerce, and Regional Culture in South China*, ed. Helen F. Siu, 59–76. Hong Kong: Hong Kong University Press, 2010.

Chinn, Thomas W. *Bridging the Pacific: San Francisco Chinatown and Its People*. San Francisco: Chinese Historical Society of America, 1989.

Chow, Rey. *Ethics after Idealism: Theory, Culture, Ethnicity, Reading*. Bloomington: Indiana University Press, 1998.

Chow Sze Sum 周仕深. "Fang Yenfeng fangxian erhuang manban han fangxian bangzi zhongban" 芳艷芬的反線二黃慢板和反線梆子中板 (Analysis of Fang Yenfeng's fangxian erhuang manban and fangxian bangzi zhongban). *Xin yanyang chuanqi*, ed. Yue Qing, 179–189. Hong Kong: Yueqing Chuanbo, 2008.

——. "Fanxianerhuang manban zaixiangang yueju jinbainian de yanbian" 反線二黃慢板在香港粵劇近百年的演變 (The Evolution of fanxian erhuang manban in Hong Kong Cantonese Opera of the Past Hundred Years [Part I]). *Journey to Chinese Opera and Drama* 53 (2006): 68–69.

——. "The Mode of Cantonese Opera." M.A. thesis, Chinese University of Hong Kong, 2007.

Choy, Philip. Interview by Christine Cushing. https://www.youtube.com/watch?t=90&v=j7hbFhV4keY.

——. *San Francisco Chinatown: A Guide to Its History and Architecture*. San Francisco: City Light, 2014.

Choy, Wayson. *Paper Shadows: A Memory of a Past Lost and Found*. New York: Picador, 2000.

Chu, Peter, Lois M. Foster, Nadia Lavrova, and Steven C. Moy, eds. *Chinese Theaters in America*. Washington, DC: Bureau of Research and Publications, Federal Theater Project, Public Works Administration, 1936.

"A Circus in Court: Four Chinese Actors Display Their Ability before Judge Hoffman." *New York Times*, August 23, 1884.

Clavin, Patricia. "Defining Transnationalism." *Contemporary European History* 14/4 (2005): 421–439.

Cox, Arnie. "Hearing, Feeling, Grasping Gestures." In *Music and Gesture*, ed. Anthony Gritten and Elaine King, 45–60. Aldershot: Ashgate, 2006.

Crawford, Richard. *America's Musical Life: A History*. New York: Norton, 2001

Crowe, Michael F., and Robert W. Bowen. *San Francisco Art Deco*. Charleston, SC: Arcadia, 2007.

Cusick, Suzanne. "Feminist Theory, Music Theory, and the Mind/Body Problem." *Perspectives of New Music* 32/1 (1994): 8–27.

Davis, James J. "How the Immigration Laws Are Working Now." *Review of Reviews* 65 (1922): 509–516.

de Certeau, Michel. *The Practice of Everyday Life*. Berkeley: University of California Press, 1984.

Delgado, Grace Peña. *Making the Chinese Mexican: Global Migration, Localism, and Exclusion in the U.S.-Mexican Borderlands*. Stanford: Stanford University Press, 2012.

Dirlik, Arif. "Transnationalism, the Press, and the National Imaginary in Twentieth Century China." *China Review* 4/1 (2004): 11–25.

Dong, Arthur. *Forbidden City, USA: Chinese American Nightclubs, 1936–1970*. Los Angeles: Deep Focus, 2014.

Donovan, Brian. *White Slave Crusades: Race, Gender, and Anti-vice Activism, 1887–1917*. Urbana: University of Illinois Press, 2006.

"Drama of Fire Ends Old Thalia Theatre: Bowery Landmark Wrecked as Roof Drops into Pit Where Crinolines Once Swished." *New York Times*, June 6, 1929.

Driscoll, Margiorie C. "Chinatown Stage Acquires Charming Star: Smile Captivating, and Dimples Delightful." *San Francisco Chronicle*, December 15, 1922.

Duchesne, Isabelle. "A Collection's Riches: Into the Fabric of a Community." In *Red Boat on the Canal: Cantonese Opera in New York Chinatown*, ed. Isabelle Duchesne, 16–69. New York: Museum of Chinese in the Americas, 2000.

Dyer, Richard. *Heavenly Bodies: Film Stars and Society*. London: British Film Institute, 1986; 2nd ed., New York: Routledge, 2003.

Edwards, Clarence E. *The Art of Elegant Dining—Bohemian San Francisco: Its Restaurants and Their Most Famous Recipes*. San Francisco: Paul Elder & Company, 1917.

Eng, David. *Racial Castration: Managing Masculinity in Asian America*. Durham: Duke University Press, 2001.

Erdman, Andrew. *Queen of Vaudeville: The Story of Eva Tanguay*. Ithaca: Cornell University Press, 2012.

Fleming, Ann Marie. *The Magical Life of Long Tack Sam*. Toronto: Riverhead, 2007.

Foster, John W. "The Chinese Boycott." *Atlantic Monthly*, January 1906, 118–127.

Foster, Lois Rodecape. *Chinese theatres in America*. Albany: [s.n.], 1943. SFPALM.

Frederick, David C. *Rugged Justice: The Ninth Circuit Court of Appeals and the American West, 1891–1941*. Berkeley: University of California Press, 1994.

Fritz, Christian G. *Federal Justice in California: The Court of Ogden Hoffman, 1851–1891*. Lincoln: University of Nebraska Press, 1991.

——. "A Nineteenth Century 'Habeas Corpus Mill': The Chinese Before the Federal Courts in California." *American Journal of Legal History* 32/4 (1988): 347–372.

Gabaccia, Donna R. "Is Everywhere Nowhere? Nomads, Nations, and the Immigrant Paradigm of United States History." *Journal of American History* 86/3 (1999): 1115–1134.

Gaboriau, Émile. *Monsieur Lecoq* [1869]. Translated by Shanxiang Lu and Shuyuan Qiu. Shanghai: Shang wu yin shu guan, 1912.

Garrett, Charles Hiroshi. "Chinatown, Whose Chinatown? Defining America's Borders with Musical Orientalism." *Journal of the American Musicological Society* 57/1 (2004): 119–174.

——. *Struggling to Define a Nation: American Music and the Twentieth Century*. Berkeley: University of California Press, 2008.

Gee, Herb B. "San Francisco's Chinese Theater Gives Occident New Slant on Drama." *San Francisco Chronicle*, October 29, 1922.

"General Review: Pantages." *Los Angeles Times*, November 14, 1916.

Gillenkirk, Jeff, and James Motlow. *Bitter Melon: Inside America's Last Rural Chinese Town*. San Francisco: Heyday, 1987.

"Glamour Gone from Chinatown." *New York Times*, September 13, 1925.

Glaucus. "China in California." *New York Times*, March 28, 1860.

Goldstein, Joshua. *Drama Kings: Players and Publics in the Re-creation of Peking Opera, 1870–1937*. Berkeley: University of California Press, 2007.

Grande, Andrew. "Rekindling Ancient Values: The Influence of Chinese Music and Aesthetics on Harry Partch." *Journal of the Society for American Music* 4/1 (2010): 1–32.

Guangdongsheng xiju yanjiushe (Center for Operatic Research of Guangdong Province), ed. and comp. *Yueju changqiang yinyue gailun* 粵劇唱腔音樂概論 (General Discussion of the Style of Vocal Music of Cantonese Opera). Beijing: Renmin Yinyue Chubanshe, 1984.

Guarnizo, Luis Eduardo. "The Emergence of a Transnational Social Formation and the Mirage of Return Migration among Dominican Transmigrants." *Identities* 4/2 (1997): 281–322.

Guy, Nancy. *Peking Opera and Politics in Taiwan*. Urbana: University of Illinois Press, 2005.

Haenni, Sabine. *The Immigrant Scene: Ethnic Amusements in New York, 1880–1920*. Minneapolis: University of Minnesota Press, 2008.

Hanan, Patrick. *The Sea of Regret: Two Turn-of-the Century Chinese Romantic Novels*. Honolulu: University of Hawaii Press, 1995.

Hardy, Lady Duffus. *Through Cities and Prairie Lands: Sketches of an American Tour*. New York: R. Worthington, 1881.

Hartigan, Royal, with Fred Ho. "The American Drum Set: Black Musicians and Chinese Opera along the Mississippi River." In *Afro Asia: Revolutionary Political and Cultural Connections between African Americans and Asian Americans*, ed. Fred Ho and Bill V. Mullen, 285–290. Durham: Duke University Press, 2008.

Hearn, Adrian. "Chinatown Havana: One Hundred and Sixty Years below the Surface." In *Chinatowns around the World: Gilded Ghetto, Ethnopolis, and Cultural Diaspora*, ed. Bernard P. Wong and Chee-Beng Tan, 163–186. Leiden: Brill, 2013.

Heriot, Angus. *The Castrati in Opera*. London: Calder and Boyars, 1975.

Hern, Frances. *Yip Sang and the First Chinese Canadians*. Victoria, BC: Heritage House, 2011.

Higginbotham, Evelyn. *Righteous Discontent: The Women's Movement in the Black Baptist Church, 1880–1920*. Cambridge: Harvard University Press, 1993.

Highmore, Ben. *Everyday Life and Cultural Theory: An Introduction*. London: Routledge, 2002.

Hill, Katherine. "Putting on Chinese Play at Mandarin." *San Francisco Chronicle*, February 25, 1934.

"Hitchcock's Chinese Actors: Comedian Said to Have Leased Tong Theatre in Doyer Street." *New York Times*, February 20, 1910.

Ho, Fred. *The Monkey: Part One*. Koch Records KOC 3-7815-2, 1996.

——. *The Monkey: Part Two*. Koch Records KOC-CD-7840, 1997.

——. *Wicked Theory, Naked Practice: A Fred Ho Reader*. Ed. Diane C. Fujino. Minneapolis: University of Minnesota Press, 2009.

Hoexter, Corinne K. *From Canton to California: The Epic of Chinese Immigration*. New York: Four Winds, 1976.

Hom, Marlon. *Songs of Gold Mountain: Cantonese Rhymes from San Francisco Chinatown*. Berkeley: University of California Press, 1987.

Hsu, Madeline Y. *Dreaming of Gold, Dreaming of Home: Transnationalism and Migration Between the United States and South China, 1882–1943*. Stanford: Stanford University Press, 2000.

Hu, William C. "The History of Cantonese Opera in San Francisco, California (1852–1941)." Manuscript.

Huang, Chun. "A New Exploration of Cantonese Opera All-female Troupes in Early Republican Period." *Journal of the Graduates of Sun Yat-Sen University* 33/11 (2012): 7–18.

Huang, Deshe黃德深. "Yueju nubande xingqi, fazhanhe shuailuo"粵劇女班的興起、發展和衰落 (The Rise, Development and Decline of Cantonese Opera All-Female Troupes). *Guangzhou Wenshi Ziliao*, no. 6. http://www.gzzxws.gov.cn/gzws../cg/cgml/cg6/200808/t20080826_4224.htm.

Huang, Jingming 黃鏡明. "Shitan yueju changqiang yinyuede xingchenghe gaibian."試談粵劇唱腔音樂的新唱和改編 (The Formation and Change of Cantonese Opera Vocal Music) *Yueju Yishuziliao* 2 (1979): 97–100.

Huang, Tao. *Yueju huibian* 粵劇彙編 (Cantonese Opera Promotion Association) [http://www.cantoneseculture.com/page_CantoneseOpera/index.aspx].

Huang, Wei 黃偉, and Shen Youzhu沈有珠. *Shanghai yueju yanchu shigao* 上海粵劇演出史稿 (A History of the Cantonese Opera Performed in Shanghai). Beijing: Zhongguo xiju chubanshe, 2007.

Huang, Zhao-han 黃兆漢, and Ying-Jing Zhen 曾影靖, eds. *Xishuo yueju: Chen Tie'er yueju lunwen shuxinji* 細說粵劇： 陳鐵兒粵劇論文書信集 (A Collection of Writings and Letters on Cantonese Opera by Chen Tie'er). Hong Kong: Guangming Tushu, 1992.

Hwang, David Henry. *The Dance and the Railroad*. In *Trying to Find Chinatown: The Selected Plays*, 53–88. New York: Theatre Communications Group, 2000.

——. *M. Butterfly*. New York: Plume, 1988.

Hwang, Jason. *The Floating Box: A Story in Chinatown*, cond. Juan Carlos Rivas. New World Records 80626 (2 CDs), 2004.

Idema, Wilt L. "Prosimetric and Verse Narrative." In *The Cambridge History of Chinese Literature: From 1375*, ed. Kang-i Sun Chang and Stephen Owen, 343–412. Cambridge: Cambridge University Press, 2010.

Irwin, Will. "The Drama in Chinatown." *Everybody's Magazine*, June 1909, 857–869.

——. "The Drama That Was in Chinatown." *New York Times*, April 10, 1921.

Izzo, Francesco. "Divas and Sonnets: Poetry for Female Singers in *Teatri arti e letteratura*," in *The Arts of the Prima Donna in the Long Nineteenth Century*, ed. Rachel Cowgill and Hilary Poris, 3–20. Oxford: Oxford University Press, 2012.

Jenkins, Michael. "Mexicali Blues: Community Organizations among the Baja California Chinese." Master's thesis, University of North Carolina Wilmington, 2011.

Jiang, Jin. *Women Playing Men: Yue Opera and Social Change in Twentieth-Century Shanghai*. Seattle: University of Washington Press, 2009.

Jones, Andrew. "The Gramophone in China." In *Tokens of Exchange: The Problem of Translation In Global Circulations*, ed. Lydia H. Liu, 214–236. Durham: Duke University Press, 2000.

——. *Yellow Music: Media Culture and Colonial Modernity in the Chinese Jazz Age*. Durham: Duke University Press, 2001.

Jones, Stephen. "Living Early Composition: An Appreciation of Chinese Shawm Melody." In *Analysing East Asian Music: Patterns of Rhythm and Melody*, ed. Simon Mills, 25–112, Musiké 4 (The Hague: Semar, 2010).

Jorae, Wendy Rouse. *The Children of Chinatown: Growing Up Chinese American in San Francisco*. Chapel Hill: University of North Carolina Press, 2009.

Jung, Moon-Ho. *Coolies and Cane: Race, Labor, and Sugar in the Age of Emancipation*. Baltimore: Johns Hopkins University Press, 2006.

Kenaga, Heidi. "Civic Pageantry and Public Memory in the Silent Era Commemorative Film: The Pony Express at the Diamond Jubilee." In *Memory and Popular Film*, ed. Paul Grainge, 42–64. Manchester, UK: Manchester University Press, 2003.

Kim, Ju Yong. *The Racial Mundane: Asian American Performance and the Embodied Everyday*. New York: New York University Press, 2015.

King, Homay. *Lost in Translation: Orientalism, Cinema, and the Enigmatic Signifier*. Chapel Hill: Duke University Press, 2010.

Kingston, Maxine Hong. *Conversations with Maxine Hong Kingston*, ed. Paul Skenazy and Tera Martin. Jackson: University Press of Mississippi, 1998.

——. *Tripmaster Monkey: His Fake Book*. New York: Vintage, 1989.

——. *The Woman Warrior: Memoirs of a Girlhood among Ghosts*. New York: Knopf, 1976.

Koegel, John. *Music in German Immigrant Theater: New York City, 1840–1940*. Rochester: University of Rochester Press, 2009.

Lai, Bojiang 賴伯疆 and Huang Jingping 黃鏡明, *Yueju shi* 粵劇史 (History of Cantonese Opera). Beijing: Zhongguo xiqu chubanshe, 1988.

Lai, David Chuenyan. "From Downtown Slums to Suburban Malls." In *The Chinese Diaspora: Space, Place, Mobility, and Identity*, ed. Laurence J. C. Ma and Carolyn Lee Cartier, 311–336. New York: Rowman & Littlefield, 2002.

Lai, Him Mark. *Becoming Chinese American: A History of Communities and Institutions*. Walnut Creek, CA: Alta Mira, 2004.

——. *From Overseas Chinese to Chinese American: History of the Development of Chinese American Society during the Twentieth Century*. Hong Kong: Joint Publishing, 1992.

Lai, Him Mark, Genny Lim, and Judy Yung, eds. *Island: Poetry and History of Chinese Immigrants on Angel Island, 1910–1940*, 2nd ed. Seattle: University of Washington Press, 2014.

Lam, Fung Shan 林鳳珊. "A Study of Cantonese Opera Scripts of the 1920s and 1930s." Master's thesis, University of Hong Kong, 1997.

Lausent-Herrera, Isabelle. "The Chinatown in Peru and the Changing Peruvian Chinese Community(ies)." *Journal of Chinese Overseas* 7/1 (2011): 69–113.

Lechner, Ethan. "Composers as Ethnographers: Difference in the Imaginations of Colin McPhee, Henry Cowell, and Lou Harrison." Ph.D. diss., University of North Carolina, Chapel Hill, 2008.

Lee, Anthony W. *Picturing Chinatown: Art and Orientalism in San Francisco*. Berkeley: University of California Press, 2001.

Lee, Erika. *At America's Gates: Chinese Immigration during the Exclusion Era, 1882–1943*. Chapel Hill: North Carolina University Press, 2003.

——. "Defying Exclusion: Chinese Immigrants and Their Strategies during the Exclusion Era." In *Chinese American Transnationalism: The Flow of People, Resources, and Ideas between China and America during the Exclusion Era*, ed. Sucheng Chan, 1–21. Philadelphia: Temple University Press, 2005.

Lee, Erika, and Judy Yung. *Angel Island: Immigrant Gateway to America*. Oxford: Oxford University Press, 2010.

Lee, H. Robert, and Judy Yung. "Boyhood Memories of the Wing Chun Laundry." *Argonaut* 27/1 (summer 2016): 6–19.

Lee, Josephine D., Imogene L. Lim, and Yuko Matsukawa, eds. *Re/collecting Early Asian America: Essays in Cultural History*. Philadelphia: Temple University Press, 2002.

Lee, Leo Ou-fan. *Shanghai Modern: The Flowering of a New Urban Culture in China, 1930–1945*. Cambridge: Harvard University Press, 1999.

Lee, Robert G. *Orientals: Asian Americans in Popular Culture*. Philadelphia: Temple University Press, 1999.

Lee, Tong Soon. *Chinese Street Opera in Singapore*. Urbana: University of Illinois Press, 2009.

Lee, William W. *San Francisco Son*. Bloomington: Xlibris, 2011.

Lei, Daphne. *Alternative Chinese Opera in the Age of Globalization: Performing Zero*. London: Palgrave, 2011.

——. "Can You Hear Me? Female Voice and Cantonese Opera in the San Francisco Bay Area." *The Scholar & Feminist Online* (2003) (Barnard Center for Research on Women, http://www.barnard.edu/sfonline/ps/lei.htm)

——. "Interruption, Intervention, Interculturalism: Robert Wilson's HIT Productions in Taiwan," *Theatre Journal* 63/4 (2011): 571–586.

——. *Operatic China: Staging Chinese Identity across the Pacific*. London: Palgrave, 2006.

——. "The Production and Consumption of Chinese Theatre in Nineteenth-Century California." *Theatre Research International* 28/3 (October 2003): 289–302.

Lew-Williams, Beth. "Before Restriction Became Exclusion: America's Experiment in Diplomatic Immigration Control." *Pacific Historical Review* 83/1 (2014): 24–56.

Li, Henbing, and Marc Leman. "A Gesture-based Typology of Sliding-tones in Guqin Music." *Journal of New Music Research* 36 (2007): 61–82.

Li, Jian 黎鍵. *Xianggang yueju xulun* 香港粵劇口述史 (Discourse on Cantonese Opera in Hong Kong). Hong Kong: Sanlian, 2010.

Li, Marjorie H. "The Cantonese Ballads Collections at the East Asian Library of Rutgers University and the Wason Collection of Cornell University," *Journal of East Asian Libraries*: 1991/92, Article 7. Available at: http://scholarsarchive.byu.edu/jeal/vol1991/iss92/7.

Li, Siu Leung. *Cross-Dressing in Chinese Opera*. Hong Kong: Hong Kong University Press, 2007.

Li, Xuefang. *Shilin jita*. Great Wall Records C-3514, C-3515, C-3516 (3 disks), n.d.

Li Xuefang dingmao youmei liuhen 李雪芳丁卯遊美留痕 (A Trip to United States). San Francisco: Mandarin Theater, 1927. UCB-HML, 2000/26 ctn 10:17.

Liang, Peijin 梁沛錦. *Yuemu jumu tongjian* 粵劇劇目通檢 (*Anthology of Cantonese Opera Titles*). Hong Kong: San lian shu dian Xianggang fen dian, 1985.

Lim, Genny. Interview of Eva Chan, San Francisco, CA, August 8, 1982, Chinese Women of America Research Project.

——. Interview of Rose Moon, San Francisco, CA, April 12, 1982, Chinese Women of America Research Project.

Linares, Maria Teresa. "Chinese in Cuba." In *Music in Latin America and the Caribbean: Performing the Caribbean Experience*, ed. Malena Kuss, 109–111. Austin: University of Texas Press, 2008.

Lionnet, Françoise, and Shumei Shi, eds. *Minority Transnationalism*. Durham: Duke University Press, 2005.

Liu, Guo-Xing 劉國興. "Yueju banzhu dui yiren de boxue" 粵劇班主對藝人的剝削 (Exploitation of Actors by the Owners of Opera Companies). *Guangdong wenshi ziliao* 3 (1961):126–146.

——. "Yueju yiren zai haiwaide shenghuo ji huodong" 粵劇藝人在海外的生活及活動 (The Lives and Activities of Cantonese Opera Actors Abroad). *Guangdong wenshi ziliao* 21 (1965): 172–188.

Liu, Haiming. *The Transnational History of a Chinese Family: Immigrant Letters, Family Business, and Reverse Migration*. New Brunswick: Rutgers University Press, 2009.

Liu, Jin-Zhi 劉靖之 and Elizabeth Sinn 冼玉儀, eds. *Yueju yantaohui lunwenji* 粵劇研討會論文集 (Papers and Proceedings of the International Seminar on Cantonese Opera). Hong Kong: Joint Publishing, 1995.

"Long Tack Sam at the Carlton Theatre: An Excellent Performance by Very Clever Troupe." *North-China Herald and Supreme Court & Consular Gazette*, February 11, 1928.

López, Kathleen. *Chinese Cubans: A Transnational History*. Chapel Hill: University of North Carolina Press, 2013.

Louie, David Wong. *The Barbarians Are Coming*. New York: Marian Wood, 2000.

Lowe, Lisa. *Immigrant Acts: On Asian American Cultural Politics*. Durham: Duke University Press, 1996.

Lui, Mary Ting Yi. *The Chinatown Trunk Mystery: Murder, Miscegenation, and Other Dangerous Encounters in Turn-of-the-Century New York City*. Princeton and Oxford: Princeton University Press, 2005.

Luo, Li. *Yueju dianyingshi* 粵劇電影史 (A History of Cantonese Opera Films). Beijing: Zhongguo Xiju Chubanshe, 2007.

Lynn, Grace. "Mr. Mei and the Local Chinese Drama." *New York Times*, April 6, 1930.

Ma, Shi-zeng 馬師曾. *Qianli zhangyouji* 千里壯遊集 (Voyage of a Thousand Miles). Hong Kong: Tongya, 1931.

Mai, Xiaoxia 麥嘯霞. *Guangdong xiju shilue* 廣東戲劇史略 (A Brief History of Opera Theater in Guangdong). Xianggang: n.p., 1974.

Mar, Lisa Rose. *Brokering Belonging: Chinese in Canada's Exclusion Era, 1885–1945*. Oxford: Oxford University Press, 2010.

Mark, Diane Mei Lin, and Ginger Chih. *A Place Called Chinese America*. Dubuque: Kendall Hunt, 1993.

Marshall, Alison. *Cultivating Connections: The Making of Chinese Prairie Canada*. Vancouver: University of British Columbia Press, 2014.

Mason, Daniel Gregory. "The Dilemma of American Music." *American Mercury* 7 (January 1926): 55–61.

Masters, Frederic J. "The Chinese Drama." *Chatauquan* 21 (1895): 434–442.

McDowell, Henry Burden. "The Chinese Theater." *Century Illustrated Monthly Magazine*, November 1884, 27–44.

McKeown, Adam. *Chinese Migrant Networks and Cultural Change: Peru, Chicago and Hawaii, 1900–1936*. Chicago: University of Chicago Press, 2001.

——. "Conceptualizing Chinese Diasporas, 1842 to 1949." *Journal of Asian Studies* 58/2 (1999): 306–337.

——. "Review of Shehong Chen, Being Chinese, Becoming Chinese American." *American Historical Review* 108/2 (2003): 537–538.

——. "Ritualization of Regulation: The Enforcement of Chinese Exclusion in the United States and China." *American Historical Review* 108/2 (April 2003): 377–403.

——. "A World Made Many: Integration and Segregation in Global Migration, 1840–1940." In *Connecting Seas and Connected Ocean Rims*, ed. Donna R. Gabaccia and Dirk Hoerder, 42–64. Leiden: Brill, 2011.

Mears, Eliot Grinnell. *Residential Orientals on the Pacific Coast*. Chicago: University of Chicago Press, 1927.

Meixi bahe: suiyue Guanghui ershinian 美西八和： 歲月光輝二十年 (Bahe of the West Coast: Twenty Brilliant Years). San Francisco: meixi bahe, 2010.

Metzger, Sean. "Charles Parsloe's Chinese Fetish: An Example of Yellowface Performance in Nineteenth-Century American Melodrama," *Theatre Journal* 56 (2004): 627–651.

Miller, Karl Hagstrom. *Segregating Sound: Inventing Folk and Pop Music in the Age of Jim Crow*. Durham: Duke University Press, 2010.

Miller, Leta E. *Music and Politics in San Francisco: From the 1906 Quake to the Second World War*. Berkeley: University of California Press, 2011.

Minnick, Sylvia Sun. *Samfow: The San Joaquin Chinese Legacy*. Keene, CA: Heritage West, 1987.

Moon, Krystyn R. "On a Temporary Basis: Immigration, Labor Unions, and the American Entertainment Industry, 1880s–1930s." *Journal of American History* 99/3 (2012): 771–792.

——. *Yellowface: Creating the Chinese in American Popular Music and Performance, 1850s–1920*. New Brunswick: Rutgers University Press, 2005.

Mooney, Ralph James. "Matthew Deady and the Federal Judicial Response to Racism in the Early West." *Oregon Law Review* 63 (1985): 615–616.

Moy, Ernest K. ed. *Mei Lan-fang and Chinese Drama*. New York: China Institute in America, 1930.

——. *The Pacific Coast Tour of Mei Lan-Fang, Under the Management of the Pacific Chinese Dramatic Club, San Francisco, Cal*. San Francisco: n.p., 1930.

Moy, James. *Marginal Sights: Staging the Chinese in America*. Iowa City: University of Iowa Press, 1993.

"The Music of Barbarian Bands—The Nerves of the Municipality Agitated—Gongs, Cymbals, Castanets and Tomtoms." *Daily Evening Bulletin* (San Francisco), August 5, 1869.

"Music, Old Favorites." *Time*, March 24, 1923.

Naden, Corinne J. *The Golden Age of American Musical Theatre: 1943–1965*. Metuchen, NJ: Scarecrow, 2011.

"A New Chinese Theater." *New York Times*, October 27, 1879.

"New Chinese Theater: A Grand Star Company of Heathen Artists on the Way." *San Francisco Chronicle*, October 13, 1877.

"New Chinese Theater: Competition in the Theatrical Circles of Chinatown." *San Francisco Chronicle*, September 25, 1879.

Newbould, Brian. *Schubert: The Music and the Man*. Berkeley: University of California Press, 1997.

Newell, Gordon R. ed. *The H. W. McCurdy Maritime History of the Pacific Northwest*. Seattle: Superior, 1966.

Ng, Poon Chew. "The Treatment of Exempted Classes of the Chinese in the U.S. (1908)." In *Chinese American Voices: From the Gold Rush to the Present*, ed. Judy Yung, Gordon H. Chang, and H. Mark Lai, 111–112. Berkeley: University of California Press, 2006.

Ng, Wing Chung. "Chinatown Theatre as Transnational Business: New Evidence from Vancouver during the Exclusion Era." *British Columbia Studies* 148 (winter 2005–2006): 25–54.

——. *The Rise of Cantonese Opera*. Urbana: University of Illinois Press, 2015.

Ngai, Mae N. *Impossible Subject: Illegal Aliens and the Making of Modern America*. Princeton: Princeton University Press, 2004.

——. *The Lucky Ones: One Family and the Extraordinary Invention of Chinese America*. New York: Houghton Mifflin Harcourt, 2010.

——. "Promises and Perils of Transnational History." *Perspectives on History* (December 2012). http://www.historians.org/publications-and-directories/perspectives-on-history/december-2012/the-future-of-the-discipline/promises-and-perils-of-transnational-history.

Obituary of Charles Thomas Parsloe, *New York Times*, January 23, 1898.

Obituary of Frank A. Cook, *New York Sun*, January 12, 1937.

Oja, Carol. *Making Music Modern: New York in the 1920s*. New York: Oxford University Press, 2000.

Okihiro, Gary Y. *Common Ground: Reimagining American History*. Berkeley: University of California Press, 2001.

"Old Chinese Stage Growing Up to Date: Younger Orientals Insist on Scenery, Jazz Music and Girl Actors." *Washington Post*, June 29, 1925.

Ouyang, Yuqian 歐陽予倩. "Shitan yueju" 試談粵劇 (A Preliminary Discussion of Cantonese Opera). In *Zhongguo xiqu yanjiu zilaio chuyi*, ed. Ouyang Yuqian, 109–157. Beijing: Yishu Chubanshe, 1956.

Palumbo-Liu, David. *Asian/American: Historical Crossings of a Racial Frontier*. Stanford: Stanford University Press, 1999.

Parsons, Neil. *Clicko: The Wild Dancing Bushman*. Chicago: University of Chicago Press, 2010.

Pearce, Nick. "Directness, Quaintness and Squalor: Aspects of Translation and Transformation in Franco Leoni's Opera L'Oracolo." In *Travels and Translations: Anglo-Italian Cultural Transactions*, ed. A. Yarrington, S. Villani, and J. Kelly, 337–352. Amsterdam: Rodopi, 2013.

"People vs. Ah Tim and Ah Luck," *Sacramento Daily Record-Union*, August 5, 1880.

Peretti, Burton W. *The Creation of Jazz: Music, Race, and Culture in Urban America*. Urbana: University of Illinois Press, 1994.

Pian, Rulan Chao. "Aria Structural Patterns in the Peking Opera." In *Chinese and Japanese Music Dramas*, ed. J. I. Crump and William Malm, 65–89. Ann Arbor: Center for Chinese Studies, University of Michigan, 1975.

Preston, Katherine. *Opera on the Road: Traveling Opera Troupes in the United States, 1825–60*. Urbana: University of Illinois Press, 1993.

Qiu, Shuang 秋霜. "Duiyu yuejulide yinyuede yanjiu" 對於粵劇裡的音樂的研究 (Study of Music in Cantonese Opera). *Xiju* 1/1 (1929): 92–110.

Quan, Bruce, Jr. "In the Shadows of History: Life and Times of Lew Hing, an Extraordinary Life in Extraordinary Times." Manuscript.

Rao, Nancy Yunhwa. "American Compositional Theory in the 1930s: Scale and Exoticism in 'The Nature of Melody' by Henry Cowell." *Musical Quarterly* 85/4 (2001): 595–640.

——. "Cantonese Opera in Turn-of-the-Century Canada: Local History and Transnational Circulation." *19th Century Music Review* 11/2 (2014): 291–310.

——. "Color of Music Heritage: Chinese America in American Ultra-Modern Music." *Journal of Asian American Studies* 12/1 (2009): 83–119.

——. "Cowell's Sliding Tone and American Ultra-Modernist Tradition." *American Music* 23/3 (2005): 281–323.

——. "The Public Face of Chinatown: Actresses, Actors, Playwrights, and Audiences of Chinatown Theaters in San Francisco of the 1920s." *Journal of the Society for American Music* 5/2 (2011): 235–270.

——. "Racial Essence and Historical Invisibility: Chinese Opera in New York, 1930." *Cambridge Opera Journal* 12/2 (2000): 135–162.

——. "Songs of the Exclusion Era: New York's Cantonese Opera Theaters in the 1920s." *American Music* 20/4 (2002): 399–444.

——. "Transnationalism and Everyday Practice: Chinatown Theatres of North America in the 1920s," *Ethnomusicology Forum* 26/1 (2016): 107–130.

Rao, Yunhwa 饒韻華. "Returning to New York: Manhattan's Chinese Opera Theaters and the Golden Age of Cantonese Opera in North America." 重返紐約!從20年代曼哈頓戲院看美洲的粵劇黃金時期. In *Qingxun zuiji erbainian: Yueju guoji yantaohui lunwenji*, ed. Chow Sze Sum and Cheng Lin Yan, 261–294. Hong Kong: Chinese University of Hong Kong Press, 2008.

Reynolds, Margaret. "Ruggiero's Deceptions, Cherubino's Distractions." In *En Travesti: Women, Gender Subversion, Opera*, ed. Corinne Blackmer and Patricia Smith, 134–151. New York: Columbia University Press, 1995.

Rice, Diana. "'Left Their Pigtails Behind Them': Common Report Has It Only One Queue Is Left in All Chinatown." *New York Times*, March 30, 1924.

Riddle, Ronald. *Flying Dragons, Flowing Streams: Music in the Life of San Francisco's Chinese*. Westport: Greenwood, 1983.

Robinson, Greg. *By Order of the President: FDR and the Internment of Japanese Americans*. Cambridge: Harvard University Press, 2001.

Rodescape, Lois. "Celestial Drama in the Golden Hills: The Chinese Theater in California, 1849–1869." *California Historical Society Quarterly* 23 (1944): 97–116.

Rodger, Gillian M. *Champagne Charlie and Pretty Jemima: Variety Theater in the Nineteenth Century*. Urbana: University of Illinois Press, 2010.

Rosenstein, Brad, ed. *Painted Men: Chinese Opera Backstage* (Catalogue for Celebrating the Amazing Legacy of Chinese Opera in San Francisco). Text by William C. Hu. San Francisco: San Francisco Performing Arts Library and Museum, 2005.

Russell, Gillian. *The Playbill and Its People: Australia's Earliest Printed Document*. Canberra: National Library of Australia, 2012.

Said, Edward. *Orientalism*. London: Penguin, 1977.

——. "Orientalism Reconsidered." *Cultural Critique* 1 (1985): 89–107.

Salyer, Lucy E. *Laws Harsh as Tigers: Chinese Immigrants and the Shaping of Modern Immigration Law*. Chapel Hill: University of North Carolina Press, 1995.

Scott, A. C. *Mei Lan-fang: The Life and Times of a Peking Actor*. Hong Kong: Hong Kong University Press, 1971.

Scott, Joan. "The Evidence of Experience." *Critical Inquiry* 17/4 (1991): 773–797.

Scott, Mary. "Chinese Opera." In *The Asian Pacific American Heritage: A Companion to Literature and Arts*, ed. George Leonard, 476–481. New York: Routledge, 1998.

Seligman, Scott D. *The First Chinese American: The Remarkable Life of Wong Chin Foo*. Hong Kong: Hong Kong University Press, 2013.

Shah, Nayan. *Contagious Divides: Epidemics and Race in San Francisco's Chinatown*. Berkeley: California University Press, 2001.

——. *Stranger Intimacy: Contesting Race, Sexuality and the Law in the North American West*. Berkeley: University of California Press, 2011.

Shen, Shaung. *Cosmopolitan Publics: Anglophone Print Culture in Semi-Colonial Shanghai*. New Brunswick: Rutgers University Press, 2009.

Shih, Shu-Mei. *Visuality and Identity: Sinophone Articulations across the Pacific*. Berkeley: University of California Press, 2007.

Shimakawa, Karen. *National Abjection: The Asian American Body Onstage*. Durham: Duke University Press, 2002.

Sinn, Elizabeth. *Pacific Crossing: California Gold, Chinese Migration and the Making of Hong Kong*. Hong Kong: Hong Kong University Press, 2014.

Smith, Icy. *The Lonely Queue: The Forgotten History of the Courageous Chinese Americans in Los Angeles*. Gardena, CA: East West Discovery Press, 2001.

Song, Zuanyou 宋鑽友. "Yue Ju Zai Jiu Shanghai De Yan Chu" 粵劇在舊上海的演出 (Cantonese Opera in Historical Shanghai). *Shi Lin* 1 (1994): 64–70.

Spottswood, Richard. *Ethnic Music on Records*, vol. 5. Urbana: University of Illinois Press, 1991.

Stallmann, Louis. "Donaldina Cameron vs. Yellow Slavery." *San Francisco Chronicle*, June 14, 1914.

Stock, Jonathan P. J. "The Application of Schenkerian Analysis to Ethnomusicology: Problems and Possibilities." *Music Analysis* 12/2 (1993): 215–240.

——. *Huju: Traditional Opera in Modern Shanghai*. New York: Oxford University Press, 2003.

——. "A Reassessment of the Relationship between Text, Speech Tone, Melody, and Aria Structure in Beijing Opera." *Journal of Musicological Research* 18/3 (1999): 183–206.

Suisman, David. *Selling Sounds: The Commercial Revolution in American Music*. Cambridge: Harvard University Press, 2009.

Sundar, Pavitra. "Meri Awaaz Suno: Women, Vocality, and Nation in Hindi Cinema." *Meridians* 8/1 (2007): 144–179.

Tate, E. Mowbray. *Transpacific Steam: The Story of Steam Navigation from the Pacific Coast of North America to the Far East and the Antipodes, 1867–1941*. New York: Cornwall, 1986.

Taylor, Diane. *The Archive and the Repertoire: Performing Cultural Memory in the Americas*. Durham: Duke University Press, 2003.

Tchen, Jack K. W. *New York before Chinatown: Orientalism and the Shaping of American Cultures*. Baltimore: Johns Hopkins University Press, 1999.

"This Chinese Actress Says She'll Never Wed: Soo Lum Mark, at 18, Is Rather Young Leading Lady, but She's Clever." *Toronto Daily Star*, July 17, 1922.

Thrasher, Alan. *Sizhu Instrumental Music of South China: Ethos, Theory and Practice*. Leiden: Brill, 2008.

Tick, Judith, and Paul Beaudoin, eds. *Music in the USA: A Documentary Companion*. Oxford: Oxford University Press, 2008.

Tillmany, Jack. *Theatres of San Francisco*. Charleston: Arcadia, 2005.

Triana, Mauro García, and Pedro Eng Herrera. *The Chinese in Cuba, 1847–Now*, ed. and trans. Gregor Benton. Lanham, MD: Lexington, 2009.

Trimboli, Daniella. "Memory Magic: Cosmopolitanism and the Magical Life of Long Tack Sam." *Continuum* 29/3 (2015): 479–489.

Tsou, Judy. "Gendering Race: Stereotypes of Chinese Americans in Popular Sheet Music." *Repercussions* 6 (Fall 1997): 25–62.

Tsui, Kitty. "Kwan Ying Lin: Kwan Yuem Sheung." In *The Words of a Woman Who Breathes Fire*. Iowa City: Iowa City Women's Press, 1983.

———. "Kwan Ying Lin, Mao Dan So & Co.: Stars of the Chinatown Stage." University of California, Santa Cruz, Asian Pacific Islander Lesbian Collection, 1980–2001, Box-folder 29:5.

Turner, Robert D. *The Pacific Princesses: An Illustrated History of the Canadian Pacific Railway's Princess Fleet on the Northwest Coast.* Victoria, BC: Sono Nis, 1977.

Urban, Greg. *Metaculture: How Culture Moves through the World.* Minneapolis: Minnesota University Press, 2001.

U.S. Census Bureau. *Chinese and Japanese in the United States 1910*, Bulletin 127. Washington, DC: Government Printing Office, 1914.

———. *Eleventh Census of the United States*. Washington, DC: Government Printing Office, [1895–1897].

———. *Fifteenth Census of the United States: 1930, Population*. Washington, DC: Government Printing Office, 1930.

Wang, Ying-fen. "The 'Mosaic Structure' of Nanguan Songs: An Application of Semiotic Analysis." *Yearbook for Traditional Music* 24 (1992): 24–51.

Ward, Barbara. "Regional Operas and Their Audiences: Evidence from Hong Kong." In *Popular Culture in Late Imperial China*, ed. David Johnson, Andrew J. Nathan, and Evelyn S. Rawski, 161–187 (Berkeley: University of California Press, 1989).

Wen, Zhi Peng 溫志鵬. "Yueju nuban zhi chutan" 粵劇女班之初探 (A Preliminary Study of Female Troupes). In *Yueju yantaohui lunsdnji*, ed. Ching-Chih Liu and Elizabeth Sinn, 367–390. Hong Kong: Hong Kong University Centre of Asian Studies, 1995.

White Powder and Neon Lights, dir. Wong Hok-Sing, prod. Joseph Sunn Jue. San Francisco: Grandview Film Company, 1946.

"Will Give 'Food' at the Orpheum." *San Francisco Chronicle*, October 28, 1914.

Witzleben, John Lawrence. *"Silk and Bamboo" Music in Shanghai: The Jiangnan Sizhu Instrumental Tradition*. Kent, OH: Kent State University Press, 1995.

Wo Foshan, Rene 我佛山人, ed. *Li Xuefang* 李雪芳. Shanghai: Dongya Tushuguan, 1920.

Wong, Deborah. *Speak It Louder: Asian Americans Making Music*. New York: Routledge, 2004.

Wong, Jade Snow. *Fifth Chinese Daughter*. [original 1945]. Seattle: University of Washington Press, 1989.

Wong, K. Scott, and Sucheng Chan. *Claiming America: Constructing Chinese American Identities during the Exclusion Era*. Philadelphia: Temple University Press, 1998.

Wong, Marie Rose. *Sweet Cakes, Long Journey: The Chinatowns of Portland, Oregon*. Seattle: Washington University Press, 2004.

Wong, Sau-ling Cynthia. "Autobiography as Guided Chinatown Tour? Maxine Hong Kingston's *The Woman Warrior* and the Chinese-American Autobiographical Controversy." In *Critical Essays on Maxine Hong Kingston*, ed. Laura E. Skandera-Trombley, 146–167. New York: Hall, 1998.

Wunder, John R. "Anti-Chinese Violence in the American West, 1850–1910." In *Law for the Elephant, Law for the Beaver: Essays in the Legal History of the North American West*, ed. John McLaren, 212–236. Pasadena: Ninth Judicial Circuit Historical Society, 1992.

Xie, Bin-chou 謝彬籌. "Huaqiao yu yueju"華僑與粵劇 (The Chinese Overseas and Cantonese Opera). *Xiju yishu ziliao* 7 (1982): 21–39.

Xie, Yinghua 謝瑛華. "Shanghai's New Stage: 1908–1927" (上海的新舞台: 1908–1927). Master's thesis, Fudan University, 2005.

Xin Zhu 新珠. "Yueju yiren zai nanyang ji Meizhou de qingkuang" 粵劇藝人在南洋及美洲的情況 (The Conditions of Cantonese Opera Actors in Southeast Asia and the Americas). *Guangdong wenshi ziliao* 21 (1965): 146–171.

Xiyang Nü 西洋女. "Xinzhu xiaozhuan" 新珠小傳 (A short biography of Xinzhu: The Wife's Memoir). *Xiju yishu ziliao* 4 (1981): 27–41.

Yan, Yuan. "Historical Transition of Chinese Theaters in Cuba." *Journal of Latin American Studies* 33/6 (2011): 37–42.

Yeung, Loretta Siuling. "Red Boat Troupes and Cantonese Opera." Master's thesis, University of Georgia, 2010.

Young, Elliott. *Alien Nation: Chinese Migration in the Americas from the Coolie Era through World War II*. Chapel Hill: University of North Carolina Press, 2015.

Yu, Henry. "Introduction: The Rhythms of the Trans-Pacific" and "The Intermittent Rhythms of the Cantonese Pacific." In *Connecting Seas and Connecting Ocean Rims: Indian, Atlantic, and Pacific Oceans and China Seas Migrations from the 1830s*, ed. Donna R. Gabaccia and Dirk Hoerder, 393–414. Leiden: Brill, 2011.

Yu, Siu wah余少華. *Yue you ruci* 樂猶如此 (Such an Unfading Sound). Hong Kong: International Association of Theatre Critics, 2005.

Yu, Yong 余勇. *Mingqing shiqi yuejudeqiyuan, xingcheng he fazhang* 明清時期粵劇的起源、形成和發展(The Origin, Formation, and Development of Cantonese Opera in the Ming and Qing Dynasties). Beijing: Zhongguo Xiju Chuban She, 2009.

*Yue ju da ci dian*粵劇大辭典(A Dictionary of Cantonese Opera). Guangzhou: Guangzhou chu ban she, 2008.

Yueju jumu gangyao 粵劇劇目綱要 (Anthology of Cantonese Opera Titles and Plots). Guangzhou: Zhongguo xijujia xiehui guangdong fenhui, 1961; repr., Guangzhou: Yangcheng Wanbao, 2007.

Yung, Bell. *Cantonese Opera: Performance as Creative Process*. Cambridge: Cambridge University Press, 1989.

——. "Muk'yu: Voices of the People." In *Uncle Ng Comes to America: Chinese Narrative Songs of Immigration and Love*. Hong Kong: MCCM Creations, 2014.

Yung, Judy. *Unbound Feet: A Social History of Chinese Women in San Francisco*. Berkeley: University of California Press, 1995.

——. *Unbound Voices: A Documentary History of Chinese Women in San Francisco*. Berkeley: University of California Press, 1999.

——. *San Francisco's Chinatown*. Chicago: Arcadia, 2006.

Yung, Judy, Gordon Chang, and Him Mark Lai, eds. *Chinese American Voices from the Gold Rush to the Present*. Berkeley: University of California Press, 2006.

Yung, Sai-Shing 容世誠. "'Jinru chengshi': wuguangshize" 進入城市：五光十色：1920年代粵劇探析 ('Entering the City and Its Bright Light': A Study of Cantonese Opera in the 1920s). In *Qingxun zuji erbainian: Yueju guoji yantaohui lunwenji*, ed. Chow Sze Sum and Cheng Lin Yan, 73–97. Hong Kong: Cantonese Opera Research Programme, Chinese University of Hong Kong, 2008.

——. "Moving Body: The Interactions between Chinese Opera and Action Cinema." In *Hong Kong Connections: Transnational Imagination in Action Cinema*, ed. Meaghan Morris, Siu-leung Li, and Stephen Chan Ching-kiu, 21–34. Durham: Duke University Press; Hong Kong: Hong Kong University Press, 2005.

——. "Mu-yu shu and the Cantonese Popular Singing Arts." *Gest Library Journal* 2/1 (1987): 16–30.

——. "Recording Cantonese Opera and Music in the 1920s and 1930s from a Viewpoint of Cultural History." *Journal of Chinese Studies* 12 (2003): 473–502.

——. "Territorialization and the Entertainment Industry of the Shaw Brothers in Southeast Asia." In *China Forever: The Shaw Brothers and Diasporic Cinema*, ed. Poshek Fu, 131–153. Urbana: University of Illinois Press, 2008.

——. *Xunmi yueju shengying: cong hongchuan dao shuiyingdeng* 尋覓粵劇聲影：從紅船到水銀燈 (From Opera Boat to Silver Screen: Visual and Sonic Culture of Cantonese Opera). Hong Kong: Oxford University Press, 2012.

——. *Yueyun Liusheng* 粵韻留聲：唱片工業與廣東曲藝 (Cantonese Opera from the Gramophone: A Cultural History, 1903–1953). Hong Kong: Institute for the Research of Humanities, Chinese University of Hong Kong, Cosmos Press, 2006.

Yung, Sai-Shing, and Chan Kowk-bun. "Chinese Entertainment, Ethnicity, and Pleasure." *Visual Anthropology* 18/2–3 (2005): 103–142.

Zhang, Yihe 章詒和. *Yizhen feng, liuxia qiangu juechang* 一陣風，留下千古絕唱 (A Gust of Wind, Leaving the Songs of the Eternal Farewell). Hong Kong: Oxford University Press, 2005.

Zheng, Luofu 張洛夫. "Yueju Congtan" 粵劇叢談 (General Discussion of Cantonese Opera) *Youxi shijie* 10 (1922): 13–16.

Zheng, Su. *Claiming Diaspora: Music, Transnationalism, and Cultural Politics in Asian Chinese America*. New York: Oxford University Press, 2010.

Zhou, Shi-shen 周仕深 and Zheng Ning-en 鄭寧恩, eds. *Qingxun zuiji erbainian: yueju guoji yantaohui lunwenji* 情尋足跡二十年：粵劇國際研討會論文集 (Search for Two Centuries of Footprints: A Collection of Papers from the International Symposium on Cantonese Opera). Hong Kong: Cantonese Opera Research Programme, Chinese University of Hong Kong, 2008.

Zhu, Bing-tan 朱炳堂. *Yuediao gequ jinghua* 粵調歌曲菁華 (Essence of Cantonese Arias and Songs). San Francisco: Sun tai lok, 1926.

INDEX

Page numbers in *italics* refer to illustrations.

NANCY YUNHWA RAO is a professor of music at Rutgers University.

MUSIC IN AMERICAN LIFE

Only a Miner: Studies in Recorded Coal-Mining Songs *Archie Green*
Great Day Coming: Folk Music and the American Left *R. Serge Denisoff*
John Philip Sousa: A Descriptive Catalog of His Works *Paul E. Bierley*
The Hell-Bound Train: A Cowboy Songbook *Glenn Ohrlin*
Oh, Didn't He Ramble: The Life Story of Lee Collins, as Told to Mary Collins *Edited by Frank J. Gillis and John W. Miner*
American Labor Songs of the Nineteenth Century *Philip S. Foner*
Stars of Country Music: Uncle Dave Macon to Johnny Rodriguez *Edited by Bill C. Malone and Judith McCulloh*
Git Along, Little Dogies: Songs and Songmakers of the American West *John I. White*
A Texas-Mexican *Cancionero*: Folksongs of the Lower Border *Américo Paredes*
San Antonio Rose: The Life and Music of Bob Wills *Charles R. Townsend*
Early Downhome Blues: A Musical and Cultural Analysis *Jeff Todd Titon*
An Ives Celebration: Papers and Panels of the Charles Ives Centennial Festival-Conference *Edited by H. Wiley Hitchcock and Vivian Perlis*
Sinful Tunes and Spirituals: Black Folk Music to the Civil War *Dena J. Epstein*
Joe Scott, the Woodsman-Songmaker *Edward D. Ives*
Jimmie Rodgers: The Life and Times of America's Blue Yodeler *Nolan Porterfield*
Early American Music Engraving and Printing: A History of Music Publishing in America from 1787 to 1825, with Commentary on Earlier and Later Practices *Richard J. Wolfe*
Sing a Sad Song: The Life of Hank Williams *Roger M. Williams*
Long Steel Rail: The Railroad in American Folksong *Norm Cohen*
Resources of American Music History: A Directory of Source Materials from Colonial Times to World War II *D. W. Krummel, Jean Geil, Doris J. Dyen, and Deane L. Root*
Tenement Songs: The Popular Music of the Jewish Immigrants *Mark Slobin*
Ozark Folksongs *Vance Randolph; edited and abridged by Norm Cohen*
Oscar Sonneck and American Music *Edited by William Lichtenwanger*
Bluegrass Breakdown: The Making of the Old Southern Sound *Robert Cantwell*
Bluegrass: A History *Neil V. Rosenberg*
Music at the White House: A History of the American Spirit *Elise K. Kirk*
Red River Blues: The Blues Tradition in the Southeast *Bruce Bastin*
Good Friends and Bad Enemies: Robert Winslow Gordon and the Study of American Folksong *Debora Kodish*
Fiddlin' Georgia Crazy: Fiddlin' John Carson, His Real World, and the World of His Songs *Gene Wiggins*
America's Music: From the Pilgrims to the Present (rev. 3d ed.) *Gilbert Chase*
Secular Music in Colonial Annapolis: The Tuesday Club, 1745–56 *John Barry Talley*
Bibliographical Handbook of American Music *D. W. Krummel*
Goin' to Kansas City *Nathan W. Pearson Jr.*
"Susanna," "Jeanie," and "The Old Folks at Home": The Songs of Stephen C. Foster from His Time to Ours (2d ed.) *William W. Austin*
Songprints: The Musical Experience of Five Shoshone Women *Judith Vander*

"Happy in the Service of the Lord": Afro-American Gospel Quartets in Memphis *Kip Lornell*

Paul Hindemith in the United States *Luther Noss*

"My Song Is My Weapon": People's Songs, American Communism, and the Politics of Culture, 1930–50 *Robbie Lieberman*

Chosen Voices: The Story of the American Cantorate *Mark Slobin*

Theodore Thomas: America's Conductor and Builder of Orchestras, 1835–1905 *Ezra Schabas*

"The Whorehouse Bells Were Ringing" and Other Songs Cowboys Sing *Collected and Edited by Guy Logsdon*

Crazeology: The Autobiography of a Chicago Jazzman *Bud Freeman, as Told to Robert Wolf*

Discoursing Sweet Music: Brass Bands and Community Life in Turn-of-the-Century Pennsylvania *Kenneth Kreitner*

Mormonism and Music: A History *Michael Hicks*

Voices of the Jazz Age: Profiles of Eight Vintage Jazzmen *Chip Deffaa*

Pickin' on Peachtree: A History of Country Music in Atlanta, Georgia *Wayne W. Daniel*

Bitter Music: Collected Journals, Essays, Introductions, and Librettos *Harry Partch; edited by Thomas McGeary*

Ethnic Music on Records: A Discography of Ethnic Recordings Produced in the United States, 1893 to 1942 *Richard K. Spottswood*

Downhome Blues Lyrics: An Anthology from the Post–World War II Era *Jeff Todd Titon*

Ellington: The Early Years *Mark Tucker*

Chicago Soul *Robert Pruter*

That Half-Barbaric Twang: The Banjo in American Popular Culture *Karen Linn*

Hot Man: The Life of Art Hodes *Art Hodes and Chadwick Hansen*

The Erotic Muse: American Bawdy Songs (2d ed.) *Ed Cray*

Barrio Rhythm: Mexican American Music in Los Angeles *Steven Loza*

The Creation of Jazz: Music, Race, and Culture in Urban America *Burton W. Peretti*

Charles Martin Loeffler: A Life Apart in Music *Ellen Knight*

Club Date Musicians: Playing the New York Party Circuit *Bruce A. MacLeod*

Opera on the Road: Traveling Opera Troupes in the United States, 1825–60 *Katherine K. Preston*

The Stonemans: An Appalachian Family and the Music That Shaped Their Lives *Ivan M. Tribe*

Transforming Tradition: Folk Music Revivals Examined *Edited by Neil V. Rosenberg*

The Crooked Stovepipe: Athapaskan Fiddle Music and Square Dancing in Northeast Alaska and Northwest Canada *Craig Mishler*

Traveling the High Way Home: Ralph Stanley and the World of Traditional Bluegrass Music *John Wright*

Carl Ruggles: Composer, Painter, and Storyteller *Marilyn Ziffrin*

Never without a Song: The Years and Songs of Jennie Devlin, 1865–1952 *Katharine D. Newman*

The Hank Snow Story *Hank Snow, with Jack Ownbey and Bob Burris*

Milton Brown and the Founding of Western Swing *Cary Ginell, with special assistance from Roy Lee Brown*

Santiago de Murcia's "Códice Saldívar No. 4": A Treasury of Secular Guitar Music from Baroque Mexico *Craig H. Russell*
The Sound of the Dove: Singing in Appalachian Primitive Baptist Churches *Beverly Bush Patterson*
Heartland Excursions: Ethnomusicological Reflections on Schools of Music *Bruno Nettl*
Doowop: The Chicago Scene *Robert Pruter*
Blue Rhythms: Six Lives in Rhythm and Blues *Chip Deffaa*
Shoshone Ghost Dance Religion: Poetry Songs and Great Basin Context *Judith Vander*
Go Cat Go! Rockabilly Music and Its Makers *Craig Morrison*
'Twas Only an Irishman's Dream: The Image of Ireland and the Irish in American Popular Song Lyrics, 1800–1920 *William H. A. Williams*
Democracy at the Opera: Music, Theater, and Culture in New York City, 1815–60 *Karen Ahlquist*
Fred Waring and the Pennsylvanians *Virginia Waring*
Woody, Cisco, and Me: Seamen Three in the Merchant Marine *Jim Longhi*
Behind the Burnt Cork Mask: Early Blackface Minstrelsy and Antebellum American Popular Culture *William J. Mahar*
Going to Cincinnati: A History of the Blues in the Queen City *Steven C. Tracy*
Pistol Packin' Mama: Aunt Molly Jackson and the Politics of Folksong *Shelly Romalis*
Sixties Rock: Garage, Psychedelic, and Other Satisfactions *Michael Hicks*
The Late Great Johnny Ace and the Transition from R&B to Rock 'n' Roll *James M. Salem*
Tito Puente and the Making of Latin Music *Steven Loza*
Juilliard: A History *Andrea Olmstead*
Understanding Charles Seeger, Pioneer in American Musicology *Edited by Bell Yung and Helen Rees*
Mountains of Music: West Virginia Traditional Music from *Goldenseal* *Edited by John Lilly*
Alice Tully: An Intimate Portrait *Albert Fuller*
A Blues Life *Henry Townsend, as told to Bill Greensmith*
Long Steel Rail: The Railroad in American Folksong (2d ed.) *Norm Cohen*
The Golden Age of Gospel *Text by Horace Clarence Boyer; photography by Lloyd Yearwood*
Aaron Copland: The Life and Work of an Uncommon Man *Howard Pollack*
Louis Moreau Gottschalk *S. Frederick Starr*
Race, Rock, and Elvis *Michael T. Bertrand*
Theremin: Ether Music and Espionage *Albert Glinsky*
Poetry and Violence: The Ballad Tradition of Mexico's Costa Chica *John H. McDowell*
The Bill Monroe Reader *Edited by Tom Ewing*
Music in Lubavitcher Life *Ellen Koskoff*
Zarzuela: Spanish Operetta, American Stage *Janet L. Sturman*
Bluegrass Odyssey: A Documentary in Pictures and Words, 1966–86 *Carl Fleischhauer and Neil V. Rosenberg*
That Old-Time Rock & Roll: A Chronicle of an Era, 1954–63 *Richard Aquila*
Labor's Troubadour *Joe Glazer*
American Opera *Elise K. Kirk*

Don't Get above Your Raisin': Country Music and the Southern Working Class *Bill C. Malone*
John Alden Carpenter: A Chicago Composer *Howard Pollack*
Heartbeat of the People: Music and Dance of the Northern Pow-wow *Tara Browner*
My Lord, What a Morning: An Autobiography *Marian Anderson*
Marian Anderson: A Singer's Journey *Allan Keiler*
Charles Ives Remembered: An Oral History *Vivian Perlis*
Henry Cowell, Bohemian *Michael Hicks*
Rap Music and Street Consciousness *Cheryl L. Keyes*
Louis Prima *Garry Boulard*
Marian McPartland's Jazz World: All in Good Time *Marian McPartland*
Robert Johnson: Lost and Found *Barry Lee Pearson and Bill McCulloch*
Bound for America: Three British Composers *Nicholas Temperley*
Lost Sounds: Blacks and the Birth of the Recording Industry, 1890–1919 *Tim Brooks*
Burn, Baby! BURN! The Autobiography of Magnificent Montague *Magnificent Montague with Bob Baker*
Way Up North in Dixie: A Black Family's Claim to the Confederate Anthem *Howard L. Sacks and Judith Rose Sacks*
The Bluegrass Reader *Edited by Thomas Goldsmith*
Colin McPhee: Composer in Two Worlds *Carol J. Oja*
Robert Johnson, Mythmaking, and Contemporary American Culture *Patricia R. Schroeder*
Composing a World: Lou Harrison, Musical Wayfarer *Leta E. Miller and Fredric Lieberman*
Fritz Reiner, Maestro and Martinet *Kenneth Morgan*
That Toddlin' Town: Chicago's White Dance Bands and Orchestras, 1900–1950 *Charles A. Sengstock Jr.*
Dewey and Elvis: The Life and Times of a Rock 'n' Roll Deejay *Louis Cantor*
Come Hither to Go Yonder: Playing Bluegrass with Bill Monroe *Bob Black*
Chicago Blues: Portraits and Stories *David Whiteis*
The Incredible Band of John Philip Sousa *Paul E. Bierley*
"Maximum Clarity" and Other Writings on Music *Ben Johnston, edited by Bob Gilmore*
Staging Tradition: John Lair and Sarah Gertrude Knott *Michael Ann Williams*
Homegrown Music: Discovering Bluegrass *Stephanie P. Ledgin*
Tales of a Theatrical Guru *Danny Newman*
The Music of Bill Monroe *Neil V. Rosenberg and Charles K. Wolfe*
Pressing On: The Roni Stoneman Story *Roni Stoneman, as told to Ellen Wright*
Together Let Us Sweetly Live *Jonathan C. David, with photographs by Richard Holloway*
Live Fast, Love Hard: The Faron Young Story *Diane Diekman*
Air Castle of the South: WSM Radio and the Making of Music City *Craig P. Havighurst*
Traveling Home: Sacred Harp Singing and American Pluralism *Kiri Miller*
Where Did Our Love Go? The Rise and Fall of the Motown Sound *Nelson George*
Lonesome Cowgirls and Honky-Tonk Angels: The Women of Barn Dance Radio *Kristine M. McCusker*
California Polyphony: Ethnic Voices, Musical Crossroads *Mina Yang*
The Never-Ending Revival: Rounder Records and the Folk Alliance *Michael F. Scully*

Sing It Pretty: A Memoir *Bess Lomax Hawes*
Working Girl Blues: The Life and Music of Hazel Dickens *Hazel Dickens and Bill C. Malone*
Charles Ives Reconsidered *Gayle Sherwood Magee*
The Hayloft Gang: The Story of the National Barn Dance *Edited by Chad Berry*
Country Music Humorists and Comedians *Loyal Jones*
Record Makers and Breakers: Voices of the Independent Rock 'n' Roll Pioneers *John Broven*
Music of the First Nations: Tradition and Innovation in Native North America *Edited by Tara Browner*
Cafe Society: The Wrong Place for the Right People *Barney Josephson, with Terry Trilling-Josephson*
George Gershwin: An Intimate Portrait *Walter Rimler*
Life Flows On in Endless Song: Folk Songs and American History *Robert V. Wells*
I Feel a Song Coming On: The Life of Jimmy McHugh *Alyn Shipton*
King of the Queen City: The Story of King Records *Jon Hartley Fox*
Long Lost Blues: Popular Blues in America, 1850–1920 *Peter C. Muir*
Hard Luck Blues: Roots Music Photographs from the Great Depression *Rich Remsberg*
Restless Giant: The Life and Times of Jean Aberbach and Hill and Range Songs *Bar Biszick-Lockwood*
Champagne Charlie and Pretty Jemima: Variety Theater in the Nineteenth Century *Gillian M. Rodger*
Sacred Steel: Inside an African American Steel Guitar Tradition *Robert L. Stone*
Gone to the Country: The New Lost City Ramblers and the Folk Music Revival *Ray Allen*
The Makers of the Sacred Harp *David Warren Steel with Richard H. Hulan*
Woody Guthrie, American Radical *Will Kaufman*
George Szell: A Life of Music *Michael Charry*
Bean Blossom: The Brown County Jamboree and Bill Monroe's Bluegrass Festivals *Thomas A. Adler*
Crowe on the Banjo: The Music Life of J. D. Crowe *Marty Godbey*
Twentieth Century Drifter: The Life of Marty Robbins *Diane Diekman*
Henry Mancini: Reinventing Film Music *John Caps*
The Beautiful Music All Around Us: Field Recordings and the American Experience *Stephen Wade*
Then Sings My Soul: The Culture of Southern Gospel Music *Douglas Harrison*
The Accordion in the Americas: Klezmer, Polka, Tango, Zydeco, and More! *Edited by Helena Simonett*
Bluegrass Bluesman: A Memoir *Josh Graves, edited by Fred Bartenstein*
One Woman in a Hundred: Edna Phillips and the Philadelphia Orchestra *Mary Sue Welsh*
The Great Orchestrator: Arthur Judson and American Arts Management *James M. Doering*
Charles Ives in the Mirror: American Histories of an Iconic Composer *David C. Paul*
Southern Soul-Blues *David Whiteis*
Sweet Air: Modernism, Regionalism, and American Popular Song *Edward P. Comentale*
Pretty Good for a Girl: Women in Bluegrass *Murphy Hicks Henry*
Sweet Dreams: The World of Patsy Cline *Warren R. Hofstra*
William Sidney Mount and the Creolization of American Culture *Christopher J. Smith*

Bird: The Life and Music of Charlie Parker *Chuck Haddix*
Making the March King: John Philip Sousa's Washington Years, 1854–1893 *Patrick Warfield*
In It for the Long Run *Jim Rooney*
Pioneers of the Blues Revival *Steve Cushing*
Roots of the Revival: American and British Folk Music in the 1950s *Ronald D. Cohen and Rachel Clare Donaldson*
Blues All Day Long: The Jimmy Rogers Story *Wayne Everett Goins*
Yankee Twang: Country and Western Music in New England *Clifford R. Murphy*
The Music of the Stanley Brothers *Gary B. Reid*
Hawaiian Music in Motion: Mariners, Missionaries, and Minstrels *James Revell Carr*
Sounds of the New Deal: The Federal Music Project in the West *Peter Gough*
The Mormon Tabernacle Choir: A Biography *Michael Hicks*
The Man That Got Away: The Life and Songs of Harold Arlen *Walter Rimler*
A City Called Heaven: Chicago and the Birth of Gospel Music *Robert M. Marovich*
Blues Unlimited: Essential Interviews from the Original Blues Magazine *Edited by Bill Greensmith, Mike Rowe, and Mark Camarigg*
Hoedowns, Reels, and Frolics: Roots and Branches of Southern Appalachian Dance *Phil Jamison*
Fannie Bloomfield-Zeisler: The Life and Times of a Piano Virtuoso *Beth Abelson Macleod*
Cybersonic Arts: Adventures in American New Music *Gordon Mumma, edited with commentary by Michelle Fillion*
The Magic of Beverly Sills *Nancy Guy*
Waiting for Buddy Guy *Alan Harper*
Harry T. Burleigh: From the Spiritual to the Harlem Renaissance *Jean E. Snyder*
Music in the Age of Anxiety: American Music in the Fifties *James Wierzbicki*
Jazzing: New York City's Unseen Scene *Thomas H. Greenland*
A Cole Porter Companion *Edited by Don M. Randel, Matthew Shaftel, and Susan Forscher Weiss*
Foggy Mountain Troubadour: The Life and Music of Curly Seckler *Penny Parsons*
Blue Rhythm Fantasy: Big Band Jazz Arranging in the Swing Era *John Wriggle*
Bill Clifton: America's Bluegrass Ambassador to the World *Bill C. Malone*
Chinatown Opera Theater in North America *Nancy Yunhwa Rao*

The University of Illinois Press
is a founding member of the
Association of American University Presses.

Cover designed by Jacqueline Thaw
Cover photos by Christine Hills

University of Illinois Press
1325 South Oak Street
Champaign, IL 61820-6903
www.press.uillinois.edu